Kimberley: Turbulent City

Brian Roberts

KIMBERLEY: Turbulent City

IN ASSOCIATION WITH THE HISTORICAL SOCIETY
OF KIMBERLEY AND THE NORTHERN CAPE

DAVID PHILIP : PUBLISHER : CAPE TOWN

PUBLISHED IN 1976 BY DAVID PHILIP, PUBLISHER (PTY)
3 SCOTT ROAD, CLAREMONT, CAPE, SOUTH AFRICA
© BRIAN ROBERTS 1976
ISBN 0 949968 62 5 (BOARDS)
SECOND IMPRESSION 1984

PRINTED AND BOUND BY PRINTPAK (CAPE)
DACRES AVENUE, EPPING, CAPE

Contents

Foreword

Kimberley has had a profound effect on the course of history in Southern Africa. The discovery of diamonds there, more than a century ago, proved to be the first step in the transformation of South Africa from an agricultural into an industrial country. When gold and other minerals were later discovered to the north, there were already in Kimberley men of vision and enterprise with the capital and technology to develop the new resources.

The Kimberley mines are still in production and Kimberley is still the headquarters of what is now a very large and complex international diamond industry. Thus the city can justly claim a permanent and important place in the history of the sub-continent, and it is entirely fitting that this book should now be produced with the help and encouragement of the Historical Society of Kimberley and the Northern Cape.

To me, having been closely associated with Kimberley for the greater part of my life, the publication of this book is especially gratifying. From his scholarly research the author has created a lively and absorbing story that captures the spirit and times of a city, which to my mind is both an institution and a place. Mr Roberts is to be congratulated.

H. F. OPPENHEIMER

FOR JUDY HOARE

Acknowledgements

The idea of writing this book was first suggested to me, several years ago, by Mrs Judy Hoare, the present Chairman of the Historical Society of Kimberley and the Northern Cape. Fascinated as I was by the suggestion, I felt at that time unequal to the task. Kimberley's history is as complex as it is exciting: it involves not only the growth of the city, but the development of the South African diamond industry and the careers of some of the most influential men in South Africa's history. I had serious doubts whether all this could be satisfactorily dealt with in a single volume. After writing my book *The Diamond Magnates*, however, many of these doubts were overcome. I recognised that there was a definite narrative thread from which the story of this extraordinary city could be developed. In attempting to follow this thread it has not been possible to cover every aspect of the city's growth or to mention every individual connected with Kimberley and the diamond industry – remarkable as many of them have been. I have, however, tried to include all the important events of the last hundred or so years, as well as the men and women connected with those events. Any omissions are due to lack of space rather than lack of recognition.

My very sincere thanks must go to the Historical Society of Kimberley and the Northern Cape who, with the co-operation of De Beers Consolidated Mines, Limited, commissioned me to write this history. De Beers especially, without in any way influencing the writing of the book, have provided me with every assistance.

In attempting to tell the story of Kimberley, I have been greatly assisted by the interest and advice of many people. My chief debt, however, is to Mrs Judy Hoare. Not only did she inspire the book, but her knowledgeable help in answering my endless queries and in researching obscure details has been invaluable. Her unflagging enthusiasm has been a constant source of encouragement and I can only trust that her faith in the book has, in a small way, been rewarded.

I am extremely grateful to Mrs Marian Robertson whose co-operation and expertise have, as always, proved most helpful. Her authoritative book *Diamond Fever* is essential to any account of the early diamond discoveries and her generosity in lending me unpublished material and books that are not easily obtainable provided answers to many of my problems. I am equally grateful to Mr G. Hawthorne, of Kimberley, for allowing me to consult his father's unpublished typescript, *Digging for Diamonds: Kimberley and Its*

Story, which contains much useful information about the later years. An additional word of thanks is due to Mr Pat Sydie, of Kimberley, whose efficiency and skill helped to provide copies of most of the photographs in the book.

I have received assistance from several public institutions, but must single out the Kimberley Public Library for special mention. I am most grateful to the City Librarian, Mrs F. van Niekerk, for allowing me access to the Library's collection of Kimberley documents and I particularly appreciate the expert advice and co-operation which I received from Mrs Muriel Macey. My sincere thanks go also to the staffs of the McGregor Museum, Kimberley, the South African Library, Cape Town, and the Cape Archives.

To acknowledge sources of illustrations reproduced, the following abbreviations have been used in parentheses after illustration captions:

C   Cape Archives
J   Jagger Library, University of Cape Town
K   Kimberley Public Library
M   McGregor Memorial Museum, Kimberley
S   South African Library

For their interest in a variety of ways – advice, additional information and the loan of books – I am most grateful to: Mrs C.H. Farrer, Miss F. Barbour, Miss O. McIntyre, Mr A.S. Hall, Mr R. Elliott and Mr H.A. Morris of Kimberley; Miss N. Henshilwood of Kommetjie; Mr P. Pitchford of Kirkwood; Mr A. Porter and Mr B. Watkins of Port Elizabeth.

I would also like to record a very special word of thanks to Mr André Bothner for his unfailing interest and encouragement, which have been of inestimable value.

I owe a lasting debt of gratitude to Mr Theo Aronson, whose patient advice, assistance and constructive criticism have aided me every step of the way.

Finally I would like to thank Miss Winifred Currey for permission to quote from the unpublished autobiography of J.B. Currey, and the Van Riebeeck Society of Cape Town for allowing me to quote from *Selections from the Correspondence of J.X. Merriman.*

PART ONE: DISCOVERY

Colesberg Kopje in 1871. An artist's impression of the activity at New Rush, shortly after the discovery of the mine. (K)

The First Finds

It was an extraordinary landscape. Lying at the geographical heart of what was to become the Republic of South Africa, it was as spacious an area as one could imagine. Nothing, not even the coming together of those two great rivers – the Orange and the Vaal – seemed able to disturb the tranquillity of its appearance. Only on the banks of these slow and muddy rivers was there a fringing of green; for the rest, the plains stretched away almost unbroken to the heat-hazed horizon. The earth was grey, stony, cindery, carpeted in long silvery grass and dotted with thousands upon thousands of umbrella-shaped thorn trees. There was something almost park-like about it. As though to make up for the serenity of the land, the skies were dramatic: sometimes untrammelled blue, sometimes piled with great clouds, sometimes a-fire with sunsets. When it rained, the normally dry watercourses became raging torrents; when it blew, the dust was choking; when, as happened for most days of the year, the sun shone, it was like an oven. In more ways than one could it be described as a no-man's-land; lying between the Great Karoo to the south, the undulating grasslands to the north-east and the Kalahari desert to the north-west.

Yet it was not uninhabited. It might be arid but it could sustain life. There were the Koranas, smeared with grease and hung with hide mantles; there were the ochre-skinned Hottentots; and there were small, naked Bushmen. More recently had come the accurately named Bastards, in whose veins flowed the blood of white adventurers, Hottentots and Bushmen. With their horses and their guns and even their wagons, bands of Bastards had joined the other tribesmen roaming the face of this harsh countryside. Together they made up a nomadic, independent, haphazard society, each group following its own chief. Even the occasional passing white men – travellers, traders and hunters – were hardly better organised.

Order, of a sort, was instigated in the early years of the nineteenth century. The London Missionary Society arrived on the scene. Uneasy about the nomadic habits of the Bastards, the missionaries urged them to settle down. Settle down they did. A spring, named Klaarwater, was chosen as their headquarters. Having altered what they considered to be the tribesmen's unfortunate way of life, the London Missionary Society, in the person of the Reverend John Campbell, now decided to change their even more unfortunate name. With a wave of an ecclesiastical pen, the Bastards became the Griquas. Klaarwater became Griquatown and, in the fullness of time, their territory became Griqualand West.

This well-meant reorganisation did not last long. Old habits dying hard, the Griqua restlessness soon reasserted itself. The tribesmen reverted to their wandering ways, they resumed their raiding expeditions, they split into factions. Ill-defined limits of both territory and authority were assumed and gradually the region developed into an arena for conflicting aims, claims and ambitions.

To complicate things still further came the Boers – farmers trekking from the Cape Colony in the south. Splashing across the sluggish waters of the Orange River, they settled in the grassy plains to the east and north-east of the Griqua lands; some fanned out and established isolated farms in the Griqua territory itself. From being a no-man's-land, the region developed into an area in which only too many people seemed to have an interest.

For all that, it remained an inhospitable landscape, desolate and lonely. One could ride for days without seeing a soul. By the 1830s, the nearest white settlement, lying almost two hundred miles south-east of Griquatown, was Colesberg. And that was no more than a village. Situated eighteen miles south of the Orange River, Colesberg had been founded on the abandoned station of the ubiquitous London Missionary Society. Colesberg was a trim, typically Karoo village. A long main street, bordered by one-storied, flat-faced houses, led up to the pivot of most South African dorps – the Dutch Reformed Church. For an outpost of civilisation, it looked singularly unexciting.

But an outpost Colesberg undoubtedly was. It remained so for some twenty years: there was no other centre of human activity between it and Griquatown. Not until 1853 did the scattered white farmers farther down the Orange River – half-way to Griquatown – decide to form a settlement of their own. Their intention was to establish a church and to build a village which would provide them with stores and the amenities of civilised life. They approached the presbytery of the Dutch Reformed Church at Graaff-Reinet for permission to form a congregation. Permission granted, they founded their village on the farm of Duvenaarsfontein the following year. The farm had been bought from a local Boer, Siewert Christiaan Wiid, for £1,125, and the new settlement was named after the acting secretary of the Cape Colonial government, Major William Hope.

Hopetown. It seemed an incongruous choice of name for this forlorn village, situated in such an unpromising stretch of land. Only the nearby Orange River relieved the miles of parched, inauspicious-looking countryside by which it was surrounded. Yet, by a bizarre turn of events, the name of the new settlement was to be amply justified. For Hopetown – or rather the district of which it was the centre – was destined to bring hope, not only to the Griqua wilderness, but to the whole of South Africa.

(2)

The establishment of Hopetown appears to have roused a flicker of interest in Cape Town. In 1859, five years after the founding of the village, the Cape authorities sent a Government surveyor, W.F.J. von Ludwig (eldest son of a well-known Cape Town personality, Baron von Ludwig) to survey the Crown Lands between Hopetown and the junction of the Vaal and Orange rivers. As a result of this survey, a number of farms along the Orange River came up for sale during the next couple of years. One of these farms, De Kalk, was sold to the same Siewert Christiaan Wiid who had once owned the farm on which Hopetown had been built. Wiid, who appears to have been living at De Kalk when it was surveyed, purchased the farm jointly with his stepson, Schalk Jacobus van Niekerk. The subdivision of the farm between step-father and -son was purely a personal arrangement: an arrangement that was to last only a few years.

Schalk van Niekerk, Wiid's stepson, was a lean-faced, intense-looking man, then in his early thirties. Not much is known about him but there is reason to suspect that he was not cut out for the hand-to-mouth existence of a struggling farmer; his mind was too often on other things. It is said that, when Von Ludwig was surveying the farms, he not only spent his Sundays with Van Niekerk but actually stayed for several months at De Kalk while finalising his map. The friendship had a profound effect on the young farmer. For, besides being a professional surveyor, Von Ludwig was a keen amateur mineralogist and his survey had led him to think that the country around De Kalk was diamondiferous. He told Van Niekerk this. He did more. When he eventually left the area, he gave his friend a book on precious stones and told him to 'keep his eyes open'.

Unlikely as Von Ludwig's theory might have seemed, it was not entirely original. Other people are known to have shown an active interest in the 'pretty pebbles' found in the Vaal and Orange River area. There were even rumours that a few diamonds had been discovered there. One story has it that there existed an ancient mission map of the Orange River region with 'here be diamonds' scrawled across it. However that may be, Van Niekerk undoubtedly took his friend's advice seriously. He soon became known as a collector of *'mooi klippe'*.

But, although his pebble collection grew, his fortunes seem to have declined. By 1866 he had decided to sell his portion of De Kalk. Among the notices of farms for sale in August of that year, there appeared one putting Schalk van Niekerk's property up for auction. As it happened, an auction was not required for De Kalk. A prospective buyer was found for it close at hand. Living on the farm, close to the boundary separating Van Niekerk's portion of De Kalk from that of his stepfather, was a Boer family named Jacobs. This family – father, mother and five children – were housed in a small, two-roomed, thatch-roofed cottage typical of the district. But their simple way of life was deceptive. By 1866 Daniel Jacobs, the father, was by no means the impoverished *bywoner* he was later made out to be. He was rich enough to offer £1,125 – the price Wiid had received for the entire Hopetown site – for Van Niekerk's portion of De Kalk. Van Niekerk accepted and a verbal agreement on these terms was reached in November 1866.

It may have been in connection with the proposed sale that Van Niekerk paid what was to prove an important visit to the Jacobs family. Calling at the cottage, probably in December 1866, he noticed the children playing the familiar game of 'klip-klip' (five stones) with an assortment of pebbles. As avid a collector as ever, he was quick to spot that one of the stones was somewhat unusual. On examining it he became even more interested. Whether it was a diamond or not, it was certainly different from any in his collection. He offered to buy it, but Mrs Jacobs laughed at the idea. She said it was just a stone picked up in the veld. One of the children – precisely which one is uncertain – had, it seems, found it in 'a hollow dug by a Bushman'. If Van Niekerk wanted the stone he was welcome to it, said Mrs Jacobs.

Despite his undoubted interest, Van Niekerk did nothing more about the stone until a couple of months later. Then, in March 1867, he showed it to a passing trader, John O'Reilly, who had stopped at De Kalk on his way south to Hopetown and Colesberg. O'Reilly was every bit as intrigued as Van Niekerk himself. In fact, he was later to claim (in one of his many contradictory statements) that he immediately recognised the stone as a diamond, although he had never seen a rough diamond in his life. Be that as it may, O'Reilly agreed to take the stone to Hopetown 'to find out what it really was'.

The storekeepers of Hopetown were far from helpful. Indeed, so sceptical were they that one of them bet O'Reilly 'a dozen of beer' that the stone was not a diamond. In a billiard room that evening, O'Reilly was chaffed unmercifully; everyone was convulsed at the idea of his finding a diamond. They laughed so much that at one stage, according to the resident magistrate, the infuriated O'Reilly was on the point of throwing the stone away.

But he did not throw it away. He took it with him to Colesberg. Here there was more laughing, more ragging. Not until he showed the stone to the Acting Civil Commissioner, Lorenzo Boyes, did anyone take O'Reilly seriously. Even the interested Boyes was somewhat dubious. He consulted a local chemist, who immediately topped the Hopetown merchant's bet of 'a dozen of beer' by offering to buy Lorenzo Boyes a new hat if the stone proved to be anything but a topaz. To settle the matter, it was decided to send the stone to the nearest geologist: Dr William Guybon Atherstone, in Grahamstown.

In many ways, Dr Atherstone was a remarkable man. Besides being the first surgeon outside Europe and America to perform an operation under anaesthetics (he amputated a leg with the use of ether in 1847), he was a keen naturalist and one of South Africa's pioneer geologists. His survey of copper discoveries in Namaqualand and the geology of the Uitenhage district had already won him considerable renown, and he had been instrumental in exposing at least one geological hoax.

Dr Atherstone was sitting in the garden of his Grahamstown house when the postman handed him the letter from Lorenzo Boyes. On opening the gummed envelope – which was neither registered nor sealed – he subconsciously noticed something small fall onto the lawn. Only when he had read the covering note did he realise what it was that had dropped. He immediately called his daughter and there was a wild scrabble in the grass until they found, what looked like, 'a dull, rounded, apparently water-worn river stone'. Experienced as he was, Atherstone had never seen a diamond in its rough state, and, unlike John

O'Reilly, he did not recognise its value immediately. Instead, he subjected it to several tests – such as taking its specific gravity and examining it by polarised light – until he was fairly certain that it was a diamond. Then he rushed to the house next door and showed the stone to his friend, Dr James Ricards, the local Catholic priest. Once Father Ricards had, with a fine sense of occasion, cut his initials and the date on one of the panes of glass in the window of his study, all doubts vanished. At a dinner in the Drostdy at Grahamstown that evening, the discovery was publicly announced and South Africa's first diamond was included among the toasts.

Atherstone lost no time in reporting to Lorenzo Boyes. The stone, he said, had ruined every jeweller's file in Grahamstown; it was a veritable diamond, weighing 21¼ carats. 'Where that came from,' he declared, 'there are lots more.'

Within hours of Boyes receiving this report, the news had leaked out and Colesberg was agog. Now it was John O'Reilly's turn to laugh. However, there were still some who were cynical. Reporting Dr Atherstone's confirmation in the *Colesberg Advertiser* the following day, the wary editor had distinct reservations. But even he felt the need to cover himself.

'Stranger things', he admitted, 'have come to pass in the world than the Discovery of Diamonds in South Africa.'

(3)

When Lorenzo Boyes sent the stone to Grahamstown, he asked for it to be returned to him. Dr Atherstone, however, held on to it. Recognising the stone's importance to the Cape, he asked Boyes if he could send it to the Colonial Secretary, Richard Southey, in Cape Town. That same day Atherstone wrote to Richard Southey and, after discussing other matters, mentioned, almost casually, that he had been sent a diamond picked up in the Hopetown district. The stone, he said, was 20 carats, and worth, in its present state, £800. He felt it was a pity that it could not be displayed on the Cape Colony's stand at the *Exposition Universelle,* which had just opened at Paris.

Southey first replied by wire, asking for the stone to be sent to Cape Town. He then wrote to Atherstone and, after dealing with the doctor's other queries, referred to the diamond. The best thing, he explained, would be for the stone to be sent to London and then, if it turned out to be genuine, it could be forwarded for exhibition in Paris. His tone, like Atherstone's, was remarkably casual. This off-handed attitude was, in fact, to characterise official reaction to diamond discoveries for a long time.

For all that, as soon as the stone reached Cape Town, Richard Southey consulted several people competent to judge its worth – including M. Ernest Héritte, the French Consul, and Louis Hond, an experienced diamond polisher. Everyone agreed that it was indeed a diamond: so confident was Louis Hond that he offered to buy the stone, there and then, for £400. But Southey decided to stick to his original plan. The stone was put into a Government despatch bag and, on 19 April, it was sent to London on board the s.s. *Celt.*

So long did it take to receive a reply by sea from Britain, that almost three months passed before the Cape authorities heard anything more about the stone. Then, on 12 July, Richard Southey had a letter from Penrose Julyan, the Crown Agent in London. All the earlier reports were confirmed. Julyan had sent the stone to Garrards, the well-known jewellers of the Haymarket, where it had been pronounced a diamond worth £500.

This, one would have thought, should have convinced even the most hardened sceptics. Garrards, who handled the Crown Jewels, were certainly competent to recognise a diamond when they saw one; their valuation could not be questioned. But, instead of dispelling old suspicions, the jeweller's confirmation only aroused new ones. Now it was not the stone, but its unlikely source, that was doubted. Nobody would believe that the impoverished Cape could produce such riches.

John Blades Currey, the man responsible for the Cape stand at the *Exposition Universelle*, discovered this all too quickly. When he tried to whip up some publicity for the stone in London, he met with unexpected opposition. The *London Illustrated News* refused to publish a picture of the 'Cape diamond' and Garrards washed their hands of it, saying that they would not be interested in the discovery until sufficient diamonds had been found to affect the market. Sir Roderick Murchison, of the Museum of Practical Geology, went even further. In an interview with Currey, Murchison frankly pooh-poohed the idea of diamonds being found at the Cape: he was willing, he said, to stake his professional reputation on there not being a matrix of diamonds in South Africa.

There was very little more that the bewildered Currey could do. But he did what he could. He had a replica made of the stone and sent it to the Paris Exhibition. Unfortunately, it arrived too late to make any real impact. It was a strange launching for a diamond that was to be known as the 'Eureka'.

(4)

Every bit as strange was the continuing indifference of the Cape authorities. For, by the time Garrard's confirmation was received, there was additional reason for them to take the discovery seriously. At the beginning of June another diamond had been found by John O'Reilly. It gave substance to what, until then, had appeared to be an unexplainable fluke.

After the finding of the first diamond, several stones had been picked up by farmers in the Hopetown district, but they had all proved to be worthless. For the most part, they were nothing more than chips of glittering quartz, in which the stony region abounded. There was, however, no mistaking the pebble which O'Reilly had obtained from a farmer named Duvenhage. It had been vouched for by none other than Louis Hond, the diamond polisher who had identified the first stone. At the end of April, shortly after the first diamond had been shipped to London, Hond had hurried to Hopetown and set himself up as the only person in the district qualified to recognise and value a diamond. He had no hesitation in certifying that O'Reilly's second discovery was a small diamond of the first water, weighing 9 carats.

On the day he received this second diamond, Richard Southey confirmed rumours of its discovery by making a short announcement in the Cape Parliament. The stone, he told the House, was smaller than the first one, but of much better quality; he estimated its value at £200. The announcement was greeted by cheers. But the flutter of excitement was shortlived. There were more serious matters on hand. The House was due to go into Committee on Estimates; there was the question of encouraging the cultivation of cotton and silk; the sale and leasing of Crown lands had to be discussed. Why should anyone bother unduly with the unlikely happenings in the barren wastes beyond the Orange River? How many members had seen, let alone interested themselves in, those heat-flattened lands? It all seemed too remote from reality.

Yet reality, in a particularly pressing form, should have aroused more than a passing cheer. The promise of riches, however hazy, was not something that could be dismissed lightly. For the Cape was far from prosperous. With few viable industries and a largely rural population, dependent for the most part on agriculture and stock farming, South Africa was ill-equipped to withstand the economic vagaries of the 1860s. Nowhere was this more apparent than in the Cape Colony. By the middle of the decade, a series of disasters – recession in Britain, a crippling drought and a serious financial crisis – had severely shaken the Cape's economy. If things were allowed to drift, there seemed precious little hope of reversing the downward trend. Indeed, with the prospect of the opening of the Suez Canal threatening to deprive farmers and merchants of their revictualling trade with ships travelling between Europe and the East, the immediate future looked far from promising. It would require a radical solution to pull the Cape out of the financial doldrums.

Cape politicians were, of course, fully aware of all this. It accounted for their interest in, among other things, the possibility of cultivating cotton and silk. In the months ahead other schemes for promoting industry were to be suggested and Government officials were to seize upon the merest rumours of copper, lead and silver discoveries with great enthusiasm. When, at the beginning of 1868, news was received that gold had been found in the Tati region of Bechuanaland (Botswana), all Cape Town marvelled. Why the early diamond finds did not cause more of a furore is something of a puzzle.

Perhaps it was the very nature of the discoveries that made men suspicious. Unlike the rumoured metal deposits – such as gold, silver, lead and copper – diamonds, picked up singly in an isolated area, had to be taken almost entirely on trust. The finding of a few stones in the veld could mean anything or nothing: there was always the possibility that the Hopetown discoveries were part of an elaborate hoax. Sir Roderick Murchison had hinted as much; and, later, it was to be openly claimed that the stones had been deliberately planted in the desolate region in the hopes of attracting immigrants and improving land values. Such thoughts may already have occurred to the Cape politicians; unexplained diamonds can have an inhibiting effect on cautious men.

Some, however, were less cautious than others. One of the bolder spirits was none other than the Governor of the Cape, Sir Philip Wodehouse. Although

Wodehouse was apparently reluctant to acknowledge the significance of the diamond finds, he was quick to recognise their value. Hardly had the second stone arrived in Cape Town than the Governor made a personal bid for it; and, as soon as Garrard's verification of the first diamond was received, he extended his offer to cover both stones. This offer was accepted by John O'Reilly, and Wodehouse eventually acquired the two diamonds, paying £500 for the first and £200 for the second.

That he might be the dupe of unscrupulous land speculators, seems not to have worried Wodehouse at all. Hoax or no hoax, His Excellency let it be known that he was in the market for any diamonds that came his way.

Not many did, in fact. The next two diamonds forwarded to Richard Southey by the Civil Commissioner of Hopetown – in July and August 1867 – proved to be of too inferior quality to interest the Governor. Another diamond, found in October, was snapped up by a Hopetown merchant for £30. Not until the beginning of the following year was Wodehouse able to add a third stone to his collection, when he succeeded in buying a beautiful three and five-sixths carat diamond for £250.

These, however, were merely the finds that were recorded. There can be little doubt that other diamonds had been picked up in the Hopetown district at this period and disposed of privately. In November 1867, for instance, John O'Reilly arrived in Cape Town with two diamonds that did not pass through official channels. That a certain amount of secrecy existed about some finds is not surprising. The Cape Government had a clause in land titles which reserved mineral rights to the Crown and, although it was announced – after the finding of the second diamond – that no action would be taken against prospectors for the time being, the very fact that there was such a clause tended to make finders wary. This may well explain why there was no immediate large-scale rush to the Hopetown district.

No one was more incensed by the general apathy than Hopetown's Civil Commissioner, William Chalmers. When, some three years earlier, he had been appointed to his post, Chalmers had despaired. He had felt then that he was being sent into exile. Hopetown, he complained, was the 'least known, most insignificant, and the most outlandish and expensive District in the Colony'. Now that the region was showing unexpected promise, the *insouciance* of officialdom turned his despair into something like anger. He was forever urging his superiors to action.

'The reason why (diamonds) are not found in greater abundance', he lamented to Southey in March 1868, 'is that no systematic search is made for them. People will not leave their business to look for surface Diamonds, for one may look a long time and not find any. I am certain that if a proper search were made, or rather if mining were carried on, by persons who understand the work a great many Diamonds would have been found. Those that have been found have been picked up by the merest chance. I should have thought that sufficient Diamonds had been found to convince people to form a company and make a proper search. Surface Diamonds, wherever Diamonds are found, are a scarce article. We all know they are principally found by mining. . . . The Colony complains about hard times; but it deserves to be hard up when it quietly hears of the discovery of the richest of all gems in one of its Districts, and takes no steps whatever to open up the vast wealth which these gems would produce. I do not think any other colony would have treated the matter with such carelessness and cool indifference.'

But it was no use. A full year had passed since the discovery of the first diamond, and Chalmers was almost a lone voice crying in the Hopetown wilderness. His complaints were echoed, with less urgency, by Lorenzo Boyes in Colesberg. Twice Boyes had set off on private prospecting expeditions that had proved fruitless. On each occasion he had hoped that Dr Atherstone would join him, but the doctor had been unable to leave his practice in Grahamstown and, having only a scanty knowledge of geology, Boyes had returned empty-handed. What was needed, both Chalmers and Boyes agreed, was an expert who could assess the region's mineral potential. Their pleas, despite Sir Philip Wodehouse's personal interest in the recent discoveries, went more or less unheeded in Cape Town.

A mineralogist did, however, arrive at Hopetown a few months later. This was James R. Gregory of London who toured the Orange and Vaal River regions, in some secrecy, between June and August 1868. Gregory had been sent to the Cape by a Hatton Garden diamond merchant named Harry Emanuel, who, it is thought, became interested in the South African discoveries after receiving some of the unrecorded diamonds that had found their way to Europe. Precisely why Emanuel employed Gregory to investigate the Cape discoveries is something of a mystery.

Certainly Gregory was not the type of expert that William Chalmers had been hoping for. Within hours of arriving at Hopetown, Gregory called upon Chalmers and blandly informed him that he did not believe that diamonds had been found there and that there were no indications that the region was diamondiferous. If any diamonds had been found in the Hopetown area, he said, they must have been carried there by ostriches. Chalmers was flabbergasted. How could Gregory be so free with such opinions on so little evidence? He had not even bothered to enquire where the diamonds had been picked up befoie reaching his staggering conclusions. 'My suspicions', reported the furious Chalmers, 'were at once aroused about him. . . . I felt perfectly convinced that he had been engaged by some person or company in England, which might be interested in diamonds from other parts, to come out here for no other purpose than to *cry down* the South African diamonds, in order to keep up the market prices of their own diamonds.'

Gregory, in turn, was to voice a few suspicions of his own. He it was who publicly announced that, if the stones had not been dropped by migrant ostriches, they had been deliberately planted near poverty-stricken Hopetown by chancy land speculators hoping to turn a quick penny. Even after exploring the Vaal and Orange rivers, he stuck to his original opinion that the region was not diamondiferous.

'I made a very lengthy examination of the districts where diamonds are said to be found,' he reported in the *Geological Magazine* on his return to England, 'but saw no indication that would suggest the finding of diamonds or diamond bearing deposits in any of these localities. The geological character of that part of the country renders it impossible, with the knowledge in our present possession of diamond bearing rocks, that any could have been discovered there.' Harry Emanuel, of course, backed his agent's findings up to the hilt.

The combined attack by Gregory and Emanuel produced a lively reaction in South Africa. Dr Atherstone, William Chalmers and John O'Reilly were among those who rushed into print to refute Gregory's accusations. In a long letter to the *Geological Magazine*, published in May 1869, Atherstone gave a detailed account of the finding of the first diamond. He traced its progress from the time it was found until it was bought by the Governor of the Cape. 'The parties concerned', he pointed out, 'were – a farmer's child, a Dutch Boer, Mr O'Reilly, Mr L. Boyes, a Government official, myself and Sir Philip Wodehouse. . . . Which of these parties is the fraudulent impostor, getting up a land-jobbing speculation?' Chalmers was equally scathing. Only Gregory, he claimed, would be foolish enough to suggest that a £500 diamond had been given the Jacobs children as a plaything. How could anyone be sure that the children would not lose it or tire of it and throw it away? John O'Reilly had his own ideas about Gregory and implied that the mineralogist was merely covering up the discoveries so that he could return to the Cape and fill his own pockets.

Heated as these recriminations were, they were soon to prove superfluous. For, while the controversy was at its height, an event occurred that was to bring all academic squabbles to an abrupt halt. In March 1869, Schalk van Niekerk arrived in Hopetown with a magnificent white diamond weighing 83½ carats. Soon to be known as 'The Star of South Africa', this diamond was to dispose of Gregory's insinuations far more effectively than any paper arguments. Not even the most sceptical mineralogist could claim that such an obviously valuable diamond was being bandied about by land speculators.

James Gregory's report to the *Geological Magazine* was soon discounted. His name, however, lived on. For a long time any misstatement or lie about diamonds was to be laughingly dismissed as a 'Gregory'.

(5)

The finding of 'The Star of South Africa' made everyone sit up. Newspapers throughout the Cape reported the discovery in their boldest type. In Hopetown, it was spoken of as South Africa's 'Koh-i-noor' and estimated to be worth £30,000. For once, there seemed little chance of this splendid diamond finding its way into Sir Philip Wodehouse's collection. No sooner had Schalk van Niekerk arrived in Hopetown than local merchants started to outbid each other in attempts to buy it. The following day, it was sold to the firm of Lilienfeld Brothers for £11,200. Schalk van Niekerk had not haggled for long over the price; he was, claimed a defeated bidder, a 'lazy man'.

Lazy or not, Van Niekerk had certainly made on the deal. He had obtained the diamond from a Griqua shepherd, named Swartboy, for 500 sheep, ten head of cattle and a horse. When, where and how Swartboy had found the stone was to be a matter of considerable controversy.

The stories told about the finding of 'The Star of South Africa' are as confusing as they are legion. As far as can be judged from the mass of conflicting evidence, however, it would seem that Swartboy picked up the stone on the northern side of the Orange River in November 1868. Suspecting that his find was valuable, he had immediately crossed the Orange lest the stone be claimed by Nicolaas Waterboer, the Griqua chief. He had then obtained work at a farm, Sandfontein, not far from Schalk van Niekerk's property, De Kalk. While working at Sandfontein, he is said to have found another, much smaller, diamond. For a while he kept both finds secret.

When eventually he decided to dispose of the larger stone, it was inevitable that he should think of Schalk van Niekerk. Since the discovery and sale of the first diamond, Van Niekerk's reputation as a collector of unusual stones had received a tremendous boost. His hobby, once considered eccentric, was now treated with respect, not only by his neighbours but throughout the territory. Swartboy therefore sent a friend of his to De Kalk to negotiate the sale. Immediately recognising the diamond's worth, Van Niekerk had offered to buy the stone for all the livestock he could muster. Swartboy accepted. The deal concluded, Van Niekerk hurried to Hopetown with the diamond.

Straightforward as it seems, this simple transaction was to lead to endless complications. The trouble started shortly after Van Niekerk had sold the stone to Lilienfelds; it came from an unexpected direction.

Towards the end of 1868, a group of professional and business men – Lorenzo Boyes among them – had defied the prevailing apathy and had formed a prospecting company, centred on Colesberg, known as the Diamond Metal and Mineral Association. One of the group's first moves had been to negotiate with the Griqua chief, Nicolaas Waterboer, for a concession to all the metal and mineral finds in the Griqua territory. The deed of concession was eventually signed on 30 December 1868; by it Waterboer was to receive a royalty of one-fifteenth of the gross revenue of the company. It was this Diamond Metal and Mineral Association that challenged Lilienfelds' right to 'The Star of South Africa'.

Although little was then known about Swartboy, rumours that he had found the diamond in Griqua territory were quick to spread. Lorenzo Boyes, for one, had no doubt about it. 'I am quite willing', he wrote to Southey on 2 April, 'to make an affidavit that I was told at the time, that the Man had come from and gone over again to Waterboer's Country, and I think the fact speaks for itself, all or nearly so, of the diamonds have with the exception of the first three or four been found ... in the Country over which we hold a Concession from Waterboer.' The fact that he was confusing Swartboy with a mysterious 'witch doctor' made no difference to Boyes's conviction. His partners agreed with him. They had, in fact, already taken legal action.

On 31 March, the Diamond Metal and Mineral Association applied to the Court at Colesberg for an interdict restraining the Lilienfeld Brothers from disposing of 'The Star of South Africa'. They had until the middle of May to establish the diamond's provenance. The first legal tussle over a South African diamond had begun.

During the next few weeks, Hopetown was caught up in a flurry of activity such as it had never known before. Agents of the Diamond Metal and Mineral Association rushed about trying to obtain affidavits from anyone to whom Swartboy had so much as mentioned his controversial find, while the equally energetic Lilienfeld brothers did their best to outwit their rivals. Poor Swartboy himself was kidnapped, in turn, by both sides and bullied into making contradictory statements: statements made all the more confusing by his deliberately mixing up the two diamonds he had found. By the time the case came before the Cape Supreme Court, on 19 May, over one hundred pages of affidavits had been submitted.

Three judges waded through the evidence and found in favour of the Lilienfelds. The affidavits collected by the Diamond Metal and Mineral Association were, they ruled, merely hearsay and it was perfectly obvious that Swartboy had been frightened into contradicting himself. Doubt was also expressed as to whether the concession, signed on 31 December, was in force when the diamond was found. The most interesting observation, however, came from the Chief Justice. Was there, he wanted to know, 'anything to show Waterboer's rights, provided the diamond was found across the Orange River?'

Mercifully no evidence was led on this aspect of the case. Had it been, there is no knowing how long it would have taken to answer such a ticklish question. The problem of defining the extent of the Griqua domains and the precise nature of Waterboer's authority was to cause endless headaches in the years ahead. It was never resolved to everyone's satisfaction.

The Lilienfeld brothers lost no time in making the most of their triumph. After exhibiting 'The Star of South Africa' at the Commercial Exchange in Cape Town, to help 'swell the funds of that very deserving institution, the Ladies Benevolent Society', they shipped the diamond to England on the ever-handy s.s. *Celt*. In England it was eventually sold, cut and polished, to the Earl of Dudley for £30,000. Over a hundred years were to pass before it again came onto the market. Then, on 2 May 1974, it was sold at a quiet auction in Geneva to an unknown buyer for the equivalent of £225,300. Swartboy had, indeed, made a staggering discovery.

His discovery put an end to the doubts about South Africa's mineral potential. The scientists had been confounded, the fortune hunters moved in. In a steady stream men began to trek across the arid wastes north of the Orange River. For a while they concentrated on the Hopetown district; but soon, when prospecting in this area proved disappointing, they drifted farther north to join the handful of speculators already at work along the Vaal River.

Even the most sceptical had to admit that Hopetown had lived up to its name. 'I can no longer', confessed the bewildered Harry Emanuel to Richard Southey, 'have any doubt of the fact of Diamonds being found in your Colony.'

2

The River Diggings

South Africa's first diamond rush was under way. But to call it a 'rush' is misleading. Only in a strictly technical sense could the increased activity along the Vaal River be described in such hectic terms. For all its exciting overtones, the search for diamonds, even after the discovery of 'The Star of South Africa', was a slow, laborious, often heartbreaking, business.

Continuing rumours of new finds did, it is true, lure more and more men to the river region. In the Orange Free State, the Cape and Natal, tradesmen and farmers, lawyers and doctors, civil servants, army officers and shop assistants loaded up ox-wagons or set off on foot to prospect for diamonds. But they did not rush; it was impossible to rush. As their heavy wagons creaked across the trackless, heat-hazed plains – often overtaken by a lone rider, or a bold walker, shouldering a shovel and a billy-can – it required tremendous optimism to keep up their spirits, let alone maintain any semblance of haste. The farther they journeyed, the more cautious they became. Visions of glittering, diamond-strewn, river beds tended to evaporate in the sweltering wilderness; stories of fabulous finds were less frequent, more improbable. The barren Griqua territory bore little resemblance to the legendary land of Sinbad.

South Africans led the way, but they were soon joined by others. Enterprising seamen deserted their ships in the Cape and Natal harbours and joined the fortune hunters; more experienced men from Europe and the goldfields of Australia and America booked passages on ships sailing to South Africa. Prospectors from all over the world began to arrive at the Cape: the purposeful, the hopeful and the adventurous fell into line and trekked across the stony veld to scratch for luck in the mud and gravel of the river beds.

Hard-up foreigners, unused to South African travel, often found themselves at a distinct disadvantage. It required a well-stocked wagon to complete the long journey up-country in anything like comfort. Those able to shoot the occasional bird or buck could at least live off the land, but the rest had to rely on what they could carry to survive the long stretches of semi-desert. Halting-places – thin-flowing streams and isolated farms – were few and far between; those that existed soon became recognised landmarks.

At the farms, the parched, dust-begrimed traveller was nearly always sure of a warm welcome from the hospitable Boers. Poverty-stricken as most of them were, these lonely farmers rarely turned a stranger away. Their houses were often little more than small clay-plastered stone huts, scantily furnished, carpeted with animal skins and built near a stream or a natural water reservoir – known as a 'pan' – with few comforts and no luxuries. Apart from meat, water and, sometimes, milk, they could offer visitors few provisions; but, what they had, they were willing to share. Guests would be fed, bedded down for the night with the family, and sent on their way with strips of biltong (dried meat) at little or no charge. In the rainy season those travelling in mule carts or ox-wagons would be allowed to water their beasts at the 'pan'. Bleak as it was, such hospitality was eagerly sought by men slogging their way to the distant river regions.

Two such farms, Bultfontein and Dorstfontein, were acknowledged stopping-places for travellers – particularly those from the Orange Free State – even before the sensation caused by the discovery of 'The Star of South Africa'. Situated to the north-west of Hopetown and some twenty-five miles south of the Vaal River, they were often visited by traders journeying to and from the north.

Both farms were typical of the district. Bultfontein consisted of 'a small mud cottage with two rooms, a hartebeeste (a little thatched outhouse) and a long upland flat sloping to a "pan" full of brack water' and was owned by Cornelis du Plooy – a somewhat querulous old man, with a deaf wife and a regrettable tendency to bicker with his neighbours. At nearby Dorstfontein lived Adriaan van Wyk and his wife, who were relative newcomers. The title to Dorstfontein had been granted to a certain Abraham Paulus du Toit in April 1860 and Du Toit had later sold the farm to Adriaan van Wyk, who built a small cottage close to a brackish 'pan' and named the place Dorstfontein. This new name, however, had not taken. To the locals the farm was known, and continued to be known, as 'Dutoitspan'.

If J.B. Robinson, one of the first men to prospect for diamonds at the Vaal, is to be believed, it was at Dutoitspan that the first diamonds in this area were found.

Joseph Benjamin Robinson was the son of a British settler who had come to South Africa in 1820. At the time of the diamond discoveries he was in his mid-twenties, having been born at Cradock in the Cape in 1840. A tall, hard-eyed, morose young man, he had left home a few years earlier and established himself as a trader at Bethulie in the Orange Free State. But his trading store, although originally described as a model of its kind, had not prospered. By the middle of the 1860s, Robinson was in a bad way financially – some say he was on the verge of bankruptcy. Not surprisingly, the news of the early diamond finds put him on the alert. On his trading expeditions across the Orange River, he kept his eyes open for likely looking stones and eventually, in July 1868, found his first diamond on the banks of a stream. This was one of the early diamond finds that was not officially recorded.

Having got off to a promising start, Robinson then began to search in earnest. But he did not search at the spot where he had found his diamond: instead he headed for the Vaal. Why he did this is not clear. He may have had doubts about prospectors' rights in the Orange River area or perhaps he had heard that tribesmen were already finding diamonds at the Vaal. In any case, it was to the Vaal he went. On his way there he camped for a night near

Dutoitspan.

In later years Robinson was to tell many stories about this overnight stop. 'It was a most marvellous thing how I struck oil at Dutoitspan.' he would say. 'I was told that an old lady had picked up some stones at the back of her house. I got up, mounted my horse (I had ten or twelve with me), took my gun and galloped over to this house. It was very early in the morning, and after a time this woman brought out two bottles of pebbles among which I found six or eight diamonds. I gave her four sovereigns for the lot, cash.' In another version, he claimed that there were no diamonds in the bottles but he found no fewer than fifteen among some white stones that Mrs van Wyk had wrapped in a piece of rag. Whatever the truth, he was insistent that he bought some diamonds found at Dutoitspan at the end of 1868 and that he held on to them for the rest of his life.

Even so, Robinson did not allow this remarkable find to detain him. Having made his purchase he went on to the Vaal, where, at the African village of Hebron, he bought a small two-carat diamond from a tribesman. He then moved to the opposite side of the river, pitched his tent, and organised parties of Africans to surface-search for diamonds. 'In six weeks,' he claimed, 'they had found 30 diamonds worth £10,000.' There was little doubt in Robinson's mind that the river was the place to pick up a fortune. He could afford to forget the happy accident at Dutoitspan.

It is doubtful whether the Van Wyks forgot it. Strangers willing to pay four sovereigns for a few stones picked up in their garden did not arrive at Dutoitspan every day. They must have continued looking for the *mooi klippe*; others appear to have joined them. After the sale of 'The Star of South Africa' the following March, more strangers passed Dutoitspan on their way to the Vaal, and the search at the farm intensified.

A few months later, probably in September 1869, diamonds were found at neighbouring Bultfontein. There was an immediate rush to the two farms.

Frederick Philipson Stow, a young Cape attorney, arrived at Bultfontein in October 1869 to find the place humming. Besides his own party, he reported, 'there were sixty or seventy others chiefly Boers with their families from the neighbourhood. These were crawling about like so many ants looking for gems on the surface of the ground on this and on the adjacent farm Dorstfontein afterwards called "Du Toits Pan".' Inexperienced as were these Boer families, they quickly learned to recognise a valuable stone. There is no record of the number of finds at the two farms at this time – the 'rush' in fact was soon to be forgotten – but there can be no doubt that diamonds were plentiful.

Another visitor to Dutoitspan that October was Fred Steytler, a government clerk from Hopetown, who had taken two weeks' leave to tour the Vaal region. On his return, he reported to Richard Southey that sixteen diamonds had been found at the farm the day before he arrived there and that no fewer than five had been discovered during his short, two-to-three-hour stop-over. His travelling companion, he said, had been lucky enough to pick up a 5¾ carat stone. At Dutoitspan, concluded Steytler, 'diamonds are found in abundance'.

With the entire neighbourhood on the alert, it was only to be expected that the search should widen. Other farmers began to scratch the stony soil surrounding their mud cottages; the Boer searchers began to fan out. There is good reason to think that other farms in the area were casually prospected in late 1869.

One such farm was Vooruitzigt, situated some two miles from Dutoitspan and owned by two brothers. The name of the brothers was De Beer.

(2)

When the Lilienfeld brothers had scampered about Hopetown trying to obtain affidavits to substantiate their claim to 'The Star of South Africa', they had been enthusiastically supported by Louis Hond, the former diamond polisher and the district's first diamond expert. The Lilienfelds and Hond knew when they were on to a good thing and were prepared to go to great lengths to prove it. Their triumph in securing 'The Star of South Africa', inspired them to branch out in another direction: they formed a land-speculating association. As a third partner in the enterprise they enlisted Henry Barlow Webb.

They were on the look-out for likely properties when stories of the finds at Dutoitspan and Bultfontein reached Hopetown. How they came to hear about the farms is not certain. Perhaps they were told of them by young Fred Steytler who arrived back at Hopetown, full of the exciting happenings in the Vaal region, at the beginning of November. However it came about, the partners were immediately interested. What better start could they have than the acquisition of two promising 'diamond farms'?

They lost no time in following up the reports they had received. On Sunday, 14 November 1869, Leopold Lilienfeld and some of his associates arrived at Bultfontein all set to negotiate a sale.

Unfortunately they arrived too late. Others, besides the Hopetown merchants, had recognised Bultfontein's potential. Only a few hours earlier, Thomas Lynch, a speculator from the Orange Free State, had inveigled Cornelis du Plooy, the owner of the farm, into selling the property to him for £2,000. Old Cornelis du Plooy, who had been eking out a miserable existence and, it is said, had been on the point of giving up 'farming and the ghost' before the diamond discoveries, no doubt thought he had done rather well for himself. What was this madness of scratching about for shiny stones compared with a firm promise of £2,000? He had had little hesitation in accepting Thomas Lynch's offer. The Hopetown group had, or so it seemed, been pipped at the post.

But the astute Lilienfeld was not one to be put off by an unconcluded sale. He knew his pious Boers and quickly spotted a loophole. The sale, he blandly informed Du Plooy, had been made on a Sunday and was therefore illegal: such business could not be conducted on the Lord's Day. If Du Plooy refused to go through with this ungodly transaction, said Lilienfeld, the Hopetown group would not only make him a valid offer of £2,000 but give him an indemnity against any damages that Thomas Lynch might claim. Faced with the wrath of both God and the law, the bewildered old Boer decided to play it safe. He cancelled his agreement with Thomas Lynch and, two days later, sold Bultfontein to Lilienfeld and his partners for £2,000.

At neighbouring Dutoitspan, Lilienfeld appears to have been unsuccessful. He did manage to obtain a ten-year lease on another (unspecified) farm in the district, but Adriaan van Wyk was not yet ready to sell. The speculators had to remain content with the purchase of Bultfontein, where for the time being they installed the pious Du Plooy as caretaker. Adriaan van Wyk continued to manage his own affairs at Dutoitspan: affairs which were soon to become extremely complicated.

News of the Lilienfelds' *coup* was not kindly received in Hopetown. Local merchants complained bitterly at having lost yet another valuable property. 'This is not a bad spec,' sulked one of them; 'the Jews have got ahead of us again.' The thwarted Thomas Lynch was even more incensed. He immediately took action. The following month he had the unfortunate Du Plooy arrested and sued him for £10,000. It did him little good. The case dragged on for months and when judgement was finally given, in August 1872, Lynch was merely awarded £500 costs. This did not prevent Du Plooy, in turn, from bringing an action against the Lilienfelds – who had not honoured their indemnity – in which he obtained judgement for £760 19s. 1d. and costs. From the very outset, diamond transactions and litigation seemed to go hand in hand.

So, for that matter, did diamond properties and trouble. This was something which the Hopetown Company (as it became known) quickly discovered.

Once in possession of Bultfontein, the company appear to have put one of the partners, Henry Barlow Webb, in charge of operations there. Webb – who later acquired Louis Hond's third share in the company – was undoubtedly the driving force behind the venture. He set a small party to work, surface-searching for diamonds, and left these men under the supervision of Du Plooy. It was not long before others got wind of what was happening and the searchers on the two farms were joined by a further influx of prospectors from the Vaal River. Then the high jinks began.

One of the newcomers was a diamond pioneer named William Alderson. Many years later he was to recall what happened when he and some friends arrived at the farms towards the end of 1869. It was a story which was to become all too familiar.

Alderson and his party had been working near Pniel, a German mission station on the Vaal, when they heard that diamonds were being found on the Van Wyk property. Immediately they downed tools, loaded their wagons, and trekked south. On reaching Dutoitspan they were met by two disgruntled Englishmen who told them that Van Wyk was allowing only Boers to search on his farm. At the same time they heard a rumour that ninety-two diamonds had just been found in a nearby furrow. This rumour, although later proved false, was sufficiently exciting to make Alderson's party defy Van Wyk's prohibition and rush to the furrow. Their mad scramble quickly brought Adriaan van Wyk, accompanied by a Field Cornet from the Orange Free State, storming onto the scene.

Van Wyk was furious. He warned the newcomers not to start digging and gave them an hour to inspan and clear off. The two Englishmen, who had been threatened earlier, needed no second telling. Alderson's party, they said, would be wise to pack up and leave. If they did not, they would be fired upon from the farm cottage. But Alderson was having none of it. Grabbing his pick and pegs, he ran towards a small hillock where he intended to stake out a claim. 'Who follows me?' he shouted. 'I think an Englishman has as much right to work as a Dutchman.'

He sounded more confident than he was. Every minute he expected the shooting to start. But nothing happened. Once he had run about fifty yards, the rest of his party joined him and, on reaching the top of the hillock, they began pegging out claims. They were watched by a crowd of open-mouthed Boers.

There were then, according to Alderson, some two hundred Boers working at Dutoitspan. Having been given permission to search, these Boers had apparently accepted Van Wyk's regulations and kept within set boundaries. The defiance of the newcomers now opened wider possibilities. 'Seeing that no shots were flying round', says Alderson, '(The Boers) rushed up with wild screams and marked out claims also.' This was too much for poor Van Wyk. Confronted with wholesale rebellion, he had no option but to give in gracefully. He let it be known that, if everyone would stop work, he would be willing to come to terms. The triumphant diggers literally swept him off his feet.

'He was immediately carried shoulder high to a wagon,' claims Alderson, 'and from that point of vantage he announced that he was by no means averse to Englishmen, and that we might all work on his place on payment of 15/- per claim per month. I acted as spokesman for the others; I told him I had been the first to rush the mine, and that I considered he would be well paid at 7/6 per claim. The Dutchmen unanimously supported the suggestions, and eventually the farmer agreed. We paid down our money, and he granted us "briefies" (written licences) in acknowledgement. This is the origin of what are known as "briefe claims". They constituted to all intents and purposes leases in perpetuity.'

In this case, however, 'perpetuity' was shortlived. After digging to a depth of five feet and finding nothing, Alderson and his party moved to Bultfontcin. Here they persuaded Cornelis du Plooy to grant them the same rights they had wrung from his neighbour. But they were given little time in which to prospect Bultfontein. Old Du Plooy, thoroughly unnerved by the upheaval, lost no time in sending for the new owners of the farm. A few days later Henry Barlow Webb drove up in a Cape cart grimly determined to put matters to rights.

Webb acted briskly. First he marched up to the farm cottage and slated his agent. 'We heard him roundly abusing Du Plooy for granting us permission to dig,' admitted Alderson. Then he started negotiating with the diggers. Two days later he presented them with a proposal. Seeing that they had found nothing, he said, he was willing to return their licence money if they would give an undertaking to leave the farm, never to return. The diggers accepted. 'We signed the undertaking in a book,' says ·Alderson, 'and left.' What Alderson does not mention is that Webb not only returned their licence money but paid them an additional 12*s*. 6*d*. for each licence. However, the first rush of Bultfontein and Dutoitspan was over.

The diggers had given up easily. There were several reasons for this: not the least being the difficulty they experienced in working the farms. It was now high summer, and the territory had barely recovered from a prolonged drought; the lack of water made it almost impossible to prospect away from the rivers. The chronic water shortage was, and continued to be, a major problem at the 'dry diggings'. Not only did the diggers require water for mining operations, but it was also needed for drinking – for themselves and their animals. With water and forage having to be transported to Bultfontein and Dutoitspan at great cost, few could afford to prospect for long at these land-locked farms.

And why should they sweat it out on the farms when the Vaal was a mere twenty-five miles away? In these late months of 1869, few diggers had faith in finding a diamond mine at Bultfontein or Dutoitspan. As far as they knew diamond deposits were linked in some way with the rivers and they regarded any finds away from the Vaal as flukes. Fred Steytler, in his report to Richard Southey, had more or less summed up the prevailing theory. 'The Vaal, there is no doubt,' he wrote, 'must some years since have overflowed its banks, brought down the gems, & deposited them all over the country in its vicinity. (Dutoitspan) may very likely have been the bed of a very large lake many years ago.'

There must have seemed little point in wasting time on freak deposits when the true source of riches was so close. As the hot summer months wore on, the slow-flowing Vaal, with its tree-shaded banks, became more and more of an enticement to the dust-caked diggers. At the river one could live and work in relative luxury: bathe, wash one's clothes, swim, fish and even hunt guinea-fowl and partridges in the surrounding bush. What is more, diamonds found near the river were regarded as far superior to those found at the farms; they were larger and of better quality, as well as being more plentiful. By the end of 1869 there were several recognised camps dotted along the banks of the Vaal. Soon there was to be little doubt in anyone's minds that the river diggings were not only more pleasant: they were decidedly more profitable.

Alderson is vague about when he and his friends finally abandoned Bultfontein and Dutoitspan. It was probably at the beginning of 1870. Their hurried departure seems, in fact, to coincide with the important discoveries made at the Vaal in the early months of that year. These discoveries were due, among other things, to an improved knowledge of working diamond claims.

While Alderson and others had been prospecting at the farms, a well-organised party of diggers had arrived at the Vaal. This party had been fitted out in Natal by an army officer, Major George Francis, who later claimed to be responsible for the first scientific search for diamonds in South Africa. Unable to get leave himself, Major Francis had sent six well-equipped men – including a Frenchman who knew something about diamonds – to explore the river. The recognised leader of the party was one of Francis's fellow officers, Paddy Rolleston.

After a false start, the men from Natal eventually reached Hebron (later renamed Windsorton) on the Vaal, where, in December 1869, they started mining by sinking a thirty-foot shaft. But it was not until 4 January 1870 that

The well-loved Mrs Catherine Jardine, hostess of the river diggings and later pro-
prietress of the Queen's Hotel, Kimberley. (K)

Erasmus Stephanus Jacobs in old age. As a young boy he is reputed to have
picked up South Africa's first known diamond, the 'Eureka'. (M)

Adriaan van Wyk and his wife. Van Wyk was the owner of the farm Dorstfontein,
later better known as Dutoitspan. (K)

they washed out their first, two-carat, diamond. Having no further luck, they soon moved along the river to join the diggers at Pniel, the German mission station. Here they struck it rich and continued to operate with great success. It is estimated that, between their first strike and June 1870, they sent something like £12,000 worth of diamonds to Major Francis in Natal.

The knowledgeable digging of the Natal party was quickly adopted by others and there was a significant increase in the number of diggers at both Pniel and Klipdrift on the opposite side of the river. News of the rush to these places soon spread.

This rush to the river – which started at the beginning of 1870 and gathered momentum throughout the year – was a decisive event in the history of the South African diamond fields. It transformed the prospecting and speculating activities of a few hundred optimists into a lucrative industry which attracted thousands to the Vaal. 'Butchers, bakers, sailors, tailors, lawyers, blacksmiths, masons, doctors, carpenters, clerks, gamblers, sextons, labourers, loafers – men of every pursuit and profession', it was reported, 'jumbled together . . . (and formed) a straggling procession to the Diamond Fields. Army officers begged furloughs to join the motley troop, schoolboys ran away from school, and women even of good families could not be held back from joining their husbands and brothers in the long wearisome journey to the banks of the Vaal.'

Almost overnight, towns throughout South Africa found themselves denuded of young men. '*These* diggings are all the rage now,' wrote a Transvaal resident in July 1870, 'and people are flocking to the banks of the Vaal from all parts of the old Colony and Natal. Potchefstroom is nearly deserted and will be quite, if the mania continues.' So drained was the Civil Service that the Colonial Secretary had his work cut out refusing requests for leave that flooded in from district officers in the Cape. 'Otherwise,' he explained, 'all would go.'

At Klipdrift and Pniel, the mass of tents and wagons cluttering both banks of the river linked by ferry boats which charged sixpence for the crossing gradually developed into sprawling canvas towns. Here and there amid the sea of canvas a few slightly more substantial buildings sprang up. On either side of the dusty main road at Klipdrift, rows of rickety wood and iron shacks served as shops, canteens, billiard rooms, eating-houses, diamond-buying offices and lawyers' rooms. Joel Myers opened the first corrugated-iron store and one of the early brick buildings was a small church which 'welcomed all comers to its Sunday services'. On the other side of the river, Mrs Jardine's hotel at Pniel, 'The Royal Arch' – 'a straggling chain of rooms, without windows but abundantly supplied with doors' – became a popular Sunday meeting-place. 'There were very few women in the camps,' remembered a digger. 'Men young and old called Mrs Jardine "Mother" and thought of her hotel as home.' At Pniel, also, the Standard Bank was to open its first branch; and both camps were to publish their own news sheets – the *Diamond Field* at Klipdrift, the *Diamond News* at Pniel – mostly filled with advertisements and in deadly opposition to each other. Civilisation, of a sort, had at last come to the diamond country.

For the time being, Bultfontein and Dutoitspan were left to a handful of

Boers who had resisted the rush to the river. These, and a party of Africans employed by the Hopetown Company, continued to scratch about in the sun-baked veld surrounding the forsaken, but not entirely forgotten, farms.

(3)

Many diggers were to look back on these early days at the river diggings as idyllic. The days were long, the work hard, supplies were uncertain and the climate veered to extremes; but it was an invigorating life, free from petty restraints, and brightened by the pleasant setting and the prospects of un-covering a fortune. Even the absence of proper medical aid and repeated onslaughts of 'camp fever' could not dampen the optimism in the newly established camps.

'We may challenge the world,' wrote a pioneer bravely, 'where a like number of people have gathered together, unaccustomed to such a rough and exposed life, to show so little sickness and so few deaths.' In his opinion, accidents and drink had proved more deadly than disease. 'Several cases of drowning have occurred on the Vaal,' he went on, 'some accidental, and many of drunkards, who, under the influence of alcohol, have sought this way of ending their days.'

That many of the newcomers were driven to despair, there can be no denying. Some, who had travelled thousands of miles to reach the diggings and were quickly discouraged by the back-breaking, often boring and unrewarding work, packed up and left, after a brief stay. The diamond boom, they reported, was a hoax; the fields would soon be played out; only fools would waste their time and money pursuing phantom fortunes on the Vaal. Others who listened to such stories did not even reach the river. One man is said to have walked all the way from Cape Town – over six hundred miles – and, after meeting some luckless diggers twenty miles from the diamond fields, promptly turned about and walked all the way back again. Success was as much a matter of faith as it was of endurance.

Luckily, the majority of diggers possessed both. They found it easier to believe in their own ability to win through than to be daunted by the mis-fortunes of others. Sunburnt, unshaven and roughly dressed – in a weird assortment of collarless, coloured and striped flannel shirts, corduroy trousers and rubber boots, riding-breeches and laced leggings, canvas suits and woollen stockings, wide-brimmed felt hats and pith helmets and, invariably, the essen-tial broad leather belt with pockets for diamonds and money – the hopeful diggers sweated away happily along the banks of the river. As one of them remarked, 'When digging for diamonds, no one has time to be dull or melan-choly.' Who knew what the next turn of the spade might reveal?

Not that diamonds cropped up all that casually. Far from it. Digging at the Vaal was a laborious business. Claims were dug in the small hills, or koppies, which lined the river and working close to the water made the washing of gravel relatively easy. The most difficult task was the removal of the iron-stone boulders which blocked many claims. Among these boulders was the gravel in which diamonds were found. Once the boulders were out of the way, the gravel – or 'stuff' as it was called – was loaded onto a cart and taken to the river to be sieved and washed.

Various sieving processes evolved but the most popular was the 'cradle', which held two or three sieves of graded mesh. 'While the stuff is being rocked in this cradle,' explained a visitor, 'one of the diggers pours buckets full of water into it. The gravel thus being thoroughly cleansed by this double process of sifting and washing, the larger stones in the top sieve are hastily glanced over, to see if perchance any *big* diamond be amongst them, and the other sieve or sieves are taken out, and the contents emptied on to the "sorting table". . . . At this table, the digger either sits or lies, according as it has legs or rests on the ground, and quickly sorts over the stuff with the aid of an iron or wooden scraper. . . . Diamonds, especially those of good quality, show out brilliantly, and can very seldom be missed on the sorting table; the larger gems, indeed, are often found in the sieve or even in the act of digging.' Invention of the most widely used sieving-cradle is attributed to Jerome Babe, an American digger, who became known as the 'only Babe to rock his own cradle'.

As a rule, work started at sunrise, after a gargantuan breakfast of steaks, chops or sausages fried over the camp fire, and, apart from a short break at midday to 'liquor up', went on until sunset. Occasionally, when a big find was made, all those in neighbouring claims would down tools and chair the lucky finder to the nearest canteen and be treated to a variety of splendidly named drinks: Pickaxes, Revivers, Shandygaffs, Nectars and, surprisingly enough, Cocktails. Otherwise most working diggers kept clear of the canteens until the evening, when they would join the inevitable groups of disheartened loafers who had spent the day in a drunken stupor, outswearing each other with stories of their bad luck. For those who could stand the pace, it was a simple, strenuous, but highly exhilarating existence.

Klipdrift and Pniel remained the chief centres, but other camps developed on both sides of the river: notably at Hebron on the northern bank, which became famous for, among other things, its amateur theatricals. There were constant new rushes which, in time, provided the Vaal with a variety of graphically designated landmarks – Gong Gong, Delport's Hope, Forlorn Hope, Poorman's Kopje, Sixpenny Rush, Moonlight Rush and many more. By the end of the year, diggers could be found working the Vaal and its tributaries in an area which stretched for a hundred or more miles. It has been said that the diamond yield from these camps eventually averaged £4,000 for every three hundred claims. Hardly surprising is it that so many diggers looked back fondly on life at the Vaal.

'The quietude of these hitherto solitary regions', wrote a pioneer of 1870, 'is now broken by the song of the happy digger as he goes forth in the morning to begin his day's labour among the huge boulders in his claim, where, throughout the day, the sound of pick and shovel is heard, or, perhaps, the shout of the lucky digger who has just succeeded in finding a diamond.'

Unfortunately, this blissful state of affairs was not to last long.

(4)

In South Africa the most harmless-seeming incident can spark off a full-scale political crisis: an event like the discovery of diamonds was therefore bound to have political repercussions. Not only was this inevitable but, considering the region in which diamonds were found, it appeared to be satanically ordained. Few spots on the South African map were more vulnerable to political pressure than was the Vaal River region.

To the east lay the Boer Republic of the Orange Free State; to the west were the ill-defined Griqua territories. Across the Vaal, to the north-east, lay another Boer Republic, the Transvaal; and to the north-west across the Vaal were the lands of the BaThlaping and Barolong tribes. It was like a jigsaw puzzle in which no pieces fitted precisely.

Attempts to make the pieces fit had not been wanting. For years there had been bickering over the fuzzily mapped boundaries and ill-defined spheres of authority. However, the discovery of diamonds had sharpened interest all round; the possibility of underground riches whetted the appetites of governments as well as individuals. The problem of deciding who in fact owned the diamond fields had become a matter of immediate importance; it was a problem as complicated as it was contentious.

There can be little doubt that the most impressive claim to the region was that put forward by the Boers of the Orange Free State. They maintained that the western limits of their republic had been established some twenty years earlier when their territory – then known as the Orange River Sovereignty – was being administered by the British. At that time the Vaal had been vaguely recognised as a natural boundary, and the lands east of the Vaal had been included in British definitions of the Orange River Sovereignty. The validity of the Vaal forming the western boundary of the Sovereignty had been further emphasised when the British made land grants to some farmers living east of the river.

In 1854 the British had abandoned the territory, and the Orange River Sovereignty had become the republic of the Orange Free State. Thus the Boers, not unreasonably, claimed to have inherited the boundaries and the land grants of the former Sovereignty. The new republican government continued to grant land to farmers living east of the Vaal and, in 1861, extended their claim to the territory when they purchased certain lands from Adam Kok, a Griqua chief: included in this purchase – or so it was argued – were the so-called Campbell Lands. These Campbell Lands lay to the west of, in other words across, the Vaal. As Klipdrift and other centres of the river diggings were situated in the Campbell Lands, the Orange Free State's claim to the diamond fields on both banks of the river appeared well founded.

But it was not as simple as that: not by any means. The Free State's claims were heatedly contested on all sides. The most prolonged and determined opposition had come from the Griqua chief, Nicolaas Waterboer – or, rather, from David Arnot, Waterboer's representative.

David Arnot was a handsome, astute and extremely able, Cape Coloured lawyer. The son of a Scots father and a coloured mother he was a convinced imperialist, dedicated to British expansion in Africa and, although he chose to deny it, passionately anti-Boer. From the time of his appointment as Waterboer's agent, he had devoted himself to frustrating Boer encroachments on Griqua territory. He regarded the westward drift of Free State farmers not only as a threat to Griqua rights in the region, but as a possible block to British expansion northwards. If, as he hoped, British influence was to spread from the Cape Colony into the heart of Africa, 'the road to the North' must be kept open.

As early as 1862, Arnot had formally requested the Cape authorities to recognise specific Griqua boundaries which lopped off the Free State's claim to a sizable portion of the territory on both sides of the river, including the Campbell Lands to the west. He followed this up by inducing British immigrants from the eastern Cape to settle in Griqua territory to the north of Hopetown (known as Albania) and thus form a 'wall of flesh' against further Boer encroachments.

Inevitably, the Orange Free State had refused to acknowledge Arnot's claims. There had been talk of submitting the dispute to Sir Philip Wodehouse, the Cape Governor and High Commissioner, for arbitration; but, although Wodehouse had been prepared to act as mediator, the argument had been so protracted that nothing had come of it. Now – with the discovery of diamonds intensifying the issue – Wodehouse was no longer available. At the beginning of 1870, the Cape Governor's term of office had ended and Lieutenant-General Charles Hay had been appointed to act for him until his successor, Sir Henry Barkly, arrived at the end of the year.

Wodehouse's departure, coming when it did, was unfortunate. Lieutenant-General Hay was politically inexperienced and the Cape Colonial Secretary, Richard Southey, was placed in a position of exceptional power. Southey, like Arnot, was an arch-imperialist. He also believed in British expansion, in promoting British commerce, and in the need to protect the Griquas against the covetous tendencies of the Boer republics. Arnot, in fact, could hardly have found a better ally: he had no difficulty in enlisting Richard Southey's support for his arguments.

These arguments were extremely involved. They referred back to treaties made years before the Orange River Sovereignty was established – treaties made between the Griquas and the Cape authorities, between rival Griqua factions, between the Griquas and the BaThlaping tribes. According to Arnot, these treaties had defined the Griqua boundaries and confirmed the authority of his client, Nicolaas Waterboer. The Boers, he maintained, were wrong in claiming that such agreements had been invalidated by subsequent events.

Arnot resolutely refused to allow that the Free State had 'inherited' accepted boundaries from the Orange River Sovereignty. Not only had Waterboer been ignored when the Sovereignty was proclaimed but, Arnot told Southey, 'the proclamation of British supremacy over *native territories* was simply of a jurisdictive effect and did not aim at their territorial acquisition'. How then could the Boers claim to have inherited the disputed land?

Johannes Nicolaas de Beer, owner of
Vooruitzigt, the farm on which the Old
De Beers and New Rush mines were
discovered. (K)

Olof J. Truter, the genial magistrate of
the Orange Free State at Pniel and the
dry diggings. (K)

Nikolaas Waterboer, the Griqua chief,
who was a central figure in the land dispute over the ownership of the diamond
fields. (K)

Arnot was equally emphatic on the question of those Campbell Lands, lying to the west of the river. Certain Griqua territory had indeed been sold to the Boers in 1861, by an agent employed by Adam Kok, but that agent had not had authority to sell the Campbell Lands. The disputed land west of the Vaal had formerly been occupied by Adam Kok's uncle, Cornelis – a subject of Waterboer's. Although Adam Kok had been acknowledged as his uncle's heir, this had not given him the right to dispose of public Griqua lands. By overriding Waterboer's authority the alleged sale of the Campbell Lands had, Arnot contended, been illegal.

Theoretically, therefore, both the Free State Boers and the Griquas had strong claims to the diamond diggings. How far these claims could be substantiated by valid documentary evidence was another matter. It was a matter to which both President Brand of the Free State and David Arnot, on behalf of Waterboer, began to give serious attention. Once the dispute developed in earnest, the arguments on both sides became more heated, more confused. Each tried desperately to back their case with written proof; each accused the other of forgery and chicanery.

But it was neither the Free State nor the Griquas who made the first tangible grab at the river diggings. It was the Boers of the Transvaal. As if things were not complicated enough, the Transvaal republic asserted – despite objections from local tribesmen – that its hazily defined borders stretched westward along the northern banks of the Vaal and took in part of the already disputed Campbell Lands. To prove this, the Transvaal government made a bold move. At the end of a session of the Transvaal Volksraad in June 1870, legislation was passed granting a diamond concession on the northern banks of the Vaal to three men – one of whom was H.B. Webb of the Hopetown Company – for twenty-one years. There was an immediate outcry from all concerned.

Nowhere was this outcry louder than at Klipdrift. When Henry Webb and one of his partners, J. Posno, arrived at the diggings to inform the diggers that they 'would be charged a tax of 10s. a month for the privilege of mining', they immediately ran into trouble. At a stormy meeting called by the locally elected diggers committee and attended by some 500 diggers, the two concessionaires were howled down. The jeering diggers refused to recognise the authority of the Transvaal republic and threatened to drag Webb and Posno 'through the river' if they did not drop their demands. This brought President Marthinus Pretorius of the Transvaal onto the scene. Arriving at Klipdrift shortly afterwards, the Transvaal President – his authority bolstered by a troop of armed burgers – attempted, somewhat ham-handedly, to proclaim the diggings as Transvaal territory. It was a grave mistake. His troops found themselves faced by a crowd of angry diggers, the Transvaal flag was snatched before it could be hoisted, shots rang out, and the President was forced into a hurried, if temporary, retreat.

It was obvious that, whoever owned the diamond fields, the diggers intended to remain in possession. Led by an ex-ablebodied-seaman, Stafford Parker, the miners of Klipdrift had formed their own committee, made their own rules, and had very definite ideas about rights and justice. If the Transvaal concessionaires showed up again, declared Parker, 'They would most certainly be "ducked" and put across the river.'

The next move came from President Brand of the Free State. Supported by President Pretorius of the Transvaal, Brand arranged to meet Nicolaas Waterboer and David Arnot to discuss the tortuous question of the Campbell Lands. The meeting was held at Nooitgedacht on the Vaal on 18 August 1870. As far as the Griquas were concerned it was a total failure. Waterboer and Arnot walked out in a huff, Brand and Pretorius settled their own differences and, a few days later, the Campbell Lands were formally proclaimed as Free State property.

To make good his claim, Brand beaconed off the appropriated territory and sent a magistrate to Pniel to uphold the authority of the Free State. The man chosen for this unenviable post was Olof Truter, a one-time policeman with experience on the Californian and Australian goldfields. Controversial as was his appointment, the new magistrate soon made himself popular with the diggers. Truter was to be remembered as 'a courteous gentleman', firm but fair, and well able to handle 'the rougher elements of the community'.

But, of course, not everyone was happy to see Olof Truter installed at Pniel. His appointment, and the Free State's seizure of the Campbell Lands, merely signalled a new round in the struggle for the diamond fields. David Arnot, who had returned to his farm near Hopetown after the Nooitgedacht meeting, now began to bombard Richard Southey with letters urging him to intervene on Waterboer's behalf. Most of the diggers, he argued, were British subjects who were now controlled by the high-handed Free State authorities. 'Their bumptiousness in their expression respecting the British Govt.', he told Southey on 1 September, 'is simply disgusting. I shall be glad if you will at once declare or get declared that territory under British Supremacy. There are already some 7 or 8000 people at the diggings. . . . The British Govt. must do something.' With somewhat suspect indignation, he protested that 'the immorality & gross life (notwithstanding newspaper reports to the contrary) is something frightful'.

Southey hardly needed persuading. He had already toyed with the idea of sending a representative to the Nooitgedacht meeting to safeguard the interests of British diggers. Arnot's request gave him a much better excuse for intervention. He declared himself 'strongly of opinion that Waterboer's only chance is to ask H.M. to take him & his country as British. . . . It would be very desirable that the diggers should at the same time express a desire for us to exercise jurisdiction over them; and if you can influence a move in that direction, you had better do so, and let there be no delay about it.' The Imperial Factor was preparing to step in.

Arnot was delighted. He assured Southey that Waterboer was willing to become a British subject and he had no doubt that the diggers would welcome British protection. While he was at the diggings, he claimed, he had seen dozens of Union Jacks waving from tents and tin shacks, but no republican flags; diggers had told him that they did not consider the Orange Free State or the Transvaal capable of governing them. 'In short,' he declared, 'they detest both republics.'

Encouraging as this was, Southey did not intend to rely entirely upon

Arnot's word or influence. He was resolved that the British should take over the diamond fields. To this end he embarked on a determined campaign: pressure was put on newspaper editors, petitions were solicited from colonial merchants, prominent citizens were urged to speak out in favour of British intervention. The campaign was undoubtedly helped by continuing unrest among the diggers. Reports of lawlessness and discontent at Klipdrift appeared regularly in the Cape newspapers and it must have been with a certain amount of relish that Southey heard that the diggers were threatening to set up their own independent republic.

By the end of October, Southey was ready to make his first move. It was announced that a Cape Town magistrate, John Campbell, had been appointed as Resident Magistrate for the diamond fields, at a salary of £1,000 a year, and would shortly be leaving for Klipdrift. 'I hope', Southey wrote to a friend, 'to be in a position to aid and support the diggers in their exertions.'

But the diggers could not wait for his help. By that time they had decided to take matters into their own hands. At a lively meeting at Klipdrift, on Friday 18 November, Stafford Parker was unanimously elected President of the Diggers' Mutual Protection Association – 'until Campbell (the magistrate) comes' – and the name of the camp was changed from Klipdrift to Parkerton.

At first nobody took either the change of name or the new President seriously. The idea of a diggers' republic was treated as a huge joke. 'Parker of the strong arm has taken possession,' wrote a newspaper correspondent, 'and he is surrounded by four lieutenants, faithful as saints, brave as soldiers, and in all things excellent. . . . I ask no questions. I look up to President Parker and his Council with admiration and awe. . . . It is certain that President Parker with as much agility and effectuality as the President of America can flourish his baton. President Grant is a tall man no doubt, but President Parker has the advantage of him in point of inches. All that Grant is to America, Parker is to these diggings. . . . We say *fiat justitia*, and date our letters Parkerton.'

But President Parker, a picaresque figure with magnificent whiskers and a taste for elegant clothes, had no intention of being laughed at. He was determined to bring a semblance of law and order to the diggings. This he had made quite clear on being elected. 'You must not lose sight', he said, 'that we have a Committee; we must not say put them in the river on the least provocation . . . if you have complaints to make come to me in the proper manner; don't ever come and say, put him in the river and all that.'

The new regime was nothing if not purposeful. President Parker ruled his republic with a firmness that doubtless surprised some of his more frivolous subjects. A butcher was placed in charge of discipline, and a bizarre set of punishments evolved: diamond thieves were flogged, prostitutes and drunks were put in stocks, card cheats were ducked in the river and pilferers placarded and paraded through the camp. Persistent offenders were expelled from the diggings, and for extreme cases there was the 'spread-eagle', the criminal being pegged out in the dust and left to the mercy of the sun and flies. Taxes were often collected at gun point.

Such measures were drastic but effective. 'In justice to Mr Parker and his counsellors,' wrote a later visitor, 'I shall declare that one whisper of cruelty, other than these eccentric punishments, never reached my ears. They did many foolish acts and perhaps committed some wrongs. It may not be well to ask closely which way their revenue all went. But their procedure answered the demands upon it. No criminal lost his life and no honest man felt terror.'

For all that, Parker was far from sure of himself. He was the leader of a faction rather than a community and, despite his show of firmness, he had grave doubts about ruling indefinitely. He, as much as anyone, was anxious for the new magistrate to arrive and for British authority to be imposed. Luckily he did not have long to wait.

John Campbell reached Pniel on 12 December 1870, and was rowed across the river the following day. On stepping ashore at Klipdrift (the name of Parkerton had not caught on) he was greeted by loud cheers from a crowd of diggers. President Parker was waiting for him under an archway 'bearing the well-selected but ancient proverb, "Unity is Strength" prettily worked in green leaves upon a white ground'. There was a mutual exchange of letters, and the rebel republic gave way, much to its President's relief, to the long arm of the British Empire. Campbell was then escorted to the Masonic Hotel by the jubilant diggers, who fired off a few random shots to show there were no hard feelings.

Everyone had hopes that Campbell's arrival would bring some sort of stability to the diamond fields. Their hopes were shortlived. A little over a week after the arrival of the magistrate, trouble broke out in a new quarter. News was received at Klipdrift that a smouldering dispute at the farm of Bultfontein was threatening to erupt in violence.

3

The Diamond Farms

In the rush to the river at the beginning of 1870, the farms of Bultfontein and Dutoitspan had been abandoned but not forgotten. As the river diggings became more crowded, many diggers began to think again about their chances at the dry diggings. Diamonds found on the farm might be inferior, but there were definite advantages in working away from the river. The prolonged drought had been broken by heavy rains and, for those without labour or equipment, surface-searching in the veld appeared an easier proposition than wrestling with the boulders which blocked claims along the river banks. The competitive and increasingly expensive life at Klipdrift and Pniel did not suit everyone.

And so, slowly, groups of poorer diggers had made their way back to the dry diggings. By the end of April there were 'a great number of people' working at Dutoitspan, where Adriaan van Wyk renewed their licences at the agreed price of 7s. 6d. a claim. But they were not allowed on neighbouring Bultfontein. The Hopetown Company, having once cleared the farm of diggers, had no intention of countenancing a second invasion. A new manager, named De Kok, had been installed in the Bultfontein farm house and, under his supervision, digging was confined to parties of Africans employed by the company. Two of the partners, Henry Webb and Louis Hond, and a new shareholder, Edgar Hurley, paid regular visits to the farm to see that the company's regulations were strictly enforced. For a while, they were.

The diggers were not looking for trouble. Most of them had slipped away quietly from the Vaal and, as was often the case with new diggings, had no desire to advertise their activities at Dutoitspan. The fewer who knew about their finds – which were later estimated to average between 60 and 100 diamonds a week – the better the diggers liked it.

But, of course; no digging could be kept secret indefinitely. Prospectors were continually roaming the area and, in August, widespread attention was drawn to Dutoitspan when a Free State newspaper reported that seventeen 'veritable gems' had been found embedded in the mud walls of the Dutoitspan homestead and kraal. This freak discovery caused something of a stir (as well as inspiring many misleading legends). Within a week an anonymous speculator had arrived at the dry diggings offering to buy Dutoitspan for £10,000, under the impression that the farm buildings 'were plastered with diamonds'. Not, he announced, that he wanted to monopolise the diggings: he merely wished to grow potatoes and vegetables on the farm to protect the diggers from scurvy. 'If that', quipped a journalist, 'is not philanthropy – what is?'

But, amusing and exciting as all this was, hard-headed diggers were probably more impressed by an accompanying report about the neighbouring farm. 'From Bultfontein,' it read, '269 diamonds – all picked up on the surface, without the aid of pick or spade – were despatched to England about six weeks ago. What will the incredulous say to this?'

Whatever the incredulous said, there was no doubt about the reaction of a great many diggers. The secret was out; once again the 'diamond farms' became the talk of the camps. More and more diggers stole away from the Vaal and applied for licences at Dutoitspan, where they staked out their claims and looked longingly across at Bultfontein. Few had any doubts that the real riches lay across the boundary. There was talk of making another rush on the Hopetown Company's property. Bultfontein, it was argued, had once been a public digging, licences had been issued there, and the fact that earlier diggers had been bought off should not prevent them from returning. 'By diggers' law the world over,' claimed one agitator, 'a farm once thrown open must always remain so to any digger who behaves himself.'

Adriaan van Wyk – evidently fearing the result of a rush on Bultfontein – decided to cash in while the going was still good. In the middle of November, his farm was offered for sale by a local attorney. An advertisement placed in *The Friend*, a Free State newspaper, described Dutoitspan as a farm of 2,580 morgen where diggers had worked successfully for more than six months; but its chief attraction – announced in bold type – was that it adjoined Bultfontein and was rumoured to be 'equally rich in diamonds'. Nothing seems to have come of this attempted sale, but it undoubtedly made Bultfontein appear more enticing than ever.

It is hardly surprising that, a couple of weeks later, the diggers at Dutoitspan suddenly discovered that the most successful run of diamonds followed a small rise crossing the Bultfontein boundary. This gave them the pretext they needed. A committee was formed and it was resolved to approach the Hopetown Company for permission to cross the dividing line. At the beginning of December a deputation of diggers duly met Louis Hond, who was staying at Bultfontein, and politely presented their request. Hond was equally polite in turning it down. Bultfontein, he explained, was private property and all diamonds found there belonged to the Hopetown Company. The diggers, as decorous as ever, then returned to Dutoitspan.

But that, as everyone was well aware, was not the end of the matter; far from it. Having observed the formalities, the diggers were now ready to take action. Hond knew what to expect. He immediately sent for his partners, Henry Webb and Edgar Hurley, who came hurrying to the farm, Hurley armed with an interdict issued by a local Free State magistrate. When the second deputation of diggers arrived, early in the morning of 19 December, Hurley and the farm manager, De Kok, were waiting for them at the Bultfontein dam.

This time the diggers were far more determined. They insisted that they had a right to dig on Bultfontein and offered to pay the recognised licence fee of 7s. 6d. a claim. If licences were refused, they said, they would dig without them;

they had already notified the Free State authorities of this and they did not consider that they were acting illegally. Hurley thought otherwise. He produced the magistrate's interdict and waved it at them. 'I am here as Justice of the Peace,' he shouted, holding up his hand, 'and I warn you of the consequences of your conduct. . . . ' The diggers were not impressed. Hurley's blustering merely brought things to a rousing climax.

At a signal from their leaders, an army of noisy diggers came marching across the boundary. Shouldering picks and spades and 'accompanied by Kafir servants and a band playing "See the Conquering Hero Comes" ' they strutted past the dumbfounded Hurley, fanned out, and began to stake their claims.

Hurley made one last desperate attempt to assert himself. He threatened that if the diggers did not leave immediately he would have them evicted by the Free State police. This produced an uproar. The diggers made it quite clear what they thought of the Free State, its government, its laws, and its police. They were more than ready to deal with any police force and, if necessary, they would call in reinforcements from Pniel. Having made themselves clear on this point, they continued their advance across the farm.

Henry Webb and Louis Hond, who had remained in the farm cottage, soon found themselves surrounded. 'Claims', it is said, 'were marked up to Mr Webb's very doorway. They used the house wall as a boundary. Big, rough fellows were tearing about with pegs in their hands, wrangling, fighting, rejoicing over the spoil. Others drove off, with many a curse and blow, the Kaffirs who had been working for proprietors' benefit. Henceforth they were to have no right to their own diamonds, excepting in two claims only.

'Mr Webb and two or three staunch friends struggled through the mob, amidst curses and threats. They attempted to plead for some small grace. . . . Active measures then were taken at the greatest personal risk. The upholders of justice drew out the pegs immediately surrounding the house. One huge fellow swore he would drive his pick through Mr Webb's foot if he dared obliterate his claim-mark. Three times the line was made, and three times was it gallantly smoothed out. . . . They threatened to hang Mr Webb and his friends on the Bultfontein tree.'

Finally the proprietors gave up. Without armed assistance they could do nothing. In an attempt to obtain such assistance Edgar Hurley and Louis Hond set off that evening for Bloemfontein, the capital of the Orange Free State. Their arrival there the following day caused a sensation.

'Mr Hurley has come to demand protection,' it was reported, 'with what results remains to be seen. We fully expect a small commando of burghers will have to be called out from the Jacobsdal and Boshof districts, in order to drive off these rioters and defiers of law. If something be not done, and that quickly, there will henceforth be no security to the holders of diamond farms.'

News of the collapse of the Diggers' Republic, a week earlier, had just reached Bloemfontein, but this was as nothing compared with the excitement created by the rush on Bultfontein. The arrival of Hurley and Hond swept all other news to the back pages of the press.

(2)

How, *The Friend* wanted to know, would the Free State authorities handle the situation? Hurley and Hond had indeed presented the Boer republic with a tricky problem. A diamond dispute had once again blown up in contested territory: the farms of Dutoitspan and Bultfontein lay just within the boundary that David Arnot was claiming for the Griquas. To deal with the conflicting claims at Bultfontein would require the utmost diplomacy. There was, in fact, far more at stake than the rights of the Hopetown Company.

One of the most frequent accusations hurled at the Free State was that its government was too weak to administer the turbulent territory. Boer officials, it was said, were too incompetent, inexperienced and ill-organised to deal with the mixed bag of diggers who had arrived on their doorstep. Their society was a rural one and as such was not geared to meeting the demands that would be made upon it by an influx of sophisticated foreigners. The truth of this had yet, of course, to be tested. Nevertheless the Boers were well aware of such criticism. They knew it was necessary for them to make a show of strength. They knew that if they did not assert themselves at Bultfontein their claim to the dry diggings would be undermined. On the other hand they could not afford to be too bold. If they came out firmly on the side of the proprietors of the farm, they would undoubtedly alienate a large number of diggers – both at the dry diggings and on the river – and this might prove disastrous. They could not afford to lose mass support for the sake of a few individuals. Nor, for that matter, could they afford to give in to mob rule. It was indeed a tricky problem.

To make matters worse, the man most competent to deal with the crisis was away. President Brand had recently left for Cape Town, where he was to meet the newly arrived Governor of the Cape, Sir Henry Barkly, to propose that the long-standing quarrel over the Campbell Lands be referred to foreign arbitration. Any decision concerning Bultfontein would therefore have to be made by his deputy. This was what worried *The Friend*. 'We are anxious', claimed the newspaper, 'to hear what decision Mr Venter will come to in this most delicate and difficult matter.'

Mr Venter, in fact, came to no decision. Politician that he was, he tried instead to delay matters. At a meeting of the Executive Council the Bultfontein problem was handed on to the popular Free State magistrate at Pniel, Olof Truter. Truter was blithely instructed to go at once to the dry diggings and 'in the name of the Government warn the diggers to depart'. It was a happy thought, but few could seriously have expected it to succeed. Nor did it.

The diggers were delighted to see Truter. They all knew and liked the magistrate and, as he rode up to Bultfontein, they greeted him by hoisting a white flag and giving a rousing cheer. But the cheers quickly changed to jeers once Truter announced why he had come. The diggers were in no mood to listen to warnings. Shouting, stamping, waving their picks and shovels, they howled the magistrate down. A few of the ringleaders pushed forward and made a pretence of reasoning with Truter. They explained that they were willing to take out licences and had, in fact, already lodged their licence fees with a committee; as soon as a settlement was reached these fees would be handed over to the proprietors of the farm. But that was as far as they were prepared to go: come magistrates or policemen they were determined to go on digging.

Truter was too much of an old hand to argue. He knew better than to start throwing his weight around with a crowd of angry diggers. In any case, his sympathies were largely with the rebels. Reporting back to Bloemfontein, he recommended that the farms be thrown open to all-comers on payment of a fair licence fee. This was hardly the advice that Mr Venter and the Council had hoped for. It put them back more or less where they had started.

All the same, things could not be left there. Something had to be done and done soon. But what? If the diggers would not listen to Olof Truter, who would they listen to? There was no shortage of suggestions. Everyone had his own ideas and everyone was eager to give advice. Why, it was asked, could not a commando be called out to send the diggers packing? This seemed the most obvious solution. It was, after all, the traditional Boer method of dealing with troublemakers and there seemed no earthly reason why it should not be used now.

Members of the Executive Council thought otherwise. They knew of at least one important reason why it would be foolish to call out a voluntary army. Such a move would be tantamount to declaring war on the diggers and that, in turn, would be an open invitation to the British to step in. The Free State's enemies would like nothing better: Richard Southey and his cronies would be given the very excuse they were angling for. There must be no suggestion of Boer aggression. Things had to be given at least a semblance of legality.

What was needed was a properly constituted police force, a much larger police force than, in fact, the Free State possessed. At their next meeting the Executive Council decided to raise such a force. Friedrich Höhne, the Government Secretary, was instructed to leave immediately for the diamond fields, investigate the position at the farms, and then 'organise, if possible, a paid force of one hundred men' to march on Bultfontein and 'clear out the unruly diggers'.

Höhne set off immediately and arrived at Bultfontein at the beginning of January 1871. He found the farm looking remarkably peaceful. There were no signs of the rioting that had been reported to Bloemfontein. Spread out across the flat, tree-studded veld, the diggers seemed more intent on looking for diamonds than looking for trouble. It was even doubtful whether they could be accused of having illegally taken possession of the farm, as most of them were still living at Dutoitspan, merely crossing the boundary to work every morning. They had pointedly avoided erecting tents or huts on the Bultfontein property and insisted that all they were claiming was the right to dig.

But things were by no means as peaceful as they seemed. One look at the ringleaders was sufficient to convince Höhne of what he was up against. They were a fearsome-looking bunch. In Bloemfontein it was firmly believed that the principal troublemakers were a group of roughnecks from Natal, but Höhne was quick to spot a few local lads – including a notorious Free State character named, rather startlingly, Doris Potgieter – among the leaders. They were certainly not men who could be reasoned with.

Höhne, wisely, did not attempt to reason. After taking a quick look round, he hurried on to Pniel and handed the problem back again to the long-suffering Olof Truter. It was to be Truter's thankless task to muster a police force and lead it, in the name of the Free State, to Bultfontein. He was authorised to offer would-be recruits a salary of £6. 10s. a month.

There was no rush to Truter's office. Indeed, he was hard put to it to raise half the force of one hundred men which the Executive Council had considered necessary. Few diggers were ready to down spades and take up batons against their former comrades. When at last the slap-happy force was assembled it consisted of hardly more than fifty loutish down-and-outs, commanded by a blustering Irish ex-army-sergeant named Brannagan. Sergeant Brannagan claimed to have taken part in every major Victorian campaign, including the Crimean war and the Indian Mutiny, and announced that he was not 'afraid of a personal encounter with anyone'. Like, it seemed, was about to meet like.

But not yet. The newly enrolled upholders of Free State law and order appeared to have little crusading spirit. Most of them were distinctly embarrassed to be on the right side of the law and were reluctant to come to grips with the diggers. So much so that, on arriving at Bultfontein and being met with a chorus of catcalls, two of the new recruits promptly deserted. The rest hovered uncertainly on the outskirts of the farm.

The diggers, on the other hand, were in their element. Recognising the policemen for riff-raff, they treated the whole affair as a huge joke. They strutted along the boundary of the farm, jeering and taunting Truter to arrest them. But Truter preferred to wait. He refused to be goaded into making a rash move. He was still waiting a week later when it was reported that he had seen 'no chance to arrest the ringleaders'.

The chance eventually came, however. The joke began to wear thin, many diggers returned to work, and even the more belligerent among them became careless. Brannagan saw his chance and took it. In a surprise move he dashed in, pounced on three or four of the leaders and triumphantly whisked them off to the nearest Free State magistrate at the little village of Jacobsdal. Louis Hond, who had recently returned to the Bultfontein cottage, obligingly lent a wagon to act as a prison van.

So successful was the *coup* that it went to Brannagan's head. Having delivered his prisoners he returned to the farm cock-a-hoop. He was determined to repeat the performance. This time, however, he ran into opposition. He managed to rope in a few more agitators but found himself without any transport. Louis Hond took fright and refused to lend his wagon for a second journey. His horses, he claimed, were exhausted. Brannagan was furious. He promptly arrested Hond for 'resisting a Government officer' and, after commandeering his wagon, hustled him off to Jacobsdal with the other prisoners.

Poor Hond was completely bemused. Only a couple of weeks earlier he had been accused of dealing in stolen diamonds at Klipdrift and a warrant had been issued for his arrest. Having talked himself out of that, he now found himself arrested on his own property and carted off to prison in his own wagon. Life could take some alarming turns on the diamond fields.

Luckily, the magistrate at Jacobsdal was singularly unimpressed by Brannagan's efficiency. Not only did he order Hond's release but, after bawling Brannagan out, he set most of the diggers free as well. This was too much for Brannagan. Olof Truter had returned to Pniel, and the purple-faced sergeant went tearing after him, demanding arrests all round – the diggers, Hond, and the Jacobsdal magistrate. He was in for another surprise.

Truter had apparently had as much as he could take from the blustering Brannagan. He put the sergeant firmly in his place. 'At Pniel,' it was reported, '(Brannagan) was insolent to the Commissioner, who after knocking him down, made him prisoner and marched him off to Jacobsdal. . . . The inspector is now undergoing two months on the Jacobsdal roads.'

At last somebody had been successfully arrested. That it was the sergeant of police was, in the circumstances, probably appropriate.

Despite Brannagan's antics, the diggers were eventually cleared off Bultfontein. It was not the Free State authorities, but a group of local Boers who were responsible for restoring law and order. Whether with the connivance, or in defiance, of the Executive Council, a number of burgers in the Jacobsdal district decided to take matters into their own hands. They organised a commando. Once the diggers at Bultfontein heard that this commando was being formed, they immediately took fright. Within a matter of hours the farm was deserted.

'The Free State boers were the first to leave,' boasted *The Friend*, 'and afterwards the uitlanders (foreigners) deemed it advisable to follow their good example. . . . They got scent of the commando coming down, and the brave thieves who were going to defy the whole State decamped in the night.'

Most of the diggers went back to Dutoitspan. A few, however, moved on to a neighbouring farm, Alexandersfontein, where the owner willingly issued them with licences. Everyone was immensely relieved that things had been settled so happily. Peace had been established, remarked *The Friend*, without 'bloodshed, or further trouble of any kind'.

(3)

But it was not peace that had been established, merely a truce. There was little chance of a lasting peace in the fight for the diamond farms. The diggers had been forced off Bultfontein but they were reluctant to admit defeat. The rights and wrongs of the issue continued to be debated in the press for weeks.

On the diggers' side it was argued that once the owners of a farm had accepted licence fees, as the owners of Bultfontein had done, that farm was a public diggings: anyone willing to pay the recognised fee had a right to dig there. In the case of Bultfontein, however, this argument was somewhat weakened by the fact that it had not been the actual owners, but their manager, who had issued licences. Once Henry Webb had arrived on the scene, he had paid off the handful of diggers working on the farm and withdrawn their licences. However one looked at it, the Hopetown Company, as the rightful owners of Bultfontein, had a fairly strong case. Had they stuck to it they might have withstood the diggers' demands longer than they did. But they ruined everything by trying to over-reach themselves.

The diggers evacuated Bultfontein at the end of January 1871. A few weeks later, on 11 March, it was announced that Adriaan van Wyk had sold the Dutoitspan farm to the 'London and South African Exploration Company' for £2,600. There were then some 5,000 diggers working on Dutoitspan, most of whom had obtained licences from Van Wyk at the accepted fee of 7s. 6d. per claim. Hardly had the sale gone through than the new owners gave notice that they intended to close the farm to the public and that all licence holders were expected to abandon their claims by 15 May. Shattering as this decree was, it was made all the more objectionable by the fact that the London and South African Exploration Company was simply the old Hopetown Company under another name. Dutoitspan had, in fact, become the property of the well-known syndicate headed by Henry Webb, Louis Hond, Edgar Hurley and the Lilienfeld brothers.

The shortlived truce between the diggers and the Hopetown merchants came to an abrupt end.

The diggers at Dutoitspan were, for the most part, a very different crowd from the rabble who had invaded Bultfontein. Many of them had been working peacefully at the dry diggings for months, had faithfully observed the restrictions imposed by Adriaan van Wyk, and in no way could they be accused of unlawful behaviour. Among them were a number of respectable professional men who were well qualified to meet the threat of eviction. Two of these men, Captain J.B. Finlayson, an ex-army officer, and Albert Ortlepp, a land-surveyor from Colesberg, immediately rose to the challenge and organised a series of protest meetings.

That their protests were well justified, they had no doubt. Dutoitspan was, and had always been, a public diggings. From the very beginning, Adriaan van Wyk had accepted licence fees and had, in fact, made more out of these fees than he had now been paid for the farm. The transfer of farm rights, they argued, in no way interfered with the rights paid for by the diggers. If anyone had acted illegally it was Van Wyk who had failed to keep his part of the bargain. A contract was a contract and it imposed obligations on both sides.

Van Wyk became the main target for the diggers' anger. Feelings against him ran high and almost resulted in a lynching. At the first meeting called by Finlayson and Ortlepp, the former owner of Dutoitspan was spotted standing on the fringe of the crowd with Henry Webb and Louis Hond. There was an immediate uproar. 'The meeting became so excited', it was reported, 'that a rush was made at Mr Van Wyk and, but for the interposition of some of the more moderate, it would have fared ill with him.'

It was an unnerving experience for Van Wyk, and after that he kept himself well in the background. Henry Webb and Louis Hond, however, brazened it out: they made a point of attending every meeting. Steadfastly refusing invitations to address the diggers, they stood at the back of the crowd muttering curses and predicting disaster. The diggers, well aware of their presence, went out of their way to taunt them. Many of the inflammatory resolutions passed at the meetings seemed, in fact, to have little point other than to enrage Webb and Hond. There can be no doubt that they succeeded. Hardly had the crowd dispersed than Webb and Hond would retire to Bultfontein and issue a strongly worded counterblast. When the diggers elected an action committee, Webb and Hond promptly declared it to be unlawful. When it was proposed to petition the Free State Government to prevent speculators from monopolising diamondiferous farms, Webb and Hond retaliated by threatening to open the Dutoitspan dam, fill in the wells, and cut off all water supplies. When the diggers hit back by announcing that they would again invade Bultfontein and get their water from there, Webb and Hond immediately posted another notice warning claimholders to leave both farms by 15 May.

And so it went on. Neither side was sure of its ground, but both were determined not to yield an inch. Bluster was met by bombast, warnings were countered by threats. The nearer the deadline drew, the higher the tension mounted.

'The eyes of all on the Fields', declared the *Diamond News* on 13 May, 'are just now fixed upon this Camp and what the diggers will do on the 15th is the question of the day.'

But it was not only a question of what the diggers would do. Dutoitspan had become a testing-ground, and the outcome of the confrontation could have far-reaching results. All sorts of rumours were afloat. Other farmers, it was said, were watching Dutoitspan and, if the owners were successful, diggers would be ejected from farms throughout the region. There was also talk of another commando being raised to settle things once and for all. More ominous was the unconfirmed report that the Free State authorities had met secretly in Bloemfontein and drafted an Ordinance which would hit at both diggers and owners alike. The precise nature of this Ordinance was a matter for endless speculation. Some maintained that the Free State Government intended to appropriate the farms outright, paying off the owners and the claimholders. Others claimed that the owners would be allowed to keep the farms but would be forced to turn them into public diggings and 'pay a royalty to the Government in consideration of which a police force would be provided' to keep the peace. Anything, it seemed, was possible.

One thing, however, was certain. Whatever else happened, the diggers were determined to have their say. On the morning of 15 May – the day of the deadline – a notice was pinned to the committee tent at Dutoitspan calling for a meeting at two o'clock that afternoon. There was a massive response. Between 2,000 and 3,000 diggers turned up at what was described as 'one of the largest assemblages of diggers that Dutoitspan – or, indeed, any other Camp – has yet witnessed'. Many of them had come armed, as usual, with picks and spades: they were evidently expecting a fight.

But there was to be no fight. This was made clear by Captain Finlayson – now regarded as the 'champion of diggers' rights' – who, having been unanimously elected chairman, surprised everyone by announcing that the meeting had been called, not by his committee, but at the request of the proprietors of Dutoitspan. He asked that all speakers be given a fair hearing and then sprang his second surprise: shouting to make himself heard, he invited Martin Lilienfeld to address the diggers. 'Mr Lilienfeld', he said, as the puffing merchant struggled onto the wagon which served as a platform, 'was as welcome as he was strange to the meeting.'

Strange as he indeed was to most of the diggers, the suave Martin Lilienfeld quickly won them over. Not only was he given a fair hearing but soon his every word was being cheered. This, admittedly, was not entirely due to his persuasive personality. He had come with good news. The farm was to be opened as a public diggings; those who already held licences would be allowed to work their claims at the agreed rate, newcomers would be charged 10s. 6d. a month; water would be provided and sanitary arrangements made. The proprietors, declared Lilienfeld, would recognise any committee elected by the diggers. To all intents and purposes the owners of Dutoitspan had capitulated.

At a meeting held two days later, a list of rules and regulations – drawn up by the diggers' committee – was agreed to and signed by Martin Lilienfeld and Henry Webb on behalf of the proprietors. The conditions laid down by the committee were, to say the least, extremely one-sided. Apart from the collection of licence fees, a tenth of which had to be handed back to the committee for administrative purposes, the proprietors had no real rights on their own farm. They became, like any other digger, subject to the rules governing the diggings. Under these rules, no one digger was allowed to work more than two thirty-foot-square claims; any person found working a claim other than his own was liable to a fine of £5; any claim abandoned for eight or more successive days could be taken over by anyone applying for a licence. Unless, therefore, the proprietors were prepared to work continually in the claims allotted to them, they had no mining rights on the farm.

Olof Truter, who attended the signing, 'expressed great satisfaction at the way things had been settled'. This satisfaction was certainly not shared by Henry Webb, who later declared that 'it was under actual duress that he consented to sign the articles; fear of bodily violence, and dread – something more certain than dread – that he would get nothing if he did not sign'. He had good reason for his fears.

For, if, Martin Lilienfeld had unexpectedly appeared as an angel of light, he had done so with badly singed wings. Both he and Henry Webb knew that they had no option but to act before they were acted against.

The rumours of a secret Ordinance passed by the Free State Government had not been without foundation. When this Ordinance was officially published two weeks later, it gave the Free State authorities sweeping powers. It decreed, in effect, that owners of diamondiferous farms would either have to sell their land to the Government at a nominal fee or be forced to open them as public diggings under the superintendence of a 'Government Inspector'. Where a Government Inspector was appointed, he would preside over a Committee of Management elected by the diggers and be empowered to collect all licence fees. The proprietors of the farms were not only ignored, but penalised. As far as they were concerned the sting came in the tail. Under Article 17 of the Ordinance, it was laid down that 'the Government Inspector shall pay over the half of the pecuniary proceeds of all licences to the owners of those farms, or their lawful agents, on receipt, and the other half shall, by those officers, be brought to account . . . in order to defray the expenses of Government, connected with keeping up an oversight over the diggings'.

Henry .Webb and his partners, for all their high-handedness, were fully justified in thinking they had been given a raw deal. The demands of the diggers and the Free State authorities placed the owner of any diamondiferous farm in an iniquitous position. As one of Webb's friends indignantly pointed out later, 'He has no privileges. He may not work more than two claims. His land is the diggers'. Of what he takes from it, 10 per cent shall go to the committee; and the Government, subsequently, robs him of 50 more.'

But there was nothing that could be done about it. The Free State Ordinance was law and its provisions were to set the pattern for all future transactions. Once it was promulgated, the Hopetown syndicate was forced to recognise defeat, albeit under protest, both at Dutoitspan and Bultfontein. The two farms were now declared public diggings.

However, there was one small consolation, if such it can be called. At that time it was confidently expected that the farms would quickly be exhausted of diamonds and that the diggers would be obliged to move on. Even before the confrontation at Dutoitspan, the diggers there had begun to lose heart and had 'pretty well decided that it does not pay to go deeper than 5 feet'. With any luck the owners of the farm would at least be free of the obligations imposed upon them by the new regulations.

There had, in fact, been a considerable exodus of diggers from Dutoitspan at the height of the recent crisis. A new discovery had not only lured away a large number of claimholders, but had robbed the diggers of some of their prominent leaders - including Captain Finlayson's former lieutenant, Albert Ortlepp.

The farm which was now attracting widespread interest - although it had so far escaped the attention of the Free State authorities - was situated some two miles from Dutoitspan. It was Vooruitzigt, the home of Johannes Nicolaas de Beer

(4)

Richard Jackson was an old man when he recalled the early rush to De Beer's farm. His memory might have been faulty and the details of his account could be open to question. But in the main the story he told appears to agree with established facts. In any case, his is the only known, first-hand description of this momentous event, and as such is worth repeating.

At the time, Jackson was a young digger working at Hebron on the Vaal River. He had arrived at the river diggings late in 1869 and, despite the excitement created by the finds at Dutoitspan and Bultfontein, had resolutely stuck to the river. In this he was by no means alone. There were a great many cautious diggers who still considered that the diamond farms would prove a nine-days'-wonder, scarcely worth the upheaval entailed in trekking to them. Not until the end of April 1871 did Jackson take an interest in the dry diggings. Even then his interest was tinged with scepticism.

While he was at Hebron, one of his African labourers told him that there was talk in the camp of a solitary white man working 'out there', to the south, 'dry-sorting and finding diamonds every day'. As 'out there' might have meant anywhere, Jackson at first paid little attention to the story. A few days later, however, his brother-in-law, E. Struben, reported that he had also been told about the lone digger by his labourers. The two of them talked it over and decided to investigate. They had been working solidly for a year and needed a break. What could they lose by a few days' sport in the veld? Taking two Transvaal friends with them – George Rex and Harry Collins – they loaded two Scotch carts and set off.

After a long, hot pull across the parched veld, they reached Vooruitzigt three days later. Apart from a tent pitched close to some thorn trees the place seemed deserted. But, sitting at a table outside the tent, there, sure enough, was a middle-aged man desultorily sifting gravel with his right hand. Jackson decided it would be best to appear innocent. He went over, shook the man by the hand, and asked him what he was doing. The man introduced himself as Corneilsa (Jackson never discovered his surname) and said he was looking for diamonds. He explained that he had been given permission to work on the farm by the owner, De Beer, on condition that he handed over 25 per cent of his finds.

It was, as Jackson quickly discovered, a fair bargain. Diamonds there were a-plenty. Even as they were talking, the man scraped up a 2½-carat diamond and handed it to Jackson. He then produced a Vesta matchbox, half full of diamonds. Jackson was staggered. 'I called my mates,' he says, 'who, like me, had never seen such a collection in one man's possession.'

It seemed too good to be true. The river diggings had never yielded diamonds – small though they were – in quantities like this. Dropping all pretence, the four men were ready to leave immediately; to seek out De Beer and obtain permission to dig. Corneilsa, however, advised them to wait. De Beer's son-in-law, he explained, would be coming shortly to value the week's finds; they could approach him. When the son-in-law, a Hollander, eventually arrived, he turned out to be a surly individual, suspicious of strangers. 'We found him', says Jackson, 'a most offensive and objectionable fellow. However we were too wise to take offence and ultimately he gave us each permission to peg out a claim, 30 ft by 30, on the 25 per cent arrangement, and also permitted us to peg for some friends we had left at the river.'

Before rushing back to Hebron, they had a quick look round the farm. To the north-east they discovered signs of full-scale mining: an eighteen-foot shaft had been sunk against a solid, hard granite reef. That this was, as they imagined, the work of Corneilsa seems doubtful. To sink such a shaft requires a certain amount of technical knowledge and Jackson had earlier claimed that Corneilsa was so inexperienced that he was not sure of the Afrikaans word for a diamond. It seems more likely that the mining had been done earlier and then at a later stage had been abandoned.

There was no time for questions. Certain that they had found a 'hole' the four men were anxious to get to work. They had doubts as to whether the mine would be workable beyond a depth of sixty to eighty feet, but even at that depth there was a fortune to be made.

Returning to Hebron they collected the friends for whom they had pegged claims and tried to sneak away as quietly as possible in the hope of forestalling the inevitable rush. It was a slight hope. The sight of eight loaded wagons trundling out of camp put everyone on the alert. 'Before we were out of sight of Hebron,' sighed Jackson, 'the majority of tents were down and oxen were being inspanned to chase after us. They forced the pace and we only managed to keep the lead, I being first wagon, the mob pretty close behind.'

At Vooruitzigt there was a mad scramble for claims. Few knew the reason for the rush but everyone was determined to grab whatever looked like a good position. Jackson and his friends were quickly surrounded; pegs sprang up on all sides. But, knowing little and expecting too much, the frantic diggers were soon disillusioned. The immediate results were far from encouraging. After a few days' hard digging, many of Jackson's immediate neighbours threw up their holdings and either went back to the river or wandered off 'prospecting, anywhere, everywhere'.

Among the first to leave was a group of diggers from Colesberg, known for their distinctive headgear as the 'Red Cap party'. Their leader, Fleetwood Rawstorne, is said to have gambled away the few diamonds he found at De Beer's, and this, together with the poor finds generally, led to his abandoning his claim and disappearing into the veld with his friends. It was some weeks before Jackson saw him again.

What Johannes Nicolaas de Beer thought of the invasion of diggers, Jackson does not say. He could not have been pleased. A dour-faced member of the puritanical 'Dopper' branch of the Dutch Reformed Church, De Beer would hardly have welcomed the ungodly disruption of his peace. He, no less than his son-in-law, was extremely suspicious of English-speaking strangers. As far as the initial rush was concerned – and there were probably fewer diggers involved than Jackson implies – he had no option but to recognise a *fait accompli*. However, once the diggers began to leave he clamped down. De Beer's soon became notorious for its exclusiveness. 'Everyone knows', reported the *Diamond News* on 6 May, 'that it is next to impossible to procure a claim at that place, owing to the determination of the proprietor to open it only to a few individuals.'

This state of affairs was not to last long. Events had a way of overtaking Johannes Nicolaas de Beer, leaving him helpless to control them. The days when he could walk peacefully round the diggings collecting subscriptions for his church (some diggers actually obtained new claims by making a timely donation) came to an abrupt end in July 1871; less than three months after the opening of De Beer's.

In the middle of July, the bearded, red-capped Fleetwood Rawstorne emerged from the veld, panting with excitement. He rushed up to Richard

Jackson and told him that he had found 'a place better than De Beer's'. After digging there for a few feet, he said, he had struck yellow ground and 'in a couple of buckets he had found 3 diamonds'. When Jackson asked him where it was, he pointed to a small hillock, surmounted by a clump of thorn trees, about a mile due west. He had named the hillock after the hometown of his party: Colesberg Kopje.

Rawstorne's discovery was meant to be a secret. It did not remain a secret for long. His arrival at De Beer's sparked off the famous New Rush.

(5)

There were to be many stories told about the discovery of Colesberg Kopje. In later years several of the pioneers at De Beer's – or Old De Beer's as it was soon to be known, for Colesberg Kopje was also on De Beer's farm – claimed to have had a hand in it. Most of these stories, however, can be easily dismissed. Only two appear to approximate to the truth; or, at least, to the circumstances surrounding the discovery.

The first of these is derived from a legend in the family of Albert Ortlepp, the land-surveyor from Colesberg who had previously been active at Dutoitspan. Ortlepp's wife, Sarah, always maintained that it was she who found the first diamond on the hillock. In proof of this her family for many years preserved, in a small packet dated 1871, the diamond she claimed to have found.

According to Sarah Ortlepp, she and her family were, in July 1871, living in a tent close to the Red Cap party and not far from the hillock, which was known then as Gilfillan's Kop. Apparently Albert Ortlepp, like Fleetwood Rawstorne and his friends, had become disillusioned with De Beer's and was wandering the veld in the hopes of a better strike. The Ortlepps had with them a small son and daughter, and one Sunday the entire family, accompanied by their dog, strolled over to Gilfillan's Kop. It was an aimless outing. On the way the dog barked at a snake, but nothing else happened until they reached the top of the hillock. There they decided to rest under a tall thorn tree, and Sarah Ortlepp began, probably from force of habit, 'sifting the surface gravel through her fingers'. She picked up several pebbles and discovered one of them to be a small yellow diamond.

Why the Ortlepps did not follow up the find by digging is something of a mystery. In fact, it throws doubt on the entire story. But then odd diamonds were picked up in unlikely places from time to time without necessarily signifying a large deposit. It was afterwards claimed that Sarah Ortlepp was advised to report her find but 'was diffident as to the publicity it would entail' and persuaded Fleetwood Rawstorne to claim the discovery. This, when one knows how fiercely competitive the diggers were, seems highly unlikely. Nevertheless, it is possible that the Ortlepps showed Rawstorne their little yellow diamond and told him where it came from.

The second, more widely accepted, version gives more credit to the Red Cap party. One of the party, Henry Richard Giddy, recorded the story shortly before he died. In essence, it substantiates a similar account given by Fleet-

Dutoitspan Village, seen from the Pan, shortly after the great rushes to the dry diggings in 1871. (K)

Fleetwood Rawstorne, leader of the famous 'Red Cap Party' responsible for the discovery of Colesberg Kopje (New Rush) in July 1871. (M)

Dutoitspan Government Offices shortly after the rush to the 'dry diggings'. This painting by McGill depicts the defiance of the Dutoitspan diggers in hoisting the 'horse' flag of the recently defunct Diggers' Republic. (M)

wood Rawstorne's mother a few years earlier.

Fleetwood Rawstorne was the son of Colesberg's first magistrate and had come to the diggings in style. He had brought with him a Cape Coloured servant, named Damon, to act as his cook. Unfortunately, Damon, who had grown up with the Rawstorne family, had a fatal weakness. Perfectly reliable when sober, he was, says Giddy, an equally perfect nuisance when 'under the influence'. He also showed considerable ingenuity: even in the wilds he repeatedly got so drunk that the long-suffering Rawstorne was driven to distraction. Eventually he became so impossible that Rawstorne was forced to order him from the camp. He was given some food and cooking utensils and sent to Gilfillan's Kop to start digging.

He returned a few nights later. Rawstorne was playing cards with his friends when his tent flap opened and Damon's face appeared.

'Fleet, I want to see you,' he hissed.

'All right,' sighed Rawstorne. 'Come inside. We are all friends here. What do you want?'

Damon came in. Without saying a word, he unclutched his hand and showed them two or three small diamonds. 'The effect on us all', says Giddy, 'was electrical.' There was a mad scramble for the door of the tent, stakes and hatchets were grabbed and, with Damon in the lead, the entire party went haring across the veld. On reaching the top of the hillock, Damon showed them a shaft he had sunk beside the tall thorn tree. There was no doubt about it: it was a beautifully clear moonlit night; Damon was sober, the diamonds were real, and the shaft was ten or twelve feet deep.

Rawstorne, as leader of the party, had first choice: he marked out his claim around Damon's shaft. The rest of them stumbled about in the grass trying to decide the direction of the pipe. They were in a quandary. Were they near the centre of the mine? How far did it extend? There was no way of telling. The grass was knee-high and there were no signs of outcropping reef. It became a matter of pure guesswork and, hoping for the best, they pegged out claims in all directions.

That, according to Giddy, was how Colesberg Kopje was discovered.

He may have been right. But so may Sarah Ortlepp. The two stories are not as conflicting as they are often made to appear. After all, why had Rawstorne sent Damon to dig on that particular hillock? Could it have been Sarah Ortlepp's diamond that put him on the trail? Damon certainly sank the first shaft on Colesberg Kopje, and the Red Cap party pegged out the first claims there, but it might well have been Sarah Ortlepp who found the first diamond. There must have been some reason why her family kept that diamond so neatly wrapped and carefully dated.

But, whoever was responsible for the discovery, there can be no doubt as to its effect. Once the news was out, there was an immediate rush to Colesberg Kopje; thousands of diggers joined the headlong race for claims. The first to arrive came from De Beer's, Dutoitspan and Bultfontein, followed closely by a frantic mob from the river diggings. They came on horseback, in Cape carts, donkey carts and tented wagons, while the less fortunate – slung about with pegs, their shoulders bruised by bumping spades – panted behind on foot. They called it New Rush, but they could just as easily have called it the Great Rush, the Great Charge, or even, the Stampede. Nothing like it had been seen before. Other rushes there had been, but they were not as instantaneous, as concentrated or, for that matter, as frenetic as the storming of Colesberg Kopje.

The first few weeks were chaotic. Not until the beginnning of August did things begin to sort themselves out. Then it was estimated that something like 800 claims had been cut out of Colesberg Kopje, many of them subdivided into halves and quarters. Between 2,000 and 3,000 men were said to be working on the hillock. But this was only a rough guess. The phenomenal rate at which claims were changing hands made any attempt at accuracy impossible. 'The claims are selling at as high as £100 each,' it was reported on 7 August. 'The finds have become so numerous that miners rarely, if ever, "shout". It is astonishing where all the people are coming from.'

But still they came. With each new influx, competition became more intense, prices soared. In little over a week the average price of a claim had risen from £100 to £500. But fewer and fewer were prepared to sell. 'The "Colesberg Rush" ', it was claimed, 'is unquestionably the richest diggings on these fields and numbers many workers who would not take less than three or four thousand pounds sterling for their respective claims.'

The frenzy of the rush threw poor Johannes Nicolaas de Beer completely off balance. He could not begin to cope with the pandemonium. Colesberg Kopje was on his farm but, once the diggers began to pour across his boundaries, he was helpless to control events. His first reaction was, it seems, one of panic: he wanted to sell up and get out. He had not far to look for buyers. Hot on the heels of the diggers came the speculators. Within a month of the discovery of Colesberg Kopje (variously recorded as 15, 16 or 17 July) De Beer had arranged to sell the Vooruitzigt farm.

For once the Hopetown syndicate held back. Having twice been outmanoeuvred on diamondiferous farms, they evidently had no wish to repeat the experience. The man who secured Vooruitzigt was Alfred Ebden, a partner in the Port Elizabeth firm of Dunell Ebden and Company. Ebden was then touring the diamond fields with his daughter. Whether or not he was on the look-out for properties is not certain, but he lost no time in approaching De Beer. On 10 August, *The Friend* announced that Ebden had arrived in Bloemfontein after purchasing 'a portion of the farm but by the post which arrived here yesterday morning, he learnt that his offer had been accepted and that his agent had closed for the remaining portion'.

In fact, Ebden had left two agents at the diggings to deal with De Beer. One was a Dutoitspan merchant named Robert Stockdale (after whom one of the first streets in the new camp was to be named) and the other was D.K. Reitz. The transaction was not to be concluded until two months later when, on 19 October 1871, D.K. Reitz formally purchased Vooruitzigt for 6,000 guineas on behalf of a syndicate which Alfred Ebden had formed with some other Port Elizabeth firms. But both Old De Beer's and New Rush were recognised as Ebden's property long before then. Ebden's agents quickly came to terms with the diggers. Albert Ortlepp, as a former member of the Dutoitspan committee, was appointed temporary General Manager at New Rush – in which capacity he issued claim licences, one of the first being taken out by Olof Truter's wife – and G.F. Stegmann was employed to survey the camp 'and afterwards lay out a town there'.

Stegmann needed to work fast. A township of sorts was already developing at New Rush. Corrugated-iron huts and canvas-framed hotels had begun to appear amid the jumble of tents and wagons and, by the end of August, the number of diggers living in the camp had doubled. 'There are at least 5,000 people digging there . . . ' it was reported on 7 September. 'Shops, stores and tents are erected in all directions. Passenger carts run between Dutoitspan and De Beers every hour of the day, and they are always heavily loaded.'

It was all highly exciting and, for some, completely bewildering. None was more bewildered than Corneilsa, the lone Boer digger who, in a way, had started it all. When the confusion was at its height, Corneilsa sought out Richard Jackson and asked him whether it was safe to stay. 'It was pathetic', says Jackson, 'to see the state of absolute fear he and his wife were in, as tents rose like magic all round them and their sheep kraal.'

Corneilsa was as much concerned for his sheep as he was for himself; he was sure the horde of newcomers would rob him of his livestock. Jackson told him not to worry; there was, he assured him, not the slightest danger. But Corneilsa was not so sure. After waiting three more days, he sold his claim for £110 and, leaving the lunatic throng at De Beer's to their own devices, trekked to the Transvaal.

How was he to know that he had seen the birth of a city?

PART TWO: SHANTY TOWN

Earliest photograph of New Rush yet traced, showing part of Main Street nearest the mine. Photographed by H.F. Gros late 1871. On the left is the notorious London Hotel and Billiard Room later owned by Harry Barnato. The New Rush Mine is in the foreground. (K)

4

'A Gentleman's Diggings'

When Frederick Boyle, an English travel writer, arrived at Cape Town in November 1871 he had great difficulty in booking a place on a passenger wagon travelling to the diamond fields. 'All the seats had been full for weeks nor was there a vacancy in the following vehicle, nor even in the third.'

Such had been the position for the past four months. Since the discovery of Colesberg Kopje, the crush of fortune seekers trying to get to the diggings had become so great that it was all but unmanageable. Hardly a ship put in at the South African ports that did not bring a fresh influx. They came from England, America, Australia, Germany, Russia, from everywhere and anywhere; all determined to reach the 'New Eldorado' in the shortest possible time.

Those docking at Cape Town were the most fortunate; they at least found some sort of organised transport already in existence. Since the beginning of November 1870, the Inland Transport Company had run a regular weekly service to the river diggings, its wagons seating eleven passengers at £12 a head. The fare was considered outrageous and the exhausting journey – then some seven hundred and fifty miles – a positive nightmare, but until New Rush the service had, *faute de mieux*, proved adequate enough for those who could afford it. Those who could not – and they were in the majority – either had to travel by ox-wagon with a private contractor or set out hopefully on foot.

At the other ports it was a different story. The shortest route from the coast to the Vaal River was that from Port Elizabeth, a distance of less than four hundred and fifty miles. Anyone studying a map of South Africa might, understandably, have chosen Port Elizabeth as the most likely port at which to disembark. Those that did so were quickly disillusioned. For, until the latter half of 1871, Port Elizabeth did nothing to exploit its obvious advantage. There were, of course, the inevitable ox-wagons leaving at odd times, there was also an erratic coach service which ran via Queenstown to Pniel, but there was nothing else. The ox-wagons were painfully slow and the coach service, when it ran, took a circuitous route at a leisurely pace. Port Elizabeth could offer neither speed nor convenience; anyone docking there was bound to reach the diamond fields weeks after those who had wisely left the ship at Cape Town.

The first person effectively to recognise the potential of the Port Elizabeth base was a young American, Freeman Cobb, who had established coaching services in his own country as well as on the gold fields of Australia. By 1871 Cobb's American business had been badly hit by the opening of the Trans-Pacific railway and he had decided to ship some of his coaches to

South Africa. But more than coaches were required to start a coaching service: it took Cobb several months to round up sufficient horses to launch his Port Elizabeth enterprise. The first of the famous Cobb coaches, which were to become such an institution on the diamond fields, did not reach Dutoitspan until March 1872. When Frederick Boyle arrived at the Cape in November 1871, the only evidence of the proposed new service was a trial-run from Port Elizabeth to the nearby town of Uitenhage by two coaches which, it was said, took the startled residents of Uitenhage 'by storm'.

Only the very rash chose to disembark at the Natal port of Durban. Here the means of reaching the diamond fields were precarious indeed. For anything vaguely resembling speed, one had to rely on Walsh's passenger carts, which travelled by way of the Orange Free State and entailed so many changes and such discomfort that few, other than hardened Natalians, ever contemplated using them.

Things being what they were, it is not difficult to imagine Boyle's frustration. Everything, in fact, seemed to be working against him. His voyage to the Cape had been horrific. Having left Southampton on the s.s. *Cambrian*, at the end of September, he had met with nothing but disaster. The officers and crew of the *Cambrian* had proved utterly incompetent; the ship had been forced miles off course; shortly after leaving St Helena one of the passengers had fallen overboard and been lost at sea; fuel had run so low that only by burning cabin doors, spars and, finally, the deckhouse, had they managed to reach the Cape at all. One needed to be tough, and determined, to reach the diamond fields.

Fortunately Boyle was both. He was also an experienced traveller, too experienced to be put off by a fully booked coach. By some judicious bribing at the offices of the Inland Transport Company, he was able to contact a passenger who, at a price, was prepared to give up his seat. 'A very few words settled the bargain,' says Boyle, 'and I left the office in possession of a pink ticket, guaranteeing a seat – and nothing more – between Capetown and Pniel.'

He travelled the first sixty miles, to the little town of Wellington, by train. The railway line ran no farther. Passengers for the diamond fields had to leave the train at Wellington and wait until their coach was unloaded from a truck. This wait at a local hotel marked, as Boyle soon discovered, the end of any pretence at comfort.

The coach was a huge covered wagon, drawn by eight horses. Three wooden benches under the awning seated nine passengers, while two others perched at the back with the guard. There was little room for luggage and, more often than not, those inside had to sit with their cases cutting into their knees. Nor was this the only torment. Loose canvas pockets for carrying food swung from the roof with every jolt of the wagon and passengers had continually to duck to escape having their heads banged to bits. This inconvenience, however, was a very necessary evil. Overnight stops were brief and food on the road practically unprocurable. The days when hospitable Boers provided meals for chance travellers were long since past. 'The farmer would be ruined,' admitted Boyle, 'were he to feed one half of the crowd that passes up, on foot or in ox-wagons ... so the voyager is bound to lay in stores of provisions,

sardines, potted meats, bread, brandy, and all actual necessaries for the road.'
Boyle had arrived with a couple of hams which, he realised too late, he
had neglected to have boiled. It was hardly an encouraging start to the
seven-hundred-mile journey.

The road immediately beyond Wellington was deserted. They passed not a
single traveller, and Boyle became bored and depressed. He found the scenery
dreary beyond words. How the Cape had gained a reputation for beauty was
incomprehensible to him. 'What a frightful wilderness!' he complained, once
they had passed the famous Bain's Kloof. But he spoke too soon. On the
second day they entered the Karoo; here the real wilderness began.

For miles ahead the monotonous veld shimmered, flat and forbidding, under
a pitiless sun. There seemed no end to the grey, stony, desolate plains. Boyle
was appalled. 'No object over six inches high, whether plant or stone, breaks
that dead level, till in the dim haze it fades against the low dusty hills,' he
moaned. 'No shadow falls here but the gloom of a passing cloud. Even the
stones that clothe the land are small and shadeless. A dusky knot of prickles
here and there, a sprig of heath, a tuft of chamomile or sage, a thin grey arm of a
nameless root, a bulb like a football broken, peeling in the heat – such is the
vegetation. . . . The sole thing real in all this landscape is that abomination
stretched before you.'

It took them the best part of a week to cross the Karoo. Sitting stiff-backed
on the wooden benches, unable to move their legs or rest their heads, plagued
by the heat, the dust, the flies – the journey was hellish. At the short stops they
snatched what sleep they could, but they dared not sleep too long; it was as
necessary to walk as it was to rest. 'My ankles had begun to swell,' explained
Boyle, 'and give some slight pain. One of us was in a terrible state from this
cause, his limbs double their size, and blotched with discolourations, another
suffered severely, and a third was lame. A three hours' walk cured my case; but
the others were too far gone for the remedy.

Occasionally they passed groups of men, slogging along on foot, who
stopped them and begged for water. At one stop they discovered two sailors
resting after being picked up senseless with thirst in the veld. 'There were, and
are,' said Boyle, 'continual discoveries of unknown dead in this wilderness.'

Not until the day after they had crossed the Orange River near Hopetown
did things begin to brighten. There was a gradual, but discernible, change in the
scenery: the scrub was taller and tinged with green, the earth was redder, grass
rippled in the breeze, and here and there low thorn trees began to appear. Even
the jaundiced Boyle had to admit that there were parts which were 'quite
pretty'. That night they were obliged to sleep in the veld, but they were on their
way again early next morning and by late afternoon they had reached Pniel,
their journey's end. They had left Wellington eleven days earlier.

The river diggings came as a distinct disappointment to Boyle. Before
leaving England he had seen a photograph of the great sea of tents and wagons
that had formed the camp at Pniel in its hey-day. Now, four months after New
Rush, the place was all but deserted. It seemed, says Boyle, like the bivouac of a
marauding army 'after the troops have left, and the camp followers are still

packing'. Mrs Jardine's famous hotel was still there and Boyle was impressed
by the decorum with which it was run. The diggers were quiet and orderly,
meals were punctual and the service unobtrusive. Most welcome of all,
however, were the mattresses spread out on the floor of a small apartment
which, closely packed as they were, offered the exhausted travellers a good
night's sleep.

But there was no point in lingering at Pniel. Dutoitspan and New Rush were
now 'the real diamond fields' and, although the Inland Transport Company
had not yet recognised this fact, new arrivals were quick to back-track to the
dry diggings. The following morning Boyle obtained a place on one of the two
rickety carts which ran daily between the river and Dutoitspan. He was
disgusted to discover that the fare for this short, bone-shaking journey was
fifteen shillings.

The road was atrocious and, for the most part, deserted. Not until they
neared New Rush were there any signs of activity. Then carts began to pass
them every five minutes; occasionally an empty wagon, returning from de-
livering produce to the diggings, lumbered by. Dotted about the veld could be
seen the isolated camps of Boers who, too poor to own a claim, eked out a living
by carrying home debris for their wives and children to sort.

Soon the camps became more numerous, the road more crowded. Tents and
canvas-framed houses took on the appearance of streets. A low rise, faintly
white against the sky, broke the horizon, and the driver, pointing his whip,
shouted – 'New Rush!'

'Through the straggling purlieus of the place we trot with crack of whip and
warning shout,' says the excited Boyle. 'The roadway swarms with naked
Kaffir and brawny white man. Dressed in corduroy or shoddy, high booted,
bare as to arms and breast, with beard of any length upon their chins, girt with a
butcher's knife on belt of leather – one could not readily believe that amongst
these bronzed fellows might be found creditable representatives of every profession. The road grows snowy white. Our wheels sink into "diamondiferous
sand".... Wooden houses show themselves, all hung about with mis-
cellaneous goods. Thicker and thicker stand the tents, closer presses the
throng. A din of shouts and laughter fills the air. We pass drinking shops full of
people; negroes go by in merry gangs. One stares amazed at such a crush of
dwellings, such a busy, noisy host. One more sharp turn, and market square
opens before us.'

Half the passengers left the cart at New Rush; Boyle went on to Dutoitspan,
bypassing Old De Beer's on the way.

The approach to Dutoitspan was more orderly than that to New Rush. The
tents were as closely packed, the streets as busy, but the roads were broader and
more regular; the hotels were larger, the shops more established. Dutoitspan,
which also acted as a centre for Bultfontein, did not sprawl to the same extent
as New Rush, and the diggings had not been allowed to intrude upon the camp.
The diggers there seemed a more reserved, less noisy, and better organised
crowd. Altogether, says Boyle, there was something staid and decent about
Dutoitspan 'which befits the elder sister, though elder she be but by six
months'.

'Woes of travelling in a Cape "spider" in the early days.' A contemporary illustration of the difficulties of reaching the diamond fields. (K)

Prospecting Colesberg Kopje (later the Kimberley Mine) shortly after the New Rush. Painting by A. E. White after J. W. George. (M)

'The Street we lived in — New Rush — Diamond fields.' Painting by Mary Elizabeth Barber. (K; Albany Museum, Grahamstown)

He decided to make Dutoitspan his base and put up at Benning and Martin's hotel, just off the market square.

Boyle's journey to the diamond fields was similar to that of many new-comers. His first impressions are also typical. What perhaps struck him as much as anything was the Britishness of the diggings. While at Pniel he had met some old friends at Mrs Jardine's hotel: one was the son of a Scottish baronet and another – 'the swellest of swells' – was a man he had known for years in London. It had made him feel at home immediately. The same clublike atmosphere was apparent also at Benning and Martin's in Dutoitspan. Snob that he undoubtedly was, Boyle was glad to note that his fellow guests in the ramshackle hotel were not only well behaved but decidedly well bred: there was a remarkable absence of crudity, the English spoken at the dinner table was impeccable. 'Boers do not come here,' Boyle observed smugly, 'and the poorer sort take luncheon at their tents or in the claim. Diamond digging is em-phatically, up to this time, a "gentleman's digging". Long may it continue so.'

There seemed no reason why it should not. Indeed, there was every likelihood that the 'outpost of Empire' flavour would become stronger. The long-drawn-out quarrel over the ownership of the diamond fields had just come to an abrupt, if not unexpected, end. Only a matter of days before Boyle landed at the Cape, the diggings had been proclaimed British.

(2)

A year earlier, at the end of December 1870, Sir Henry Barkly had arrived in South Africa to take up his position as Governor of the Cape. At Cape Town he had been met by President Brand of the Orange Free State. Brand and a member of his Executive Council, C. W. Hutton, had come to the Cape to tackle the new Governor about the ownership of the diamond fields. Even then the dispute had been dragging on for months and they were hoping that Barkly would see reason and that the matter would be settled amicably. They soon discovered how wrong they were.

The first formal meeting between the Free State delegates and the Governor was held on 3 January 1871. It lasted three hours. All the old arguments were trotted out. From the very outset Barkly, primed by Richard Southey, insisted that Nicolaas Waterboer had a firm claim to the territory. He suggested that the entire controversy be submitted to arbitration. This immediately put the Free Staters' backs up. There could be no question, they argued, of Water-boer's claiming land east of the Vaal, where the dry diggings were situated. The boundaries of that territory had been decided in the days of the Orange River Sovereignty and passed on to the Free State in 1854. Few, if any, Griquas lived in the region and Waterboer had never exercised his jurisdiction there. Most of the farms east of the Vaal had been transferred to Free State burgers, and the Free State had continued the Sovereignty's practice of issuing land grants there. There could be no doubt as to the Free State's right to the territory.

The vexed problem of the Campbell Lands across the river was another matter. Here there were a number of claimants, including the Transvaal. As far as these lands were concerned, the Free State was prepared to allow the arbitration of a foreign court but, as Waterboer had offered to cede his territory to the British Government, Barkly was not sufficiently impartial to act as umpire in the matter.

Not surprisingly, the meeting ended in deadlock. So did subsequent meetings, at which the legality of various farm transfers was contested. Eventually Brand recognised that his hopes of an amicable settlement were doomed. It was a hard pill for him to swallow. Hutton, on the other hand, was later to claim that he had recognised the futility of the discussions from the very beginning and would not have remained at the Cape twenty-four hours had he not been persuaded to do so by Brand.

But obviously things could not be left there. At the end of February Sir Henry Barkly visited the river diggings, on his way to Basutoland. He was met at Klipdrift by President Pretorius of the Transvaal Republic, Nicolaas Waterboer – accompanied by David Arnot – and chiefs of the Barolong and Ba-Tlaping tribes. All had claims to the Campbell Lands on the north bank of the Vaal and all agreed to submit their claims to an arbitration court presided over by Robert Keate, the Lieutenant-Governor of Natal. In the meantime the disputed diggings were to be administered jointly by the Cape magistrate at Klipdrift and a Transvaal magistrate at Hebron.

Encouraged by this success, Barkly continued his journey and stopped off at Bloemfontein in the hopes of persuading President Brand to follow the example of President Pretorius. He was asking a great deal. Not only did he want Brand to accept arbitration in the matter of the Campbell Lands – the Free State still had its magistrate at Pniel on the south bank – but to 'submit to the decision of arbitrators the right of the state to all the ground claimed by Mr Arnot for Waterboer'.

President Brand, of course, would have none of it. He wanted nothing to do with Arnot's sweeping claims. His attitude was much the same as it had been at Cape Town. The Free State, he maintained, had every right to the dry diggings and if anyone tried to interfere with those rights they would be met with 'measures of resistance'. He was still prepared to agree to arbitration in the Campbell Lands' dispute, but not to an arbitration court presided over by the Lieutenant-Governor of Natal. The question must be decided by an impartial judge. He suggested either the President of the United States or the King of Holland. Alternatively, the Free State was prepared to sell its title to the Campbell Lands on fair terms or exchange it for the Albania district, near Hopetown. Barkly turned all these proposals down.

The Cape Governor was encouraged in his uncompromising attitude by the ever-watchful Richard Southey. 'I was glad to find that you had succeeded with Pretorius so well,' wrote Southey on 11 March. 'Brand must ultimately come to some arrangement of the kind, but his case is so weak that I am not surprised at his resisting it by all means in his power.' He promised to send Barkly a draft reply to Brand's latest arguments.

There could be little doubt as to what President Brand was up against. With David Arnot constantly at Waterboer's elbow and Richard Southey breathing down the Governor's neck, the chances of a moderate solution were slim indeed.

Nor was this backstairs influence confined to South Africa. Reports sent to London from the Cape undoubtedly coloured the views of the Secretary of State for the Colonies, Lord Kimberley. These views were expressed in a despatch which Kimberley wrote on 17 November 1870. 'Her Majesty's Government', it read 'would see with great dissatisfaction any encroachment on the Griqua territory by those republics, which would open to the Boers an extended field for their slave-operations.' Such an attitude was hardly conducive to mutual trust.

All the same, Lord Kimberley was by no means eager to fall in with Southey's plans entirely. He was, he declared, reluctant to sanction any extension of British dominion beyond the Cape Colony if it entailed additional responsibility and cost. But, as so often happened, the pace of events made it impossible for Whitehall to stand aloof indefinitely. Hardly had Barkly left Bloemfontein than an attempt by a few individuals to defy Free State authority on the diamond fields led to President Brand's calling out a commando to uphold law and order. Barkly responded by ordering a Colonial force to concentrate on Hopetown, while a troop under Commandant Bowker marched to Klipdrift to support the British magistrate there.

This confrontation appears to have spurred Kimberley into action. On 18 May 1871, he authorised Barkly to accept the cession of Waterboer's territory in order to safeguard the interests of British subjects on the diamond fields. However, his despatch emphasised that the responsibility for the territory would rest with the Cape parliament, which would have to consent to the annexation. Any force sent to preserve order, he said, would 'not consist of British troops but be a force raised and supported by the colony'.

But which precisely was Waterboer's territory? This was a problem which worried the Cape parliamentarians. Few doubted the advantage of securing the diamond fields for the Cape, but some members had doubts about taking over such an ill-defined possession. How, they argued, could the territory be properly administered when the question of land rights had not been settled? How would the Free State and the other claimants react to such a move? It would not do to act rashly.

When, in July 1871, Southey moved in the Assembly that Waterboer's territory be annexed, he was given only lukewarm support. The matter was debated until the beginning of August and then Southey's motion only scraped through on a single vote. It was passed on the understanding that nothing other than what belonged to Waterboer would be annexed. This, Southey blithely assured the House, was all that was intended.

Yet Barkly hesitated to act. He was, he informed President Brand, reluctant to fix boundaries in direct opposition to the Free State's claims. Would not the Free State accept arbitration? He had reason to think that the Free State might. Already the Boers had made an important concession. In April, when the diamond farms were in the news – the Dutoitspan diggers were then defying Henry Webb and Louis Hond – the Free State legislature had agreed to allow arbitration on the question of the dry diggings. It had been proposed that Britain choose between the German Emperor, the King of Holland and the President of the United States as an arbitrator. The proposal had been turned down. Barkly had no intention of allowing outside interference.

However, by the time Southey's motion was squeezed through the Cape Assembly, things had changed. Colesberg Kopje had been discovered and backs had stiffened all round. President Brand recognised the futility of trying to negotiate with Sir Henry Barkly. He decided instead to appeal over the Governor's head. At the beginning of October he informed the Cape authorities that he had sent a special representative to England.

Unfortunately this move was made too late. Not only did the Free State delegate receive short shrift in London but, a few days later, Barkly was presented with a substantial prop for his plans. On 17 October the findings of Lieutenant-Governor Keate's arbitration were made public.

In effect, the publication of the Keate Award, as it was known, decided the fate of the diamond fields.

The Keate Award was to come in for much criticism. It gave the Barolong and BaThlaping tribes certain land, cut the Transvaal off from the diggings, and made acceptance of the boundary claimed by David Arnot east of the Vaal – encompassing the Dutoitspan, Bultfontein and Vooruitzigt farms – inevitable. The only person to gain substantially by it was Nicolaas Waterboer.

But Keate, with whom the final decision rested, was not entirely to blame for what looked like a prejudiced judgement. The case presented by the Transvaal was muddled and unreliable; the Free State had refused to take part in the arbitration. Acting on the evidence before him, Keate had little alternative but to decide as he did.

No one was more surprised at the outcome than David Arnot. 'I had not a single trump card in my hand,' he later declared, 'but I won the game.'

His jubilation rang hollowly in the ears of the Transvaal and Free State Boers. The loss of the diamond fields was for them a bitter and lasting blow. 'To this transaction', wrote the historian G.M. Theal, 'more than to any other is due the feeling of suspicion of English policy mingled with enmity towards it, which for the next thirty years was entertained by many residents of the secluded farms in the republics.'

The falsity of Arnot's claims was not acknowledged until some five years later, after a more thorough investigation. Then the Free State was persuaded to relinquish its claims on payment from Britain of £90,000. But the harm had been done. No amount of compensation could soften the hostility of those Boers who considered that they had been robbed of untold riches.

Once the Keate Award had been published, Nicolaas Waterboer lost no time in swearing allegiance to the British crown. Sir Henry Barkly was just as hasty in accepting his submission. In a proclamation issued ten days later and signed by Barkly, Her Britannic Majesty Queen Victoria graciously acknowledged Nicolaas Waterboer and his people as British subjects. The boundaries of Waterboer's territory, known as Griqualand West, were then set out. The dividing-line between Waterboer and the Transvaal was that defined by the

Keate Award. As far as the Free State was concerned, it was pointed out that President Brand had refused to accept arbitration and therefore 'Her Majesty is compelled to determine the said boundary line between the said territory and the said Orange Free State upon the best evidence which she has been able to obtain'. This meant that Barkly, accepting the claims of David Arnot, had formally grabbed the dry diggings. The long dispute had been ended by a stroke of the Governor's pen.

Further proclamations issued on the same day laid down the means by which the territory would be governed. Griqualand West, it was declared, would be subject to the same laws and usages as the Cape Colony 'so far as the same shall not be inapplicable'. To administer these laws three commissioners – John Campbell, the magistrate at Klipdrift, James Henry Bowker, commandant of the frontier force, and John Cyprian Thompson, a Cape lawyer – were appointed. Barkly's proclamation announcing these appointments ended: 'I hereby command all Her Majesty's loving subjects in the said territories of Griqualand West to be aiding and assisting the said Commissioners.'

He was asking a lot from Her Majesty's loving subjects on the diamond fields.

(3)

Market Square, New Rush, was a large space cleared amid the jumble of tents on the east side of Colesberg Kopje. From one corner of the square, a more or less straight road, known as Main Street, ran direct to the diggings. At the end of this road was a huge pile of debris from the mine which the diggers had nicknamed 'Mount Ararat'. The square, the street and the debris heap were, during the early months, the only really distinguishable features of the new camp. Mr Stegmann's attempts to impose some sort of order in New Rush had, for the most part, been defeated by the wild scramble for claims and living space. Once the diggers had pitched their tents or positioned their wagons, it had become all but impossible to shift them. Whatever other roads existed were merely rutted tracks which wound haphazardly through the maze of tents; the so-called streets of New Rush, it was claimed, simply followed the course of the wheelbarrows.

From the very beginning the market square provided a natural centre for the diggers. Surrounded mostly by tents, wagons and rickety, canvas-framed structures, it also boasted a few hastily erected wooden shacks, built by the more enterprising merchants as makeshift stores, diamond-buying offices and canteens. Anything of significance which happened at New Rush tended to happen in or around the dusty market square. Here meetings were called, announcements were made and demonstrations were held.

One of the first of these demonstrations occurred on the morning of 17 November 1871, when a mob of diggers crowded into the square to await the arrival of the newly appointed Cape commissioners. They were, for the most part, in a holiday mood and gave a great cheer when, at eleven o'clock, two of the commissioners – John Campbell and John Cyprian Thompson – came riding into the square at the head of fifteen armed and mounted police.

The little procession threaded its way through the jostling diggers and came to a halt outside S.A. Mons's wooden store. Dismounting, the two commissioners climbed on a wagon and John Campbell solemnly read out Sir Henry Barkly's edict declaring the diamond fields to be British. His final words – 'God Save the Queen' – were drowned by the deafening cheers which broke out as the Union Jack was slowly hoisted.

The performance was repeated in Dutoitspan at midday (where Sheriff Buykes also read the proclamation in Dutch) and an hour later at Bultfontein. On all three farms the British flag was unfurled without a dissenting voice being heard. 'There was not an obstacle raised,' claimed a journalist, 'nor the slightest opposition shown; but, on the contrary, the diggers as a body, seemed delighted with the change. Du Toit's Pan, which we have been led to believe all along had such Free State proclivities was the most enthusiastic in its reception of the Commissioners.'

But all was not as it appeared. Widespread rejoicing at the British take-over was only superficially apparent. By no means all the diggers were carried away at the sight of the new commissioners. At New Rush, for instance, one digger was seen shaving outside his tent when the Union Jack was raised and, as the crowd roared its approval, he merely glanced up, grunted, and went on lathering his face. Later that day, an American digger showed his disapproval by hauling down the British flag. These were small, isolated incidents which passed almost unremarked; but, as everyone knew, they were symptomatic of a very definite and deep-rooted hostility towards British rule. The prediction of trouble from diggers with 'Free State proclivities' was not without foundation.

It was not merely the change of flag that was resented; more important was the anticipated change of law. Although the Free State Boers were by no means the 'slave dealers' of Lord Kimberley's imaginings, they had strong reservations about Cape laws which did not distinguish between people of colour. Until now the regulations of the diggers' committees, backed by the Free State, had effectively excluded all but whites from owning claims; Africans had not been allowed to buy or sell diamonds, had been prohibited from roaming the streets at night, and had been forbidden to buy liquor without a written permit from their employers. Now it seemed more than likely that these restrictions would be abolished. 'All contemplated with alarm the probable results of British law upon their industry,' said Frederick Boyle. 'They feared difficulties with the negro, needless interference with their rules.' There were many, in fact, who still hankered after an independent republic governed by a diggers' committee.

Not for nothing did one of the commissioners, speaking at a banquet that night, remind his audience that Cape law would only apply on the diggings 'in so far as the same be not inapplicable to the circumstances existing'. His speech was, in a way, the first public acknowledgement of the ugly racialistic whispers that were then gathering momentum.

One of the few remaining hopes of the dissidents was that, if the Free State law no longer applied, they would at least have the benefit of a Free State magistrate. Olof Truter, who had earlier been transferred from Pniel to Dutoitspan, had proved as popular at the dry diggings as he had been on the river. Although he complained bitterly about his incapable and largely corrupt police force, he had managed to administer a 'rough-and-ready sort of justice' which satisfied most of the diggers. Hope that he would be retained by the new regime was, however, shortlived.

The day after the reading of the proclamation, a prisoner named Duffy, who had been arrested for theft by the Free State police, appealed to some passers-by for the protection of the English authorities. That same afternoon orders were given for his release by Inspector Gilfillan of the Cape Mounted Police. On receiving these orders, Truter rose from his bench, violently protested against such interference and broke up his court. Inspector Gilfillan was immediately appointed to take his place.

During the next few weeks tension mounted. At the end of the month the commissioners dissolved the standing diggers' committees, abrogated their rules and proposed that new committees be elected. The diggers responded by holding a boisterous meeting in the market square at Dutoitspan. Frederick Boyle, who was present, gave a graphic account of the speeches. 'Something in this style the oratory ran,' he says: ' "Did we invite this 'ere English annexation, brother diggers? No we didn't: we didn't ask for it, and we don't want it. We was content with the old Committee and its rules, wasn't us, brothers? Those gentlemen understood the wants of the diggers, and provided for 'em. These Commissioners don't know nothing about us. I ask you, brother diggers, was there ever a diamond digging like this afore? No! Well, then, what do these Commissioners know about it? What does the Cape Parliament, or what does the English Parliament know about it? Nothing! Very well, then, let us be ruled by them as does know; and if we are to vote, let us vote for the old Committee back again, and all the old rules. That's your ticket, brother diggers! The old Committee and the old rules!" '

The meeting broke up in confusion, but at an adjourned session the old Dutoitspan committee was re-elected. The commissioners, not surprisingly, refused to acknowledge it. They maintained that the election was the work of irresponsible agitators. Taking comfort from the fact that the more established leaders – men like Stafford Parker and Captain Finlayson – had refused to oppose the Cape authorities, they apparently thought they could afford to ignore the rabble rousers. How wrong they were. The rabble rousers had no intention of being ignored: the trouble, in fact, had only just started.

A climax was reached two weeks later. On 17 December, after a month of British rule, the diggers of New Rush went on the rampage.

The riot, for that is what it amounted to, was not entirely unexpected. For some time there had been rumours that a number of canteen keepers at New Rush were trading in stolen diamonds. Illicit diamond buying was already a serious problem but the fact that the canteen keepers were suspected of enticing Africans to steal stones from the diggings in return for brandy made their crime doubly outrageous: it flouted the mostly strongly enforced rules in the diggers's book. However, prevalent as the rumours were, it had been impossible to pin any of the suspected men down. It was not until a coloured servant confessed to having seen his master – a man named Ascher – purchase a stolen diamond from an African that a little more substance was given to the rumours. The diggers immediatedly sprang into action. At a hurriedly convened meeting, held in the old committee tent at New Rush, the unfortunate Ascher was confronted by his servant and publicly accused of theft. The servant's word was enough to convict him. There were fifty influential diggers present and their verdict was unanimous: Ascher had violated their code and *they* would punish him, not the law.

Storming out of the tent, they frog-marched Ascher along Main Street. By this time all New Rush was alerted and some two thousand determined diggers joined the march to Ascher's canteen. Things began to get out of hand. Although there had originally been no intention to harm Ascher personally, in a scuffle outside the canteen one of the mob hit the helpless prisoner over the head with an empty bottle, while others attacked his servants. Then orders were given to ransack the canteen; the flimsy canvas structure was ripped down, furniture smashed, liquor bottles shattered and the ruins set on fire.

There was no holding the mob after this. Rushing along Main Street, they went from canteen to canteen, dragging out suspects, holding mock trials and dealing out indiscriminate punishment. Four or five more canteen keepers were pronounced guilty and their premises were burnt down one after another.

While the rioting was at its height, Inspector Gilfillan arrived from Dutoit-span. He was given a tremendous cheer. There was, as everyone knew, nothing he could do. Most of his police had joined the mob and he only added to the confusion by sympathising with the rebels. Jumping onto a cart, he shouted, 'I am a digger myself, and I understand you.' However, he insisted that enough had been done and begged the crowd to disperse. Gradually they did. After setting light to an empty tent and attacking odd individuals here and there, the majority of diggers called it a day. Only the thugs refused to give up; they contented themselves by 'chasing negroes round about, aimlessly punching their heads when caught'.

A further attack was expected at Dutoitspan the following day, but it proved a false alarm. The Dutoitspan diggers had their own way of dealing with things. On 29 December they held another mass meeting in the market square and passed a number of fiery resolutions. 'By the action of Government,' they declared, 'not only does disorder and confusion reign in the Camp, by disallowing our Rules etc., but by issuing of licences to dig for diamonds to coloured persons of more than one fourth black blood – an act totally opposed to diggers Regulations – a pretext is given by which our native servants can wrongfully and lawfully dispose of our property.'

The distinction of one-quarter black blood was thought to be significant. Many diggers were to argue that they were not motivated entirely by racial prejudice. The trouble was, they claimed, once a recognisable black man was allowed to dig legitimately he could sell diamonds legitimately. If this happened it would be impossible to distinguish between black diggers and black labourers who stole from claims. The fact that non-claimholding white men, however disreputable, could trade in diamonds did not enter into it. What they were admitting, in fact, was that their undoubted prejudice did not enable them to differentiate between a respectable black digger and a potential thief. The blatant racialism of most of the demonstrations was all too obvious.

In the middle of January there was another ugly eruption at New Rush. This time a white youth, employed by a highly respectable merchant, was suspected of using 'a Kafir by the name of Charley' as a go-between for buying stolen diamonds. Once again a huge crowd gathered outside the merchant's store in Main Street; once again there were demands that the store be burnt down. It was only when the merchant assured the mob that he had sacked Charley that morning and was prepared to surrender the suspected youth to the law, that reason prevailed. 'The boy was handed over to the tender mercies of several diggers,' it was reported, 'and the Kafir Diamond Merchant and the boy together were marched off to the new gaol. The crowd then dispersed.'

With each new incident racial tension mounted. 'Nigger,' a new term of abuse for the black man popularised by American diggers, was shouted at meeting after meeting. Only a few were brave enough to stand out against the bigotry of the mob; even then their defence of the black man was somewhat equivocal. 'A man having a white face, who can pay his way here,' one digger wrote to the *Diamond News,* 'has all the rights of a digger. Surely, the misfortune of having a black phiz does not make such an enormous difference as to exclude its ill-starred possessor from those rights. I'm not one of those who believe the black is our equal. . . .All I advocate is the impartial justice that the Englishman is so fond of talking tall of so often.'

(4)

Appeals to Sir Henry Barkly produced little in the way of constructive reforms. The Governor was hardly in a position to take strong measures. Southey's narrowly passed motion in the Cape Assembly had merely recognised the desirability of annexing Waterboer's territory; a bill formally claiming Griqualand West for the Cape had still to be debated by Parliament. It was introduced in the House in April 1872 and came up for a second reading on 5 June. Opposition to it was strong and heated. All the doubts expressed earlier were vigorously repeated. Barkly's blithe acceptance of David Arnot's claims was regarded with suspicion. Some members wholeheartedly supported the Free State view that Waterboer had no right to the dry diggings and were in favour of rejecting the annexation outright. Others wanted a fuller investigation into the conflicting claims and were not prepared to vote for the annexation until such an investigation had been carried out. As the Cape was then moving towards responsible government, it was thought that it would be foolish to complicate matters by taking on such a trouble-fraught territory. Faced by such resolute opposition, Barkly instructed Richard Southey to withdraw the annexation bill without putting it to the vote.

The diggers were delighted. Barkly's climb-down gave extra strength to the arguments that Cape rule was too weak and indecisive to bring order to the diggings. Evidence of lawlessness was being accumulated almost by the day. At the beginning of May there had been a sensational daylight robbery at New Rush. A respectable-looking Englishman, named John William Harding, had strolled up to the post office and, finding the counter unattended, had coolly reached through the delivery window and removed a bag of letters containing 2,381 diamonds. His eventual capture owed more to luck than to the efficiency of the police. He was arrested in a Cape Town hotel, on 4 June, on a charge of stealing money from a fellow passenger from England some three months earlier. As he had already booked his passage home on the s.s. *Syria,* the police boarded the ship and examined his luggage; they discovered 2,347 diamonds – some stuffed down the barrel of a rifle – and over £1,000 in cash. At his trial, Harding confessed to robbing the New Rush post office. An equally daring, but unsuccessful, attempt was made shortly afterwards to steal a postbag of diamonds from a mail wagon. It is hardly surprising that few diggers had faith in the diamond fields police force.

Soon, what little faith they had was to be effectively snuffed out. On 16 July the most serious riot in the history of the diggings broke out. It started when a mob of diggers at New Rush rushed a tent belonging to an Indian suspected of illicit diamond buying. The tent was torn down, diamonds discovered, and the Indian stripped, flogged and kicked out of the camp. The following evening an enormous procession of diggers, headed by a makeshift band, marched through the camp, wrecking tents, burning canteens and beating up anyone who got in their way. 'Bottles of French brandy, wines and bitters were ruthlessly smashed,' it was reported, 'casks were stoved in, and every article of value destroyed. The crowd could not have numbered less than four thousand, and it was momentarily increasing.'

When a little band of mounted police eventually showed up, the situation was completely out of control. As the police held the mob back at rifle point in front of one tent, the diggers darted behind them and set light to a tent in the rear. Flames rose throughout the camp; it was no longer a question of guilt or innocence, canvas was fired in all directions. A perfectly blameless butcher was forced to stand by as his shop and stock roasted to a cinder. At another tent a terrified woman and child only escaped burning when one of the mob shouted, 'Save the female.' When Inspector Gilfillan made a desperate attempt to reason with the rioters, he was seized by a hefty digger, lifted shoulder high, and 'threatened with closer proximity to the flames than appeared to be pleasant'. After this undignified treatment, commented a journalist, 'the gallant officer retired'.

A cry went up for the mob to move on to Dutoitspan. There was an immediate surge along Main Street and a 'dense living mass, many persons being carried along with the stream', headed for the Dutoitspan road. On the outskirts of New Rush they were met by another contingent of mounted police. Whether it was the presence of the policemen or whether, as seems more likely, it was the shout 'Too late to go Dutoitspan!' that turned them back is not clear. In any case, turn back they did. They returned to the market square and, after a short, rowdy meeting, dispersed.

The following afternoon, R. W. Giddy – who was acting as the Resident Commissioner at New Rush, in place of Commandant Bowker – invited a group of influential diggers to meet him. He appealed to them to help him maintain law and order and persuaded most of them to enrol as special constables. That same afternoon some of the leading rioters were arrested. Once news of these arrests leaked out, a huge crowd gathered outside the Commissioner's office in the market square demanding that the prisoners be released. Giddy gave in. Standing on a chair outside his office, he assured the crowd that the arrested men would be released on bail. He went on to explain that he was enrolling special constables not, as was thought, to turn digger against digger but 'for increasing the means whereby rascally native servants and dishonest diamond buyers may be brought to justice'.

But clearly more was needed than this. Things had reached a stage where, if outright rebellion was to be avoided, the commissioners would have to come to terms with the still-active diggers' committees. Realising this, Giddy sent for the other two commissioners, John Campbell and John Cyprian Thompson, who were stationed at Klipdrift. A meeting was arranged for Monday 19 July.

It took place in the Resident Commissioner's office at New Rush at three o'clock in the afternoon. The market square was packed. Over a thousand diggers milled around Giddy's office. They were joined by a deputation from Dutoitspan, which marched into the square behind a Scotsman carrying a red flag. As their representatives conferred with the commissioners, the diggers held their own impromptu meeting. Speaker after speaker climbed on to a buckwagon and harangued the crowd. Somewhat to everyone's surprise, one of the speakers was Captain Finlayson. Having so far kept aloof from the demonstrations, Finlayson now turned around and denounced British rule as 'weak, bad, revengeful, despotic, and cruel'. Not only was his speech loudly cheered, but it was most likely heard by the commissioners.

(5)

The outcome of the meeting was more favourable to the diggers than any of them had expected. In a proclamation issued four days later, the commissioners agreed to most of their demands. The most important of these demands was, of course, that all licences held by 'natives' be scrapped. The proclamation was signed by John Campbell and R.W. Giddy; the third commissioner, John Cyprian Thompson, would have no part in it.

Thompson was a lawyer and his objections to the proclamation were based not only on humanitarian grounds, but on justice and logic. The dry diggings had, in theory, been ceded to Britain by the Griquas. If people of colour were to be denied their rights on the diamond fields, the British Government would rightly be accused of betraying a trust. Such a move, Thompson argued, would open the door to a great many evils; it would initiate class legislation and lay the foundation for future trouble. There could be little doubt that Sir Henry Barkly would refuse to sanction it.

And so it turned out. When the proclamation was referred to Cape Town,

Barkly disowned it. Like Thompson he was not prepared to condone a blanket ban inspired by colour prejudice. As he later explained to the diggers, while he was aware of the trouble caused by some dishonest servants, he could not accept skin colour as the criterion of honesty. 'I have met men', he said, 'whom you would call off-coloured of most estimable and admirable qualities. It is very unjust that all these classes of persons should be placed in the same category. You have here the industrious and honest Malay from the Cape Colony, and, on the other hand the wild Bechuana, and both are placed on the same footing, which I do not think is just.'

Fairminded as his attitude was, the Governor's rejection of the proclamation simply sparked off a fresh wave of violence at the diggings: there were more mass meetings, more demonstrations, more tent burnings. The shaky rule of the three commissioners was brought to the point of collapse.

Barkly was forced to realise that he would have to intervene in person. At the beginning of September - the earliest he could get away from Cape Town - he hurried to Dutoitspan. It was a brave move. Few men were more unpopular in Griqualand West than the Governor of the Cape; there was every reason to think that his appearance at the diggings would prove disastrous. 'The idea then prevailed at Capetown', says Dr Matthews, 'that the diggers would think no more of chopping off a governor's head than they would of decapitating a domestic fowl.' But Barkly did not arrive unprepared: he had an important card to play. Far from being a disaster, his visit ended as a huge success.

Shortly after his arrival, a 'Tiffin' (an informal meal) was held in his honour in the Mutual Hall at New Rush. About one hundred and forty diggers were invited, as well as the visiting Bishop of Bloemfontein and the newly elected President of the Transvaal, Thomas Burgers.

Addressing the guests, Barkly produced his ace. He admitted frankly that he had been over-hasty in imposing government by commission on the diamond fields. The mining community could not be ruled from Cape Town, seven hundred miles away. The diggers objected to such rule and the 'antiquated Conservatives' in the Cape House of Assembly were opposed to an alternative form of government. He had therefore, he said, decided to drop his plan for annexing the territory to the Cape. Instead he intended to apply to the imperial authorities to proclaim Griqualand West a Crown Colony. This meant that the territory would, like Natal, be administered by a Lieutenant-Governor in consultation with a small legislative council elected by the diggers.

He ended his speech by acknowledging the presence of the Transvaal President and praising President Brand of the Orange Free State. If the new constitution proved acceptable, he declared, he hoped that Griqualand West would be 'among the first of the States' to enter into a South African federation, a federation which would include the Boer republics. He was given a standing ovation.

It seemed, on the face of it, a simple enough solution. There was, however, one unforeseeable snag. The man whom Barkly intended to appoint as the first Lieutenant-Governor of Griqualand West was Richard Southey.

5

Dust, Drought and Flies

'The four great mines (New Rush, Dutoitspan, Bultfontein and Old De Beers) were roughly circular in shape, the claimholders erecting their dwellings as close to the mines as possible, and traders, storekeepers and publicans put up their buildings in any vacant spot . . . thus each mining camp was composed of a central group of workings surrounded by a ring of shacks, shanties, huts and shelters constructed of any material that would keep off the rain or the scorching heat of the sun.'

This is how one digger remembered the dry diggings of 1871.

Of the four mines, New Rush was undoubtedly the best organised. For, although it had been impossible to create a planned township around Colesberg Kopje, order of a sort had been imposed within the New Rush diggings themselves. Hard experience had taught the diggers the need for such order. The haphazard way in which the Dutoitspan and Bultfontein mines had been opened had resulted in a jumble of holes, pits and burrows, with narrow, winding paths leading to the perimeter where and how they could. This had proved not only unsatisfactory but downright dangerous. Few diggers had been prepared to give up part of their claims to allow others access to the centre of the mine, and the occasional roads that had been established were constantly being whittled away. There were frequent fights over right of way, the roads soon began to cave in, and accidents, often fatal, occurred daily.

To prevent the same thing happening at Vooruitzigt, a Free State mine inspector had insisted, from the very outset, that the claims at both the De Beers diggings be properly organised. Provision had been made for fourteen roads to run north to south across the mine at Colesberg Kopje. These roads, fifteen feet wide, had been cut from the claims – diggers on either side of them surrendering seven and a half feet of surface soil – and were regarded as common ground. As each claim was a standard thirty foot square by Free State measure (thirty-one foot square, English measure) and no one was allowed to own more than two claims, road-making demands at New Rush entailed a considerable sacrifice on the part of individual diggers. But it was a sacrifice most of them were ready to make. The roads were essential for carting soil to the sorting-tents at the edge of the mine; without them early digging on Colesberg Kopje would have been chaotic.

The system worked well enough as long as the diggings were relatively shallow: unfortunately they did not remain shallow for long. Within a matter of weeks Colesberg Kopje had disappeared under a thousand picks and spades – the hillock, as became apparent later, was simply the cone of a deep volcanic pipe – and by the middle of 1872 the mine was fifty to eighty feet deep. The road-ways between the claims became walls, the walls began to crumble, and digging at New Rush quickly became every bit as precarious, every bit as dangerous, as it was in the other mines. The accident rate was alarming. Mule carts and wheelbarrows crashed daily into the deepening chasms, taking diggers and labourers with them; huge chunks of rock were dislodged and fell, burying men working below; chains and ladders – often insecurely fastened – were needed to scramble in and out of the deeper claims. Eventually the badly cracking roads had to be abandoned and replaced by a system of hauling-ropes which carried swaying buckets of soil to and from stagings dotted about the mine. Deaths, disablements, lucky escapes and near-misses became gruesome talking-points throughout the camps.

'This time last year,' observed a digger, looking down into the New Rush mine at the beginning of 1873, 'there were roads leading across the vast abyss, and connecting the sides and roads with each other. Carts and horses and men crossed and recrossed daily. Now the roads have gone; the stuff of which they were made has been reduced to fine sand. . . . It needs a firm nerve to stand upon the brink alone where I am now standing, and look through the running gear – the great network of ropes that cover the face of the Kopje, as it were a spider's web spread over the whole – and, in the midst of the great buzz, to take a calm survey of the work going on. I have seen strong men tremble and clutch the staging whilst they looked into this great human ant-hill. . . . The giddy heights, the noise, the bustle, the elbowing, are sufficient to bewilder anyone. . . . Some of the men get to work in these awkward and dangerous places by means of ladders, some rope-ladders, and some the ordinary builder's ladder. Never has a native met with an accident in going to and from his work by means of holes cut in the rock; but there have been many accidents from climbing up rope and chain-ladders. . . . Men have had frightful falls without being much injured. One man fell over fifty feet, and came up only a little bruised. A man yesterday, aggravated by another, threw him down his claim, between forty and fifty feet deep. The fellow came up again as lively as a cricket; he was not even scratched. The greatest danger to be now apprehended is the falling in of the reef. Several pieces have fallen in, and men have been buried in the ruins. It has been predicted that the staging will yet fall in; and if that were to take place, thousands of lives must be sacrificed.'

The possibility of accidents in the mine was only one of the diggers' worries. There were others, perhaps not so serious but equally dispiriting. Optimists who arrived at the diggings, fed on stories of fabulous finds, quickly discovered that more than luck, or even hard work, was needed to make a fortune on the diamond fields. It required stamina, determination and, above all, good health, not to succumb to the primitive conditions of Griqualand West. This was particularly true of the summer months, when the crippling heat, the lack of sanitation and the scarcity of fresh water made life in the camps a living hell.

The greatest curse of camp life during the early months was the complete absence of any sanitary arrangements. This was due, almost entirely, to the

New Rush in 1872. (C)

Colesberg Kopje in 1873. (C)

R. W. H. Giddy, the Resident Commissioner at New Rush during the early riots.(K)

The saintly Father Anatole Hidien, who died while nurisng a sick digger at Dutoits-pan in November 1871. (K)

New Rush in 1873, showing surface operations and diamond sorting. (J)

hasty way in which the camps had been established. Thousands of diggers had flocked to the dry diggings and gaily settled around the mines without giving a thought to the necessities of everyday living. When Dr Atherstone–the man who had identified the 'Eureka' diamond–visited Dutoitspan at the end of 1871, he was appalled by the unhealthy state of the camp.'Just fancy,' he snorted, 'the organic *débris* of 20,000 persons with their belongings, canine, equine, asinine, and bovine deposited on the edge of a pan without outlet.'

The same was true of the other camps. Closepacked and overcrowded, they festered in the sun and stank to high heaven. Drainage was impossible and no attempt was made to dispose of even the most foul-smelling rubbish; the carcasses of slaughtered oxen, sheep and goats were left to rot outside tents, and the only lavatories were huge open trenches, often dug within the camp itself. In certain sections of the camps the stench was so great that they were avoided by all but the more insensitive or impoverished of diggers.

Flies there were by the million: big flies, small flies, black flies and green flies. They were a plague. The very thought of the flies was enough to make diggers shudder years later. 'And the flies!' groaned one of them. 'Oh, yes! the flies that buzzed in one's ears, settled on the plates, and kept dropping into the dish of melted butter, or dashing into one's coffee or tea.' At one canteen visited by Frederick Boyle the canvas walls were black with flies. 'Dishes and drink choked with them,' he gasped. 'They actually bit our flesh and drained our mortal juices. . . . The horror of illness was more than doubled by this plague.'

Not until July 1872 were some elementary sanitary regulations drawn up at Dutoitspan and New Rush. They were only partly successful. The scarcity of water made any semblance of hygiene all but impossible. Most diggers were unable to wash themselves, let alone keep their surroundings clean.

The water shortage was chronic. It had been since the discovery of the dry diggings. The natural reservoir at Dutoitspan had proved totally inadequate–it quickly dried up and the stagnant water became polluted by debris from the camp–and the two dams built subsequently were soon exhausted. In an effort to eke out the water supply, the diggers' committees at Dutoitspan and Bultfontein had sunk wells and charged one shilling a month for water rights. This entitled diggers to two buckets of water a day which they had to draw from the wells themselves. 'The wells', it was said, 'were nearly always crowded, and the water muddy.' A more serviceable well, providing pure water, was eventually sunk by private enterprise, which for four shillings a month allowed a limited number of subscribers to draw four buckets daily. At New Rush the charge was threepence a bucket, but the water there was notoriously bad. 'The newcomer', advised a visitor, 'should be careful not to drink too much water at first, it is apt to give diarrhoea. A little – a very little – brandy in it is an improvement and a corrective in this respect.'

Even so, diarrhoea was a common complaint throughout the camps, as were dysentery and various types of skin disease. More serious was the malarial 'camp fever' which prostrated many diggers during the summer months and often proved fatal. That more did not die from the fever was due largely to the nature of the mining community. Most diggers were healthy, hearty young men who, having survived the gruelling journey to the fields, were strong enough to recover from their periodic bouts of illness. They undoubtedly needed to be robust: there was, in the early days, very little in the way of medical aid to cure them.

The first - and for some time the only - hospital at the dry diggings was a tent at Bultfontein, known as the Dutoitspan Hospital, which was erected and run by a saintly Roman Catholic priest, Father Anatole Hidien. Almost single-handed Father Hidien laboured among the sick and dying, visiting diggers in their tents and nursing the worst cases in his makeshift infirmary. It was a daunting task. The hospital tent was pitifully ill-equipped; there were no beds - patients lay huddled together on the dusty floor - few medical supplies, even fewer nurses and, as far as is known, Father Hidien was not a trained doctor. The most sick men could hope for was some well-meant but inexpert attention, solace and shelter.

At the beginning of September 1871, it was realised that, with summer approaching, a much larger hospital was needed. For all Father Hidien's devotion he could not alone be expected to cope with the increasing numbers of sick and maimed. A joint meeting of the Dutoitspan, Bultfontein and Vooruitzigt diggers' committees was held and it was decided to erect a central hospital which would serve all the camps. Almost £70 was collected at the meeting towards the cost of the new hospital and a week later it was announced that donations had risen to £400 'and more promised'.

The Diggers Central Hospital was a marquee erected near the Dutoitspan gaol. It was managed by a man named Dowdle; and Dr Patrick Considine, helped by a medical orderly, Alfred Aylward - who later gained considerable notoriety at the diggings - was employed to attend the sick. Despite its size, financial backing and doctor, the new hospital was not a great improvement on Father Hidien's tent. There were still no beds, little in the way of comforts, and the staff was seriously overworked. Nor did it last long. During a ferocious duststorm which lashed the camps at the beginning of November, the marquee was ripped to pieces and rendered useless.

Once again Father Hidien came to the rescue by turning over his own tent to the hospital committee. It was the last of his many unselfish gestures. He was, at that time, slowly dying of typhus which he had contracted while nursing 'a poor man who was full of worms and covered with horrible ulcers'. He died on 19 November. Throughout his own illness, he had continued to wash the sores of his patient twice a day, and for hours after his death the diseased man could be heard calling his name. When told of the priest's death, the man himself died almost immediately.

Remarkable Christian that he undoubtedly was, Father Hidien deserves to be better remembered.

Nothing was done to relieve the pressure on the Dutoitspan tent until early in 1872. Then agitation by the diggers prodded the government into making a grant towards a new hospital. At a meeting in New Rush on 8 March, plans were put forward to build three wattle-and-daub huts, roofed with strong canvas, near the Bultfontein racecourse. It was intended that each of the huts should accommodate ten patients. This far-from-satisfactory arrangement was hailed by the government-supporting *Diamond News* as a tremendous step forward. 'These primitive buildings', it reported with more hope than accuracy, 'can be erected at small cost, and they will serve the purpose for which they are intended as well as the finest hospitals in the colony.'

That was expecting a great deal, particularly in Griqualand West. By the time the building was completed the original plans, simple as they were, had been considerably modified. The new hospital consisted of nothing more than two long huts with twenty beds and a large tent which acted as a mortuary. It did, however, have the distinct advantage of being served by three visiting, fully qualified physicians: Dr William Grimmer, Dr John Dyer, and Dr Josiah Matthews.

Just how horrific conditions at the hospital were, is graphically illustrated by a story told by Dr Matthews. Shortly after his arrival he went to the mortuary tent to examine the corpse of one of his patients who had died in the night. On entering the tent, he says, he discovered 'merely the trunk of the poor fellow's body left; the prowling, ravenous dogs which then roamed about, having devoured the poor man's limbs, which they had torn in pieces from his body'.

The erection of a wood-and-iron building some months later did little to improve matters. Apprehensive as most diggers were of accidents and ill-health, they were no less alarmed at the thought of entering hospital.

(2)

The duststorm which wrecked the Dutoitspan hospital tent was by no means exceptional. The high winds of Griqualand West which regularly battered the camps throughout the year were as notorious as they were destructive. There was not a digger who did not come to recognise and dread their approach.

For an hour or so before the storm broke, there would be an ominous, unnatural calm. Then a slight breeze would rustle among the tents, lifting paper, worrying canvas flaps and growing stronger by the second; soon tent ropes would begin to creak and strain, tent poles begin to wobble, corrugated-iron roofs begin to shake, until the gale crashed into the camps carrying everything before it. It was, said one terrified woman, like a dense 'brown wall coming on in the distance'. And the closer the squall got to the camps, the more dust it gathered, the thicker it became. Huge clouds of fine sand and grit, whipped from the debris heaps, engulfed the mines; tents were sent flying; shacks and shanties flattened; furniture, buckets, pots and pans scattered and even heavy carts and wagons overturned. In a severe storm families suddenly found themselves sleeping in the open, their canvas roofs ripped from over their heads; it was not unknown for a storekeeper, venturing out at the height of a storm, to find his corrugated-iron shop following him down the street.

Even the mildest onslaught left layers of dust behind. For hours after a storm, the camps reverberated with the sound of scraping spades, as diggers battled to clear their tents of dirt. There was no escaping the dust: it coated the skin, clogged the eyes, dried the mouth, powdered food and penetrated clothes and bedding. 'The dust of the dry diggings', moaned a journalist, 'is to be classed with plague, pestilence and famine, and if there is anything worse, with that also.'

Newcomers to the fields remarked more on the dust, the flies and the heat than they did on the diamonds. 'My nose is peeled, and my nails chipped,' complained Dr Atherstone, on his second visit, 'and my skin feels dry and brittle, and the·ink dries faster than I can write. . . . I drink all day, I drink at night, but the thirst will never give in, and the flies drink too from each welling pore in my skin.' Rhyming, he continues: 'The dust lies here and the dust flies there, when I move or sneeze aloud, I breathe it in and I breathe it out, like visible steam from a kettle spout, in a fine implacable cloud. Hot, sultry, and dry, not a cloud in the sky, save the dust cloud stalking along, solemn and slow, whilst its hot blasts blow, with a force irresistibly strong.' It was more than he could bear. He caught the next coach back to Cape Town.

The diggers, however, had to learn to live with the discomforts of tent life. With any luck a duststorm would last only a couple of hours and be followed by deep rolls of thunder and the promise of refreshing rain. But even this could prove a mixed blessing. A really vicious thunderstorm was every bit as alarming as a duststorm. Many diggers tried to insulate their tent poles from lightning by covering them with the necks of broken bottles, but this did not prevent them from being struck, nor did it prevent their tents from being flooded in a heavy downpour. All too often the rattle of rain on canvas was a far from welcome sound: water would seep in through the cracks and joins in the roof, puddles would form, and the steamy heat of the tents would become stifling. Inexperienced diggers, caught unawares, often found it impossible to live in their tents for days after a rainstorm. The ground would be sodden, the animal skins on which they slept damp and green with mildew. 'Fancy sleeping in a puddle! . . .' one of them wrote in a mournful letter home. 'You can hardly conceive how miserable, wet, and filthy everything looked. We managed to get some dry clothes and boots on (my sea boots had about a quart of water in each) and then fled the place in disgust, and went to an iron hotel, where we breakfasted, dined, and at night slept on the table, very comfortable and *dry*. The hotels and canteens were full of· washed-out diggers.'

The degree to which diggers suffered depended, to a certain extent, upon their luck in the mines. Those who struck it rich, the 'swells' of the diggings, were able to afford a minimum of luxury. Many of them lived in large well-furnished tents, surrounded by a thorn-bush fence, and usually pitched on a rise, close to a convenient tree. Some bachelors at Old De Beers and New Rush clubbed together and turned these enclosures into 'messes'. This meant that they were not only able to share food, expenses and servants but more often than not were able to commandeer a good-sized tree which, it is said, was 'used as a larder, its branches tastefully hung with legs of mutton and other joints of meat, so that it looks like a very substantial Christmas Tree'. But such establishments cost money and were rarely within the reach of the poorer diggers who had wives and families to support.

Women at the diggings found camp life particularly tough. Most of them spent their days sweating over the sorting-tables and then, dead beat, had to return to the tents and attend to the needs of their families. Unlike the men, respectable women were unable to escape to the canteens after a hard day's work; for them it was a wretched, bleak and, above all, lonely existence. 'We had many nice gentlemen friends,' said Alice Stockdale, who arrived at New Rush with her husband in 1871, 'but I had not a lady friend for six months.'

Many of the women came from good Colonial families and were totally unprepared for the primitive conditions with which they had to cope. Though they were accustomed to efficiently run households with plenty of servants, they found it practically impossible to get domestic help at the diggings. There were very few female servants available and those men who were willing to work outside the mine often proved more of an embarrassment than a help. Coming straight from their kraals, these tribesmen were quite unaware of the niceties of Western civilisation and roamed the camps as naked as they roamed the veld. 'The consequence is', fumed the *Diamond News,* 'that no respectable female can walk the street . . . without having her sense of sight shocked.' And if it was unnerving for respectable women to walk the street, it was positively unthinkable that they should employ fully exposed black men in their tents.

Nor, it should be added, was this the only source of female embarrassment. Unclothed as most of them were, the tribesmen made no attempt to disguise their curiosity about European dress. At least this is what Alice Stockdale discovered when she eventually hired a 'raw Kafir', named Master Jim, to do her washing. She says that after giving Master Jim his instructions she went into her tent and was startled, some time later, to hear screams of laughter coming from the yard. Dashing out she was horrified to see 'the boy holding up one of my garments and letting the wind blow it into shape'. With every gust of wind, Master Jim doubled up. The outraged Alice was far from amused. 'I rushed at him,' she says primly, 'pulled it out of his hands and told him, he was to wash the things but not look at them.' By and large it was safer, and more seemly, for women to do their own housework.

Feeding a family was a problem in itself. There was no shortage of food: meat, eggs and milk were plentiful, but many children, as well as adults, suffered from scurvy because of the lack of fresh vegetables, which, even when they could be bought, were ruinously expensive. The stores were usually well stocked with tinned food but again, owing to the cost of transport, such luxuries were far from cheap. Most poorer families existed on a staple diet of rice and mutton, supplemented occasionally by dried fruit.

Meals were invariably cooked out of doors at a fireplace (a shallow pit, crossed by iron hoops which served as a grating) dug close to the tent. But as all drinking-water, as well as food, had to be boiled, firewood was soon in short supply. As early as September 1871, the owners of Vooruitzigt were forced to prohibit the cutting down of trees on their farm. 'It is perfectly barbarous,' commented the *Diamond News,* 'the way in which beautiful trees within the precinct of the camp, which should form a most grateful shelter during the coming summer months, are being hacked and hewn to pieces.' Consequently firewood had to be transported to the camps and could cost anything up to £3 a wagonload.

It is hardly surprising that men who had sold up everything, bundled their families into a wagon, and started for the diamond fields hoping to return as millionaires, quickly became disillusioned. Life at the dry diggings could be grim indeed for those–and there were many of them–who had neither the resources nor the fortitude to sit out the bad times. 'I would advise no one to come to this country,' warned an American digger, 'unless they have a capital, or can stand hard work. . . . It is the worst place in the world for a penniless man.'

(3)

But it was not all moans and misery; not by a long chalk. For a great many diggers these were the palmy days, days of optimism, ambition and excitement, days when, for all its drawbacks, life was worth living. Indeed, how could it be otherwise? Miserable as the overcrowded, foul-smelling and badly organised camps might be, there was always the chance that things would brighten, that the hardships would pass and that one could emerge from the squalor a very rich man. It could happen to anyone at any time. All that was needed to transform poverty into prosperity was a lucky turn of the spade. This was the tantalising thought that kept the majority of diggers buoyant; the camps were full of Micawbers.

Nor was it entirely a matter of wishful thinking. Stories of fluke finds, of unexpected strikes and surprising reversals of fortune, were told all the time. They were the favourite talk of the canteens. Nothing delighted diggers more than to hear of some poor wretch who, driven to despair, had sold his claim for a song and then watched the new owner uncover a huge diamond the very next day. So often was this said to happen that one suspects it was more of a cautionary tale – the means by which some diggers kept heart against all odds – than the common occurrence it was made out to be. Nevertheless, there were enough verifiable stories to give hope even to the most hardened cynics. Supposedly barren claims did suddenly produce riches, big diamonds were stumbled upon, overnight fortunes were made: every camp had its wealthy men to prove it.

Diggers took hope not only from each other but from the mines in which they worked. In time the camps developed into distinct entities, each with its own community spirit, its own loyalties, and its own collective personality.

New Rush was the most crowded and the most turbulent of the camps. The diggers there tended to be younger, brasher, noisier, and more hot-headed than their neighbours. It was at New Rush that the worst rioting broke out, that tents were burnt, policemen assaulted and the law contemptuously defied.

On the other hand New Rush was known to be remarkably friendly. Some of the most spectacular finds had been made at Colesberg Kopje, money was plentiful and, in their less aggressive moments, the New Rush diggers were an open-handed, happy-go-lucky crowd. There was something peculiarly endearing about the raffish, undisciplined atmosphere of the place. 'Every visit', declared Frederick Boyle, 'impresses one more strongly with the size of the camp and the energy of its population. . . . It is a forest, a labyrinth of tent poles and a billowy sea of canvas. To seek therein for any one person, or any one tent, is more hopeless than to wander through the streets of London on that same errand. Roads everywhere, of every fashion and repute, from the broad street lined with iron stores, and pretty canvas houses, to the scrubby path between Kaffir huts. . . . Pretentious canteens or low drinking-tents meet the eye every step. . . . But the hospitality of the Colesberg Kopje! It is irresistible.'

In contrast to this lively bustle, neighbouring Old De Beers–a mere mile away–was positively sedate. Regarded as 'by far the most pleasant camp on the Dry Diggings', Old De Beers was a refuge for those wishing to escape the rough and tumble of New Rush. The camp itself was widely scattered, it had few shops or business places, and life there, if not so lucrative, was altogether more leisurely. So much so that the professional men of New Rush often preferred to build huts for their wives and families at Old De Beers, where (because the diggers were more law-abiding) there were more trees, more shade and consequently slightly less dust. The camp was noted for its many domestic features, not the least being the tiny garden patches which surrounded some of the tents and huts. Visitors to Old De Beers were often startled to find tough, burly diggers taking endless trouble with a puny geranium plant or a twig of fuchsia, or trying to grow a few lettuce and a sprinkling of cress. 'It is a pretty, loving sight,' remarked one journalist, 'to see the trowel, the spade, and the watering-pot going in some of these cottage plots at eventide.' Unfortunately, Old De Beers was not to retain its rustic seclusion for long. By 1872 its outlying tents were beginning to merge with those around New Rush; soon it became impossible to tell where one camp ended and the other began.

A similar merger between Dutoitspan and Bultfontein had taken place much earlier. The Bultfontein diggings, despite their original promise, had proved somewhat disappointing. Diamonds found there had a beauty of their own, and some rich strikes had been made, but the Bultfontein mine was considered a difficult mine to work. There were occasional spurts of activity at the diggings, but the camp never really became a prosperous centre. The old Bultfontein farm cottage remained the headquarters of Henry Webb and the London and South African Exploration Company, and a few shops and offices had been built nearby, but there was very little else. It was too close to Dutoitspan to claim an independent existence. If Bultfontein could be said to have any individuality it was merely that of a poor relation.

Dutoitspan, on the other hand, was looked upon as the hope of the dry diggings. Not only was the camp itself thought to be more solidly established than New Rush, but few doubted that the Dutoitspan diggings would prove more durable. New Rush, for all its dash and glitter, was not expected to last long.

From the very outset confidence in the potential of Colesberg Kopje had been very shaky. The early rush there had been so frenetic and had resulted in such overcrowding that it was widely predicted that the mine would soon be exhausted. 'Such an immense number of hands are now at work at the Colesberg Kopje', wrote Charles Payton in 1871, 'that many people say it will

H. Carter's house, looking deceptively trim, amidst the rough and tumble of New Rush in about 1873. (K)

Typical digger's home in early days. This was the residence of a digger named Tom Bell, whose mother is seen at the sorting-table. (K)

be entirely worked out in from six to twelve months' time.' Nor did the diamonds found at New Rush provide much encouragement. Plentiful they might be, but they were often of inferior quality, badly shaped and off-colour. Everything, in fact, seemed to indicate that it would be only a matter of time before Dutoitspan–with its steadier, more reliable output–came into its own again.

It was this underlying faith in Dutoitspan's future that gave the camp a prosperous air. Most of the important business places were centred there. When, at the end of 1871, the professional men of Pniel and Klipdrift had finally decided to move to the dry diggings, it was to Dutoitspan that they flocked. The speed with which they had descended upon the camp was little short of marvellous; the number of offices, stores and hotels in or near the Dutoitspan market place had doubled almost overnight. 'Even the *Diamond News* with all its presses and type, offices and editor and all,' gasped a journalist in September 1871, 'has gone to Dutoitspan which . . . . has become a scene of such bustle and activity as is to be seen nowhere else in South Africa.· . . . The *Diamond News* office is erected in the middle of the Market-square and the erection of this building last Friday shows how rapidly such work is done. On Thursday morning the site on which it now stands was vacant, on Friday evening the offices were up, and on Saturday the first issue took place.'

Hot on the heels of the *Diamond News* had come Stafford Parker, one-time President of the Diggers' Republic, bringing with him a huge iron building from Pniel. Known as Stafford Parker's Assembly Rooms, this building had quickly become one of the wonders of Dutoitspan. The main hall was used for concerts, lectures and dances during the week and for church services on Sundays – Anglicans in the morning, Roman Catholics in the evening – while a smaller room served as a diggers' club. No less impressive was Benning and Martin's sprawling hotel, where smoking-concerts were held twice a week and which boasted a billiard room and a dining-room where, it was said, 'there are never less than fifty – sometimes nearly a hundred – at dinner'. Such grandeur was as yet unknown in the other camps.

By the end of 1872, Dutoitspan had developed into a thriving, spacious settlement. Its broad main street, with its plate-glass shopfronts and fine merchants' offices, was considered to be as handsome as that of any colonial town in South Africa. 'Many of the residences here', it was said, 'are built with much taste–neat villas with verandahs and trellises; well regulated hotels and taverns; and there are all the characteristics of a township on every side of you, go where you will.' How could anyone doubt that Dutoitspan was destined to become the capital of the dry diggings? Beside it New Rush, for all its pretensions – it had an Oxford Street, a Piccadilly, a Regent Street and a Cheapside – seemed very second-rate indeed.

It is hardly surprising that the Dutoitspan diggers thought that the future was theirs. Many agreed with them. 'The centre of a country', noted Frederick Boyle, 'is that point to which the most and the largest interests converge. This point, in Griqualand West, is Dutoitspan, and, so far as we can see, will continue to be. . . . Every business man in the colony feels sure that Dutoitspan is destined to be an important centre.'

But, as is apt to happen, the business men were to be proved wrong.

(4)

Stafford Parker's contribution to the religious life of the dry diggings was merely a stop-gap. His splendid hall was not used by the Anglicans and the Roman Catholics for long. They, like other denominations, soon had their own meeting-places. The speed with which churches sprang up was, in fact, one of the remarkable features of the South African diggings. Such instant piety was practically unheard of in the mining camps of the world.

Lay preachers there were a-plenty. In their tents, or under trees, they held meetings every Sunday both at the river diggings and the dry diggings. Mostly non-conformists, their hectoring sermons and unaccompanied hymn-singing had a chastening effect on the godly and ungodly alike. Few diggers were brave enough to be seen in their claims on the Sabbath. 'It is true that they visited bars and liquored up on a Sunday all the same,' observed an astonished visitor, 'but there was neither card nor billiard playing. They left off work and put on a Sunday appearance which was the extent of their Sunday observance, but still observance of the day, which was very remarkable seeing that everyone of them was engaged in a race for wealth.'

As early as November 1870, Archdeacon Kitton had arrived at Klipdrift, where an Anglican brick church was to be built. Father Hidien was the first Catholic priest, and Lutheran pastors from the mission station at Pniel frequently visited the diggings. Soon there was scarcely a religious denomination that was not represented by a minister or a lay preacher. Churches - often no more than tents or shacks - rose cheek by jowl with the bars, the brothels and the gambling-houses.

By September 1871, Church of England services were being held regularly in a tent at New Rush. Three months later the foundations of an Anglican and a Dutch Reformed Church were laid at Dutoitspan and a wood-and-canvas Wesleyan chapel was built there at about the same time. The Anglicans and Wesleyans were also active at Old De Beers, where in 1871 each had a flimsy, canvas-framed church. At the beginning of 1872, the Catholics of New Rush met at Hurley's Reading Room and 'subscribed *at once* the whole sum necessary for the erection of a church'. If not all the diggers were devout, it was certainly not for the want of incentive.

Nevertheless, attendance at church was not something to be undertaken lightly. One needed to be strong in constitution as well as faith to withstand the rigours of a lengthy service. Seated bolt upright on backless benches, pestered by the maddening, omnipresent swarms of flies, and sweating in the dank heat of a tent lit by candles or paraffin oil lamps, even the staunchest of churchgoers were apt to faint away during a wordy sermon. But the most excruciating torment was that inflicted by the host of fleas that seemed to infest the sandy floor of every church. There was no escaping them; they turned every act of worship into an endurance test. It was by no means unusual to see an entire congregation sitting with their feet on the benches in front of them to escape the fleas hopping underfoot; to kneel at prayer was, of course, asking for trouble.

Nor were the frequent duststorms an aid to meditation: the wrath of God seemed only too real when a tent collapsed about a preacher's head. This happened to the canvas-framed Anglican church at Old De Beers. 'There was a goodly congregation at the time in church,' says John Angove, 'including several ladies, who all had to scramble out from beneath the fallen canvas and light wood-work in the best manner they could.' Only the speedy action of servers, who covered the candles with their hats, prevented the place from going up in flames.

Yet, for all their hazards, the Sunday church services brought a whiff of civilisation to the diggings. Women in particular welcomed the opportunity to escape the daily grind of diamond-sorting. Sunday was the one time they could relax, forget about money-grubbing and exchange their faded print dresses and coalscuttle *kappies* for slightly more fashionable bustles and bonnets. Such occasions were rare indeed.

(5)

Novelists, trying to breathe romance into early camp life, have often portrayed the bars of New Rush as hives of sexual intrigue. Flashily dressed women are depicted hanging onto the arms of hard-drinking diggers as they gamble away a fortune; pimps and prostitutes abound and every rich diamond dealer has his mistress. It is a conventional enough picture, easy to imagine, but far removed from the truth.

White women, in fact, were seldom seen in the bars and canteens. Hard-working and highly moral, the diggers' wives had little time, let alone inclination, for the gayer side of camp life. There were very few single girls on the diggings and, surprisingly, even fewer white tarts. Diggers often complained bitterly about the lack of available females. 'A shipment of these', sighed a frustrated New Rush bachelor in 1872, 'would command extreme rates, in fact it is the most virtuous place in the world.' This, however, was an exaggeration. New Rush was far from being virtuous.

Prostitutes there were, but they were mostly black girls employed in sleazy back-street brothels. Easily picked up, they did a brisk trade and were far more procurable than female servants. 'A great many of them', sniffed a disapproving digger, 'are too lazy to work, and prefer to get money more quickly and easily, as is soon apparent, by their bolder and richer apparel, their constant promenading about the camp, and their impudent looks.' A few of the less conventional diggers had coloured mistresses but, more often than not, such attachments were shortlived and rarely flaunted. South Africa being what it was, prejudice invariably tended to temper passion.

It was some time before white prostitutes put in an appearance. Those who did arrive were mostly discreet, often working as part-time barmaids in the more disreputable canteens. Not that all barmaids were prostitutes; far from it.

Many of them – such as Australian Annie and Natal Sue – were brassy, but fundamentally decent, working-girls who became as much an institution in the early days as the famous Cockney Liz and Biddy McCree were to be later. Far more outrageous than any part-time barmaid was the notorious 'Blonde Venus', whose much-heralded arrival had all the men of New Rush panting. Making no secret of her profession, this somewhat blowsy blonde announced her arrival by mounting an empty liquor crate in a canteen and inviting offers from diggers who wished to spend a night with her. In the frantic auction which followed, the diggers – some of whom were in evening dress for the occasion – went berserk. Within a matter of minutes the bidding rose from £5 and a box of champagne to £25 and three boxes of champagne. The successful bidder was a lusty diamond merchant who lost no time in whisking his prize back to his tent, only to have his expectations shattered when, with perfect timing, a crowd of his rivals lifted the tent from over his head and turned his expensive private treat into a public exhibition.

But, for the most part, diggers were forced to live a barrack-room existence: in a predominantly male society sex inevitably took second place to drink. And in drinking they were able to indulge themselves to the full. For scarce as were women, there was certainly no shortage of liquor. Every street, every back alley, had its canteen, pub, bar or refreshment room. In a survey conducted in 1874 it was estimated that there were at least forty canteens to every forty people, not counting those on the outskirts of the camps. Indeed, it was almost easier to obtain a liquor licence than it was to think up a new name for a drinking-den. The outlandish names given to some of the better-known canteens never failed to fascinate visitors: The Blue Posts, The Scarlet Bar, The Red Light, The Cat and Gridiron, The Hard Times, The New Found Out, The Perfect Cure, Hand-in-Hand, Café Francaise, Uncle Tom's Cabin – the list was endless.

One of the more popular pubs was The Pig and Whistle, which, although it lacked the ultimate attraction of a barmaid, did have a fully fledged army captain as a barman. Another was The Old Cock in Jones Street, off Market Square at New Rush; the street – later to be well known – taking its name from the owner of the pub, W.T. Jones. These were the haunts of affluent diggers, places where a lucky find was celebrated by drinking champagne from a bucket, where cigars were lit with five-pound notes, and where customers stood ten deep at the bar counters offering to stand drinks all round.

There were other bars, equally lively, but distinctly less attractive. Housed in squalid tents or tin shanties, many of them were simply dives, centres for illicit diamond buying and shady deals of all sorts. Down-at-heel diggers could be seen reeling out of them at all hours of the day, blind drunk on a vicious cheap brandy known as 'Cape Smoke'. Bar-room brawls were run-of-the-mill, fights broke out at the bend of an elbow, and it was a foolish barman who did not keep a heavy stick handy to deal with obstreperous customers. Most of the New Rush riots had been sparked off in one or other of these low-class canteens, and this, as much as anything, had made diggers in the other camps wary of joining in these demonstrations: they could never be sure whether it was a justifiable

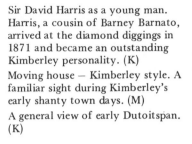

Sir David Harris as a young man. Harris, a cousin of Barney Barnato, arrived at the diamond diggings in 1871 and became an outstanding Kimberley personality. (K)

Moving house — Kimberley style. A familiar sight during Kimberley's early shanty town days. (M)

A general view of early Dutoitspan. (K)

cause or a drunken orgy that they were being asked to support.

Smug Dutoitspan diggers were particularly suspicious of the drunken goings-on at New Rush. 'The sudden riches of Colesberg Kopje', sniffed one of them, 'have turned a few heads, and brought the canteen-keepers some too good customers. . . . One white man I saw seated in the middle of the road, leaning upon·a naked Kaffir scarcely less drunk, while both sang, shouted, threatened and alaughed at the crowd that surrounded them, and passed the bottle of "Cape Smoke" freely from one to the other . . . (they) had to be dragged out of the way of an advancing waggon. I never saw black and white so equalised by any other medium.' Worse he could not say.

But drink broke more than accepted taboos: it literally destroyed hundreds of otherwise healthy diggers. Dr Matthews was to claim that at least seventy per cent of the white diggers he attended had succumbed to 'excessive indulgence in alcohol'. This is hardly surprising. Bars were open all day during the week. When a committee was eventually set up to investigate the drinking problem on the diggings, one of its strongest recommendations was that no canteen should be allowed to open before five o'clock in the morning. Is it to be wondered at that Dr Matthews denounced intemperance, in resounding Victorian phraseology, as 'the curse of the diamond fields'?

Gambling, in the eyes of many, was another curse. Even Dr Matthews, who was somewhat over-fond of a flutter himself, coupled gambling with drinking as 'the two great social evils' of the mining camps. It was perhaps only to be expected. Men who lived by the turn of the spade were, as Matthews pointed out, equally ready to chance their luck on the turn of a card. 'The difference', he claimed, 'between the precarious business of digging for diamonds and gambling at a faro table, in fact, being a moral difference only.'

Fine as this difference was, some diggers found it very much to their advantage. The story is often told of two diggers who, despairing of their claim, opened a gambling-saloon at New Rush and retired a few months later with a fortune of £40,000. Nor did such luck run entirely one way. David Harris, a young cockney who had borrowed £150 from his mother, set out for South Africa and, landing at Durban, had walked 600 miles to the diggings, won a small fortune at Dodds Canteen in New Rush, almost by accident.

Harris was not a gambler and, having been lured into the canteen by a friend, had stood primly by the roulette table without making a bet until he was given a free drink on the house. 'Just as I had finished my glass of champagne,' he said, 'one of the proprietors remarked significantly that some men only visited the rooms for the purpose of getting free drinks. This remark aroused my ire, as I thought it was meant for me. So purely out of pique, I put a sovereign on number thirteen with the intention of losing it and clearing out.' But he did not lose: number thirteen came up and paid off at 35-1. Harris went on gambling until the early hours and eventually left the canteen richer by £1,400. That, he says, was the last time he entered a gambling-saloon.

His win was to become part of a legend. Not only was it rare, but it produced astonishing results. On Harris's return to London, his two stagestruck cousins, Henry and Barnett Isaacs - known on the boards as Harry and Barney

Barnato – were so dazzled by his luck that they began to have second thoughts about their rather tatty conjuring act. If cautious David Harris could make so much money so easily, what was to prevent them from doing the same? They decided to investigate the diamond diggings. First Harry, then Barney, followed young Harris back to South Africa; the roulette tables at Dodds Canteen had whisked up more than a small fortune.

Dodds Canteen was one of the more reputable gambling-saloons. There were plenty of others. One could always join a card school in a private tent and 'gambling hells' were as numerous, and every bit as chancy, as the drinking-dives. Such places tended to spring up overnight and disappear as quickly as their customers' money. 'It is desirable', warned a bitten digger, 'to exercise a good deal of caution in playing with comparative strangers, for some very sharp practitioners are to be found among the card playing fraternity on the Fields.'

Card-sharps and tricksters were also very much in evidence at the dry-diggings racecourse. Horse-racing was extremely popular with the diggers. The first race on the fields was run at Pniel in January 1871; such a success was it that a group of sporting diggers banded together and formed the Diamond Fields Turf Club. A course was laid out near the Dutoitspan and Bultfontein mines, and a gala race-meeting, lasting three days, was arranged for the middle of 1872. It was widely advertised, racehorses were brought to the diggings from as far afield as Colesberg and Cradock in the Cape, and substantial prize money was offered. Exciting as the event promised to be, it was remembered not so much for the races as for the sleazy sideshows it attracted.

Crooks of all sorts converged on the course. The main bar, beneath the rickety grandstand, was run by an American negro, whose tender of £200 was the highest offered. Other canteen keepers set up their own bars, gambling-booths proliferated and small-time chisellers had a field day. 'The over-and-under tables were there in galore,' it was said; 'thimble-rigging and three card tricksters were vigorously prosecuting their devices to swindle an easily-gulled public.' It was at this race-meeting that a sprinkling of flashy 'hostesses' first appeared in public, presiding over roulette wheels and fleecing the sex-starved diggers.'Some of those women', snorted an outraged client, 'were of foreign extraction, but they answered the purpose for which they were employed, and brought much gain to the men who employed them.'

Unfortunately, horse-racing at the diggings was always to be plagued by confidence men, fly-by-night bookies and horse-nobblers. So much so that, a few years later, the Turf Club was forced into temporary liquidation as a result of the chronic 'turf swindling'. On the whole diggers found it safer to confine their sporting activities to the many billiard rooms, or to risk an odd bet on a boxing bout – where well-known prize fighters, such as 'The Ladies' Pet' or 'Cockney Bill', could be relied upon to give fair value for money.

(6)

There were, of course, more innocent forms of amusement. Dances were held from time to time in Stafford Parker's Assembly Rooms at Dutoitspan and in the Mutual Hall at New Rush. The only trouble here was that the heavily chaperoned girls were invariably outnumbered by the men. Indeed, a young woman, whatever she looked like, would have had to suffer from a highly infectious disease not to have found a partner. 'There were no sitting out places,' one of them explained. 'We all went to dance–and dance we did. . . . Once the dance started five or six men would make a rush for a girl . . . We all had admirers.' For all that, the girls were far from blasé about their easy conquests. It took them days to prepare for a dance, weeks to get ready for a ball.

Young Flora Brown and her sister Jeannie were among the few single girls on the diggings in the early 1870s, and were much in demand at the dances. But this, according to Flora, did not lessen their problems. 'What with white ants and the size of the dresses,' she sighed, 'you can imagine the trouble we had keeping things for the dances.' Their first invitation to the Mutual Hall threw them into a complete flap. 'We were greatly excited,' remembered Flora. 'But we were equally distressed when we found that it was to be "full dress". We could not get white shoes in the camp for love or money. But we were not beaten yet. We wore elastic-sided boots at the time, and so Jeannie cut them down to shoes and covered them with white calico. We felt that we really were in the fashion then, and away we went to our favourite dances – the Sir Roger de Coverly, the Caledonians, the Mazurka and the Quadrilles.' For all the diggers would have noticed, they could as well have worn sky-blue gumboots.

Every bit as popular, and almost as respectable as the dances, were the theatres. It is true that performances in the early theatres were often drowned by the noise from the bar–which was part of the building–fights would break out and some actors replied to heckling by threatening to beat up members of the audience, but, by and large, most diggers considered the theatre a respectable enough entertainment for their wives and daughters. Knock-about farces, operettas and Christy Minstrel shows were particularly popular. So were circus acts; when Signor Marcellino, the 'Fire King', and Madame Pauline D'Esta, the 'celebrated danseuse', first appeared with the New Rush Circus Company in March 1872, they played to packed houses for weeks.

Amateur theatricals had always flourished at the diggings, and Stafford Parker had employed professional performers at his imposing brick Music Hall in the main street at Klipdrift. Shortly after the rush to the dry giggings, a permanent repertory group, known as the Harper–Leffler Company, was established at Dutoitspan, with Mr Leffler and his versatile wife Madame Leffler playing most of the leads–musical or dramatic–supported by a variety of amateur acts and actors, at the grandiloquently named Theatre Royal. The name of the theatre was, in fact, the most impressive thing about it. No more than a suffocatingly hot tin shanty, with the audience seated on 'planks, having gin boxes for legs', its only real claim to distinction was a luridly painted stage backdrop depicting a brilliant sunset, lit by spluttering paraffin lamps. Nevertheless, it more than served its purpose. 'This dramatic first born', claimed one of the performers, 'was received with open arms by its nurse the public.'

So well attended were performances at the Theatre Royal that, in March 1872, the Harper-Leffler Company was prosperous enough to erect 'a very fine hall of wood and iron' at Dutoitspan. This new theatre, the St James's Hall, was only a slight improvement on its predecessor - it was built in a week - but was said to 'supply a want that has long been felt'. Noisy, stuffy and invariably overcrowded, it did at least attract a wide range of professional talent and the regular one-act melodramas and operettas were backed by an assortment of ballad singers, dancing duos, violin virtuosos, ventriloquists and performing animals. Performers from all over the world began to make their way to the diamond diggings.

An early solo act at the St James's Hall was a conjuror who, billed as a 'Great Wizard', claimed to have performed before 'the Royal Family'. Wisely, he was careful not to say which royal family for, unless royalty had been in the habit of frequenting the slums of London, it is extremely doubtful whether he could have backed up his claim. The 'Great Wizard' was, in fact, young David Harris's chancy cousin Henry Isaacs, who, in his role of Signor Barnato, had arrived in South Africa with nothing more than a few stage props, a certain dexterity, and a great deal of smooth talk.

Henry Isaacs's father, Isaac Isaacs, was a second-hand clothes dealer and, before arriving at the diamond diggings, Henry - or Harry as he was called - had not, at twenty-three, travelled much farther than London. For the most part, his life had been largely divided between his occasional appearances at cheap music halls and his more permanent employment as barman and chucker-out in a rowdy East End pub owned by his brother-in-law, Joel Joel. Neither profession had proved particularly lucrative. Harry had shared his stage act with his younger brother Barney. They were known as the Barnato Brothers, a name which is said to have been inspired by a stagehand who, resenting the way in which Harry always hogged the applause for their act, had one night pushed young Barney forward and shouted 'Barney too'. The shout had stuck. 'Barney too' sounded more exotic than Isaacs and after trying out some variations - Barnyto and Barneto - the brothers had adopted the name Barnato. Unfortunately, the change of name did nothing to improve their mediocre conjuring act; they still found it difficult to get bookings. David Harris's return to London, rich from Africa, had been all that was needed to entice Harry to the diggings.

His act at the St James's Hall was a huge success. He opened on 29 October 1872 and played to packed houses for two weeks. Hackneyed his tricks might have been, shabby his dress suit was, but Harry Barnato undoubtedly had a way with him. He had a good stage presence, and his enormous handlebar moustache and dark, lively eyes made him appear every bit the romantic Italian he pretended to be. The diggers were captivated. Even hardened cynics had grudgingly to admit that he was clever.

'The wizard's performance', one of them claimed, 'consisted of doing a few sleight-of-hand tricks, as old and verdant as the hills, accompanying the finale of each illusion by ejaculating "A la me!" which was accepted by the majority of the audience as positive proof of the exotic ability of the "Seggnor". . . . Without doubt he brought forth eggs from nowhere, cards from anywhere, and goldfish in glass dishes from the region of his coat-tails – value for money indeed! The night I attended the show the "Seggnor" in the course of his amazing feats borrowed from me, as one of the audience, a sovereign which he duly returned. Now that was truly marvellous!'

'The cry is "Still They Come!",' it was announced when Harry switched his act to the Mutual Hall in New Rush in the middle of November. He continued at the Mutual Hall until the end of the year. On Boxing night he gave a 'Grand Christmas Festival', including 'His Great Feat of *Aerial Suspension of a Human Being,* Sleeping in Mid Air! (Must be seen to be believed.)' But after that his popularity declined and he was eventually replaced by a Christy Minstrel troupe. Soon the 'Great Wizard' was reduced to staging sparring exhibitions with an ex-policeman in the Market Square.

Forced to give up his hotel room and live in a tent, things looked bleak indeed for Harry until David Harris took pity on him and found him a job with a diamond dealer in Dutoitspan. Once he had settled down he wrote home urging Barney to join him. With the arrival of Barney Barnato, at the end of 1873, the diamond diggings gained a colourful personality. However, it took some time for Barney to make his mark. In the early days he had plenty of competition; the one thing the diggings did not lack was colourful personalities.

6

A Collection of Characters

Outlandish characters of all types had, from the very beginning, been the delight of the diamond fields. Many of them, like Stafford Parker – the ex-able-seaman, ex-President of the Diggers' Republic and ex-Music-Hall-proprietor – not only cultivated, but traded on, their eccentric reputations. In fact, Parker, with his grey top-hat, frock coat and dark glasses, was remembered more for his incongruous elegance than for his shortlived achievements. Others, like the notorious 'Champagne Charlie', had less reputable claims to distinction.

'Champagne Charlie' was a deserter from a sailing-ship who arrived at Dutoitspan 'still sporting his sea-going togs' in 1872. A huge, big-mouthed man, he made an immediate impression. For the first few days after his arrival he was seen in every bar and canteen, drinking heavily and treating everyone. However, his greatest triumph came when he pegged out a claim and, within a matter of days, unearthed a large dark-green diamond. Such a stone had never been seen before; it was estimated to be worth a small fortune. 'Champagne Charlie' became the toast of the canteens, diggers fell over themselves to congratulate him. His popularity rose by the hour and so did his credit. Then, as suddenly as he had arrived, he disappeared. His creditors were left with the remarkable green diamond which, not surprisingly, they soon discovered to be nothing more than a carefully filed-down glass bottle-stopper.

The ruse of 'salting' an unproductive claim with dud diamonds was by no means original. 'Champagne Charlie's' fame rested more on his choice of name and his audacity in passing off such an unlikely coloured stone. He was one of the first really bold confidence tricksters to appear on the fields. Those who came later were more subtle, more painstaking and decidedly more ambitious. They fooled many more diggers and assumed much grander pseudonyms.

Almost every bar and billiard room had its bogus baronet or lord, at one time or another; a few even boasted an odd earl or two. So plausible were these impostors that they often worked the camps for months before they were exposed. It is possible that some escaped detection altogether. In such a mixed community, it was impossible to vouch for anyone's background: a pompous manner and the right accent could work wonders.

Who, for instance, was the mysterious Russian princess working at the diggings in 1872? Nobody seemed quite sure. She arrived from the Cape 'in a sort of menagerie van', complete with a maidservant and a young black boy, and settled at Dutoitspan. But little else was known about her. It is not even certain whether she was digging for diamonds or buying diamonds. 'This lady', says Frederick Boyle, 'whoever she be, is an unaccountable person. . . . Armed with an autographed letter from Lord Granville, supplemented by the recommendation of Sir H. Barkly, she receives the greatest attention from our magistrates and officials. . . . The common story makes her out a lady of very high rank, exiled from Russia for four years. The Foreign Office letter gives no clue at all, nor do I think the authorities at Capetown are better informed than we.' But for all her mystery, she did not – as far as is known – attempt to defraud anyone.

Which is more than can be said for the *soi-disant* 'Lord Darnley'. This fast-talking charlatan was probably the most successful, although not the most accomplished, pseudo-aristocrat ever to hit the diamond diggings. 'Lord Darnley' appears to have been only one of his many titled aliases, but his methods, simple as they were, never varied. He would arrive at a camp, ingratiate himself with rich diggers and canteen owners, borrow money and run up bills, and then, when his creditors began to get suspicious, disappear. More often than not, he would take a temporary job with a local farmer and lie low until he thought it was safe enough to return to another camp and start all over again. If, as sometimes happened, he was recognised by his old creditors in his new disguise, he would swear that he had reformed – even taken to religion – and was trying to earn enough to pay off his debts. The amazing thing is that he got away with so much for so long. His manner seems to have been unmistakably vulgar and his accent atrocious, but his line of talk was such that he was able to convince naive diggers that he was very much the English 'gentleman'.

However, the time came when, having done the round of the camps once too often, he was forced to transfer his activities to other South African towns. When Lord Rossmore arrived in Cape Town in 1876 without a letter of credit, he found it difficult to cash a cheque, 'Lord Darnley's' recent spree in the town had made the banks and shopkeepers extremely suspicious of anyone calling himself a lord. This was not the last that Lord Rossmore was to hear of his fellow 'peer'. On their way to the diggings, Rossmore's party camped one night on a farm owned by a Boer. While they were eating their supper they were approached by a seedy white man whom they took pity on and invited to share their meal. It soon became clear that their guest was the dubious 'Lord Darnley'.

'He was certainly very down on his luck,' says Rossmore, 'but after some Congo brandy he became quite talkative, and seating himself beside me he opened the ball by saying in a confidential aside, "I say – tell me as a pal – who the 'ell are you really?"'

Lord Rossmore, an opinionated and extremely peppery peer, was outraged. He gave his impertinent guest a short, explosive, but decidedly aristocratic, answer. 'Lord Darnley' was most impressed.

' "Oh come now, I say, draw it mild," he said admiringly. "That's jolly good;" then, regretfully, "I only wish I could have done it like that, I'd have lasted longer – if only I could have bluffed like you." '

But 'Darnley's' bluffing days were drawing to a close. Shortly afterwards he was arrested at the diggings and brought to trial. As far as Lord Rossmore was concerned the last straw came when, he says, the unabashed prisoner 'had the audacity to speak of me in court as "my friend Rossmore".'

'Lord Darnley' was sent to gaol. Whether he, like some of the other local criminals, ended up on the breakwater at Cape Town is not clear. But, wherever he served his sentence, he no doubt enjoyed the company of many another phony nobleman from the diamond diggings.

(2)

Not every flamboyant character at the diggings was a crook. Some, it must be admitted, sailed very close to the wind but they were still able to keep up a show of respectability. Moritz Unger, one of the best-known diamond buyers in the early days, successfully lived down a shaky reputation and became, if not respected, at least trusted.

Even the most casual visitor to the camps soon became aware of the jaunty Moritz Unger. It was impossible to ignore him. His huge advertisements, which announced that his was 'the only Establishment where Diamonds of High Value are Purchased for CASH', were splashed across the front pages of both local newspapers. When not in his office he could invariably be found in one of the bars or canteens touting for business. Dressed in a bright velvet jacket, white cord breeches and highly polished long boots, he was unmistakable and always available. Anyone with diamonds to sell was advised to try Moritz Unger first. Not only was his firm known to be backed by an influential 'Amsterdam house' but he had the rare reputation of offering fair prices. 'He is not famed', remarked a digger, 'for excessive politeness, but is somewhat cheeky and slangy. This, however, is no serious drawback to business.'

Unger was the first diamond buyer from Europe to reach the diamond fields. He arrived in South Africa from Hamburg at the beginning of 1870 and started business at the river diggings. His energy and enthusiasm quickly attracted the diggers. 'He seems', declared one of his early customers, 'to be in a perpetual state of excitement and declares the Vaal country to be the finest in the world for diamonds.' Once he had established himself, Unger sent for his wife and daughter, who with his brother-in-law arrived at the diggings in November 1870. Shortly afterwards he built himself a handsome house and glass-fronted office at Klipdrift and added to his reputation by acquiring an impressive stable of thoroughbred horses. In the eyes of most diggers he was one of the most influential and reliable diamond buyers on the fields. But unfortunately his past caught up with him.

Born in Austria, Moritz Unger had, prior to living in Hamburg, worked for several years in Scotland. Starting as a wine merchant and jeweller, he had later branched out and revived the neglected, and somewhat surprising, Scottish industry of pearl fishing. According to his own statements this new venture was, for some years, highly successful. He estimated that, during the summer of 1864 alone, divers recovered pearls for him worth £10,000. 'The Empress Eugénie, Queen Victoria, and other Royal ladies,' it was reported at the time, 'as well as many of the nobility, have been making purchases of these Scottish gems.' The truth of these claims was never fully established, but certainly Unger's luck did not last. By 1867 he was bankrupt. He left Scotland hurriedly, owing over £3,000, and went into hiding at Hamburg.

'If I had not allowed myself stupidly to speculate on the Stock Exchange,' Unger was to claim, 'my Scottish affairs . . . would have been settled long since.' These unsuccessful speculations were made during the three years he was in Hamburg and it was when they failed that he decided to try his luck in South Africa. Apparently his creditors had no idea of where he had disappeared to until, as one of them put it, 'his name as Unger the great diamond merchant of the great diamond fields had been listened to by one half of Europe'.

Moritz Unger was a distinctive-enough name for the trustee of his insolvent Scottish estate to send an agent out to the river diggings to ascertain whether Unger the diamond merchant was in fact Unger the missing pearl merchant. The agent chosen for this mission was Leopold Lowenthal, who as a boy had known Unger well. He arrived at the diggings, calling himself Mr Lowe, recognised Unger, and then returned to Scotland for the necessary authority to take proceedings against the diamond merchant.

Unger's trial was held at Klipdrift at the begining of September 1871. From the very outset doubts were expressed about the court's competence to try the case as the diggings were then still disputed territory. This, and the fact that the evidence presented by Lowenthal 'appeared to have been drawn up largely from memory' resulted in the magistrate's dismissing the action with costs. Lowenthal appealed against the judgment without success. Unger remained as popular with the diggers as he had ever been.

His popularity is not all that surprising. Despite his dubious past, Moritz Unger was a highly engaging character. He had the rare knack of appealing to the diggers' love of novelty. Shortly before his arrest, for instance, the whole of Klipdrift was riveted by his scheme to repeat his Scottish experience and employ a man to dive for diamonds in the Vaal. Unfortunately, just as he had got his diving-apparatus in working order, the diver went on strike and nobody could be found to take his place. 'It is to be regretted', complained the *Diamond News,* 'that Mr Unger's enterprising spirit had a wet blanket thrown on it so soon. It is quite possible that, had he gone on, he might have been the means of doing as much for the diggers on the Diamond Fields as he did for the pearl fisheries of Scotland.'

Unger never lost his love for the river diggings. Even after he moved to New Rush he was full of plans for building a bridge between Pniel and Klipdrift. But it was at New Rush that he made his real fortune. He established his main office close to the mine and opened a branch in Dutoitspan. Few men were better known in the camps than Moritz Unger; it was widely predicted that he would be one of the first elected members of the proposed Legislative Council. Everyone was surprised when he did not offer himself for election. They were even more surprised when, in December 1873, he put his offices up for sale and announced that he was returning to Germany. What prompted his sudden departure nobody knows. It did not end his association with the diamond fields – in the 1880s he was largely responsible for building the long-promised bridge across the Vaal – but he was never again a big name in the camps. Moritz Unger, however, left behind him more than a fleeting reputation: he left Leopold Lowenthal who, in time, was to become very much a personality in his own right.

One of Unger's great rivals in the early days – as a character, rather than as a merchant – was the inimitable Ikey Sonnenberg. There were no secrets about Ikey's past. His life's story, as he told it, was an open book – with a joke on every page. To listen to Ikey talk was a treat in itself; he was always sure of an audience. The trouble was, it was impossible to know when he was being serious.

His name was really Isaac Sonnenberg, but he was always known as Ikey. He was the eldest son of a German Jewish trader and was born in the village of Floersheim, near Mainz, in 1833. While still a boy of fifteen, in 1848, he decided to emigrate to America. The general unrest which followed the revolution in Germany of that year had aroused strong anti-Semitic feelings, which, it is said, was responsible for young Ikey leaving home. He landed in New York shortly before the great Californian gold rush and began his new life by selling matches on street corners, or, as he put it, 'started as a timber merchant in a small way'. But gold fever was running high and it was not long before Ikey had saved enough to join the 'Forty-niners' in California.

His career as a gold miner was fatally influenced by his weakness for gambling. By the time the American Civil War broke out he had lost more money than he had made, and learned as much about cards as he had about mining. During the war he fought with the Northern forces, although not, it seems, from any strong conviction. Later he went out of his way to sympathise with both sides to show, as he said, 'there was no ill feeling'. On the battlefield at Gettysburg he met up, quite accidentally, with his brother Charlie who had been sent to America to find him and, having no luck, had also joined the Northern army. The brothers ended the campaign together, Charlie as a colonel.

Restless as ever, Ikey sailed to the Cape shortly after news of the diamond finds there began to be noised about. He went straight to the river diggings but, having little success, soon abandoned digging and started a small trading-store at Jacobsdal in the Free State. Once the rush to the dry diggings got under way Ikey, who had recently married a Cape girl from Queenstown, Jeannette Rosenblatt, started a regular passenger-cart service between Jacobsdal and Dutoitspan. He extended his business and advertised himself as an importer of provisions and mining-tools from London, a buyer of diamonds, ostrich feathers, ivory, wool and 'any other produce'.

But for all his versatility Ikey was no great shakes as a merchant. The partnership which he and his brother Charlie, who joined him in South Africa, established on the diggings never came to much. Ikey was too much of a gambler, too fond of a joke, and far too good-natured to make a good businessman. 'Although he was as cunning as a fox in some things,' said one who knew him well, 'he was in others simple as a child.' His shrewdness never outstripped his sense of humour. Anecdotes about Ikey are legion; one of the best concerns the deal he made with a Boer.

It seems that Ikey had agreed to buy some wool from this Boer at so much a pound, but when it came to payment there was an argument about the total amount due. Ikey's mental calculation was much lower than that worked out by the Boer. They haggled until the Boer, in desperation, produced a ready reckoner to prove his point. Ikey was undeterred. He took one look at the ready reckoner and burst out laughing. 'Good God, man,' he shrieked, 'you have last year's reckoner, its worthless this year.' Needless to say, Ikey got his price.

Stories like this, told by himself, often gave people the wrong impression of Ikey; he was thought to be a little too slick to be trusted. When Lord Rossmore was at the diggings, for instance, his brother gave him a stern warning never to play cards with Ikey Sonnenberg. 'I felt', says Rossmore, 'that my brother had his reasons for speaking so strongly, and I therefore promised I would follow his advice.' Instead of playing cards, his lordship accepted Ikey's invitation to dine, got drunk, and then boasted of repeatedly throwing one of the guests out of the window. If this, as it appears, tickled Rossmore's aristocratic sense of fun, his attitude towards Ikey did him little credit. Ikey was indeed an inveterate gambler - his card-schools at Dutoitspan were an institution - but those who played with him regularly swore to his honesty. You could, they said, trust Ikey with your life. J.B. Taylor, who knew Ikey for many years, considered that he was incapable of faking cards but, Taylor added, he was 'a match for anyone who tried to cheat him'.

All the diggers knew Ikey. It was impossible to miss him. Tall, lanky, with 'the biggest feet ever seen', he loped about the camps wearing a tall white hat and a ready grin. He had a word or a nod for everyone and was looked upon as an easy touch - anyone down on his luck could go to Ikey for a hand-out. 'The whole town', declared an admirer, 'loved him. All the dogs in Dutoitspan wagged their tails as Ikey slouched by.'

Ikey Sonnenberg was not the only character in the camps with a quick wit, a kind heart and remarkable feet. Alfred Augustus Rothschild, the popular auctioneer, could claim all these distinctions and more. Rothschild, or the 'Baron' as he was inevitably called, had arrived at the river diggings, aged twenty-one, in 1869. His career as a diamond prospector does not, however, appear to have lasted long. With disappointed diggers constantly selling up and leaving the fields, to be replaced by optimistic newcomers, he soon realised the opportunities open to an astute auctioneer and set up business, in partnership with A. Berlyn, at Pniel. Shortly after the rush to the dry diggings he had transferred his main auction rooms to Dutoitspan and later established himself at New Rush, where for many years his Saturday afternoon sales were among the recognised entertainments of the camps. The Baron, with his rapid racy patter and his flair for languages - he could speak German, French, English and Dutch - was, in the words of a contemporary, 'a noted "card" '.

He was a dapper little man with curly, heavily greased hair, a nattily trimmed beard and, as he said himself, 'strongly marked oriental features'. But his greatest pride was his tiny feet. 'So intent was he on retaining their shape', claimed David Harris, 'that he always put his slippers on with the aid of a shoehorn!' Mounted on an ox-wagon, a chair, or even a wobbly box, the Baron could keep an enormous crowd of diggers amused for a whole afternoon in the scorching sun.

Like most auctioneers, Rothschild had a remarkable gift for repartee. Fast-talking and nimble-witted, he could, and did, sell everything, from a tent full of furniture to a box of paper collars, from a bullock-wagon to a bottle of pickles – anything remotely marketable came under the Baron's hammer. His sales were always well advertised, well attended and, more often than not, hilarious. Whatever he had to sell, be it a sorting-table or a pair of trousers, he would invariably describe as 'diamondiferous'. The number of diamondiferous oxen he auctioned off in the course of a single afternoon was said to be astonishing. 'Whenever he was selling any diggers' tools,' remarked Charles Payton, 'the article he was selling was sure to be the "very identical sieve in which the 93 carat was found last week", or, "here's a nice little pick, a dear little pick, a diamondiferous little pick – it picked out a 40-carat stone two days ago, and is warranted to do the same again".'

Attending a Rothschild sale could, at times, be quite bewildering. Few doubted the Baron's honesty but his quick-fire sales talk was often obscure, if not downright misleading. On one occasion, for instance, while selling a horse, he casually mentioned that the near-perfect animal had only two faults. As this was made to sound like a recommendation, rather than a criticism, it in no way affected the bidding. It was only after the horse had been sold for £20 that the new owner thought to inquire what the two faults were. 'Well,' explained the Baron, 'he is apt to break out of hand and is difficult to catch, and secondly, when caught he is not much good.' Not until the horse had proved its worth did the apprehensive buyer appreciate the joke.

The joke, in fact, was typical of the man. A.A. Rothschild, for all his foolery, was never known deliberately to cheat anyone. His long success as an auctioneer owed as much to his reputation for fair dealing as it did to his fame as a wit. When, many years later, ill-health forced him to leave South Africa, his honesty as well as his generosity had earned him a respect which few other pioneers enjoyed. The newspapers were full of his praises. 'Gentle in manner, vigorous in deed,' reads one report, 'scattering sunshine upon everyone with whom he came in contact, he has secured a hold upon the hearts of the people such as a King might envy.'

Flowery the tribute might be, but it was nonetheless sincere. Men like the Baron and Ikey Sonnenberg are not easily, or quickly, forgotten.

(3)

But the camps were not entirely inhabited by rogues, colourful characters and jokers. There was another side to camp life, a more sober side, a side which all too often has been ignored or overlooked because it does not fit romantic conceptions of what life in a mining-camp should be. Diggers recalling the early days were inclined to remember and record the exciting times, the bizarre happenings, the rough and tumble. This is only natural, but it is far from being the entire story. It has, in fact, resulted in many false legends, fanciful stories, and a distorted idea of what the diggings were really like.

It has been said, for instance, that the diggers were 'the derelicts of other worlds and other occupations; men reckless, feckless, unable to work for themselves, unable to work for a master, with nothing to lose and only luck to hope for'. There were, of course, many diggers who fitted this description but they certainly did not constitute a majority.

The rougher, more irresponsible element was, in the early days, confined largely to New Rush; it was this element which, from time to time, tried to settle the diggers' grievances by violence. That they received so little support from the other camps is significant. The diggers at Dutoitspan, Bultfontein and Old De Beers – and, indeed, many at New Rush – felt just as strongly about the unrest but drew a line at anarchy.

It is important to remember that the diggings, isolated in the wilds of Griqualand West, were for a long time effectively cut off from the civilising influences of the established South African colonies. Whatever restraint was exercised in the camps came from the diggers themselves. That there should have been any restraint at all was due to the fact that, from the very beginning, there was a solid core of upright citizens at the diggings who, if not always successful, acted as a corrective to the wilder, lawless factions. Such men, by their very nature, were rarely regarded as outstanding personalities, but they undoubtedly contributed much to the overall tone of the camps. They were far from being shiftless outcasts.

A man who typified the earnest, serious-minded digger was George Bottomley. Stern-faced, with beetle-brows and a large spade beard, Bottomley looked more like an Old Testament prophet than a diamond hunter. And a prophet of sorts he was. He had a mission: George Bottomley was always to regard diamond digging as secondary to his self-appointed task of instilling a fear of God into the diggers. A more dedicated, more conservative man one could not hope to find.

He was middle-aged by the time he arrived at the river-diggings in 1870. For a man of such set, orthodox views, his early life had been strangely unresolved. Some twenty years earlier he had left England and settled in Natal as a farmer near the Congella River. But, like so many other emigrants to Natal at that time, he had met with little success. When, shortly before the diamond rushes, gold had been discovered at Tati, beyond the Limpopo River, Bottomley had led a party from Durban to the new goldfields, only to meet once again with disappointment. He had then made his way south to the river diggings.

Once established as a diamond digger, he quickly drew attention to himself by his religious activities. A devout Presbyterian, he started the first Sunday School at Pniel, organised a church choir, and was well known as a lay preacher. The announcement that 'Mr Bottomley will preach in the Diggers Church Tent at 11 a.m. and 7 p.m.' became a regular feature of the 'Local' column of the *Diamond News*.

1870

1882

The jaunty young Barney Barnato photographed shortly after his arrival at Kimberley (S)

Rhodes as an undergraduate at Oxford. (J)

The dapper 'Baron' A.A. Rothschild, Kimberley's famous auctioneer. Drawing by A. Hirsch taken from one of Rothschild's amusing advertisements. (K)

Following the rush to Dutoitspan, Bottomley combined his religious zeal with a passion for politics. He was an active member of the diggers' committees – doing his utmost to curb the extremists – and gave sterling support to various charitable organisations. Dour, priggish and a fanatical teetotaller, he was nevertheless highly respected and gained a surprising number of adherents. His opponents might jeer at his puritanical views, but they never questioned his integrity. 'As a public man,' it was said, 'there was no citizen so frequently, and with so much credit to himself, before the inhabitants . . . as Mr Bottomley.'

When, in September 1873, a Temperance organisation known as the Good Templars opened its first lodge – 'The Hope of Du Toit's Pan, No 1' – it had no more convinced nor fervent champion than George Bottomley. His championship, however, was well rewarded: throughout his long political career he could always rely on the support of the Good Templars. The remarkable thing is that, on the supposedly dissolute diggings, this support was often influential enough to ensure Bottomley's success at the polls.

Another darling of the Good Templars was the formidable J.B. Robinson. It was Robinson, of course, who claimed that on his way to the Vaal River in 1868 he had bought the first diamonds found at Dutoitspan from Mrs van Wyk. This had launched him on his astonishing career, first as a diamond prospector and then as a diamond buyer. Although Robinson was not a total abstainer, his notorious meanness had made him sufficiently abstemious to win the favour of the Good Templars. Certainly he deserved to rank among the austere, serious-minded diggers. By no stretch of the imagination could he be considered frivolous or irresponsible. 'If ever', declared a journalist, 'a man "scorned delights and lived laborious days" that man is Mr J.B. Robinson.'

A combination of shrewdness and hard work had ensured his success at the river diggings. He was one of the first men to arrive at the Vaal and had quickly learnt all there was to know about surface-searching for river diamonds. In no time he had acquired extensive properties on both sides of the river, from which he recovered diamonds in large quantities. By the time Pniel and Klipdrift were established, J.B. Robinson was a man to be reckoned with on the banks of the Vaal.

He was active in many spheres. At the time when the Free State was trying to assert its authority over the river diggings, Robinson had been appointed as a special magistrate, instructed to 'put down the rioting in the Free State Territory' and he had also served as a Free State delegate on the committee which elected Stafford Parker as President of the Diggers' Republic. His close association with the Free State, where he had once been a trader, had earned him the reputation of being 'pro-Boer'. This had not made him popular with the diggers, but it had been a decided advantage to him as a land speculator. Until the Free State's claim to the territory had been challenged, Robinson had been able to snap up properties on the river with comparative ease. He had taken full advantage of his privileged position. As a land-owner, digger and diamond buyer he had few equals at the river diggings.

Robinson, working in partnership with Maurice Marcus, became the first claim-holder to export diamonds direct to London. His initial consignment was taken to England by Marcus in a red flannel belt which he wore around his waist. 'Night and day he wore them,' claimed Robinson, 'until he got to London, preferring the pain to the risk of having them stolen.' For a long time afterwards, Marcus is said to have borne the marks of this uncomfortable belt.

The London connection served Robinson well when he moved to New Rush. He set up a shop in one of the first buildings in the cluttered, dusty main street – a single-storied wood-and-white-plaster affair – and advertised himself as a 'Diamond Merchant . . . having entered into arrangements with London and Paris Houses'. Soon he was acknowledged, along with Moritz Unger, as one of the most important diamond buyers in the camp. It was impossible not to recognise his person or his position. His above-average height, his cultivated military stride, his cold-eyed stare and the white pith helmet that he always wore, singled him out as a notable personality and earned him the nickname of 'The Buccaneer'. Not the least of his virtues was his dependability – diggers with diamonds to sell did not have to comb the bars and canteens for him. He also had an enviable reputation for fair dealing. 'Mr J.B. Robinson. . .', it was said, '(trades) like a Christian and a gentleman. He gives the highest prices for diamonds, and hands over his cheque promptly and politely to all his customers.' This was more than could be said for some of his rivals.

In some respects J.B. Robinson could claim to be New Rush's first civic dignitary. He served on various diamond trade committees and was the elected president of the Diamond Fields Chamber of Commerce and Mutual Protection Society. When Sir Henry Barkly visited the diggings in 1872, Robinson was a prominent member of the diggers' reception committee. Indeed he was later to claim most of the credit for the Cape Governor's success with the diggers. 'I remember,' he boasted, 'just before the tiffin on that occasion that Sir Henry Barkly asked me what reception he would probably meet with. I replied that all would depend on his speech. Previous to the tiffin Sir Henry Barkly was the most unpopular man in the country; half an hour afterwards he was the most popular.' The Governor's plan to annex Griqualand West as a Crown Colony was, it would seem, as nothing compared to J.B. Robinson's timely, if rather obvious, warning.

But for all his airs and pretensions – or perhaps partly because of them – Robinson was not popular with the diggers. They respected him, but they did not like him. He was far too aloof, too surly and, above all, too tight-fisted to endear himself to the free-and-easy crowd at New Rush. His meanness was proverbial. Rich as he was, he made a point of getting up at dawn to scratch for bargains on the early-morning market and he would never enter a bar without first making sure that he would not have to buy anyone a drink. Nor did his uncertain temper help matters. As touchy as he was pugnacious, he was liable to take offence at the most unintentional slight. There was, in fact, no telling when his pompous facade would crack and reveal an even less attractive side of his character. His temper when roused could be terrifying: only the very rash or the very foolish went out of their way to provoke J.B. Robinson.

One man silly enough to cross Robinson was a dapper little dentist named Ernest Moses. In addition to extracting teeth, Moses wrote an occasional column for the newspaper and ran an amateur diamond-buying business. As a dentist his services were unremarkable, his newspaper column was scurrilous and his reputation as a diamond buyer dubious. He had done many unwise things, but his greatest mistake was to offend J.B. Robinson.

His offence was twofold: first he ridiculed Robinson in the press, and then he sold him a dud diamond. He could not have acted more foolishly. To puncture both Robinson's pride and his pocket was simply asking for trouble. It was not long coming. On the morning of 30 September 1872, as Moses strolled along the dusty main street of New Rush, the door of Robinson's office flew open and the proprietor rushed into the street flourishing a horsewhip. Grabbing Moses by the scruff of the neck, he began to beat the little dentist unmercifully. 'The pliant whip', it was reported, 'came down one, two, three, fitting the plump shoulders of Mr Moses as though it had been made for them. . . . Mr Moses took the one, two, three, and then tried to run off, but Mr Robinson is swift of foot, as well as smart of hand . . . and down came the pliant whip again, one, two, three across the Mosaic buttocks.'

The incident caused something of a stir. Fights were common enough in New Rush, but a public horsewhipping was considered a huge joke. For days the newspapers carried reports of impending lawsuits, Moses threatening to sue Robinson and Robinson declaring that he would defend any action brought against him. Eventually, however, the matter was settled out of court. In an exchange of letters, Moses apologised to Robinson, and Robinson apologised to Moses and, much to everyone's disappointment, the somewhat ludicrous affair fizzled out.

Trivial as it was, Robinson's action of taking the law into his own hands is not without significance. While the controversy lasted, the newspapers tended to take Robinson's side: he was publicly congratulated for exposing Moses's fraudulent methods of diamond dealing. For all that, there was no insistence that Moses be formally charged for attempting to palm off a dud diamond.

Once the matter had been settled to everyone's satisfaction it was quickly forgotten. This is in marked contrast to the diggers' attitude when a black man was discovered to be dealing in suspect diamonds; then no punishment was harsh enough for the offender, and wild generalisations were made against all black men who traded in diamonds.

On the other hand, the incident did nothing to increase Robinson's popularity. Not everyone at New Rush was favourably impressed by his display of righteous indignation. The diggers' standards of justice might be one-sided but they did not include the public horsewhipping of a man half one's size. For a man of Robinson's pretensions there were other ways of settling an argument, even in the rough-and-tumble of the diggings. If J.B. Robinson was a man to be reckoned with, so it seemed was his temper. Diamond dealing had a way of exposing the weaknesses of even the most responsible men in the camps.

(4)

Men like Moritz Unger, Ikey Sonnenberg, A.A. Rothschild, George Bottomley and J.B. Robinson dominated the diggings in the early days. But, for the
most part, their fame was to be shortlived. They were, with one exception, to be
either forgotten or dimly remembered as typical characters of the pioneering
days. The real men of power had yet to make their mark.

Most of these men were still finding their feet. Some were already on the
diggings but they were either too young or too poor to make an immediate
impression. The diamond industry at this stage was not stable enough to
command the talents of the men who were eventually to control it. There was
still a lot to be learned about the intricacies of what in effect was a revolutionary process.

That many bright young men had been attracted to the dynamic new
industry is hardly surprising. Diamond mining had brought the industrial
revolution to South Africa and consequently offered enterprising youngsters a
novel challenge and hitherto undreamed-of opportunities. Many rose to the
challenge, others faced it by arriving at the diamond fields with their families.
Not all of them were to succeed as claim holders but the diggings undoubtedly
played an important part in shaping their ambitions. There were, for instance,
no fewer than four future South African Prime Ministers living in the camps
during the early 1870s.

Of these four, only one had so far embarked on a political career. He was
John X. Merriman, the tall - six foot four inches - lanky, aesthetic-looking son
of the Bishop of Grahamstown. Merriman was almost thirty when he arrived at
New Rush. He had been born in Somerset, England, and had come to South
Africa as a boy when his father, Nathaniel Merriman, had been appointed the
first Anglican Archdeacon of Grahamstown. At the age of fifteen, John X.
Merriman had been sent back to England to complete his education at Radley
College, near Oxford, and had then worked for three years as a clerk in a
London tea- and silk-importing firm. Returning to the Cape in 1862 he had
qualified as a land-surveyor and seven years later had been elected to the Cape
Legislative Assembly as the member for Aliwal North. His election marked the
beginning of his long and distinguished political career.

As the representative of a rural constituency, Merriman came to have a great
sympathy for the Afrikaners. During the debates which preceded the annexation of Griqualand West by Sir Henry Barkly he had emerged as a champion of
the Orange Free State. By that time he was one of the few Cape politicians who
could speak with authority on matters concerning the diamond fields.

Merriman, like so many others, had been drawn to the diggings in 1871,
when the diamond fever was at its height. He went first to Klipdrift, where he
set up as a diamond buyer, and then moved to New Rush and tried his hand as a
digger. He was not particularly successful in either occupation.

Throughout his life Merriman was to be torn between a desire to succeed as a
businessman and a determination to shine as a politician. The two goals were
not always reconcilable and, more often than not, it was the businessman that

lost out. His chances of making good on the diamond fields were exceedingly slim. Apart from anything else, his temperament was against him. Witty, volatile, but fundamentally studious, he was more suited to browsing in a library than to burrowing in a claim; the mechanics of diamond buying bored him; he had little in common with men who were totally obsessed by money-making. In the camps he was very much an odd man out.

While most diggers enthused over the camaraderie of New Rush, Merriman felt strangely isolated. 'The camp', he wrote to a friend in February 1872, 'is an awful place. About two or three miles long. No order or anything else – a sort of canvas London, for no-one seems to know their next-door neighbour.' He regretted the scarcity of women and, though no prude, was frankly disgusted by the lawless behaviour of many drink-sodden diggers. 'Nothing is more common', he complained, 'than to see the canteens adorned with a row of dead-drunk corpses at ten a.m. Policemen there are none, and they never appear in the streets unless three parts gone, but quarrels are generally settled by a stand-up fight.' The camps had precious little to offer a man who admitted to having many 'governing class' prejudices.

Merriman battled on at New Rush for three years and then gave up. He went back to Cape politics, which, with his occasional business ventures, occupied him for the rest of his life. The peak of his political career was reached in 1908, when he became Prime Minister of the Cape. But his departure from New Rush did not end his association with the diggings. Both as a politician and as an aspiring financier, Merriman continued to take a lively, often active interest in the diamond industry – but he never again tried his luck as a digger.

Whether Merriman knew young Will Schreiner while he was at New Rush seems doubtful. There was very little chance of them meeting. Like Merriman, William Philip Schreiner was to become Prime Minister of the Cape – Merriman, in fact, would one day serve in his Cabinet – but at New Rush their worlds were far apart.

Will Schreiner, son of a German-born missionary, was still a schoolboy in the early 1870s. He had arrived at the diggings at the age of thirteen with his elder brother Theo. After a few months' unsuccessful digging on the Vaal, Will had been taken back to the Cape and packed off to school, but Theo later returned to the dry diggings. Both at Dutoitspan and New Rush, Theo Schreiner and his sister Ettie – who kept house for him – were to become well known as fervent supporters of various Temperance organisations. During the school holidays they were invariably joined by young Will, who, it is said, 'picked and sweated' in Theo's claims.

This appears to have been the limit of Will Schreiner's experience as a practical digger. In 1878 he went to England, where he read law in London and Cambridge and was admitted to the English bar before returning to the Cape. But the diggings never lost their fascination for him; the diamond industry was to play an important part in shaping his political career.

Another, even more remarkable, member of the Schreiner family was also fascinated by life in the mining-camps. In December 1872, Olive Schreiner, the brilliant, complex novelist and one of South Africa's most outstanding women, joined her brothers and sister at the diggings. The seventeen-year-old Olive, then recovering from an unfortunate love affair, lived at New Rush for about ten months. They were ten very important months in her life: her experience on the diamond fields was to have a profound effect on her writing.

She had, it seems, already succumbed to a form of literary diamond fever. At the age of sixteen she had started writing her first novel, *Undine*, which was set partly in New Rush, and a month before she arrived at the diggings she was working on an essay about diamonds. While living in the camp she was to begin work on a new novel, the unfinished *From Man to Man*, and the influence of the diamond fields can be traced in many of her other writings, both published and unpublished. It was at the diggings, says one of her biographers, 'that she first began seriously to think of herself as an authoress'.

Few diggers were able to convey as vividly as did Olive Schreiner, the confusion, the dust, the vitality, the variety, the whole pulsating and kaleido-scopic atmosphere of the camps. Perhaps her most evocative description, however, is that of a night visit paid by the heroine of *Undine* to the ever-deepening mine at the centre of New Rush.

'When the camp below was aglow with evening lights and the noise and stir in its tents and streets became louder and stronger, she rose and walked into the Kop in the bright moonlight. It was like entering the city of the dead in the land of the living, so quiet it was, so well did the high-piled gravel heaps keep out all sound of the seething noisy world around. Not a sound, not a movement. She walked to the edge of the reef and looked down into the crater. The thousand wires that crossed it, glistened in the moonlight, formed a weird, sheeny, mistlike veil over the black depths beneath. Very dark, very deep it lay all round the edge, but high towering into the bright moonlight rose the unworked centre. She crouched down at the foot of the staging and sat looking at it. In the magic of the moonlight it was a golden castle of the olden knightly days; you might swear as you gazed down at it, that you saw the shadows of its castellated battlements, and the endless turrets that overcrowned it; a giant castle, lulled to sleep and bound in silence for a thousand years by the word of some enchanter.'

Only a highly gifted novelist could weave such romance into that vast, prosaic pit. For those who sweated in the mine every day, it was a hell-hole; it inspired no whimsical visions, it engulfed, rather than liberated, men's souls. There were some, in fact, who regarded the mine as a chasm of the damned, an infernal abyss radiating an evil which infected every aspect of camp life. The white men worked there to make a fortune and live for pleasure; the black men merely wanted to earn enough to buy a gun. It was a godless place.

That, at least, is how one young Afrikaner boy saw it. He felt so strongly about the materialism of the camps that he tried to express his disgust in verse. Unlike Olive Schreiner, his poems did not conjure up eerie castles and phantom enchanters. They were written, says his biographer, simply to express 'his indignation at the supplying of weapons to natives while Boers were refused permits'.

The boy was James Barry Munnik Hertzog. In time he was to become a Prime Minister, not Prime Minister of the Cape, but of the Union of South

Africa. Throughout his political life he was to champion the Afrikaans language and strive to promote South African nationalism. His ideal was to be the unity of the two white races in South Africa but his suspicion of outside interference in the affairs of the country made him, in the eyes of many, the personification of an exclusive Afrikanerdom. There can be little doubt that the seeds of his future creed were sown during the years he spent at the diggings.

Young Barry Hertzog arrived at Dutoitspan with his family in 1872. His father, a somewhat free-and-easy farmer who had been badly hit by an agricultural depression in the Cape, started life at the diggings as a claim-holder and later established himself at New Rush as a butcher and baker. The six-year-old Barry was sent, with his brothers and sister, to a school run by Mrs Pohl van Niekerk. He was a reserved, studious little boy. His teacher was to remember him mainly for his impeccable behaviour. 'No, I never birched the future Prime Minister of the Union!' she giggled. 'He was always a good worker, quiet and retiring. Everything he attempted, he did well; his school-work was always neatly done. He was a real little gentleman, and very fond of his books.'

There were not many boys like young Barry at the diggings. He seems, by all accounts, to have been a model child. This was largely his mother's doing. His father was a tough, good-natured man who taught his sons to use their fists and stand up for themselves, but Mrs Hertzog was exceedingly prim. She did all she could to protect her children from the coarser influences of the diggings. So strongly did she disapprove of the uncouth diggers that she would not allow any of the family to play cards or attend dances and adamantly refused to speak English in the home. Barry was very much his mother's son.

Any form of loose behaviour shocked him to the core. One day, watching some diggers greet a crowd of rowdy women who had arrived on the passenger cart from Cape Town, he was overcome with disgust. 'The vicious language he heard on that occasion', it is said, 'convinced him that these money-grubbing foreigners who had invaded his homeland were nothing but a noisy, insensitive crowd, in spite of their superior attitude towards his own people.' If anything had been needed to reinforce his prejudices, the raffish side of camp life provided it. He returned to his books, studied the history of the Afrikaner, and cultivated his dislike for the *uitlanders*. By the time his family moved from the diggings, in 1879, says his biographer, 'his course was set'.

It was a very different course from that of another young man then living in the camps. Cecil John Rhodes was to have little in common with Barry Hertzog. He too had come to the diggings as a youngster – he was older than Hertzog, but still young; he too was to have his prejudices confirmed by life in the camps; he too was to translate those prejudices into a political creed which inspired his life's work: but there any similarity between Cecil Rhodes and Barry Hertzog ended. For Rhodes's prejudices were very different from those of Hertzog: he, in the eyes of many, was to become as much the epitome of the plutocratic Englishman as Hertzog was the personification of exclusive Afrikanerdom. These views of both men were, to a greater or lesser degree, mistaken, but there is no denying the conflict between their basic ideals. The nationalism engendered in Hertzog at the diggings would always be opposed to the imperialism which Rhodes sucked from the same roots.

Rhodes, like Merriman and Schreiner, was to become Prime Minister of the Cape; like them, also, he was a parson's son. His father, the Reverend Francis William Rhodes, was the vicar of Bishop's Stortford in England, where Cecil Rhodes was born on 5 July 1853. Even as a boy Rhodes was rarely called Cecil outside the family circle. He was a moody, solitary lad whose aloof manner did not invite intimacy. He was also far from robust. After leaving the local grammar school, at the age of sixteen, he fell ill and, upon being examined by the family doctor, was found to be tubercular. The doctor advised that he should leave England for a while and, as his elder brother Herbert had recently emigrated to South Africa and was sending home enthusiastic reports concerning his prospects as a cotton grower in Natal, it was decided that Cecil should join him there.

This interruption to his scholastic career was a sad disappointment to Rhodes. He had set his heart on attending university; it was then his ambition to become either a barrister or a clergyman. Ill-health, which was to plague him throughout his life, had forced him to change his plans. But the change was, for Rhodes, merely a temporary measure: he was determined, once he was well enough, to return and continue where he had left off. Come what may, he would go to university.

When Rhodes – 'a tall, lanky, anaemic, fair-haired boy' – docked at Durban on 1 September 1870, his brother was not there to meet him. Like many another adventurous young man in Natal, Herbert Rhodes had gone to try his luck at the river diggings. But he was soon back again. Restless and irresolute, Herbert was not the type to stick at anything for long. His finds at the Vaal did not match his expectations and, within a matter of weeks, he returned to Natal. He found Cecil waiting for him at Pietermaritzburg.

Herbert's cotton plantation was in the Umkomaas Valley, a few miles from Pietermaritzburg. It had so far yielded little. The first crop, which Herbert had planted with more enthusiasm than knowledge, had been almost totally destroyed by sub-tropical insects. Now the two brothers set to work again. They cleared more ground and soon had a hundred acres of cotton under cultivation. Manual work suited Cecil. It not only improved his health but added to his philosoph. Throughout his life he was to admire men who worked by the sweat of their brow – they were the 'decent chaps', the rest were loafers. 'Shouldn't do that,' he once told a friend who wanted to write, 'it is not a man's work – mere loafing. Every man should have active work.'

Herbert found the work less agreeable. His experience at the river diggings had unsettled him and when, a few months later, news of the rush to the dry diggings reached Natal, he became extremely restless. He waited until March 1871 and then decided to try his luck at Dutoitspan. This time he was more fortune. He was among the first diggers to peg out claims on Colesberg Kopje and struck it rich immediately. In a list of early returns from New Rush 'Mr Rhodes of Natal' was reported to have found '110 carats, including stones of 14, 16 and 28 carats'. He had little difficulty in persuading Cecil to join him.

Cecil Rhodes left Natal for New Rush in October 1871. He travelled in a Scotch cart drawn by oxen, and took over a month to complete the 400-mile journey. His luggage reflected his ambitions: alongside an assortment of digger's tools were stacked volumes of the classics and a Greek lexicon. Fired as he was by Herbert's enthusiasm, he was taking no chances. The glitter of diamonds could prove deceptive. He was still preparing himself for university, preferably Oxford.

Hardly had he reached New Rush than he found himself alone. On the spur of the moment, Herbert decided to return to Natal and then take a holiday in England. Cecil, eighteen years old and completely inexperienced as a digger, was left in sole charge of three diamond claims, estimated at that time to be worth £5,000. This worried him not at all. He worked the claims as energetically as he had cultivated cotton. Soon he was writing home giving expert opinions on the value of diamonds. He found that the big yellow-tinged ones were often deceptive: they had 'a nasty habit of suddenly splitting all over'. On the other hand, every stone had some value: 'the great proportion are nothing but splints', he reported, 'but still of even these you very seldom find one that is not worth 5s.'.

He took his brother's place in one of the fenced-off bachelor 'messes' at New Rush, living with a group of young men known as 'The Twelve Apostles'. But he was by no means as popular as his brother had been. Lacking Herbert's gregariousness, he kept himself very much to himself. Descriptions of Cecil Rhodes during these early days invariably picture him sitting alone at his claim on an upturned bucket, with one eye on his African labourers and the other on a text book. He took very little part in the social life of the camps. When he did attend the occasional dance, he made it clear to his unfortunate partner that he was only there for the exercise.

One of the few friends he made was Charles Dunell Rudd, a 28-year-old Englishman who, like himself, had originally come to South Africa to recuperate after an illness. While Herbert was still in England, Cecil Rhodes and Charles Rudd had found themselves working in adjoining claims and had decided to pool their resources. The partnership prospered. The two of them not only worked side by side in the diggings, but devised schemes for improving their capital, including the erection of an ice-making plant from which they supplied the thirsty diggers with cold drinks.

Rudd was one of the first men to succumb to that rare charm which Rhodes reserved for those he wished to win over. Having been educated at Cambridge, Rudd fully entered into a plan which would allow Rhodes to go to Oxford while he looked after their joint interests at the diggings.

Another man to be impressed by Rhodes was John X. Merriman. Although twelve years Rhodes's senior, Merriman found that he had much in common with the moody young man. The two of them would often ride into the veld discussing the classics, history and South African politics. Merriman was later to say that they had come to an agreement that the only intellectual pursuit open to a colonist was an active interest in public affairs; it was an agreement which they both took to heart, although with differing results.

That Rhodes was already taking a keen interest in public affairs there can be little doubt. His arrival at New Rush had coincided with Sir Henry Barkly's annexation of the diamond fields to the Cape. He had lived in the camp throughout the chaotic rule of the three commissioners and had witnessed the disastrous New Rush riots. He was still there when Barkly arrived with his plan to make Griqualand West a Crown Colony. For Rhodes this solution held a special significance: his experience in the camp had even then convinced him that it was the duty of Britain to control, not only Griqualand West, but as much of the world as possible. In his opinion only a strong, benevolent authority could bring peace to turbulent situations such as existed on the diamond fields. He had already given testimony to this belief.

A few months earlier, while he was still preparing to go to Oxford, he had suffered a slight heart attack. By that time Herbert had returned to the diggings and, restless as ever, was planning to investigate rumours that gold had been discovered in the Transvaal. Alarmed at his brother's illness, Herbert had decided to take Cecil with him on the gold-prospecting expedition. It was hoped that the invigorating air of the highveld would prove beneficial to the invalid. The expedition proved fruitless as far as gold was concerned, but it did give Cecil time to think about his role in life. It was on this journey that he made his first will. Writing on an odd scrap of paper, the young digger bequeathed his small fortune to the Secretary of State for Colonies; the money was to be used for the purpose of extending the British Empire. As one of the trustees he named the Attorney-General for Griqualand West, Sidney Shippard.

The brothers returned to the diggings and a few months later Cecil left for Oxford. He, like Barry Hertzog, was now set on his course. It was a course largely decided upon during his years at New Rush.

The discovery of diamonds has long been recognised as a turning-point in the economic life of South Africa. What is not generally appreciated is the extent to which the diggings influenced the men who were to dominate the politics of the country. More than diamonds had been unearthed in Griqualand West.

7

Governor Southey

Richard Southey, the former Colonial Secretary, arrived at New Rush to take up his appointment as Lieutenant-Governor of Griqualand West on 9 January 1873. It was a great day for the diggings. A reception committee had been formed and much energy expended to welcome the new administrator. Flags and bunting fluttered from most tents and shanties, triumphal arches were erected and brass bands rehearsed to precede Southey's entry into the camp.

In true South African fashion, it was decided that the Lieutenant-Governor should be met a few miles outside New Rush so that he could be suitably escorted into the camp. The place chosen for the rendezvous was Alexandersfontein, then a favourite picnic spot for diggers which boasted a hotel 'where bridal pairs went to get their first taste of connubial felicity'. Southey and his recently married second wife were expected to arrive at four o'clock that afternoon, but hours beforehand huge crowds were seen flocking towards Alexandersfontein. J. B. Robinson, as owner of the finest equipage in the territory and a prominent member of the reception committee, lent his carriage and horses to carry Southey and his wife into the camp.

By two o'clock, says R.W. Murray, New Rush was 'all hustle and bustle, and by three o'clock, the horsemen were in their saddles, the drivers were in their seats cracking their whips, and the vehicles were loaded up. . . . At three thirty the road was crowded. Every inch of it was covered with well-mounted horsemen and well-laden vehicles, and by four o'clock, when His Excellency arrived, before or behind him was one living mass of people. . . . He was received at Alexandersfontein with such cheering, loud and hearty, as might have been, and I was told at the time, *was*, heard at Bultfontein. The run into town was done at a splitting pace, the people cheering as they went.'

For the new Lieutenant-Governor, the arrival in his future capital must have been both rewarding and forbidding. After a hot, dusty, seemingly endless journey across hundreds of miles of featureless countryside, the sight of the white tents and flashing roofs of the diggings must have come as something of a relief. But once inside New Rush, with its rutted, haphazard streets, its treeless Market-square and its ramshackle shops and offices, Southey might well have had second thoughts about the task he had undertaken. Like most newcomers, he must have found the bleakness of the camp singularly uninspiring. Nor could the first glimpse of her new home – a small wood-and-iron building lent by a merchant for the occasion – have given his bride much pleasure. But, *faute de mieux*, the Lieutenant-Governor and his sad-eyed lady were obliged to make the best of things.

They were probably slightly cheered by the magnificent 'Tiffin' that had been arranged for them. This welcoming meal was given in one of the new wonders of New Rush: a splendid refreshment room, known as Parker's Pavilion, which the enterprising Stafford Parker had built 'just in the nick of time, for the reception of the Governor' and which, it was claimed, had been 'fitted up upon the London model', complete with experienced London barmaids and waiters. The barmaids were not in evidence during the Tiffin – in fact they were kept discreetly out of sight until the Governor had left for his official visit to Klipdrift – but there was an excellent spread and several stirring speeches by old residents.

That evening Southey, imposing in plumed hat and lavishly embroidered uniform, was present with his wife at a firework display in the Market-square. The place was packed and it was claimed that the Lieutenant-Governor 'met with good wishes from everyone'.

Altogether, this first day was an impressive, if deceptive, start to Richard Southey's turbulent term of office.

(2)

The new constitution which Sir Henry Barkly had promised the diggers had not yet been drawn up. For the first few months of his reign Southey, like the three commissioners before him, had to rule by Proclamation. To assist him three officials – a government secretary, a crown prosecutor and a treasurer general – had been appointed. But hardly had Southey arrived when, somewhat ominously, both the crown prosecutor and the treasurer general fell sick and applied for leave. This meant that most of the initial work had to be shouldered by Southey and the healthy, but unfortunate, government secretary. It was asking a lot of them. As things turned out, it might well be thought that it was asking too much.

Southey's government secretary was John Blades Currey – the man who, some six years earlier, had tried to publicise the 'Eureka' diamond in Europe. On his return to South Africa, Currey had worked as a civil servant in Cape Town, eventually becoming Southey's confidential clerk. His appointment as government secretary of Griqualand West was not entirely unexpected, nor was it particularly welcomed.

Currey was not popular with the diggers. When his appointment was announced, at the beginning of December 1872, it was greeted with sneers in the local press. These sneers were soon to develop into open hostility. In time Currey was to be described as the evil genius of the diggings. All the mistakes of the Southey regime were to be attributed to him. 'Currey made the bullets,' snorted one digger, 'and Southey fired them.' There was some truth in the accusation.

If the diggers did not like Currey, he was not exactly in love with all of them. He had little time for the disorderly, dirty townships which called themselves camps and even less time for the lawless element so conspicuous in New Rush.

He considered these diggers to be totally irresponsible, nothing more than play-acting miners. Their tough, cynical behaviour was, in his opinion, simply a pose. 'By common consent,' he claimed, 'and almost insensibly the manners and even the speech of American Mining Camps as depicted by American Humourists were copied.' Nor did the blatant racialism of the camps appeal to him. He was disgusted, he says, to discover that at New Rush 'for the first time in my experience of South Africa the black and even the coloured man was called a Nigger'.

For all that, he was no advocate of complete equality. Far from it. One of his main objections was to the rabble-rousing cries of the diggers' committees which sought, in his opinion, to destroy the privileges of affluent miners and replace them by mob rule. The rules drawn up by these committees were evidence of their determination to curb capitalist enterprise. Why else did they insist that no digger should own more than two claims? It was obvious that the ultimate goal of the New Rush agitators was a white proletarian republic.

This was a strange ambition for men employed in unearthing stones to decorate duchesses, but that is how Currey saw it. In his view the diggers' committees were both dangerous and subversive. He openly admitted to his 'object of curbing or getting rid of the Diggers Committees' and establishing 'Mining Boards with defined and limited powers' in their place. In many ways this was a legitimate enough aim but, in view of the past history of the diggings, it was not something that could be achieved easily. It required patient and tactful handling. Unfortunately tact and patience were not Currey's strong points. His influence on Southey was apparent from the outset.

Hardly had the new Lieutenant-Governor arrived on the diggings than he issued his first controversial edict. In a Proclamation dated 31 January 1873, he suspended one of the long established diggers' rules. This was the rule by which any claim left unworked for eight or more days could be seized, or 'jumped', by anyone proving such neglect. That Southey's action was approved by the majority of diggers there is little doubt. The 'jumping' system was never popular and had cost many a man dearly. Nevertheless it was a direct blow to the authority of the diggers' committees and was recognised as such by some of the committee members. There could be no doubt as to the direction in which Southey was moving.

To soften the blow, Southey then announced his intention to set up a commission to 'determine more definitely what officers or bodies should be entrusted with the control of matters' on the diamond fields. Five prominent diggers, including leading members of the diggers' committees, were appointed to the commission. This was to be the first step towards establishing Mining Boards. Significantly the commission was headed by J. B. Currey.

Currey also played an important part in framing another controversial law. In March Southey issued a Proclamation making it illegal 'to keep or to frequent a gaming house or gaming table within the territory of Griqualand West'. Police were empowered to raid any hut or tent where gambling took place, and anyone caught gambling was liable to fines ranging from £10 to £500. These conditions, says Currey, were drawn up one Sunday by himself

'A leading man in the Government.' A typical cartoon of the Southey era showing J.B. Currey pulling Southey along by the nose. (K)

Lord Kimberley. A cartoon of the British Secretary of State for the Colonies, after whom Kimberley was named in July 1873. *Vanity Fair*, 16 July 1869. (K)

Henry Tucker. Diggers' leader during the notorious 'Black Flag Rebellion' in 1875. (M)

Sir Richard Southey and members of the first Legislative Council of Griqualand West, 1874: seated left to right, J.B. Currey, Richard Southey, J. Cyprian Thompson; standing left to right, David Arnot, Henry Green, R.W.H. Giddy, Francis Thompson, P.J. Hardman Graham. (M)

and young Cecil Rhodes. The twenty-year-old Rhodes, who had not yet left for Oxford, had, it appears, a good knowledge of the harm done by gambling.

Once again there was widespread support for the new law. Gambling was, as Dr Matthews pointed out, one of the 'great social evils' of the camps and many were glad to see it finally stamped out. An earlier attempt to suppress the vice by prohibiting public lotteries had merely made the 'hell keepers' more cautious. Instead of keeping open house they had formed clubs and sent out invitations to old friends and new to attend private 'At Homes'. The new legislation was more positive and, according to Currey, decidedly more effective. 'The Americans who had the largest business', he says, 'packed up their traps and left with, it was said, the modest sum of £50,000 and the smaller fry submitted without a murmur.' This is not quite true. An attempt was made to reopen the gambling-dens across the Free State border but it failed because all but the most ardent gamblers refused to travel so far for a flutter. It is extremely doubtful whether all the diggers accepted the outlawing of one of their few diversions as meekly as Currey suggests.

But it was not so much Southey's repressive edicts as the absence of more constructive action that incensed the diggers. Sir Henry Barkly had promised them representative government and, as the months went by without any sign of the new constitution being proclaimed, they began to grow more and more impatient. The fault, however, was not Southey's. The letters patent declaring Griqualand West a Crown Colony were being held up in London. Lord Kimberley, the Secretary of State for the Colonies, was insisting that before electoral divisions could be defined, the places 'must receive decent and intelligible names'. His Lordship, it appears, 'declined to be in any way connected with such a vulgarism as New Rush and as for Vooruitzigt . . . he could neither spell nor pronounce it. Klipdrift and Griquatown were not much better and he requested that English sounding names might be given to the Districts round the Mining Camps.'

The request was passed on to Southey who promptly handed it over to Currey. This was something which Currey felt very able to deal with. Klipdrift he changed to Barkly 'to perpetuate the name of the Governor who promised the Constitution', and Griquatown became Hay, partly as a tribute to General Hay, the former acting Governor, and partly in memory of a Scottish town that Currey had known in his youth. When it came to renaming New Rush, he proved himself a worthy diplomat. He made quite sure that Lord Kimberley would be able both to spell and pronounce the name of the main electoral division by, as he says, calling it 'after his Lordship'.

The new names were announced in a Proclamation, dated 5 July 1873. New Rush, with all its boisterous associations, was no more.

It was now known, and continued to be known, as Kimberley.

(3)

Although most diggers were agreed that the name New Rush was inelegant, they were not all prepared to accept Currey's new designation. The *Diamond*

Field newspaper, which had recently moved to the camp from Klipdrift and was rapidly becoming the mouthpiece of the diggers' committees, regarded the change of name as a bad joke. For months the newspaper stubbornly refused to use the new name on its banner heading, insisting that it was still printed in New Rush.

But this was a matter of minor concern. The real shock was contained in the fine print of the new constitution. It had been generally assumed that the Legislative Council promised by Sir Henry Barkly would give the diggers an effective say in their own affairs: that members elected by a popular vote would be assisted by one or two Government nominees. To their utter amazement and disgust, the diggers now discovered that the Council was to be constituted on a deadlock principle. There were to be only four elected members – two for Kimberley and one each for the Barkly and Hay districts – and four Government nominees, the Lieutenant-Governor having the casting vote. This meant that, with Southey empowered to veto legislation, the diggers were scarcely better off than when they had been ruled by Proclamation. Southey was still the effective master of Griqualand West.

The *Diamond Field* was completely bewildered. 'We certainly do not know what to make of it. . . . ' the newspaper declared. 'We had dreamed of a possible Institution wherein we should have found satisfaction for all our long continued discontent and restlessness. . . . Some twelve chosen men, in this dream of ours, sat with three or four officials there. This was the sort of Assembly we dreamed of. But we went to sleep in New Rush and waked up in Kimberley, and so our dream was gone – faded in the light of common day.'

So resentful were the majority of diggers that it was doubted whether anyone would accept nomination for the elections. Eventually, however, several candidates came forward and preparations for the registration of voters went ahead. At New Rush the more vocal malcontents pinned their hopes on two men, Henry Tucker and David Buchanan, but the nomination of Buchanan was rejected by the authorities on the grounds that the requisition asking him to stand contained a trifling legal inaccuracy. This made Henry Tucker the sole candidate of the disgruntled members of the once powerful diggers' committees.

Tucker was well liked. Black-bearded, genial, with a forceful personality and a strong sense of justice, he was not only well-educated but an experienced politician. From 1861 to 1866 he had been a member of the Cape Legislative Council, but had resigned and left the Colony when his business went bankrupt. Since coming to the diamond fields he had had little luck as a claimholder and was chiefly known for his passionate advocacy of 'diggers' rights'. It was as a champion of these rights that he entered the election contest. He embarked on his campaign by promising cheap bread and cheap meat and committing himself to the 'encouragement of properly organised Detective Societies and the punishment of diamond thieves'.

He could not have chosen a more popular platform. The cost of living at the diggings had risen astronomically over the past couple of years. Goods destined for Griqualand West were heavily taxed by the Cape customs, and the cost of transport was crippling. All goods coming to the diamond fields had to be carried by ox-wagon, and the transport of building-materials, machinery and provisions from the Cape could cost anything between thirty and fifty shillings per hundredweight. Plans were under way to extend the railway line in both the western and eastern Cape, but it would be years before these lines could reach the diamond fields. Until that happened all transport was dependent on grass. A severe winter, when the roads hardened and there was insufficient grass for the draught oxen, could prove ruinous. During the second half of 1873, at the time of the elections, a bad drought had brought transport practically to a standstill. Prices had soared. Even the most affluent diggers felt the pinch and many of the newly arrived civil servants had to take on extra clerking jobs to supplement their meagre salaries. Two months after his arrival at the diggings Southey had found living so expensive that he applied for an additional £500 to his recently agreed salary of £2,000 a year. Henry Tucker's demand for cheap bread and meat was more than just a vote-catching slogan.

Every bit as welcome was Tucker's determination to stamp out illicit diamond buying. The crime of I.D.B., as it was called, was as rife as ever. Sir Henry Barkly's half-hearted attempts to control the sale of diamonds by increasing the penalties for illicit diamond transactions and prohibiting canteen keepers from trading in diamonds had proved singularly ineffective. Scores of African labourers were hauled into court every week, charged with selling stones to shady white 'fences'–buyers of stolen diamonds–and things had been made decidedly worse by slick lawyers who often got their clients acquitted on a technicality. Even the most loyal diggers tended to look back with longing to the rough justice of Orange Free State rule.

'I could', one of them wrote, 'say a good deal on the subject of diamond stealing; under Truter, if such a thing occurred, the thief had but scant grace shown him – if he were a black man it was proof enough of his guilt and punishment was severe, and no doubt the decision in nine-tenths of the cases was correct. . . . To be sure there was no organised system of fences in those days – but now . . . after weeks of suspicion and finally catching a thief, you bring him before the magistrate, to find him defended by quibbling lawyers. . . . Is it not absurd to apply the niceties of English law when dealing with savages?'

This, for all its racialism, was the view of the majority of diggers. Few would have argued with Tucker's proposal to organise detective societies and apply arbitrary punishment to diamond thieves. The normal Cape laws were regarded as totally inadequate for dealing with the crime.

Yet, popular as his sentiments were, Henry Tucker lost the election. The Kimberley division was contested by three candidates: Henry Green, a former civil servant and staunch supporter of the Government, Dr P.J.H. Graham, a well-known physician, and Henry Tucker. On the day of the election, 25 November, things were surprisingly quiet. Most diggers found it impossible to realise that they were being asked to vote in the first election the camps had known. A few carts sporting the candidates' colours were seen darting about - mostly in Dutoitspan - but it was not until Henry Green turned out with a brass band, seated in a horse van and playing lively Irish airs, that any life was injected into the campaign. 'Then', it was reported, 'many men forsook their jobs and, in real electioneering spirit, made a day of it.' Even so it was a lack-lustre affair. The contest was notable for its sedateness: there were no argu-ments, no street fights and, most astonishing of all, no drunkenness. Kimberley's first election can hardly be said to have set a pattern for those to come.

The result, published the next day, showed Dr Graham heading the poll with 850 votes, Henry Green came second with 802 votes, and Henry Tucker finished a poor third with 652 votes. The real significance of the election, however, was revealed when the voting was broken down into districts. At New Rush, Henry Tucker soundly beat both his opponents but lost out to them at Dutoitspan, where he managed to pick up only 36 votes. The rivalry between 'gay New Rush' and the 'toiling Pan' was still very much a factor to be reckoned with.

So, for that matter, were Henry Tucker's irate supporters. Hardly had the results been announced than a group of New Rush diggers issued a strongly worded protest, challenging the legality of the election. In a lengthy letter to Sir Henry Barkly they pointed out that the Proclamation which made provision for the election had been signed by J.B. Currey on 24 October - a date when Currey had been absent from the diggings. They also complained about the rejection of David Buchanan as a candidate. On the face of it, these objections were trifling and no doubt Barkly felt justified in ignoring them. What he failed to recognise was the threat they posed to the new constitution. The New Rush agitators were, in effect, giving warning that they had no intention of allowing a puppet government to ride rough-shod over them.

Had Barkly been a little more familiar with the diggings the names of those who had signed the letter might have made him think twice. The protest had been organised by William Ling, an active member of the New Rush Diggers' Committee. He was well known for his outspoken opposition to the Southey regime. Earlier he had been associated with a stormy meeting that had been called to defy the Lieutenant-Governor's suspension of the 'jumping' system. He was also involved in litigation with the syndicate which owned the Vooruitzigt farm. William Ling was not a man who could easily be ignored.

Like many of the rebel diggers, Ling had come to the diamond fields from Natal. He was a man who could inspire vehement hostility or tremendous loyalty. His opponents regarded William Ling as 'little above the peasant class . . . shrewd, dogged and overbearing'. But his many admirers had nothing but praise for his 'uprightness and integrity . . . his bold and un-flinching advocacy of sound political principles.' He was, they said, 'warm-hearted and public spirited to a remarkable degree'. What both sides admitted was his undoubted qualities as a sportsman. In time William Ling was to be revered as the 'Father of Kimberley cricket'. When not engaged in political agitation he was tireless in arranging cricket matches between bizarrely named diggers' sides - Handsomes *vs* Uglies, Home *vs* Colonial - and it was largely due to his efforts that an open space, known as the Natal Cricket Ground, was acquired at New Rush. But this did nothing to endear him to Kimberley's new rulers. Richard Southey had no more bitter and determined enemies than William Ling and Henry Tucker.

The opposition forces had yet to become properly organised. For the most part, both Southey and Currey were pleased with the election results. They could count on the support of Henry Green and expected little trouble from Dr Graham. The Barkly (Klipdrift) division had returned Francis Thompson, a popular advocate, and the unopposed representative for Hay (Griquatown) was none other than Southey's old friend and confidant, David Arnot. There seemed no reason to doubt that the new Legislative Council would function smoothly.

And so it proved. When the Council met for the first time, on 30 December 1873, all was sweetness and harmony. In due course J.B. Currey made his first Budget speech and introduced legislation to abolish the diggers' committees and replace them with carefuly controlled Mining Boards. There was no opposition to these measures. 'All', thought Currey, 'seemed to be going well.'

Not until later did he realise how wrong he was. What happened in the Council chamber was no real reflection of the growing resentment in the camps. The fiery members of the old diggers' committees were even then preparing to hit back. They had been too powerful for too long to accept such high-handed treatment by the newly arrived officials. 'It was', Currey later admitted, 'the destruction of their power by the new Mining Ordinance which became law in 1874 that led in no small measure to the troubles of 1875.'

(4)

It would be wrong to dismiss Richard Southey as an unprincipled charlatan. This is how his opponents saw him, and this, to a greater or lesser degree, is how his traducers have judged him. He has been depicted as a grasping Imperialist, determined to cheat the Boer republics out of the diamond fields. It has been implied that he was an arrogant, self-righteous autocrat whose unsympathetic attitude towards the diggers invited trouble. His motives, his manner and his actions have come in for severe criticism. As is often the case, there is an element of truth in all these accusations. But his faults have been grossly exaggerated.

That Southey was a convinced Imperialist there can be no doubt. That he schemed to secure the diamond fields to the British interest is also true. Like many another man of his time, he considered that only Britain had the power to ensure peaceful progress in southern Africa. Strength, as well as goodwill, was required to overcome the racial antagonisms which plagued the sub-continent. Events were to prove him wrong. But if his motives were misguided, they were not necessarily mean. History has a way of cheapening idealism: it is always easy to recognise mistakes once they have been made, it is also easy to scoff at those whose convictions have been proved false. Southey did not have the benefit of hindsight. In this he was no better and no worse than most men.

His attitude towards the diggers must be balanced by their attitude towards him. Those opposed to him were determined to bring about his downfall. They would have been satisfied with nothing less. If at times he took refuge in his official status, it was from the conviction that deliberate attempts were being made to undermine his authority. Who can say he was wrong?

He was not always aloof and unapproachable. He could, when necessary, 'talk over and conciliate the most rampant radical'. What he would not compromise were his principles. Prominent among these principles was the responsibility he felt towards all the citizens of Griqualand West, irrespective of colour. His attitude towards colour prejudice was far more enlightened and commendable than that of his self-seeking opponents. It was this, as much as anything, that made his position impossible from the outset. Perhaps the worst that can be said of Richard Southey is that he was the wrong man, in the wrong place, at the wrong time.

Certainly the times could hardly have been less auspicious. The problems that faced Southey when he arrived at New Rush were legion. There was scarcely a disaster–political, economic or natural–that he did not have to cope with at one time or another. Not all of them were of his own making. Some he inherited, others were sprung upon him. It would have required a superman to handle them all successfully.

Politically he faced not only the hostility of the rebel diggers but the under-standable bitterness of the neighbouring Boer republics. Barkly's annexation had by no means ended the controversy over the ownership of the diamond fields. President Brand was still valiantly disputing the boundaries and demanding foreign arbitration. Nor had things been helped by the way in which the diamond discoveries had disrupted the labour force of the Boer republics. Africans, lured by extra money, had deserted the farms and flocked to the diggings. Serious as this was, in the eyes of the farmers, it was made all the more alarming by the fact that the Africans had little difficulty in obtaining guns in the camps. The sight of armed Blacks marching home from the diggings infuriated the Boers. Attempts were made to prevent some Zulu and Basuto from reaching the diamond fields. A few Africans returning home with guns were shot on sight: eventually they took to travelling across country in armed bands. Shortly after Southey arrived, a crisis arose when the Boers seized a consignment of guns destined for the diggings. Strong complaints were also made by the Natal authorities who had recently faced an armed rebellion.

Southey refused to entertain such protests. He maintained that most of the Africans at the diggings came, not from the republics or Natal, but from the north. The sale of guns to them represented an important avenue of British trade to the interior. 'I should consider it', he told Barkly, 'very undesirable to purchase the friendly feeling of those Boer republics at the expense of injustice or oppression toward her Majesty's own subjects or unfriendly acts toward the aboriginal inhabitants of the country.' He was convinced, in any case, that if the government prohibited the traffic, the guns would be smuggled to the interior by unscrupulous traders.

The wisdom of Southey's attitude is certainly open to question, but he

Young Cecil Rhodes (in black hat, sitting right, with a dog) at an early diggers' encampment. (K)

Digging for diamonds at the Cape Colony. A contemporary drawing showing the arrival of African labourers at Kimberley as tribesmen, and their departure after having acquired clothes and guns. (M)

literally stuck to his guns. It is estimated that in 1873 some 18,000 guns were introduced into Griqualand West, for which nearly 10,000 permits of sale were issued. The Boers felt they had good reason to object.

In yet another dispute Southey at least had the wholehearted support of the diggers. This was the continuing quarrel between the owners of Vooruitzigt and licensed claim-holders. On his way to New Rush, Southey had passed through Port Elizabeth and had there been met by a deputation from Alfred Ebden's syndicate. As purchasers of a farm that was yielding untold riches, members of the syndicate were incensed by the fact that all they received was a miserable ten shillings a month for each claim; they informed Southey that they intended to raise the monthly licence fee to ten pounds. But they had come to the wrong man. Southey had no intention of supporting their demands. In his view the owners had relinquished their right to a share in the mineral wealth of the farms by issuing licences to dig for diamonds instead of demanding rent. This meant that they had tacitly admitted that they had only surface rights and, as far as mining was concerned, they 'were really quitrent tenants under the crown . . . and that the ownership of minerals and precious stones was vested in the Government'.

Once he was installed at New Rush, Southey had his opinion legally confirmed and, to the diggers' delight, not only refused to pay the farm owners any of the licence money collected, but demanded a refund of that which they had already received. This started a long legal tussle which only ended on 31 May 1875, when the owners finally gave in and sold the farm to the Government for £100,000.

Fifteen years later it was estimated that the value of the Vooruitzigt Estate, originally sold by the De Beer brothers for 6,000 guineas, had risen to £14,500,000.

(5)

This was one of the few battles that Southey won. There were others that he could do nothing about. Perhaps the greatest problem facing the mining industry at that time was the serious decline in the price of diamonds. This was something that the wiser diggers had long feared. They were fully aware that the most formidable threat to the industry was the diamond itself. For most diamonds are useless. Their value is artificial and depends largely upon their scarcity. Before the opening of the South African mines they *were* relatively scarce. By flooding the market with stones the diggers had cheapened the product of their labours. The decline in the price of diamonds was inevitable.

Frederick Boyle had recognised the danger in 1872. 'You cannot drown the market with an article appertaining to the highest luxury,' he wrote, '– you cannot popularise a traffic in such articles – without sudden and swift catastrophe. These things require the most delicate manipulation, they exact the strictest reticence, they need a hand to hold them back or to loose them as the occasion asks. . . . By royal monopoly alone, or by means of great and powerful companies, can jewel digging be made a thriving industry. Into the hands of a company all these public fields must fall, and, thus used, they may benefit the country for generations to come.'

But there was no hope of either the Government or a powerful company controlling the output of diamonds in 1873. This was a problem which it would take many years to resolve. When Southey first arrived on the fields few diggers were ready to predict that the diamond industry would benefit future generations, however it was organised. It seemed then that Boyle had been over-optimistic. For not only had the price of diamonds declined, but there seemed every likelihood of the stones petering out altogether.

This was the time of the 'blue-ground scare'. Having worked to a considerable depth through arid yellow soil, the diggers suddenly struck much firmer, more compact, blue-coloured ground. At first this new ground seemed unproductive. For many diggers this was the last straw. Life in the 'hell-holes' had never been easy and now that it seemed that the mines were almost exhausted they gave up in despair. Claims were sold for a song; the diggings were left to those who could afford to take chances. The outlook was gloomy indeed.

So gloomy was it that many a hopeful newcomer arriving at Cape Town was dissuaded from travelling any farther. The diggings, they were told, had been played out. One such newcomer was young Barney Barnato, who docked at the Cape in August 1873. He was on his way to join his brother Harry in Kimberley. Years later he was to tell of an encounter at the Masonic Hotel the morning after his arrival. He was, he said, sitting on the hotel verandah when he was accosted by a prosperous-looking man who asked him where he was going. When Barney told him, the man looked sceptical. 'Too late, boy, too late,' he said. 'Nothing left. I struck it rich, but the sands are dry now. Best take the next boat back.' But Barney was not easily discouraged. Having come so far he had no intention of turning back. For £5 he was allowed to load his luggage onto an ox-wagon travelling to Kimberley; he walked beside the wagon during the day and slept under it at night. The journey, which lasted nearly two months, was, he recalled, 'one of the jolliest times I ever had'.

Before Barney left England his brother-in-law, Joel Joel, had supplied him with forty boxes of poor-quality cigars. It was hoped that with these Barney would be able to found an exporting business in Kimberley. But, as he soon discovered, the times were wrong for commercial enterprise: the diggers were not interested in his dubious cigars. Instead, Barney was obliged to start life at the diggings as a 'kopje-walloper'. It was a demoralising occupation. Most 'kopje-wallopers' were simply small-time opportunists who, without claims or much capital, toured the diamond-sorting tables in the hopes of picking up (or fiddling) a bargain. Respectable diggers had little time for such scroungers. Nevertheless, Barney persisted. Blue ground or no blue ground, he was determined to make a fortune.

In fact, the blue ground scare did not last as long as is generally supposed. By the end of 1873 things had begun to look more hopeful. On 3 December the *Diamond Field* was able to announce that at Dutoitspan and Old De Beers 'diggers have gone down into the blue and report the finds are improving'. They continued to improve. The blue ground proved far from unproductive; the deeper it went, the richer it seemed. Those who had held onto their claims had good reason to congratulate themselves.

But just as one bogey was disappearing, another was discovered. The hopeful report in the *Diamond Field* ended on an apprehensive note. Although the diggers' finds were improving, it said, 'the water bothers them a good deal'. This was an early mention of a new hazard. Water had begun to seep into the mines and the deeper they were sunk the worse this water menace became. Soon mining was brought almost to a standstill. The disastrous drought of 1873 was followed by heavy rains in February 1874 and the four mines were quickly flooded. Primitive pumping equipment had to be hastily rigged up to make it possible for work to continue.

At Dutoitspan pumping operations were carried out by Cecil Rhodes and his partner Charles Rudd. Rhodes had recently returned from Oxford. His second term at university had been cut short when, while rowing on the river, he had caught a severe chill which had affected his heart and lungs. The doctors had given him less than six months to live. He had been advised to return to South Africa. Two years were to pass before he was fit and ready enough to continue his studies in England. In the meantime he had to content himself with dreaming his dreams of British expansion while he watched over the rickety pumping-machines. This, as Charles Rudd later explained, did not make him the most efficient of partners.

One night as Rudd was clearing debris at the edge of the crater, he glanced down and saw that Rhodes, who should have been working the pumps, had left his post and was walking up and down abstractedly. Seconds later there was a loud explosion as the boiler burst – Rhodes had forgotten to supply it with water. They appear to have patched up the plant for, shortly afterwards, it was working sufficiently well for them to make a bid for a contract with the Old De Beers Mine.

But the mine most seriously affected by the flooding was the Kimberley (formerly New Rush) Mine. The damage done by the water in this mine was not fully appreciated until a few months later. Pumping operations at Kimberley had been undertaken by Messrs Walsh and Company. So successful were they that, by 6 October, some three to four thousand men were able to resume work after an enforced idleness of nearly nine months. Their good fortune did not last long. They had been digging for only a couple of weeks when a huge crack of twenty-five to thirty feet was discovered under the staging on the south side of the mine. Immediately, all work was stopped by the newly formed Mining Board. Further examination proved that the mine was in an extremely shaky condition.

The first of the many great landslips in the Kimberley Mine occurred at half-past nine in the morning of 20 November 1874. Within a matter of minutes thousands of pounds worth of claims were buried in the debris. Had the crack not been discovered earlier the death toll would undoubtedly have been enormous. As it was, over a thousand men were thrown out of work. This was probably the greatest disaster the diggers had yet faced. The future looked bleak indeed. What with heavy taxation, low diamond prices, flooded mines and falling reef, there seemed little prospect of the diamond industry thriving. Everyone was on the point of despair.

'I have read with much regret', Sir Henry Barkly wrote to Southey, 'of the great fall of earth that has taken place on one side of the Colesberg kopje, and of the fissures which threaten even greater landslips. Misfortune seems to thicken around you, and I must own that I am beginning to feel some alarm as to the future state of affairs at the diamond fields. . . . Ominous rumours of heavy overdrafts at the local branches of the banks are current here, and I cannot contradict them. Let me learn what really is the truth, for there is no use shutting our eyes to it.'

There was little chance of Southey shutting his eyes. He was only too conscious that disaster was staring him in the face.

(6)

The extraordinary thing was that at this time – when the economic depression had reached a new low, political agitation a new height, and natural disaster threatened the entire industry – the camps had never looked more prosperous, more settled.

In truth, they could no longer be called camps. They were rapidly evolving into townships. New Rush and Old De Beers had merged to become Kimberley; Bultfontein had long since been swallowed up by Dutoitspan. The untidy conglomeration of tents and wagons was giving way to neat rows of galvanised-iron houses. Advertisements in the newspapers offered sizable residences, some with four or more rooms, for sale. Here and there could be seen the substantially built homes of rich diggers and merchants.

In Kimberley the tone was set by the grandiloquently termed Government House. This unpretentious, two-windowed, corrugated-iron cottage, fronted by a simple wooden verandah, was hardly a mansion but, situated as it was in a street off the Market-square, it did at least give a semblance of permanence to the place. Southey and his wife had moved there after living for the first few months in a small house on the outskirts of the camp, lent by a merchant. The central Post Office had been built next to Government House and soon other similarly designed houses, shops and offices had sprung up on all sides. Kimberley not only had a new name and a new status, but a new centre.

The diggers had welcomed these outward signs of stability. More and more of them had been joined by their wives and families; there was now a more domestic atmosphere in the new townships. Even the dust began to settle when, in 1874, a system for regularly watering the streets was inaugurated. The place was still as hot as ever, still plagued with flies, still shaken by the unpredictable gale-force winds, but many of the primitive discomforts of everyday life were disappearing. Southey had plans for channelling water to Kimberley from the Vaal River which would irrigate the surrounding countryside and enable the diggers to grow their own vegetables. Once this happened it was hoped that one of the worst health hazards, scurvy, would be overcome.

The primitive wood and iron Carnarvon Hospital in 1874. (K)

Kimberley during the 1874-5 period, showing Main Street, with Government House to the right of the Post Office and R.W. Murray's auction rooms extreme left. (K)

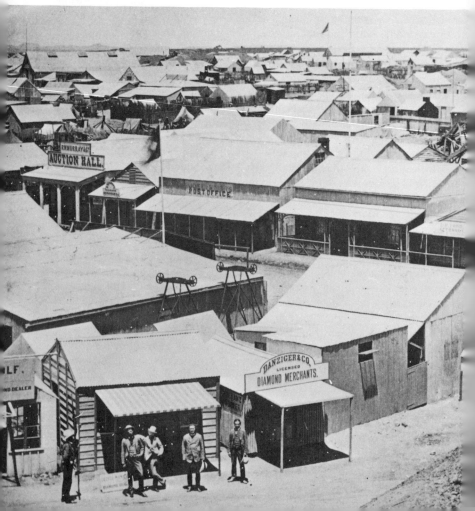

J.B. Currey had been particularly concerned about the prevalence of disease in the camps. It was largely through his efforts that the Government had granted £3,000 towards the building of a new wood-and-iron hospital for paying patients. This was the Carnarvon Hospital – named after Lord Carnarvon, the Colonial Secretary who succeeded Lord Kimberley in February 1874–erected next to the Diggers Central Hospital in the Dutoitspan Road. Unfortunately it got off to a bad start. At the end of September 1874, just as it was nearing completion, it was gutted by fire. 'To see this fine structure in flames', reported the *Diamond News,* 'was a sickening sight. No body of men ever felt more helpless than did the great mass surrounding this blazing pile.' All that remained of the hospital was the brick lining of one of the wings. 'The worst feature of the catastrophe', declared a journalist, 'is the impossibility of rebuilding the hospital before the fever season sets in.' However, by the beginning of November an iron roof had been put over the brick work and part of the hospital had been made serviceable. The rebuilding then went ahead.

The Dutoitspan Road, in which the Carnarvon Hospital was situated, was rapidly becoming one of the most important thoroughfares in Kimberley. It was the road that connected the two main centres and was already lined with straggling houses. A visitor driving into Kimberley along this road at the beginning of 1874 noticed 'a large Roman Catholic church, built of corrugated iron, and which had schools attached to it; a Wesleyan chapel stood nearly opposite to it, and then came several large stores and hotels'. And as work went ahead on the rebuilding of the hospital, plans were being made to build a Synagogue a little farther along the road. This, it was generally thought, would answer a longfelt need.

The Jewish community on the diggings was, during the early years, rather badly served. In 1871 it was estimated that there were some 1,400 Jews on the diggings, of whom about 600 were adult males. At that time the only form of religious organisation for the Jewish community was 'a temporary or loose congregation called "The Griqualand West Hebrew Association" '. This congregation had to rely on the infrequent visits of Rabbis from Cape Town and Port Elizabeth for circumcisions and marriages; services on High Holidays being conducted by lay members. Not until 1873 was a permanent congregation formed, and even then they had no full-time minister. When the Reverend Samuel Rappaport from Port Elizabeth visited Kimberley in November 1874, the *Diamond News* felt obliged to comment on the neglect. 'We are astonished,' it exclaimed, 'considering the number of Jewish residents in our midst, that they have not a regular ordained minister, and a properly constructed place of worship.'

The newspaper was being a little premature. Even then, it appears, plans were under way to build the Synagogue in Dutoitspan Road and to appoint the Reverend Berthold Albu as Kimberley's first Rabbi. The synagogue, like all the township's buildings, was a simple corrugated-iron structure, designed to hold 250 people. It cost £3,000 to build and the foundation stone was laid in 1875 by Mrs C. Sonnenberg, wife of the first President of the Congregation. Respectability was fast catching up with the diggers.

Other institutions marking the religious and cultural advance of the diggings were already established. In December 1873, for instance, the Good Templars had extended their activities by founding the 'Star of Kimberley' lodge above R.C. Gowie's store. A few weeks earlier Richard Southey, as the District Grand Master of South Africa, had assisted at the consecration of a new Masonic Temple; and a Masonic lodge, 'Peace and Harmony', had been opened in Dutoitspan. In Kimberley's Main Street the Craven Club, with its comfortable reading-room, card room and billiard room, was the recognised meeting-place for well-to-do diggers, and the nearby Varieties Theatre, managed by Sidney Colville a popular entertainer, was considered the last word in theatrical elegance. 'It looks exceedingly neat and comfortable,' reported the *Diamond News* when the theatre was opened in November 1874. 'The walls are papered and decorated with handsome pictures. The stage has been erected upon the latest principle, so as to afford everyone present a full view of the actors. On either side of the stage is a splendid mirror seven feet in height, draped with red and white damask curtains.' The suppression of gambling had not left the diggers without alternative diversions.

Not the least of these diversions was the existence of a Public Library which had been opened 'next door to Sangers Bowling Alley' in October 1873. Of the library's popularity there can be no doubt, but financially it was not an immediate success. At the first annual general meeting of the Library Council, in October 1874, it was reported that public subscriptions amounted to £522, and to this the Government had added a grant of £300. Excellent as this was, it barely covered the library's expenditure, rent alone costing £300. After considering various alternatives, it was decided to move the library to a stationer's shop in Main Street. The reduction in rental and other expenses allowed the Library Council an additional £20 a month to be spent on books. It was a modest enough start for a library which, in time, was to include among its subscribers some of the most celebrated men in South Africa's history.

But Kimberley was a South African town and, not surprisingly, the diggers' favourite recreation was sport. Horse-racing, which had started with such a flourish, failed to live up to its initial promise owing to the sharp practice of many of its followers. Even the presence of Richard Southey and his wife at the annual Spring Meeting failed to make the sport popular. 'The ladies', it is said, 'were conspicuously absent, and with not much fashion and less of beauty, the grand stand appeared dull and uninteresting.'

There was no lack of spectators, however, for other sports. William Ling's cricket matches, which soon became regular fixtures, always drew large crowds. By 1873 there was sufficient support for a group of enthusiasts to form Kimberley's first Rugby Football Club. Less reputable, but every bit as popular, were the barefist boxing bouts and the back-alley cockfighting contests. At weekends hundreds of diggers rode to the Vaal River, or into the veld, for a day's fishing and shooting.

The great sporting event of 1874 was the 'series of athletic sports, swimming, shooting and horse racing' held at Alexandersfontein and Wessels farm during the Christmas holidays. This was the first big holiday function to be organised at the diggings. It was very much a family affair and, by all accounts, an unqualified success. 'The Christmas season 1874', it is claimed, 'saw the beginning of true home life at the diggings, with the boyish spirits of the men chastened by the presence of wives, sisters and mothers. Crowds spent the holidays on the Vaal River, whilst mine host Kelsey at Alexandersfontein Hotel ran an Athletic Sports Meeting, extending over three days.'

A stranger at that meeting would have found it difficult to realise that, even then, the diggers were in the throes of a serious political crisis.

8

The Black Flag Rebellion

At one o'clock in the afternoon of Saturday 15 August 1874, a horse-drawn van paraded solemnly through the streets of Kimberley. Seated in the van was a string band, above which fluttered a flag bearing the inscription 'The Earth is the Lord's and the fulness thereof'. But what riveted the attention of most spectators was the pile of diggers' implements, ominously topped by a rifle, stacked at the foot of the flagstaff. The symbolism of the gun covering the mining equipment was unmistakable. Kimberley was being treated to its first whiff of organised revolution.

All that morning men had been distributing handbills calling upon citizens to attend a mass meeting in the Market-square. The object of the meeting was to demand a change of Government policy in Griqualand West. The Lieutenant-Governor was to be respectfully requested to 'repeal, alter or mutilate many of the recently passed ordinances. Failing satisfaction, the promoters promised to exert themselves to the utmost, to watch over and protect the liberties and rights of the people.' Precisely who these public-spirited promoters were, was not immediately clear. The handbills gave no indication as to who was organising the protest. Not until the meeting was about to start did the leading agitators put in an appearance. Few diggers, however, could have been surprised to find that prominent among them were Henry Tucker, the defeated candidate for the Legislative Council, and his chief lieutenant, William Ling.

The meeting was well attended and, for the most part, orderly. Several fiery speeches were made: the recent actions of the Lieutenant-Governor were heatedly denounced, the diggers' many grievances were magnified, doubts were expressed about Southey's ability to maintain law and order. Surprisingly all this hot air drew little response from the crowd. The majority of diggers seemed strangely unmoved by the speakers' eloquence. Not that this in any way deterred the speakers. The protest had been organised for a specific purpose and, come what may, they were determined that that purpose should be fulfilled. It was. At the end of the meeting a 'Committee of Public Safety' was formed. Henry Tucker was nominated chairman, and William Ling and several well-known personalities, such as John Birbeck, J.J. 'Dan' O'Leary and M.M. Steytler, were elected to serve under him.

Oddly enough, the name of the principal speaker at the meeting – the man who had made a passionate appeal to his 'brother diggers and brother sufferers' – did not appear on the list of committee members. 'Dr' Alfred Aylward, for all his fervent rhetoric, was not elected. But this did not mean that he had no further part to play. Far from it. He, more than anyone, was to be responsible for whipping up the revolutionary fervour of the next few months.

Alfred Aylward was one of the most colourful and mysterious men ever to arrive at the diggings. Who he was and where he came from, no one was quite sure. Most of the stories told about Aylward's early life were told by Aylward himself and are, to say the least, suspect. He was to claim that, among other things, he had once been employed in a publishing office in Edinburgh, and edited various papers in America ('I was on a Yankee paper', he once bragged, 'the proprietor of which was in a lunatic asylum, and all the contributors were lunatics – and troth I was the biggest lunatic of the lot') and had served as a volunteer under Garibaldi in Italy. As he was only in his thirties when he arrived on the diggings, he would appear to have packed a great deal into a short life.

The truth about Aylward is less romantic. As far as is known, he was born in Kilkenny, Ireland, and educated at a Jesuit college in County Kildare. For some time he worked in an attorney's office in Dublin, where his mother kept a small stationer's shop. At one period of his life he was associated with the Fenian organisation – the Irish Republican movement which originated in America – and this landed him in trouble. There seems, however, to be little truth in his claim that he was forced to flee England after being involved with other Fenians in the murder of a Manchester policeman. An official inquiry into his origins was later to state that the 'Fenians were afraid to trust him and tried to assassinate him; and finally the Government sent him out of the country deeming him a mischievous man to be at large, and not sufficiently dangerous to warrant his being kept in custody'. He was well known to the police both in Dublin and London.

Aylward first became known to the diggers when he acted as Dr Considine's assistant at the Diggers Central Hospital in 1871. According to Considine he had a good knowledge of medicine and surgery and this had earned him the nickname of 'Dr' Aylward. He was a huge man, over six feet in height, stout, with jet-black hair, a flowing beard and 'eyes of a dark, sinister aspect'. He was full of Irish blarney and everyone who met him remarked on his quick wit and apparent good humour. Everyone, that is, except those Africans who were unfortunate enough to annoy him. His colour prejudice was as notorious as were his anti-British sentiments. He was a great admirer of the Free State policy of keeping 'the nigger in his place'. This was what first brought him to grief.

At the end of October 1872 Alfred Aylward was arrested on a charge of attempted murder. The events leading up to his arrest were not particularly unusual for Kimberley; it was Aylward's uncontrollable temper that landed him in court. He had gate-crashed a party which some young English diggers were holding in Moss's store. Finding himself unwelcome he had first angered the diggers by making a virulently anti-British speech and had then seized a leather strap and tried to attack two of the African servants who were serving drinks. He was thrown out of the store and pursued by the diggers, who, failing to catch him, returned to their party. Later that night one of the diggers, W.H.

Dixon, had been hauled out of bed and taken to the police office charged with having attempted to burn down Aylward's tent. The police refused to accept the charge and Dixon was released. Hardly had he returned to his tent than he heard Aylward shouting outside, 'Up the Free State police and at them!' Rushing into the yard he was joined by some other diggers and in the fight that followed Aylward accidently shot one of the diggers in the arm and stomach. His offer to dress the man's wounds was refused; he was beaten up and dragged to the police station.

While he was awaiting trial some of Aylward's friends tried to persuade him to make a bolt for it. This he refused to do and was duly tried by jury, found guilty of common assault, and sentenced to eighteen months' hard labour. The sentence so infuriated his friends that two of them – Dr Considine and a young German adventurer, Conrad von Schlickmann – conceived an elaborate plan to help Aylward escape. Unfortunately the plot was betrayed by a gaoler they attempted to bribe and Considine only escaped arrest himself by fleeing the diggings in disguise. Aylward was punished by being given fourteen days in chains: none of which increased his love for British justice.

His friends, however, continued to agitate for his release and organised a petition signed by 470 Kimberley residents that was presented to the Lieutenant-Governor in September 1873 by Dr Graham, the soon-to-be-elected member of the Legislative Council. It was largely due to Graham's intervention that Southey agreed to remit five months of Aylward's sentence and set him free in December 1873. Had he but known it, this was one of Southey's more serious mistakes.

Aylward had lost no time in contacting the rebel diggers. His aim was either to have the diggings returned to the Free State or to establish another independent diggers' republic. Whatever happened, he was determined that British control of the diamond fields should end. Southey had few more dedicated, or reckless, opponents than Alfred Aylward.

Once the 'Committee of Public Safety' had been formed at the mass meeting, the disaffected diggers had a basis to work from. During the next couple of months more meetings were held in secret and letters appeared almost daily in the *Diamond Field* vilifying the Southey regime. J.B. Currey's high-handed attitude provided them with plenty of ammunition. Even his close friends had to admit that Currey showed little tact when dealing with opponents of the Government. 'What an abominable, unhappy manner he has,' wrote George Paton in September 1874, 'and yet how agreeable he can make himself when he chooses – he has done more to damn Southey's administration than all the other men put together.' But Currey was immune to all criticism. 'A little bloodshed', he remarked, when the crisis was at its height, 'would put the diggers in their places.'

The *Diamond Field* had long since been recognised as the mouthpiece of the rebel diggers. Any doubts about the newspaper's policy were finally settled at the beginning of October 1874, when it was taken over lock-stock-and-barrel by the 'Committee of Public Safety'. The paper's new proprietor was William Ling, its editor was Alfred Aylward. From now on leading articles in the

Diamond Field became progressively more outspoken, more inflammatory and, it must be admitted, decidedly more lively.

However, Southey was not without his champions. Every attack upon him in the *Diamond Field* was answered extremely effectively in the Government-supporting *Diamond News*. R.W. Murray, the editor of the *Diamond News*, was every bit as capable and experienced as his vitriolic rival Alfred Aylward. Murray was an old hand at the newspaper game. Born in London, he had worked on several newspapers in England before sailing, in 1854, for Australia. But he never reached Australia. The ship in which he was sailing had been wrecked off the South African coast and he had settled in Cape Town, where, three years later, he and a partner had established the *Cape Argus*. He had later edited the *Great Eastern* in Grahamstown and was over fifty when he arrived on the diamond fields. In Kimberley Murray was as well-known as an auctioneer - his auction rooms were a stone's throw from Government House - as he was as a newspaper editor. Nevertheless, it was as the editor of the *Diamond News* that he made his mark.

Of Murray's journalistic talents there can be no doubt. He was a genuine ink-in-the-blood newspaperman who, in time, was to work on practically every Kimberley newspaper. There was nothing he liked better than a rip-roaring editorial battle. So much so that, it is said, at one time he edited two rival newspapers, attacking himself in the columns of one and answering in the leading articles of the other. For Murray, it was the fight more than the cause that mattered. But there can be no doubt that he fought Southey's battles from conviction. He genuinely admired the Lieutenant-Governor. To know Richard Southey, he was to say, 'was to admire and respect him'. And he said this long after the fight was over.

When Alfred Aylward embarked on his anti-Government campaign, he must have known that Murray would dog him every step of the way. Had the possible outcome been less serious, the diggers might have been greatly amused at the ding-dong battle between the *Diamond Field* and the *Diamond News*. As it was, the abuse that was flung from one to the other only added fuel to an already crackling fire.

(2)

James Anthony Froude, the historian, was the first distinguished man of letters to visit the diggings. He arrived at Kimberley at the end of 1874 and was not particularly enamoured of the place. About the town's inhabitants he was cynical; he described them as 'diggers from America and Australia, German speculators, Fenian head-centres, traders, saloon keepers, professional gamblers, barristers, ex-officers of the Army and Navy, younger sons of good family who have not yet taken to a profession or have been obliged to leave; a marvellous motley assemblage, among whom money flows like water from the amazing productiveness of the mine; and in the midst of them a hundred or so keen-eyed Jewish merchants, who have gathered like eagles over their prey, and a few thousand natives who have come to work for wages, to steal diamonds and to lay their earnings out in rifles and powder'.

Mr Froude was allowing his facile pen to run away with him. His description is often quoted, but it is more colourful than accurate. Wrong on several counts, he was never more wrong than in thinking that money was flowing like water. Kimberley's finances could not have been in a worse way. There was little scope for professional gamblers even if any of them remained, which is doubtful. The trouble was, Froude listened only to what he wanted to hear. In Kimberley he found precious little to please him.

The historian had not come on a sightseeing tour. He had been sent to South Africa on a political mission by Lord Carnarvon, the new Secretary of State for Colonies. The purpose of his supposedly unofficial visit was to examine the possibilities of Confederation in South Africa. He was to report to Carnarvon on his return and he was forming some very positive, if one-sided, views. Just how one-sided were those views was not apparent during his stay in Kimberley. J.B. Currey, in fact, was convinced that he had succeeded in winning Froude over completely. 'The great creature', Currey skittishly informed J.X. Merriman, 'stayed a week with old Southey and of course I saw a good deal of him, and had many interesting conversations, which are supposed to have deeply impressed him. At all events he sent off a very voluminous despatch to Earl Carnarvon very soon after I had given him *my* ideas at a little dinner here, when I had produced some of that famous old wine.'

The wine was more celebrated than potent. Froude completely fooled Currey. Far from siding with the Southey regime, he was to denounce the annexation of the diamond fields as 'a crime and a blunder'. His sympathies were with the Orange Free State; he had a great admiration for the stabilising influence of Boer conservatism. He certainly did not like Southey. Part of the trouble in Kimberley, he was to tell his daughter, was that 'Mr Southey the Governor believes in niggers'.

Here at least he had hit a nail obliquely on the head. Although later it tended to be glossed over, there can be no doubt that foremost among the diggers' many grievances was Southey's non-racial policy. 'The only point', observed George Paton, 'on which the malecontents join issue is niggers being allowed to hold claims.' Barkly's earlier pleas to them, not to judge a man by the colour of his skin, had had little effect. They still considered that the only way to stamp out the continuing evil of I.D.B. was to deprive all black men Africans, Coloureds, Malays and Griquas – of the right to trade in diamonds on their own account.

No one was more aware of this than Alfred Aylward. He used the common prejudice as a clarion call in one of the first leaders he wrote for the *Diamond Field*. 'Ruin, financial ruin for the whites, moral ruin for the natives, these are the results of the attempt to elevate in one day the servant to an equality with his master . . . ' he thundered. 'Class legislation, restrictive laws and the holding in check of the native races, till by education they are fit to be our equals, is the only policy that finds favour here.' It was an all-too-familiar cry. The so-called 'class warfare' of Europe was distorted into racial friction in South Africa.

It is to Southey's credit that he adamantly refused to yield to such pressure.

He informed Barkly that he was not prepared to grant 'privilege to white persons purely because they are white'. Nor would he receive a deputation from the Committee of Public Safety. The diggers, he maintained, had been given a legitimate means of expressing their grievances - through the Legislative Council - and it was up to them to make use of it. He was perfectly willing to meet individuals but refused to acknowledge 'a political organization which had neither law nor executive authority for its basis'. In any case, he was convinced that the rebels did not have the support of the law-abiding majority.

And he might, at that stage, have been right. But by taking up such an uncompromising stand he played into the hands of his enemies. The times were against him. The diamond market was depressed, money was tight, and the future of the industry was uncertain. What in more prosperous times might have been shrugged off as the inevitable irritations of authority were now magnified into intolerable high-handedness. There can be no doubt that resentment of the unrepresentative Legislative Council was widespread. In sticking to the letter of an unpopular law, Southey was asking for trouble. It was not long in coming.

More meetings were organised by the rebel faction. The Committee of Public Safety gave way to the more purposeful Diggers' Protection Association - or the 'Associationists' as they were generally known. There was open talk of resorting to arms. So menacing did the situation become that the possibility of enrolling loyal citizens to maintain law and order was discussed in the Legislative Council. It needed only a trivial incident to bring things to a head.

The Associationists cast about to fix upon such an incident. Their cause was greatly helped by the legal dispute between William Ling and the Ebden syndicate which then still owned the Vooruitzigt estate. Ling had refused to pay rent for his house, maintaining that 'diggers' rights' entitled him to a dwelling-place and the fact that a town had grown up around his original shanty in no way affected the value of the site or his occupation of the building. He was vigorously supported by Alfred Aylward in the *Diamond Field*. Aylward went even further. He broadened the attack by implying that the Government was conniving at the sale of Crown Lands. In a particularly vitriolic editorial he accused 'our nefarious rulers' of 'holding a land jobbing sale'. This led to the immediate arrest of I.R. Taylor, the publisher of the newspaper. 'The paper appeared at 6 a.m.,' says one of Taylor's sons; 'at 10.30 my father, as the publisher, was arrested and placed in jail.'

The Associationists now had their long-sought incident. On 3 March 1875 a fiery meeting, chaired by Henry Tucker, was held in the Kimberley Hall. Ostensibly the purpose of the meeting was to protest about I.R. Taylor's arrest and to challenge a High Court judgment that had ordered William Ling to vacate his house. But Alfred Aylward, one of the main speakers, was determined to push things further. He ended his impassioned speech by calling on the audience 'to assemble with their weapons in the name of Heaven and the Country, to protect themselves from injustice whenever he should hoist a (black) flag at the mine'.

As was intended, the meeting caused widespread alarm. The call to revolution, long in the air, had at last been openly proclaimed. 'These are stirring times! Yes sir-ee!' J.X. Merriman wrote to Currey when the news reached Cape Town. 'Went not my soul with thee when . . . Tucker and . . . Ling carried on their absurd public meetings. G—d d—n them all is the fervent prayer of yours truly!'

But more than prayers were needed to combat the rebels. They were geared for action, and action they were determined to have. More meetings were called, seven armed companies – trained by Aylward's military friend, Conrad von Schlickmann – were formed. Sentries were posted outside the Associationists' offices and men paraded the streets shouldering guns.

Southey reacted swiftly and typically. On 19 March 1875, he issued a Proclamation warning all people against 'taking illegal oaths or assembling in arms'. The following day the rebels replied with a Proclamation of their own. They swore loyalty to Queen Victoria and announced their intention to protect life and property and maintain order. Two days later J.B. Currey drafted a long memorandum to Sir Henry Barkly, outlining the situation and asking for troops to be sent, or held in readiness, and requesting permission to enrol local volunteers.

Barkly refused to be panicked. 'I am glad to find that Aylward is so openly resorting to violent measures', he wrote cheerily to Southey, 'as to alarm the respectable part of the community and this strengthens your hands sufficiently to admit of his arrest. . : . I should be loath to send soldiers, excepting only *after* an outbreak had occurred, or at the urgent solicitation of the bankers, merchants, and shareholders. The expense of their transport and support, which would have to be borne by the Province, would be very heavy.'

(3)

Southey was not so foolish as to arrest Aylward. He had no intention of presenting his opponents with such an obvious martyr. On the other hand, he was careful not to allow the Associationists to think that he was weakening. When, at the end of March, Henry Tucker tried to arrange for a deputation to meet him 'to discuss eleven matters of grave importance', Southey again took refuge in his official status. As Lieutenant-Governor, he said, he was prepared to receive individuals, but not a deputation.

Negotiations for the proposed meeting had been carried out by Kimberley's senior citizen, J.B. Robinson. Until then Robinson, conscious of his dignity as a prominent diamond buyer, had done his best to remain aloof. His sympathies were largely with the Associationists but his respect for established authority would not allow him openly to defy Southey. This, his first attempt at intervention, resulted in yet another *impasse*. Things came to a head in a more violent fashion.

At the beginning of April, William Cowie, a canteen keeper, was charged with unlawfully supplying twenty guns to Alfred Aylward. Whether, as was suspected, Cowie courted arrest on the instructions of the Associationists is not certain. What is beyond doubt is the Associationists' reaction to his arrest. They quickly let it be known that any attempt to carry out a conviction would be resisted by force of arms. Even then, it is said, a group of diggers were busy stitching away at a black flag.

The case against Cowie was heard in the Resident Magistrate's Court at Kimberley on the afternoon of 12 April. The canteen keeper was found guilty and sentenced to a £50 fine or, alternatively, three months' hard labour. Probably acting on the advice of the Associationists, Cowie refused to pay the fine and was led from the dock to serve his sentence. Immediately sentence was passed, spectators in the Court began to leave. 'It was apparent from the noise outside the Court', reported the Acting Resident Magistrate, 'that some movement was on foot.'

Some movement was indeed on foot. No sooner had the verdict been announced than Alfred Aylward, with two revolvers strapped to his belt and a cavalry sword swinging from his waist, had galloped down Main-street to the foot of Mount Ararat, the huge debris heap. Standing on top of the debris was one of his friends, Albany Paddon, who, when Aylward unsheathed his sword, hastily unfurled the black flag. Some three hundred armed men were waiting for the signal. Led by Henry Tucker and William Ling, they stampeded down the road to the Magistrate's Court. They were met by a handful of constables who, with drawn revolvers, managed to hold them in check.

The police decided to act swiftly. Four Justices of the Peace were summoned to accompany the policemen detailed to escort Cowie to the gaol, some 250 yards away. As they approached the entrance of the prison, they were overtaken by the armed diggers who blocked their path. At that moment a small band of police reinforcements, armed with rifles with fixed bayonets, appeared at the lower corner of the gaol. They took up a position in front of the rebels. It was a tense moment. Some 3,000 people, armed and unarmed, were swarming about the gaol. Had either side opened fire it might well have resulted in a mass slaughter.

It was the coolness of the Resident Magistrate, R.K.H. D'Arcy, that saved the situation. Surrounded by the jostling diggers he remained amazingly calm. Even when Conrad von Schlickmann accidentally fired a shot close to his ear, he did not flinch. 'I addressed the armed men,' he reported, 'and asked who was their leader. Upon this Mr William Ling stepped forward and said that he was. I asked him if he knew what he was doing, and he called on Mr Henry Tucker to come forward. Mr Tucker then advanced. Ling said they had been goaded into their present action, and asked if they could see the Governor. I said that, in hope of avoiding a collision, I would go with them and communicate with his Excellency, who was at the Legislative Council.'

Southey, stiff as ever, refused to grant an interview. He said that anything the rebels wished to bring to his notice should be communicated in writing. However, J.B. Currey proved more amenable. After talking the matter over with D'Arcy and the Acting Attorney General, Sidney Shippard, he agreed that Cowie should be released if someone would stand bail for him. Henry Tucker immediately offered a cheque for £50, on the condition that it should not be cashed until the sentence had been properly reviewed. With that the 'Black Flag Rebellion' fizzled out. Cowie was set free and the crowd dispersed.

Not all the participants in the rebellion were there to see it end. Notable among the absentees were the two men who had sent the armed mob to the Court House. Alfred Aylward, who had given the signal, and Albany Paddon, who had hoisted the flag, had both bolted. Aylward had fled to the Transvaal, where, hearing that his plans had failed, he published his own death notice in a local paper. Where Albany Paddon went to nobody knows; he was never seen in Kimberley again.

J.B. Robinson had also missed the fun. On the afternoon of the rebellion he had been conveniently confined to his bed by illness. He was quickly informed of what had happened. A group of businessmen hurried to his house and asked him to attend a meeting which was being called to send a deputation to the Governor of the Cape. Robinson claimed that he was not well enough to take any part in the proceedings, but he let it be known that any move to consult the Cape authorities had his blessing.

(4)

It was an uneasy peace that descended on Kimberley. The Associationists had secured William Cowie's release but had achieved nothing more: their loudly proclaimed grievances were still unsettled. The more militant among them, led by William Ling, resolutely refused to disarm. They were in no mood to admit that the rebellion had failed. Southey also was far from complacent. On 17 April he reported that he feared there would be a violent outbreak before troops could arrive. In a heavy-handed attempt to assert himself, he made things worse by enrolling volunteers as special constables. Then he took 'the insanely injudicious step of beginning to arm natives'. Once again things became tense.

Southey's action was undoubtedly unwise. Knowing as he did the colour prejudice which existed among the rebels, he should never have made that prejudice an issue in trying to maintain law and order. It should, however, be said in his defence that he had good reason to suspect the sincerity of those who were claiming that they wished to discriminate against men of colour only in order to stamp out diamond thieving. On 22 April he had received a report from Gilbert Percy, the Inspector of Police, giving 'a few names of the persons now taking a prominent part in the armed demonstrations at Kimberley'. The list showed that no fewer than thirteen of the rebel leaders had criminal records and that seven of them – including Conrad von Schlickmann – were suspected of, or had actually been imprisoned for, illicit diamond buying. If Southey considered that colour prejudice was an excuse, rather than a cause, for revolution, it is hardly surprising.

Southey's repeated requests for troops to be sent was backed by a group of civic dignitaries. On 1 May this group published a 'Protest' in the *Diamond News*. They deplored the existing state of affairs and demanded militant action from the Cape authorities. J.B. Robinson was quick to associate himself with the 'Protest'.

At a packed meeting in the Kimberley Hall, four days later, Robinson acted as chairman. The meeting had been called to consider the 'Protest' and Robinson opened the proceedings with a slashing attack on Richard Southey. 'It is much to be regretted', he declared, 'that all our endeavours were in vain and nothing would induce His Excellency to throw off his official grandeur. Owing to his repeated refusals to receive deputations, the Associationists first enrolled, and then the Government armed its volunteers, which was more deplorable still . . . the Lieutenant-Governor committed a grave error in forcing his subjects to take up arms. From the action of the Government the community is now thoroughly unsettled, and the moderate men must come forward and place themselves between the two parties.'

The meeting resulted in the formation of Kimberley's first properly constituted political party. Called the Moderate Party, it was headed by the odd combination of dour J.B. Robinson and A.A. Rothschild, Kimberley's dapper auctioneer. Although the members of the party styled themselves 'moderates', they were undoubtedly biased in favour of the rebels. In his initial speech, Robinson had made it quite clear where his sympathies lay. This was not lost on Richard Southey's supporters. As the mouthpiece of the Lieutenant-Governor, the *Diamond News* immediately began sniping at the Moderate Party and its leaders.

The newspaper's editor, R.W. Murray, was scornful of the new party's impartial pose and implied that Robinson had been financing the Associationists from the outset. Robinson heatedly denied the accusation. His fury was such, in fact, that he eventually resorted to his usual tactics and threatened to horse-whip Murray. Only by seeking the protection of a magistrate was the petrified editor able to escape a public thrashing.

For all that, Robinson did his utmost to calm the rebels. He contacted Sir Henry Barkly by telegram and tried to persuade the Associationists to disarm. His efforts were unsuccessful. The matter was settled by the arrival of troops at Kimberley on 30 June. There had been talk of the Associationists marching out to prevent the troops reaching the town but, as in the case of the Black Flag Rebellion, words spoke louder than action. 'Troops arrived yesterday,' it was reported on 1 July. 'They paraded on the Market-square, and were much surprised at being pelted with oranges instead of bullets.' That afternoon a crowd of red-coated soldiers were seen outside 'The Old Cock' in Jones Street, playing leapfrog over barrels of beer that had been rolled out for their benefit. There could be no doubt about the sincerity of their welcome.

With the arrival of the troops, the last flickerings of revolt petered out. The Diggers' Association was dissolved and an amnesty granted to those who had illegally acquired arms. Even the five leading Associationists who had been arrested when the troops took over soon realised they had nothing to fear. So obvious was this that the truant Alfred Aylward decided to come to life again and claim his place in the dock as one of the ringleaders. The trial, when it took place, was a mere formality and ended in a wholesale acquittal.

Richard Southey was not so fortunate. In August, Lord Carnarvon sent a long despatch to Sir Henry Barkly complaining about the administration of Griqualand West. He was gravely concerned about the declining finances of the territory and insisted on a cut in expenditure. One of his suggested economies was that Southey be replaced by a less highly-paid official. The post of Lieutenant-Governor was to be abolished and an Administrator appointed. His Lordship was also of the opinion that J.B. Currey should retire as Government Secretary. He intended, he said, to appoint a competent person to report on the financial position of the mining community and to recommend further economies.

Lord Carnarvon's suggested reforms were thought to be not so much a result of the rebellion, as of the report presented to him by James Anthony Froude. In fact it amounted to the same thing. Froude was known to have consulted the rebel leaders, and his views were undoubtedly coloured by their opinions. However it came about, both Southey and Currey were sacked. Southey retired on a pension and later entered Parliament as the member for Grahamstown. Currey was to try his hand at various commercial ventures until 1883, when he returned to Kimberley as the manager of the London and South African Exploration Company.

With Southey's departure Griqualand West entered a new phase. In November 1875, Major William Owen Lanyon arrived to take over as the new Administrator. He was joined shortly afterwards by Colonel Crossman, the man appointed to enquire into the territory's finances. By the end of the year the diggings had more or less settled down again.

The extent to which the Associationists accepted the change-over was illustrated when, on Christmas Day, William Ling set off with a cricket team for Bloemfontein. The team left in great style from Dutoitspan and were cheered all along the way. At Bloemfontein they were given a champagne reception by the Free State authorities and, to add to their glory, they won their match by a comfortable margin of an innings and 68 runs. Ling, in white flannels and a tall top hat, looked anything but a rebel leader.

9

Civic Beginnings

Colonel Crossman, the Royal Commissioner appointed by Lord Carnarvon, opened his official enquiry in the Kimberley Hall on 5 January 1876. Ostensibly the purpose of the enquiry was to ascertain the financial position of the mining community; in effect it was an investigation of the many grievances that had led up to the Black Flag Rebellion.

The first day of the hearing was lively. Among the first to give evidence were a group of former Associationists. William Ling set the ball rolling by vehemently protesting about the composition of the newly established Mining Boards. These, he maintained, were completely unrepresentative; most of the members were capitalists who did not have the ordinary diggers' interests at heart. He was followed by J.J. 'Dan' O'Leary, an estwhile member of the Committee of Public Safety. Dan O'Leary, a red-headed Irish-American, was even more outspoken. He said that 'he had been told by some hot-headed people that if they did not get satisfaction from the Government they would resort to Lynch Law'. There was an immediate burst of applause from the audience. Crossman had considerable difficulty in restoring order. Once he could make himself heard, however, he sharply informed O'Leary that he had no intention of listening to 'what he considered an implied threat'.

This show of firmness did not prevent other diggers from speaking out. Throughout the enquiry accusations and counter-accusations were hurled from one witness to another. Crossman, caught in the cross-fire, needed all his wits about him to prevent an uproar. Most of the complaints were little more than unsubstantiated generalisations, stemming more from heat than injury. Not until late on the first day did Crossman get around to examining specific charges. One of these concerned the flooded claims and the inefficiency of the water-pumping system. It was said that a Mr Huteau, who had charge of the machinery for pumping water from De Beers Mine, had been offered £300 by a speculator if he would stop the machinery by damaging it in some way. Huteau was sent for and, after some hedging, reluctantly agreed to write the name of the speculator on a piece of paper. He insisted that he had given his word not to speak the man's name in court. By writing the name Huteau kept his word, but not his secret. No sooner had Crossman read the name than he sent for the man concerned – Cecil John Rhodes.

Rhodes was nowhere to be found. Instead, his partner, Charles Rudd, arrived and told Crossman that he was prepared to give evidence that Huteau was lying. Cecil Rhodes, he declared, 'was the last man to attempt bribery'. By the time Rhodes turned up, the court had adjourned. Not until the next session, two days later, was he able to answer the charge. He did so with characteristic firmness. After taking legal advice, he said, he had decided to charge Huteau with perjury and had handed the case over to the public prosecutor. Crossman had no option but to let the matter drop.

Rhodes did not proceed with the case. Having deftly removed the issue from the court of enquiry, he made a show of prosecuting Huteau and then quietly withdrew the charge. Whether or not he had attempted bribery was never legally established. But not everyone was fooled. A good many diggers were ready to believe Huteau and regarded the affair as another example of capitalist duplicity. Rhodes, who had steered clear of the recent upheavals, was placed squarely in the enemy camp. Writing from Oxford a few months later, he was to say: 'My character was so battered at the Diamond Fields that I like to preserve the few remnants.'

Colonel Crossman's enquiry continued throughout the best part of January. He heard innumerable witnesses, examined available documents and made on-the-spot investigations. One of the last cases to come before him was that of William Cowie, whose arrest had sparked off the Black Flag Rebellion. The canteen keeper claimed that he had been wrongfully convicted of buying firearms without a licence; the guns discovered on his premises had been sent by a mistake on the part of the suppliers.

In a speech made at a public dinner given in his honour before he returned to England, Crossman poured cold water on the rebel's hopes. He admitted that he had found many grievances, but these were not serious enough to warrant a Royal Commission. Most of the accusations of land swindling were completely without foundation. The real importance of Crossman's enquiry was revealed in the reports he submitted to Lord Carnarvon in February and May 1876. Much of what he had to say was to prove prophetic.

Griqualand West, he claimed, should not have been proclaimed an independent colony. It was centred on a mining community which could be administered as little more than a municipality. He was of the opinion that the territory and its debts should again be taken over by the Cape Colony. Control of the mining industry should be in the hands of an organisation created by the mining interests themselves. As far as the Government was concerned, all that was needed was the appointment of a capable Civil Commissioner to ensure law and order. The newly proclaimed Ordinance 10, which disqualified any individual or company from holding more than ten claims, should be rescinded. The way would thereby be prepared for company control and operation. Like many others, Crossman was aware of the harm that was being done to the diamond industry by indiscriminate competition.

The immediate results of Crossman's investigations were to change the face of Kimberley. 'There was an end now', says Professor de Kiewiet, 'to the grogshops and the black prostitutes that had made a Kimberley Saturday night a scene to marvel at. Gone too were the native gun shops that encouraged stealing and the "swell niggers" who were the "go-betweens" of the illicit diamond dealers. But equally was there an end to the rights of natives as

Southey had conceived them. They could no longer be permitted to hold claims or wash debris. In the interests of efficiency and economy natives on the diamond fields could henceforth only have one status–that of labourer.'

It is necessary to emphasise the implications of these sweeping 'reforms'. The discovery of diamonds had brought the industrial revolution to South Africa. As a result of racial prejudice the black man was now prevented from contributing anything, other than his labour, to industrial development. The pattern set on the diamond fields was to be followed by other South African industries. The full irony of this legal discrimination was only to become apparent later. The time was to come when later racialists would argue that black men had only minimum claims to the fruits of industries built up by the initiative of white men. Few of them recognised that any attempt at black initiative had been effectively blocked from the very outset of the industrial boom.

'It is perhaps idle to wonder', Professor de Kiewiet goes on to say, 'what might have been the possibilities of Southey's liberal interpretation of the native's place in South Africa's first industrial community. It is sufficient to say that it was at the diamond fields that the gate to all but low paid unskilled labour was slammed against the native in industry.'

The rebel diggers had won one of their most important points. But this did not satisfy all of them. There were those who still hankered for revenge against the officials who had opposed them. Just how determined such diggers were was shown when Inspector Gilbert Percy – the man who had revealed the criminal activities of some of their leaders to Southey – was himself arrested on a charge of illicit diamond buying. The proceedings which followed were long and tedious. They ended with Percy being cleared of the charge by a judge and jury. In a perjury case which resulted from Percy's acquittal, several African witnesses were sentenced to long terms of imprisonment after admitting that 'they were induced to make the charges on the promptings of white men'.

Justice on the diamond fields was slow and not always sure.

(2)

For the majority of diggers in Kimberley life went on much as usual. Once the excitement of rebellion had died down, the town returned to its humdrum ways. Newcomers to the diggings were constantly surprised at just how placid day-to-day life was on the diamond fields. To those used to the raffish mining camps of America and Australia, the increasingly tame atmosphere of Kimberley was difficult to credit. It was not, of course, entirely a matter of chance. Definite steps had been taken to curb the more dissolute element. Southey had effectively stamped out gambling, Crossman's enquiry had clamped down on prostitution, and under Major Lanyon the issuing of liquor licences became so restricted that many canteens were forced to close down.

Yet, domesticated as it had become, Kimberley was far from dull. Its population was still largely cosmopolitan and lively; it could still boast a splendid assortment of flamboyant, unconventional characters. It was these characters who gave the town its individuality. Their like was not to be met anywhere else in South Africa. So *outré* were they that many a staid colonist was profoundly shocked by their seemingly outrageous behaviour. Set against other South African towns, Kimberley seemed a veritable centre of sin.'All that is revolting in human nature may be found there,' sniffed one tight-lipped visitor. 'The libertines, the forgers, bird catchers, and outcasts of Europe found asylum there, as in Alsatia of old. . . . The vices of drinking, swearing, cursing, bullying, lying, cheating, and all kinds of other abominations permeate society.' Extreme as was this judgement, it was widely held. There seemed something positively immoral about a community dedicated to enriching itself.

For there was no escaping the fact that Kimberley society was essentially materialistic. Most diggers had been lured to the place by the prospect of making a fortune and, for all their churches, temperance societies and fumbling pretensions to culture, it was this prospect that kept them going. All other considerations were secondary. Many, admittedly, had been discouraged by the disasters that preceded the Black Flag Rebellion, but those who remained still clung to their dreams of riches. And, elusive as those dreams often were, they could still be unexpectedly realised. The days of the big diamond finds were, in fact, only just beginning. The year 1876 was, for some diggers, a year of renewed hope.

Hardly had the political disturbances died down than the financial outlook showed signs of brightening. Unemployment was still rife, the diamond market was still depressed and it was estimated that well over a thousand white men and some eight thousand blacks had been forced to leave the diggings because of the crippling slump, but there was reason to hope that the industry would eventually recover. The main reason for the growing, if deceptive, optimism was the now proven richness of the blue ground.

Those who earlier had panicked and sold their claims were cursing themselves. Their lack of confidence had cost them dearly. A visitor to the Kimberley Mine in 1876 was startled by the astronomical rise in the price of claims. He gave examples of claims that had been sold for as little as £300 having risen to anything up to £3,000. 'The first holders', he observed, 'feeling inclined to go out and weep bitterly on discovering that with all their cleverness they had allowed fortunes to slip through their fingers.'

The increase in the value of claims had become the great talking-point of Kimberley. At the Saturday auctions, A.A. Rothschild and his partner Goodchild 'sales by the children', they advertised did a roaring business selling off claims. The rise in price was most spectacular in the Kimberley Mine, but even at the neglected and unpromising Old De Beers the value of claims rose from £80 to £305 in three months. For anyone with capital the chances of success looked rosy indeed.

Considerable progress was also being made in clearing the debris caused by the great land-slip in the Kimberley Mine. The damage in some cases was not as serious as had at first been supposed and within a matter of months large numbers of the owners of buried claims were back at work again.

A further boost to trade came on 12 February 1876, when Kimberley was at last linked directly with the outside world. For years all news, all business and all private transactions had been dependent on post carts and passenger coaches which, at best, took six to eight days travelling from Cape Town. 'The want of telegraphic communication', sighed a digger, 'was severely felt.' Not surprisingly then, the opening of a telegraph office next to the Resident Magistrate's Court was regarded as a great event.

A huge crowd gathered for the launching ceremony which was attended by Major Lanyon, Colonel Crossman and members of the Legislative Council. Unfortunately, just as the first message was about to be sent, news was received that the line had broken down beyond Fauresmith in the Orange Free State. Nothing daunted, the Civil Commissioner, R.W.H. Giddy, gamely sent a glowing telegram to the magistrate of Fauresmith. 'Cordial greetings and best wishes from the Diamond Fields,' he wired. 'May the link that now unites us be welded into a chain of strong affection to bind South Africa together.' A breathless hush followed as the crowd waited for a reply. It was signalled by the tinkling of a little bell and informed Mr Giddy that the citizens of Fauresmith would have 'much pleasure in drinking your health at one p.m.' There was an immediate whoop of delight.

The opening of the telegraph line brought Kimberley at least a week nearer to Europe. But it was not cheap. To send twenty words, including name and address, to Colesberg cost 5*s*; to Port Elizabeth 10*s*.; to Cape Town 15*s*. One needed to be very rich, or desperate, to send a telegram.

For all that, this first link with the world of affairs was a source of pride to many Kimberleyites. No longer were they a neglected community, more or less isolated from civilisation. Their importance had at last been recognised. The telegraph poles spaced out across the wilderness not only connected them with the coast towns but provided visible proof of the permanence of the diamond industry. Almost overnight the town acquired a new dignity.

This dignity might, however, have been difficult for a stranger to appreciate. Kimberley in 1876 did not, at first sight, appear to have progressed far from its origins as a mining camp. The buildings of the town were certainly more substantial – Market-square even boasted one of two storeys – and only the poorest diggers now lived in tents. The shops were much better supplied and living conditions were, on the whole, less primitive. But when one had said that, one had said almost everything. Civic pride was more theoretical than evident.

The trouble was that no control had been exercised over the town's development. Corrugated-iron houses had sprung up haphazardly; the streets were still little more than footpaths, unpaved, pot-holed and ankle-deep in dust. There were no gutters to carry away storm water and after a heavy rain the roads were slimy with mud. 'Comparatively poverty-stricken hamlets of the Colony', it was being said, 'maintained better streets than did the wealthy township of Kimberley.'

The main thoroughfares were, if anything, in a worse condition. Dutoitspan Road, for all its importance, was so rutted by heavy traffic that to drive along it was a nightmare. Bumpy, dusty, strewn with stones and full of holes, it often became unusable in the rainy season. Nor had anything been done to regulate the traffic. It was estimated that besides the constant stream of private vehicles – bullock wagons, goods carts and coaches – some sixty cabs travelled back and forth between Kimberley and Dutoitspan every day. There were no restrictions on these cabs, the drivers being free to charge and carry what they liked. Official interference was kept to a minimum. The upkeep of the roads depended entirely on the availability of convict labour, which, more often than not, was fully occupied in digging sanitary pits.

In the townships sanitation remained very much a matter of chance. Major Lanyon had tried to improve things by proclaiming a Cape Act which, among other things, provided for the 'cleansing of slaughter-houses, and the disposal of filth and night-soil', but the Sanitary Board lacked the necessary powers to enforce these regulations. Alleyways between the shanties were still the main dumping-ground for rubbish, flies still swarmed on the rotting carcasses of dead animals, and packs of unlicensed, scavenging dogs still roamed the streets. In the summer months 'camp fever' was rife.

The need for some sort of local governing body had long been apparent. As early as January 1872 a public meeting had been called at New Rush to discuss 'whether municipal regulations should be adopted'. But despite the widespread concern nothing came of this and similar efforts to clean up the townships. It was the old and all-too-familar story of passing the buck. The diggers looked to the Government, and the Government waited for the townspeople to show some initiative or offer some assistance; the result was that nothing was done.

Nothing, that is, until J.B. Robinson decided to make a move. In May 1876, he and some other leading citizens petitioned the Resident Magistrate to call a public meeting 'to consider the advisability of moving in the matter of a Municipality for Kimberley'. The meeting, held in the Magistrate's Court, was well attended and after several indignant speeches it was resolved to ask the Government to approve the institution of a Town Council. A number of other meetings followed and it was not until 27 June 1877 that the Kimberley Municipality was formally constituted.

In the meantime Major Lanyon made a few necessary reforms. The danger of fire in a township of flimsy, carelessly constructed buildings was a constant hazard. This was made dramatically apparent at the beginning of 1876, when a huge fire destroyed two large canvas houses and badly damaged a nearby iron store. The volunteer Fire Brigade proved worse than useless and it was left to a group of determined citizens to bring the fire under control. Partly as a result of this fire, Lanyon initiated a scheme of brickmaking, 'the bricks being used in public buildings, or sold at a small profit to builders and others'. Nothing, however, was done to remedy the lack of proper fire-fighting equipment. Later that year a dog tax was imposed and attempts were made to improve the sanitary arrangements. But, by and large, the Administrator refused to accept responsibility for the absence of public amenities.

It was becoming increasingly obvious that Kimberley needed not only a Town Council but more public-spirited representatives in the Legislative Council. Here, once again, the indomitable J.B. Robinson decided to step in.

(3)

Kimberley's second election of members to the Legislative Council was held in July 1876. It was a much livelier affair than the first. The campaign lasted three weeks and was fought with considerable bitterness. So much so that, shortly after it started, two of the candidates were forced to give up, leaving the other three–J.B. Robinson, Henry Tucker and Mr Advocate Halkett–to battle it out. One of the retiring candidates was Dr Graham, a former member for Kimberley, who became so alarmed at the prospect that Henry Tucker, 'a rebel against the Queen', might win that he withdrew in favour of Advocate Halkett. Another medical man, Dr William Murphy, was effectively knocked out of the race when J.B. Robinson, belligerent as ever, threatened to sue for a vicious personal attack.

Personal attacks, if not always vicious, were very much a feature of the campaign. Since Southey's removal, candidates for the Legislative Council had very little in the way of political principles to fight about. This, in the eyes of some, tended to make Kimberley's early elections somewhat trivial and dull. 'Whether it is in the air or in the soil no one can tell,' declared R.W. Murray, a few years later, 'but there is something somewhere in or about Kimberley that is not congenial to healthy political growth. . . . There were cliques, cabals, and revolutionary combinations plotting against law, order, and authority. There never has been a good, sound, healthy, active public opinion, without which politics are a snare and a delusion.'

This is only partly true. Public opinion might not have been politically sound, but it was undoubtedly active. The diggings had never before seen such enthusiasm at an election. Cape carts decorated with rosettes dashed about Kimberley and Dutoitspan, flags and bunting flew from electioneering offices, and the candidates' meetings, held almost daily, were invariably packed. J.B. Robinson, distinctive in his white pith helmet, was very much in evidence. His red, white and blue colours and rather improbable slogan 'Robinson for Ever' were displayed throughout the town.

On the day of the election betting was brisk. In Kimberley, Robinson was the hot favourite. Not only had he spent more on his campaign than the others but he had received considerable support from the *Diamond News*. But he proved to be a bad bet. The results showed Halkett heading the poll, after collecting most of the votes in Dutoitspan; and Henry Tucker came a close second with the support, rather surprisingly, of the Good Templars. J.B. Robinson ended up a rather poor third. 'Could bunting have carried the day,' commiserated the *Diamond News*, 'Mr Robinson had been certain of success.'

Robinson's defeat came as a blow to the Kimberley financiers. They had backed him as their spokesman and had fully expected him to romp home. 'Shows one can never tell,' commented Cecil Rhodes from Oxford.

Defeat did not discourage Robinson. He had set his heart on becoming a public figure and he soon found another outlet for his energies. There were other things to consider besides politics. Not the least of these was the need for some sort of military organisation. Kimberley, for all its riches, was still a frontier outpost and, as the Black Flag Rebellion had proved, was badly in need of a defence force. Lanyon had realised this and early in August 1876 had formed the Griqualand West Rifle Volunteer Corps. This was soon supplemented by a more mobile unit. At a meeting held at the Varieties Theatre four days later it was resolved to form a volunteer calvary corps to be known as the 'Kimberley Light Horse'. Lanyon was elected to the honorary position of Colonel, and effective command as Captain went to J.B. Robinson. After a great deal of discussion it was decided that the uniform of the corps would be a blue patrol jacket, Bedford cord breeches, riding-boots, spurs and a forage cap with a puggaree.

On Saturday afternoon, 19 August, Captain Joseph Benjamin Robinson, K.L.H., proudly led his men on their first mounted drill and paraded them at sunset outside Government House. Major Lanyon solemnly inspected the troop and complimented it on 'its very smart appearance'. Not to be outdone, thirty-five Dutoitspan diggers, commanded by Captain L. Rolleston–a pioneer of the river diggings–formed the Du Toit's Pan Hussars a month later. Rolleston was a tall handsome man with an impressive presence. In his blue-cloth ceremonial uniform, with its elaborate silver trimmings, he was more than a match for J.B. Robinson. The friendly rivalry which sprang up between the two units provided the diggers with endless fun. Their formation, says John Angove, served as 'a source of amusement, as well as recreation, and it was also a means of breaking the monotony of the digger's everyday life'.

But the winter of 1876 was to be remembered for more than the elections and the formation of Kimberley's fighting force. It was the time of the never-to-be-forgotten 'Great Snow Storm'. Obsessed as the diggers were with the vagaries of Griqualand West's climate, they were never more surprised than when, on the morning of Sunday 25 June 1876, they woke to find the diggings covered in snow.

It was not the first time snow had fallen. In July of the previous year there had been an overnight snow-storm which had caused several tents to collapse, but it had lasted only a matter of hours. By the middle of the following morning the snow had already begun to turn to slush. The 1876 fall was much more dramatic. For over twelve hours, from before midnight on Saturday 24 June, until afternoon the following day, the snow came drifting down onto Kimberley. In the streets it lay a foot deep. The effect on this normally duncoloured town was extraordinary. Roads, roofs, canopies, carts and wagons glistened white in that Sunday afternoon sunshine. But the most magnificent sight of all was the Kimberley Mine. With its intricate lacing of ropes and wires all covered with snow, it looked like some gigantic and glittering spiderweb.

Although the tent dwellers and shanty dwellers–the impoverished whites and the Africans–suffered real hardship from the cold and the inconvenience, the rest of the population enjoyed themselves hugely. Snowball fights raged for days. Hurling snowballs made the streets positively unsafe and apprehensive shopkeepers were forced to put up their shutters. These battles reached their climax when two teams, respectively led by the magistrates of Dutoitspan and

Kimberley, staged a 'battle royal' halfway between the two townships. 'Those were the rough old days,' sighed one old townsman, 'and no one thought it *infra dig* for such dignitaries to engage in a mêlée of this kind.'

(4)

Henry Tucker's career as a member of the Legislative Council did not last long. Shortly after the election he was arrested for buying diamonds without a licence. The arrest shocked everyone. It was regarded as little more than a snide political move. This could well have been true.

Whatever might be said about the motivations of some of the rebel leaders, Henry Tucker's honesty and sincerity were unquestioned. He was genuinely concerned about the failings of Southey's administration and welcomed Colonel Crossman's suggested reforms. If Tucker had a fault it was that he allowed himself to be used by lesser men.

That Henry Tucker should have fallen foul of the new diamond-buying regulations was ironic. Not the least of his ambitions as leader of the Associationists had been to have the laws concerning illicit diamond buying made more effective. Now that attempts were being made to tighten up those laws, he was one of the first to be arrested. What made his arrest so suspect, however, was the fact that his offence was a technical one – his diamond-buying licence had just expired. This did not prevent his opponents from crowing. As far away as England, hostile magazines published cartoons of the unfortunate Tucker captioned 'Hoist with his own petard'. It was considered a huge joke.

But very few in Kimberley laughed. No one was more distressed by the affair than the man who had sold him the diamonds, Lou Cohen. 'When it became known', wrote Cohen, 'that Mr Henry Tucker had committed an offence against the Diamond Law – even though a technical one – his political enemies pounced down on him, and he was at once arrested. . . . I did all that was possible to help him, but the trial was a foregone conclusion, and, to my intense sorrow, goodhearted, honourable Harry Tucker was sent to prison for nine months.'

This, in the circumstances, was a generous observation. The acidulous Lou Cohen was not usually given to making kind remarks. His vitriolic pen was to cut more than one Kimberley personality down to size. Many years later J.B. Robinson was to sue him for defamation and to insist that his libellous *Reminiscences of Kimberley* be legally suppressed. But the man to suffer most from Lou Cohen's scurrilous comments was his one-time partner Barney Barnato.

Lou Cohen, who came from Liverpool and claimed to have been educated in Belgium, had arrived at the diggings in 1872. He first met Barney Barnato in the Scarlet Bar canteen. At that time they were both young newcomers and both scratching a living as 'kopje wallopers'. Cohen, whose writing was often more colourful than accurate, has left an amusing account of their first meeting. It has, at least, a ring of truth about it.

He claims that he was sitting in the canteen when Barney breezed in and, after throwing his cloth cap on a hat rack, plonked himself down between two of the customers. Cohen could not take his eyes off him. 'It rather interested me', he says, 'to see the way in which he beamed on everybody in general but nobody in particular, without taking the slightest notice of the frowns and muttered curses of the two foreigners he had separated. He was a strongly built young fellow, wore a pair of spectacles on his uninviting dust-stained face, and had the ugliest snub nose you could imagine.' Barney introduced himself after choking on his soup and bespattering everyone within radius. 'You'll excuse me,' he apologised to Cohen, 'but a fly fell on my nose.' It was the beginning of a somewhat erratic friendship.

Shortly after their meeting, the two of them went into partnership as diamond buyers. They set up office in a corrugated-iron shanty next to a canteen on the Dutoitspan Road. It cost them a guinea a day in rent, but Barney considered it a bargain. 'If you can make two pounds a day out of it,' he argued, 'it ain't dear for a guinea.' They certainly needed to do things on the cheap. Their assets amounted to £90 in cash and the remainder of Barney's unsaleable cigars. Had anyone arrived with a large diamond to sell they would have been completely stumped.

For the first month or so they slept on the floor at the back of the office and ate a nightly meal of curry and rice by the light of two candles stuck in beer bottles. When business finally began to pick up they were able to move into the canteen for bed and board. But the good times did not last long. Events were against them. They had set up their office shortly before the Black Flag Rebellion, and the political turmoil, coupled with the depressed state of the diamond market, soon forced Barney to have second thoughts about the joint venture. He finally persuaded Cohen to take over his share of the office for £125. It was a rather depressing end to a business which Cohen liked to refer to as 'the cradle of the Barnato millions'.

After the break Barney went to stay with his brother Harry, who was then the proprietor of the grandiloquently named London Hotel. This large corrugated-iron hut, squeezed between merchants' offices at the edge of the Kimberley Mine, was more of a canteen than a hotel. A few theatrical families boarded there, but it depended more on its notoriety as a rendevous for illicit diamond buyers than on its fame as a hostelry. The police, it is said, took a disconcerting interest in both the hotel bar and its habitués. If a policeman showed up at the London, claimed Lou Cohen, 'some of the most eminent customers would scatter like rats that had seen a cat'.

Not that this bothered the Barnato brothers unduly. By fair means or foul, Harry Barnato managed to scrape enough money together for him and Barney to start up another diamond-buying business. This new venture–doubtless helped by the clientele of the London Hotel–proved more successful than Barney's previous partnership. At the beginning of 1876, when the value of claims was still uncertain, the Barnatos managed to snap up four claims in the Kimberley Mine for £3,000. This was one of their many strokes of luck. Within a matter of weeks prices began to soar. Barney was to take the credit for this timely investment: it was he, or so he claimed, who persuaded Harry to buy the claims. However that might be, the gamble certainly paid off. Kimberley was to know few more successful diamond buyers than the Barnato brothers.

According to Barney, he and Harry sweated 'day and night' to make their new venture pay. This seems somewhat doubtful. A great many people believed that most of the spectacular diamonds unearthed by the Barnato brothers were put into their claims before they were discovered. Certainly Barney spent very few nights working in the family business. More often than not he was kept fully occupied at the Theatre Royal formerly the Kimberley Hall where for some months he had been a regular performer.

He seems to have started as a stage manager: designing scenery, organising costumes and acting as a property master. Before long, however, he was appearing on the boards. He was not easy to cast his size, his youth and his appearance were against him but in time he built up a repertoire of character parts which were in constant demand. His performances in contemporary melodramas and farces *The Ticket of Leave Man* and *The Two Orphans* were highly praised. He was equally at home wringing his hands as Fagin in *Oliver Twist* or overacting Iago in *Othello*. But Barney's greatest triumph was as Mathias in *The Bells*. He had learnt the part long before he arrived in South Africa. The role had been created by his idol, Henry Irving, and, having studied Irving's interpretation down to the last gesture, Barney was able to give a passable impersonation of the great actor. It made his own performance appear surprisingly professional. 'When we saw the piece,' wrote a critic in January 1876, 'we joined most heartily in the well merited applause which the really good acting of Mr Barnato elicited. . . . Mr Barnato in delineating "Mathias" was as unlike an amateur as it is possible to imagine, and he must we feel certain have studied the character for months, otherwise he could not have rendered it as perfectly as he did.'

Not everyone was so impressed. Lou Cohen, who dabbled in the theatre himself, claimed that Barney's Mathias was ruined by his appalling accent and a lack of sound effects. His dramatic ' 'ow the dogs do 'owl', smirked Cohen, was 'a monstrous inexactitude considering the animals were as absent as his h's.'

But then Cohen, who for a while acted as a dramatic critic, was very sparing in his praise of Kimberley's actors. His biting reviews made him far from popular in theatrical circles; often they proved downright dangerous. Never more so than when he made the mistake of slating a performance given by Miss Flora Miller in a farce called *A Kiss in the Dark*.

'The lady, who was very tall and muscular,' Cohen recalled ruefully, 'announced to her friends and admirers, after she had read the notice, her fixed determination to thrash me at sight.'

She was as good, or almost as good, as her word. Cohen foolishly came within Miss Miller's sight at the Theatre Royal that very morning. Snatching a gingham umbrella, the infuriated actress made a running jump at him. 'The Junoesque goddess of war', admitted the far from confident Cohen, 'looked formidable enough. I received the onset at first with great elegance like a matador, then dodged . . . and bolted, with the Amazon in full chase.' He dashed into the auditorium 'upsetting two chairs, a nigger, and Mrs Cox's poodle, and by the skin of my teeth reached the stage, the fair artiste holding her petticoats with one hand and beating nothing in particular with (the) green and white umbrella. Almost at the last hurdle, when victory was in her grasp, the huntress fell . . . displaying a lavish amount of hose and lingerie.'

Cohen managed to escape but only made things worse by gleefully reporting the incident in his newspaper column. This immediately aroused the anger of a beefy, red-faced stage carpenter, who stormed into the newspaper office and challenged Cohen to a fight. 'I fought him without much damage to myself,' bragged Cohen, 'but while I was engaged with the man a parcel of diamonds worth seven hundred pounds, which I carried in my back pocket, fell to the ground. I saw Barney Barnato–who was seconding me–pick them up, and recovered them politely from his hands.'

Encounters like this were by no means uncommon at the Theatre Royal. A theatre critic needed to have his fists ready and his wits about him before breaking into print in Kimberley.

The Theatre Royal and the Varieties Theatre provided the diggers with most of their stage entertainment. It was at the Theatre Royal that the first important visiting performer appeared on the diggings. In the middle of 1876, Madame Anna Bishop, the celebrated singer, braved the still very uncomfortable journey across the veld to give a series of concerts for the music-starved diggers. The fact that Madame Bishop was by then a little *passée* made no difference to her reception. Accompanied by her own pianist, she sang to packed houses and was given a standing ovation at every performance.

Encouraged by this cultural enthusiasm, Messrs Lloyd and Abel decided to open a new theatre on the corner of Jones Street and the Dutoitspan Road on 22 July 1876. Named after the Administrator, the Lanyon Theatre cost £5,000 to build and was considered the height of theatrical *chic*. Unfortunately it was not destined to last long. One of its few claims to fame was the staging of Lou Cohen's five-act play *The Land of Diamonds*–featuring Barney Barnato in a character part–which, Cohen boasted, was 'the first drama ever written in South Africa'. He was extremely proud when, after the first performance, Major Lanyon 'called me into his box, and I received congratulations on what was then only a successful failure'.

Giving his name to the new theatre was not Major Lanyon's only contribution to the town's cultural life. He became more personally involved when he set about smartening up Kimberley's dusty and neglected public park. Few people knew about, let alone used, the park until Lanyon–in an effort to absorb some of the unemployed labourers from the mines–decided to make it more attractive. Trees were planted, paths were defined and tennis and croquet courts were laid out. Within a matter of months the park, though sadly lacking in grass, became a popular meeting-place. At the weekends, crowds would gather there to watch Captain J.B. Robinson put his mounted troops through their paces or to listen to Bandmaster Saunders conducting the Philharmonic Society's brass band at a Sunday afternoon concert.

It was one of the few reforms initiated by Major Lanyon that won the wholehearted approval of the townsfolk. For the new Administrator, like his predecessor, was proving to be far from popular.

10

Enter Doctor Jim

The choice of Major William Owen Lanyon as Richard Southey's successor was unfortunate. A melancholy, reserved and autocratic man, he had many of Southey's faults and added to them by attempting to rule Kimberley as if it were a military barracks. Cecil Rhodes was later to sum up Lanyon's administrative abilities by accusing him of conducting 'business on the lines of a second-rate line regiment'.

To make matters worse, before coming to South Africa Lanyon had served for several years in Jamaica, and this, together with his swarthy complexion, gave rise to the rumour that he was a half-caste. The fact that he was the son of a well-known English engineer and architect, had an Irish mother and had been born in Belfast, made no difference to the local gossips. In Kimberley, where skin colour was an explosive political issue, there was little hope of the dark and temperamental Lanyon overcoming local prejudice.

And if Kimberley did not like its new Administrator, he was every bit as prejudiced against the town. From the time of his arrival, Lanyon made no secret of his distaste for the crude living conditions at the diggings, and his impatience with local dignitaries earned him many enemies. In some ways he was at a greater disadvantage than Southey had been. Whatever some diggers had thought of Southey, he at least commanded a certain amount of respect as a man who had lived most of his life in the Cape Colony and was therefore fully conversant with South African problems. Lanyon, on the other hand, was regarded as an outsider whose main concern was to ingratiate himself with the authorities in England. This alienated him from even the more conservative diggers. R.W. Murray, the former editor of the *Diamond News* and Southey's great champion, was scathing about his idol's successor. Richard Southey and Major Lanyon, he declared, 'were two very different men; as different as chalk and cheese, and the Major was not quite the cheese'.

R.W. Murray came to know Lanyon well when he worked with him on the Legislative Council. Murray was then the elected member for Hay on the Council, and this gave him an insight into Lanyon's autocratic methods of government. It also made him appreciate just how undemocratic was the constitution that had been imposed on Griqualand West. The Council was still equally divided between elected and appointed members, with the Administrator having the casting vote. 'His Honour', says Murray, 'could turn the scale whichever way he chose, and we may be sure he would choose the official side of the question.'

The Queen's Hotel in 1881. For many years this hotel, run by the popular Mrs Catherine Jardine, was considered the most pleasant in Kimberley. (K)

R.W. Murray (senior), the well-known Kimberley newspaper editor and auctioneer. (M)

Major Owen Lanyon, Administrator of Griqualand West, and his Executive Officers. Lanyon is seated, centre. (K)

This was one of the diggers' grievances that Colonel Crossman's enquiry had not remedied. It played a decisive part in determining the future status of the diamond fields.

In the middle of 1876, the long-drawn-out dispute over the ownership of the diamond diggings came to an end. With a show of reluctance, President Brand agreed to waive the Free State's claim to the territory in exchange for a money payment of £90,000. Lord Carnarvon, the British Secretary of State for Colonies, made the concession not so much as an admission of the Free State's rights as in the hope of winning President Brand's support for his plan to federate the various states of South Africa. Once the agreement had been reached pressure was brought to bear on the Prime Minister of the Cape Colony, John Molteno, to have Griqualand West again annexed to the Cape. Molteno was told that, if he would agree to the annexation, 'the Home Government would engage itself to override any objection by the Griqualand West population'.

Molteno was not keen – particularly when he learned that £90,000 had now been added to the territory's debt – but he eventually yielded and the Griqualand West Annexation Act was passed by the Cape Assembly, after some opposition, on 27 July 1877. A time limit of three years was allowed between the proclamation of the Act and its implementation.

In Kimberley there was widespread opposition to the proposed annexation. Few diggers relished the idea of being taken over by the Cape. Memories of the unfortunate reign of the three commissioners were still very much alive. It was thought that the laws of the Cape Colony could not properly be applied to the peculiar circumstances of Griqualand West and would make for continuing conflict. In the Legislative Council, both R.W. Murray and Advocate Halkett maintained that a more satisfactory solution would be to unite Griqualand West with Bechuanaland in the north and that the two territories should be ruled as a Crown Colony.

But probably, more than anything else, the diggers resented the high-handed way in which their future was being decided. They were to be handed over to the Cape simply to save the British Government further embarrassment. Dr J.W. Matthews put it all down to the Black Flag Rebellion. That act of defiance, he claimed, had made Britain determined to get rid of 'so troublesome a crown colony as Griqualand West'.

However that might be, Major Lanyon had his orders and was resolved to carry them out. In the Legislative Council, both R.W. Murray and Advocate Halkett were equally resolved to fight him every step of the way. The struggle was to bring all legislation in Griqualand West to a standstill.

When Lanyon introduced the Annexation motion in the Legislative Council, the elected members spoke strongly against it. They proposed that 'the question be considered this day six months'–which, in effect, was an outright rejection of the motion. Lanyon remained undeterred. 'The Imperial Government', snorted Murray, 'wanted annexation, and if he could say to the people at head quarters "Alone I did it" it would give him a stronger claim than before on his Imperial masters.'

But Lanyon's determination was matched by the obstinacy of his opponents. So strong was their challenge that, on Saturday 8 December 1877, Lanyon was forced to dissolve the Legislative Council. Once again constitutional government in Griqualand West had broken down.

The fight against annexation went on, however. In desperation, Lanyon tried to organise petitions in favour of the move. He was answered at stormy meetings called by the diggers. The dispute was still raging when, in March 1879, Lanyon was promoted to colonel and transferred to the recently annexed Transvaal. He was not greatly missed in Kimberley.

(2)

But if Major Lanyon was never very popular with the diggers, he did not lack admirers. Among these was the colourful and eccentric Captain (later Sir) Charles Warren.

Warren had been sent to South Africa in October 1876 to represent Britain in the final demarcation of the boundary lines between Griqualand West and the Orange Free State. By the middle of 1877 he had completed his survey and arrived in Kimberley to take up an appointment as a special land claims commissioner. He immediately warmed to Lanyon. 'I like Major Lanyon,' he declared; 'he is so sensible.'

By 'sensible' Warren meant that he considered Lanyon a good army officer. He gave him full credit for pulling Kimberley's defence force together so quickly. At a parade given in honour of Sir Arthur Cunynghame – commander-in-chief of the Cape regiments – in September 1877, Warren was astonished at the efficiency of the local fighting units.

'We had a good show of Volunteers,' he noted in his diary, 'mounted and foot, Du Toitspan Hussars, Kimberley Light Horse, and Griqualand Infantry, all in resplendent uniform. They performed nothing but parade movements, but their precision was excellent, and when they advanced in line to Sir A. Cunyinghame (sic), with Lanyon at the head, and gave him a general salute, it was done so well that I felt quite proud of our little Province. I don't know what they can do in the field, but if diggers, who are supposed to be under no control, can disguise themselves as soldiers with such good effect on parade, I think they have the chance of doing well also in the field.'

He was soon to find out just how good their chances were. At the beginning of the following year he was appointed to command one hundred and ten men who volunteered for a campaign against rebel tribesmen in the eastern Cape. The troops, who were given a rousing send-off by a huge crowd at Dutoitspan, acquitted themselves well in this their first campaign. Their greatest triumph came in a stiff fight at Debe Nek, outside King William's Town, when a small force successfully withstood a determined attack by some 1,500 warriors. 'The news of this gallant defence filled the inhabitants of the Diamond Fields with exultation,' says Dr Matthews. 'Congratulations were telegraphed down to Colonel Warren and his men, while friends of the brave band under him were highly delighted. The back of the rebellion had been virtually broken.' Their success set the pattern for future campaigns against rebel Griquas, when they would be commanded by Warren and Lanyon. In just over a year, the supposedly unruly diggers had raised and trained a fighting force which matched up to any in the country.

Sir Arthur Cunynghame had been every bit as impressed by the parade of the Kimberley volunteers. In a lengthy speech he made to the troops, he claimed that in all his years as a general officer 'he had seen nothing equal to this display'. The compliment, admittedly, had to be taken with a pinch of salt: 'War Horse' Cunynghame was inclined to say much the same thing to any troops he reviewed. Nevertheless he could not help but notice the way discipline had tightened up in Kimberley since his last visit. Then he had commanded the troops sent from the Cape immediately after the Black Flag Rebellion. Things were very different now.

At a masonic ball given in his honour that evening, Cunynghame had great fun spotting the former rebel leaders as they waltzed sedately pass his box. He bluffly told Warren that the rebellion 'was due to the claim of the diggers to be able to "wallop their own niggers"'. Warren considered this too epigrammatic, although he was convinced that the blacks had been far too 'uppish'. He had obtained most of his information about the rebellion from Alfred Aylward. What struck Warren most forcibly about the dancers was how strange the deeply tanned men looked in evening dress. They were in marked contrast to their pale-skinned partners who, for the most part, seemed to keep their complexions.

Warren enjoyed life in Kimberley. By the middle of 1877 things seemed altogether much brighter at the diggings. 'Diamonds are looking up just now,' reported Warren, 'and everybody in a good humour. I am having a very pleasant time here, plenty of hard work and everybody very jolly.'

Unlike many other visitors, Warren was not unduly bothered by the discomforts of the diggings. This was largely due to the fact that he was staying at the Queen's Hotel, which then ranked as the 'premier on the Fields'. It was run by Mrs Jardine, the well-loved hostess of the river diggings. Mrs Jardine's reputation for mothering lonely diggers was well established before she moved to Kimberley; at the Queen's Hotel it became legendary. 'Whether a man had money or not,' says one of her many admirers, 'he dined at Mrs Jardine's on Sunday, and she accumulated good-fors, I.O.U,'s and promissory notes amounting to many thousands of pounds, for she never sued any of her guests. . . . She was of the "salt of the earth".' It is said that when she finally retired to Scotland, Mrs Jardine took a huge pile of unpaid bills with her and made her son burn them ceremoniously shortly before she died. That she was remembered with such affection is hardly surprising.

But, for those who could afford to pay, living at the Queen's Hotel was not cheap. Warren discovered this when he decided to give a little dinner party one evening. He invited young Cecil Rhodes and four other men and the modest entertainment cost him £15. 'Prices here', he commented feelingly, 'are awful.'

Rhodes was then paying one of his fleeting visits to the diggings during the long vacation from Oxford University. He was in Kimberley only a matter of weeks and was kept extremely busy.The activities of the Rudd–Rhodes partnership now extended far beyond their water-pumping contracts. A great deal of money could be made in Kimberley from ancillary mining enterprises, but there was no escaping the fact that it was in diamonds that the substantial fortunes were made. To own and work claims was the ambition of every Kimberley entrepreneur. Rudd and Rhodes, for all their profitable sidelines, were no exception.

They had taken full advantage of the slump and subsequent boom in the value of claims. And, like other capitalists, they had been further encouraged when–following Colonel Crossman's recommendations–clause 18 of the Diamond Ordinance, which prevented anyone from owning more than ten claims, had finally been revoked. The time was ripe for enterprising young men and there were few more enterprising young men than Cecil Rhodes and his partner.

Starting with a valuable block of claims at Baxter's Gully in the Old De Beers Mine, they had gradually increased both their holdings and their influence. At one time, it is said, they had the opportunity of buying the entire mine for a mere £6,000. They had been forced to decline the offer because 'they could not afford the capital as well as the licence fees'. This was something which they were later to regret. At the time, however, they had not been deterred. By taking others into their partnership they had extended their mining interests and were now claim-holders of considerable importance.

Charles Rudd, of course, had been largely responsible for the growth of their diamond concern. With Rhodes away at Oxford for long periods, he had handled the direct negotiations. But Rhodes had not been idle. Both by letter and on his visits to Kimberley, he had been actively involved in every move his partner made. His visit in 1877 was no exception. During the few weeks he was there he seemed to be everywhere at once.

In fact, he crammed too much into too short a time. His heart could not stand the strain. Some time during this visit he suffered another heart attack, an attack which left him shaken and frightened. He was staying, as always, in the bachelor quarters of the 'Twelve Apostles'–the young men with whom he had shared from his earliest days at the diggings–and his behaviour after his heart attack was most strange. 'His friends', says Sir Lewis Michell, 'once found him in his room, blue with fright, his door barricaded with a chest of drawers and other furniture; he insisted that he had seen a ghost.'

Rhodes was incurably superstitious and no doubt believed what he said, but the spectre which really frightened him was the glimpse he had had of death. He saw death not in terms of his own mortality, but as the end of his championship of a far greater cause. The time he had spent at Oxford had confirmed his earlier belief in the need for Britain to civilise the world. He had tried to express this belief in the will he had made as a young obscure digger. Now, shaken by the thought that he might soon die, he decided to make a second will. This time he had more money to leave and more definite ideas on how it should be spent. His second will was more comprehensive than the first and decidedly more peculiar.

Written in the sweaty heat of a Kimberley shack, it sets out to reorder the world. He dated it 19 September 1877 (the day he was due to return to England) and described himself as Cecil John Rhodes of 'Oriel College, Oxford, but presently of Kimberley in the Province of Griqualand West, Esquire'. As executors he named Lord Carnarvon and Sidney Shippard, the Attorney General of Griqualand West. These two unsuspecting gentlemen were to be responsible for the establishment of a Secret Society whose aim and object would be the extension of British rule throughout the world. No less. A clandestine and dedicated brotherhood was to bring the entire continent of Africa under its sway and to populate South America, the Holy Land, the seaboard of China and Japan, the Malay Archipelago, the islands of Cyprus and Candia, and any islands in the Pacific not possessed by Britain, with British settlers. As if this was not enough for any underground movement to be going on with, the Society was also instructed to recover the United States for Britain, consolidate the Empire and inaugurate a system of Colonial Representation in the Imperial Parliament for the foundation of 'so great a power as to hereafter render wars impossible and promote the best interests of humanity'.

It all made Griqualand West's constitutional struggles seem as nothing. Having signed his will, Rhodes returned to Oxford.

(3)

'Anthony Trollope has arrived here, and has given us great entertainment,' wrote Charles Warren on 16 October 1877. 'He is writing about this country, and I hope will prove to be an antidote to Mr Froude. . . . He is a dear old man, full of contradiction, and very snappish when he chooses, but most good hearted: he has a wealth of human kindness welling up out of his rugged nature.'

Warren's hope that the famous novelist would give a more balanced view of South Africa was, as far as the diamond fields were concerned, only partly realised. Trollope's short visit was to be a landmark in the history of Kimberley, but his description of the town is hardly flattering. He found it hot, enervating and hideous; the dust and the flies almost drove him mad. 'Dust so thick', he exclaimed, 'that the sufferer fears to remove it lest the raising of it may aggravate the evil, the flies so numerous that one hardly dares slaughter them by ordinary means lest their dead bodies should become noisome.'

The fact that these twin plagues had once been much worse, and even now were not as bad as they would become when the really hot weather set in, impressed Trollope not at all. He was in no mood for excuses; he simply became more and more exasperated. 'I sometimes thought', he snorted, 'that the people of Kimberley were proud of their flies and their dust.'

Widely travelled though he was, Anthony Trollope was not the right person to appreciate the struggles of a pioneering community. Attuned to the cosy simplicities of English country towns, the bleakness of Kimberley depressed him immensely. 'I do not think that there is a tree to be seen within five miles of the town,' he moaned. 'When I was there I doubt whether there was a blade of grass within twenty miles, unless what might be found on the very marge of the low water of the Vaal river. Everything was brown, as though the dusty dry uncovered earth never knew the blessing of verdure. To ascertain that the roots of grass were remaining, one had to search the ground.' Griqualand West was, indeed, a far cry from Barchester.

He found living conditions in Kimberley equally unpleasant. The mean-looking corrugated-iron houses were, in his opinion, completely devoid of comfort. Only the linings of the houses were made of brick, he explained, because there was no fuel to burn bricks, and sun-dried bricks would not withstand the weather. Lath and plaster for ceilings were unheard of. 'The rooms are generally covered with canvas which can be easily carried,' he noted. 'But a canvas ceiling does not remain clean, or even rectilinear. The invisible dust settles upon it and bulges it, and the stain of dust comes through it. Wooden floors are absolutely necessary for comfort and cleanliness; but at Kimberley it will cost £40 to floor a moderate room.' He asked his readers to imagine a town in which every plank used had to be dragged five hundred miles by oxen. What chance was there of ornamentation? Was it surprising that the famous Diamond City was so unspeakably dreary?

When asked to admire the spaciousness of the Market-square - the town's most impressive feature - he could only stare in disbelief. A woman, recently out from England, told him that she had at first considered the square to be ugly but had gradually come to appreciate its magnificence. 'I could but say', declared the astonished Trollope, 'that corrugated iron would never become magnificent in my eyes. In Kimberley there are two buildings with a storey above the ground, and one of these is in the square. This is its only magnificence. There is no pavement. The roadway is all dust and holes. There is a market place in the midst which certainly is not magnificent. Around are the corrugated iron shops of the ordinary dealers in provisions. An uglier place I do not know how to imagine.'

Yet, for all his aesthetic distaste, Trollope was extremely impressed by Kimberley. Not by its houses, or its streets, or with the way its citizens made their money. He considered grovelling in the earth for diamonds a degrading occupation. When he learned that women and children took a hand in diamond sorting he was disgusted. 'I thought', he exclaimed, 'that I could almost sooner have seen my own wife or my own girl with a broom at a street crossing.' What did excite him was the Kimberley Mine. He visited the mine during the day and, like Olive Schreiner, marvelled at its 'peculiar strangeness' in the moonlight. He was lowered 230 feet to the bottom of the mine and clambered about inspecting the way in which the 408 claims were separated from each other. He was intrigued by the network of wires which twanged over his head, carrying the buckets of diamondiferous soil to the surface.

All this, however, was incidental to what he considered the real wonder of Kimberley. He had little time for diamonds as such, but he rejoiced in the workings of the capitalistic system. In his opinion, the flesh-pots of Kimberley were succeeding where missionaries had failed; in the glitter of the diamonds he saw reflected the 'civilisation of the Savage'.

'The simple teaching of religion has never brought large numbers of Natives to live in European habits; but I have no doubt that European habits will bring about religion . . .' he maintained with smug Victorian hypocrisy; 'when I have looked down into the Kimberley mine and seen three or four thousand of them at work – although each of them would have stolen a diamond if the occasion came – I have felt that I was looking at three or four thousand growing Christians.' This it was that made him hail Kimberley as 'one of the most interesting places on the face of the earth'.

He even thought it possible that Kimberley might one day develop into a respectable town. If the diamond finds continued; if the railway line from the Cape reached the diggings; if water could be piped from the Vaal River; if planks and bricks became easily available; if trees could be planted; and if something could be done about the dust and the flies – there was just a chance that the place would become livable. 'And,' he added, 'as the nice things come the nasty habits will sink. The ladies will live far away from the grit, and small diamonds will have become too common to make it worth the parents' while to endanger their children's eyes. Some mode of checking the Kafir thieves will perhaps have been found–and the industry will have sunk into the usual grooves.'

It was an encouraging thought, but it is unlikely that the jaundiced Trollope really believed it. He had little faith in the diamond mines being productive for more than twenty years.

(4)

For all his criticism, Trollope was not entirely oblivious of Kimberley's more worthy institutions. He was delighted to find that churches were plentiful and admitted to hearing some sermons that were above 'sermon par'. He was also tremendously impressed by the Carnarvon Hospital and its new matron. As he spoke to this calm and efficient nurse he felt, he said, 'that I was speaking to one of the sweet ones of the earth'.

The new matron of the Carnarvon Hospital was a nun, Sister Louise. She was a member of the Anglican Community of St Michael and All Angels which had been founded at Bloemfontein three years earlier. A Dublin-trained nurse, Sister Louise had been sent a year before Trollope's visit, to take over as matron of the Carnarvon Hospital–which, unlike the adjacent Diggers Central Hospital, was reserved for paying patients. Her appointment reflected the serious efforts then being made to improve the medical services on the diggings.

The disastrous fire in September 1874 had badly hampered the progress of the Carnarvon Hospital. It was not until the beginning of the following year that Dr William Grimmer, a former district medical officer of the Cape, took up his formal appointment as Resident Surgeon, at a salary of £300 a year. He was assisted by his colleagues Dr Matthews and Dr Dyer, who acted as hospital consultants. Aware of the crying need for trained nurses, these doctors had persuaded Major Lanyon to apply to Bishop Webb of Bloemfontein for the services of the sisters of the Community of St Michael and All Angels to staff the Carnarvon Hospital.

Bishop Webb and one of the nuns, Sister Henrietta, had arrived in Kimberley on Passion Sunday 1876 to make the necessary arrangements. It was agreed that the sisters would work without remuneration (only board and lodging being provided), would be under the supervision of the doctors and would serve all patients irrespective of religious denomination. Shortly afterwards Sister Louise and two lay women took over all the nursing duties at the hospital, while Sister Henrietta acted as 'Lady Visitor'. With the arrival of Sister Henrietta, Kimberley gained the services of one of the most remarkable women ever to come to the town.

Henrietta Stockdale, the eldest daughter of an impoverished Anglican clergyman, was born in Gringley, Nottinghamshire, on 9 July 1847. Inspired by a visit to her father's parish of a South African Bishop, she had decided to devote her life to missionary nursing. In 1873, at the age of twenty-six, she had left home to train at the hospital of the Clewer Sisterhood, an Anglican community, and at the Great Ormond Street Children's Hospital. The following year, she and five other young women had arrived in Bloemfontein, where they founded the Community of St Michael and All Angels. While serving her novitiate, Sister Henrietta started a school but, it is said, 'teaching was not her real interest. She longed to tend the sick.'

Kimberley provided her with the opportunity. Besides being attached to the Carnarvon Hospital, she worked as a district nurse under the Canadian-born Dr James Perrott Prince, who taught her elementary midwifery. Unfortunately her first stay in Kimberley did not last long. After working for a few months with Dr Prince she became ill with typhoid fever and was sent back to England to recuperate. On returning to Bloemfontein she was appointed matron of the St George's Hospital, thus becoming the first hospital matron in the Orange Free State. But Kimberley was yet to claim her. At the outbreak of the Zulu War in 1879, Sister Louise was sent to Natal and Sister Henrietta took her place at the Carnarvon Hospital. It was the beginning of an outstanding career.

The nursing discipline created by Sister Henrietta at the Carnarvon Hospital was to bring an unexpected fame to Kimberley. Under her supervision the reputation of the hospital became such that patients 'came from all parts of the country for treatment and nurses trained there were sought as matrons of new hospitals started in other places'. Tall and willowy, with dark-brown hair and blue eyes, Sister Henrietta was as beautiful as she was dedicated. Lady Frere, wife of the newly arrived Governor of the Cape, considered her 'the most beautiful person she had ever seen'. Many thought of her as a saint.

But, like so many saintly people, the grave and reserved Sister Henrietta was a formidable personality. Her cool, controlled manner made patients speak of her as 'an angel carved in marble'; doctors, whom she always addressed as 'Sir', found her quite frightening; more than one of her pupil nurses was to remember her as 'a real tartar'. None of this, however, detracted from the respect which she commanded from admirers and critics alike. Her achievements were too great to suffer from any lack of personal warmth. 'The

Kimberley system', says E.H. Burrows, the medical historian, 'was the foundation of modern nursing in South Africa and Sister Henrietta herself might well be looked upon, with due regard for altered circumstances, as the country's Florence Nightingale.'

Certainly Kimberley needed the services of dedicated medical assistants such as Sister Henrietta. With sanitary conditions as appalling as they were and camp-fever still rampant, the death rate among both black and white diggers was still alarming. Even the improvements to the Carnarvon Hospital made little difference to the all-over situation. During the hot, unhealthy summer months, the handful of local doctors could not begin to cope with the hundreds of patients they were called upon to attend. The need for more trained medical practitioners was obvious and urgent.

Having lost the support of Sister Henrietta in the middle of 1877, Dr James Perrott Prince had to look elsewhere for assistance. He applied to University College, London, for a partner. It was some time before a suitable candidate presented himself. Not until the middle of January 1879 did an advertisment appear in the local press announcing: 'Dr Prince begs to notify that he has associated with himself in practice L.S. Jameson, M.D., B.S., London M.R.C.S., late Demonstrator of Anatomy at University College, London, and Resident Medical Officer at the Hospital . . . Dr Prince having obtained assistance, patients will receive prompt attention at all hours.'

Dr Prince's new partner was Dr Leander Starr Jameson, a short, perky and extremely able young Scotsman. Then twenty-five years old, Jameson had been born in Edinburgh and had abandoned a promising career as a London surgeon to answer Dr Prince's appeal. What decided him to do so is not certain: it was widely believed that, like so many other professional men in Kimberley, he emigrated to South Africa to cure a weak lung. However, his biographer, Ian Colvin, implies that it was a diamond which his brother Julius sent home from South Africa that prompted his decision. 'The diamond', says Colvin, 'may have flashed in his mind as well as in his cravat.' Yet another version has it that he intended to make enough money in Kimberley to pay for a course of medical studies in Vienna.

But, whatever his reasons, Jameson's arrival in Kimberley was both fortunate and timely. Talented, charming and boyishly handsome, he was able to take full advantage of the town's crying need for doctors. From the very outset he proved immensely popular with the mining community and quickly established himself as one of the leading medical practitioners on the diamond fields.

Not a great deal is known about Jameson's early career in Kimberley. Nor is it possible to pin down precisely the secret of his undoubted charm. Some claim that the diggers welcomed him for his forthright bedside manner. He was a doctor, they say, who stood no nonsense: if anyone went to him complaining of a vague backache they were told to go away and rub their back with a brick. This was the type of humour that the down-to-earth diggers appreciated. Kimberley gossips, however, tended to regard him as a smooth-talking ladies' man. 'With the fair sex,' sniggered the scurrilous Lou Cohen, 'although he

The dashing young diamond merchant. An early, little-known, photograph of
Barney Barnato taken by J.E. Middlebrook in Kimberley. **(M)**
Dr Leander Starr Jameson, Kimberley's popular medical practitioner. (M)

A group of Kimberley's leading citizens, purportedly: Cecil Rhodes, standing
with umbrella, J. B. Robinson, hand in pocket, Sidney Shippard, Attorney-
General, seated. (J)

wasn't particular about complexion, he was undeniably most popular.'

Jameson's amatory exploits, real or imagined, were a source of never-ending fascination to Cohen. In the highly libellous reminiscences he was later to write, he returned time and again to 'Dr Jim's' popularity with his female patients. Doubtful as most of his legends are, they were to become part of the Kimberley legend. Many a digger's child, proudly boasting of having been brought into the world by the famous Dr Jameson, was to have second thoughts after reading the snide Lou Cohen.

'I knew a chap once,' mused Cohen, in a typical aside, 'who had been very successful in life, and whose only trouble was that his charming wife had not presented him with a tiny image of himself. He confided in me, and on my initiative he consulted Dr Jim with the result that, hey presto! before the year was out, and on the first of April too, he became the proud pater of bouncing twins. The Doctor was, indeed, a life giver.'

No one laughed more heartily at Cohen's heavy-handed humour than Jameson himself. By the time the scandalous reminiscences were published, the dashing little doctor had withstood much deeper thrusts than Lou Cohen's pinpricks. Dr Jim's contribution to Kimberley history was not confined to his medical practice.

11

Company Mining

Kimberley was now the second-largest town in South Africa. Census figures for 1877 showed that the town had 13,590 inhabitants. When Dutoitspan and Bultfontein were added to this, the total population of the dry diggings was seen to be 18,000: 8,000 whites and 10,000 'non-whites'. In a mere six years, the capital of Griqualand West had outstripped in growth all other Colonial towns with the exception of Cape Town. There could no longer be any doubts about Kimberley's importance.

The census figures are interesting, not only because they illustrate the rapid rise of this new South African urban centre, but also because they reflect the now established predominance of the former New Rush camp. The incredible richness of the Kimberley Mine had finally ended the long-standing rivalry between New Rush and Dutoitspan. Those knowing Dutoitspan diggers who at one time had been inclined to write off New Rush as a temporary, get-rich-quick phenomenon had been forced to admit they were wrong. Dutoitspan and the other camps were now regarded as nothing more than suburbs of Kimberley. Anthony Trollope had made this clear during his visit. He had dismissed Dutoitspan and Bultfontein as mean little villages 'very melancholy to look at, consisting of hotels or drinking bars, and the small shops of the diamond dealers'. Old De Beers he had not even bothered to explore. It was the town that had developed around the long-vanished Colesberg Kopje that was now – and would continue to be – the heart of the diamond diggings.

And Kimberley was jealous of its superiority. Its citizens saw their town as an independent entity, a place quite capable of running its own affairs. When the time came for the town to be proclaimed a municipality, the poorer 'suburbs' were excluded. The election of town councillors was confined to six wards within a two-mile radius of the Kimberley Court House; this included Old De Beers but not Dutoitspan and Bultfontein. Qualifications for voting were simple. An elector had, irrespective of race, to be an adult male who owned or occupied immovable property valued at £20 a year. Candidates for the twelve council seats – two to each ward – had to possess similar qualifications as well as claiming a previous residence of at least six months.

It was a rough-and-ready arrangement, and the first municipal elections, held on Tuesday 11 December 1877, showed the town to be far more rough than ready. In some of the wards voting was chaotic. Hardly were the polling-booths open than they were besieged by huge crowds who blocked the roads and refused to let any but the supporters of favoured candidates vote. Touts, claiming to assist innocent voters, were seen to grab openly at voting-papers and tear them up. 'Even the candidates', it was reported, 'collared all comers and brought them to the poll by force of arms. . . . More coolies and kafirs were brought to the poll than were ever seen in the streets before, whilst the coloured gentry were never so cuddled, coaxed and treated as they were on that day.'

The hastily compiled voters' rolls proved totally inadequate. Many of the black voters, claiming to be property owners, arrived at the polling-stations with hardly a rag to their backs. African labourers were herded from their claims to vote and domestic servants were marched to the booths by their employers. So long as a man was vouched for and could make a cross on his voting-slip he was passed by the polling-officers. Drinks were handed out freely and more than one drunken voter was seen to leave the back of a booth, be handed a fresh voting-slip, and then rushed to the front to vote again.

So blatant was the bribery in Ward 1 – where the rakish Leopold Lowenthal headed the poll – that a second election had to be held ten days later. It made little difference to the result or the corruption, the four candidates merely adding two or three hundred votes each to their totals. The entire town went on a drunken spree after the announcement of the first results. Candidates were expected, win or lose, to stand drinks all round. When one of the winners in Ward 2 refused to join in this 'liquoring up', his shoes, socks and hat were taken off and hoisted mast-high at the polling-office. Kimberley's municipal elections were undoubtedly far more fun than those for the Legislative Council had ever been.

But, boisterous as were the elections, the fact that Kimberley now had its own Town Council was seen as a big step forward. Among the new councillors were a number of solid citizens – men like George Bottomley, Alexander McGregor and A. Stead – who were to contribute much to the development of the town. That such men were prepared to offer themselves for election was an encouraging sign in itself. 'It was evident', says Sydney Hawthorne, 'that there were many men who had come to regard Kimberley as their future home, and were willing to devote both time and money to make it a creditable town.'

On 27 December the Town Council met for the first time to elect a mayor. Only two men were nominated for the office: John Birbeck, a diamond buyer at Old De Beers, and the fiery Dan O'Leary. Both nominees had at one time been members of the controversial Committee of Public Safety and were well-known Kimberley personalities. But O'Leary, although the more colourful of the two, had a reputation for recklessness which appears to have undermined his chances. After a hat had been passed round the Council table and the votes had been counted, John Birbeck emerged as Kimberley's first mayor with a majority of two votes.

The new Council had a tough job ahead of it. There was much that needed to be done to pull the town into shape but, as always, the means were sadly wanting. Major Lanyon agreed to hand over a certain amount of revenue – from dog and cat taxes and hawkers' licences – to the new body but, until a proper system of property valuation was instituted, there could be no real municipal reforms. The Council was hamstrung almost from the outset. During its first year of office it was beset by the all-too-familiar plagues of Kimberley.

At the beginning of the year a frightening fire completely destroyed two drapers' shops and seriously threatened the Theatre Royal. A prolonged drought resulted in one of the worst epidemics of horse flies and house flies the town had ever known. The lack of rain caused the price of water to soar and the Administrator adamantly refused to consider a plan submitted by a civil engineer for pumping water from the Vaal River. Rarely had the roads been in a more appalling state. The enthusiasm shown during the Council elections soon began to wane. When an attempt was made to revise the ludicrous voters' rolls, so few citizens registered that the new returns showed that there were 600 voters fewer than on the previous lists. Government by a local body was proving no more effective than that of the much-despised Imperial authority.

Not until new elections were held at the end of 1878 was any real interest shown in municipal affairs. Much of this renewed interest sprang from the surprising intervention of Barney Barnato. To everyone's astonishment, the hitherto frivolous Barney suddenly announced that he intended to contest the seat held by George Bottomley in Ward 5. He could hardly have chosen a more formidable or unlikely opponent. Bottomley, backed by the Good Templars, had recently been elected to the resuscitated Legislative Council, where he had announced his intention of introducing an act amending the liquor laws and preventing the sale of alcohol 'to any native'. This, and a private bill authorising the supply of water from the Vaal, had won him wide support. Barney's chances of unseating him seemed slim indeed.

So much so that, at first, nobody took his candidature seriously. One newspaper went so far as to say that he had only been nominated 'for the mere sake of bringing the whole Municipal Council into contempt'. But Barney was not playing games. And he soon let them know it. A couple of days later the newspaper apologised for saying his candidature had been a joke.

Barney's first venture into public affairs is instructive. It provides a glimpse of the growing Barnato power. The firm of Barnato Brothers was still in its infancy, but it was sufficiently well established to swing a local election. Admittedly all that was needed to do this was money.

The second municipal contest was by no means as riotous as the first. By comparison it was almost sedate, but there was still plenty of scope for a smooth operator like Barney Barnato. 'It is well known', claimed the *Diamond News*, after the election, 'that . . . some of the contests were largely affected by voters who came to the polling stations provided with receipts for rates which had been openly and without concealment paid by the aspirant for Municipal honours or his accredited agents. Now there can be no doubt that this is bribery in its most direct and objectionable form.' There can also be no doubt that Barney was one of the offenders. He not only headed the poll in Ward 5 but saw to it that his running-mate, James Lawrence, was also elected. Poor George Bottomley, conscientious and honest as he was, had not stood a chance.

For all that, Barney proved a worthy councillor. He took his duties very seriously and rarely missed a council meeting. In his election manifesto he had promised to give urgent attention to the infamous drainage and water supply of the town and at an early meeting he was, in fact, elected to the sanitary committee. But his heart was not really in water affairs. The workings of the Municipal market were far more to his taste. He was convinced that not only could he make the market pay but that he could set an example to the council's employees. Many an eyebrow was raised at his antics in the marketplace.

'An edifying spectacle may be observed on the Market every morning,' it was reported in April 1879. 'A full fledged Town Councillor, clad in check trousers etc., touting for the assistant Market master, holding up cabbages and other vegetables to the gaze of an admiring public, and finally returning home with a cabbage under each arm, a pocket full of carrots, or some other presents contributed by grateful sellers, who seem to appreciate the efforts of this worthy controller of our roads and morals to get them the highest prices for their products.' Bribery in Kimberley could, it seems, work both ways.

Barney was in his element on the Town Council. He adored an audience, be it in the theatre, the marketplace or the council chamber. If he had a fault as a councillor, it was his tendency to let his tongue run away with him. His speeches were often as irrelevant as they were irreverent. He regretted that council meetings often clashed with his work at the mine and that he consequently had to cut his speeches short at times. In fact, one of the first resolutions he moved was that council meetings be held in the evening instead of in the heat of the afternoon. The Mayor was quick to oppose this. Looking fixedly at Barney, he pointed out that 'members who had a glass of wine for dinner, would want to air their eloquence before the public'. A poker-faced Barney then 'gravely assured the Mayor that he had no wish to air his eloquence'. The motion was, nevertheless, defeated.

For all his fooling, Barney did a competent job. At the elections held at the end of 1879 he was returned unopposed.

(2)

For most visitors Kimberley's main attraction was still the Kimberley Mine, the ever-deepening hole around which the town had developed and from which the diggers drew their lifeblood. Colesberg Kopje, the cone that had once covered the fabulous diamond deposits, was a dim memory by the end of the 1870s. Only the long-established pioneers could recall the days when De Beers farm was merely a stopping-place on the way to the river diggings. It seemed impossible that there had once been a time when the barren veld had stretched undisturbed to the distant horizons. The mine had become Kimberley and, for most people, Kimberley was the mine.

To stand at the edge of the vast crater was a sobering experience. 'You immediately feel', observed Trollope, 'that it is the largest and most complete hole ever made by human agency.' This was what impressed most visitors: it was the size of this man-made hole, rather than its riches, that made an immediate impact. Some people were unable to look down into the mine without becoming dizzy. Others were struck dumb when trying to describe the bewildering maze of claims. 'The ground, which was once a hill, is cut into–whereto shall I compare this labyrinth of pits?' an early visitor had gasped. 'Nothing in the world, I think, suggests the like.' Whether seen by day or by night, under snow or in sunshine, the Kimberley Mine was breathtaking. Never, however, had it looked more impressive, more magnificent, than during the visit of Sir Bartle Frere, the latest Governor of the Cape, in May 1879.

The Governor's visit to Kimberley has been described as 'a red-letter day in the annals of the Diamond Fields'. Preparations for his arrival went on for days. Kimberley, it was felt, should show its loyalty to a man who was then struggling to uphold British prestige in South Africa. Certainly Sir Bartle Frere needed all the encouragement he could get.

From the time he had taken over at the Cape from Sir Henry Barkly, in March 1877, Frere had been battling against tremendous odds. He had been specially chosen for the post by Lord Carnarvon, who hoped that he would guide South Africa towards federation. But from his arrival Frere had been beset by tribal wars: first the frontier wars of the Cape Colony and then the disastrous Zulu war which started with the unprecedented massacre of British troops at Isandhlwana in January 1879. The Zulu war was still raging when Frere made a tour of the recently annexed Transvaal and faced the growing hostility of the Transvaal Boers. It was on his return from this tour that the Governor paid his visit to the diamond fields.

Of the approval of the Griqualand West community for his policies, Sir Bartle Frere was left in no doubt whatsoever. Flags fluttered in the sunshine, bunting flapped in the breeze, triumphal arches spanned the roads, the press of people was so thick that His Excellency could barely mount, or leave, the platform in the Market-square. He was even presented with a bouquet–no mean achievement 'on account of the great difficulty there was at that time in raising flowers'. Every speech, every archway, every banner extolled his 'native policy'. In the name of the 'natives' themselves, he was thanked for the 'rights' and the 'good government' they enjoyed.

The climax to all this exhuberance came with His Excellency's visit to the mine. Escorted by hundreds of Africans carrying flaming torches, Frere passed through the inevitable, illuminated, triumphal arch and took up his position on the Grandstand. Before him was a magical sight. Thousands upon thousands of tins, filled with paraffin-saturated stuffing, had been fastened to the intricate webbing of cables and set alight. The effect of these different-coloured flames, travelling to and from the hauling-gear, was dazzling. And in the middle of it all blazed an illuminated balloon that had been fashioned in the shape of a huge diamond. It was not surprising that Sir Bartle Frere should afterwards advise a visitor to go to Kimberley, 'for there you will see one of the wonders of the world when you look into that mine of diamonds'.

The visitor was Stephen Massett, an American actor who was touring South Africa with a theatrical company. He arrived in Kimberley at the beginning of 1880 and was overwhelmed by the hospitality of the town's 'generous and good natured' inhabitants. 'Money is plentiful,' he enthused, 'and they spend it freely; there is nothing mean or small about the Kimberleyites, and an El Dorado indeed it is to public performers, for they are patronised most generously.'

But with the mine he was disappointed. Sir Bartle Frere's description had led him to expect too much and he regretted that he was not important enough to be treated to illuminations and fireworks. It came as a great disappointment when he was told to climb into a bucket which was to carry him to the bottom of the 'diamondiferous pit'. Nor was the mine the glittering Aladdin's Cave he had expected. As he scrambled about the claims, ankle-deep in dust, he looked in vain for diamonds: all he could see was dreary blue earth, muddy water and stones. He was thankful to leave - even though it meant another frightening journey in a swaying bucket.

Surprisingly enough, he was far more impressed by the town itself. At first glance the straggling streets and one-storied iron houses reminded him of 'San Francisco in the early days, or some of the interior California mining towns'. Main-street on Saturday night awoke other memories. It put him in mind, he says, 'of the Edgware Road, London! and really when you think that every thing here has actually been brought by ox wagons, it is indeed a wonderful place. Here are three or four large, and even elegant haberdashers or dry goods stores, stationers' shops, chemists and druggists, boot and shoe makers, toy shops, a well appointed club, called the "Craven", billiard saloons, all lighted up brilliantly. There is a Theatre Royal and an Odd-Fellow's Hall . . . and altogether there is a life and bustle about the place which is good to behold.'

It needed someone like Massett, used to the rough-and-tumble of a theatrical company, to appreciate the gaiety of Kimberley. He had none of Trollope's fastidious complaints; what discomforts there were he took in his stride and he made friends galore. Staying at the Queen's Hotel he was enchanted by the kindhearted Mrs Jardine and was delighted with the food and service. 'I was really surprised,' he admitted, 'to find away out here in the deserts of Africa so many luxuries and comforts.'

But perhaps what pleased him more than anything was the carefree spirit, the lack of violence and fear, the feeling of wellbeing that seemed to pervade the town. This he thought truly remarkable. Perhaps not all the town-proud citizens would have agreed with him when he said that they were possessed by 'diamonds and money-getting, and the idea of clearing out as soon as your "pile" is made' but they would undoubtedly have basked in his description of them as a 'jolly, happy and lighthearted' community. Certainly, by the beginning of 1880, most Kimberleyites had good reason to be cheerful. The price of diamonds was continuing to rise, the crippling drought had been broken and more determined attempts were being made to smarten up the town. Massett, in fact, was full of praise for Kimberley's civic institutions (he thought the prison the most perfect of its kind in South Africa - an opinion not shared by everyone) and was perfectly charmed by the vegetable gardens of 'Mr Rothschild . . . Mr Rudd and Mr. R.W. Murray'.

Many of the improvements had been brought about by the recently elected Council. For the benefit of his American readers, Massett gave a breakdown of

Griqualand West's system of government, ending with the administration of
Kimberley itself. 'There is a Municipality for the town of Kimberley,' he
explained, 'administered by a Town Council, who elect their Mayor: J.B.
Robinson is the present popular chief.'

(3)

Whether J.B. Robinson was as popular a Mayor as Massett imagined is, to say
the least, debatable. His election had been strongly opposed by a group of
councillors and many doubted whether he was entitled to hold office at all.
Civic dignity had, in fact, come to J.B. Robinson as so much else came to
him – cloaked in controversy and delivered in a court of law.

Of Robinson's determination to occupy the mayoral chair there can, however, be no doubt. After his defeat in the Legislative Council elections he had
become firmly resolved to obtain political office of some sort. That he had set
his sights on the Town Council is not surprising. The running of Kimberley's
municipal affairs had far greater significance than was immediately
apparent. Since the lifting of the Ordinance restricting claim holders to ten
claims, the running of the diamond industry had become more complex, more
competitive; rivalry in local politics reflected a good deal more than the usual
parochial animosities.

By the end of the 1870s, it was becoming increasingly obvious that, sooner or
later, there would be a powerful struggle for control of the mines. Most of the
capitalists in Kimberley were aware of this and, in their various ways, were
beginning to muster their forces. Even the most trivial jostling for position had
a financial significance. Control of the Town Council strengthened an
ambitious financier's hand immensely. Now that the Legislative Council had
proved more or less ineffective, Kimberley had no greater political prize to
offer. It was this, as much as anything, that had determined J.B. Robinson to
become Kimberley's third mayor.

By careful planning he had placed himself in a strong position to achieve his
ambition. Not only was he one of the richest diamond merchants in the town
and effective commander of Kimberley's defence force, but he had the
advantage of controlling the most influential newspaper on the diamond fields,
the *Independent*. He had taken over this recently established newspaper from
William Ling shortly after his first political defeat. His success as a press baron
had astonished everyone.

To run a newspaper in Kimberley was no easy matter. Even experienced
journalists like R.W. Murray had found this out. A satirical magazine, *Fun,*
which Murray launched in September 1877, had failed to live up to its name
and collapsed within a matter of months. A more ambitious venture, the
Kimberley Observer – published the following year – had met with a similar fate.
But under Robinson's guidance the *Independent* had flourished. He put his
bookkeeper, Lionel Phillips – a young Jewish clerk, recently out from
England – in charge of the printing works and appointed his attorney,
Mortimer Siddall, as editor. With his natural flair for controversy, J.B.

Robinson saw to it that the *Independent* became essential, and entertaining, reading.

So immediate was the *Independent's* success that, in July 1877, the long-established *Diamond Field* was forced to close down. This left the stolid *Diamond News* as Robinson's main rival until the following year, when a third newspaper, the *Diamond Fields Advertiser,* was founded. During the turbulent years ahead, it was to be these three papers – the *Diamond News,* the *Independent* and the *Diamond Fields Advertiser* – that kept Kimberley politicians on their toes.

But it was Robinson's paper that made the running at the outset. Hardly a week went by without someone or other threatening to sue the *Independent* for libel. Charges against Robinson, as the proprietor, and Mortimer Siddall, as editor, were frequently heard in the law courts and, more often than not, it was the newspaper that had to foot the bill.

The most scandalous of these libel cases was that which arose from an editorial written shortly after Robinson took over the paper. At that time the action taken against Henry Tucker for buying diamonds without a licence was still very much a public issue. So was the unpopularity of Major Lanyon as Administrator. Siddall cashed in on the controversy by publicly accusing Lanyon of the same offence as Tucker. The legal proceedings which followed were widely reported and the case became a South African *cause célèbre.*

For the most part, public opinion in Kimberley was solidly behind Robinson. This became evident when the criminal charge brought against Siddall, as the author of the libel, was thrown out of court by a sympathetic jury. Robinson was not so lucky. There was no jury in the civil action he faced the following month and he was found guilty. Only by agreeing to publish an apology did he escape paying £10,000 damages. For all that, the case did much to improve Robinson's public image.

But if the libel had been an astute political move, financially Robinson lost out badly. Although he had escaped paying damages, he had to meet the costs of both his own and Siddall's case; these, in Griqualand West, were heavy. Running a newspaper was proving an expensive hobby. It unsettled both Robinson's miserly habits and his staff of novices. Siddall resigned as editor and Lionel Phillips requested a transfer from the printing works to the firmer ground of J.B. Robinson's mining company. Shortly after this, Robinson let it be known that he intended selling the newspaper to Casper H. Hartley. The sale, however, was only nominal. Robinson retained his controlling interest and the *Independent,* as every well-informed newspaperman knew, remained Robinson's political mouthpiece.

It provided him with a powerful weapon in his campaign to become Mayor. By the time the campaign opened, the influence of the *Independent* was unquestioned. Previously it had, like its rivals, appeared three times a week; but towards the end of 1879 it changed its name to the *Daily Independent* and became the first Kimberley paper to appear regularly every weekday. To advertise in the *Independent* cost as much as to advertise in the London *Times.* 'I should imagine the income of the *Independent,* looking at the advertisements, to be something wonderful,' declared Stephen Massett. 'I am told that Rothschild, a celebrated auctioneer here, pays something like £500 a month for his advertisments.' With this kind of backing Robinson could count on swaying public opinion in his favour. More difficult was the problem of getting his fellow councillors to elect him as mayor.

Much depended on the outcome of the council elections. In 1879 several seats were unopposed and Robinson was among those returned without a fight. So were Barney Barnato and a number of other financiers who could be depended on to vote for Robinson as mayor. Only two wards, in fact, were contested; of these the voting in Ward 4 was expected to produce the most interesting results. Here three newcomers had been nominated for the two seats. Two of the candidates – Henry Chapman and William Thompson – were known to be Robinson supporters. The third was Cecil Rhodes, whose sympathies were extremely uncertain.

Rhodes had been late entering the lists. Since his most recent return from Oxford, at the end of 1878, he had been kept busy with his mining concerns. His protracted university studies – interrupted by illness and the constant journeying between two continents – were almost complete. He had, in fact, to attend Oxford for only one more term before taking his degree. Now his mind was turning to the serious work he had set himself. Like Robinson and Barnato, he had recognised the importance of local politics and allowed himself to be nominated for Ward 4. Then, quite unexpectedly, he changed his mind. Three days before the election he wrote to the Town Clerk and withdrew his candidature.

Rhodes's withdrawal had farcical and far-reaching results. It confused the entire issue of the election and landed J.B. Robinson – inevitably – in court. In the first place his withdrawal lulled his two Ward 4 opponents into such a state of complacency that they were late in handing in their requisitions. The Ward 4 election was consequently postponed for two days. Thus, with the other elections having taken place as planned, the two Ward 4 members were missing when the new council met to elect a mayor. But not for long. Their postponed election having taken place on the very day of the mayoral election, they came haring across to the Council Chamber, in Main-street, just in time to vote for a mayor. This, the Town Clerk assured them, they would not be allowed to do: their election to Ward 4 had not yet been gazetted.

The Town Clerk's ruling accepted, the remaining councillors applied themselves to the all-important business of electing a mayor. Barney Barnato proposed Robinson. Barney had an eye to business. The diamond industry was by no means in the majority on the council and he recognised the importance of supporting an influential diamond merchant like Robinson. His proposal was seconded by his old rival, George Bottomley, who approved not so much of Robinson's business connections as of his abstemious drinking habits. There was only one other nomination. This was for the re-election of Kimberley's first mayor, John Birbeck, who, as was well-known, was an old political opponent of Robinson's.

A hat was passed round the council table for the votes. When a count was made, it was found that the two members for Ward 4 had defied the Town Clerk and voted for Robinson. The voting-slips were promptly torn up and the hat passed round again. This time the chairman kept a close watch on the voting and refused the slips presented by the recalcitrant members for Ward 4. The vote this time was five for Birbeck and four for Robinson. John Birbeck was again declared Mayor of Kimberley.

But J.B. Robinson had no intention of accepting the result. He maintained that he had been fairly elected on the first ballot. His views were faithfully echoed in the *Independent*. 'Whether Mr Robinson was elected by a combination of Good Templars and the diamond trade or not,' thundered the newspaper, 'he was elected.' Supported by Barney Barnato and those who had voted for him, Robinson applied to the High Court for the election of the new mayor to be set aside.

As always in legal actions brought by J.B. Robinson, the case attracted country-wide attention, and when it came up for hearing the court was packed. The verdict was in Robinson's favour. The judge found that John Birbeck was an 'usurper' and ruled that 'Mr Robinson should be declared Mayor for the ensuing year'. The decision was not well received. But there was nothing anyone could do about it. Like it or not, J.B. Robinson had achieved his ambition and was now the Mayor of Kimberley. 'It is to be hoped', said the disgruntled *Diamond News,* 'that the battle which has been fought in the High Court will not be renewed in the Council Chamber.'

Surprisingly enough it was not. Although far from being a universal favourite, Robinson – backed by Barney Barnato and the other diamond merchants – proved a capable and efficient mayor. He was extremely proud of his position and did his utmost to weld the council together. Slight as his victory might appear, he regarded it as one of the landmarks of his life. In time J.B. Robinson was to become one of the richest men in the world and would have much to boast about, but he never failed to rate his term as Mayor of Kimberley among his great achievements.

(4)

The year 1880 was to be remembered in Kimberley for more than Robinson's controversial mayoralty. It was the year that saw the beginning of the end of the small digger.

The fusion of mining interests was a gradual process. In the early days, when the ownership of claims was severely restricted, there could be no question of mining companies being formed. Each digger worked for himself, selling his finds to individual diamond merchants on an open market. This arrangement had worked well enough so long as diamond digging was confined to pick-and-shovel operations. But as the mines went deeper it became more and more apparent that such simple digging methods could not continue indefinitely. The soil became harder to work—particularly when the 'blue' ground was reached—heavy equipment was needed to tackle the deeper levels, water seeped into the claims, and pumping was an expensive and perpetual necessity.

The French Company's offices in the Diamond Market, Kimberley. (K)

The Mayor of Kimberley. The steely-eyed J.B. Robinson in the early 1880s. (S)
Sir Julius Wernher, influential diamond magnate and partner of Alfred Beit. (K)

Mining, even when it involved valuable claims, became impossible for the man who lacked financial or co-operative backing.

The need to combine was obvious. It was for this reason that, first the two-claim restriction and then, in 1876, the ten-claim restriction had been abolished. The final lifting of restrictions had immediately led to greater enterprise. At the beginning of 1877, a group of diggers backed by a London syndicate had made a determined effort to amalgamate their claims in the Kimberley Mine. This bid had failed because the group was unable to buy up certain claims essential to their scheme. The obstructing claims were owned by J.B. Robinson, who adamantly refused to sell out to the group. As a result, a legend arose that Robinson was opposed to amalgamation. Nothing could have been further from the truth. Robinson was wholeheartedly in favour of amalgamation; but it had to be an amalgamation which he controlled. He had, in fact, already launched his own amalgamation scheme and was to accuse his rivals of obstructing *his* company. Whoever was to blame, the tactics of the opposing groups had prevented any significant attempt at amalgamation.

But not for long. In other parts of the mine, interests had been joined and a few potentially powerful companies had been formed. When Anthony Trollope visited the diggings at the end of 1877, he noted that one of the most prosperous concerns in the Kimberley Mine was the firm of Messrs Baring-Gould, Atkins and Co. The head of this company, Francis Baring-Gould, had been long established on the diamond fields and had been quick to recognise the advantage of co-operative mining. By combining his claims with those of a neighbouring digger, he had not only taken control of fifteen claims but, as Trollope remarked, had 'gone to the expense of sinking a perpendicular shaft with a tunnel below from the shaft to the mine–so as to avoid the use of the aerial tramway'. The shaft, in fact, did more than that: it helped to safeguard Baring-Gould's claims from falling debris. In time the sinking of shafts was to play an important part in the diamond-mining industry.

The abolition of the ten-claim restriction not only encouraged enterprise, it also opened the way to the international money market. Banks were now more ready to give credit, and the opportunity was provided for attracting foreign investors and speculators. Groups of diggers were now able to turn over their claims to joint stock companies.

At first European investors showed little inclination to rise to the bait of South Africa's diamonds. Shareholders in the early registered companies were largely Kimberley residents. By 1880, however, at least one recently formed company had foreign backing. This was the *Compagnie Francaise des Mines de Diamant du Cap,* or, as it was popularly known, the French Company.

Jules Porges, the man responsible for the formation of the French Company, was the head of one of the largest and richest diamond concerns in the world. He had been the first international diamond merchant of substance to recognise the importance of the South African discoveries and, in 1871, had sent out Julius Wernher - a huge, handsome ex-Prussian Dragoon - to represent his firm in Griqualand West. It was largely through Wernher's efforts that the firm had acquired interests in all four mines. Four years later Porges himself had arrived at the diggings and, once the claim restrictions had been lifted, he and Wernher had concentrated on buying up properties in the Kimberley Mine. Starting with a few valuable claims, for which they paid £120,000, they later amalgamated with another group and formed the French Company. From this base, Porges and Wernher were soon to strike out in a quest for further financial conquests.

Others were also seeking foreign backing. Not the least among them being the ambitious Barnato brothers. In June 1880, Barney and Harry Barnato left Kimberley for a visit to England. The main purpose of this visit appears to have been to open a London office of their firm. The office, which was to handle the marketing of their diamonds in Europe, was established at 106 Hatton Garden as 'Barnato Brothers, Diamond Dealers and Financiers'. Before they left South Africa it had been rumoured that Barney was to take charge of the London office, but he seems quickly to have abandoned the idea. The brothers arrived back in Kimberley in December 1880, bringing two of their nephews, Isaac and Solly Joel, with them. A third nephew, Woolf Joel, had come out to South Africa earlier, at the age of fifteen, and was already an experienced diamond buyer. Barnato Brothers was very much a family concern.

It was also, as soon became apparent, a concern to be reckoned with. Kimberley cynics who had been inclined to dismiss the Barnato brothers as frivolous, rather shady, theatrical upstarts now had to change their tune. Harry and Barney were emerging as astute, hard-headed businessmen. Nothing emphasised this more than their new venture, embarked upon three months after their return from England. 'Messrs Barnato Brothers have started four Mining Companies within the last fortnight,' reported the *Independent* in March 1881. 'The total capital subscribed was considerably over half-a-million, and covered the amount asked for many times over. The shares for all four companies are at a premium, and the undertakings may be regarded as a wonderful success.' Success was not the word everyone used. But that the Barnatos had entered the 'company-boom' stakes there could be no doubt.

The struggle for control of the Kimberley Mine was beginning. Two of the main contenders – Baring-Gould and the French Company – were already well established; the Barnato Brothers and others were just limbering up. Everyone recognised the inevitability of a single company controlling the mine. When, in October 1881, the *Independent* was accused of secretly trying to bring about an amalgamation, it replied: 'To secure the amalgamation of the Kimberley Mine will require no conspiracy on our part; come it will in the end, whether we fight against it or no.' It was merely a question of which faction would come out on top. At this stage of the game there was certainly no shortage of contestants.

Nor was the struggle confined to the Kimberley Mine. Similar moves were being made in all the mines, nowhere with more success than at Old De Beers. This was largely due to the determined efforts of Cecil Rhodes. His plans to take over Old De Beers were already well advanced.

By the beginning of 1880, the Rudd–Rhodes partnership had established a firm foothold in old De Beers. After combining with other claim holders they had built up a syndicate which controlled an important section of the mine. On

1 April 1880, they were able to announce the formation of the De Beers Mining Company, with an authorised capital of £200,000. This was not, as is often supposed, Rhodes's only mining interest at this time. By the end of 1880, Rhodes was a director of the Lilienstein Mining Company, which operated at Bultfontein; his name appeared as a director of the International Diamond Mining Company and both he and Rudd were directors of the Kimberley Coal Mining Company.

But it was on the De Beers company that he focused his ambitions. The mine, it is true, was not the richest nor the most important but to control it would place him in a position to match up to his rivals. While others spent their money and energies jostling for position in the Kimberley Mine, Rhodes intended to establish a sound base for any future struggle. And he was convinced that a much tougher struggle lay ahead, a struggle which would involve not merely the control of individual mines but control of the entire diamond industry.

There was no longer any doubt in Rhodes's mind about the enormous potential of the South African diamond fields. His confidence was reflected in a letter he wrote to J.X. Merriman shortly after floating the De Beers Mining Company. Griqualand West, he said, had seen some 'wonderful changes' since Merriman's day. 'There is every chance', he went on, 'of our prosperity lasting; the old fear of the mines working out is rapidly fading . . . what I want to impress on you is the fact that this is now the richest community in the world for its size and that it shows every sign of permanency. The present proved depths of our mines alone would take at our present rate of working a hundred years to work out, and of course we cannot tell how much deeper they may go.'

Kimberley had indeed become a prize worth fighting for.

PART THREE: PROGRESS

Crushing blue ground on the Bultfontein Mine floors, about 1884. (K)

12

Progress and a Threat

'In redemption of the undertaking given by the Colonial Legislature and confirmed by the Colonial Governor,' Sir Bartle Frere announced at the opening session of the Cape Assembly in 1880, 'we relieve Her Majesty's government of the responsibility of the administration of the affairs of Griqualand West. The bill passed for that purpose . . . will shortly be proclaimed.'

This announcement is said to have 'electrified' the citizens of Kimberley. Although the bill annexing Griqualand West to the Cape had been passed by the Cape Assembly in 1877, nothing had been done about it. There seemed, in fact, every reason to think that the vehement protests made in Kimberley had had the desired effect. Indeed, only a matter of months before Sir Bartle Frere made his announcement, the Prime Minister of the Cape had visited the diamond fields and assured the diggers that he had no intention of proceeding with the annexation against their wishes. This, according to Dr Matthews, had lulled the inhabitants of Kimberley 'into a sense of false security'.

But Dr Matthews was probably exaggerating. To any observant Kimberleyite it must have been obvious that the Imperial authorities fully intended to abandon the troublesome Crown Colony. Since Major Lanyon's departure for the Transvaal in March 1879, no attempt had been made to replace him with a responsible Administrator. For a short period the former Captain Charles Warren had acted as Administrator – causing much indignation when he attempted to sack the Attorney General – and he had been followed by the equally unpopular Mr Justice de Wet. Finally a junior Cape magistrate, James Rose Innes, had been sent to Kimberley to preside, as his son put it, over 'the expiring stage of the old regime'. How, in the circumstances, could anyone have felt secure?

But angry the majority of diggers undoubtedly were. Frere's abrupt announcement sparked off yet another round of exasperated protests. In the Legislative Council, Dr Matthews and George Bottomley, the elected members for Kimberley, tabled a formal motion objecting to the annexation. Such a move, they maintained, 'would be detrimental to the best interests of the province, and opposed to the wishes of the inhabitants'. They were solidly supported by a crowded meeting held in the Theatre Royal a fortnight later. The arguments put forward were much as before: the public had not been consulted; the Cape laws could not be applied to an industrial community; Griqualand West would be inadequately represented in the Cape Assembly.

Of these various objections it was probably the last which caused the greatest concern. Under the terms of the annexation act, Griqualand West was to have much the same representation as it had had in the much smaller Legislative Council: a mere four seats–two for Kimberley and two for the Barkly district. This, for a community acknowledged as the richest and most progressive in the country, was considered ridiculous. It was something which worried even the most amenable of Kimberley's citizens. Cecil Rhodes had pleaded the point in the letter he wrote to J.X. Merriman shortly after Frere's announcement.

'We are evidently to be annexed,' Rhodes had said. 'I hope if there is a chance of increased representation for this place you will not oppose it . . . when the Griqualand West question comes up, show a consideration for this Province–the community here always thinks that whenever you get a chance you abuse them and never give them fair play. There will be two opportunities . . . namely, an increased representation and railway extension here, both of which are fairly due, you *must* remember that the Griqualand West of 1880 and that of 1877 are two very different places.'

But neither pleas nor protests made any difference. The Act passed in 1877 remained intact. There was nothing that could stop its acceptance in the Legislative Council: the casting vote, as always, was in the hands of the acting Administrator and, sympathetic as Rose Innes might have been, he, like others before him, had his orders and carried them out.

When the matter was finally debated, on 30 September 1880, Dr Matthews made one last despairing protest. It was, as he well knew, a futile gesture. Turning to Rose Innes at the end of his speech, he said: 'I feel like a man who has been wrongly convicted, but the jury have given their verdict and it remains with you, sir, as judge today to pass the sentence. As the mouthpiece of the law you must do its behests, but I protest against the passing of a sentence of capital punishment.'

The sentence was passed. Rose Innes gave his vote in favour of annexation and, on 15 October 1880, Griqualand West was formally incorporated with the Cape Colony.

The first parliamentary elections were announced for March 1881. There was no immediate rush of candidates for the four seats. Kimberley had had more than its share of elections over the past few years. There had been elections for the Legislative Council, elections for the Town Council and various by-elections for both councils. The novelty of voting was wearing exceedingly thin.

But there was more to the prevailing apathy than that. Election to the Cape Assembly lacked the attraction of local politics. Not only was the election contest costly but the successful candidates would be forced to spend lengthy periods in Cape Town, and their business interests could suffer. To the money-conscious inhabitants of Griqualand West this was a serious consideration. While the importance of the diamond industry's being strongly represented at the Cape was generally recognised, most local politicians were prepared to hand over this responsibility to others.

From the outset it was acknowledged that, whatever the competition, the Kimberley seats were likely to attract more candidates than those of the Barkly

The Members for Barkly West, Cecil Rhodes, aged 28, and Frank Orpen, photographed shortly after taking their seats in the Cape House of Assembly. (J)

Dr J.W. Matthews and his son. Matthews, a popular Kimberley physician, was the first senior member for Kimberley to be elected to the Cape Assembly, in March 1881. (K)

Pniel Road photographed from the Kimberley Mine Dumps about 1880. The building on the right-hand side, where the office of Julius Pam is clearly visible, also bears the name Barnato Brothers. Note how the Kimberley Mine is encroaching upon the town — some buildings nearly covered by debris. (M) district. Kimberley was the heart of the diamond industry, big business was centred there, and electioneering in the town was easier than canvassing the widespread rural area. As it happened, the Barkly seats were not contested. Only two candidates stood. One was Frank Orpen, an Irishman whose family had long been active in South African politics; the other was Cecil Rhodes. That Rhodes should have chosen Barkly rather than Kimberley, came as something of a surprise. He had had little to do with the river diggings and his interests were bound up with the town. However, it proved a wise choice. Although he was not opposed at Barkly in 1881, Rhodes was later to hold the seat against fierce competition. Even when his reputation in South Africa was at its lowest, nothing could dislodge him from his entrenched position. He represented Barkly – or Barkly West as it became – until the day he died.

The first candidates to offer themselves for the Kimberley seats were the two former members of the Legislative Council, Dr Matthews and George Bottomley. Several other names, including that of Barney Barnato, were bandied about as possible contestants. In the end, however, it was the indefatigable J.B. Robinson who rose to the challenge. He accepted nomination with a show of reluctance but, once the contest opened, his diffidence disappeared. With Barney Barnato as his campaign manager, and backed by several other financiers, he went all out to win.

As election day drew near, some of Kimberley's old fighting spirit reasserted itself. Robinson's supporters, led by 'a capital brass band' paraded the town touting for votes and Dr Matthews's supporters retaliated by forming a torch-light procession and pelting their opponents with stones. None of this was Dr Matthews's fault. Personally, he fought a clean campaign against what he considered to be overwhelming odds. His rivals seemed to have all the advantages. 'The unlimited expenditure of money by the one (Robinson)', he complained, 'and the pertinacious sectarian adherents (the Good Templars) of the other, proved a formidable opposition.' But Dr Matthews's own popularity was not to be discounted. In the end he finished top of the poll, with Robinson coming a close second. It was the abstemious George Bottomley who again lost out.

(2)

Having packed their representatives off to Cape Town, the Kimberley capitalists went on with the serious business of company mining. The 'share mania' was as frenetic as ever. Lou Cohen, who had been absent from the town for some months, returned shortly after the elections to find 'the place strangely altered'.

'The old time digger,' he says, 'the farmer-digger, the gentleman-digger had almost disappeared, and in their place had sprung up a mushroom breed of financiers, who were destined in the near future to put their hands deep in the pockets of the British public, and form the cradle of a brood of costers and aliens, whose business methods later made South African company promoting a vehicle for wholesale plunder and chicanery. In 1881, that bubble year, there were in Kimberley more than a dozen companies.'

Cohen was jaundiced. Like many another unfortunate speculator he had invested badly and missed out on the 'company boom'. It riled him to see his former, more astute, colleagues thriving. Not the least of these newly prosperous financiers was Cohen's old partner, Barney Barnato.

It was impossible to miss Barney in Kimberley: he was to be seen everywhere–at the Diamond Market, at the diggings and on the stage. Always a dandy, he was now in a position to indulge his passion for clothes to the full. He always looked immaculate. The heat might be gruelling but, with his pince-nez, his starched collars, his bow-ties, his buttonholes and his spats, he cut a jaunty figure. And he had every reason to be jaunty. The Barnato companies were flourishing. In June 1881 the brothers published their first quarterly report which showed that they had mined 10,328¼ carats of diamonds in three months and sold them for £17,478. 6s. 3d. This, Barney assured his shareholders, had been no fluke. 'There is every prospect of a much larger dividend next quarter,' he boasted. The following month saw the opening of the Barnato Stock Exchange: the second of its kind in Kimberley. (The Kimberley Royal Stock Exchange had opened a few months earlier on 2 February 1881.) It is hardly surprising that Lou Cohen was scathing about the 'mushroom breed of financiers'.

But if business was being conducted on a different scale, the town itself looked much the same. It was still as hot, still as dusty, still as plagued with flies and still as unlovely as ever. The majority of its buildings were still mere corrugated-iron sheds; one could almost count the straggling dry-leaved trees. The bars were packed with bragging customers, the shops crammed with expensive goods; hopeful traders were still dreaming of the day when the arrival of the railway would solve their transport problems. Complaints about the drainage, the water supply, the pot-holed roads and the local politicians were as loud as ever. Four years of municipal rule had, to outward appearances, made precious little impression on Kimberley.

Lady Florence Dixie, a spirited English journalist, visiting the diamond fields in 1881, had little to say in favour of the 'vast straggling town'. Admittedly she did not see it at its best. 'Our first impressions of Kimberley', she wrote, 'were made in a whirlwind of dust, which continued to blow about in large clouds the whole of that day.' As these were not only her first, but her sole, impressions of the town her report was naturally prejudiced. Nevertheless, her host did his best to impress her. She was taken on a tour of the Carnarvon Hospital, which she, unlike Trollope, found far from perfect. Not even Sister Henrietta's efficient organisation could offset her feeling of claustrophobia in the wards. In the adjoining general hospital for non-paying patients conditions were nothing short of appalling. The place, she discovered, was run entirely by an old man and his wife who were expected to do all the cooking and cleaning as well as the nursing. The wind and rain beat into the ward for white patients, and the walls were damp and unhealthy looking. But what shocked her most was the 'room or out-house set aside for Kaffirs'. This, she said, 'more resembled a barn, as indeed it was, than anything else; and the miserable aspect

Dr and Mrs William Grimmer. Dr Grimmer was the first medical superintendent of the Carnarvon Hospital, and his family played an important part in the development of Kimberley. (M)

The middle-aged J. B. Robinson. (S)

Jones Street, Kimberley, in 1881, showing Dutoitspan Road intersection and the first Theatre Royal in Dutoitspan Road. In the background can be seen that all-too-familiar Kimberley menace — an approaching dust storm.

of the poor sufferers therein was pitiable to behold. Many lay on mattresses on the ground, where the cold draughts swept over them night and day, and on which they were stretched out, helpless to move or assist themselves.'

Disgraceful as conditions at the hospital undoubtedly were, Lady Florence was wrong in thinking that nobody cared. The overworked medical staff had long been concerned about the non-paying patients and even then plans were going ahead to build an extra wing onto the general hospital. The foundation stone for this wing was to be laid by Kimberley's new Mayor, Mr Moses Cornwall, the following year and in October of that year the amalgamation of the old Diggers Central Hospital and the Carnarvon Hospital was finally agreed to. The combined hospitals became the Kimberley Hospital, which was not only to achieve fame as the training school for Sister Henrietta's remarkable nurses, but as the largest and best-equipped hospital in the Cape Colony. Soon it could boast a working staff of nearly 50 and had '66 surgical and 42 medical beds for the Bantu, 20 for poor Whites and 20 for paying Whites and an isolation ward of four beds'.

But of this Lady Florence knew nothing. Nor was she aware of the long fight that had been put up to improve the Kimberley gaol. On being conducted over the prison by the governor, she had some tart observations to make about the institution which Stephen Massett had so lavishly praised. She was horrified to find that the prisoners, whatever their crime, were herded together indiscriminately, the only distinction being that murderers were kept chained hand and foot (even the less critical Trollope had protested that there should be separate rooms for those awaiting trial and those committed). Most of the prisoners were serving sentences for illicit diamond buying and Lady Florence was surprised to discover among them 'men as well as women, some of whom were respectable people of the upper class in Kimberley'. But this was something which would only have shocked a stranger. As everyone on the diggings was fully aware, I.D.B. knew no distinction of race, sex or class.

The trouble with ill-informed critics of Kimberley was that, for the most part, they were blissfully ignorant of the tremendous burden placed upon the local authorities. No sooner was one problem overcome than another appeared. A graphic example of this was given when a fire broke out in Mainstreet, shortly after Lady Florence's departure. Everybody, one would have thought, was only too alive to the persistent threat of fire during the summer months. But when, on Sunday 11 December 1881, flames were seen coming from Mr Caples's boot-shop, the Volunteer Fire Brigade proved worse than useless. For a long time, the fire-engine–which had cost £400–could not be found. When it was eventually discovered, carefully covered over in a stable, there were no horses, no harness and no men to move it. Luckily there was no wind that day to fan the flames. As it was, the fire was brought under control only by the efforts of the Mayor, the Town Clerk, the Sanitary Inspector and his staff of Zulu labourers, who formed a chain along which buckets of water were passed from a nearby well.

It was partly as a result of this conflagration that the Town Council hit upon the novel idea of offering a reward of £5 to the first person to arrive at the scene of a fire with a load of water.

Lack of water remained Kimberley's most pressing problem. Not only was water needed for fire-fighting and drinking, but it was essential for washing blue-ground in the mines. It was to overcome this last problem that Thomas Lynch founded the Griqualand West Railway and Water Company in 1880. Lynch proposed to build a railway between Kimberley and the Vaal in order to convey the blue-ground to the river. Later, however, this scheme was scotched. It was decided it would be much better to bring water to the mines and also ensure a water supply for the town. This was an enlargement of Richard Southey's original plan which had been frustrated by subsequent Administrators. Now a more determined effort was made. Lynch promoted the Kimberley Waterworks Company to undertake the work.

Machinery was obtained from London, specially designed by Mr G.A. Cowper of Westminster, and work went ahead on laying the main line – which was to stretch from a reservoir at Newton, on the outskirts of Kimberley, to the Vaal. The scheme was initiated by the Mayor, Moses Cornwall, who turned the first sod of the works on 19 May 1881. It was a festive occasion, accompanied by hilarious speeches and the drinking of bumpers of champagne. 'Mr Lynch', trumpeted the *Independent,* 'may safely be called the first and greatest public benefactor Kimberley has ever been able to claim as its own.'

In April the following year, Moses Cornwall again wielded his ceremonial silver-bladed spade when the first inlet pipe was laid at Newton. The scheme was justly hailed as little short of remarkable. One of its most unusual features was, in a way, typical of Kimberley: to avoid the high cost of transportation, the pipe line was constructed of wrought-iron instead of the conventional, but much heavier, cast-iron pipes. The first trial of the pumping-system took place in October 1882, and at the beginning of the following month the Waterworks Company announced that it would shortly be prepared to supply Vaal River water at the rate of 1s. 3d. per 100 gallons. 'Soon', claimed a proud citizen, 'there would be no reason to fear, when drinking what was known as "Adam's ale", that there was any chance of imbibing a solution of dead Kaffir.'

That great day came at the beginning of the following year. First, early in January, water was pumped to the mines, and two months later the town was supplied. Kimberley, plagued for years by drought and dryness, was at last able to drink freely and without fear. The gardens of the town suddenly took on new life and colour. So brightly did they bloom that two years later, in April 1884, a group of enthusiasts were able to form the Griqualand West Horticultural Society. The barren veld could at last yield more than diamonds.

But this was not the only marvel of 1882. By the time water reached the town, Kimberley had already taken another enormous stride forward. It had become the first town in the southern hemisphere to have its streets illuminated by electric arc lamps.

The idea of lighting Kimberley's dark, often dangerous, streets by electricity had long been debated. It seemed only right that South Africa's most go-ahead town should pioneer such a novel scheme. What could be more fitting than that the centre of the diamond fields should glitter at night? So insistent was the agitation that, at a public meeting held towards the end of 1881, it was agreed that the matter be decided by popular vote. The result of a poll taken on Saturday 17 December showed a majority in favour and the Town Council was authorised to negotiate a lighting system.

Within a matter of weeks a contract was arranged with the Cape Electric Light and Telephone Company, who undertook to maintain thirty-two lamps of two thousand candle power at the cost of £7,000 a year. There was only one snag: the contract could not be ratified until the lighting system was in working order. This, at first, looked like undermining the entire scheme.

The first experimental trial, held on municipal grounds in February 1882, was a dismal failure. It was discovered that most of the lamps had been damaged in transit and, instead of the expected flood of light, there was merely a spluttering sparkle. The lamps were eventually repaired; further experiments were made; and finally one or two public buildings were successfully illuminated. For all that, public confidence had been severely shaken.

At a series of lively public meetings, held after the first failure, protests against the scheme were loud and vehement. A vote taken at one of the meetings showed that 162 were in favour of continuing with the street lighting and 133 were against. Accusations were made against certain councillors who were said to have an interest in the Cape Electric Light Company. In July an unsuccessful attempt was made to test the matter in court. Not surprisingly, the Town Council became extremely wary. It decided to cut the original plan by half and, in August 1882, cautiously agreed to the erection of sixteen electric light standards.

Four of the new lamps were installed in the Market-square and the rest dotted about the town. They were unceremoniously switched on on 1 September 1882. The result might not have been quite as dazzling as the Town Council had bargained for, but of the astonishment of the African population there was no doubt whatsoever. Here, indeed, was a brilliant illustration of the white man's magic.

Less spectacular, but every bit as welcome, were the improvements being made to Kimberley's erratic transport system. The need for cheaper, more reliable transport between Kimberley and Dutoitspan had long been recognised. At the beginning of 1882, an attempt was made to introduce a horse-drawn omnibus service which would serve the two centres. This widely advertised venture – launched after several projected schemes had been abandoned – was made to sound far grander than in fact it was. The much acclaimed 'buses' were nothing more than a string of carts – one equipped with bars for the conveyance of convicts–roped together and pulled by eight horses. However, by charging a maximum fare of one shilling each way, it cut costs considerably and, to the chagrin of profiteering cab-drivers, proved extremely popular. But ultimate success was defeated by the appalling state of the Dutoitspan road. Jolting, lurching and often swaying in the most unpredictable manner, the string of carts was difficult to control and eventually the service had to be abandoned. Nevertheless, it was fun while it lasted.

Culturally, also, Kimberley was advancing. Nothing emphasised this more

BARKLY POST & PASSENGER CARTS
Run Daily to and from Kimberley to Barkly.

Advertisement for the Barkly Post and Passenger Carts, which appeared in the *Diamond Fields Advertiser*, January 1882. (K)

The first Kimberley Club building, with one of Kimberley's original electric light standards opposite it, about 1883 or 1884. (K)

A group of early members of the Kimberley Club photographed outside temporary premises in 1881: left to right, seated, C.E. Nind, E.W. Tarry, George Hull, Henry Dunsmure, Pat Sim, Bob Graham; standing, George Rowe, F.R. Despard, , James Benningfield, Maynard, George Richards, Dr J.A.J. Smith. (M)

than the founding, in August 1881, of the Kimberley Club. Clubs had always featured prominently in life at the diggings. By the early 1880s the town could boast several social and sporting clubs, the best known being the Craven Club in Main-street. But, plush, popular and well patronised as the Craven was, it could hardly be called exclusive. Often overcrowded, sometimes downright rowdy, it had never really shaken off its pub-like origins. The need for a more dignified club – a club on the lines of the London prototypes – had long been felt. As far back as 1876, attempts had been made to acquire suitable properties for such a club, but not until the advent of company mining and the rise of a Kimberley élite did the vaguely discussed plans become more purposeful.

The idea is said to have originated with some leading members of the Craven Club. At a time when company promoting was fashionable, they decided to launch the new venture as a joint-stock company. An advertisement was placed in the press calling for designs for a new club-house, the cost not to exceed £6,000. The first meeting of the company was held in May 1881 and seventy-four well-known citizens duly pledged themselves to take one debenture share of £100 in the proposed Kimberley Club. Prominent among the shareholders were Cecil Rhodes and his partner, Charles Rudd; J.B. Robinson and his company manager, Lionel Phillips; John Birbeck, the former Mayor, and several prosperous merchants. There were also a fair number of professional men, such as Theodore Reunert, a successful young engineer; J.H. Lange, an attorney and former Clerk of the Legislative Council; and those popular physicians, Dr Josiah Matthews and Dr Leander Starr Jameson. The new Club had got off to a promising start.

It took the best part of a year to complete the double-storied building in the Dutoitspan road; members did not move into the Club until August 1882. But the wait had been worth while. The new premises exceeded everyone's expectations. 'It beats anything of the kind I was ever in,' enthused young Neville Pickering, the newly appointed secretary of the De Beers Mining Company, on 14 September 1882. 'We have our dinners and dances – one finds oneself in evening dress every night. It's ruination to health and pocket. And then our Club is such perfection. Electric bells wherever you like to touch. Velvet pile and Turkey carpets to walk upon and then one loses oneself in a luxurious lounge. This reminds me of an advertisement I remember seeing at home: Call a spade a spade, but call our new velvet lounges the very essence of luxury and extreme comfort.'

Neville Pickering was in a position to appreciate such elegance. It was in marked contrast to his own living-quarters. He had only recently arrived in Kimberley and, besides being appointed secretary of De Beers Mining Company, he was sharing a cottage opposite the Natal Cricket Ground with Cecil Rhodes. Now that Rhodes had taken his degree at Oxford and had been elected a member of the Cape Assembly, his time was divided between Kimberley and Cape Town. The cottage he shared with Neville Pickering was, to all intents and purposes, his permanent home. Visitors to it never ceased to be amazed. One such visitor was James Rose Innes, the son of the last acting Administrator. He was taken on a tour of Kimberley when he visited Griqualand West during the last days of his father's term of office. 'After a morning of sightseeing,' he says, 'I lunched at the club with Robert Dundas Graham, who prided himself on his knowledge of Kimberley. He would show, he said, one sight which I had not seen. He took me to a wood and iron house of the usual pre-railway type; an outside door opened from the street into the small shabby bedroom, on the iron stretcher an old Gladstone bag sagged in the middle, served as a bolster for a dingy pillow. "That is the bed of a man worth £100,000, and I consider it one of the sights of Kimberley," said Graham. We were in the bedroom of Cecil Rhodes.'

In fact there was nothing so unusual about Rhodes's spartan way of life. This is how many rich Kimberley bachelors lived. But that men like Rhodes and Pickering should have welcomed the luxury of the new club is not surprising. There, at least, they could forget the dust and grime of the diggings and relax in some sort of style. Mercifully the Kimberley Club was never to become as sedate as its founders may have intended. The rough-and-ready, hard-drinking habits of the mining magnates died hard; they did not make for stodginess. But what it lacked in propriety, it more than made up for in prosperity. 'The place was . . . ' as a later visitor remarked, 'stuffed with money – more millionaires to the square foot than any other place in the world.' This, in itself, tended to make the Club a typical, if exclusive, Kimberley institution.

The 'company boom' which launched the Kimberley Club was also responsible for reviving another aspect of the town's cultural life. In 1880 a group of concerned citizens had met to discuss the sorry state of the Public Library. This literary venture, started so hopefully seven years earlier, had failed to live up to its initial promise. Lack of books, lack of funds and lack of interest had made it a poor rival to Mr George Goch's fashionable Circulating Library, which proudly informed prospective subscribers: 'Books to suit all (except vicious) tastes will be found on the shelves.' While not wanting to fill the only gap on Mr Goch's shelves, the meeting of 1880 set out to rescue the Public Library by forming it into a joint-stock company. A trust deed was drawn up, shares were issued and an ambitious new building was planned. Unfortunately the shareholders ambitions outran their assets. At the first annual meeting held under the new trust deed, on 15 March 1882, it was announced that 'the public had not come forward in support of the Institution as anticipated, the income being £40 per month and expenditure £71 per month'.

For all that, the shareholders refused to give up. There was a crying need, it was maintained, to provide a 'resort for young men and others, where light literature and periodicals would be found to beguile an hour or so, that would otherwise be spent in billiard saloons and other places'. Thanks to these worthy sentiments a proposal that the company be dissolved was defeated. At a second meeting, held a few days later, the secretary was able to report that the Government had agreed to give an immediate grant of £500, and an annual grant of £200. If private enterprise had failed to resolve the library problem, it had at least succeeded in pricking the conscience of officialdom, which, with so many changes of regime, had become lax.

However, Kimberley decided not to rely entirely on the Cape Government.

At the first Town Council meeting in July 1882 it was confirmed that the municipality was to purchase the Kimberley Public Library and Institute Building. The shareholders agreed to transfer the property to the Town Council without delay and use the purchase money to discharge its liabilities, which then amounted to £4,200. The Mayor and Councillors intended, as soon as the affairs of the joint-stock company had been settled, 'to accept charge of the Library in the interest of the public of Kimberley'.

This transaction, unimportant as it might appear, is not without significance. As much as anything it reflects the growing sense of civic responsibility which was now becoming apparent. The old taunt that Kimberley was a place where men 'made their pile' and then cleared out was no longer as true as it had been in the early days. Admittedly there was still a floating population of adventurers who, having dabbled unsuccessfully in diamonds, quickly departed. It was also noticeable that few really rich magnates seemed prepared to build themselves a Kimberley home worthy of their wealth and status. They would, for the most part, have agreed with Anthony Trollope's observation: 'Why try to enjoy life here, this wretched life, when so soon there is a life coming which is to be so infinitely better?' That notion had long consoled Christians, said Trollope, so why not the rich men of Kimberley?

But while this remained the attitude of some, it was no longer true of everyone. There was a solid core of citizens – not necessarily rich, not necessarily remarkable – who were beginning to regard Kimberley as their permanent home. And it was from their ranks that men were now being attracted to the Town Council. They were the plodding, earnest committee men who form the backbone of every established town or city; it was they, probably more than their colourful predecessors, who became the real pioneers of Kimberley.

Civic pride, however, was not confined to Kimberley. Even neglected Dutoitspan took on a new lease of life. It started when its inhabitants petitioned the Cape Governor to change its status to that of a municipality. 'The name of such Municipality', stated the petition, 'shall be Beaconsfield.' This was a belated tribute to the former British Prime Minister, Lord Beaconsfield (Benjamin Disraeli), who had died in April 1881. The petition was granted and, on 16 August 1883, Dutoitspan officially became Beaconsfield.

Not everyone welcomed the change. It took some time for the new name to catch on. Newspapers continued to report the doings of Dutoitspan, and most of the old inhabitants referred to the place affectionately as 'the Pan'.

Two months later, in October 1883, the recently elected Village Management Board was replaced by a Municipal Council. This heralded the beginnings of the new township. At the first meeting of the Council, held in the Good Templars Hall, Mr S. C. Austin was elected Mayor, and Mr C. K. O'Molony became Town Clerk. Plans went ahead for laying out streets, for bringing water and for installing a more efficient sanitary system.

To accomplish all this was not, as John Angove remarks, 'the work of a few days'. Several years were to pass before the neatly planned township was pulled into shape. Not that there was a lack of enthusiasm; far from it. So lively were

New Main Street, Kimberley, in 1881, showing original Presbyterian Church, and Kimberley Public Library building under construction. The Library later became the old Town Hall. (K)

Bultfontein and Dutoitspan villages. (K)

the early meetings of the Beaconsfield Council that a policeman had to be stationed in the Council Chamber to eject unruly members. It is hardly surprising that one of the first public buildings to be erected was a handsome Court House 'built of rough cut stone of the most durable quality'.

Yet, ominous though it might have appeared, the new Court House did symbolise the emergence of Beaconsfield from the straggling, once proud, camp of Dutoitspan.

(3)

But the outward signs of progress, permanency and prosperity, which typified the early 1880s, were deceptive. All was not what it seemed. While Kimberley appeared to be growing, the diamond industry was once again on the point of decline. The main cause of this sudden change of fortune was the unexpected collapse of the 'company boom'.

It had been too frenetic, too undisciplined to last. Within a matter of months–between the end of 1880 and the beginning of 1881–the number of companies floated in the various mines had risen from half-a-dozen to seventy-one. Who or what was responsible for the launching of these often worthless, sometimes bogus, companies is difficult to fathom. Some claim it was the work of unscrupulous promoters trying to offload worked-out claims on an un-suspecting public. Others say it was inspired by the success of the early companies started by Francis Baring-Gould and Jules Porges: everybody suddenly wanted to cash in on a good thing. The more flippant put it down to Kimberley's unquenchable gambling spirit. Whatever the cause, the effects were as extraordinary as they were inexplicable. Nothing in Kimberley's history was to equal the mad scramble for shares during the height of the boom.

'The various offices of companies in formation', says Dr Matthews, 'were simply stormed, and those who could not get in at the door from the pressure of the crowd, threw their applications for shares (to which were attached cheques and bank notes) through the windows, trusting to chance that they might be picked up. It is difficult to picture the eagerness, the plots, the rage of the excited multitude bent on securing this, the magic scrip, which was to make the needy rich and the embarrassed free.

'It was astonishing how the mania seized on all classes in Kimberley, from the highest to the lowest . . . how every one, doctors and lawyers, masters and servants, shop-keepers and workmen, men of the pen and men of the sword, magistrates and I.D.B.'s, Englishmen and foreigners, rushed wildly into the wonderful game of speculation.'

It was all a snare and a delusion. Many of the companies were formed without capital, some were blatantly fraudulent. To attract investors, some promoters lavishly 'salted' their claims with diamonds before inviting would-be shareholders to inspect them. The story was told of one rash speculator who, going down a shaft to examine a possible investment, 'had a hail-storm of little diamonds showered on him (some of which lit on the brim of his hat) which were meant for him to unearth in the loose ground at the bottom'. He was lucky. Some of the companies floated did not even have claims for their investors to inspect. While the mania lasted all that was needed to spark off an indiscriminate buying spree was an office and a crowd.

It was the local banks that first took fright. Many bank managers had initially been carried away by the general excitement and had freely advanced money on doubtful security. But when the scramble for shares showed signs of getting out of hand they had quickly drawn in their horns. In the middle of 1881 the banks clamped down on loans, refusing to make any more advances on scrip for mining companies. There was an immediate outcry from frustrated speculators, many of whom had mortgaged their original shares to purchase more. The action of the banks was condemned as 'arbitrary and injudicious'. The banks, however, stood firm: it quickly became apparent that, protests or not, they intended to stand by their decision.

This was all that was needed to set the entire sharebuying process in reverse. The rush to invest was quickly turned into a stampede to sell up. By the end of the year most of the dubious companies had collapsed and shares in the more reputable concerns began to decline. Kimberley was heading for the most serious financial crisis in its history.

Shaky as the financial situation had become, it was made much worse by conditions in the mines themselves. There was something uncanny about the onslaught of disasters that rocked Kimberley throughout 1882. In February of that year the diggings experienced one of the most destructive storms they had ever known. Heralded by tremendous claps of thunder and flashes of lightning, the heavens opened and a deluge of rain was followed by a terrifying whirlwind. Buildings were ripped in half, roofs were torn from offices, sheets of iron were sent hurtling through the air, shacks, shanties and tin huts were flattened. It took days to clear the debris from the streets; the entrances of some business premises were blocked and the top of the Barnato Chambers was piled high with mangled corrugated iron. What made the storm appear all the more ominous was the fact that, by some freak, most of the damage occurred within a two hundred yards' radius of the Kimberley Mine. It was as though that particular mine had been singled out – that a sinister warning had been sounded.

Certainly later events seemed to bear out this superstition. Throughout 1882 reef fell in the Kimberley Mine with alarming regularity. Hundreds of claims – including those of the Barnato Company and J. B. Robinson's Standard Company – were buried in the land-slips and work in the centre of the mine came to a standstill. Many of the smaller companies, which had barely survived the financial hazards of the year before, were finally put out of business by the falling reef of 1882. The large brigade of ruined speculators was now joined by a veritable army of unemployed diggers and labourers.

It was a year of frightening signs and portents. Not only Kimberley but the entire Cape was threatened with disaster when, in the middle of the year, a smallpox epidemic broke out in Cape Town. The disease – originating from a visiting steamship, the *Drummond Castle* – quickly spread throughout the southern Cape. Within a matter of weeks cases were being reported from

Worcester and the railway camp at Victoria West. The Kimberley Town Council immediately sprang into action. A wire was sent to the Secretary of the Medical Board at Cape Town asking for permission to proclaim the Contagious Diseases Act. Once the act was published, on 11 July, a vaccination campaign was launched; by the end of the month some 7,000 people had been vaccinated. Unfortunately the campaign appears to have been conducted with more haste than skill. The newspapers were soon reporting cases of people – the Secretary of the Sanitary Board among them – who had died as a result of 'blood poisoning consequent upon vaccination'. Not that this deterred the authorities. On the last Sunday in August, no fewer than 2,000 African servants of the mining companies were vaccinated in a single day by two doctors working from daybreak to sunset.

Fear that the infection would spread among the mine labourers, and so threaten the entire diamond industry, was not the least of the Town Council's concerns. On the grounds that prevention could be as effective as vaccination, it was decided to set up a quarantine station at Modder River, some twenty odd miles south of Kimberley. Most vehicles entering Griqualand West from the Cape crossed the Modder; to prevent traffic crossing other river drifts, police patrols were sent out to divert all vehicles to the quarantine station. Come what may, the authorities were determined to keep the dreaded disease away from Kimberley.

The man in charge of the quarantine station was a young, newly arrived, Afrikaans doctor, Hans (Johannes) Sauer. Having recently qualified as a physician, Sauer had leapt at the opportunity to demonstrate his skills. His only reservation was the legality of his position. Did he really, he asked Denis Doyle, the Sanitary Inspector of Kimberley, have the right to place people in quarantine? Was this not interfering with the rights of travellers on the Queen's highway? Doyle had no doubts whatsoever. Pointing to a troop of mounted police, he said, 'There's your law, and behind them is the Kimberley Town Council.'

Sauer remained at the Modder River station for fourteen months. During that time he examined thousands of men, women and children. Travellers from the Cape had either to produce a valid certificate of vaccination or be vaccinated at the station and then pass through a shed to be fumigated by burning sulphur for three minutes. Anyone refusing to submit to Sauer's decrees was forcibly vaccinated and detained in the quarantine camp. This, as Sauer fully realised, was utterly illegal. He says that at one time he had as many as nineteen actions for assault and battery taken out against him, but they were all subsequently dropped. What he could congratulate himself on was the success of the scheme. During his term of duty he spotted fourteen genuine cases of smallpox (two of whom died) and, despite several false alarms, prevented the disease from invading Kimberley.

It was later estimated that well over two thousand cases of smallpox were dealt with in Cape Town alone before the epidemic was brought under control. Hundreds of victims, mainly Coloured, died of the disease. By its prompt action the Kimberley Sanitary Committee – financed entirely by subscriptions raised in the town – had saved the diggings from further disaster. The knowledge gained by Dr Sauer at the Modder River station had made him something of an authority on smallpox. Altogether, one would have thought, some salutary lessons had been learned. Unfortunately this did not prove to be the case.

13

I.D.B.

Had anyone in Kimberley been asked to explain the latest economic depression, he would have had his answer ready. The greatest financial evil of the diggings, it was firmly believed, was the loss sustained by the diamond industry through illicit diamond buying. I.D.B. was made to account for every type of failure. Such things as barren claims, unstable markets, business incompetence and sheer bad luck, did not exist as far as Kimberley bankrupts were concerned. Every ruined digger, speculator or company promotor attributed his downfall to the army of thieves and crooked diamond buyers who plagued the diggings. Nothing would convince them otherwise.

'It is the fashion', commented the *Independent* in 1881, 'to ascribe the failure of many companies to work profitably claims which have always yielded a handsome return in the days of individual diggers to the depredations of the I.D.B. and, no doubt, these scoundrels are responsible for a large portion of the want of success. But they are not the only causes of failure. There is much mismanagement on the part of the companies themselves.'

Eminently sensible as this observation was, it went unheeded. As companies continued to collapse, the hysterical rantings against I.D.B. mounted. Until this evil was stamped out, it was said, there could be no prosperity for Kimberley. Had not I.D.B. been responsible, directly or indirectly, for every crisis that had rocked the diggings? Had it not led to the early riots and tent burnings at New Rush? Had it not contributed to the discontent that sparked off the Black Flag Rebellion? Had it not been the albatross around every Administrator's neck? How could an industry that was undermined by criminals be expected to prosper?

But loud as were the complaints, the remedy remained as elusive as ever. All attempts to deal with I.D.B. by legislation had failed miserably. There was not a Government official who had not tried, in one way or another, to find a solution to the problem. They had all been forced to admit defeat.

It was Sir Henry Barkly who had first introduced a law which attempted to regulate diamond-buying transactions. On 16 April 1872 he had issued a proclamation requiring all sellers of diamonds to hold a £10 licence and all buyers of diamonds to keep 'intelligible Registers'. Realising how inadequate this legislation was, he had tightened it up the following month by making all unauthorised diamond dealers liable to a fine 'not exceeding three times the value of the diamond or diamonds so brought or received, and in default of payment of the same, to imprisonment, with or without hard labour, for any period not exceeding two years'. This had had little or no effect. Nor had further proclamations which debarred canteen keepers from dealing in diamonds and prohibited diamond transactions during daylight hours when African labourers were free from curfew restrictions.

Barkly, and those who followed him, were soon made to realise that unlawful activities could not be regulated by half-hearted laws. Not that this stopped successive Administrators from trying. As late as 1880, James Rose Innes was still using much the same methods with much the same results. In the last session of the old Legislative Council he had introduced two ordinances aimed at controlling I.D.B. The first of these ordinances (No. 8 of 1880) raised the penalty for illicit diamond transactions to £500 and five years' imprisonment for a first offence, and £1,000 and ten years' imprisonment for subsequent offences. The second ordinance (No. 11 of 1880) made provision for a properly organised detective department. Resolute as these moves at first appeared, they did little to improve matters.

The newly formed Detective Department and its star operator, Detective Izdebski, were nothing if not zealous. Once it went into action the number of I.D.B. arrests rose impressively. Much of the department's success, however, resulted from the way in which the notorious 'trapping system' was now perfected. This method of catching criminals, although highly effective, was to become one of the most controversial aspects of the long battle against I.D.B. Anyone wishing to hit at those who professed to uphold law and order in Kimberley could always win sympathy by attacking the 'trapping system'.

In essence, the system was as simple as it was obvious. An African would be thoroughly searched and then given diamonds to take to a suspect buyer. He would be followed by detectives who, at a given signal, would close in and arrest the buyer in the act of taking the diamonds. This method of operating was, of course, wide open to abuse. The African runner was often used purely as an *agent provocateur,* and many an otherwise innocent dealer was lured into a police trap before he had had time to test the runner's credentials. Stories abounded of men who had been forced into seemingly illicit transactions. It earned the Kimberley police a bad reputation. Harry Graumann, who arrived at the Cape in the early 1880s, for instance, says he was afraid to visit the diamond diggings. 'I had been intimidated into believing', he says, 'that anyone was liable to get into trouble at Kimberley in connection with the illicit diamond trade. . . . On all hands one heard stories of detectives putting diamonds into the pockets of innocent people, and then charging them with an offence which has always been punished very severely.'

Trying to defend the 'trapping system' was to give Kimberley legislators many a headache. Nevertheless, even the most disinterested citizens were willing to spring to its defence. Not only did they regard it as essential to the stamping out of I.D.B. but, for the most part, they insisted that it was employed with the utmost caution. 'I can conscientiously say,' declared the fairminded Dr Matthews, 'I have never known one single man found guilty who did not well deserve his punishment.' Stories of wrongful arrest and police persecution originated, in his opinion, from the I.D.B.s – or 'the fraternity of the mystic three letters' as he called them: innocent people had nothing to fear in Kimberley.

Almost as harmful to the Detective Department was the effect their activities had in blunting the public's conscience. The more arrests that were made, the less serious the crime tended to appear. Not only acknowledged criminals, but seemingly highly respectable citizens were soon being hauled before the magistrates. The guilty included, as Lady Florence Dixie had remarked, men and women in every stratum of Kimberley society–from Louis Hond, that well-known character of the pioneering days, to an African known as 'Bloody Fool' whose deadly assault on his wife was represented as secondary to his I.D.B. offence. So many people seemed to be involved in stealing diamonds that the illicit traffic seemed less like a crime and more like a way of life. A popular joke had it that the population of Kimberley was made up of 'those in prison, those who had been, and those who should have been'.

The stigma attached to I.D.B. was no longer as effective as it had once been. The battle of wits waged between members of 'the trade', as it was known, and the Detective Department became a popular topic for table talk. Many an upright citizen was known to dine out on stories of diamonds hidden between the pages of books, in a plate of soup, in the heel of a shoe, or down the bosom of a well-filled dress. Initial expressions of shock quickly dissolved into giggles as one guest tried to top the story of another. Every visitor to Kimberley came away with his favourite I.D.B. story. So many of these stories were told that it is impossible to vouch either for their veracity or their origins. Two, however, were so often repeated that they can be regarded as classics. Both concerned women.

One of these quick-witted ladies was said to be the wife of a somewhat dubious market gardener. She and her husband lived on the outskirts of Kimberley and attracted the attention of the police when their fortune seemed to outgrow their produce. On the day detectives arrived to search their cottage the woman was baking bread and, hearing a knock on the door, quickly stuffed a parcel of diamonds into the dough before putting it into the oven. By the time the police had completed their fruitless search the bread was baked. According to one version of the story the woman then handed the loaf to the detectives and asked them to admire its lightness. Others claim that she actually served tea to the exhausted raiding-party, calmly cutting slices of bread from the diamond-less end of the loaf. In either case, it was considered a huge joke.

The other woman was the landlady of a dubious hotel. When the police called on her she was entertaining a party of I.D.B.s who had gloatingly spread their latest haul on one of the diningroom tables. As the detectives entered the front door of the hotel, the landlady deftly gathered up the tablecloth and hurried out to the kitchen. Once again the police search revealed nothing. The I.D.B. party was delighted. But not for long. When they asked for their diamonds back, the landlady stared at them blankly. She knew nothing, she said, of any diamonds and politely suggested that they enquire about them at the police station. The I.D.B.s were not amused but the rest of Kimberley rocked with laughter.

But if such stories were typical, they bore little relation to the true nature of the crime. They only involved minor offenders; men and women who dealt in a handful of diamonds at a time. It was well known that I.D.B. was often organised on a much larger scale. The failure of the police to trap the men behind such large-scale operations had resulted in a general lack of confidence in police methods; ways were sought to tackle the problem un-officially. In March 1880, for instance, the Kimberley, Dutoitspan and De Beers Mining Boards held a joint meeting to explore the possibility of financing a private detective system. This immediately raised a number of delicate questions. In his opening address, the chairman wanted to know whether the meeting 'had for its object the detection of this (I.D.B.) traffic, whether amongst licensed diamond buyers, brokers or diggers'? Everyone was well aware of what he meant: an efficient detective system was bound to uncover a good deal more than petty pilfering. How many prominent citizens might not then be implicated?

J.B. Robinson, who was very active in the fight against I.D.B., underlined what they were all thinking. He told them that the British Government had recently sent out an officer to enquire into the official detective system in Kimberley. 'I had a long discussion with him on the subject,' said Robinson; 'as I understood him his view was this: "Your detective system as worked at present is not efficient, as I find from some enquiries that only the small ones are caught here and the large ones escape," and he said "a system like that isn't in force anywhere in the world." ' Robinson proposed that they should act on the officer's advice and employ special detectives from Scotland Yard who, he said, would cost them about £12,000 a year.

One important result of this meeting was the establishment, on 15 June 1881, of the Diamond Mining Protection Society, in which J.B. Robinson played a prominent part. The object of the society was to agitate for an amendment of the laws governing the diamond trade and to assist the detective force then operating in Kimberley.

But this, as they soon discovered, was easier said than done. At a public meeting held by the society in March 1882, it was reported that of the ninety I.D.B. cases that had come before the magistrates in the previous six months no fewer than thirty had been withdrawn because key witnesses had been 'spirited' away or other irregularities had occurred. To trap I.D.B.s was one thing but, so long as sharp lawyers were in practice, to bring them to justice was quite another. There were also loud complaints about the way in which Government ordinances were being subverted. What was needed, it was argued, was a system whereby mine labourers could be searched before leaving work, and a law making it illegal to supply Africans with liquor. So long as black men were tempted to steal diamonds in order to buy drink, I.D.B. would flourish.

There was more to it than that, however. Not only the Diamond Mining Protection Society, but most diggers, were agreed that there was an urgent need to tighten up the I.D.B. laws. Only in this way could the real criminals, the large-scale operators, be caught. As things stood it was virtually impossible to track down large quantities of stolen diamonds. Claim-holders did not have to account for the stones they sold: it could be assumed that stones in their possession had been found in their claims. The more claims a digger worked, the more safely could he dispose of large quantities of diamonds. If a claim holder was also a licensed diamond buyer, the disposal of stones–wherever they came from–was a simple matter indeed. 'The licensed diamond buyers,' says John Angove, 'although sometimes run in, yet too often bamboozled the detectives on account of their being duly licensed buyers of diamonds, when they shielded behind their licence.'

The problem needed to be tackled at its roots. Those roots were embedded in the existing legislation. Now that Griqualand West had its own representatives in the Cape Assembly, it was up to them to get the laws changed.

(2)

The Cape Assembly was not unaware of its obligations. In September 1881 – a few months after the Griqualand West elections – a Mining Commission, under the chairmanship of J.X. Merriman, had been set up to investigate the state of the diamond industry and to make recommendations for improvements. Both Cecil Rhodes and J.B. Robinson had been appointed to serve on it.

Not everyone in Kimberley had welcomed the announcement of Merriman as chairman. Now well established as a Cape politician, the lanky, intellectual and somewhat cynical Merriman was regarded as a disappointed digger who was prejudiced against the diamond industry. His liberal political views were looked upon with suspicion and it was thought that he would influence other members of the Commission, particularly his friend Cecil Rhodes. 'Mr Rhodes' appointment', complained the *Independent,* 'appears to be the one most open to objection . . . everyone knows that so long as Mr Merriman is Chairman of the Commission, Mr Rhodes will follow him as a blind man follows a dog.'

These misgivings were to be proved unnecessary. Rhodes played little part in the deliberations of the Commission. Shortly after his appointment he had departed for his last term at Oxford. It had been left to J.B. Robinson and the Diamond Mining Protection Society to draft the bill that was to be presented in the Cape Assembly. Not only, as might have been expected, were the provisions of this bill most stringent, but Robinson had succeeded in winning Merriman's full support for the proposed legislation. Merriman had seen it simply as a matter of ensuring honesty and fair dealing in an industry vital to the Cape.

The proposed Diamond Trade Act of 1882 came up for discussion when the Cape Assembly met in March of that year. Rhodes was in his seat when the debate opened. Having lost ground to Robinson during the drafting stages of the bill, he was determined to make himself heard in parliament. He was given plenty of opportunity. The debate was nothing if not lively.

The main opposition speaker was James Leonard, a former Attorney General. He commenced his attack by denouncing the Special Diamond Court, the court that dealt with I.D.B. offences. Cases coming before this court were heard by three officials–not always magistrates–and the sentences passed were sometimes reduced or quashed on appeal to the Supreme Court. In Kimberley such reversals were attributed to the quibbles of pettifogging lawyers. Leonard thought differently. 'I have seen cases', he thundered, 'appealed before the Supreme Court in which convictions have been obtained upon evidence which I am certain no jury in the country would convict the commonest black man of the most ordinary crime. . . . The Illicit Diamond Court of Griqualand West is a blot on the judicial system of the country which should not be allowed to remain.'

He went on to denounce, with equal vigour, the notorious trapping system. This system, he maintained, coupled with the judgements of the Kimberley courts, had resulted in the 'grossest injustice' being perpetuated in Griqualand West.

Answering Leonard's attack, Rhodes put up a spirited defence of the Special Courts but was somewhat cornered on the trapping system. 'As regards the system of trapping,' reads a report of his speech, 'he admitted that if one was to argue generally that was a system which no-one could approve of. But the circumstances were very exceptional. . . . He would like anyone to show him any method or means whereby this crime could be checked except by this exceptional and obnoxious system.' He was enthusiastically supported by J.X. Merriman who claimed that something like £40,000 worth of diamonds were stolen every week. Merriman was also in favour of mine workers being searched. All attempts to introduce a searching-system, he said, had been foiled because white men objected to being searched in the same way as black men. Nevertheless he was convinced that such a system was both necessary and possible.

The debate ended with Rhodes moving for a Select Committee to enquire into the whole subject of illicit diamond buying. The motion was approved and Rhodes was appointed chairman of the Select Committee. There were no objections to his appointment. The only other possible chairman would have been J.B. Robinson but unfortunately Robinson was not available. He was still in Kimberley, tied down by one of his never-ending libel suits. However this did not prevent him from making his views known.

As soon as reports of the debate reached Kimberley, Robinson sprang into action. That same afternoon he called a public meeting at the office of the Kimberley Mining Board. George Bottomley was in the chair, but Robinson did most of the talking. A huge crowd turned up to hear him.

He quickly let it be known that he considered Rhodes's defence of the trapping system to be feeble. Unless this system was employed, he told his approving audience, 'you might as well hand over your claims to the illicits themselves'. He went on to read out the proposals which he and the Diamond Mining Protection Society had made. These proposals advocated, among other things, that the police be given powers to search suspects without a warrant and that anyone found in possession of a rough diamond, without a permit, should be liable to a minimum of five years' imprisonment. There was also a strong recommendation that the Cape liquor laws should be amended to prohibit the sale of liquor to Africans in Kimberley.

This last suggestion created an uproar. Canteen owners and shopkeepers saw it as a threat to their trade. Immediately after the meeting a whispering campaign began. It was rumoured that plans were under way to herd Africans into compounds where they would be served by mine-owned shops. There was also talk–inspired by Merriman's contribution to the debate–of an extension of the searching-system. Once the Africans were isolated, it was said, the mining companies would tighten their grip. Everyone employed on the mines would be searched before they left work; white overseers, as well as black labourers, would be forced to strip and be subjected to an undignified examination. It was all the work of the money-grubbing Robinson and that pillar of sobriety, George Bottomley.

A few days later placards attacking Robinson and Bottomley were posted throughout Kimberley. They called upon mine overseers to attend a mass protest meeting. To the older inhabitants it must have seemed like a repetition of the early stages of the Black Flag Rebellion; the posters appeared anonymously and no indication was given of who was organising the meeting. The slogan 'Justice for Licensed Victuallers' did, however, smack strongly of vested interests.

On the evening of the meeting several thousand people packed the Market-square. Robinson arrived early. Determined to have it out with his anonymous opponents, he stamped about defying them to appear. He was stoutly supported by an 'imposing assemblage' of mine overseers who had met at the Kimberley cricket ground and marched in procession to the meeting. They had come not to do battle for the canteen owners, but to support their employers. This unexpected display of loyalty threw the meeting completely out of gear. There was no sign of the nameless organisers. The sight of the grim-faced overseers had, it was said, struck terror 'into the hearts of the demagogues who would fain have misled them'. When it looked as if the crowd would disperse for want of a speaker, Robinson and a few others mounted a platform and made rallying speeches. There was no need for them to say much. A petition to the Cape Assembly–opposing trial by jury and the sale of liquor to Africans–was presented and approved and the meeting fizzled out.

'The 19th of April, 1882', trumpeted the *Diamond Fields Advertiser,* 'will remain a red-letter day in the history of the Diamond Fields, for the reason that on the day named certain infamous combinations against the mining interests were defeated on their own ground, and taught a lesson for all time to come.' This, considering the poor showing of the opposition, was somewhat over-stating the case.

In the Cape Assembly the fight went on. Robinson hurried to Cape Town to play his part. He left Kimberley the day after the Market-square fiasco and was in the House of Assembly when the Select Committee, appointed to investigate illicit diamond buying, reported back. Its findings came as no surprise. The crime of I.D.B. was shown as a formidable threat to the diamond industry and stringent legislation (including 'searching overseers and other employees') was forcefully recommended. Rhodes and Robinson, in rare partnership, teamed up to push the draconian laws through parliament.

Central Company's depositing floors in 1881. Ground left to disintegrate in the sun was broken up by gangs of African labourers. (K)

A typical Kimberley scene in the 1880s, showing teams of oxen in the Market Square. (K)

They had to fight for practically every clause of the bill. Only Rhodes's attempt to retain flogging as a punishment for buyers, as well as stealers, of illicit diamonds was rejected outright. Dr Matthews, the liberal senior member for Kimberley, was largely responsible for this defeat. 'I decidedly objected', he said, 'to flogging being inflicted for what was not a crime against the person but against property. I was so far successful that such brutal ideas were expunged from the act.' Not everyone regarded such humanitarian principles as admirable, however. Dr Matthews was later to be vehemently attacked in sections of the Kimberley press for his 'sensational and somewhat imaginative' ideas on the flogging question.

For his part, Robinson fought the suggestion that three qualified judges should be appointed to hear I.D.B. cases. He had much experience, but little faith, in the courts of Griqualand West. In his opinion, knowledge of the diamond industry counted for more, when dealing with cases involving stolen diamonds, than did knowledge of law. He was only partly successful in his objections. A compromise was reached whereby one judge and 'two others' were appointed to the Special Court.

There were very few other compromises. Most of the recommendations of the Diamond Mining Protection Society were adopted without modification. Detectives were authorised to search for rough diamonds without a warrant; all diamonds passing through the hands of dealers had to be registered and a monthly return made; any diamond buyer suspected of an illicit transaction could be stopped, searched and have his books impounded; the onus of proof of legal possession of diamonds was thrown on the individual in whose custody they were found. The penalty for nearly all the offences listed was fifteen years' imprisonment or a fine of £1,000.

By and large the Griqualand West contingent in the Cape Assembly had good reason to congratulate themselves. When they returned to Kimberley in July 1882, Rhodes and Robinson were hailed as heroes. It had been a tough battle but they had fought it manfully. 'We had great difficulty in passing the Diamond Trade Act,' Robinson was to say. 'This Bill took weeks and weeks–nearly the whole session of 1882.' Only Dr Matthews was in disgrace. His objections to the flogging clause earned him much criticism and this, combined with a decline in his personal fortune – he was on the verge of bankruptcy – proved too much for him. Shortly after the Cape Assembly met again, the following year, Dr Matthews resigned.

There was still one matter outstanding. The new laws did not cover the sale of liquor to Africans. J. B. Robinson, cheered on by Rhodes and George Bottomley – who was soon to become Kimberley's new Mayor – tackled this issue during the next parliamentary session. He proposed that the Cape liquor laws be amended to prohibit the sale of alcohol to Africans within a five-mile radius of any mine. The amendment was favourably received, but was unexpectedly defeated by a majority of nine votes. Robinson fumed; the canteen keepers rejoiced.

The canteen keepers had reason to be pleased. The man largely responsible for the defeat of Robinson's amendment was Dr Matthews's successor,

George Garcia Wolfe. As was well known, Wolfe owed his election, in no small measure, to the support he was given by the Licensed Victuallers Association. He proved a worthy choice. In a brief, but telling speech, he pleaded with the House not to be misled by false reports in the Kimberley press. Robinson had quoted these reports 'in an endeavour to prove the terrible prevalence of drink among natives in Kimberley'. Wolfe maintained that such reports were merely veiled attempts to injure honest tradesmen. If Robinson's amendment was allowed, he declared, it would be 'the first step towards a fatal injury to the real commercial interests of Kimberley'.

Wolfe's accusations were to be echoed in subsequent Kimberley elections. It would take a long time to eradicate the mutual suspicion that was developing between the merchants and the mining magnates.

But, suspicions aside, the Diamond Trade Act of 1882 could be regarded as a triumph for Rhodes and Robinson. Both were proud of the Act and both claimed full credit for having it passed. In Kimberley their supporters were prepared to divide the honours equally. This they did at an impressive ceremony in the Kimberley Town Hall, on 25 September 1883. Rhodes and Robinson were each presented with an 'influentially signed' address which congratulated them on their efforts on the Liquor Bill and regretted that their amendment had not been accepted. They both made long and pompous acceptance speeches. It was a memorable occasion. Never again were these two rich and powerful magnates to share such popular acclaim. 'By their efforts', cooed the *Independent,* 'in the cause of morality and general well-being of the community, Messrs Robinson and Rhodes have well earned the mark of regard which is conferred upon them.'

That was one way of putting it. Others felt differently. The Diamond Trade Act did not always inspire admiration. Many regarded it purely and simply as a capitalist charter. Visitors to South Africa were constantly shocked by its provisions and by the sentiments that inspired it. 'A law of exceptional rigour punishes illicit diamond buying, known in the slang of South Africa as I.D.B.ism,' wrote Lord Randolph Churchill ten years later. 'Under this statute, the ordinary presumption of law in favour of the accused disappears, and an accused person has to prove his innocence in the clearest manner, instead of the accuser having to prove his guilt . . . this tremendous law is in thorough conformity with South African sentiment, which elevates I.D.B.ism almost to the level, if not above the level, of actual homicide.'

But perhaps the most telling criticism of the Act was that its effectiveness proved transitory. New ways of evading the laws were discovered; I.D.B. continued to be a menace. It still is.

(3)

It took some time before loopholes were found in the new laws. When the Diamond Trade Act was passed it seemed foolproof, or as near foolproof as it could be made. It was hailed as the answer to the diamond industry's major problems and for a short period the ships to Europe were said to be crowded with frustrated I.D.B. agents. This exodus, however, could not be attributed entirely to the workings of the Act; much of the credit was undoubtedly due to Kimberley's new police chief, John Larkin Fry. Few men were as active, or as successful, in combating I.D.B. as the zealous Mr Fry.

Born at Rondebosch in the Cape, John Fry was the son of an Anglican clergyman. He had arrived at Dutoitspan in 1871, at the age of thirty-four, after a somewhat chequered career in the Cape Civil Service. Having no luck as a digger, he had eventually been forced to find other employment. At one time he was the acting manager of the London and South African Exploration Company and then served on various Mining Boards until he was appointed Kimberley's Clerk of the Peace. In April 1882—while Rhodes and Robinson were busy pushing the Diamond Trade Act through the Cape Assembly—he had been selected by the Diamond Mining Protection Association to act as the head of the revitalised Detective Department. Efficient, energetic and enterprising, John Fry was considered to be just the man to see that the new laws were implemented as forcefully as they had been framed.

And, for a while, it seemed as if the choice was a wise one. No sooner was the Diamond Trade Act promulgated than Fry sprang into action. For a month or two passenger coaches leaving for Port Elizabeth and Cape Town were stopped at Alexandersfontein and all passengers—including two outraged Anglican Bishops—were systematically searched. This procedure, however, proved more harmful than helpful. So loud were the protests and so few the arrests, that Fry was advised to act more discreetly. He did. Working on the theory that it took a thief to catch a thief, he employed a team of 'reformed' I.D.B.s as traps and succeeded in luring some of the most elusive Kimberley criminals into his net. Backed by the stringent new laws, he was not only able to make arrests but to secure convictions. There was a sharp increase in the number of cases coming before the Special Court and an equally sharp increase in the terms of imprisonment that were handed out.

Nobody felt safe. Long-suspected illicit operators—such as the notorious Mrs Pound, the slippery Annie Penton, the wealthy Harris Philip and Elias Jacobs and another well-known licensed diamond buyer (whose wife later tried to reclaim his confiscated diamonds)—were deftly cornered, found guilty, and given severe sentences. Neither age nor ignorance was accepted as an excuse. At the beginning of 1883, the elderly Mrs Johanna Ventura of Dutoitspan was sentenced to ten years' hard labour for a second offence and a few months later an eleven-year-old boy, Joseph Lange—who was discovered with diamonds hidden in the false pockets of his coat—was sent to a juvenile reformatory for five years. The trapping methods used by John Fry might at times have been questionable (one of his best agents was the suspiciously named Mrs Diamond) but his success was undoubted. 'He showed remarkable astuteness in all his operations. . . .' it was said, 'his prevention of diamond thefts were marked and carried out with an intelligence and vigilance which frequently won for the (Detective) Department the highest encomiums.'

But there were certain areas in which even the astute Mr Fry had to admit defeat. Clever as he was, his powers were limited. The provisions of the

Diamond Trade Act applied only to Griqualand West. Any diamond thief, any dealer in illicit diamonds, any middle man, was safe once he had smuggled his stolen stones across the border into the Orange Free State, the Transvaal, Natal, or even–until 1885–other parts of the Cape Colony. And as, at places, the Free State border merely skirted the diamond diggings, the Free State soon became a refuge for I.D.B.s.

The Free State authorities were not unaware of this. In the year that the Diamond Trade Act was promulgated they had passed an ordinance of even greater severity by which illicit diamond transactions were made liable to a maximum penalty of £2,000 fine, twenty years' hard labour and a hundred lashes. But this was rendered largely ineffective by Free State judges who interpreted it as applying only to areas within six mile of proclaimed diamond diggings. Consequently when the aptly named village of Free Town sprang up across the Free State border, just beyond the prescribed limits from Dutoitspan, it provided a convenient bolt-hole for escaping diamond thieves. Once Free Town had been reached the most notorious I.D.B.s were able openly to ply their trade happily humming the chorus of a popular ditty:

'Over the Free State line,
Whatever is yours is mine.
If I've a stone
It's all my own.
No "John Fry" shall make me groan.'

The story is told of a homestead built on the Cape – Free State boundary. The front room ('voorkamer') was in the Cape, the kitchen in the Free State. Often it is said the police were thwarted in I.D.B. cases because the transaction took place – quite openly – in the Free State section.

Infuriating as all this was for the Detective Department, it at least provided Kimberley with a new source of entertainment. Visitors to the town were often startled when whistles blew and crowds flocked into the street to cheer as a posse of puffing policemen pursued some fleetfooted thief heading for the border. Bets were taken on who would win; more often than not the odds were against the police.

But not all thieves evaded the law in such an obvious manner. Some decamped quietly when things became too hot and a few even managed to escape after their arrest. It was, in fact, the non-appearance in court of a particularly well-known illicit diamond buyer that led to John Fry's downfall.

On Thursday, 20 March 1884, two detectives called upon Isaac Joel, the eldest of Barney Barnato's nephews, at his diamond-buying office in the Barnato Building. Empowered by the new legislation, they demanded to examine his diamond register. Their inspection showed that, of the 1,003¼ carats of rough and uncut diamonds on hand, no entry had been made for the receipt of three 10-carat stones. Joel was arrested and taken to John Fry for interrogation. Failing to convince Fry with his weak explanations, the young man was formally charged with two contraventions of the Diamond Trade Act.

When, on 8 May, Joel came before the Special Court on the first of the two charges, he was found not guilty. No evidence was led; he was acquitted on a legal technicality. As he stepped down from the dock he was immediately rearrested on the second charge. Bail of £4,000 was granted and the second hearing was fixed for 27 May. The case was never heard. Joel was not there to face the charge. He had bolted. Somehow or other he escaped to England, changed his name to Jack Joel, became very rich, and was never seen in Kimberley again.

How much his uncles, Barney and Harry Barnato, had to do with his escape is not known. The brothers were in England when their nephew was arrested and had come haring back to Kimberley immediately they received the news. Barney was in a terrible state. He went weeping to J.B. Robinson – who was then the chairman of the Diamond Mining Protection Association – in an attempt to have the case dropped. Finding there was nothing Robinson could do, he then tried, rather clumsily, to bribe John Fry. But he had picked the wrong man. Fry considered the case to be one of the clearest and strongest he had brought to court and refused to have anything to do with the distressed Barney. Isaac Joel was left to take the only way out open to him.

The affair might have been quickly forgotten had Barney not been so vindictive. Unable to forgive John Fry he set out to ruin him. It proved a costly business. It involved Barney in an expensive libel case against the *Cape Argus* - which reported his bribery attempt and lost him much of his popularity in Kimberley. But he continued his campaign, even going so far as to finance a newspaper, the *Diamond Times*, in order to vilify the Detective Department. John Fry had no hope against the Barnato millions. Strings were pulled in Cape Town and eventually, in February 1885, Fry was dismissed from the Kimberley police force. The reasons given for his dismissal were, to say the least, unconvincing. They amounted to nothing more than a charge of negligence in keeping the Detective Department's books: not even his most determined opponents were able to accuse him of misappropriating official funds for his personal use.

Fry was replaced by Henry Basil Roper, who, during the four years he headed the Detective Department, was also subjected to vilification. It was not the most popular post in Kimberley. Nevertheless sympathy for John Fry was not lacking. Among his fervent champions was George Garcia Wolfe, who fought unsuccessfully in the Cape Assembly to have him reinstated. When, in 1886, it became obvious that these appeals would fail, Fry accepted a job on the Tati goldfields. But he was a doomed man. The following year he became seriously ill with a facial cancer and eventually returned to Kimberley, to be nursed at the hospital. He died, aged fifty-one, in November 1888. The Detective Department, headed by Henry Roper, turned out in full force at his funeral. Obituaries in the local press described him as a dedicated and zealous public servant. They might have added that it was his attributes that led to his downfall: when fighting I.D.B. it did not pay to be too dedicated, too zealous.

14

The Great Strike and Smallpox

By the beginning of 1883, Kimberley could claim many important 'firsts' in South African history. Among other things it had become the first large inland settlement to develop away from a river, the first town to depend solely on South Africa's mineral wealth, the first major industrial centre. It had attracted an army of foreign capitalists and artisans and was the first South African town to have its streets lit by electricity. To many its glitter and enterprise symbolised South Africa's entry into the modern world.

But if Kimberley had brought the benefits of the industrial revolution to the country, it had also brought its troubles. It had already witnessed the first industrial riots and inspired the first racial, or class, legislation in industry. Before the end of 1883 the Diamond City was to chalk up yet another controversial 'first' by becoming the scene of South Africa's first large-scale industrial strike. This strike was, in many ways, typically South African. It had nothing to do with wages or working-hours: its purpose was to uphold the dignity of the white man. What sparked it off was the enforcement of the new laws permitting mine-owners to search their employees.

Outrageous as it was later made to appear, there was really nothing new about the searching-legislation. As far back as July 1880 the Legislative Council had passed an ordinance providing 'for the searching of natives and others employed in the various mines'. But nothing had been done about it. Unable to agree on a workable searching-system, the four Mining Boards had let the matter drift. Not until the Diamond Trade Act was passed did the need to search mine employees become urgent. Then it became obvious to everyone that there could be no hope of stamping out I.D.B. until thieving was stopped at its source. That meant that something would have to be done to prevent stolen diamonds from leaving the mines. So long as workers were allowed to come and go as they pleased, the illicit trade would flourish. Harsh penalties and an efficient Detective Department might make thieves cautious but the temptation would remain: a stone once stolen would always find a buyer.

But how would the searching-system work? Would it be confined to black labourers? Were only black men dishonest? What was to prevent a black digger passing a stone to a white overseer? Who could be trusted? What would be gained by sowing unnecessary suspicion? The Mining Boards had no wish to alienate long-standing employees. But to search some men and not others would make any system unworkable. Obviously there could be no half measures. It was a ticklish problem.

Nevertheless it was a problem that had to be faced. While the Mining Boards dithered, others became impatient. Finally the Diamond Mining Protection Association decided to step in. On 10 January 1883, they published a list of 'Rules and Regulations for the Searching of Mining Labourers'. These were not as comprehensive as they might have been but they did provide a working basis. They decreed that all the mines should be fenced in and that anyone entering the enclosure would have to pass through a searching-station. All employees below the rank of sub-manager would be liable to be searched and no employee would be allowed through unless he was wearing a regulation uniform, the design of which was left to the mine owners. Any employee leaving a mining enclosure during working-hours would have to produce a properly authorised permit.

All in all, the proposed regulations were very much what might have been expected. Anything less would have been hopelessly inadequate. The Mining Boards had little hesitation in accepting them. However, for a short period, the mine owners were apprehensive. They had every reason to expect an outcry: if not from the low-ranking white overseers, then certainly from the commercial sector. The fencing-in of the mines could well be regarded as the thin edge of a wedge which would isolate black labourers from the town traders.

Surprisingly enough, there was little immediate reaction. The only notable move by a Kimberley merchant showed more enterprise than umbrage. A couple of weeks after the rules were published, Mr John Foote, a 'Fashionable Tailor' of Stockdale Street, placed advertisments in the newspapers inviting mine managers to inspect his specially designed suits 'for wear by Native labourers and others in the Mines'. These suits, he declared, were 'all of one piece and by pressing a spring at the back the dress can be very expeditiously unloosened at will'.

Encouraged by such signs of co-operation, the mine owners went gleefully ahead with the scheme. By the end of February most of the mines were enclosed, searching-houses were established, and arrangements made with the Detective Department for teams of suitable searching-officers. According to Dr Matthews it was a costly business. 'The number and expense was ridiculous,' he protested, 'eighty (80) searchers were employed in the four mines, and the expense was nearly two thousand pounds per month.' Nevertheless the mine owners considered it a sound investment. At last it seemed as if a major problem would be solved.

But, of course, it was not. The reason for the seeming docility of the white overseers quickly became apparent. As far as the black workers were concerned the searching-system worked reasonably well. They went through separate searching-houses and were thoroughly examined. On entering the mine they changed into their new uniforms, leaving their own clothes behind. At the end of the day they were stripped of their uniforms and, before they could put on their own clothes, were made to parade naked through the searching-house. As most diamonds were small enough to be concealed in any orifice of the human body, every orifice of the human body was then systematically probed. It was an uncomfortable, embarrassing and, above all, undignified procedure. To expect the white overseers to submit to the same treatment was asking a great deal. In fact, it was asking too much.

Even the most diligent searcher was reluctant to insist on a thorough examination of the overseers. An attempt to do so at the Bultfontein Mine brought such a sharp reaction that it was hastily abandoned. In the white searching-houses the system was 'looked upon as farcical'. The men merely sauntered through, joked with the searchers as their pockets were patted, and went on their way. This was not at all what the Diamond Mining Protection Association had had in mind.

To make matters worse, not a single diamond was found on black or white. That the system would have to be tightened up soon became obvious. Rumours that this was what the mine owners intended immediately put the white workers on their guard. On 9 March – a week after the system came into operation – a group of overseers met outside the Kimberley Mine and insisted on being told exactly how they would be searched. They were given an evasive answer. But the rumours persisted. A few weeks later the De Beers Mining Board received a petition, signed by sixty-three overseers, complaining that 'it would be a disgraceful and degrading thing if they should be compelled to disrobe in the searching house, and so lowered in the eyes of the natives'. Once again the members of the Mining Board refused to commit themselves.

They should have known better. By repeatedly evading the issue they were simply asking for trouble. Although Kimberley was by no means as rebellious as it had once been, it was not lacking in spirit. Agitators were still ready to seize upon popular grievances, to sow suspicion, and to crusade for justice. Now they quickly got to work. During the next few months a number of meetings were held, mostly behind closed doors; the overseers of the four mines joined forces and an organised protest meeting got under way.

Things came to a head with a mass rally of 'mechanics, engine drivers and overseers' in the Market-square on Sunday 14 October 1883. There was really no need for the few speeches that were made: everyone was prepared for the outcome. When, at the end of the meeting, it was proposed that all work stop until the searching-rules were rescinded, hardly a dissenting voice was heard.

The following day the four mines were deserted. Only a handful of brave or – depending how one looks at it – subservient white and black workers reported for duty. That evening a huge torchlight procession formed in the Market-square and, headed by the inevitable band, set out on a tour of the four mines. First the Kimberley and De Beers mines were visited. Here the leaders called upon the few remaining night workers to down tools and, after a few rocks had been hurled into enclosures, they were quickly obeyed. At Dutoitspan things became more rowdy. Carts were overturned, horses were let loose, picks and shovels were smashed and the manager of the Griqualand West Company was badly beaten up. Throughout the night excited crowds packed the streets of Beaconsfield and did not disperse until the early hours of the morning.

The strike lasted for over a week. Apart from an abortive attempt to rush the Bultfontein and Dutoitspan mines, there were very few incidents. A few mining companies managed to continue working with the help of a skeleton staff, and valiant efforts were made to keep the pumping-machines going and so prevent the mines from being flooded. But there was no escaping the seriousness of the situation. Something had to be done, and done quickly. Meetings of the four Mining Boards were hurriedly called and a joint committee was formed to negotiate a settlement.

Among the representatives of De Beers Mine was Cecil Rhodes. For once Rhodes, the great mediator, had to admit defeat. There was nothing he could do to get his colleagues to come to terms with the strikers. The joint committee was, as always, hopelessly divided. It was more by luck than agreement that the committee members were finally persuaded–by that former firebrand turned peacemaker, Dan O'Leary–to pass a resolution calling for the removal of the 'stripping' clause. But passed it was. At a meeting of mine employers, held on the third day of the strike, it was clearly stated that it had never been intended that white men should strip and that such searching-methods would not be employed.

To convince the strikers of this was not easy. There was widespread resentment of the high-handed attitude adopted by certain mine owners and it was thought that such men could not be trusted. One of the more vocal groups of strikers was all for breaking off negotiations until their employers approached them with greater respect. But they were in a minority. Most of the men could not afford to stand out for what appeared to be an irrelevant quibble. A deputation was sent to meet the mine owners and it was eventually agreed that the men should return to work on certain conditions.

'The objection to stripping had been met,' reported the deputation. 'With regard to the uniform adopted, there was no degradation in wearing it. It was understood there should be no victimization, but those men who had threatened or used violence to their employers, could expect to be taken back.'

This did not please everyone. The malcontents remained suspicious. A group of them, dressed in sacks stamped 'Mechanics Uniform', paraded through Beaconsfield in a cart in an attempt to keep the strike going. 'Whenever a crowd collected,' it was reported, 'they were addressed by Mr Jackson one of their number who often remarked–"See here (pointing to the sack) white men have travelled 8000 miles to wear a thing like this. . . . I am frightened to get out of this cart lest a guard searches me and besides I have no pass." ' They were cheered on their way by the laughing crowds, but were given little support. To all intents and purposes the strike was over.

Hardly had work been resumed, however, than the French Company went back on its word and sacked thirteen mechanics and enginedrivers. Before the end of the year Baring-Gould's Central Company was to follow suit by sacking more than twenty of its white employees. Those who had trusted the mine owners began to have second thoughts. Had their grievances really been settled by the strike? How long would it be before the other promises they had been given were broken? They were soon to find out.

But before that happened another crisis arose. For a few months the industrial unrest was pushed into the background as Kimberley faced a more serious threat.

(2)

Shortly after the strike ended, Dr Hans Sauer returned to Kimberley from a hunting expedition in the Transvaal. Since the closing of the quarantine station at the Modder River some months earlier, he had been on holiday. Once the smallpox scare had fizzled out in the Cape, there had seemed no reason for Sauer to remain in Griqualand West. He had put all thoughts of the epidemic behind him until he arrived at Lydenburg in the Transvaal. There he had heard rumours of an outbreak of the disease in neighbouring Mocambique. The local authorities had consulted him and he had advised them to set up isolation posts on the Transvaal-Mocambique border. This, he had said, would prevent the disease from spreading. But his advice had come too late. He did not discover this until he returned to Kimberley.

As the passenger coach in which he was travelling drove into Kimberley, Sauer noticed a number of lads running about the streets offering pink slips to passers-by. One of these slips was handed to him as he stepped down from the coach. Glancing at it, he saw that it was a notice assuring the public that a disease that had been reported at nearby Felstead's farm was not smallpox but 'a bulbous disease of the skin allied to pemphigus'. This mystified him. 'In the first place,' he says, 'I did not know where Felstead's farm was, nor did I know there was any disease there, and, finally, I had never heard of a bulbous disease of the skin allied to pemphigus.' These mysteries were cleared up when Sauer reached his sister's house. Fred Stow, a neighbour, hurried round to explain the situation.

A week or so earlier, at the beginning of October, it had been reported that smallpox had broken out at Klerksdorp in the Transvaal. As Klerksdorp was on the direct route to and from the diamond fields, the Kimberley Town Council had immediately contacted the Transvaal authorities to ask what action they should take. They had been told not to worry. In his reply the Chief Medical Officer of the Transvaal, Dr Dyer, had assured them that the disease was not *variola* (smallpox) but *varicella* (chicken-pox). But this comforting message had been offset by a private letter from a Kimberley businessman who was visiting Klerksdorp: the disease, he wrote, 'is smallpox as we expected'.

Who was right? The Council decided to take no chances. Whatever the disease was it could only spell trouble. 'I gather from these letters', sighed the Town Clerk, 'that it is pretty clear that the supply of labour will partially fail - at least for a time-which will be a great blow to the mining industry.' If this happened, not only the mine owners but everyone in Kimberley, black and white, would suffer. In an attempt to keep a check on the disease, the Town Council wired Cape Town asking permission to set up a Board of Health. Once permission was received seven doctors were appointed to the Board and precautionary measures were taken. Strict sanitary regulations were enforced at the mines, African labourers were examined and a fumigation shed was erected at Halfway House, between Kimberley and Beaconsfield.

By that time the authorities had good cause for alarm. Reports were received of Africans who had passed through Klerksdorp on their way to Kimberley and who were suffering from a skin disease. All the cases reported were packed off to Felstead's farm, where they were kept in isolation. Soon no fewer than 177 Africans were in quarantine. Unfortunately the local doctors who examined the sick men were unable to agree about the nature of the disease. A majority refused to admit that it was smallpox. Some claimed it was 'Kaffir pox', which was relatively harmless and did not affect Europeans. Others – led by Dr Jameson and Dr Matthews – diagnosed it as the mysterious disease allied to pemphigus.

Dr Sauer, however, had no such doubts. Shortly after his arrival he issued a report, quoting chapter and verse, and stating positively that the disease was smallpox. This started what Sauer describes as 'The Great Smallpox War'.

Writing about this controversy some fifty years later, Sauer seems to have muddled his facts. He implies that most of the doctors, including Jameson, recognised the disease as smallpox but then tried to cover it up in order to prevent a panic that would harm the diamond industry. He also implies that little was done to check the disease before he issued his report. Neither of these insinuations is strictly true. Both Dr Grimmer and Dr Otto had already declared two of the cases they examined to be smallpox and action had been taken to isolate the disease. And when Sauer issued his report he was publicly supported by some of the doctors he claims had opposed him. But it is true that neither Dr Jameson nor Dr Matthews agreed with Sauer. Both of them were to stick to their anti-smallpox theories throughout their lives. They were backed up by a number of other Kimberley doctors.

According to Dr Sauer there was a great deal of reluctance on the part of the mine owners to have their labourers examined. He says that it was only by obtaining an order from the Civil Commissioner that he was able to enter the Dutoitspan Mine. He took an army of sanitary police with him and conducted an extensive investigation. 'Needless to say,' he writes, 'I found a disgusting state of affairs. . . . I found a large number of cases embracing all (stages of the disease) also the bodies, still unburied, of several men who had died of the disease. How many had been buried under false certificates I never knew.'

There is undoubtedly a great deal of truth in this. In the report he issued at the time, he complained bitterly about the negligence of the Dutoitspan and Bultfontein mine owners. He was also justified in condemning the virulent opposition he encountered from the doctors opposed to his findings. This opposition did much to encourage the spread of the disease. The townsfolk, afraid of being deprived of their livelihood, clung to the reassurances given by Dr Jameson and Dr Matthews. Even after Dr Falkiner, a Government inspector, had visited the quarantine stations in November and confirmed that 65 out of 70 patients treated had died of smallpox, the majority of citizens remained unconvinced.

Mass meetings were held at Dutoitspan and resolutions were passed expressing confidence in the theories of Dr Jameson and his colleagues. At one of these meetings, held at the Dutoitspan Club on 6 December, Lionel Phillips expressed the feelings of the mine owners. 'Ruin', he declared, amid sympathetic murmurings from the audience, 'stared us in the face.' He read a report from a Dr Crook who stated that he had treated patients for chicken-pox, syphilis and other skin diseases but 'not a single case of smallpox, and this I state most emphatically'. There was loud cheering when Phillips announced that this report had been confirmed by Dr Jameson. What would happen, Phillips wanted to know, if farmers refused to enter the town with their produce? 'On Saturday,' he thundered, 'we might have a starving population to support, which was a fact more dangerous even than smallpox.' The meeting was unanimous in voting for a Medical Commission to be appointed 'to investigate the disease prevalent among the natives'.

But the disease was not confined to the blacks. On 26 December a white man, George Wallace, died of smallpox in the Dutoitspan Lazaretto. Other cases of white people contracting the disease were reported. Vaccination was carried out with more haste than competence–at least one African died through being left too long in a fumigation shed. The disease soon began to spread from the mining areas to the town. Even the doctors opposed to the smallpox theory agreed to join in the vaccination campaign. But they were fighting against hopeless odds. In Kimberley there were too many danger spots, too many congested areas where it was impossible to control the epidemic.

One of the most vulnerable locations was the squalid, tightly packed Malay Camp which had sprung up on the outskirts of the town, just off the Dutoits-pan road. This camp had been started by the Malay transport drivers who had flocked to the diggings in the early days. Since then it had grown consider-ably. Not only the Malays but Cape Coloured and Indians–who had drifted to the diamond fields from Natal–lived in the makeshift hovels that made up the camp. Barred from owning claims and often unable to make a respectable living, they existed in the utmost squalor. Even in the best of times the Malay Camp was a breeding-place for disease.

The most poverty-stricken were probably the Indians. Few of them worked in the mines, most scratched out a living as hawkers. They could be seen any time of the day wandering about the town with their scanty, unsaleable wares, often openly begging for food, sometimes on the verge of collapse. Always they were a pathetic sight. Charles Warren described a typical Indian family who had crept into his yard searching for weeds.

'The woman', he said, 'has her head tied up, but the children have theirs surrounded by most glorious masses of matted jet black hair. They have funny ragged clothes on, made of bright coloured pocket-handkerchiefs, and silver bangles. They are picking up a morning salad. . . . They are quite covered up, for the coolies here do not go naked as the Kaffir children do. A handkerchief in front and one at the back over the shoulders, tied at the waist, and then two or three to make up a skirt.

'And where do you think some of the people live? They live in houses made of jam pots. They take the tin jam pots, beat them out flat, fasten them together and sheet over their houses with them; and then you see a bright silver looking house, glowing dazzling in the sun.'

But the glitter was only discernible from afar. The conditions under which most Indians lived were appalling: the filth, the stench, the crawling poverty of parts of the Malay Camp had made it one of the plague-spots of the town. There were, it is true, sections of the camp in which well-to-do Malays lived in relative comfort. The Malays were, for the most part, noted for their honesty and sobriety. Some of them owned passenger carts and had built up respectable businesses. Others were skilled masons and earned good money as builders. But such men were exceptions. Kimberley, in the 1880s, could not be proud of the way in which the majority of its black citizens were housed.

Nor were things helped during the smallpox epidemic by the fear that some Malays had of vaccination. Many refused outright to be treated by doctors, and put up a fight when attempts were made to remove them to isolation posts. Dr Matthews, sceptical of what he termed 'the so-called small-pox scare', was delighted when he was able to prevent one of his Malay patients from being dragged from his house by a health officer. 'I happened', he crowed, 'very fortunately to arrive on the scene, just as this illegal attempt was being made by that officer, who assisted by about thirty police was dragging the sick man amidst the hoots and execrations of an infuriated mob through the streets into an ambulance.' Knowing the law, Matthews immediately applied to a magistrate for a restraining order. It was granted. 'To my intense delight,' says Matthews, 'these myrmidons of the law who would not, who dare not, have attempted such officious illegality in the case of a European, had to slink away completely crestfallen.'

The well-meaning doctor was even more pleased when his patient recovered and presented him with a silver cup 'for his successful efforts in protecting the Mussulman interests'. He could well feel that his timely intervention was a triumph for civil liberties. Whether such behaviour aided the fight against smallpox is another matter. There can be little doubt that Dr Sauer had grounds for complaining about the attitude of some of his colleagues.

Certainly all attempts to control the plague failed. By the end of 1883 hundreds of cases had been reported and the death toll continued to rise. It was a grimly fitting finale to one of the most disastrous years in the town's history. Looking back on it, many must have seen an uncanny significance in the fact that, as early as January, a group of charitable ladies had launched the macabrely named 'Coffin Fund'. Appalled by the neglected state of the cemeteries and the fact that many destitute whites were being buried in blankets, the women had determined that the poor be given decent burials. They had little realised then how urgent their efforts would soon become. And those who looked for portents could also point to the untimely death, at the age of fifty-five, of the presiding Mayor, Mark Foggitt, in October–the month of the strike and the outbreak of smallpox. George Bottomley took over as Kimberley's first citizen in the midst of the crisis.

Sympathy for the hard-pressed townsfolk was widespread. There seemed no end to their miseries. The way in which they coped with their endless troubles evoked unstinted admiration. 'With many disasters to contend against,' declared the editor of a Port Elizabeth newspaper, 'Kimberley has had to undergo a severe ordeal in the collapse of mining scrip speculations, the fall of the price of diamonds, and heavy falls of reef in the Mine; but the inhabitants of the Fields are no ordinary community, possessing indomitable courage and dauntless resolution. Difficulties and obstacles which would have the effect of disheartening and discouraging ordinary communities seem only to have the effect of nerving them to greater resolutions and effort. Just as prosperity was returning after the lengthened period of forced depression and inactivity, the new danger of small-pox had occurred, which appears as a new trying and difficult calamity to be borne.'

Would 1884 see a turn for the better? Many must have asked the question. They had not long to wait for an answer.

(3)

The new year opened with a bang: such a bang as had never been heard in Kimberley before.

For a long time dynamite had been used in mining operations. The sound of periodic blasts had become commonplace. But the 'thunderous and fearful roar' that shook the four camps at two-fifteen on 10 January 1884 was no blast: it seemed more like the wrath of the gods. The entire population rushed panic-stricken into the streets. 'The violent trembling of the earth', claimed a petrified citizen, 'for a moment suggested that it was caused by an earthquake; immediately after there was a second explosion, followed by a third, which were far less severe than the first.'

As the rumbling died away, the crowds in the streets became aware of a huge column of smoke towering 'like a sullen ghost fiend' above the De Beers Mine. So dense was the smoke and so high did it rise that, it was said later, it could be seen forty miles away. There was an immediate stampede to the danger spot. For a danger spot it was. As the ever-growing crowd surged about the De Beers enclosure, thousands of cartridges whizzed and exploded over their heads. The cause of the explosion was soon understood, if not explained. Somehow a number of dynamite magazines had blown up. How this had happened was anyone's guess. Not that anyone stood around guessing for long. There was fresh panic when it was learned that there was a great stack of dynamite hidden behind some iron sheets that had not exploded. The crowds fled as quickly as they had gathered.

It was some time before any attempt was made to approach the mine. Everyone was tense, waiting for further explosions. Only when it seemed the danger had passed was a team of wagons sent in to remove the stack of dynamite. The unexploded magazines were discovered buried beneath layers of twisted iron sheets. How they had escaped detonation nobody knew. Nearby, a huge hole several feet deep and broad told its own story.

Mercifully the casualties were few. The broken and scattered remains of two bodies – thought at first to be those of a white man and a black man, but later identified as two Africans – were picked up and buried. A number of people had been injured by the flying cartridges. It could have been a lot worse. There were thousands of men regularly employed at De Beers.

What had caused the explosion? Everyone had his own ideas. The most common theory was that the two dead men had been smoking near the magazines and had carelessly tossed a lighted match into some inflammable material. Another was that the galvanised iron against which the dynamite had been stacked had become red-hot in the fierce sun. But there might have been a more sinister explanation. Could the explosion have been the result of spite? That is what many people thought when Jacobus Schwartz, a notorious horse-thief who boasted that no gaol could hold him, was arrested at the scene of the disaster.

Whatever the cause, the tremendous blast gave everyone a nasty shock. It must have been something of a relief when, two days later, the Civil Commissioner formally opened the Kimberley Park Swimming Club. Many a citizen felt the need to cool off.

Throughout January reef continued to fall in the mines, several fires broke out–including one in the Town Hall–and the number of illicit diamond buyers appearing before the Special Court increased. Kimberley's troubles in 1884 seemed to be following the pattern set in preceding years. But, in fact, they became worse.

On 27 February the town was shattered to hear that the smallpox epidemic had invaded the Kimberley Hospital. The disease had been detected on an African working in the Carnarvon wing and unmistakable symptoms were found on the corpse of another African in the mortuary. Dr Sauer claimed that the situation was much more serious than it first appeared. He accused Dr Wolff, the acting Medical Superintendent of the hospital, of deliberately falsifying the death certificates of patients who had died of smallpox.

The first case that Sauer heard of concerned a Mrs Greenhough, one of Dr Wolff's private patients. Suspecting that the woman had died of smallpox, not pneumonia as stated on her death certificate, Sauer obtained an exhumation order. On examining the body, he says, 'it was evident that she had died of confluent smallpox of the most severe type'. He immediately turned the matter over to the Public Prosecutor. Hardly had he done so than he received a visit from a young Irishman who told him that a friend of his named Gallety was lying dead in the Kimberley Hospital and that he had died from smallpox. Aparently before he had died he had been operated on by Dr Jameson and Dr Wolff. The young man also claimed that there were several other dead bodies in the hospital, all from the same cause.

As Kimberley's Medical Officer of Health, Sauer decided to act immediately. He sent for Deñis Doyle, the Sanitary Inspector, and instructed him to place a cordon of police around the hospital at dawn the following morning. Nobody was to be allowed to enter or leave the hospital until Sauer had carried out an inspection. This, however, was easier said than done.

On arriving at the hospital, after breakfast the next day, Sauer ran bang into the formidable Sister Henrietta. He does not say it was Sister Henrietta, but it obviously was. The sister who tried to prevent him entering the hospital, he says, was 'a woman of strong character, handsome, well-bred, very popular, and much respected on the Fields'. That described Sister Henrietta to a tee. Certainly the fight she put up was typical. She adamantly refused to allow

Sauer to inspect the medical staff until he threatened her with his band of policemen. Unless he was allowed to examine the nurses, he said, they would all be carted off to a lazaretto. She finally gave in. The nurses were paraded before Sauer who found that they had all been carefully vaccinated and were therefore immune from smallpox. He then insisted on being shown over the wards. 'This request', he claims, 'was reluctantly consented to, and with bad grace two nurses were detailed to show me over the wards.'

Just as Sauer was starting his tour, Dr Wolff turned up. He was fuming. 'If you move to another bed,' he hissed at Sauer, 'I will have you thrown out.' Taking no notice of him, Sauer moved on. Wolff then ordered two male attendants to seize Sauer. When they hesitated, a nurse was sent for further assistance. But before she could return, Sauer called in six of his policemen and told them to turf Wolff out. This they did. To the astonishment of patients and nurses alike, the acting Medical Superintendent of the Kimberley Hospital was frog-marched out of one of his own wards.

Sauer claims that he not only discovered cases of smallpox in the wards but, on entering the mortuary, 'found several dead men, all of whom had died of confluent smallpox'. Among the dead was the friend of the young Irishman. The next day Sauer made a formal report of his finding to the Sanitary Board.

Although Sauer's account varies somewhat from the official findings, there can be no doubt that smallpox had invaded the Kimberley Hospital. On 10 March Dr Wolff was charged at the Magistrate's Court for neglecting to inform the Hospital Board of the infectious disease. The case lasted for several days. The court was packed throughout the hearing. Wolff conducted his own defence, with Dr Jameson as his principal supporting witness. They were severely cross-examined by a group of other doctors, led by Dr Sauer. Judgment was given on 23 April. In finding Wolff guilty, the Resident Magistrate declared 'he had no hesitation in asserting the Crown had succeeded in proving the disease to be smallpox'. Wolff was fined the maximum penalty of, surprising as it seems, £10.

This was the first of the sensational court cases which were to rock Kimberley throughout 1884. Most of the town's doctors were involved in the legal battles that followed. Not only personal but professional reputations were at stake as the opposing medical theories on the smallpox epidemic were publicly debated.

Dr Wolff set things going by appealing against his sentence. The appeal was heard in May and Wolff was acquitted on a technical point. There was great jubilation among the anti-smallpox brigade. So carried away were they that, at a celebratory dinner, both Dr Jameson and Dr Wolff threw medical etiquette to the winds and roundly denounced Sauer as a charlatan. In highly libellous speeches they accused Sauer of trying to make money out of the smallpox scare. Sauer's immediate reaction was to sue the newspapers that had reported the speeches. He won both the cases that came before the courts and was awarded token damages.

Not content with this he then sued Jameson and Wolff for slander. They countered by claiming that Sauer had damaged their reputations in the report that he had submitted to the Hospital Board. These cases were heard by the High Court in July. The result of the protracted, lively and, at times, highly humorous hearing was a stalemate. The judges regretted that the actions had ever been brought, found both sides wrong, and awarded equal damages to the plaintiff and defendants alike. 'This judgement,' complained Sauer, 'in my opinion, was all wrong.' Jameson, however, treated the entire affair as a joke. 'Why does the Board of Health not fumigate me?' he quipped. 'I have been rubbing my hands over a smallpox patient and sitting on him.'

Amusing it might have been, but the legal wrangle did nothing to check the spread of smallpox. The epidemic raged for two years; there were some 2,300 cases and 700 deaths, of which 400 cases and 51 deaths occurred among the white population. Dr Sauer's diagnosis was correct but it came too late. Even the most fervent of Dr Jameson's admirers had to admit that he had acted foolishly. Whatever the disease was, says his biographer Ian Colvin, 'it was not "a bulbous disease allied to pemphigus" '

The smallpox controversy divided the whole of Kimberley. It had not only the doctors but the mine owners at each other's throats. Everybody wanted to blame everybody else. Some mining companies accused others of deliberately hampering the work of the Sanitary Department. In the Cape Assembly J.X. Merriman claimed that 'the spread of the disease in Dutoitspan (the centre of the anti-smallpox agitation) was entirely the fault of the inhabitants who had behaved in a disgraceful way'. J.B. Robinson played a prominent part in advocating measures to fight the epidemic, but he did not help matters by blaming Rhodes and the De Beers Mining Company for failing to control the movements of their African workers. Disunity in the mining industry was as evident in this crisis as in everything else.

But the greatest division was that which existed between the mine workers and their employers. In the early months of 1884 it was this division, rather than the smallpox debate, which occupied most people's minds. Kimberley's second industrial strike was a much more serious affair than the first.

(4)

The mine owners had given a solemn promise that no white employee would be forced to strip. How they expected the searching-system to work if this was really their intention is puzzling. It is hardly surprising that many strikers doubted that they would keep their word. And, of course, they did not. Searching after the strike was no more effective than it had been before. No diamonds were found; I.D.B. agents continued to be caught; the increase in fines in no way compensated for the lack of finds. The mine owners began to have second thoughts and it was not long before those thoughts were translated into action.

On Friday 28 March 1884, fourteen white employees of the Bultfontein Mining Company were stripped and searched. There was an immediate outcry. Once again the overseers, mechanics and enginedrivers met to organise a protest. It was now obvious that they would have to act more decisively. They could no longer rely on promises. So long as the 'stripping-clause' remained law the mine owners could claim that they were acting within their rights. There was nothing for it but to get the obnoxious clause revoked. In April, first a telegram and then a petition–signed by over 2,000 workers–was sent to the Cape Governor asking him to suspend the stripping-clause until the Cape Assembly met at the beginning of May. The Governor (then Sir Hercules Robinson) wired back to say that he had referred the matter to the appropriate Cape Ministers.

Apparently this made the mine owners sit up. If their employees could flex their muscles, so could they. A few days later the De Beers Mining Company announced that they intended to lock-out all workers not wearing the prescribed uniform and who refused to abide by the searching-regulations. The French Company made a similar announcement. When the employees of these two companies arrived for work on 24 April they found all mining operations had stopped. Things were decidedly uneasy throughout the four mines. Some of the other mine owners, not wanting to force a direct confrontation, had tried for a compromise. Searching-officers were told to stop every fifth man entering the mine and ask him to submit to a thorough search. Not surprisingly, most of those pulled out of line adamantly refused to strip. As the searching-officers had not been instructed as to what action they should take in such cases, these objectors were allowed to pass. On their return from the morning shift, however, they were politely informed that they had been sacked. Then the real trouble started.

'The outcome of all this', says W.W. Chatterton, the head searching-officer at the Kimberley Mine, 'was intense excitement all over the mine. Men could be seen gathering together in groups, both above and below, discussing the situation. The upshot was that at noon every whistle on the mine, lustily and lengthily blew the signal for a strike. The "Great Strike" had begun.'

At a meeting held by the strikers the following day, a telegram said to have been sent from Cape Town by Cecil Rhodes was read out. 'If the searching rules could not be carried out in entirety,' it said, 'they should be abolished altogether, and the old system of compounds for kafirs resorted to.' But when tackled by George Garcia Wolfe in the Cape Assembly, Rhodes refused any compromise. 'As an employer of labour,' he declared, 'I will not budge one inch.' This apparent contradiction was typical of the attitude of many employers. It only added to the confusion.

For a couple of days nothing was done about the men who continued to work. A few companies, protected by armed police, were still operating on Friday 25 April. An armed force of mounted men with drawn swords also patrolled the North Circular Road. The strikers made threatening noises, but hesitated to act against the 'blacklegs'.

But the threatening noises were frightening enough. Among the men still working for the Central Company in the Kimberley Mine there were two youngsters, Albrecht Dietrich, aged sixteen, and Moritz Dietrich, aged twelve. They came from a poor family and continued to work because they needed the money. Their elder sister, Elsa, had the terrifying duty of taking food to the

Kimberley Mine in April 1884.
View from the top of the French
Company's shaft. Four days after
the photograph was taken, this
was the scene of the second great
strike, during which six men
were killed. (K)

Barney Barnato photographed in
Kimberley in his mid-thirties. (K)

J. B. Robinson's workshop. Robinson manufactured wagon
wheels and barrels as a sideline.
He is seen sitting on a barrel,
right foreground, wearing a
white pith helmet. (M)

boys twice a day. 'I used to dread those journeys,' she later recalled. 'Our house was some distance away and I had to walk through a district crowded with strikers. Groups of sullen-looking men were loafing at the street corners and as I passed carrying my *decker* they would scowl and shout insults after me. I tried to take no notice but all the time my heart was pounding against my ribs.'

On Monday 28 April, the first mass meeting of strikers was held on the Kimberley racecourse. It was attended by over 2,000 people, not all of them mine workers. The canteen keepers and 'Kafir-store' owners, hearing fresh rumours of an all-embracing compound system, were loud in their protestations that the mine owners intended to deprive them of their livelihood. Several angry speeches were made and the cry 'Who were to search the searchers?' had the crowds cheering. This, as far as many of them were concerned, seemed to sum the matter up. But, on the whole, the meeting was orderly and ended with resolutions calling for a complete stoppage of work being passed.

Very few men reported for work the next day. Those who did came in for some rough handling. 'A party of strikers came to our house,' says Elsa Dietrich, 'to persuade my mother to keep the boys at home from work. They were a rough crowd and Mama tried to be conciliatory. "What am I to do?" she said. "I am a poor woman, but if you will guarantee my sons their billets for the rest of their lives, they can go on strike." The only reply of the gang was to threaten to bombard the house. After this episode the company gave us a guard, but we still had to make our daily journey to the mine. . . . One morning some men seized my decker and threw the food on the ground; they left me alone, but that evening Mama was fired at as she passed through the same street. Fortunately the shot missed and she escaped with a fright.'

By that time, however, some more deadly shots had been fired. The strikers' committee had given orders that the men were to keep clear of the mines where work was continuing. But this was asking too much. The morning after the mass meeting, a huge crowd of white and black men gathered on the debris heaps surrounding the Victoria Company at the De Beers Mine. The manager of the company, Francis Oats, came out to reason with them. After a long discussion, Oats agreed to suspend all operations until twelve o'clock the following day.

Not every company was as obliging. At the Kimberley Mine the French Company made a determined attempt to keep the strikers at bay. This was not entirely a matter of obstinacy. The French Company was largely responsible for the pumping-machinery in the mine and had been instructed to keep their pumps going at any cost. 'The reason for this', explained W.W. Chatterton, 'was that if it stopped the mines would be flooded, and when the men wished to resume work they could not do so.' To guard the pumping-machinery, a semicircle of empty trucks was placed around the French Company's works and a band of armed special police were stationed behind them. These guards, commanded by a Captain Christian, had orders to fire on anyone attempting to stop the pumps.

They were soon put to the test. An hour or so after work had been stopped at

De Beers, a huge crowd–some accounts say 600 strong, some say 300– of white and black strikers marched from Dutoitspan to the Kimberley Mine. Led by Phillip Henry Holmes, they were armed with 'pick-handles, crow-bars, knobkerries, sticks and some knives, and at least one was armed with a revolver, possibly more'. As they marched, more crowds gathered to watch; many people fell into line behind the grim-looking procession.

'When Schute and I rode up at about 2:45,' said a newspaper reporter, 'to the south side of the Kimberley Mine, we found a large crowd extending from Main Street right up to the barrier of the trucks formed for the defence of the water-gear then working. Close at the barrier was a dense crowd, mostly white, about 200 to 250 strong. Christian talked to the crowd warning the men who threatened him with kerries and pointed a revolver, that to strike him was to strike the law, and that if they crossed the barrier . . . they would be fired upon.'

At first it seemed as if the leaders were prepared to negotiate with Captain Christian. But they were given little chance. The strikers at the back of the crowd began to push forward shouting, 'Rush the bastards, rush them!' The pressure was too much for Philip Holmes. He broke through the ranks, dashed towards the trucks, wrenched two of them apart and knocked down one of the guards with his kerrie. He was followed by two others. As they struggled to seize the guard's rifle, a shot rang out. Holmes dropped dead. At that most of the Africans bolted, leaving the whites to storm the trucks. Whether by order or not, the police opened fire as the men tried to push through the opening made by Holmes. Three more men were killed and several badly wounded before the strikers retreated.

The wounded were rushed to the Kimberley Hospital for treatment. At the mines the guards put down their rifles and acted as stretcher-bearers. Philip Holmes had died immediately, shot through the eye. One of the wounded was a seventeen-year-old boy, Paul Roux, whose brother had been one of the firing-party. 'This poor fellow's grief', says Chatterton, 'was sad to behold.'

The whole of Kimberley was stunned by the catastrophe. That afternoon every shop closed; groups gathered aimlessly at the streetcorners. The next day a Sabbath-like hush enveloped the town. A funeral service was held for the four dead men in the Odd-fellows' Hall and some 1,400 silent people, dressed in deep mourning and marching four abreast, followed the hearses to the cemetery. Behind them came a party of mounted horsemen and a procession of Cape carts. Special prayers for the dead were offered at the Anglican, Roman Catholic and Lutheran churches.

But the tragedy did not end there. The day after the funeral, Joseph Sablich, one of the wounded men, died after having his arm amputated. Five weeks later, on 7 June, young Paul Ròux, who had been shot between the eyes, also died in the Kimberley Hospital, bringing the total number of deaths to six.

At an inquest held immediately after the strike it was found that the men had died while 'unlawfully and riotously' attempting to stop the water-pumping gear. Precisely who was responsible for their deaths was impossible to establish. Three of the guards were arrested on 1 May, but were later released owing to lack of conclusive evidence.

Gradually the strikers began to drift back to work. By 5 May–a week after the shooting–most of the mines had resumed operations. An attempt by a group of white workers in the Kimberley Mine to prolong the strike fizzled out. The majority of men could not afford to hold out indefinitely.

The entire affair was heatedly debated in the Cape Assembly. Cecil Rhodes declared that 'he was personally in favour of instructing the Chief of the Detective Department to issue an announcement that Government was prepared to promise the stripping regulations should not be carried further than they were at present: that nothing more should be attempted than divesting men of hats, boots and coats'. But neither Rhodes nor the Cape ministers would agree to the stripping-clause being suspended from the Diamond Trade Act. Replying to a monster petition sent to the Government by the people of Kimberley, the Prime Minister insisted that no searching-system which did not include 'the white as well as the black servants employed in the Mines' could possibly be effective.

To all intents and purposes the strike had achieved nothing. Six men had been killed and many more wounded, only to have their demands cursorily brushed aside. Once again they were forced to rely on the vague promises of their employers. But if those promises were vague, they were by no means as fickle as they had once been. The strike had given the mine owners a nasty shock. They were to think twice before breaking their word in the future.

Another significant result of the strike was the tightening up of the compound system. Africans arriving at the mines had long been housed and fed by their employers but, for the most part, they had been free to wander about the town at will. Now it was decided to establish closed compounds where black labourers would be confined for the duration of their contracts. In this way they would be isolated not only from illicit diamond buyers but from the notorious 'Kaffir-canteens'. The idea, it was argued, was to ensure that 'the employer got more of his diamonds, and his natives were always fit for work instead of being incapacitated by poisonous liquor'.

While living in the compounds the Africans were to have all their needs supplied by their employers. Mine owners were authorised to open stores which sold food and clothing, but it was stipulated that these stores should operate on a strictly commercial basis. There was to be no question of wages being paid partly in goods. In this way, it was thought, the labourers would benefit both in health and pocket. Kept away from the demoralising influences of Kimberley, they would leave the mines well fed and clothed and take home the best part of their earnings. To many it seemed a sensible, safety and philanthropic measure.

The opening of the first closed compound by the Central Mining Company in April 1885, a year after the strike, was treated as a gala occasion. Public inspection was invited and elegantly dressed women sauntered about the enclosures, twirling parasols and cooing with delight. The arrangements made for housing the Africans were considered nothing short of marvellous. Even the sceptical Dr Matthews was favourably impressed. 'I attended the opening ceremony,' he says, 'and to my surprise found a large yard some 150 yards square inclosed partly by buildings and the remainder by sheets of iron ten feet high. Within this inclosure were sleeping rooms for 500 Kaffirs, a magnificent kitchen and pantry, large baths, guard room, dispensary and sick ward, stores and mess rooms. There is no doubt that this arrangement will be the means of greatly decreasing the thieving by natives.'

But the system did not, of course, please the Kimberley traders. For years they had been protesting against the introduction of such a scheme. They saw it merely as the means by which the mine owners intended to deprive them of 'the native trade'. Now it looked as if their worst fears had been confirmed. It was to take a long time to resolve the dispute between the mining and commercial sectors of Kimberley.

Almost from the outset it was agreed that every article sold in the compounds should be bought in the Kimberley district. The mine owners were not allowed to import goods or to be involved in any trading concern in the town. In 1887 an Act was passed in the Cape Parliament to restrict the buying of goods for the compounds to Kimberley firms. This was done to protect the local merchants and to ensure strict impartiality. Unfortunately doubts were to persist about the way in which compound supplies were bought and sold. The traders also objected to the mine owners selling goods at cost or a little over cost. Worthy as this non-profitmaking system at first appeared, it tended to bring the Kimberley merchants into disrepute. 'When the natives' time expired in the compounds,' it was said, 'the traders in the town were accused by them of overcharging.'

However, a compromise was eventually reached. The mine owners agreed to charge the town retail prices and use the profit for charitable purposes. This more or less settled the matter. Agitation against the compound system continued for many years but even the most determined traders were finally forced to realise that they were fighting a losing battle. The system was not without its faults – one of the worst being, of course, that it reflected a distinct racial bias – but, in the circumstances, it seemed to many the lesser of many evils. Ten years after the introduction of the closed compounds, Cecil Rhodes was able to announce that the annual profits from the stores was something like £10,000. Every penny of this profit had been used to benefit Kimberley: donations had been made to the hospital, the library and to various public schools. 'I do not think', he declared, 'anyone need object to these payments. They have, I think, been fairly well disbursed; they have been given to good objects'. When set against this announcement, the complaints of the traders seemed hollow indeed.

15

The Railway Arrives

'The suicidal mania is seizing the community here . . . ' Cecil Rhodes wrote to J.X. Merriman from Kimberley in April 1883, 'the doctors say it is almost like an epidemic. I do not despair of the place, as the wealth in diamonds, if regulated, must eventually become a source of profit to the holders.'

To have this sort of confidence in the diamond industry in the early 1880s one needed to be an incurable optimist, plain pig-headed or something of a visionary. Rhodes was fortunate in being all these things. Not everyone shared his obstinacy or his gifts. The 'suicidal mania' of which he spoke had then only just begun. As diamond companies continued to fold, shares to plunge, and reef to fall, the suicide rate in Kimberley rose alarmingly. Throughout 1883 and 1884 hardly a week passed without an announcement of some well-known businessman taking his own life. Clergymen and rabbis lectured their congregations on the crime of self-murder, and newspaper editors, weary of the sameness of their reports, lost all sympathy for the victims. 'The fact is that this mania for suicide taints the whole moral atmosphere,' grumbled the *Diamond Times* at the beginning of 1885, 'and it is questionable whether it is good for the safety and morality of Society that such acts be recorded with tenderness. . . . There is never a hero without a struggle and a battle, and the battle of life is worth fighting, though a man may sometimes have to fight against desperate odds.'

Everyone was fighting against desperate odds. Even those who did not resort to suicide were driven to near despair. The ghastly depression affected every stratum of Kimberley society. Dr Matthews, who resigned his seat in the Cape Assembly to fight off financial disaster, found it impossible to survive and was declared insolvent in 1883. 'The decline in the value of shares in the market was enormous,' he confessed. 'Central shares in the Kimberley mine, which had an easy sale in March, 1881, at £400 per share were in 1884 almost unsaleable at £25. Rose-Innes shares which were sought after at £53 sank to £5, and a similar fall also occurred in the shares of all the companies in the other mines in the province.' A.A. Rothschild, the dapper little auctioneer, lost a fortune through reckless investments. Years later he was to joke about his downfall in one of his droll advertisements.

At the beginning of the decade he had been sitting pretty. 'Scrip rose,' he explained gaily, 'and so did the Baron's ambition. Instead of being satisfied to sit on one chair he required two; one cigar at a time was not sufficient, so he smoked a "Rothschild" on the one end and an "Alfredo" on the other; balance in the Bank was enormous. Managers dined with him, General Managers stayed with him and all was glory and halleluyah. He woke one morning, scrip was down, and gradually he went low. No more managers, no more cigars and no more two chairs. Down! down! down!'

But at the time it was no laughing matter. Plucky as he was, the nimble-witted Baron never fully recovered his losses. For a few more years he struggled along on promissory notes and what he could make in his auction rooms. Then, in July 1886, crippled by ill-health and bad luck, he was obliged to sell-up and retire to England. He was given a rousing send-off. When he died in Hertfordshire, in 1917, the Kimberley papers remembered him with affection. 'A kindlier man', they said, 'it would be difficult to imagine.'

Several other old-timers were badly hit by the depression. Some were luckier than others. At the beginning of 1884, J.B. Robinson was forced to quit politics when his claims in the Kimberley Mine were buried by a landslide. Only by drawing huge loans from the Cape of Good Hope Bank was he able to survive. Nor did the cocksure Barnato brothers escape entirely. Some of their most valuable claims became unworkable and in August 1884 they announced their intention of dissolving the Barnato Company. It was only the determination of their desperate shareholders that prevented them from doing so.

The established diamond buyers were hit the hardest. They, more than any other section of the community, accounted for the rising suicide rate. To withstand the increasing pressures required courage as well as financial backing. It was all too easy for the faint-hearted to give in to despair once their diamond stocks dwindled. The survivors were often men of stamina rather than men of substance.

One such survivor was Bernard Klisser. Well known and highly respected, Klisser had arrived at Dutoitspan with his uncle Mark in 1870. He was then a youngster of seventeen. Starting as koppie-wallopers, the Klissers had toured the diggings buying diamonds from individual diggers and selling them at the Exchange and Auction Mart in the St James Hall. By the time old Mark Klisser died, his nephew was well-enough established to found his own diamond-buying company. He did well. Although not as rich as some, Bernard Klisser was a prosperous diamond merchant at the beginning of the 1880s. But he was not prosperous enough to stand up to the great depression. In 1883, while still in his twenties, he was declared insolvent.

In later years the modest, somewhat shy, Klisser was fond of telling stories of the fortunes that had been made and lost in Kimberley. Of his own fortune he rarely spoke. Precisely how he recovered the money he lost in 1883 is not clear. But recover it he did. He was a very rich man when he died in 1922. He was also a very generous one. Among his bequests he left over £44,000 to the poor and needy of Kimberley. 'I wish to let the money I made', he told a friend, 'go back to where it came from, where I have been happy, and where most of my friends are.' It is hardly surprising that he was known as 'The Great Kimberley Philanthropist' or that, for many years, the Kimberley Council had a special wreath placed on his London grave on the anniversary of his death.

That men like 'Baron' Rothschild and Bernard Klisser should have succumbed to the economic slump is an indication of its insidious effect. Both were honest, hard-working and popular, but this was not enough to save them. Indeed their very virtues might have contributed to their downfall: one needed to be canny and more than a little devious to escape unscathed.

Yet many did. The diamond industry did not collapse completely. Strikes, smallpox, suicides and slump were looked upon as evils that had to be borne until better times arrived. Things, it was said, could hardly get worse. There had to be an answer to Kimberley's many problems somewhere.

Some, like Rhodes, saw the answer in regulating the output of diamonds. So long as the industry remained competitive, so long as diamonds were thrown indiscriminately onto the market, there could be no hope of financial stability. While the price of diamonds continued to fluctuate, the majority of sellers were bound to suffer. Only if some stopped selling would the market improve. But who could be expected to stop selling? Who could be expected to sacrifice a small profit, so that others could make a larger?

It was J. B. Robinson who first tackled the problem publicly. At the beginning of July 1883, he called a meeting to discuss the possibility of controlling the output of diamonds. Opening the discussion he spoke at great length about 'the ruinously low prices induced by the enormous over-production'. The only solution, he said, was to restrict the output of the mines by common agreement. Rhodes disagreed. He took the view that it was first necessary to fix a price below which diamonds could not be sold. They must agree among themselves, he said, not to sell for less than the cost of production. As so often happened when Rhodes and Robinson met, the discussion developed into a heated argument. Finally they agreed to hand the matter over to a committee formed from representatives of the four mines. But nothing more seems to have been done about it.

There was, in any case, little hope of either plan working. To try to regulate the price or the output of diamonds on a voluntary basis was to try the impossible. Competition was too keen and corruption too rife for a gentlemen's agreement to work in Kimberley. Any form of regulation would have to be enforced; this could only be done by a company or a combination of companies which controlled the entire industry; no dissension could be allowed. The answer was amalgamation. But that raised more spectres than anyone was yet prepared to face.

They preferred, instead, to look elsewhere for salvation. By the end of 1884 it began to look as if a solution of sorts was in sight. There seemed every possibility that Kimberley would soon be linked to the coast by railway. Surely then trade would pick up?

*   (2)

Linking Kimberley by rail to the coastal ports–Cape Town, Port Elizabeth and East London–had proved no easy matter. Work had started on the various railway extensions a few years after the discovery of diamonds but, although most people recognised the value of the link-up, progress had been hampered by a multitude of problems. Doubts, difficulties and suspicions had been met all along the line. The construction had been debated stage by stage in the Cape Assembly.

There had been geographical problems: mountain passes to be traversed, numerous rivers crossed. There had been economic problems: even those in favour of the railway had, at times, blanched at the cost. There had been political problems: Afrikaners in the Cape Assembly had seen the northward extension as a threat to the Transvaal's independence. There had also been the sheer cussedness of those responsible for the work. This, at times, had driven J.X. Merriman–an ardent champion of the railway–to distraction. 'I have had an interview with the "Railway Extension Committee" this morning,' he wrote despairingly to the Cape Prime Minister from Port Elizabeth in July 1882. 'Really, how grown men can make such donkeys of themselves I dont know! Not one of them had been up the line, nor did one of them know anything about it, and they got me there to lecture *me* on the slow rate of progress! It is hard to keep one's temper sometimes.'

Not only the slow progress of the line, but the slowness of the trains had made the railway something of a joke. Even when the line had advanced miles into the Karoo many visitors found it speedier to travel all the way from Cape Town in one of the Gibson brothers' efficient coaches. 'Crawling Trains and Flying Coaches', the *Cape Times* had headed a report of a mail coach arriving two hours ahead of a train.

Endless stories were told about the slowness of trains crossing the Karoo. A favourite story was that of a passenger who, after a long halt in the wilds, put his head out of the window and shouted to the guard to ask what was wrong. He was told that cattle were crossing the line. Eventually the train started, but twenty minutes later it stopped again. Once more the irate passenger rushed to the window. 'What, *more* cattle!' he helled to the guard. 'Oh no, sir,' came the blithe reply. 'Same cattle.'

But, despite all opposition, the construction of the line had gone ahead. By the end of 1884 it had reached the Orange River, just beyond Hopetown. On 12 November the Governor of the Cape, Sir Hercules Robinson, accompanied by his wife and daughter, had formally opened the gaily decorated Orange River station. It was a great occasion for the diamond fields. After the opening ceremony the Governor and his party had been lavishly entertained in Kimberley for a week: there were banquets, balls, a special race meeting and a display by members of the Kimberley Gymnasium. All thoughts of the depression were temporarily cast aside. Nothing, it seemed, could prevent the railway reaching Kimberley within a year to two at the most.

In fact it was to take less time than even the optimists anticipated. George Garcia Wolfe, that indefatigable champion of commerce, persuaded a well-known contractor, George Pauling, to undertake the last stages of the line construction; Pauling promised to complete the job in a matter of months. He was not quite as good as his word, but almost.

In the meantime visitors to Kimberley could travel to within striking distance of the town in relative comfort. Not that everybody appreciated this.

When the American entertainer, G.A. Farini, boarded the train in Cape Town in June 1885, he was distinctly disappointed with the widely advertised 'Pullman sleeping-car'. It bore, he sniffed, 'as distant a resemblance to the sleeping-car of the American railroads as the yellow skins of the Malay boys did to the ebony face of Sambo. On one side of the gangway was a row of seats for one person, and on the other side a row of wider seats to hold two. Over each of these latter the attendant – or "steward" as he is called – suspended from the roof of the car a piece of canvas, on which he placed a thin, dirty mattress; and this constituted the "bed". There was no covering whatever.'

More seasoned travellers, those who remembered the swollen legs and aching backs of the early coaching days, could be forgiven for thinking of these primitive arrangements as a luxury. Even the snooty Mr Farini came near to thinking the same when, after leaving the train, he found himself sleeping in the veld at a night stop on his way to Kimberley.

But such discomforts were soon to be a thing of the past. Pauling was pushing ahead with the line, laying about a mile of rail a day. The official opening day was scheduled for 28 November 1885. Unfortunately not everything went as planned. Pauling found himself bogged down by bungling officialdom and had some tart things to say about the bureaucrats of Kimberley. The main stumbling-block was the Kimberley station. This, when complete, was to be 624 feet long and about 150 feet broad. The goods shed was to be the largest in the Cape, and the engine shed would house nine locomotives. It was an ambitious project; too ambitious for the time allowed. As opening day drew near it became obvious that the station would not be ready and a temporary platform of railway sleepers was built in the Natal Cricket Ground, at the side of the Public Gardens.

None of this discouraged the excited Kimberleyites. They were beside themselves with anticipation. Crowds flocked to inspect the daily progress of the line, and over 1,500 special tickets were issued for seats on the trial excursion trains. The town began to blossom with bunting. Every shop, every office, every public building was draped with flags. Merchants in the Market-square vied with each other to produce the most outstanding display, the palm going, it was agreed, to Messrs Peat & Co. Ltd, whose 'excellent model of an express train, a work of considerable mechanical ingenuity and skill', was a wonder to behold.

Opening day was a Kimberley scorcher. From early morning the sun beat down mercilessly on the huge crowd gathered on the De Beers debris heaps overlooking the temporary platform. By eleven thirty, when the opening train was due to arrive, most of the spectators were wilting. But there was no sign of the train: not a puff of smoke could be seen on the cloudless horizon. Two more hours passed before the faint chugging of the engine was heard. Then there was a mighty roar as the train, gaily decorated with evergreens, came into sight and steamed slowly up to the temporary platform. It had been delayed at the Orange River station to allow Mrs de Wet time to break a bottle of champagne on one of the girders of the 'Good Hope Bridge'.

Stepping down from the engine, Sir Hercules Robinson tactfully kept his speech short. As he spoke, the officials accompanying him looked longingly for shade. They looked in vain. Heatwave or no heatwave, Kimberley was not to be cheated of its great day. The answering speeches went on unabridged. Only after the Mayor had solemnly smashed another bottle of champagne on the engine was the Governor's party ushered to a luncheon tent in the Public Gardens. But no sooner had they reached the tent than they had to retreat. The sun had turned it into a furnace. Nor were things helped by the arrival of the Fire Brigade, who, trying to cool the canvas with their hoses, succeeded only in drenching the guests. The official luncheon was eventually eaten with several of the diners crouched 'under the shelter of hastily procured umbrellas'.

The spirit of Kimberley remained undampened, however. Kimberleyites had a hard-earned reputation for resilience and they were determined to live up to it. They had had enough gloom, enough despair and enough, heaven alone knew, of moaning about the depression. The train had arrived and good times were on the way–they must be.

For a week the town indulged itself, made merry, and went a little wild. There were more balls, more banquets, more race meetings and more athletic displays. There were cricket matches (the Eclectic Cricket Club Pavilion had been opened on the same day as the railway), children's parties, picnics at Alexandersfontein and excursions to Riverton on the Vaal River. At a special exhibition of Griqualand West produce, one the great attractions was the De Beers Mining Company's stand, where the full name of the company was spelt out in 'sparkling gems set on a background of black velvet'. The Kimberley Mine was illuminated at night with a chain of lights designed to resemble 'a huge necklet of gold with a diamond pendant attached'. The band of the Kimberley Scots was in attendance everywhere and Frank Fillis's ever-popular circus did a roaring trade. Who could doubt that a new era had dawned?

And so, for a while, it seemed. By the time that Alexander McGregor took over as Mayor in mid-December, Kimberley had every reason to congratulate itself. The effects of the railway link were as immediate as they were amazing. Vegetables and tinned goods became more plentiful and cheaper, building materials more easily available, and the delivery of mail decidedly more reliable. The drop in the cost of fuel was remarkable–within a matter of weeks the price of coal had fallen from £24 to £6. 7s. 6d. a ton. Everyone was now able to contemplate a holiday at the coast, and those suffering from 'camp fever' were given new hope. 'The railway,' reported Dr Matthews, 'even in this matter has come to our help, as on the first approach of the fever, the desired change (of climate) can be obtained in a couple of days, or even less, and a threatened attack possibly averted.'

Ironically enough, the coming of the railway also encouraged the development of Kimberley's long-neglected road transport. Credit for this was due almost entirely to the enterprising Gibson brothers – John, James and Fred – whose famous 'Red Star Line' had been one of the most popular coaching services to and from the Cape. Recognising the futility of trying to compete with the railway, they turned their attention to the local transport system. In July 1885, it was announced that they intended to start a new bus

Arrival of the first official train in Kimberley, 28 November 1885. (K)

From a Gibson Brothers letterhead. (K)

service between Kimberley and Dutoitspan. Two of their 'stylish omnibuses' were put on display in Cape Town before being taken to the diamond fields.

The service, launched at the beginning of August, was an immediate success. In no way could the Gibson Brothers' coaches be compared with the jolting string of carts that had once plied between the two camps. 'The seats', it was reported, 'are luxuriously cushioned with crimson plush, and the conveyance is provided with a lamp and mirror, as well as a bell to intimate a desire to stopping the driver.' Each bus carried twenty-six passengers at the cost of one shilling each way. This, as the local newspapers observed, was progress indeed.

The local cab-drivers thought otherwise. They started to agitate against the new service, which, they claimed, was undercutting them. But the Gibson Brothers were not to be frightened off. In September they applied for permission to build a tramline between Kimberley and Dutoitspan 'to be worked either with horses or silent engines as used in large towns in England'. This resulted in the founding, in 1887, of the Victoria Tramway Company, the company which for many years monopolised passenger traffic between the main townships. Once the three-foot-six-inch-gauge line had been laid, ten four-wheel single-deck cars 'of the open cross bench type' – horse-drawn and imported from America – went into service. These brightly painted vehicles were to prove extremely efficient until, in 1890, Kimberley became the first town in South Africa to experiment (at first not too successfully) with an electrically-powered tramway. If nothing else, the diamond diggers richly deserved their reputation as a progressive community.

The railway certainly ushered in a new era. There was, as one old resident remarked, no longer any doubt that 'the Diamond Fields would become a part of the country that would be worth living in'.

(3)

The Kimberley railway station was eventually completed and formally opened on 31 July 1886. Crowds thronged the platform, and the mail train steamed in to a fusillade of fog signals. It was a merry enough occasion but, compared with the opening of the railway proper, something of an anticlimax. This was not entirely the fault of the railway authorities. The delay in completing the building of the station had, it is true, caused considerable annoyance (George Pauling, the contractor, had actually come to blows with some of the local officials) but, in the ordinary way, this might have been forgotten. Kimberley, given the slightest excuse, was always ready to celebrate. But, by the middle of 1886, excuses for celebrations were wearing a little thin. The majority of Kimberleyites were far too preoccupied to go on a spree. They had more serious things on their minds. Startling new events had occurred.

A couple of weeks before the opening of the station, Fred Alexander, a Kimberley merchant, had returned from the Transvaal with specimens of gold-bearing rock. His arrival created much excitement. He had picked the rock up on the Witwatersrand and, to prove it was auriferous, he invited several prominent Kimberley men to see a panning. The demonstration took place behind Alexander's shop on 16 July. It was a great success. It confirmed the vague rumours which were already current in the town.

One of the first to hear about the Transvaal gold discoveries had been J.B. Robinson. He had, or so he said, received a telegram from a former diamond digger telling him of the finds and urging him to leave for the Transvaal immediately. A couple of days after Fred Alexander's panning, Robinson was on his way. His sudden departure on the Transvaal coach was regarded as significant. 'It may be relied upon', commented the *Diamond Fields Advertiser,* 'that the nature of the gold fields is of a particularly attractive nature, or else Mr J.B. Robinson would not be going off to the new Eldorado.' The wily 'Buccaneer' was not, as everyone knew, a man who would waste his time chasing rainbows.

Reports of the astonishing finds being made on the Witwatersrand filled the Kimberley newspapers for the next week or so. Diggers were said to be flocking to the Transvaal from all over the country, and crowds of local men joined in the rush. The capital of the Boer Republic, Pretoria, was a whirl of activity. 'There has seldom', it was reported, 'been so much excitement in the town as at present as regards gold-mining in this district. . . . The new Gold Field is somewhat distant being thirty to thirty-five miles away from Pretoria. . . . It is difficult to say at present how far the auriferous deposit extends. Some people assert that it can be traced a distance of fifty to sixty miles.'

On 30 July, the day before the station opened, Kimberley received news of J.B. Robinson's activities. He was reported to be in the thick of things, buying up properties right, left and centre. He had made some incredible bargains and few doubted that he was on to a good thing. What must have puzzled those who knew him well was how he could afford to speculate so lavishly. When he had left Kimberley, he had, so to speak, been on his uppers.

J.B. Robinson's finances were indeed a mystery. To all outward appearances he had weathered the depression by obtaining huge loans from the Cape of Good Hope Bank. But, as a handful of Kimberley financiers knew, all was not what it seemed. The Cape of Good Hope Bank had itself been badly hit by the depression and for some months had been threatening to sell off the shares that Robinson had pledged as security. There had been, or so it seemed, nothing Robinson could do to stave off what looked like certain disaster. Most of his diamond investments had failed; landslides had put paid to all but two of his companies; he was up to his neck in debt. All his attempts to borrow money locally had been unsuccessful. Not only was he without security but he was no longer the powerful political figure he had once been. At the beginning of the year he had made a desperate attempt, in a hard-fought by-election, to regain his seat in the Cape Assembly but had been decisively beaten by the redoubtable Dan O'Leary. He had taken his defeat badly. As truculent as ever, he had petitioned to have the election declared invalid. He had accused O'Leary of not being a citizen of the Cape Colony and of employing corrupt practices. It was while he was awaiting the results of this petition that news had arrived of the gold finds in the Transvaal. How he had been able to cash in on those finds was anyone's guess.

The mystery was not cleared up until some years later. It then emerged that Robinson had been rescued by the enigmatic Alfred Beit. That Beit–or 'little Alfred' as he was affectionately known–should have taken the risk of financing Robinson was typical both of the man and of the way he operated. There were few men in Kimberley quite like 'little Alfred'.

Shrewd, shy and secretly generous, Alfred Beit was not given to showy gestures. One can search the early Kimberley newspapers and find very few mentions of his name. When it does appear it is merely as a member of some mining committee or, more frequently, heading the list of contributors to some struggling charity. Other than supporting worthy causes he played little part in the public life of the town. It was not that he did not care: he simply preferred to work behind the scenes.

Born in Hamburg, Germany, Beit had come to South Africa in 1875. He was then twenty-two and had spent the previous two years as an apprentice to a diamond dealer in Amsterdam. To look at, he was singularly unimpressive. A dumpy young man, whose head seemed too large for his body, he gave the impression–with his bulbous brown eyes, receding chin and tiny moustache–of being weak-willed and not over-bright. He was exceptionally retiring; a mass of nervous mannerisms. He would tug at his collar, twist his moustache and bite the corner of his handkerchief. With strangers he could rarely relax. But his seeming diffidence was deceptive. When it came to business, Alfred Beit was not only extremely gifted but remarkably determined.

Arriving at the diggings at the time of the Black Flag Rebellion, he had been quick to recognise the potential of the ailing diamond industry. With trade depressed and the market uncertain, many diggers and diamond buyers were beginning to lose confidence in South African diamonds. They felt that the stones being unearthed in Griqualand West could never compete with those sold from the long-established mines in Brazil. Beit knew enough about diamonds to realise how mistaken this attitude was. For him the loss of confidence provided a wonderful opportunity. 'When I reached Kimberley,' he said, 'I found that very few people knew anything about diamonds; they bought and sold at haphazard, and a great many of them really believed that the Cape diamonds were of an inferior quality. Of course, I saw at once that some Cape stones were as good as any in the world, and I saw, too, that the buyers protected themselves against their own ignorance by offering generally one-tenth part of what each stone was worth in Europe. It was plain that if one had a little money there was a fortune to be made.'

He went ahead and made his fortune. Starting as a representative of a Hamburg diamond-importing firm, he soon branched out on his own. He bought a piece of land and on it he built twelve or thirteen offices, keeping one for himself. This provided him with the base he needed. By offering high prices for diamonds, he quickly established himself as a diamond buyer. He did not have to look for sellers. His reputation for honest dealing soon spread. So did his reputation for generosity: any digger down on his luck could always be sure of a handout from Alfred Beit. In 1880 he had joined forces with Julius Wernher–the impressive-looking manager of Porges's French Company. This partnership was to prove one of the most successful in Kimberley. Beit's exceptional business acumen–he was said to have a mind like a ready-reckoner–was neatly complemented by Wernher's cool judgement. Together they prospered exceedingly.

It was probably Beit's uncanny intuition that made him answer J.B. Robinson's appeal for help. He had no earthly reason to involve himself in Robinson's affairs, although Robinson thought otherwise. At that time Robinson was ready to blame anyone and everyone for his downfall, including Alfred Beit. When he first approached Beit for a loan he did so with character-istic bluster. He did not so much ask for assistance as demand it. He accused Beit of being in league with others to 'squeeze' him out of the diamond industry and insisted on a loan as compensation. Beit was dumbfounded.

'I did not know what to say,' he later confessed. 'At last I asked him how much he wanted. He said he would leave that to me.

' "If I give you twenty thousand," I said, "will that do?" Of course, I was not obliged to give him anything at all. "Oh, yes," he said; "how good of you. I can win with that." From his manner I saw I had offered too much. I went on – "I suppose if I give you this twenty thousand, you will use it on joint account?" He said "Yes." So I gave him a cheque for twenty thousand or twenty-five thousand – I forget which – and he went off to the Rand.' Beit had no reason to regret his gamble. The investments made by Robinson proved, quite literally, to be gold mines. Within a matter of weeks Robinson was saved from bankruptcy and was well on his way to making a second, much larger, fortune. His partnership with Beit did not last long, but long enough for Beit to obtain a firm foothold in the goldfields. By the time that Johannesburg was established as the centre of the gold-mining industry, both Robinson and Beit were in new positions of power.

They were soon joined by other diamond magnates. Not all of them took part in the first mad rush to the Transvaal, but they were not far behind. The lure of gold proved irresistible; it attracted the successful and unsuccessful alike. Men who had become moderately rich in Kimberley went on to become the multi-millionaires of Johannesburg. Some of them had prospered on the diamond fields, others had felt the pinch of events: a handful had tried their luck at the Barberton gold diggings before moving to the Witwatersrand.

Included in the great exodus of the next few years were many Kimberley pioneers: men like Sigismund (later Sir Sigismund) Neumann, one of the early diamond buyers; young J.B. Taylor and his brother William, whose father had once owned the *Diamond Field;* George (later Sir George) Albu and his brother Leopold, who had set up as diamond buyers in 1877 and worked profitable claims at Dutoitspan and Bultfontein; George Goch, an active Member of the Cape Assembly; Henry 'Beetles' Bettleheim, a colourful diamond merchant and theatrical personality; Lionel (later Sir Lionel) Phillips, the former employee of J.B. Robinson who had married spirited Florrie Ortlepp, daughter of Sarah Ortlepp – the 'discoverer' of Colesberg Kopje; Hermann Eckstein, one of Alfred Beit's protégés. . . . The list is endless.

All these men who, in varying ways, had contributed to the development of

Corner of the Diamond Market, Kimberley, showing Alfred Beit's first diamond-buying office on the left. (K)

Bar of the Craven Hotel in 1890. Established in the early 1870s, the Craven was one of the oldest, as well as the most fashionable, of Kimberley's public houses. (K)

Kimberley were claimed by Johannesburg. It is ironic that just as the Diamond City was reaching maturity, when the hardships and primitive living conditions were rapidly becoming things of the past, so many talented men should disappear from its streets. Numbered among those who remained were some of the great names of South African history, but in the dramas that lay ahead they would be supported by a much smaller cast.

Johannesburg quickly eclipsed Kimberley as South Africa's foremost industrial town. Its rapid rise to prominence was a thing to marvel at. But behind the glitter of its gold there could always be detected the sparkle of diamonds. Kimberley men and Kimberley money supplied the knowledge and materials necessary to develop the gold mines: if Johannesburg was Kimberley's successful rival, it was also Kimberley's wonder child.

(4)

The town which the gold prospectors left behind bore little resemblance to the dust-blown camps in which they had lived on arriving at the diggings. For one thing, it had grown considerably. The last of the tents and wagons had long since disappeared; they had been replaced by substantial houses which spread in all directions. The time when Kimberley (or New Rush) and De Beers had been independent settlements was all but forgotten; buildings dotted the Dutoitspan Road and although old-timers still spoke of Beaconsfield as the 'Pan camp' most Kimberleyites regarded it as a suburb. Only the mines distinguished one centre from the others.

Not even the most loyal inhabitants could call the centre of Kimberley an attractive place. Its narrow, unpaved streets followed no pattern, its buildings claimed little architectural merit, its open spaces boasted few trees. It was crowded, close-packed and all higgledy-piggledy. With bricks still in shorter supply than diamonds, the town was built, almost entirely, of corrugated iron. This did not add to its charms. 'Corrugated iron', as one visitor remarked, 'is exceedingly serviceable and easy to handle by the builder; but, frankly, it is not pretty; and what a lot of corrugated iron has been used in the construction of Kimberley!' Some of the wealthier homes were enhanced by complicated trellis-work; a one-storied brick facade, pompously pedimented and pilastered, might screen the front of a corrugated-iron shop; but the all-over impression remained that of a 'tin town'–the very flower pots lined up on the verandahs were fashioned from old meat tins. Outwardly, in fact, Kimberley had not changed much since Anthony Trollope had described it as one of the ugliest places on earth.

Yet there were indications that it harboured some of the richest men in South Africa. Here and there, in the sprawling suburbs, the turrets of ornate private homes rose above the carefully nurtured gum trees. Richly patterned cast-iron pillars and balustrades graced an occasional public building. One might catch a glimpse of a superb carriage, a fern-hung conservatory, even a uniformed servant. The interiors of the most humble-looking iron houses could be, and often were, lavishly furnished. In his *roman-à-clef, Mixed Humanity,* one of the few Kimberley novels of the period, J.R. Couper – the town's celebrated prize-fighter–gives a graphic description of a diamond buyer's living-room in the mid-1880s. He pictures it as oppressively opulent – crammed with mahogany furniture, thick Persian rugs, velvet table covers, lace curtains and heavy silver. Not everyone, it seems, had the spartan tastes of Cecil Rhodes.

Kimberley had grown and many of its inhabitants had prospered; the town prided itself more on its progressive spirit than on its outward charms. There was much to boast about. Most of the town's public services – its water supply, its street lighting, its hospital, library and railway–had been established against great odds. Kimberley's isolated pioneers had had much to contend with and, even now, not all of the plagues of the past had been vanquished. Sanitary conditions were certainly better, the general standard of health had improved, there were fewer flies about and the roads, if far from perfect, were not as hazardous as they had once been; but it was still as hot as ever, duststorms still bombarded the town and the threat of fire remained a constant menace.

There were several serious fires in 1886, one of the worst occurring one evening in November, when the Kimberley Club was burnt to the ground. How the fire started no one was quite sure. It was thought that an oil-lamp had fallen in one of the upstairs rooms (members in the dining-room later claimed to have heard the thud). But whatever the cause, the result was disastrous. By midnight all that was left of the building–one of the 'most pleasing' in Kimberley 'with a great deal of wood in its construction'–was a shapeless mass of smouldering ruins. No time was lost in the rebuilding, but the fire hazard remained. Nine years later the Club was again gutted by fire and only then did a newspaper suggest 'that the time was ripe for the thorough re-organisation of the Fire Brigade'.

In other respects, however, Kimberley's forward-looking reputation was well deserved. Nowhere was this more apparent than in the field of education. The 1880s saw the foundation of the town's best-known schools. Humble as their origins were, these schools did credit to their founders. They, as much as anything, reflected the townsfolk's fundamental faith in the future during the great depression.

The few schools that existed during the early days had been started by various churches. One of the first was a primary school at Dutoitspan, established in 1871 by the Dutch Reformed Church. Originally a mere tent with a handful of pupils, it was somewhat enlarged when the municipality of Beaconsfield came into being. In 1885 a new building was erected and the Church Council, unable to meet the expense, handed the school over to the local authorities. The Beaconsfield Public School, as it was called, was one of the first truly undenominational schools on the diggings.

In Kimberley itself schools had been started by the Anglican and Roman Catholic churches and, in 1881, the Methodists opened a primary school for coloured children in New Main Street. Two or three private 'academies', run by overworked women, were already in existence, but it was not until the end of 1886 that determined efforts were made to establish a proper high school for boys and girls. At a well-attended meeting, held in the Town Hall on 25

November and supported by leading churchmen, it was formally resolved to form a committee for the founding of Kimberley's first public undenominational school.

The committee was elected and went to work with enthusiasm.By April 1887, thirty-four boys were temporarily installed in a warehouse in De Beer's Road, and a girl's school, with twenty-one pupils, was opened in Woodley Street. There was tremendous public interest in the new venture. Some £4,000 was collected locally – to which the Government later added £2,000 – for the erection of a permanent school building in Lanyon Terrace. The Kimberley High School, under its first headmaster W.A. Norrie, became fully active in July 1888, when the pupils were transferred to the new building.

One of the driving-forces behind the new school was Canon William Thomas Gaul. A tiny, plain-spoken, witty Irishman, Canon Gaul was one of the most popular churchmen in Kimberley. Arriving on the diamond fields in 1880, he had first served in the small Anglican church at Dutoitspan. So well attended were his sermons that, it is said, 'many of the mining congregation had to stand outside and listen at the window'. And after his appointment as rector of St Cyprian's, attendance at the morning and evening services more than doubled. Not that everyone regarded the packed pews as a tribute to Canon Gaul's eloquence as a preacher. Some years later there was to be an outcry among the parishioners of St Cyprian's over the number of coloured people attending the church. The majority of these seemingly devout worshippers, it was maintained, were 'young females of doubtful character . . . who make no secret of looking upon St Cyprian's as a *rendezvous*'.

This might simply have been prejudice. Canon Gaul was known to be a great champion of the coloured people. Three years after his arrival at the diggings, he had started the hopefully-named Perseverance School for coloured children and student teachers and was active in other branches of welfare work. But, prejudice or not, nothing seemed to interfere with Canon Gaul's popularity among all sections of the community. Even his suspicious High Church tendencies were offset by his down-to-earth manner. High Church he might have been, admitted one wary parishioner, but he and his clergy were not 'of an emasculated or hysterical type, men indulging in man millinery or ritualistic playthings, but honest, earnest workers'. Canon Gaul remained an influential figure in Kimberley until 1895, when he became Bishop of Mashonaland – or, as he put it, 'the smallest bishop with the largest diocese in Christendom'.

Another remarkable churchman involved in the founding of the Kimberley High School was the minister of the Dutch Reformed Church, John Kestell. Then a young man in his thirties, Kestell was every bit as active as Canon Gaul. One of his most lasting contributions to the town was the building, in the mid-1880s, of the imposing Dutch Reformed Church in the suburb of Newton. This chaste and elegant structure, pillared and arched in what was loosely termed the 'Roman style', cost the then considerable sum of £6,000. But it was not until after he had left Kimberley in 1894, that his true talents revealed themselves. The son of an 1820 Settler from Devon, John Kestell became a fervent and revered champion of the Afrikaans language. He not only wrote novels and short stories in Afrikaans, but was chairman of a commission which translated the Bible into Afrikaans he being responsible for the translation of the New Testament.

The Jewish community of Kimberley was also to produce an outstanding contributor to South African literature. This was Sidney Mendelssohn, the eldest son of the Reverend Meyer Mendelssohn, who in 1878 had replaced the Reverend Berthold Albu as the town's permanent minister. The Mendelssohn family claimed a distant relationship to the famous composer and as a young man Sidney (or Sydney, as he then spelled his name) Mendelssohn was involved in many of Kimberley's cultural activities. He was, for instance, one of the most enthusiastic promoters of the Musical, Literary and Debating Society which was formed in November 1885. After amassing a fortune as a diamond buyer, he became a director of a diamond-mining company which was established on the Vaal River in 1902; the township laid out on the company's estate was named Sydney-on-Vaal after him. It was during his years as a company director that he became interested in Africana. The huge library that was built up years later at Sydney-on-Vaal helped to inspire his massive and invaluable *South African Bibliography,* which was published in two volumes in 1910.

But it was probably Kimberley's many sporting events that were missed most by those who trekked to the Transvaal. By 1886 the town was able to offer sports enthusiasts a wide variety of entertainment. Regular fixtures ranged from the conventional horseracing, cricket, rugby, swimming and athletics to the more sensational 'assault-at-arms' boxing matches staged by Jack Couper at the Theatre Royal (with himself and Coverdale 'The Ladies' Pet' as star attractions) and even, until the police put a stop to it, deadly contests between fighting dogs.

For years cricket had been Kimberley's favourite sport. Saturday afternoon matches in the Public Gardens, with the Eclectic Cricket Club playing against visiting teams or a Kimberley Club side, had always drawn huge crowds. More recently, however, rugby had shown signs of taking over. Since the formation, in 1884, of the Pirates Rugby Football Club the standard of Kimberley rugby had improved enormously. The town could now field a team which could hold its own with any of the established clubs in the Cape. In August 1885, for instance, a Kimberley team had taken part in a rugby tournament held in Grahamstown and, although beaten by Cape Town by one goal and three tries to nil, had redeemed their honour by winning the match against Port Elizabeth by a goal and three tries.

But the town's most memorable rugby battle was that between the Pirates and the Kimberley Club in September and October 1887. 'Nothing in the annals of Rugby Football', it was said, 'had ever quite equalled this long-drawn-out struggle.' The first of these matches was played on Saturday 17 September, with Pirates winning by a try to nil. Kimberley Club immediately lodged an appeal against this try and demanded a re-play. The appeal was upheld and led not merely to one re-play but five - each of them ending either in a draw or further appeals against the score. The whole thing developed into a farce. 'The Rugby Union', snorted one reporter, 'displayed lamentable weakness in granting each appeal, and became the laughing-stock of every Rugby centre in the country in allowing individual bias to sway its judgement.' It was only after each side had agreed to abide by the decision of umpires and referee, that the Pirates finally walked off with the cup in the sixth re-play.

This struggle, for all its controversy, was more amusing than deadly. The same cannot be said for all Kimberley conflicts. Compared with the financial war then being waged on the diamond fields, the rugby battle was as nothing.

16

Amalgamation

Cecil Rhodes is said to have been among those Kimberley businessmen who witnessed Fred Alexander's gold-panning demonstration in July 1886. If he was, it did not inspire him to join the rush to the Rand. At that time he was far too caught up with his Kimberley concerns to risk embarking on what might have proved a wild goose chase.

Encouraging as the gold-panning undoubtedly was, it had not impressed everyone. There had, in the past, been too many wild rumours about gold finds, and even unsuccessful gold rushes, for these latest developments to convince the more hardened of Kimberley's sceptics. Even after glowing reports of extensive finds began pouring in from the Transvaal, there were still those who felt it wiser to hold back for a while. Not least among them was Cecil Rhodes.

There were many reasons for Rhodes's caution. Apart from anything else, he was then involved in a very personal crisis. His closest friend, Neville Pickering – or 'Pickling' as he was affectionately known – was seriously ill. He had, in fact, been ill for some time. Two years earlier he had been thrown from his horse while riding in the veld. He had fallen into a clump of thorn bushes and had been badly cut and bruised; 'some of the thorns', it was reported, 'entering below the knee of both legs'. The poison from the thorns, added to the after-effects of a bout of 'camp fever', had weakened him considerably. He never fully recovered; his health was permanently impaired.

Throughout his friend's long and depressing bouts of illness, Rhodes's devotion was unquestioned. All that could be done to ease Pickering's suffering, he did. When the news of the Witwatersrand gold finds reached Kimberley, Pickering had just returned from staying with his family in Port Elizabeth. He was far from well. Had any persuasion been necessary to convince Rhodes that it was not worth forsaking his Kimberley interests to chase after gold, his friend's health would undoubtedly have provided it.

Even when, some two weeks later, Rhodes did decide to visit the Transvaal, his investigation of the Witwatersrand was extremely superficial. He gave himself little time in which to study the reef. Hardly had he arrived in the Transvaal than he received a message to say that Neville Pickering had taken a turn for the worse: he was thought to be dying. To everyone's astonishment Rhodes announced that he was returning to Kimberley immediately. He left that evening, propped up among the mail bags on top of a fully booked coach.

His haste was not strictly necessary. Neville Pickering lingered on for a few more weeks. Rhodes never left his side. At times he was joined by Neville's brother William, who was then the manager of a bank of Dutoitspan, or Dr

Jameson, who had tended the sick man from the beginning. The three of them were in attendance when, on 16 October 1886, young Pickering died in Rhodes's arms.

After the death of his friend, Rhodes moved from the cottage they had shared. He went to live with Dr Jameson in another little corrugated-iron house opposite the Kimberley Club. His way of life did not change much. Jameson was a successful doctor and Rhodes was a diamond magnate, but they lived like impoverished diggers. The house was sparsely furnished and always untidy; the sitting-room, claimed one astonished visitor, looked 'like that of an undergraduate at college'. Most of their meals were eaten at the Club across the road.

With the Pickering family Rhodes remained friendly for the rest of his life. It was Neville's brother William who took over the post of Acting Secretary to De Beers and he worked for the company all his life. In the years to come William Pickering and his family were to play an important part in the social life of Kimberley and to contribute much to the later development of the town.

How much Rhodes lost by neglecting the Witwatersrand in the vital early stages of the gold rush, it is difficult to say. He had agents working for him in the Transvaal and he kept in touch with them throughout Neville Pickering's illness. In February 1887 he and Charles Rudd founded a gold-mining company, The Gold Fields of South Africa Limited, with a capital of £125,000. Although this company by no means equalled the concerns controlled by men like Alfred Beit and J.B. Robinson, it more than compensated Rhodes for his initial tardiness. By 1892, when it was renamed The Consolidated Gold Fields of South Africa, its capital had been increased by a million and a quarter, and three years later the dividend had risen by no less than fifty per cent. For all that, Rhodes was essentially a diamond magnate and Kimberley remained his effective base.

Indeed, it was his determination to control the diamond industry, as well as his concern for Neville Pickering, that had made him wary of becoming too involved in the Witwatersrand. He could not allow himself to become distracted. During the opening months of 1886 some significant moves had been made towards amalgamating the diamond mines. Although Rhodes had been only indirectly involved in these moves, he was fully aware of their importance. So, for that matter, were others. They may well have accounted for the fact that Barney Barnato did not join the stampede to the Transvaal.

Kimberley's long-delayed power struggle was about to begin. Already the main contestants were sizing each other up and measuring out their ground. Each of them was aware of the need to stick close to the field of battle. 'Nature', Rhodes was fond of saying, 'abhors a vacuum.' He was determined not to create one in Kimberley.

(2)

A story is told of the coming together of Cecil Rhodes and Alfred Beit. There could be some truth in it. One evening, it is said, Beit was working late in his

Kimberley office. Rhodes happened to be passing by and looked in on him.

'Hullo,' said Rhodes, 'do you never take a rest?'

'Not often,' answered Beit.

'Well, what is your game?' asked Rhodes.

'I am going to control the whole diamond output before I am much older,' said Beit.

'That's funny,' said Rhodes, 'I have made up my mind to do the same; we had better join hands.'

And join hands they did.

They became business partners and they became friends. They drank champagne and stout together at the Craven bar. They played poker–badly–at the Kimberley Club. Occasionally they were seen together at a Bachelors' Ball, Rhodes vigorously twirling the plainest girl in the room and Beit prancing beside the tallest. The diminutive Beit had a *penchant* for tall ladies. To watch him dancing was one of the sights of Kimberley: he appeared to run round his lofty partners rather than dance with them. But, above all, Rhodes and Beit worked to solve the problems of the diamond industry to their own advantage.

In Rhodes, Beit found a dynamic and purposeful hero. From the time of their meeting he devoted his life to Rhodes's interests. Together they made a formidable team. Beit, the financial wizard, was precisely the man Rhodes needed to further his grandiose schemes. When they undertook to monopolise the mines, they set the pace of the race towards amalgamation. Nevertheless, they were given a good run for their money.

Several attempts at amalgamation had already been made, of course. In 1875, at the time of the Black Flag Rebellion, the diggers of the Kimberley Mine had initiated a scheme of their own. They had pooled the bulk of their claims and appointed a representative to offer the mine for sale in London. But the English lawyers who examined the scheme found that the existing claim restrictions prevented such a sale. As soon as these restrictions were removed, the diggers tried again, only to be thwarted by J.B. Robinson, who had his own scheme for amalgamation. In 1881, Rhodes had tried to interest Baron Erlanger, the international financier, in a plan for amalgamating the De Beers Mine, but this had fallen through. The following year Rothschilds of London had taken a hand in the game. They had sent a Mr Gansl to Kimberley to investigate the possibility of amalgamation, starting with the Dutoitspan Mine. Gansl had been enthusiastically championed by J.B. Robinson, but had been no more successful than the others. To weld the dissident elements of Griqualand West into a prosperous whole was a thankless and frustrating task. Even with such a glittering prize at stake, few had the heart to pursue it.

But, as everyone realised, somehow or other amalgamation had to come. Until unity and a common purpose were achieved, there could be no stability in the diamond industry. This was something which politicians as well as financiers recognised. It was not merely the Kimberley capitalists who suffered from the periodic slumps: the export of diamonds had become vital to the Cape's economy.

That astute politician, J.X. Merriman, had long been toying with the idea of

Sir Joseph Benjamin Robinson in old age, wearing his famous pith helmet. (S)

Old before their time, Cecil Rhodes and Alfred Beit were both in their late forties when this photograph was taken. (S)

Alfred Beit's office in the Diamond Market, Kimberley, photographed in 1888. (K)

amalgamation. As early as 1883 he had approached J.B. Robinson in the hopes of devising a co-operative scheme. Robinson had been full of suggestions but none of them had proved workable. However, Merriman had persisted. The following year he had entered into discussions with C.J. Posno, a member of the well-known South American family, long connected with the Brazilian diamond mines. The discussions were fruitful. In August 1885, Posno sent Merriman details of a syndicate which had been formed in London. This was the Unified Diamond Mines Ltd, established with a share capital of £10,000, for the purpose of buying as many properties as possible in the four mines of Griqualand West. Those companies which sold out to the Unified Company were to receive a corresponding proportion of shares. Two French banks had backed the enterprise with a guarantee of £600,000. Merriman was appointed the company's South African representative; A. Moulle was nominated as the overseas representative.

Merriman hailed the plan as a 'message of salvation' for the diamond industry. In January 1886, he and Moulle went to Kimberley to start negotiations. The first person they contacted was J.B. Robinson. 'Personally I am very anxious to see you take a leading share in the matter,' Merriman wrote to Robinson. There can be little doubt that Robinson was equally anxious to take that share. But, of course, he was unable to: by that time Robinson, as Merriman discovered to his amazement, was practically bankrupt. This was the first serious blow to Merriman's plan. There were more to come.

After a month of negotiations Merriman found himself caught up in the deadly rivalries that had strangled so many good intentions in Kimberley. He found it impossible to get one mining company to move without the others. They all held back until, eventually, mutual suspicion turned into outright hostility. At a public meeting held on 30 January, Merriman's proposals were unanimously rejected. But, bad as this was, the final blow was not delivered until two weeks later.

On 13 February, the Kimberley newspapers carried large advertisments detailing a new plan for amalgamating the mines. In essence it was simplicity itself. The principal mining companies in the four mines were invited to exchange scrip with each other at a commonly acceptable valuation. In this way a joint interest would develop among the various companies which, in effect, would amount to amalgamation. This new plan was sponsored by the De Beers Mining Company and was the brainchild of the company's chairman, Cecil Rhodes. It took Merriman completely by surprise. Until then he had more or less counted Rhodes among his few supporters. Now, faced by such powerful opposition, he had no alternative but to telegraph C.J. Posno calling off his still-born scheme.

Whether Rhodes seriously intended to go ahead with the advertised plan is open to doubt. He kept his exchange-of-shares idea alive for a few more weeks and then let it drop. It was hardly the type of union for which he was angling. He intended that the mines should be controlled, not mutually, but by a single company: that company was De Beers Mining Company, with him at its head. His main concern at that time was to undermine Merriman's proposals and, in that, he was certainly successful.

Merriman's intervention, brief as it was, alerted others besides Rhodes. Not least among them was Barney Barnato. Until Merriman arrived on the scene, Barney had shown little apparent interest in amalgamation. Only then, it seems, did he realise that the formidable J.B. Robinson was no longer in the running. Even after Merriman had departed, Barney continued to make a great show of opposing all plans for unification. This pretended opposition, however, was a matter of tactics. Once he saw how Rhodes had dealt with Merriman, Barney Barnato was quick to rise to the challenge.

(3)

The next few months saw a great deal of back-stairs activity in Kimberley. Once Merriman was out of the way, the race towards amalgamation started in earnest. It was led by Cecil Rhodes and Alfred Beit. They started at a distinct advantage.

For some years Rhodes had been working for the unification of the De Beers Mine. While most people considered the Kimberley Mine as the key mine on the diamond fields, Rhodes placed his faith almost exclusively in De Beers. He argued, and continued to argue, that two shares in the De Beers Mine were worth three in the Kimberley Mine. What he meant, in fact, was that control of the De Beers Mine was a simpler proposition than control of the Kimberley Mine and that whoever controlled De Beers would be in a strong bargaining position when it came to the final take-over of the four mines. Reasoning in this way he had quietly set out to amalgamate De Beers. One by one, the De Beers Mining Company had succeeded in buying out, or incorporating, most of the smaller companies in the mine. By the beginning of 1887, the monopoly was all but complete. Only one company remained outside the De Beers net: this was the Victoria Company, headed by Mr Francis Oats.

It was Alfred Beit who came up with a plan for undermining the resistance of Francis Oats. He suggested that his own firm should combine with De Beers to buy shares in the Victoria Company in London. 'We felt that if they were bought in the London market,' Rhodes explained, 'it would excite no remark.' They bought the shares at the end of 1886 and kept quiet about them. Negotiations with one or two other companies had to be tied up before they were ready to close in on the Victoria. 'However,' said Rhodes, 'in pursuance of our policy of amalgamation we at last thought the time had arrived to inform the Victoria that we were their largest shareholders . . . and that amalgamation was necessary in our interests.'

That was at the end of April 1887. A few days later, on 6 May, Rhodes was able to report on their success at a general meeting of the De Beers Mining Company. He was thanked by Alfred Beit. They had good reason to congratulate themselves. By taking over the Victoria Company they had achieved what others had dreamed of: De Beers was the first mine in Griqualand West to come under the control of a single company. Amalgamation had, in part, become a reality.

In the meantime, Barney Barnato had not been idle. He was concentrating his considerable energies on the Kimberley Mine. Like many others, he was convinced that whoever controlled this mine would eventually dominate the diamond industry. He was aiming high, but then he was not one for half measures. The bigger the challenge, the more he warmed to it. Barney had been accused of many things, but no one had ever called him timid.

Luckily, he still had a firm foothold in the Kimberley Mine. Pressure from his shareholders had prevented him from abandoning the buried claims of the Barnato Company. Instead, in 1884 he had agreed to a merger with a small neighbouring company and then enlarged his holding by buying six more claims in the mine for £180,000. He had also set to work on his buried claims. He had solved this problem by sinking a shaft and commencing underground mining. The first load of diamondiferous ground to come from the old Barnato claims in three years was hauled on 15 July 1885. 'I feel now', he had enthused at the official hauling ceremony, 'like a father elated at the birth of his first child, scarcely even yet believing that once more we are actually pulling out our ground.' That child was soon to be followed by a whole tribe of others. As Barney well knew, there was nothing like solid family backing when a fight was in the offing.

He did not beget children, he snatched them. His first victim was the Standard Company, once controlled by J.B. Robinson. When, in the middle of 1886, Robinson accused his rivals of 'squeezing' him out of the Kimberley Mine, he might well have been right. Someone was definitely buying up the shares which he had pledged to the Cape of Good Hope Bank as security. But it was not, as he thought, Alfred Beit. At the next annual general meeting of the Standard Company, in December 1886, it was Barney Barnato who emerged as the largest shareholder.

For the first time since the formation of the company Robinson was not in the chair; he was not even at the meeting. The chair was taken by a Mr Pistorius, but this was a mere formality. The longest and most authoritative speech was made by Barney Barnato. He lectured the shareholders on the running of the company and urged them to agree to the recent proposals for an amalgamation with the Barnato Company. There was considerable opposition to his proposals, but this did not bother him unduly. Another, much larger, meeting was held two months later and Barney packed it with his own supporters. The merger was pushed through and the new concern took the name of the larger of the two companies. For the short period of its existence, it continued to be known as the Standard Company.

This was Barney's answer to Rhodes's moves in the De Beers Mine. The combination of his own claims and those of the Standard put him in a powerful position in the Kimberley Mine. He also had a strong base for future operations.

His attention was turned next to the most important company in the Kimberley Mine: Baring-Gould's Central Company. This was the company which Merriman had regarded as vital to the success of his unification scheme. His failure to win over the Central shareholders had placed him at the mercy of

Rhodes. Barney took no chances. Some of the more influential shareholders in this company were former diggers who were now living in great style in London. Immediately the amalgamation with the Standard was tied up, Barney and Harry Barnato left for London. Their nephew, Woolf Joel, remained behind to look after things in Kimberley.

It did not take long to bring the new powerful Standard and the Central together. Events were speeded up by Barney's recent *coup*; there were few people in Kimberley who did not recognise the way things were going. At the end of June 1887, Woolf Joel sent Barney a cable to say that negotiations were coming to a head in Kimberley. Barney rushed back.

The amalgamation of the Standard and Central Companies was formally decided upon at two meetings held on 7 July 1887. By the end of the day the Standard Company no longer existed and the new Central Company was in possession of the greater part of the Kimberley Mine. Barney attended both meetings. He had obtained all the backing he required in London and the result undoubtedly delighted him. In little over a year he had accomplished what it had taken Cecil Rhodes the best part of six years to achieve. At the beginning of 1886 there had been four powerful companies in the Kimberley Mine: the Central, the French, the Standard and the Barnato. Of these four the Barnato had been the smallest. Now only the French Company and a few minor concerns stood between Barney and complete control of the richest diamond mine in Griqualand West.

Always a showman, Barney knew how to dramatise his latest triumph. At the conclusion of the Central Company's meeting, a series of loud explosions were heard in the vicinity of the Kimberley Mine. People passing were said to be startled out of their wits. It sounded, claimed the *Diamond Fields Advertiser*, as if 'the Transvaal Navy had suddenly appeared and were bombarding dear old Kimberley. Hundreds of people rushed towards the mine, where the cannon, that is the dynamite shots, were being fired all round the edge, while the Companies' flags were seen waving from the Central and Standard Companies works. It was an "Amalgamation Salute" and it sounded quite gay and joyful, but nervous persons did not like it at first.'

One nervous person would not have liked it at all. That was Cecil John Rhodes. Those dynamite shots were aimed right at the heart of his great vision. Fortunately, he did not hear them. He had sailed from Cape Town the day before. He was on his way to organise a counterblast. The siege of the French Company – the company whose claims ran across the Kimberley Mine, dividing the holdings of the Central from those of the former Standard – was about to begin. So long as these claims remained outside the Barnato net, the amalgamation of the Central and the Standard was, to all intents and purposes, a financial union only. Barney knew this. Rhodes knew this. All Kimberley watched and waited for the next move.

(4)

Rhodes had a slight edge on Barney. The French Company was represented by Wernher and Beit, and Beit was Rhodes's ally. It was not much of an edge. Beit only represented the French Company, he did not control it; but at least he was able to keep Rhodes informed of any moves made against him.

All the same, Rhodes needed to act swiftly. His only hope of blocking a complete take-over by Barnato was an outright purchase of the French Company. This presented a formidable problem. As the battle for control of the mine had intensified, so had the French Company's shares risen. Rhodes was a rich man but his money was tied up in his holdings; he dared not release his grip on any of the shares he held. He needed extra capital. He needed to negotiate a very large loan.

Once again it was 'little Alfred' who came to his rescue. Beit suggested that they approach Rothschild's of London. As the largest financial house in Europe, Rothschild's had both the name and the resources to give the backing they needed. Rhodes had leapt at the suggestion. Supplied by Beit with the necessary introductions and accompanied by Gardner Williams – the newly appointed manager of the De Beers Mining Company – he set off for London immediately.

On reaching England Rhodes lost no time in contacting Lord Rothschild. A meeting was arranged and the plan for buying the French Company discussed. Rothschild was cautious, but encouraging. 'Well, Mr Rhodes,' he said at the end of the interview, 'you go to Paris and see what you can do in reference to the purchase of the French Company's property, and in the meantime I will see if I can raise the £1,000,000 which you desire.' This, from a man who had recently advanced no less than four million pounds for the purchase of shares in the Suez Canal, was good enough for Rhodes.

In Paris he was again helped by Beit's influence. Beit had already prepared his associates for Rhodes's coming. He had persuaded Jules Porges that amalgamation of the mines was a sound financial move, and Porges, in turn, had recommended to his fellow directors that Rhodes's provisional offer be accepted. The French directors agreed to the sale of the company for £1,400,000. Rhodes, confident that with the help of Alfred Beit he could raise the balance, was delighted.

The sale of the company was only provisional, however. It had to be confirmed at a meeting of the French shareholders in October. This, in a way, was merely a formality. As the majority of the directors were in favour, any opposition at the shareholders' meeting could be easily overcome. Or so it was thought. Barney Barnato had other ideas.

Suspecting what Rhodes was up to, Barney had acquired a substantial interest in the French Company. When he heard of the deal that Rhodes had negotiated, he lost no time in countering it. He topped Rhodes's offer by £300,000. The Central Company, he said, was prepared to pay £1,700,000 in cash for the French Company. This, together with the shares he held, put him in a strong position.

But it was not quite strong enough. Rhodes's allies in Paris stood by him. Barnato was told that a provisional agreement had been negotiated and that he, like the other shareholders, would have to abide by it. Needless to say, Barney was not prepared to do any such thing.

On 21 September he called a meeting of all the Kimberley shareholders. It was a mammoth gathering. Barney did most of the talking; he had little difficulty in winning over his audience. With a wealth of facts and figures, he explained how the take-over would prove detrimental to the smaller share-holders. The company was being sold, he said, by people who had no real knowledge of the Kimberley Mine. He was loudly cheered and the meeting ended with a cable being sent to the directors in Paris, protesting against the sale to Rhodes 'as a better offer has already been made by the Kimberley Central Company'. Cecil Rhodes was in for some tough opposition – that much was clear.

Rhodes was quick to scent danger. He tried to snuff it at its source. On his return to Kimberley, he arranged a meeting with Barney Barnato in the hopes of calling his bluff. He said that, if the Central Company went ahead with their offer to overbid him for the French Company, then he would simply raise his bid. 'You can go on and bid for the benefit of the French shareholders *ad infinitum*,' he warned Barney, 'because we shall have it in the end.'

Barney was not impressed. Why should he have been? He knew the difficulty that Rhodes had had in raising the purchase money. In any game of beggar-my-neighbour he felt that the Central Company was a match for De Beers. Rhodes knew this as well. He was wise enough not to attempt to better the Barnato offer.

Instead, he graciously bowed out of the race. At least, that is what he appeared to do. To everyone's surprise (Barney's not least) he agreed to hand over the French Company. He made Barney a splendid offer. He said that if he was allowed to purchase the French Company without interference, he would re-sell it to the Central for £300,000 cash and the remainder in Central shares. Barney was delighted. The deal was closed. Barnato had pulled off another spectacular *coup* – or had he?

Barney should have known Rhodes better. He should have known that Rhodes did not act without a calculated motive. He soon discovered what that motive was. By seeming to give in to Barnato, Rhodes had achieved something that he had long been angling for: he had gained a firm foothold in the Kimberley Mine. Once the French Company was amalgamated with the Central, new shares were issued. Of these Rhodes held one-fifth. Now he was in a position to block Barnato's moves in the Kimberley Mine, while Barnato was powerless against him in De Beers. It was to obtain such an interest in the Kimberley Mine that he had wanted to buy the French Company in the first place. Barnato had merely given him a helping hand.

Essentially, however, the battle line remained unchanged. Tactics aside, it was still a matter of the De Beers Mine against the Kimberley Mine. In any amalgamation, the controlling interest in one mine would have to yield to the controlling interest in the other. Which mine could hold out longest? That, when it came down to it, was to be the deciding test.

The gloves were off and the battle between the two mines started. Barney was determined to crush competition from De Beers. Rhodes was equally determined to prove that he could withstand any attempt Barnato made to undercut De Beers. Production was stepped up. The market price of diamonds plummeted to eighteen shillings per carat. It was the worst kind of financial madness.

Rhodes claimed that he tried to negotiate a truce. He several times approached the Central Company with plans for a fusion which would bring the suicidal price war to an end. It got him nowhere. Neither side was prepared to accept the valuation of their property by the other side; and, until they could reach agreement on this score, there could be no fusion.

Finding Barnato immune to pressure, Rhodes decided to revert to tried and tested methods. In his take-over of the De Beers Mine, he had successfully crushed his opponents by obtaining a shareholding majority in their companies. He would do the same with Kimberley Central. It would not be easy. It would require a great deal of money. Since the amalgamation with the French Company, the value of Central shares had soared. A battle between Rhodes and Barnato for Central shares – and Rhodes knew it would be a battle – would push the price up even further. It would, indeed, require plenty of money: he estimated the cost at two or three million pounds. How was he to get it?

He got it, of course, from Alfred Beit. He and Rhodes held a council of war at Poole's Hotel in Cape Town at the end of February 1888. 'If only we can have the pluck to undertake it,' Rhodes argued, 'we must succeed.' Beit agreed. Then Rhodes asked where the money was to come from. 'Oh!' replied Beit, 'we will get the money if we only can buy the shares.'

And get the money they did. Beit himself put up £250,000 with no strings attached. The rest he obtained from international financiers: Jules Porges, the Rothschilds of Paris and London, and Rodolphe Kahn, the head of a powerful financial house in France.

Now the battle opened on a new front. Barney was no novice at scrambling for shares and, once he realised what was happening he came out fighting. Rhodes made the first moves; Barnato followed suit. They bought up shares with reckless determination. And they bought at a time when diamonds were at an all-time low; the prices they fetched hardly covered the cost of production. The value of Kimberley Central shares increased out of all proportion. When the struggle began they stood at £14, soon they had risen to £49. This created new problems.

Some of Barney's fair-weather supporters could not resist the temptation to make a quick profit. As the value of the shares rose, they stopped buying for Barnato and started selling for themselves. Rhodes's allies, on the other hand, stood firm. Soon his holdings in the Kimberley Central had increased from one-fifth to three-fifths. This proved too much for Barney. He was forced to capitulate. There was simply no point in his holding out any longer. In March 1888 he accepted Rhodes's terms. He agreed to give up the Central in exchange for De Beers shares.

It is said that there were certain provisos attached to Barney's surrender. Popular legend has it that he insisted that Rhodes use his influence to have him elected, first to the Kimberley Club, and then to the Cape Assembly. This seems extremely doubtful. Barney Barnato was quite capable of securing his election to both places, with or without the help of Cecil Rhodes. To think otherwise is to underestimate both Barney and the nature of the amalgamation battle.

But the legend persists. So does another, even more colourful story. It is said that, after introducing Barney to the Kimberley Club, Rhodes made a request. 'Well, you've had your whim,' Rhodes is supposed to have said; 'I should like to have mine, which you alone in Kimberley can satisfy. I have always wanted to see a bucketful of diamonds; will you produce one?' This is thought to have flattered Barnato. It is claimed that he shovelled all his available diamonds into a bucket and that Rhodes, plunging his hands into the bucket, 'lifted out handfuls of the glittering gems and luxuriously let them stream back through his fingers like water'.

It makes a good story, but it is most unlikely. Had Rhodes wanted to indulge such a whim, he had had plenty of opportunities for doing so. Buckets of diamonds are apt to dazzle the imagination.

One would like to believe that the deal was brought to such a glittering climax. It would have made a fitting end to one of the greatest financial transactions in history.

(5)

The war was over. All that remained was to arrange the peace. A new company had to be formed, a trust deed drawn up. The full implications of Rhodes's victory had yet to be revealed.

The amalgamation was not, as far as Rhodes was concerned, merely a business venture. He saw it as the means by which he could accomplish his political ambitions. The new company was to provide the money he needed to pursue his vision – the vision of all Africa united under the British flag. The terms of the trust deed would have to allow for this. Barney had other ideas. He wanted nothing to do with visions. He was a businessman, he insisted, and his business was diamonds, not politics. They argued the point for several days. In the end, Rhodes again had his way.

The last round was played out in the corrugated-iron cottage which Rhodes shared with Dr Jameson. Barney brought his nephew, Woolf Joel, with him; Rhodes was backed by Alfred Beit. The four of them argued all night. They became tired and irritable, but neither side would give in. Rhodes won eventually because he had to. For him this final stage was the most vital. Amalgamation meant little or nothing if he could not use it for his own ends. He brought all his powers of persuasion to bear on Barnato. He produced facts, figures and maps to support his arguments. He appealed to Barney's business instincts as well as his imagination. There was no telling what riches might be found in central Africa, he contended; Barney owed it to himself as well as to the new company to make provision for exploiting those riches.

Night gave way to morning. They were all exhausted. At last Barney, struggling to keep awake, gave in. It was then he made his famous submission. 'Some people', he shrugged, 'have a fancy for *this* thing and some for *that*; you have a fancy for making an Empire. Well, I suppose I must give it to you.'

And so it was settled. In a bleak, comfortless Kimberley cottage, the future, not only of the diamond industry, but of an entire continent was decided. The town had been in existence for less than twenty years; the eldest of the four men was thirty-five. If Kimberley was, according to Trollope, one of the ugliest places on earth, it was also one of the most extraordinary.

The new amalgamated concern was called De Beers Consolidated Mines. It was incorporated in March 1888 with a modest capital of £100,000 in £5 shares. The trust deed, drawn up later, gave Rhodes all he needed. His victory was complete. On 31 March 1888, he outlined each stage of his struggle with the Central Company to the shareholders of De Beers. The speech was one of the longest – it ran to nine thousand words – and one of the most remarkable he ever made. He spoke without notes and held his audience enraptured. Towards the end, he referred to the 'poorer mines', Dutoitspan and Bultfontein. He said that De Beers intended to make them fair offers, which they would be wise to accept. 'If they do not,' he warned, 'there may be a period of antagonism – on the most friendly basis – but we are bound to win, gentlemen, if we get your support as De Beers shareholders.'

And, of course, win they did. The take-over of these two mines was speeded up by disastrous reef falls in 1888. Rhodes had prophesied that this would happen and he was ready to act when it did. He was lunching at the Kimberley Club when one of the important owners of the Bultfontein Mine arrived to announce the disaster. A cab was called and Rhodes, accompanied by a few friends, rushed to view the scene. After sitting for an hour on the edge of the mine, Rhodes presented his proposal for amalgamation. The owners of the two mines had no option but to commence negotiations. These negotiations were protracted (some companies held out for years) but De Beers Consolidated Mines triumphed in the end. It was always accepted that they would. They had no alternative. Things had reached the stage where only amalgamation could prevent the complete collapse of the diamond industry.

Yet, obvious as this was, many found it a difficult pill to swallow. There was one last attempt to prevent amalgamation. It almost succeeded. In August 1888, a group of Central shareholders challenged the decision to merge their company with De Beers. They argued that, under their deed of association, such a merger could only be effected with a 'similar company'. The trust deed drawn up by Rhodes showed that De Beers Consolidated Mines, whatever else it might be, was vastly different from the Central Company. They took their case to the Cape Supreme Court.

The action was successful. The Chief Justice of the Cape agreed that the new corporation was an entirely new undertaking. Diamond mining in Kimberley formed only an insignificant part of the powers acquired by De Beers Consolidated Mines. The company, observed the judge, was free to mine

The last portrait photograph of Barney Barnato, taken in Johannesburg shortly before his death. (S)

The famous cheque for £5,338,650, paid by De Beers for the Kimberley Mine in July 1889. (S)

Barnato Buildings, Kimberley (Diamond Market), photographed during the 1880s. (M)

anywhere in the world. It could mine diamonds, gold or coal; it could carry on banking operations and financial obligations for foreign governments; it was free to annex territory and maintain a standing army. 'The powers of the Company', he said, 'are as extensive as those of any Company that ever existed.' His judgment was in favour of the plaintiffs.

At the same time he recognised Rhodes's difficulty and suggested a way out. Rhodes acted upon it. He and Barnato held the majority of shares in the Central. They now used this majority to put the company into voluntary liquidation. This done, they bought the assets of the Central for £5,338,650. A cheque for this amount was passed on 18 July 1889 and the amalgamation was complete.

The passing of this cheque meant more than the extinction of the Central Company; it marked the end of an era. After almost twenty turbulent years, diamond mining in Kimberley ceased to be an adventure and became a stable, less romantic industry.

Not only mining, but Kimberley itself changed. 'This town,' noted a visitor a few years later, 'once humming with speculation, business, and movement (is) now the essence of sleepy respectability and visible prosperity. . . . The stranger soon perceives that the whole community revolves on one axis, and is centred, so to speak, in one authority. "De Beers" is the moving spirit, the generous employer, and the universal benefactor.'

But this, although true enough, was not the entire story. Kimberley had changed, but it was far from dead. There were still exciting days ahead.

PART FOUR: A NEW ERA

A group of De Beers Directors: Cecil Rhodes and Barney Barnato, seated with legs crossed, centre; Woolf Joel, extreme left. (J)

17

The Fifth Mine

Barney Barnato got his wish. In November 1888 he was elected to the Cape Assembly. Whether or not his election had anything to do with the amalgamation deal he had made with Rhodes, he undoubtedly received the full support of Rhodes's colleagues. Not that he relied entirely upon this support; when it came to putting on a show Barney needed no assistance – his election campaign was one of the most flamboyant ever conducted in Kimberley.

He toured the streets in a carriage decorated in gilt, drawn by four silver-harnessed horses and attended by outriders wearing jockey caps and breeches. Two young boys, dressed in olive-green velvet coats and sporting cockaded hats, accompanied him wherever he went. He was elected with a large majority, but not without a tough fight. At almost every meeting he addressed he was heckled mercilessly, bottles were thrown, and often the proceedings ended in a free fight. He was continually taunted about his connection with I.D.B.; the case against his nephew, Isaac Joel, was dragged up; and so was his heartless persecution of John Fry. Many agreed with the fiery rector of Beaconsfield, who declared that Barney was not 'a fit and proper person to represent us in the House of Assembly'.

Barney never fully recovered his former popularity. He was not a success as a Member of the Legislative Assembly. The Kimberley newspapers were constantly attacking him for being flippant and irresponsible. In a political demonstration in 1891, both he and Rhodes were burnt in effigy by an angry Kimberley mob. This hostility, however, was not entirely political. It had much to do with the economic depression which engulfed the town after amalgamation. Not everyone welcomed the advent of De Beers Consolidated Mines.

Nor, for that matter, did everyone expect amalgamation to solve Kimberley's problems. Many considered that its ushering-in had been ominous. In July 1888 – a month before the Central shareholders challenged the merger in the Supreme Court – a fire in the De Beers Mine resulted in what was described as 'the worst mining disaster yet recorded in South Africa'.

How the fire started remains a mystery. Gardner Williams, the General Manager of De Beers, suspected that it was caused by a carelessly placed candle in a disused engine-room. An African worker is thought to have sneaked off to the engine-room, lighted a candle, and then fallen asleep. The first warning of the fire came at half-past six in the evening of 10 July. Williams was about to leave the mine when he received a message telling him that one of the mine

Barney Barnato, with supporters, in his carriage complete with liveried postillions, photographed outside the Barnato house in Kimberley during the 1888 election. (S)

Coffins of victims of the disastrous fire in the De Beers Mine in July 1888. (K)

shafts was alight. A few minutes earlier Clarence Lindsay, the Mine Manager, had taken six miners down the shaft to inspect some repair work. As soon as the alarm was given, two other miners attempted to warn Lindsay but already the smoke was so dense that they were driven back after descending a mere hundred feet. On reaching the surface they collapsed, completely exhausted. Lindsay and his party are thought to have been so overcome by the smoke that they were unable to signal for help, let alone attempt to hoist the skip in which they had descended.

Efforts to rescue the men from the surface proved useless. When Williams eventually decided to risk hoisting a skip through the billowing smoke it was too late. The hauling-wire had become so hot that it broke, sending the skip with four men in it plunging to the bottom of the mine. The shaft had become a death trap for the 66 white men and 619 Africans underground.

Tense crowds waited throughout the night. It was a harrowing vigil. At ten o'clock a white man and six Africans managed to scramble through a ventilation shaft. Rescuers battled heroically to clear more outlets, but were only partly successful: 24 white men, including Lindsay, and 178 Africans died in the fire which raged throughout the following day. Such a catastrophe did not augur well for the future.

Yet, as expected, the amalgamation did benefit the diamond industry as a whole. The ruinous competition between rival companies was halted, the output of diamonds was regulated and steps were taken to control fluctuating market prices. But even these badly-needed reforms were not achieved lightly. To reduce the diamond output the mines at Dutoitspan and Bultfontein had to be closed down and hundreds of diggers and overseers were thrown out of work; small company owners who had stood out against amalgamation soon found themselves out of business; once again unemployment became a serious problem. In Beaconsfield work was practically unobtainable.

Nor was the gloom confined to the diamond fields. Amalgamation had coincided with a country-wide slump; from almost every town in South Africa came reports of depression and shaky share markets. In March 1889 faith in the Witwatersrand had been badly shaken when shafts on the Main Reef had struck pyritic ore. It was then realised that gold mining was likely to prove a far more complicated and costly business than had been anticipated. The resulting panic led to a collapse of the gold market which affected the entire country. Three banks in the Cape Colony failed and many leading citizens were ruined. Everyone had second thoughts about the value of South Africa's mineral wealth.

'Gold Mines are all very well,' sighed J.X. Merriman in October 1890, 'but I confess I wish I could get people out here on the land as they go out in California or in Australia. Everyone in S. Africa wants to become rich by some wonderful speculation, or to sit down and see the "lazy nigger" work. It is all very disheartening.'

But in Kimberley the depression was seen purely in local terms. Amalgamation was blamed for the town's ills and Barnato and Rhodes – particularly Rhodes – were judged the villains of the piece. Demonstrations against Rhodes were whipped up and encouraged by a militant organisation known as the Knights of Labour. In their manifesto they attributed the stagnation of business to the 'existence and domination of one great Monopoly, one giant Corporation, as well as to the overweening greed and ambition of one wealthy, overestimated, disappointing politician'.

By that time the overestimated and disappointing politician had become Prime Minister of the Cape. He had been elected to office in July 1890, shortly after his thirty-seventh birthday. Caught up as he was in his political activities, Rhodes was by no means indifferent to the accusations made against him in Kimberley. His reply to his critics was as logical as it was maddening. He had done all he could to alleviate hardship in the town and supported the efforts being made to find work for the unemployed. What more could he do? If there had been no amalgamation, he argued, not only the diamond industry but all Kimberley would have been ruined. Only the pig-headed could deny that.

But Rhodes's arguments were cold comfort for Kimberley's unemployed. They were more concerned with events, than with eventualities. The demonstrations continued. For a time, Rhodes had to be given police protection whenever he was in the town.

Yet, even during this crisis, Kimberley remained a place of contradictions. With unemployment rife, agitators active and finances low, the town had rarely appeared more prosperous. When, in April 1890, Sir Henry Loch, the newly appointed Governor of the Cape, paid his first official visit to the diamond fields, he was given a traditional Kimberley welcome. The town bristled with triumphal arches, every building was festooned with flags and bunting. Banquets, levees and garden parties followed each other in rapid succession. Tim Tyson, the popular, highly efficient secretary of the Kimberley Club, surpassed himself in arranging a magnificent ball for the town's élite: the mad scramble for tickets being equalled only by the heartburnings of the excluded. Even so the place was packed.

'The handsome rooms of the Club', smirked one of the privileged, 'were none too large for the guests who attended. That it was a splendid affair and an unqualified success goes without saying.' Some Kimberleyites, at least, were learning to live with economic depressions.

Another, more impressive, indication of the town's resilience was the building boom which followed amalgamation. If nothing else, the advent of De Beers Consolidated Mines provided Kimberley with a sense of stability. Despite its teething troubles, few doubted that the new corporation was there to stay. It inspired confidence not only in the diamond industry, but in the town itself.

'At the present time,' boasted the *Diamond Fields Advertiser* in May 1890, 'when we are all suffering more or less from dull times that have been prevalent all over the Colony, the building trade in Kimberley would appear to be unusually brisk, judging by the number of new buildings in the course of erection and by the improvements being effected in the old ones. . . . That brick buildings are being built where very modest shanties were demolished only proves the truth of the assertion that Kimberley is not dead yet, but on the contrary very much alive and sanguine of a prosperous future.'

No fewer than 144 buildings, including a new fire station, were erected in 1890 alone.

De Beers Consolidated Mines was largely responsible for the new building craze. In 1889, shortly after amalgamation, it had set the ball rolling by housing its white workers in a model village on the outskirts of the town. The idea had come from Cecil Rhodes. He was determined that the employees of De Beers should live up to their new status. They were to be removed from what he called, 'those wretched, God-forsaken, and sun-burnt habitations . . . the rents of which were on the basis of pawn-brokers' charges' and given moderately priced houses in decent surroundings. With the help of Sydney Stent, a local architect, he set about planning Kimberley's most ambitious housing scheme.

The result was the famous village of Kenilworth. Some three miles from the centre of Kimberley, on land which had been described as 'a desert', the township was laid out. Broad avenues were lined with double rows of eucalyptus, beefwood or pepper trees; semi-detached houses of red brick, gabled and verandahed, were set in plots big enough to allow for fruit and vegetable gardens. At the junction of the two main avenues was a circle around which were erected the settlement's main buildings. Here was the post office, the club and the school. In time, a handsome church – the Anglican Church of Saint Edward the Confessor – was built. The foundation stone, laid by Mrs William Pickering, bore – confusingly – two dates: 26 June 1902 and 9 August 1902. The laying was planned to coincide with the date of King Edward VII's coronation; when the coronation was postponed, the date had to be altered.

Within a very few years Kenilworth ('my hobby' Rhodes called it) had developed into a show place. Water-carts trundled along its leafy streets, its villas rested in luxuriant gardens, the Club – having changed into an Institute – became a lively social centre. At the turn of the century the old mule-drawn trams were replaced by a steam-tram – the famous 'Puffing Billy'. Bordering the village was the De Beers orchard, where over 8,000 fruit trees – oranges, lemons, apricots, peaches, plums, pears, apples and quinces – as well as trellised graperies, flourished in spite of the frost and the hail and the locust. 'To see the orchard in full bloom', wrote one observer, 'is an experience never to be forgotten.' All in all, Kenilworth was an oasis. It became a favourite spot for outdoor fêtes, the first being the mammoth picnic which De Beers organised in December 1889 to celebrate amalgamation.

The improvements to Kimberley itself were hardly less impressive. Until this time, the only building of any real architectural pretensions had been the Gowie Brothers building at the corner of Dutoitspan Road and Jones Street. Built in 1886 (although the firm had been established as early as 1871) Gowies' was one of the town's landmarks. A two-storied building of red brick, it boasted a clock tower which could be seen from almost anywhere in the town.

But from now on, the one-storied corrugated-iron stores began to be replaced by altogether more ornate and substantial shops and offices. Brick frontages sported elaborate cast-iron balconies; decorative wooden pillars supported curved corrugated-iron canopies; facades were topped by urns, gables and broken pediments. Every style of robust, uninhibited, late-Victorian architecture was represented; every public building – whether it be the Library, or the Masonic Temple or the Magistrates Court – had its Corinthian pillars or its balustrades or its wooden fretwork or its ornamental lamp-stands. And to add to the exuberance of the architecture, the streets were thronged with clattering trams, tented Cape carts and strolling pedestrians.

And the town was spreading. Its wealthier citizens needed homes to suit their new-found dignity. In a suburb called – inevitably – Belgravia, scores of large, elegant houses were being erected. Built of clay-coloured Kimberley brick with elaborately pitched corrugated-iron roofs, they were rich in intricate white-woodwork verandahs. With water still in short supply, few gardens had lawns; instead, trees and shrubs shadowed carefully raked gravel surfaces. Within the cool, high-ceilinged, over-furnished rooms of these spacious villas, Kimberley's rich townsfolk could escape the still stark realities on the diggings.

Amalgamation ushered in a new era for the town. It provided not only stability, but a touch of elegance, to the once turbulent and sprawling settlements that had emerged from the squalor of the early camps. But it was to take time for these blessings to be fully appreciated. There were still pressing problems to overcome.

(2)

The building boom helped, but did not solve, the unemployment problem. Mostly it was the Malay artisans and bricklayers who benefited: too few labouring jobs were provided to make any real difference to the vast army of jobless, unskilled, African mineworkers. Nor did it help the out-of-work white overseers. The building trade was, for the most part, able to supply its own foremen and managers. Other outlets had to be sought to relieve the depressed labour market.

The most promising of these outlets was debris washing. This required neither skill nor knowledge of any trade outside the diamond industry. It had, in fact, once been a recognised and legitimate occupation for poor diggers and had assisted in relieving unemployment during previous financial slumps.

In the early days, diamond sorting had often been a rushed and haphazard business. Many diggers, with more enthusiasm than experience, had failed to appreciate the necessity for fine combing of the soil when searching for smaller stones. Impatient for quick riches and spectacular finds, they had been inclined to discard the solid lumps of earth which could not easily be broken up or which took too long to disintegrate in the sun. Even the most scrupulous of sorters, suffering from eye-strain, were known to miss valuable diamonds in moments of tiredness, or through distraction. For years Kimberley residents were to pick up diamonds from the debris soil they had used to cover their gardens.

Debris washing, in the early 1870s, had been one of the most profitable and popular industries on the diamond fields. It required no capital and little equipment. Primitive 'washing machines' could be knocked-up cheaply by a

A typical house at the 'model' village of Kenilworth, Kimberley. The village was designed to house the employees of De Beers Consolidated Mines after the amalgamation of the mines in 1889. (K)

Debris-washing in 1896. Licences were issued to wash debris during the 1890s to help relieve the unemployment problem caused by the amalgamation of the mines. (K)

carpenter and a debris washer's licence cost only ten shillings a month. Often the washers were allowed to cart away debris from the heaps without payment or would be charged a nominal fee of sixpence a load. Stories of remarkable finds made in discarded debris were legion; many a successful digger is said to have started life on the fields as a debris washer; some even made a fortune without changing their lowly occupation. At one time, the passenger coaches arriving at Kimberley were reported to be packed with penniless optimists whose sole intention was to wash debris.

'The debris heaps', says John Angove, 'were a lively scene, teeming with people, both white and black, busy with their buckets scooping up loose ground, or shovelling it into sacks to take away to the washing machines. In the scooping and shovelling operations many diamonds, some of considerable value, were found.' Debris washing was at its height in 1874, shortly before the Black Flag Rebellion. It continued for a few more years and resulted in the flattening, among other heaps, of the camp's most famous landmark – Mount Ararat. But the drive against I.D.B. had put a stop to it. For obvious reasons, diamonds said to have been 'found' on the debris heaps had become suspect and the issuing of debris-washing licences had been curtailed.

Inevitably the mine owners were accused of acting unjustly. Not all debris washers were involved in the I.D.B. traffic; many of them were hard-working men and women who were making a living honestly and legitimately. Resentment against the debris-washing prohibitions had never completely died out. In 1890, this resentment was revived by the Debris Washers Association. Throughout the early part of the year, several public meetings were called to agitate for a properly controlled system of debris washing which would provide work not only for white licence holders but for the gangs of black labourers they could employ. The meetings drew wide support; many old-timers – such as R.W. Murray and George Bottomley – actively campaigned for the renewal of debris-washing licences. The Town Council was sympathetic and eventually agreed to issue 'permits to wash diamondiferous debris on municipal land'. The sale of any diamonds found was carefully supervised; in the first year of operations the Council received £2,200 commission on the stones unearthed in debris heaps.

Welcome as this was, it merely scratched the surface of the unemployment problem. There were many white men, particularly the younger ones, who regarded debris washing as a demeaning occupation. They refused to consider such work. Accustomed to large salaries and positions of authority, they saw no future for themselves scrambling about the dusty debris heaps. That the type of position they sought no longer existed in Kimberley was difficult for them to accept. The get-rich-quick philosophy of the early days was beginning to take its toll.

What could be done about Kimberley's idle, feckless young men? It was a matter of great concern. Endless newspaper articles and editorials were devoted to the subject. The town seemed full of parasitic youngsters, living off their families or their dwindling savings. Some took part-time jobs to keep up appearances, but few showed any real initiative. In December 1890, the

Independent published a scathing description of 'The Kimberley Fashionable Young Man'.

'He is not as well off as he was when the market was booming,' it began, 'but he has his little salary, and perhaps something saved out of the last share flutter. He dresses just as well as he ever did, and if he does not drink champagne he makes a very creditable show on whisky. He belongs to the Kimberley Club of course – he would rather live on bread and butter than drop out of that great institution and he loves to drive about in a dog cart, either his own or borrowed from a friend. . . . ' But he would not get down to hard work.

The problem was not confined to Kimberley, nor indeed to a particular generation. It was the price paid by an affluent society in decline. The poor would always find work because they had to, but a challenge was needed to stir the spoilt children of the rich. How or where it would come from was anybody's guess. Once again it was Cecil Rhodes who seemed most likely to provide the answer.

Rhodes at that time was busy with many things. He had just amalgamated the diamond mines, he had become Prime Minister of the Cape and, as if this was not enough, he was in the process of taking over a new country. His insistence that the trust deed of De Beers be geared to his political ambitions had been more than a theoretical whim. Shortly before the trust deed was drawn up, he had made his first grab at central Africa.

In August 1888, Rhodes had sent his partner, Charles Rudd, north to obtain a mineral concession from Lobengula, the Matabele chieftain. There had been considerable opposition to the move. Lobengula was besieged by fortune hunters trying to secure mineral rights in Matabeleland and its vassal state Mashonaland. Rudd and his two companions had set off in the greatest secrecy. 'The people of Kimberley', says one of the party, 'were most inquisitive about whither we were bound, but I believe that not a soul there guessed our destination.' They were soon to find out. A few months later Charles Rudd, exhausted by his perilous homeward journey, limped into Kimberley with the mineral concession, bearing Lobengula's elephant seal, in his pocket.

Whether Lobengula realised the full implications of the concession is questionable. But there can be no doubt that Rhodes knew what he was about. He intended to take over Lobengula's domains and populate them with white settlers. Matabeleland and Mashonaland were the two countries that were to bear his name when they became Rhodesia.

Once he had the concession, Rhodes formed the British South Africa Company – for which, in 1889, he obtained a Royal Charter – and started to plan the occupation of Lobengula's territory. Most of the planning was done in Kimberley. It started in the Kimberley Club. There Rhodes met a young adventurer named Frank Johnson, who offered to organise a pioneer column for the northward march and, after the details had been hammered out in Dr Jameson's cottage, Rhodes accepted his offer.

According to Frank Johnson, the recruiting of the young men who were to form the pioneer column was left to him. Rhodes's only stipulations were that the corps should be made up largely of South Africans and that it should comprise a cross-section of artisans and tradesmen so that, on arrival, the skills required for establishing a civil settlement would be available. There were, however, twelve young men whom Rhodes personally selected for the column. Known as 'Rhodes's Angels' – or sometimes 'Rhodes's Lambs' – they were selected more for their friendship with Rhodes than for their qualifications as settlers. Among them were two youngsters from well-known Kimberley families, Bob Coryndon and Jack Grimmer.

Bob Coryndon was the son of Selby Coryndon, a long-established Kimberley attorney. In the early days Selby Coryndon had been one of the most popular lawyers in the town and had featured in several *causes célèbres*. Bob Coryndon had been born in Queenstown, but had spent much of his early life on the diamond diggings. His selection by Rhodes was to mark the beginning of a spectacular career – he later became Governor of Uganda and then of Kenya, and High Commissioner of Zanzibar.

Jack Grimmer was a particular favourite of Rhodes. He was the son of Dr William Grimmer, first medical superintendent of the Carnarvon Hospital. The Grimmer family had arrived at the diggings in 1872; they were old friends of Cecil Rhodes. The eldest of Dr Grimmer's eleven children, Irvine Grimmer, joined De Beers as a youngster and was to serve the company for forty-nine years, eventually becoming Assistant General Manager. Passionately devoted to Kimberley, he was regarded in later years as an authority on the town's history. He and his family, like William Pickering's family, were to play an important part in the social life of the town. Jack Grimmer's association with Kimberley was of shorter duration. A hefty, good-natured young man, he was to be remembered mainly for his lifelong devotion to Rhodes.

At the time the pioneer column was being mustered, Jack Grimmer – or Johnny, as Rhodes liked to call him – was working as a junior clerk at De Beers. He was one of the first to answer the call for volunteers. The story is told that Rhodes teased him by at first refusing to consider his application. 'No,' Rhodes is reported to have said, 'I only want men with beards.' But he was not serious and Jack Grimmer was enrolled as an early Kimberley recruit.

The town supplied many more volunteers. Kimberley's young men might have been idle, but they were not all lacking in a sense of adventure. Recruiting for the pioneer force appears to have started in Kimberley in November 1889. By the beginning of the next year men were flocking to the town from all over South Africa. The first batch of volunteers – twenty-five men, commanded by Lieutenant Roach of the Diamond Fields Horse – left Kimberley on 21 March 1890. They were followed periodically by other detachments. On 18 April, for instance, Rhodes and Sir Henry Loch inspected an artillery troop of some thirty men who departed from Hill and Paddon's store. At a banquet the evening before, the Cape Governor had given the enterprise his qualified blessing. 'The expansion of British interest', he declared amid great cheering, 'up to the very banks of the Zambesi takes its rise from Kimberley. I feel called upon, so far as I can legitimately support the interests of a private company, to give my support to that great British South Africa Company.' Eighteen days later, on 6 May, a much larger force of 140 men – 'a remarkably fine set of young fellows they are', declared the *Diamond Fields Advertiser* – left from a temporary camp at Kenilworth.

The entire force mustered at Camp Cecil, some eighty miles from Palapye in Bechuanaland (Botswana). By the end of June they were ready to start on their long march northwards. It took them over two months to reach their destination. They hacked their way through dense bush, waded across swamps, bridged rivers and marked new roads on their maps. Towards the end of August they emerged on the open plains of Mashonaland; they struck camp early in September. Tents were pitched, guns were fired and the Union Jack hoisted. They named the place Fort Salisbury after the British Prime Minister, and an express letter was sent to Rhodes.

'When at last I found that they were through to Fort Salisbury,' said Rhodes, 'I do not think there was a happier man in the country than myself. ' He was in Cape Town at the time. Earlier that month he had visited Kimberley to attend a special banquet given by the Town Council to mark his election as Prime Minister. Now both he and Kimberley had further cause for celebration. The success of the pioneer column was a triumph not only for Rhodes but for the town that had made him. Kimberley men had played an important part in the march to Mashonaland; other Kimberley men would surely join them. Thousands of settlers would be needed in the new territory, rumoured to be rich in minerals. Not merely artisans and tradesmen were wanted, but farmers, prospectors and miners. Here, it seemed, was a very real challenge to the town's jobless, disillusioned young men.

And so it was for some: but not all. Fate had a way of clouding vital issues in Kimberley. It did so now. Just as the cry 'Go north, young man!' was being raised, events took a completely unexpected turn. The need to move on suddenly seemed less urgent.

In that same September a new mine was discovered on Wessels farm, some four miles from the centre of Kimberley.

(3)

Many stories are told about the discovery of the Wesselton Mine. One of the most popular is that told by, among others, Irvine Grimmer. This has it that a prospector working on the farm accidentally stumbled upon indications of diamondiferous gravel in a heap of soil thrown out by an antbear. 'He followed it up,' claimed Grimmer, 'with the result that the Wesselton Mine was discovered.' However, Gardner Williams gave another version. According to him the prospector – an Afrikaner named Fabricius – was wandering aimlessly about the farm and sank 'a hole at random, without any apparent reason, through ten feet of limestone and found yellow ground'.

A few months after the discovery, Fabricius gave yet another account to a newspaper reporter. He said that he was 'riding over the veldt (and) observed something glittering in the sand and dismounting from his horse, picked up a handful of surface soil, containing, as he thought, the shining particles. On arriving at home he carefully washed up the soil and was surprised not only at finding a small diamond but still more at the large amount of carbon and garnets in so small a quantity of ground. Further prospecting led to the almost certain surface indications of a diamond mine.' How he was attracted to the spot in the first place is not clear.

What is even more puzzling is why the mine remained hidden for so long. Neither Irvine Grimmer nor Gardner Williams appear to have been aware that significant diamond finds on Wessels farm were nothing new. The farm, in fact, had been 'rushed' in 1871, shortly before the discovery of Colesberg Kopje. The fabulous riches of New Rush no doubt distracted the diggers on Wessels farm at that time, but many of them must have remembered the finds that were made there. It seems extraordinary that for twenty years – through every kind of slump, depression and crisis – no serious attempt was made to prospect the farm and that the mine was eventually discovered by accident.

'It was always recognised of course', the *Independent* was to say, 'that new mines might be discovered, but we had all grown weary of waiting for something good to turn up in that line.' Had there been less waiting and more looking, it might have turned up much sooner.

That details of the discovery remained vague is not surprising. In the first place Fabricius was extremely cagey. He later admitted that he deliberately 'kept the spot secret' for two months until he had come to an agreement with the owners of the mine. That agreement was not signed until 29 November 1890. Even then the owners tried to hush things up. Another two months were to pass before the news leaked out. Nevertheless rumours began to circulate and a great many people were involved in behind-the-scenes activity.

J.J. Wessels, the original proprietor of the farm, called Benaauwdheids-fontein, had long since left the district. He had retired to Wellington in the Cape and leased the mineral rights on his property to Henry A. Ward, an old resident of the diamond fields. Apparently Ward had been prospecting in a desultory fashion for some years: it was he who had employed Fabricius. Once a shaft had been sunk, Ward employed a Kimberley firm, Messrs Armstrong Brothers, Kimble and Clarkson, to start extensive digging. Naturally this activity did not pass unnoticed.

There was a great deal of talk about digging on Wessels farm. The *Diamond Fields Advertiser* even published a short article speculating on the possibility of a new mine at Benaauwdheidsfontein. Soon it was being said that the Armstrong Brothers were hauling ground which yielded half-a-carat per load. Henry Ward had little hope of keeping the discovery secret for long.

The farm was rushed on 5 February 1891. Long before day-break that morning, a stream of 'carts, pedestrians and vehicles of every description' were seen heading for Wessels farm. It was a planned operation, instigated by the Reverend A.F. Balmer, secretary of the Labour Bureau at Beaconsfield. Balmer, alarmed at the high rate of unemployment, had been determined to get the farm declared a public diggings.

Within a matter of hours, some four hundred claims had been pegged out on Benaauwdheidsfontein. The rush continued throughout the following day and the number of pegged-out claims doubled. 'The excitement', reported the

Independent, 'reminded old residents of the early days when "rushes" were frequent, and many are in hopes that the new mine will be the means of supporting a large digging community.'

Not everyone had such hopes. The directors of De Beers Consolidated Mines viewed the rush with considerable alarm. The opening of a new competitive mine would ruin all that had been achieved by amalgamation. It would result in over-production, a fall in the price of diamonds and a return to the uncertainties that had long bedevilled the diamond industry. They lost no time in approaching Henry Ward in an attempt to take over his lease.

The day after the rush, it was reported that Ward had left for the Cape to consult J.J. Wessels. It was said that he had refused the De Beers offer and was in favour of the mine being declared a public diggings. How true this was, nobody knew.

However, the Reverend A.F.Balmer and the Knights of Labour were taking no chances. As soon as it was known that De Beers were intervening, they set about organising a huge protest rally. On 23 February 1891, a huge crowd gathered outside the Memorial Hall at Beaconsfield and fell into line to march to the Kimberley Market-square. On the way they were joined by others, until the procession was estimated to number over two thousand. On reaching the Market-square, the leaders drew up two empty wagons to serve as a temporary platform. 'The huge crowd surged all round,' it was reported. 'Lit up by flaring torches, the scene was quite imposing, and it needed no very great stretch of imagination to imagine oneself back in the old days when public meetings were held in the Market Square.'

There was something familiar also about the men who addressed the meeting. They were by no means all representatives of the unemployed. What was represented as a straight fight between capital and labour quickly became a free-for-all. Old financial, as well as political, feuds and animosities came to the fore and tended to obscure the more pressing issues. Prominent among the speakers, for instance, was the redoubtable Dan O'Leary, one of the leaders of the Black Flag Rebellion. He was backed up by Dr William Murphy, a crony of J.B. Robinson and a former partner of Barney Barnato. Both men had reasons of their own for encouraging the protesters. They were vehement in attacking the recent amalgamation. Dr Murphy claimed that he had 'begged Mr Barnato, almost on his knees, not to sell their interest to De Beers' but he had lost out to Rhodes. Now, he said, the time had come for more resolute action. A resolution denouncing 'the influence of powerful monopolists' was passed unanimously.

The following day a deputation, headed by the Reverend Balmer, left for the Cape. They intended to present a petition to the Government requesting that the Wesselton Mine be thrown open to the public. Their case was later strengthened when it was discovered that the farm had been proclaimed a public diggings shortly before it was rushed in 1871.

The indignation of Kimberley's unemployed is understandable. The discovery of the Wesselton Mine did, at first sight, appear to be a heaven-sent answer to their distress. That they should put up a fight to keep the mine from being taken over by De Beers was only to be expected. But there were other considerations which, in the heady atmosphere of mass meetings, tended to be pushed aside. Just how far would the opening of Wesselton Mine go towards solving Kimberley's problems? This is what a correspondent, signing himself 'Argus', asked in a letter published in the *Diamond Fields Advertiser* shortly after the mass meeting.

'It is contended', he wrote, 'that the opening of the new mine would give employment to hundreds at present idle. No doubt it would, but would the employment last? I doubt it. It is a fact which no one can dispute that for months before the great amalgamation took place, every single Company in the four mines was barely paying expenses owing to the low price of diamonds; that in the majority of cases, it was all they could do to hold their own and would undoubtedly have had to stop work had not the De Beers grand scheme come to their aid. Hundreds of men who are now at work would have been thrown on their own resources. No sane man will for a moment contest that the state of affairs existing 18 months ago could have continued. It was just a question whether we should become one huge machine worked locally or by foreign agency.'

He went on to point out that De Beers employed over a thousand whites and several thousand blacks. The first result of opening the new mine would be a fall in the price of diamonds. This would mean that De Beers would have to restrict operations further and more men would be thrown out of work. How long would finds at the Wesselton Mine last? How many unemployed could a single mine absorb? 'There are scores of men', he declared, 'talking gleefully of the possible downfall of De Beers if the new mine is opened. Do they stop to consider the results? De Beers would only be effaced to make way for a foreign syndicate, which would mean such ruin and disorder to South Africa as is really appalling to contemplate.'

These unpalatable facts could not be ignored. They were backed by the long, precarious history of the diamond industry. While the opening of Wesselton might cure some of Kimberley's immediate ills it would undoubtedly pose greater problems for the future. This, more or less, was the opinion of the Special Committee set up by the Government to investigate the position. How far that Committee was influenced by the Prime Minister, Cecil Rhodes, was a matter of controversy. But, all things considered, it is difficult to see how even the most unbiased men could have arrived at any other solution. The finances of the Cape were too shaky to endanger them further.

De Beers were therefore able, after lengthy negotiations, to purchase Benaauwdheidsfontein. They first acquired half control of the mine and then, in December 1891, took over the farm completely. The sale was complicated by the fact that part of Wessels's property lay within the Free State boundaries. It took months of legal wrangling to sort out the Free State rights. Equally involved were the negotiations with Henry Ward concerning his mineral concession. This dispute was settled in the Cape Supreme Court. In the end Ward agreed to cede his interest in the mine on condition that he be allowed to haul 5,000,000 loads of yellow ground for a period of five years. It was Ward who then suggested that the mine be renamed the Premier, in honour of Rhodes – a name it retained for some years.

Thus the fate of Kimberley's fifth mine was decided. But the future of Kimberley's unemployed remained as uncertain as ever. The Government Select Committee had no answer to that crucial problem. Its report noted that, between 1888 and 1891, the population of Kimberley had halved and property values in Beaconsfield had fallen by a third, but a minority plea for Government intervention was rejected.

(4)

Yet all was not gloom. Kimberley still knew how to celebrate its high days and holidays. There was nothing dreary, for instance, about the letter which Sister Henrietta wrote to the *Independent* in January 1891, thanking 'kind friends' for donations to the Kimberley Hospital's Christmas festivities. The town had responded splendidly. Cases of whisky, brandy and wine had been showered on the patients.

The Mayor, E.H. Jones, had given a dozen bottles of port, a ham and a tin of biscuits. Dr Lea had sent 'a little pig, a goose and pineapples'. A dozen bottles of wine and two jars of preserves had come from C.A. Blackbeard. Messrs Jones and Warner had contributed pipes and tobacco bags. And the firm of Rolfes and Nebel had outshone everyone by supplying 'tobacco, one dozen champagne, a cask of sherry, two cases of stout, two cases of beer and five hundred cigars'.

'Our tree was very large,' reported Sister Henrietta, 'and covered with fruit, or ornaments, sweets and gifts and two large tables were covered with presents besides. Everyone had as many good things to eat and drink all through the day as they could possibly want, and we all kept Christmas royally.' Whatever Kimberley might have lacked, it was neither spirit nor generosity.

The town was in a holiday mood four months later when it welcomed Lord Randolph Churchill. It was one of the few light-hearted occasions of the year.

Churchill was on his way north to visit Mashonaland. His expedition had been widely publicised; the South African newspapers had, for some months, been full of reports of his coming. He was one of the most eminent British politicians ever to have toured the country. Although it was said that he was investigating the possibility of British emigration to Mashonaland, he was known to be interested in the new country's mineral potential. An English newspaper, the *Daily Graphic*, had commissioned him to send back reports of his South African journey.

When it was learnt that Churchill would be staying a few days in Kimberley, as a guest of Alfred Beit, the Town Council decided to put on a show. The form this show would take was the subject of much debate. Finally it was decided that he should be fêted at a public banquet. But, much to everyone's disappointment, the highly abrasive Lord Randolph turned the suggestion down. His tour, he explained curtly, was a private one and he could not agree to an official reception. This, however, did not prevent his being met at the station, on 29 May, by a delegation of local worthies and welcomed by an effusive speech from the Mayor.

Churchill's reports to the *Daily Graphic* were to cause widespread offence. He was critical of everything he saw and almost everyone he met in South Africa. Kimberley proved no exception. The buildings that were springing up here, there and everywhere impressed him not at all. His description of the town might have been written ten years earlier. The renowned Diamond City, he said, was a 'straggling, haphazard collection of small, low dwellings constructed almost entirely of corrugated iron or of wood, laid out with hardly any attempt at regularity' and was quite unworthy of its international fame. The place did, he admitted, boast a number of excellent shops, a comfortable club and an admirable race-course, but it was entirely lacking in 'municipal magnificence'.

The conducted tours arranged for him were far from inspiring. 'At Kimberley,' he wrote, 'the diamond is everything.' It was an observation made from tedious experience. Apart from a day's organised hunting in the veld he saw little of the town other than the diamond industry. He was taken on tours of the De Beers sorting-sheds, conducted through the mine compounds, bombarded with statistics and photographed at the bottom of a 900-feet-deep mine shaft. He found it extremely boring.

Only when writing about I.D.B. did he manage to work up a little enthusiasm. The searching of African workers fascinated him. 'On returning from their day's work,' he wrote, 'they have to strip off all their clothes, which they hang on pegs in a shed. Stark naked, they then proceed to the searching room, where their mouths, their hair, their toes, their armpits, and every portion of their body are subjected to an elaborate examination.' White men, he added with more truth than he appears to have realised, 'would never submit to such a process'. He was frankly astonished at the rigorous laws imposed by the Diamond Trade Act. 'If a man walking in the streets or in the precincts of Kimberley', he explained, 'were to find a diamond and were not immediately to take it to the registrar, restore it to him, and to have the fact of its registration registered, he would be liable to a punishment of fifteen years' penal servitude.'

Even so I.D.B. continued to flourish. Every visitor to Kimberley left with a story illustrating the lengths to which men would go to smuggle diamonds out of the town. Churchill had his. He was told of a notorious diamond thief who was seized by the police when he was leaving Kimberley for the Transvaal. A thorough search of the man revealed nothing and he was allowed to go on his way. A detective, still suspicious, followed him until he had crossed the Transvaal border where he immediately shot his horse and extracted a large parcel of diamonds from the animal's intestines. There was nothing the detective could do: once in the Transvaal the thief was safe.

But Churchill, like Trollope before him, was not interested in diamonds. Summing up his views on the diamond industry, he found little to say in its favour. Unlike the mining of gold, coal, tin, copper and lead, the unearthing of diamonds, in his opinion, brought no real benefit to mankind.

'At De Beers mine,' he said, 'all the wonderful arrangements I have described are put into force in order to extract from the ground, solely for the wealthy classes, a tiny crystal to be gratification of female vanity in imitation of a lust for personal adornment essentially barbaric if not altogether savage. Some mitigation of cynical criticism might be urged if the diamonds only adorned the beautiful, the virtuous and the young, but this, unhappily, is far from being the case, and a review of the South African diamond mines brings me coldly to the conclusion that, whatever may be the origin of man, woman is descended from an ape.'

This rather weak attempt at humour was to bring a storm about his head when it was published. With all the solemnity that Victorians could bring to a flippancy, outraged editors of quite serious journals denounced Churchill as an unspeakable woman-hater. But it was a quick-witted Kimberley female who really cut him down to size.

It is said that while touring the sorting-sheds, Lord Randolph was accompanied by the wife of a De Beers official. They got on well enough until the end of the tour. Then Churchill stopped and glared contemptuously at a pile of diamonds.

'All for the vanity of woman,' he snorted.

'And for the depravity of man,' came the tart reply.

18

The Exhibition

It was R.W. Murray – former newspaper editor, former member of the Legislative Council and one of the oldest residents on the diggings – who first
thought of staging an exhibition in Kimberley.

Then in his early seventies, Murray was as nimble-minded and as public-
spirited as ever. Few men knew Kimberley better than he did; he had devoted
the best part of his life to the town. As a newspaper man he had reported the
early riots and rebellion; as a councillor he had fought valiantly for Griqualand
West's independence; in one way or another he had participated in every
financial slump and crisis. He, as much as anyone, realised how precarious life
could be on the diamond fields. Yet he never lost heart. Cynical and somewhat
disillusioned he might be, but he could still rise to a challenge. The most recent
economic depression had brought him back to the public platform. Together
with that other Kimberley stalwart, George Bottomley, he had actively
campaigned on behalf of the debris washers. Now he came up with the idea of a
Kimberley Exhibition.

The idea was not entirely original. It seems to have been inspired by the
successful Centennial Exhibition which had been held in Australia a few years
earlier. The world-wide publicity given to this Australian exhibition had made
South Africans envious. There was hardly a town in the country which did not
want to put on a similar show. However, Murray's suggestion was a good one.
If a South African exhibition was to be staged, where better to stage it than
Kimberley? Not only was the Diamond City now linked to the Cape by rail but,
it was pointed out, 'being situated on the borders of the Orange Free State, it is
practically, if not geographically, the centre of South Africa'. Gold and diamonds were the country's main industrial attractions and, as work was going
ahead on railway extensions to the north, visitors to the Kimberley Exhibition
would be able to reach Johannesburg in little over forty-eight hours. Everything, in fact, seemed to point to Kimberley as the ideal focal point for
advertising South Africa to the world.

This, at least, is what most people thought. The Town Council seized upon
the idea and received enthusiastic support from De Beers and the local
merchants. The Cape Government 'promised to give every assistance in its
power'. In the middle of 1891 an Executive Committee was formed to promote
the exhibition and a fund-raising campaign was launched. The response was
spectacular; money poured in from every quarter. And as the subscription lists
filled, ambitions rose. Why, it was asked, should the show be confined to

Kimberley or even South Africa? Why not broaden its scope to attract foreign trade? Why not an international exhibition? The Executive Committee agreed. Towards the end of the year the name of the project was changed to the South African and International Exhibition.

Then things really got going. Mr Lewis Atkinson – 'a gentleman with much prior experience of exhibitions' – was appointed General Manager and packed off to London to drum up European support. T.W. Goodwin, an ex-Mayor of Kimberley, was sent on a similar mission throughout South Africa. Once Atkinson arrived in England, a London Executive Committee was formed under the chairmanship of Sir Charles Mills, the Agent-General for the Cape Colony. Enthusiasm mounted.

At an early meeting in London, Sir Charles Mills outlined his committee's plans. 'The object of this Exhibition', he explained proudly, 'is to place the exhibitors of this country (England) in direct touch with those who are their customers in South Africa, and also to induce visitors to South Africa to go and see one of the wonders of the world – the Diamond Mines of Griqualand West, of which you have heard so much, and which are so extremely well managed by our grand young man of South Africa, Cecil Rhodes.'

The exhibits called for were nothing if not comprehensive. Following Sir Charles Mills at this meeting, Lewis Atkinson attempted a short list. 'Haberdashery and millinery, apparel, cotton goods, hardware and ironmongery, leather, boots and shoes, saddlery, machinery, cabinet ware, carriages, guns, locks, cutlery, jewellery, musical instruments, etc., were all in demand,' he said, 'and exhibits would be required, in particular, of light transport machinery, rock drills, crushers, well borers, dynamos, motors, tents, transport wagons, travelling equipment, and gasmaking apparatus to utilise mineral oil and Colonial coal.' Prospective exhibitors were promised special rail facilities in South Africa, and the free return of any unsold goods. Thomas Cook, the travel agent, agreed to arrange sea voyages and tours of the country. Kimberley, it was explained, could be reached in three weeks from London, even allowing for the thirty- to thirty-six-hour journey from the Cape.

How were all the exhibits to be housed? That was the main headache of the Kimberley Committee. At the end of November they met to consider the various designs submitted for an exhibition building, to be erected in the Public Gardens at a cost of £7,000. Several members thought this was a niggardly sum. 'If a shed was all that was required,' quipped Gardner Williams, General Manager of De Beers, 'they might approach the Government, and get the loan of a railway goods shed.' The more romantically minded Albert Holt, chairman of the entertainment committee, was in favour of a handsome building 'which might subsequently be utilised as a winter palace'.

The design eventually accepted – that submitted by a local architect, D.W. Greatbatch – was a cross between the two: it was part shed, part winter palace. Set in the Public Gardens and covering an area of over 50,000 square feet, the building comprised one main hall with four separate wings leading off it. In these wings were housed the British, Continental, Canadian, American and Fine arts sections. All in all, with its two-storied facade, its steeply pitched roofs and its dozens of fluttering flags, the Exhibition Building was not unimpressive.

Equally impressive was the list of patrons supporting the exhibition. In his tour of South Africa T.W. Goodwin had succeeded in interesting every dignitary in the country. The result was a catalogue of names which read rather like a South African *Who's Who*. Sir Henry Loch, the Governor of the Cape, agreed to act as president; Cecil Rhodes was vice-president. The Governor of Natal, the Administrator of Bechuanaland, the Commissioner of Basutoland, two former Cape Prime Ministers, and a host of mayors, judges and foreign consuls, all lent their names to the project. But perhaps Goodwin's most outstanding achievement was to rope in the Presidents of the two Boer republics – Paul Kruger of the Transvaal, and F.W. Reitz of the Orange Free State. Both Presidents were well known in Kimberley; the town had fêted them at banquets, Kruger in 1883, Reitz in 1890. By giving their blessing to the exhibition they ensured that it would be a truly South African affair.

But the greatest boost came at the end of 1891, when James Lawrence was re-elected as Mayor. Bearded, handsome James Lawrence was one of Kimberley's most popular citizens. He was regarded as the epitome of the self-made man, a glittering product of the diamond diggings. Born at George in the Cape, Lawrence had arrived at Kimberley in 1878, aged twenty-six, with 'the proverbial half-crown in his pocket'. For some time he had assisted his uncle as a digger and then started up on his own as a blacksmith. By 1886 he was well-enough established to open the provision store which he was to develop into one of the leading trading concerns in the town. A skilled and amusing debater, he was highly regarded as a politician not only by his fellow merchants but by the local farmers and, perhaps more important – Kimberley being what it was – by the mining community. The widespread allegiance he commanded had led to his first election as Mayor in 1888. Now that a dynamic figure was needed to pilot the exhibition, it was inevitable that James Lawrence should again be elected. Certainly no better man could have been chosen.

Lawrence threw himself wholeheartedly into the scheme. In April 1892, he arrived in London full of proposals and enthusiasm. 'We are very anxious', he told a reporter, 'that people here should know something of our progress and that the fullest information should be given to the English people with regard to Kimberley.' By the time he left a few months later there was hardly a person in England who did not know about the exhibition. He rushed up and down the country giving interviews, encouraging exhibitors and whipping up support. Editorials praising the exhibition appeared in every leading newspaper. 'On the whole,' declared the London *Times*, shortly after his arrival, 'this is a courageous and patriotic enterprise, to which the subjects of the Queen at home are bound to wish every success.' In the middle of May it was announced that all available space in the Exhibition Building had been taken up and extensions were being built. Few doubted the wisdom of electing James Lawrence as Mayor.

Of course, not everything went smoothly. There were the inevitable rows, muddles and jealousies. Overclouding all other squabbles was the bitterly

James Lawrence, popular Mayor of Kimberley at the time of the Kimberley Exhibition in 1892. (M)

D.W. Greatbatch, well-known Kimberley architect who designed the central hall of the Kimberley Exhibition in 1892 and St Cyprian's Cathedral in 1907. (K)

Gardner F. Williams, the American-born mining engineer who became manager of the De Beers Mining Company in May 1887. (K) fought controversy surrounding the musical arrangements. This battle was fought out for weeks in private and in public. It reached its peak with the announcement that a Herr Eberlein of Durban had been engaged to supervise the exhibition music. This had every singer, every pianist and every fiddler in Kimberley up in arms. What, they demanded to know, was wrong with the local musicians? What, in particular, was wrong with Mr Heubner, the conductor for the recently resuscitated Kimberley Philharmonic Society? And if Mr Heubner was not good enough, why was it necessary to employ a musician from another colony? Surely the Cape could provide an equally qualified man? Nor were patriotic feelings soothed when it was reported that negotiations were going ahead to bring out a Viennese band. This was considered downright disloyal. Endless meetings were called, angry letters were written to the press. But the Executive Committee stood firm. 'Ah well,' sighed James Lawrence, when he was tackled about the quarrel, 'you know it is always said that musical people are the most unharmonious of folks to deal with.'

The other arts were not without their problems. Grave doubts were expressed about the plan to bring valuable paintings on loan to Kimberley. What with the heat and duststorms, it was said, they were bound to be damaged. Assurances that all works of art would be carefully looked after were of no avail. The insurance companies demanded more positive protection. Eventually it was decided to transfer the Fine Arts section from the main building to a specially built brick hall. (This hall, with its pretty cast-iron portico, was later converted into the Kimberley Drill Hall.) Once the transfer had been arranged and it was learnt that Queen Victoria was sending the famous Winterhalter portrait of the Royal family, all doubts disappeared. By the time the exhibition opened, a remarkable collection of pictures, valued at £30,000, had been amassed.

But the doubts and the squabbles were secondary to the general excitement. For the most part, fun-loving Kimberley was determined to enjoy itself. Everyone had had more than enough of depression recently. The severe winter of 1892 had added to the misery of unemployment – an outbreak of influenza had killed off many old-timers, including the doughty George Bottomley – and the town was badly in need of a diversion. As much as anything, it needed a few sunny months of relaxation. Not everyone was interested in the educational and trade advantages of the exhibition; most Kimberleyites were hoping for a good old-fashioned spree.

That, at any rate, is what they had been promised. Asked whether entertainment would be a feature of the exhibition, a committee member had given a prompt reply. 'Rather!' he exclaimed. 'There will be a perfect *embarras de richesse* in this line. Music and merriment will be the order of the day and night. There will be a string and brass band from Europe; a choir of 200 voices under Herr Eberlein, who will give three concerts weekly; and for the more frivolous there will be switchback railways, electric trams, a camera obscura, and fireworks by Pain and Company; in fact all the features of the European exhibition up to date.' More, one could not ask for.

(2)

The South African and International Exhibition was officially opened, on 8 September 1892, by Sir Henry Brougham Loch, Governor of the Cape Colony and High Commissioner for South Africa.

It was, by Kimberley standards, a most triumphant ceremony. At noon precisely, with guns thundering out a royal salute and an escort of the Diamond Fields Horse jogging behind, Sir Henry and Lady Loch drove up to the entrance gates. They were received by a guard of honour under the command of Major David Harris. The National Anthem having clashed out, His Excellency led a procession of notables – berobed, uniformed and decorated – through the main hall and onto the stage. Watched by over 2,500 'fashionably dressed ladies and gentlemen' the inauguration took place. James Lawrence, as Mayor and Chairman of the Executive Committee, having read out the illuminated address with 'considerable emphasis', presented it to the Governor. His Excellency, with less emphasis, replied. Then Lawrence presented 'the Governor with a diamond-studded golden key; various officials of the Executive Committee were introduced to His Excellency; a cable to be sent to the Queen, to inform Her Majesty of the opening of the Exhibition, was duly read out'; and when the Governor presented the cable to Mr Henry, the Postmaster, for despatch, 'a ringing cheer ran round the building'. The cheering over, Sir Henry and Lady Loch turned to face the choir, the audience rose to their feet, the controversial Herr Eberlein lifted his baton, and the choir burst into the 'Hallelujah Chorus'.

It was, remarked one observer, extraordinary to witness such a magnificent spectacle 'here, some seven hundred miles in the interior of South Africa, and on ground that not a quarter of a century ago was an arid desert'.

There were spectacles throughout the day, the grand finale being staged that night in the lantern-hung Public Gardens, where a huge crowd gathered to watch a dazzling fireworks display. Starting with the sparkling portraits of Sir Henry Loch and John Davis-Allen (Vice-Chairman of the Executive Committee), each item – 'vessels in action, and a bicycle race' – drew loud gasps and tremendous cheers. Nothing like it had ever before been seen in Kimberley: the crowd, it was said, were 'simply astounded'.

Somewhere among that crowd was an old familiar face. The Exhibition had enticed the recently knighted Sir Richard Southey, former Lieutenant-Governor of Griqualand West, back to Kimberley. He was treated as an honoured guest. At a banquet held earlier that evening, the ageing but still sprightly – he lived to be ninety-three – Southey had been one of the principal speakers. Much had happened to the town since he left it, under a cloud, seventeen years earlier.

Throughout the Governor's two-week stay, Kimberley was packed. Every hotel, every boarding-house, every private residence was bursting with guests. On the eve of opening day, the agitated staffs of an Admiral and a General were seen scurrying desperately about the town trying to find accommodation. However, Southey could have had little difficulty in finding a bed. He still had many friends in Kimberley, not least among them being his former Government Secretary, John Blades Currey. In 1883, Currey had been appointed manager of the London and South African Exploration Company, which still owned much of the land in Kimberley. Once again he had become an influential, if less controversial, figure in the town. His elegant red-brick villa in Belgravia, 'The Lodge', was one of the most impressive houses built during the recent building boom. From the very outset, Currey had been one of the most enthusiastic promoters of the Exhibition.

That the Exhibition put Kimberley on the map again, there can be little doubt. For the three months it was open, thousands of visitors flocked to the town. At the inspiration of John Davis-Allen, South Africa's first Medical Congress was held in the town to coincide with the festivities, and in November James Lawrence was host to a group of South African mayors attending the country's first Mayoral Congress. On the whole, the Exhibition itself was a huge success. Apart from the inevitable fire which broke out in the Main Hall during the second week – and, for once, was promptly put out with the help of a newly acquired, bright-red fire-engine – things went off without a hitch. As nearly everyone agreed, the South African and International Exhibition was one of the most ambitious and important undertakings ever staged in Kimberley.

But financially it was a failure. At the outset local tradesmen had been approached to give written guarantees of money to safeguard the promoters. These guarantees, they had been assured, were mere formalities. The Exhibition was expected to make a large profit and the guarantees would never be taken up. They soon discovered otherwise. 'Instead of the profit foreseen by the promoters,' claimed a shocked merchant, 'after everyone had paid up their guarantees, which took some time to collect, a deficiency of something like £40,000 stared everyone in the face.' Gloom was widespread until Cecil Rhodes stepped in and undertook to pay off the entire debt. He considered it money well spent and everyone breathed a sigh of relief.

For all that, the Exhibition was a great boost to morale. 'I have a very firm conviction in the future and stability of our township,' James Lawrence noted in the Mayor's Minutes at the end of the year. 'De Beers pays annually upwards of one million pounds for labour and supplies. (We) also have expenditure of other Diamond Mining Companies, River Diggers, wealthy speculators, Transport Riders and others which add greatly to the money put into circulation in Kimberley. . . . The glory of Kimberley may for the time being be dimmed . . . but I firmly believe Kimberley will hold its own as one of the most important centres in South Africa.'

(3)

Many agreed with James Lawrence. Among the 399,950 visitors to the Exhibition were a number of old diggers who had known the town in the early days. Some of them had struck it rich in the 1870s and had left Kimberley when it was little more than a mining camp. Returning now they were astounded at the progress that had been made. How could it be said, asked one of them, that Kimberley was 'going to the dogs'?

Rarely had the town appeared more prosperous, more lively. Everyone knew about the unemployment but this was dismissed as a passing phase. Kimberley had experienced similar depressions and recovered; it would do so again. One only had to be taken on a tour of the town to recognise its essential vitality. The idea that the Exhibition was its 'last kick' was absurd. Loyally, these former Kimberley residents were loud in their protestations. The South African newspapers were bombarded with articles and letters recalling the old days and praising the new.

Nor was this praise confined to the town's showplaces: the pretty Kenilworth village and the posh Belgravia suburb. Everywhere one looked there was evidence of progress. Beaconsfield, for instance, had been badly hit by the closing down of the Dutoitspan and Bultfontein mines, but it could hardly be described as a depressed area.

'This little town has developed rapidly,' exclaimed a surprised visitor. 'Twelve years ago not a building was to be seen near the spot; now it is quite a large place, with 10,478 inhabitants, good houses, and several public buildings, one of which is the Jubilee Memorial Town Hall.'

Other suburbs were also expanding. The old West End, divided from the centre of the town by the Kimberley Mine, had a flourishing community of its own. Most Afrikaners lived in Newton, where they were served by their own market-square and the handsome Dutch Reformed Church. The building of the railway station had boosted land values in the suburb of Gladstone, which now boasted its own church and an impressive hotel.

The famous Kimberley Market-square, with its busy lines of ox-wagons and closely packed produce stalls, was one of the liveliest spots in town. It too was almost unrecognisable to the old-timers. On one side were the large new Government Buildings, on another was the spacious new Post Office; hotels and huge wholesale stores completely dwarfed the few remaining wood and iron shops and offices. The noise and bustle of the early morning market was enough to convince anyone of Kimberley's powers of recovery.

Progress was noticeable also in the town's cultural and spiritual life. Every main thoroughfare seemed to have a church: there was St Cyprian's in Jones Street, the Presbyterian church in New Main Street, the Methodist chapel and the Roman Catholic cathedral in Dutoitspan Road. Various church societies and secular organisations, such as the Good Templars and the Freemasons, were actively engaged in charitable work. Nazareth House, started by Catholic nuns and supported by local funds, cared for the town's waifs and strays; and the renowned Pirates Club provided every type of sporting facility for the town's idle young men.

The Pirates Club was, in fact, one of Kimberley's most successful charitable ventures. It had been founded, almost accidentally, in the early 1880s by G.J.A. Danford, the 'Pirate King'. Danford, an indefatigable organiser of charity concerts, is said to have thought up the idea of the club after staging a special production of *The Pirates of Penzance* (a play, not the operetta) with a group

of youngsters. So successful was this show that the funds raised from it had
been used by Danford to establish a gymnasium for his 'Pirate Children'. Later
a clubhouse had been built in the Public Gardens; the sports teams fielded by
the Pirates became a source of pride to the town. Unfortunately, the original
sports pavilion in the Public Gardens had been temporarily dismantled to
make way for the Exhibition Buildings, but the fame of the Pirates Club
remained undimmed. It was to serve as a model for similar clubs throughout
South Africa.

Visitors to the Exhibition were invariably impressed by Kimberley's sporting
activities. There was no escaping them. Tennis courts, cricket pitches and a
swimming-bath had long been features of the dusty Public Gardens and, in
1890, the town's first bowling-green – the grass planted, it is said, 'blade by
blade' – had been fenced in there. In September 1890, also, the Kimberley Golf
Club had been formed and a rough-and-ready golf-course had been laid out on
the outskirts of the town, behind the double-storied Nazareth House. Horse-
racing had again become fashionable and the late-Victorian bicycling craze
was very much in evidence on the town's flat roads. For those who remembered
the sleazy drinking dives and gambling hells of the early days, it all seemed a
remarkable change for the better.

But the most memorable sporting event held during the Exhibition period
was the first Currie Cup rugby tournament. Kimberley had a special interest in
the Currie Cup. The donor of the trophy was the shipping magnate Sir Donald
Currie, who at one time had owned important claims in the Kimberley Mine.
He had taken an active interest in the affairs of the diamond fields and was well
known in Kimberley. In 1891, when the first British rugby side had toured
South Africa, Currie had donated a gold cup to be presented to the team that
gave the visitors the best game. It had been won by Kimberley men, who then
handed the 'Currie Cup' (a similar one had been presented to South African
cricketers two years earlier) to the recently formed South African Rugby
Board. It was accepted as a floating-trophy. The launching of the famous
Currie Cup tournaments was one of the highlights of the Exhibition festivities.
Four sides competed: Griqualand West, Border, Natal and, the victors,
Western Province. Kimberley could claim another 'first' and another change to
its own traditions.

Changed also were the methods of mining. Not only had amalgamation
regulated the output of diamonds, but it had completely revolutionised digging
operations. Driving past the still-active De Beers and Kimberley mines, one old
digger had been astonished at the transformation.

'What scenes of life these holes have shown in the past,' he marvelled. 'The
aerial tramlines whizzed and sang like a million Aeolian harps, while the
hordes of workers on the floors were hardly distinguishable from ants. All is
changed; the men are working still, but they are out of sight in the tunnels, and
the "blue" is shot up the long shafts in huge buckets that tip themselves as if
moved by the hands of unseen giants.'

Visitors taken on conducted tours of the mines often found them singularly
lacking in romance. Now that the excitement of a chance find and overnight

riches had disappeared, the diamonds themselves seemed hardly worth burrowing for. 'We have spent our time in going down the Kimberley diamond mine,' wrote Alice Balfour, sister of the future British Prime Minister, 'wonderfully arrayed in canvas jackets and sou'wester hats, and being shown all the different processes for securing the diamonds. Such disappointing things they are when you see them in the rough!'

And if the town and the diamond industry had changed, so, to a certain extent, had Kimberley's leading citizens. Among the many shifts of emphasis noticeable during the Exhibition was the growing importance of Kimberley's merchant class. This was not commented upon by casual observers, but many must have been aware of it.

In the early days most important functions in the town had been dominated by men directly connected with the diamond industry: the diggers, the claim holders and the diamond buyers. Professional men – doctors, lawyers and journalists – had influenced much of Kimberley's development but they had never controlled the town. The role of the independent merchant had, for the most part, been a minor one. If anything, the commercial section of the town had been noted mainly for its hostility towards the mine owners. This hostility had not entirely disappeared but it had been considerably modified by amalgamation. The promise of economic stability had given the merchants new confidence. It was they, as much as anyone, who had been responsible for the recent building boom. They had extended their business premises and built themselves new homes. The Exhibition highlighted their rise in status.

Typical of Kimberley's influential merchants was, of course, James Lawrence – the driving-force behind the Exhibition. He had taken over as Mayor from E.H. Jones, a builder and ironmonger who had come to Kimberley in 1882. Equally representative was Albert Holt, the chairman of the entertainment committee. Albert Holt and his brothers, David and Hillier, were – like James Lawrence – outstanding examples of Kimberley's self-made businessmen. The two elder brothers, Albert and David, had arrived at the diggings in 1878 and had been joined by Hillier four years later. Albert had started life in the town as a law agent but had soon branched out and established himself as a merchant. In partnership with his brothers he had built up a large tobacco and furniture business in the town. At the time of the Exhibition Albert Holt was President of the Kimberley Chamber of Commerce, and the firm of Holt and Holt had extended to Johannesburg, Pretoria and Bloemfontein. A few years later the Holt brothers were to form the Acme Cigarette Company and other subsidiaries and to become well known throughout South Africa. David Holt's son Harold was to achieve fame as a music impresario in Britain, and his daughters, Hilda and Mattie, reigned for many years as leading Cape Town hostesses.

Another rising Kimberley merchant, soon to gain nation-wide recognition, was a young Irishman named John Orr. Born in Benburb, County Tyrone, John Orr had come to South Africa in 1881 and started his career as a general merchant in Stellenbosch in the Cape. Moving to Kimberley in 1887, his original small business had gone ahead by leaps and bounds. Although still on the threshold of his highly successful career in 1892, he was already regarded as one of the town's most promising merchants. Two years later he was to open a business in London and eventually to establish himself in Natal. According to local legend, the extent of John Orr's business was limited only by an agreement he had made with another prominent South African merchant, John Garlick. At the outset of their careers, it is said, the two of them had made a pact never to compete with each other in the same town. Whether true or not, this unusual arrangement appears to have worked out in practice. Few department stores in South Africa were to be better known than John Orr's and Garlick's but, for many years, they never encroached on each other's territory. For all that, John Orr's first love remained Kimberley. He was to devote much of his life to the town, both as a merchant and as a public servant; his handsome, two-storied, villa in Belgravia (built originally for Gustave Bonas) became a Kimberley showplace.

It was the prosperity of the Kimberley merchants that made visitors hopeful for the future. If the character of the town was changing, the chances of making good there had by no means disappeared. 'Of course,' admitted one old-timer, 'the diamond market is not the scene of the rampant excitement it was wont to be, nor do the flashier shops flourish on the lightly spent gains of I.D.B.s. But, allowing for these changes, a great deal of solid business is done in Kimberley, and will continue to be done.' The merchants themselves agreed. 'I met my old friend Mr James Hill yesterday,' he went on, 'and he took me over the large store belonging to his firm, Messrs Hill and Paddon. There is no sign of decay about that store. The goods, from floor to ceiling, on the endless rows of shelves, are fresh from the manufacturers. No old stock disfigures this busy mart. . . . Ask Mr Hill if Kimberley is departing into the land of shadows, and observe his look. The answer is sufficient.'

(4)

In the end the unemployment problem solved itself. Or rather it was solved, for the most part, by the long-established workings of the diamond industry. A sizable majority of those whose jobs were threatened by the closing of the Dutoitspan and Bultfontein Mines were unskilled African labourers. As had always been the case, these labourers had been brought to the town to work for a specified period. Once their contracts had expired they returned to their kraals and were replaced only when work was available. This resulted in a sharp drop in the unemployment figures over the next few years.

Disposing of the jobless white workers was not so easy. Many of them were their own worst enemies. Their refusal to work as debris washers or, for that matter, to accept any type of manual labour lost them much sympathy. How serious was their plight? Some thought it greatly exaggerated. J.X. Merriman, for instance, dismissed the agitation for the opening of the Wesselton Mine as 'a demand for the support of every loafer who tramps to Kimberley'. Others agreed with him. Indeed, the longer the agitation lasted the more the scepticism grew. Compassion gave way to ridicule or outright hostility. At a lively meeting organised by the Knights of Labour in June 1892, one of the principal speakers was a man who had arrived in the town only a week before. His complaint that he had been unable to find work drew little but sneers. 'I know nothing of this man,' fumed a member of the audience, 'but I simply ask what on earth is his business in Kimberley? . . . (The) business of finding work for the unemployed has been discussed over and over again. The newspapers have again and again given publicity to these proceedings, and surely every one in South Africa knows, or ought to know, that just now Kimberley is the very place to be avoided by those who are seeking employment.'

But, in fact, Kimberley was being avoided. The odd trouble-maker might pitch up there, but it was no longer the Mecca of fortune hunters. Anyone willing to work now went to Johannesburg. This was something that even the malcontents of Kimberley were eventually forced to recognise. Slowly, sometimes sadly, they began to leave the town. Some of the younger men went to try their luck in Mashonaland, but the majority trekked to the Witwatersrand. Within a matter of three or four years, all the unemployable whites had disappeared from the street corners of Kimberley. This was perhaps the most profound effect that amalgamation had upon the town.

'One powerful corporation,' noted Lord Bryce, when he visited Kimberley in 1894, 'with its comparatively small staff of employees, has taken the place of independent adventurers of the old days . . . there are now only about 10,000 people in the town, and some of the poorer quarters are almost deserted, the stores and the taverns, as well as the shanty dwellings, empty and falling to pieces. In the better quarters, however, the old roughness has been replaced by order and comfort.'

It had to happen, of course. Johannesburg or no Johannesburg, Kimberley had to change. The romantic notions which strangers often had about the diamond diggings were nothing more than romantic notions. Reality had proved them false time and time again. Admittedly the change had caused distress, but the distress would have been far worse had it not taken place. Whether the change could have been brought about in some other way is a matter for speculation. But, given the political and economic thinking of the day, it is doubtful whether the end result would have been much different. Indeed, there is every reason to think that Kimberley gained far more than it lost.

In taking control of the diamond industry, De Beers Consolidated Mines made itself responsible for the town. It did so willingly and effectively. This was something which impressed every visitor to Kimberley. 'De Beers', claimed one enthusiast, 'is the good parent to whom every one in Kimberley looks for an allowance and a line in its will. Papa De Beers must do everything for Kimberley; give her roads and trees and electric light, water, model villages, and heaven knows what else.' De Beers, in fact, set the pattern for Kimberley's future growth.

Olive Schreiner, the famous novelist, who
for some years lived at 22 Otto Street, the
Homestead, Kimberley. (K)

The Head Office of De Beers Consolidated
Mines, Stockdale Street, in 1904, shortly
after the building had been extended to
Southey Street corner. (K)

19

Preludes to War

While the migration to Johannesburg was in progress, at least one former resident decided to return to Kimberley. In the middle of 1894, Olive Schreiner arrived in the town to stay with her sister Ettie, who was then living on the Homestead Estate. Whether at that time Olive intended to settle in Kimberley is not certain. For years she had been plagued by asthmatic attacks, and her prime motive for visiting her sister appears to have been to seek relief from her crippling complaint.

Kimberley's dry air had long been recognised as beneficial to invalids suffering from respiratory ailments, and efforts were being made to promote the town as a health resort. However, Olive Schreiner probably needed no such recommendations; her short stay at New Rush, some twenty years earlier, must have convinced her of the advantages of Griqualand West's climate. She was soon proved right. Within a matter of months she was feeling so much better that, after Ettie's departure, she decided to buy the Homestead property. Kimberley was to be her home for the next four years.

Olive Schreiner was then, in 1894, a woman of thirty-nine. Short, dumpy and dynamic she was a very different person from the moody girl who had once sat dreaming on the edge of the crater at New Rush. Moody she still was but her moods were of a far more positive nature. Since leaving New Rush her life had been transformed. During the years she had worked as a governess in the Cape, after leaving the diggings, she had written her famous novel *The Story of an African Farm*. The book had won her international fame. She had lived in Europe for eight years, returning to South Africa as a celebrity in 1889. At a literary conference held during the Kimberley Exhibition the Reverend John T. Lloyd had paid special tribute to her as South Africa's foremost writer. But she was far more than a writer. Her espousals of unfashionable causes – her support for the Transvaal Boers, her sympathy for the African people and her passionate feminism – were rapidly making her one of the most controversial figures in the country. Her notoriety was to reach a new height during her stay in Kimberley.

In Kimberley, also, Olive Schreiner experienced the most tragic loss of her life. A few months before arriving in the town she had married Samuel Cronwright, a Cape farmer. Cronwright shared his wife's political views to the full; it was in deference to her belief in equal rights for women that he agreed to change his name to Cronwright–Schreiner. He also agreed to change his way of life: to be with Olive he sold his farm at Cradock and moved to Kimberley.

He was present when their only child, a daughter, was born on 30 April 1895. The baby, delivered by a leading Kimberley doctor, lived only a matter of hours. Healthy when born – it weighed nine pounds nine ounces – it was discovered dead the following morning, apparently having choked in the night.

The tragedy of her baby's death was to haunt Olive. It took years for her to become reconciled to her loss. 'Life', she wrote in December 1896, 'has never been so beautiful to me anywhere as here (Kimberley), in spite of the one great desolating sorrow which has visited me here and of which I cannot even yet think or speak calmly.' The child's coffin, buried first in their Kimberley garden, was to follow the Cronwright Schreiners to their various homes in South Africa – finally being laid to rest in Olive's own grave, near Cradock, some twenty-five years later.

It was her intense interest in politics which helped sustain Olive in the months immediately following the tragedy. This interest centred on the great man of Kimberley, Cecil Rhodes. Once an admirer of Rhodes – whom she had first met in Cape Town in 1890 – Olive had in recent years become increasingly suspicious of his political methods and motives. Her disillusionment had set in when, in 1891, the notorious Masters and Servants Act had come before the Cape Parliament. Commonly known as the 'Strop Bill' or, more bitingly, as the 'Every Man to Wallop His Own Nigger Bill', the proposed legislation contained a clause which entitled an employer to administer corporal punishment to his black labourers. To an ardent humanitarian like Olive Schreiner, the idea of legalised brutality was horrifying. She never forgave Rhodes for supporting it. Since coming to Kimberley her hostility had, if anything, deepened. Soon her detestation of Rhodes, which was shared by her husband, was to be publicly proclaimed.

In August 1895, Samuel Cronwright–Schreiner was invited to address the Kimberley Literary Society on the current political situation in South Africa. It was a tall order. At that time the political situation in South Africa could not have been more complex or more tense. The Transvaal, in particular, was seething with unrest. The conflict which for years had existed between the Uitlanders (foreigners), who controlled the gold industry, and the Transvaal Government headed by President Paul Kruger had reached a critical stage.

From the time that gold had been discovered in the Transvaal, President Kruger had treated the army of fortune hunters who invaded his country warily. He was prepared to allow them to mine the gold but had no intention of allowing them to take over the Transvaal. Consequently he had severely restricted their civic rights and their industrial operations. The Uitlanders had protested vehemently on both scores. They claimed a right to a say in the running of the country – which they argued was supported by their money and labour – and greater industrial freedom. The conflict had led to continual strife. There had been demonstrations and counter-demonstrations, threats and counter-threats. Neither side had been prepared to make any significant concessions and it was becoming increasingly obvious that the dispute would result in some form of violence. It was rumoured that the Uitlanders were arming themselves. It was said that they intended to seize the Transvaal.

Behind all this talk of rebellion loomed the commanding figure of Cecil Rhodes.

Olive Schreiner had no doubts about Rhodes's unscrupulousness. To her he was an unprincipled capitalist who was using his sinister influence to further his own ends. She helped her husband prepare the address he delivered to the Kimberley Literary Society. In it Rhodes was attacked unmercifully. He was accused of political cynicism and opportunism. His alliance with J.H. Hofmeyr and the Afrikaner Bond in the Cape was derided. He was merely using the Afrikaner Bond, said the Cronwright–Schreiners, to implement retrogressive legislation against the blacks. As soon as the alliance had served its purpose the Bond would be cast aside. They urged all South Africans, regardless of race or colour, to unite against him.

It had required considerable courage for Cronwright–Schreiner to read his explosive address in the crowded Town Hall. For such an attack to have been launched against the all-powerful Rhodes was bad enough; that it had been launched in Kimberley – 'the stronghold of the enemy', as Cronwright–Schreiner called it – was staggering. It was something which neither Rhodes nor his political allies could ignore. J.H. Hofmeyr, the spokesman for the Afrikaner Bond, was asked to find a speaker to deliver a counterblast. He did not have to look far. There was, as it happened, a promising young politician handy who was only too ready to mount a public platform. This was a brilliant, 25-year-old Afrikaner named Jan Smuts.

Smuts had just returned from completing his law studies in England. He was then what was known as a 'Cape Colony man' and was critical of President Kruger and his policies in the Transvaal. Like Hofmeyr, he considered that political union was essential to the future of South Africa and that, by opposing Rhodes, Kruger was obstructing that union. Anxious to make his mark politically, he leapt at the chance to answer the Cronwright–Schreiners. His speech in the Kimberley Town Hall, on 29 October 1895, was his political début.

According to the *Diamond Fields Advertiser* young Smuts was given an enthusiastic reception. His audience, it reported, was 'large and representative' and listened to his speech 'with great attention . . . frequently applauding'. Cronwright–Schreiner disagreed. He claimed that the hall was half-empty and the speech so boring that even the chairman fell asleep. Neither report could be described as objective (the *Diamond Fields Advertiser* was staunchly pro-Rhodes) but Cronwright–Schreiner's was probably more accurate. Certainly the speech was long – the report of it filled several columns of fine newspaper print – and it was not particularly inspired or original. What Smuts had to say had been said many times before.

He attempted to cover all the points made by the Cronwright–Schreiners. He defended Rhodes's 'native policy' by calling upon the whites to close their ranks against 'prolific barbarism'. The democratic theories of Europe and America, he argued, could not be applied to the coloured races of South Africa. That Rhodes, the capitalist, was corrupting political life for his own gain, he vehemently denied. 'In the conduct of political controversy has he resorted to a single weapon which might not have been used by his non-capitalist predecessors and contemporaries?' he asked. 'In what way then does the accident of his being a capitalist disqualify him from being a political leader?'

Cronwright–Schreiner considered such arguments too feeble to warrant an answer. Even the partisan *Diamond Fields Advertiser* had to admit that Smuts was politically immature. It would take time, said the newspaper, for him to develop 'as a legislative and not merely a theoretical politician'. Nevertheless he was thought to show promise. With more practical experience he might well emerge as an effective speaker 'under the Rhodes–Bond–Hofmeyr banner'.

They were all wrong, of course. Cronwright–Schreiner was wrong in implying that Smuts was a boring nonentity. The *Diamond Fields Advertiser* was wrong in predicting Smuts's political future. But more wrong than anyone was Smuts himself. He was not only wrong in his arguments but it was wrong of him to have made the speech at all. He had little knowledge of Rhodes and even less of Rhodes's intentions. His Kimberley speech must rank as one of the most unfortunate of his controversial career.

If he wondered why the Cronwright–Schreiners did not reply he did not have to wonder for long. Two months later the answer came from a quite unexpected quarter. It was Rhodes himself who proved to Smuts how wrong he had been. Only then did the startled Smuts realise, as he later confessed, 'that a politician of such standing and influence as Mr Rhodes would openly and shamelessly deceive, not his enemies, but his very friends and associates'.

Another of those friends and associates was to put it more graphically. Rhodes's betrayal, J.H. Hofmeyr was to say, made him feel 'as though the wife of his bosom had been torn from his side'. He was referring to events in the Transvaal, but Kimberley was also involved.

(2)

On 30 December 1895 the citizens of Kimberley read with a mixture of incredulity and admiration that Dr Jameson and a contingent of Chartered Company's police had invaded the Transvaal. How or why the invasion had occurred was not clear. The newspaper reports were as garbled as they were vague. But this did not lessen the shock. 'No upheaval of Nature', claimed a visitor, 'could have created greater amazement . . . than this sensational news.'

A huge crowd gathered outside the offices of the *Diamond Fields Advertiser*. As they milled about in the stifling heat, waiting for further news, the excitement grew. There was talk of mass meetings, of preparations for war and of uprisings among the local farmers. Bewildering as the news was, it was not entirely unexpected. Everyone knew of the tensions in the Transvaal – most Kimberley families had a relative in Johannesburg – and an explosion of some sort had been expected for weeks. Now that it had come every man in Kimberley was anxious to play his part.

Few, however, could understand how Dr Jameson was mixed up in it. Some five and a half years earlier Jameson had more or less abandoned his Kimberley medical practice and accompanied the Pioneer Column on its northward march; since 1891 he had been the acting Administrator of Mashonaland. But Kimberley had by no means forgotten him. Not only did he pay frequent visits to the town but his role of Administrator had added a certain glamour to his name. His success in vanquishing the Matabele ruler, Lobengula, in the so-called Matabele War of 1893 had turned him into a military hero. So proud was Kimberley of the plucky little doctor that, in 1894, it was decided to honour him with a public banquet. Unfortunately, Jameson had declined the honour; he regretfully informed the Mayor that he would be unable to attend as 'he was too uncertain of his movements'. Now everyone was aware of his mysterious movements.

Even so, it was all very puzzling. Quelling a threatened 'native rebellion' was one thing, starting a rebellion in the Transvaal was quite another. The idea of Dr Jim leading an invasion force was as startling as it was incomprehensible. When it was learned that nearly all the officers accompanying him held Imperial commissions, the first flush of enthusiasm gave way to anxiety. 'One heard perfect strangers', says the visiting Lady Sarah Wilson, 'asking each other how these officers could justify their action of entering a friendly territory, armed to the teeth.'

Lady Sarah Wilson – a sister of Lord Randolph Churchill – was staying at 'The Lodge' with J.B. Currey. She was well placed to take the pulse of the town. The Curreys, like so many Kimberley families, had sons working in Johannesburg and were beside themselves with worry. What, everybody wanted to know, would happen to Englishmen in the Transvaal? Would they be commandeered to fight for the Boer Government? Would Kimberley men be forced to oppose Kimberley's popular doctor? For the next few days the town was in uproar.

The offices of the *Diamond Fields Advertiser* were permanently besieged by crowds clamouring for news. There was a growing demand for action on the part of Kimberley's leading citizens. A group of hot-heads offered to form a volunteer brigade to go to the assistance of Dr Jameson. Trains arrived at the station crammed with refugees from the Transvaal; there were even two women carrying babies that had been born on their nightmare journey. 'The Mayors of Kimberley and Beaconsfield', it was reported, 'are anxious to make arrangements for their (the refugees) accommodation, the hotels being full.'

Then came the most stunning news of all. Dr Jameson and his men were reported to have been surrounded by a Boer force and taken prisoners. At first the town refused to believe it. Whatever they felt about the invasion, they could not bring themselves to accept the fact that it had been turned into a fiasco. When a telegram was read out at the newspaper office denying Jameson's surrender, the huge crowd went wild 'and the town resounded with the refrain of "Rule Britannia".'

But they were wrong. Johannesburg had not risen, as was expected. Jameson had been captured and it was President Kruger who ruled as firmly as ever.

Gradually more news began to filter through. The invasion had been meant to spark off a rebellion in Johannesburg. Jameson had been provided with a letter calling upon him to come to the 'rescue' of his fellow-countrymen in the Transvaal. Once he had crossed the border from Bechuanaland, he was to have been joined by a force of well-armed Uitlanders. Preparations for the rising had been under way for months. Shipments of arms and ammunition had been sent to Johannesburg via Kimberley. They had been smuggled into the town and then concealed in the false bottoms of oil drums and bags of coke, stored in the diamond mines. Smuts's defence of Rhodes as a disinterested politician had been delivered within a stone's throw of a positive arsenal of illegal weapons.

But at the last minute the conspiracy had gone haywire. Jameson had ignored all warnings and jumped the gun. The Transvaal authorities had got wind of the plan, and a Boer force was waiting for the invaders at Doornkop, some twenty miles outside Johannesburg. After a short fight Jameson had surrendered and he and his men were taken to Pretoria as prisoners.

When Jameson's capture was confirmed, on 4 January 1896, the citizens of Kimberley rose to the occasion with an admirable, if misplaced, display of loyalty. Without waiting for further explanations, they closed their ranks and rallied to their local hero. A petition – signed 'by everybody in Kimberley' – was immediately sent to the British High Commissioner: 'We the undersigned Cape Colonists', it read, 'desire earnestly to represent to your Excellency that in the interests of general reconciliation a peaceful settlement is now happily in progress after the late deplorable bloodshed. Your Excellency should treat for the release of Dr Jameson and his comrades with full honours of war as of more importance than any other condition which the Government of the South African Republic is asked to grant.'

They were no less decided when it came to identifying the villains of the piece. Everyone was convinced that the mining magnates of Johannesburg were responsible for the whole sorry business. 'Loud and deep were the execrations levelled at the Johannesburgers,' says Lady Sarah Wilson, 'who, it was strenuously reiterated, had invited the Raiders to come to their succour and who, when the pinch came, never even left the town to go to their assistance.'

One mining magnate, however, they refused to blame: they could not, or would not, believe that Cecil Rhodes was in any way responsible for the misadventure. Rumours that Jameson had embarked on his 'raid' on instructions from Rhodes were dismissed as nonsense. Even after Rhodes had partly admitted his guilt by resigning as Prime Minister of the Cape, Kimberley remained loyal. When it was learnt that he was to visit the town before leaving for England, as crowd of 'several thousands' gathered at the station to welcome him. As he stepped off the train, he was greeted by 'deafening and repeated cheers'.

The demonstration touched Rhodes deeply. 'In time of political adversity,' he declared, when he was able to make himself heard, 'people come to know who their friends are, and I am glad that at this period I can count on so many friends on the Diamond Fields.' He told the crowd not to listen to rumours that his career was finished. He knew this was being said, but it was completely untrue. 'On the contrary,' he assured them, 'I think it is only just beginning and

I have a firm belief that, encouraged by the confidence and good wishes of my friends in Griqualand West and elsewhere, I will live to do much good and useful work on behalf of this community.' The crowd was still cheering as he drove away. They cheered Rhodes and they cheered Jameson. The old camaraderie of the diamond diggings was far from dead.

But the cheering could not drown the truth. Rhodes, as soon became apparent, had been in the conspiracy up to his neck. After leaving Kimberley he went to England to 'face the music', as he put it. Jameson was also sent to England to stand trial. He was found guilty and sentenced to fifteen months' imprisonment – of which, owing to ill-health, he served only just over four months. The conspirators in the Transvaal were not so lucky. A few days after the raid the members of the Johannesburg 'Reform Committee' were arrested and, as Transvaal residents, sent to gaol in Pretoria. At their trial in April, four of the leaders were sentenced to death, and the rest to two years' imprisonment and a fine of £2,000.

The severity of these sentences shocked South Africa. Nowhere was this shock more keenly felt than in Kimberley. Two of the men sentenced to death – Rhodes's brother Frank, and J.B. Robinson's former manager, Lionel Phillips – were well known in the town. Once again Kimberley showed its loyalty. In May a monster petition was forwarded to President Kruger urging that 'clemency be shown to political prisoners'. The following month the Mayor, William Willis, joined other colonial mayors in deputation to Pretoria to present a similar plea. How much good this did is uncertain. Kruger was being bombarded with similar petitions from all sides. In any case, it is doubtful whether he seriously intended that the sentences be carried out. The death sentences were quickly commuted and, by the middle of June, every prisoner had been pardoned on payment of a substantial fine.

But the full price of the Jameson Raid had yet to be paid. When the final reckoning came, Kimberley would help to foot the bill.

(3)

Kimberley was rapidly changing. Every year new buildings, new commercial enterprises and new institutions were being established. The haphazardly planned town still bore unmistakable traces of its mining-camp origins, but these were fast being overshadowed by the more substantial shops, offices and houses.

Not that this was immediately apparent to visitors to the town. Many, like Stuart Cumberland the fashionable 'mind-reader', who visited the diamond fields in the mid-1890s, liked to refer to Kimberley as a 'tin-town'. 'It has', claimed Cumberland, 'a run-up-in-a-night appearance, and, although some may find its general jerkiness of architecture quaint, no one, I take it, would find it either picturesque or imposing.' But Cumberland had not known the diggings in the early days. He had come to South Africa, like so many others, with preconceived ideas of what a mining town should look like and saw only what he wanted to see.

Kimberley's old inhabitants thought otherwise. While there was no denying that the place was still as exposed as ever, still as unbearably hot and still plagued by fires and vicious duststorms – 'it takes about ten consecutive Turkish baths to get the effects of one Kimberley dust-storm out of the pores of your skin', complained Cumberland – there could be no denying that amalgamation had radically changed the face of the town. Kimberley, in fact, was at last developing into the modern, progressive mining centre that its citizens had always hoped it would be.

Nothing emphasised Kimberley's advanced outlook more than the founding, in the fateful year of the Jameson Raid, of a training school for mining engineers. In August 1896 the South African School of Mines was formally inaugurated in Kimberley. It was the first such school to be established in South Africa.

A firmly-rooted legend has it that the South African School of Mines was the brainchild of Dr P.D. Hahn, a professor of chemistry at the South African College, Cape Town. It is said that in 1893 Professor Hahn and one of his colleagues visited the Witwatersrand to investigate the possibility of training young mining technicians. They were given every encouragement. Before leaving the goldfields they had secured £6,000 towards the launching of their project. Although there is undoubtedly some truth in this story, the idea of the school did not originate with Dr Hahn. It had been freely discussed in Kimberley some three years earlier.

It seems, in fact, to have been yet another outcome of the amalgamation. Once mining had been placed on a stable footing, it was inevitable that thought be given to instructing young men in mining techniques. Most mining engineers in South Africa came from overseas – particularly from America – and any youngster hoping to embark on a mining career had to go abroad to receive his training. Why, it was asked, should local lads be put to this unnecessary expense? Why could not young South Africans be trained in South Africa? Would it not be better for them to receive instruction in the proximity of the mines on which they would eventually work?

In the middle of 1890, several letters urging that a training centre be established appeared in the Kimberley press. The idea quickly caught on. On 3 July it was publicly announced that a petition in favour of the scheme had been started and was awaiting signatures in the office of the Town Clerk of Beaconsfield. This petition was 'to be sent to Parliament praying that the Government will take into immediate consideration the establishment of a School of Mines, and that seeing Kimberley is the centre of our mining industry, steps should be taken to establish the department here'.

Unfortunately, having got off to a promising start, the project then seems to have hung fire. It was not until four years later, when James Lawrence, the former Mayor, was elected to Parliament, that things began to move. As enthusiastic about the School of Mines as he had been about the Kimberley Exhibition, Lawrence introduced a motion in the Cape Assembly which led to the establishment of the school. Both the Cape Government and De Beers gave financial support, and an executive committee under the chairmanship of

Gardner Williams was formed in 1895.

The school was opened in temporary premises donated by De Beers on 10 August 1896. Earlier that year Professor J.G. Lawn, a lecturer at the Royal School of Mines in London, had been engaged to conduct the Kimberley mining course. The first five students had already completed part of the course at the South African College, Cape Town, and were to spend a year in Kimberley and then go to Johannesburg for a final year. That was how the course was to be conducted: two years at a college in the Cape, a third year in Kimberley and a fourth in Johannesburg. But the Jameson Raid more or less put paid to this plan. The Transvaal Government was no longer interested. It was left to the mining houses to provide elementary education on the Rand, and the idea of higher education had to be dropped. After a trial period of two years, it was decided to extend the Kimberley course by another six months, and only the last half year was spent on the mines in Johannesburg.

In 1898 a new site was found for the school in Hull Street, Kimberley. Once again De Beers supplied the land and gave £2,000 towards the erection of buildings; the Cape Government gave a further £2,000, and £5,000 was borrowed. The buildings, consisting of lecture- and class-rooms, an assay laboratory and a boarding-house for students, were completed and occupied in February 1899. This was to be the home of the South African School of Mines for the next five years. In 1904 it was transferred to Johannesburg, merged with the Transvaal Technical Institute and later developed into the famous University of the Witwatersrand. Kimberley had given birth to another great and lasting South African institution.

Three of the members who served on the committee of the School of Mines – Gardner Williams, James Lawrence and Barney Barnato's cousin, David Harris – were also very active in promoting another Kimberley venture of the mid-1890s. They were all directors of the Kimberley Theatre Company. This company, under the chairmanship of Tim Tyson (secretary of the Kimberley Club) was responsible for the building of the new Theatre Royal, which, until its destruction by fire in February 1930, was regarded as one of the most impressive theatres in South Africa.

The need for a new theatre in Kimberley had long been felt. Since the days of the old Theatre Royal and the Lanyon Theatre, several theatres had with varying fortunes come and gone. But love of the theatre had remained strong. Few important actors, musicians or theatrical companies visiting South Africa failed to play at Kimberley. There, perhaps more than anywhere else, they were always sure of good houses and an enthusiastic audience. At times, in fact, the audiences tended to be a little too lively. Unsuspecting patrons of the stalls, as well as actors, were often startled by the barracking that came from the upper balconies of a Kimberley theatre.

'Speaking of performances in Kimberley,' Stuart Cumberland observed ruefully, 'no one who hasn't given a show in that town can form the slightest idea what the "gods" are like there . . . your Kimberley "god" pays his half-crown like a sportsman, and goes upstairs, not because its cheaper – for in some cases he could just as well take a stall – but solely because he can have more fun there. He generally commences by passing a running comment upon those down below, and winds up by an attempt to draw the performer. . . . One requires the self-possession of well, a De Beers director to be able with equanimity, to run the gauntlet of the witticisms of the Kimberley "gods" .'

It all helped to make theatre-going an hilarious social occasion. Indeed, many Kimberleyites went to the theatre 'simply to hear the "latest" about the poor mortals below from the "gods" above'. Not to be seen in the stalls was tantamount to admitting you had something to hide. This might have had something to do with the invariably packed houses. For packed they were and, by the early 1890s, the need for a new theatre was becoming increasingly obvious.

But it all took time. In 1895 a group of interested citizens formed a theatre-building committee and launched a fund-raising campaign. As always, the call for funds was promptly answered by the ever-generous directors of De Beers, who guaranteed to subscribe £4,000 on a pound-for-pound basis. With this guarantee the committee had little difficulty in raising further funds, and the Kimberley Theatre Company was eventually formed with a capital of £15,000. Once the site of the old theatre in Dutoitspan Road had been leased from the Town Council, the building plans went ahead.

The new theatre - designed by D.W. Greatbatch, the architect of the Exhibition Hall - was not, as far as its exterior went, particularly remarkable. Its glory was its interior. It boasted what was probably the largest stage in the southern hemisphere, and its seating ranged from elaborately curtained boxes, through the stalls, a dress circle, a family circle and the famous 'gods'. The whole effect was elegant and spacious.

Elegant also was the grand opening on 26 October 1897. A performance of 'The French Maid' - a musical comedy direct from London - was attended by the new Governor of the Cape, Sir Alfred Milner, and every notability in Kimberley. Only one familiar face was missing. Barney Barnato, the town's most celebrated theatrical personality, was not there. Four months earlier, Kimberley had been shocked by the news of Barney's death. Weighed down by financial worries and personal misfortunes, the seemingly irrepressible Barney had, in a fit of hysteria, thrown himself from the deck of the s.s. *Scot* and drowned. 'Always', he had once said, 'wind up with a good curtain, and bring it down before the public gets tired, or has time to find you out.' His death, if tragic, was perhaps fitting.

(4)

When Sir Alfred Milner visited Kimberley, in October 1897, he had been Governor of the Cape for only a matter of months. Since his arrival in South Africa he had spent much of his time in getting to know the country. The enthusiastic welcome he had been given on his tours had greatly impressed him. 'My reception everywhere', he wrote shortly before setting out for Kimberley, 'was tremendously cordial and the impression I derived was that the country people are well affected – the English absolutely so, the Dutch quite disposed

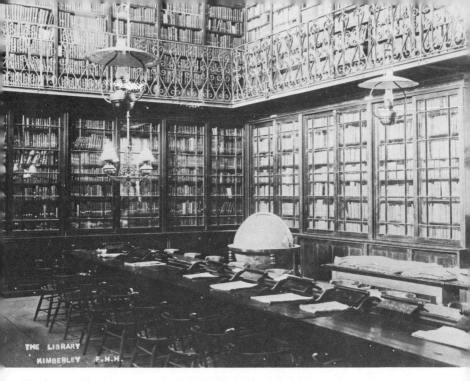

The front hall of the Kimberley Public Library, 1897. (M)

Interior of the Theatre Royal, Kimberley — erected in 1897 and destroyed by fire in 1930. The stage was said to be the largest in the southern hemisphere when it was built. (K)

to be so if they are left alone.'

Coming to South Africa in the wake of the disastrous Jameson Raid, Milner needed to be assured of support. The suspicion and hostility which now existed between Boer and Briton would not be simply overcome. Whether or not Milner was suited to his role of peacemaker had yet to be proved. He was, at this time, still testing the ground. As convinced as Rhodes of the importance of upholding British supremacy, he welcomed all signs of loyalty to the Queen and Empire. Kimberley did not let him down.

Indeed, he could hardly have chosen a better time to arrive in what had been described as this 'most English – that is, British – town in Cape Colony'. The year 1879 was the year of Queen Victoria's Diamond Jubilee. The event had been celebrated throughout South Africa. For Kimberley it had held a special significance: where better to honour a Diamond Jubilee than in the Diamond City? The official festivities had lasted for two days in the middle of June. There had been a review of the Kimberley troops, a huge sports meeting, a promenade concert and a subscription ball in the Drill Hall – the funds going towards the building of a Maternity Home for the hospital. But perhaps the most touching event was the tea-party given by the Mayor for over 8,000 white and coloured children. When, at the end of the party, the band led the youngsters in a rousing chorus of 'God Save the Queen', there was hardly a dry eye among the spectators.

Hearts were still beating loyally when the Governor arrived on 23 October. He was met at the station by a special reception committee and drove through the gaily decorated town in a coach drawn by four white horses, accompanied by a contingent of the Griqualand West Brigade. A formal address was read in the Market-square. Two days later, Milner was guest of honour at a ball given in the Queen's Hotel, and the following evening he attended the opening of the Theatre Royal. What was to have been the glittering climax of his visit – a ball in the Drill Hall – was, however, overshadowed by the death of the Duchess of Teck. As the Queen's representative, the Governor was obliged to decline his invitation. But this was the only disappointment. By the time he left for Rhodesia on 28 October, Milner could have had no doubts about Kimberley's loyalty.

The Governor's visit was to be remembered for another reason. He was one of the first distinguished visitors to stay at Kimberley's smart new 'hotel'. This was the Sanatorium, which had been built close to J.B. Currey's house, 'The Lodge', in Belgravia. An extremely handsome, double-storied, red-brick building, with graceful wooden pillars and balustrades, the Sanatorium was intended to serve partly as an hotel and partly as a health resort. It was another of Cecil Rhodes's pet building projects, partly sponsored by De Beers from compound profits. Explaining this to his fellow directors, Rhodes said: 'The Sanatorium is a bit of a hobby of mine. I have always thought that Kimberley would be an admirable place for people with chest complaints from Home, if only there were sufficient and proper accommodation. The experience of many has been that this climate has been very successful in such complaints, and doctors all agree that Kimberley is a good place for a Sanatorium.' It was one of the few of Rhodes's enterprises of which Olive Schreiner might have approved.

De Beers continued to subsidise the Sanatorium out of profits made in the compounds. The subsidy – like that given to the School of Mines – was justified by Rhodes as serving two important purposes: it benefited invalids and attracted new life to Kimberley. 'The number of young fellows who come here to learn the business of mining', he argued in 1898, 'will add to the prosperity of the place in the same way as visitors staying at the Sanatorium.' That he would soon be one of those visitors – that the Sanatorium would soon be his temporary home in Kimberley – had then not occurred to him.

The generosity of De Beers in supporting new developments in the town was boundless. There was hardly a public building erected in Kimberley during the 1890s that was not financially backed by the company. One of the most impressive of these was the large new Town Hall that was built in the Market-square in 1899.

For years the Town Hall in New Main Street had been considered hopelessly inadequate. Ramshackle, cramped, and badly in need of repair, it in no way reflected the town's growing civic pride. However, the decision to build a more spacious home for the Town Council was not taken until all the arguments for and against were settled by an all-too-familiar Kimberley catastrophe. On 29 March 1898, the old Town Hall was destroyed by fire. How or when the fire started was never satisfactorily explained. It was discovered at one o'clock in the morning by a police officer and before it could be brought under control most of the offices and all but a few of the Town Clerk's records had gone up in flames. Temporarily housed in the old Stock Exchange, the Council was then forced to its long-postponed decision. On 13 April 1898, it formally resolved to build a new Town Hall 'to meet the growing requirements of the Town, in a more suitable locality'.

Once again De Beers was prompt to offer assistance with an initial donation of £3,000. The design of the new building was decided upon by competition. Architects from all over South Africa were invited to enter – the first prize being £100, the second £50. The winner was a well-known Kimberley architect, F. Carstairs Rogers. The design he submitted was decidedly impressive.

Planned to stand in the middle of the Market-square, the building was described as being 'Roman Corinthian' in style. By the standards of its day, it was admirably restrained: a classic, honey-coloured, harmonious arrangement of pillars, pilasters, pediments, urns and balustrading. It would boast a large entrance hall, a main hall, a supper room, a council chamber, a mayor's parlour, committee room, Town Clerk's office and several municipal administrative offices. Behind would stand the Market House, open on three sides and sheltered by a corrugated-iron roof.

The Mayor, Moses Cornwall – who in his previous term of office during the early 1880s had initiated the town's electricity and water supply – laid the foundation stone on Wednesday, 16 November, 1898. The impressive ceremony, witnessed by a huge crowd and followed by a banquet at the Queen's Hotel, was regarded as a landmark in the town's history. When complete, the new Town Hall would be one of Kimberley's most imposing buildings. It would serve not only as an administrative centre but as a dignified setting for civic receptions. Many must have regretted that the building of it had been so long delayed; it would certainly have added tone to the recent reception given to the Cape Governor.

There may also have been regret that it was not ready in time for Kimberley's next important social function. This was the visit of one of Lord Hawke's famous cricket sides which was then touring South Africa. Few sporting events were to cause so much excitement as the arrival, at the beginning of 1899, of the British cricketers. The matches played during their short stay in Kimberley were to be remembered for years. Local sportsmen were to speak of them with a mixture of awe and chastened humour. 'We batted eighteen men and fielded fifteen against the English eleven,' recalled Wilfred Seymour some seventy years later. 'It was heartbreaking for me to see my Kimberley cricket heroes bite the dust one after the other, staying only a short time at the wickets.'

One of the greatest of those heroes was Jackie Powell, a famous Kimberley all-rounder. Powell had distinguished himself both as a rugby player and a cricketer, and everyone was expecting fireworks when he went into bat. But Lord Hawke's underhand bowling completely bewildered him. So much so that he let every ball pass. There was a good deal of consternation when, at the end of the over, the Kimberley side met in the middle of the pitch and then marched off the field in a body. Eventually Lord Hawke decided to go to the dressing-rooms to find out what was wrong. Powell soon told him. 'We know', he snorted, 'we can't play cricket out here but we try, and if you think you are going to bowl underhand to us, we're not taking it.' Only after the astonished Lord Hawke had agreed to abide by local custom was the game allowed to proceed.

But not all South African squabbles ended so diplomatically. Outside Kimberley another British representative was finding it difficult to satisfy local objections. Sir Alfred Milner was faced by a more determined opponent. His attempts to resolve the long-standing Transvaal dispute had failed miserably.

Things came to a head in June 1899. At a conference in Bloemfontein, the capital of the Orange Free State, Milner met President Kruger for what appeared to be an eleventh-hour attempt to settle their differences. There was little hope of a settlement and they both knew it. It was not a question of underhand bowling, but of underhand methods. Milner was determined to uphold what he considered to be the rights of British subjects in the Transvaal, and Kruger was equally determined not to yield to outside pressure. The conference was in many ways nothing more than a political front. Neither side intended to give way to the other.

Nor did they. Milner's attempt to force the issue was clumsy and disastrous. When he demanded that the Transvaal franchise be drastically reformed to give the Uitlanders an immediate voice in the Volksraad, Kruger cried, 'It is our country you want!' Kruger's own attempts to bargain were imperiously rejected and, as was expected, the conference ended in stalemate. 'This Conference', declared Milner, 'is absolutely at an end and there is no obligation on either side arising out of it.'

All that arose out of it, in fact, was the certainty of war. It was now obvious that there would be no compromise. Both sides began to prepare. As the Boers amassed arms in the Transvaal, British troopships began to arrive at the Cape. Talk of whether or not war could be avoided gave way to speculations as to when the fighting would start.

Nowhere was that speculation more rife, or more urgent, than in Kimberley. Few doubted that, once hostilities broke out, the town would be an immediate target for attack. 'I was convinced', says David Harris, 'that war was looming on the horizon, and I trembled to think what might happen, in that event, to defenceless Kimberley, 500 miles from the nearest port, bounded on the one side by the Free State, and on the other by the Transvaal. I feared that the Republican forces would make a dash for Kimberley, where Rhodes housed the bulk of his fortune, which would have made a rich haul for the invaders.'

Harris was a seasoned soldier. He had served in several local campaigns and had recently been promoted to Lieutenant Colonel of the Griqualand West Brigade. He was also a member of the Cape Assembly and a director of De Beers. As much as anyone, Harris was in a position to know what he was talking about. It had been at his suggestion that, as far back as 1896 – at the time of the Jameson Raid – the directors of De Beers had agreed to obtain and store a quantity of arms and ammunition 'for the sole purpose of defence'.

However, with the break-up of the Bloemfontein Conference the question of defence had become more urgent. At the beginning of June, a public meeting, attended by over 5,000 citizens – white and black – was called to express sympathy for the Uitlanders in the Transvaal. Deputations of anxious townsfolk began to wait on the Mayor, R.H. Henderson, urging him to petition the Government for guns, rifles and ammunition. The Kimberley volunteers, it was pointed out, were ill-equipped to withstand a full-scale attack.

This display of 'Kimberley jitters' was openly scoffed at in the Cape Assembly. Why, it was asked, was the town panicking? Who was expected to attack? 'Are you afraid of a Kafir rising?' sneered a Government spokesman. Officialdom was obviously not prepared to admit what was on everybody's mind. The Prime Minister made this quite clear. Replying to a cable sent to him in July, he declared that 'he did not see his way to lend colour to such alarming rumours by moving arms and ammunition through the Colony at the present time'. It was cold comfort to defenceless Kimberley. As rumours began to circulate that the Boers were arming 'disloyal British subjects' in the nearby Vryburg district, the town became increasingly alarmed.

But, amidst the uncertainty, the life of the town went on. By 20 September, the new Town Hall was ready for occupation. It had taken almost a year to build and cost an estimated £26,000. The official opening of the gaily decorated building was performed by the Mayor. That night the adults of the town were entertained at a masked fancy-dress ball, and the following evening a party was given for the children. This, as many must have realised, was to be Kimberley's last uninhibited fling for many months.

A week earlier, a balding 45-year-old army officer had arrived in the town. He was Lieutenant-Colonel Robert George Kekewich of the 1st Loyal North

Lancashire Regiment. His arrival was meant to be secret, but everyone realised he had been sent to organise the defence of the town. He was assisted by three regular officers, who had arrived some time before. The Cape Government had at last answered Kimberley's repeated requests for assistance. Whether the answer had come in time was another matter.

An experienced soldier who had spent most of his life in the army, Kekewich was appalled to find Kimberley dangerously vulnerable. 'At this time,' says one of his officers, 'the Volunteer units were much below establishment, and the forces in Kimberley for the defence of the Diamond Fields wholly inadequate.' With no time to lose, Kekewich briskly set about putting the town on a war footing.

'The need for troops is, I think,' he wrote to Cape Town, 'very great.' For once the response to this appeal, if not spectacular, was at least prompt. A week later Kekewich was joined by half a battalion of his own regiment, a company of Royal Garrison Artillery, and a detachment of the Army Service and Medical Corps.

A call went out for volunteers to form a Town Guard for Kimberley and Beaconsfield. There was a rush to the recruiting offices. Within a few days some 2,500 civilians had signed on and started training.

For the next couple of weeks Kimberley was caught up in a flurry of stocktaking, sandbagging, fort building and trench digging. The directors of De Beers gave Kekewich every assistance. Particularly helpful was the technical knowledge of George Labram, the company's chief engineer.

Then in his late thirties, George Labram had been born in Detroit, Michigan. He had been sent to South Africa in 1893 to erect and run a crushing plant for De Beers. Three years later he had been appointed chief engineer and electrician of the company. Inventive, resourceful and enthusiastic, Labram was to prove invaluable to Kekewich during these days of preparation. He it was who designed the 'conning tower' on the headgear of the De Beers Mine which was to serve as Kekewich's look-out. He also repositioned searchlights around the town to guard against possible night attacks. The military authorities soon came to recognise and rely upon Labram's remarkable ingenuity.

But time was all too short. There was little hope of Kimberley catching up with outside events. As Kekewich battled to prepare for war, British and Boer politicians were ensuring that those preparations were needed. All attempts at a negotiated peace failed. The quarrel was not Kimberley's but Kimberley, like the rest of South Africa, would be forced to fight. Hostilities opened with a dramatic suddenness.

On Saturday 14 October 1899, Colonel Kekewich was in the Kimberley Telegraph Office receiving instructions from his superiors in Cape Town. Suddenly the line went dead. There followed what one observer called a 'silence of death'. Everyone in the office was aware of what had happened. Three days earlier war had been declared. The telegraph line to the south had been cut. Kimberley was besieged.

20

Besieged

'*Fearful* excitement,' wrote Constance Scott on 15 October, 'the wires cut and rails taken up at Spytfontein last night. We are now quite cut off. . . . We expect an attack at any moment. Everyone at his post and all keeping a keen look out.'

One of those keeping a keen look out was Constance Scott's husband, Robert – one of Kimberley's most distinguished soldiers. Some twenty years earlier Robert George Scott, then a 22-year-old officer of the Cape Mounted Rifles, had shown considerable courage during a skirmish with the Baphuthi clan near the Basutoland border. His bravery and self-sacrifice had earned him the Victoria Cross. Few military men in Kimberley were as highly respected as Robert Scott, V.C. He had been one of the first to answer Kekewich's call for volunteers for the Town Guard and had immediately been given command of the 1st Division. Since then his wife had seen little of him.

'Men on horseback rush up to the house at all hours,' she had written the day before the siege began, 'asking for Capt. Scott, Major Scott, Col. Scott (they have not reached General *yet*). "Where is he to be found. Most important despatches." Oh! these are troublous times.'

But, as she fully realised, the troublous times were only just beginning. They were times which Constance Scott, like many other women in Kimberley, would have to face alone. Earlier she had sent her four children to Cape Town for safety and with her husband continually on duty (he was soon to enlist as a captain in the Kimberley Light Horse) she could expect little companionship or support. 'I do feel so anxious,' she sighed, 'it is hard to be a woman and have to stay at home and *wait*.'

Nor was the waiting made easier by the alarming rumours that swept Kimberley during the first days of the siege. There was talk of impending attacks, of spies being active in the town, of treachery and betrayal. When, at eleven o'clock on Sunday the 15th, the De Beers hooter sounded – calling the Town Guard to their posts – there was open panic. Clergymen stopped their services with a hasty prayer and sent their congregations hurrying home. In some streets women 'ran around frightening each other as to the number of Boers who could be seen advancing and how very easily they could take Kimberley'. It proved to be a false alarm, but was none the less frightening for that. 'The three death-like moans given out every few seconds', declared one woman, 'were enough to shake the nerves of the strongest.'

This was not the only scare that day. An hour earlier slips had been sent from house to house advising people to conserve water, as the main supply from the

Vaal had been cut off. At first it was believed that the pumping-machines at Riverton had been blown up, but this rumour, like so many others, proved to be unfounded. A Boer commando had, however, taken possession of the pumping-station and put the machines out of action. For dry, water-conscious Kimberley this was bad enough. All over town, people hastily filled tanks, baths and buckets in the hopes of preserving what little water they had. The following day it was announced that the water supply would only be turned on from nine to eleven every morning and that anyone found using water for anything other than domestic purposes would have their supply permanently cut off. 'The poor garden', winced Constance Scott, 'will have to go.'

The water supply remained precarious for three weeks. Then De Beers came to the rescue. An underground spring had been discovered at the Wesselton Mine and for the past couple of years had been used for washing blue-ground. By diverting this supply to the main pipeline, the company was able to provide the town with free water. Limited as this water was, there was sufficient to meet Kimberley's essential needs. It also meant that any rainwater collected by gardeners could be used to grow vegetables.

The initial panic over, Kimberley settled down to face the siege. The proclamation of martial law was accepted with something approaching relief. 'No one is allowed out between 9 p.m. and 6 a.m.', noted Constance Scott, 'which as *our* men are out all night is a great protection.' There was relief also when Kekewich clamped down on profiteering. In the first few days of the siege there had been a rush on the shops. Tinned food, flour, dried fruit – anything that could be preserved – had been snapped up by food hoarders and prices had soared beyond all reason. 'Paraffin,' it was said, 'which had been selling at sixteen shillings and sixpence, went up to three pounds for a ten gallon can, and other things in proportion.' This was quickly stopped. After being consulted by the Mayor, Kekewich issued a proclamation prohibiting the sale of goods beyond their normal price. Only those who had spent a fortune on groceries the day before complained.

But if Kimberley was growing calmer, it was no less apprehensive. As days passed without a glimpse of the enemy, the original sense of panic gave way to bewilderment. What were the Boers up to? Why did they not attack? Little news reached the town and what was received was heavily censored. Most people could only speculate. Inevitably the speculations were as contradictory as they were ill-informed.

That an attack would be made, few doubted. The importance of both the railway and the diamond mines could not be ignored. Nor, for that matter, could the presence in town of the Boers' *bête noire* – Cecil Rhodes.

Rhodes had arrived in Kimberley on 10 October, the day before war was declared. He had been warned not to come. A week earlier he had received a telegram from the Mayor, R.H. Henderson. 'Citizens generally', it read, 'feel that your presence here would serve to induce a rush with view to do the town, your Company, and all our joint interests great damage. Under all circumstances would ask you kindly to postpone coming in order to avert any possible risks.' Others had written to him in the same vein. There seems to have been good reason for these fears. It was well known that the Boers were anxious to capture Rhodes and it was said that they planned to exhibit him in a cage throughout the Transvaal. But Rhodes would have none of it. When it looked as if war was imminent, his thoughts had turned immediately to the cradle of his fortunes. Kimberley represented his great beginnings and De Beers Consolidated Mines was still the main source of his continuing wealth. It was, for him, both natural and inevitable that he should take his place among the citizens of Kimberley if the town were threatened. And so to Kimberley he came.

He was accompanied by his friends, Rochfort Maguire and his wife and Dr Thomas Smartt, and his private secretary Philip Jourdan. On arriving he made straight for the Sanatorium – which had already been fortified with sandbags and sheets of corrugated iron – and took over two small rooms on the ground floor. He seemed not in the least concerned. 'We dined with Mr Rhodes at the Sanatorium,' wrote Constance Scott on 14 October, 'met Mr and Mrs Maguire and one or two others. Had a very pleasant evening. After dinner played fives. Mr Rhodes very excited over it, he was *very* nice, and said he did not know why people here did not want him. He did not think he had done much harm in coming. In fact has sent for more guns and so done a great deal of good.'

Many others felt the same. When R. H. Henderson came to write his memories of the siege, he conveniently forgot his warning telegram. He made it appear that everyone was waiting to welcome Rhodes. The burning question on the eve of the siege, he says, was whether or not Rhodes would come. 'Without his presence,' he claimed 'all would not be well.' His change of heart is significant. Rhodes's presence in Kimberley was to cause a great deal of controversy. But whatever might be said by his detractors – and much has been said – there can be no doubt that to a large section of the Kimberley populace Cecil Rhodes emerged from the siege a hero.

'I really do not know what we should have done without Mr Rhodes during the siege,' gushed one young woman. 'He does not need my small "meed of praise", although I could fill this book were I to begin; but his name will ever mean that of a true friend to everyone who was in Kimberley.' Despite their initial objections, R.H. Henderson and his town councillors came to share these sentiments. They could hardly have done otherwise. Rhodes relieved them of many a pressing burden.

One of the first problems the council faced was that posed by refugees and unemployed. Thousands of black, coloured and white men, women and children had poured into the town before the siege. The night before the telegraph lines were cut, over four hundred people were sleeping in the new Town Hall alone, others were scattered throughout Kimberley. They had, as the Mayor pointed out, 'little means. No homes. No friends. Yet all must be cared for.' What was to be done with them? And for the unemployed? How could they be fed? How could they be occupied? They could not be left to wander about the town, jobless, homeless and penniless. The Mayor went to consult Rhodes.

In a half-hour interview the problem was largely solved. Rhodes agreed to employ all the able-bodied men – at an estimated £8,000 a week initially – to repair the neglected roads and parks of Kimberley. A relief committee of clergymen and women workers was set up to provide shelter for the homeless and to assist the women and children. By the end of the year De Beers had paid over £6,390 in relief wages for 185 whites, 730 coloureds and 1,457 Africans. Not only the refugees but Kimberley benefited by this relief work. 'Gardens were laid out,' says David Harris, 'trenches dug, new roads made, and a trellis-vinery, three-quarters of a mile in length was erected.'

This was only a start. Throughout the siege De Beers played an important part in relieving distress, supplying equipment and aiding charitable organisations. Had Rhodes confined himself to these activities all might have been well. Unfortunately he did not. Regarding Kimberley as his own domain, he was determined to play his part not only in relief work among the civilians but in the defence of the town. It was this that brought him into conflict with the hard-pressed military commander. Colonel Kekewich.

Rhodes had lost no time in raising a mounted corps of the Kimberley Light Horse. Not only did he help equip this corps but he regarded it as being under his command. He had a long-standing contempt for army officers and had no intention of being bound by the dictates of the military. This was further emphasised by, as Constance Scott noted, his sending direct to Cape Town for more guns. He had not consulted Kekewich about this request; nor had he informed the military of other messages he had sent out of the town. When an answer to one of these messages was received, the battle between Kimberley's two 'commanders' began.

On the second Sunday of the siege, R.H. Henderson received a message from Rhodes asking him to call at the Sanatorium at ten o'clock that morning. He says that, as he entered the gates of the hotel, he met Colonel Kekewich coming out. 'I told him,' says Henderson, 'Mr Rhodes had sent for me. He replied "Yes! I have just left him." ' If Henderson is right – another version of the incident says that Kekewich did not go to the Sanatorium but sent a staff officer – Kekewich's terse reply is understandable. His interview with Rhodes could not have been pleasant.

It appears that a dispatch-rider had just arrived from Cape Town with a coded message from Sir Alfred Milner. The message had been handed to Kekewich but, when it was decoded, it was found to be addressed to Rhodes. Not surprisingly, Kekewich found this somewhat alarming. A strictly enforced security system decreed that only messages authorised by the military authorities could be sent out of the town. As Milner's communication was obviously an answer to one sent by Rhodes, it meant that Rhodes was ignoring Kekewich's decrees.

What was Kekewich to do about it? He was placed in a difficult position. With Kimberley besieged and under martial law, it was vital that his authority be observed. On the other hand Rhodes was a powerful man whose co-operation was essential. Kekewich had no wish to alienate him. He tried instead to win Rhodes over. Tactfully he suggested – either personally or through a staff officer – that any messages Rhodes sent to Milner should either be written in the Chartered Company's code or channelled through the military authorities. But Rhodes would allow no interference. He made it clear that he would communicate with the outside world in his own way and in his own words.

According to Henderson, he was even then planning to send out further messages without informing Kekewich. He had summoned Henderson, as Mayor, to help draft an appeal to Cape Town for the early relief of Kimberley. When the reply to this appeal was intercepted by the military authorities, there was a stand-up row between Kekewich and Rhodes. Henderson was called to Kekewich's office at the Kimberley Club to witness a scene he would never forget. Throughout it Kekewich remained cool, but Rhodes stamped about the office in a towering fury demanding that the intercepted messages be handed over. When Kekewich refused, Rhodes stormed out of the office. 'I was so glad', admits Henderson, 'to see the back of Mr Rhodes. He was literally frothing at the mouth.'

So started the bitter feud between the bachelor soldier at the Kimberley Club and the bachelor politician at the Sanatorium. It was a feud that was to divide Kimberley and test many a loyalty. The people of Kimberley, it was said, admired Kekewich but worshipped Rhodes. To take sides was not always easy.

There were partisans in both camps. One of the more controversial was Major W. A. J. O'Meara, one of Kekewich's officers. Many considered O'Meara to be a troublemaker. Henderson was to describe him as 'an evil influence'. David Harris thought him boorish. 'Suspicious and cynical,' says Harris, 'and deficient in diplomatic tact, he caused much friction, and at times made matters rather difficult for Kekewich.' True or not, O'Meara's partisanship did not help matters. Several ill-informed accounts of the siege of Kimberley have been based on his biased observations.

(2)

On the morning of 4 November 1899, a large party of Boers were sighted approaching Kimberley. As they neared the outskirts of the town, one of them was seen to be carrying a flag of truce. The guards manning the barricades eyed them warily. However, before the party had come within gun range it halted; the flag bearer then broke away and advanced to the nearest outpost. He announced that he had a message from the local Boer commandant, C.J. Wessels, for Colonel Kekewich.

The message, when it was delivered at military headquarters, turned out to be an ultimatum. In polite but firm phraseology, Commandant Wessels demanded the unconditional surrender of Kimberley by 6 a.m. on Monday 6 November. It was, as everybody realised, nothing more than gesture. Wessels could have had little hope of his demand being met. The underlying purpose of the ultimatum was contained in the following paragraph. 'In case', wrote Wessels, 'your Honour should determine not to comply with this demand, I hereby request your Honour to allow all women and children to leave Kimberley, so that they may be placed out of danger. . . . I shall be ready to receive all Afrikander families who wish to leave Kimberley, and also to offer liberty to depart to all women and children of other nations desirous of leaving.' This magnanimous proposal was to intensify the feud between the Rhodes and Kekewich partisans.

According to Major O'Meara, Kekewich decided to inform the townsfolk of the ultimatum in a public statement. Before publishing this statement in the *Diamond Fields Advertiser* he showed it to Rhodes for approval. Rhodes did not approve. He said that to announce that *all* women and children had been requested to leave would cause unnecessary alarm and suggested that notice of Wessel's invitation be confined only to Afrikaner families. Kekewich altered his statement accordingly. However, Rhodes's supporters were to deny this. They claimed that Kekewich was responsible for distorting Wessels's offer and blamed him for imperilling British women and children.

Whatever the truth, the published statement had little effect. When it appeared in the newspaper, two days after the ultimatum had expired, only one Afrikaner family took advantage of the invitation to leave. Would more have gone, had the full text been published? It is extremely doubtful.

The arrival of the Boer envoys was the first real sight the townsfolk had had of the enemy. They were, however, fully alive to their presence in the surrounding district. Eleven days earlier, on 24 October, a reconnoitring party of 300 mounted men under the command of the popular Major H. Scott Turner – assisted by an armoured train – had met up with a Boer commando. Finding himself outnumbered, Scott Turner signalled for reinforcements. His signal was received by Kekewich in the 'Conning Tower'. Immediately two companies of the Loyal North Lancashires were dispatched by train, while two artillery guns and two Maxims, escorted by seventy Cape Police, were sent up by road. In the brisk battle that followed, three British soldiers were killed and twenty-one wounded. Much of the action was fought in an encroaching mist and it ended with the Boers retreating. They left behind them their dead field-cornet, Petrus Botha, in whose pocket was found a letter from an ex-Kimberley schoolboy – J.B.M. Hertzog. At the outbreak of war, Hertzog – now an Orange Free State judge – had joined the Boer forces in the Kimberley district. In his letter he had instructed Botha to capture cattle in the neighbourhood of Kenilworth; his distrust of the money-grubbing Uitlanders was as strong as ever.

The people of Kimberley had been proud of their little 'victory'. It had increased their confidence and taught them much. Not only their troops but their doctors had been tested. Tending the wounded had been a salutary experience for many of the hospital staff. 'We had a pretty busy time at the hospital when the wounded came in,' wrote Dr E. Oliver Ashe, a senior surgeon at the Kimberley Hospital. 'I got five of them under my hands, but only two were more than trifles – an officer shot through the chest and a sergeant shot through the arm, splintering up the bone. We doctors had all of us seen a few bullet wounds with revolvers and such like, but had no experience of the modern rifle bullet, and it was a revelation to us.'

Ashe, a big, bluff physician, was a comparative newcomer to Kimberley. He had arrived there in 1892. In time he was to become one of the most highly respected doctors in the town. The siege established him as a formidable Kimberley personality.

Two shells fired into the town on 6 November signalled the expiry of Wessel's ultimatum. Both of them landed on high earthworks near the Wesselton Mine, without causing any damage. They came, if anything, as an anticlimax: everyone had been expecting much worse. A couple of days before the Boer envoys arrived, the entire town had been shaken by a tremendous explosion when some of the De Beers emergency dynamite dumps on the outskirts of Kimberley had been blown up. Compared with that terrifying blast – which contributed to the final closing down of the mines – the two badly aimed shells seemed as nothing.

Nevertheless most people were on edge. If nothing else, the wail of the hooters warning them to take cover had been enough to make them jittery. In an attempt to calm the town, Kekewich ordered that the existing alarm system be stopped. The 'weird, ghastly sounding' hooters, he maintained, were more frightening than enemy action. But hooters or no hooters, nerves became increasingly frayed as everyone waited for the next onslaught. They did not have to wait long. The next day the bombardment of Kimberley began in earnest. Some fifty shells were fired into the town, most of them falling – ironically – in the 'Dutch' suburb of Newton. Again little damage was done. The shells were of low explosive content – many failed to explode at all – and fell, for the most part, in the streets or in open spaces.

In a surprisingly short time, the townsfolk became accustomed to the periodic bombardments. 'No one felt particularly nervous,' says young Annie Kingwill, 'as they appeared to be doing very little damage. The favourite time for bombarding seemed to be between six and eight in the morning, after which we would have peace for the rest of the day.' Even after the Boer guns had been repositioned and more shells fell in the centre of the town, there were remarkably few casualties. Most people built shelters and learned to take cover quickly; only pedestrians were seriously endangered. An African woman was killed by shrapnel, while passing the Catholic Church in Dutoitspan Road, but her two companions escaped. Another shell killed a cab-horse and wounded two men. There were many near-misses and miraculous escapes – one shell crashed into the Queen's Hotel where thirty people were dining but only killed two cats – but, by and large, Kimberleyites 'soon began to treat the bombardment with calm indifference'.

Some, particularly the children, made a game of it. Annie Kingwill, who was staying in an hotel, found the antics of these youngsters amusing. 'There was quite a small trade going on in fragments of shells,' she says, 'and crowds of urchins would congregate in the likeliest spots, ready to gather the pieces as the shell burst.' It was a dangerous but lucrative pastime. A good-sized fragment could be sold for a few shillings, and the bottom of a shell, or the conical point with the brass fuse in it, would fetch anything up to two pounds. According to Dr Ashe, there were instances when law suits were threatened over the ownership of pieces of a shell.

A good many of the shells were directed at Kekewich's 'Conning Tower' and at the Sanatorium, where it was known that Rhodes was staying. Neither target was hit. Attempts have been made to depict Rhodes as cowardly when the Sanatorium came under fire. The shelling, it is implied, was largely responsible for his bombarding the military authorities at the Cape with demands that Kimberley be speedily relieved. Nothing could be further from the truth. Certainly Rhodes kept up a stream of complaints about the slowness of the relieving forces – these complaints were soon appearing in London newspapers and driving Government officials to distraction – but this had nothing to do with personal fear. Whatever else he might have been, Cecil Rhodes was no coward. He had earlier proved his indifference to danger during a Matabele uprising. His courage during the siege was obvious to everyone. When the shelling of the Sanatorium was at its height, he publicly announced that he felt as safe there as in Piccadilly.

'We were, of course,' says Philip Jourdan, 'all very anxious about Mr Rhodes during the siege. He was most indifferent as to how he exposed himself, and it was a marvel to me that he was not shot.' Others also marvelled. Unmistakable in his white flannel trousers, brown tweed coat and narrow-brimmed felt hat, he was to be seen everywhere: chatting to the soldiers, organising work parties, arranging for the distribution of food and the super-vising of bomb-proof shelters. The very sight of him riding about the town was sufficient to inspire the faint-hearted with confidence.

But he was undoubtedly a thorn in the side of the long-suffering Kekewich. His obstinacy in refusing to collaborate with the military led to blunder after blunder. An illustration of his high-handedness was given shortly after the bombardment began. The mines had stopped work and, to relieve the pressure on the town's supplies, Rhodes gave orders that some 3,000 labourers be released from the compounds and sent home. This, in itself, was nothing unusual. Africans were to be sent out of besieged Mafeking for the same reason. Had Kekewich been consulted about the move, he would, says O'Meara, have been 'in every way willing to assist the De Beers Company to carry (it) out'. But he was not consulted. The first he knew of the exodus was when one of his officers spotted a huge mass of men moving across the veld north of Kenilworth. Not knowing who or what they were, the military opened fire. Fortunately the mistake was soon realised and no one was hurt. But it all made life extremely difficult for the commander of the garrison.

'If you had had any other British Commander but Kekewich,' Joseph Chamberlain said to R.H. Henderson after the siege, 'Rhodes would have been in gaol.' Loyal as he was, Henderson did not disagree.

(3)

'One Saturday morning,' wrote Annie Kingwill, 'we were awakened by the sounds of cannon and rifle fire, and knew that something unusual was happen-ing. We dressed as quickly as possible, and arrived at the corner of the street just in time to see a batch of about thirty prisoners passing. Next came a section of the Light Horse, which the crowd lustily cheered. We walked as far as the

The barricaded Sanatorium, headquarters of Cecil Rhodes during the siege. Seated left to right, Rochfort Maguire, C.J. Rhodes, Major Scott-Turner, Mrs Maguire; standing left to right, Dr Thomas Smartt, C.M.C. Luard (Reuters special correspondent). (M)

Family dugout and shelter in West End, Kimberley, during the siege. (M)

barrier and met the ambulance wagons with the wounded. As several of us had relatives amongst the men, it was an anxious time until we discovered our own, safe and sound.'

The troops were returning from a dawn attack on Carter's Ridge, west of Kimberley. News that a relief force, under Lord Methuen, was approaching the town had prompted Kekewich to arrange a 'demonstration in strength' against a Boer gun-emplacement. At 4 a.m. on Saturday 25 November, contingents of the Kimberley Light Horse, the Cape Police and the North Lancashire Mounted Infantry, had left the town under the command of the redoubtable Scott Turner, now a Lieutenant-Colonel. In the early morning light, they had stormed Carter's Ridge and attacked a drowsy Boer force at bayonet-point. Thirty-three Boers had been captured, several had been killed and the rest had fled. A couple of hours later the attackers abandoned the captured gun emplacement and returned to Kimberley, having lost seven killed and twenty-nine wounded. Among the wounded was Scott Turner, who had been hit in the shoulder and had his horse shot from under him.

It was another small, if somewhat more costly, victory for Kimberley. The fact that the Boers quickly reoccupied Carter's Ridge, and soon started shelling the town again, seemed of minor importance. For the townsfolk already knew that the relieving force was nearing Kimberley. Lord Methuen's troops were said to be approaching the Modder River. They were expected to reach Kimberley within a matter of days.

At midday on Monday 27 November, says Annie Kingwill, 'news that the Relief Column had been sighted, and our men were going out to harass the enemy, spread like wild-fire through the town. All was excitement and joy.' At three o'clock the following afternoon, huge crowds gathered to watch the Kimberley troops depart. Kekewich had decided to make another sortie in an attempt to assist Lord Methuen's force. This time it was to be a much more determined effort. Some 2,000 men, assisted by guns of the Diamond Fields Artillery and an armoured train, were being sent out to engage the enemy. The recently wounded Scott Turner was commanding the right column of over 600 men.

'Our hearts were heavy,' reports the watching Annie Kingwill, 'for well we knew there were many amongst those brave defenders whom we should never see again. As our gallant leader passed, the remark "I wonder if he will return," went from lip to lip.' There was apparently good reason for these misgivings. Gallant Scott Turner undoubtedly was, but he had a reputation for recklessness. According to Dr Ashe, some of the men under his command were wary of following him in battle. 'Of course they all knew', says Ashe, 'that any of their sorties were very risky, but Turner always seemed to go in for unnecessary risks, and the men naturally did not like it.'

That afternoon Kimberley was tense. The crackle of rifle-fire and the boom of guns could be heard in the distance, but news reaching the town was scrappy and often contradictory. Colonel Kekewich had taken up a position on the outskirts of the town to watch the advance. He was little better informed than most people. Earlier he had arranged to meet up with Scott Turner and

Lieutenant-Colonel Chamier – who commanded the centre column – but when the light began to fail and neither of the officers turned up he sent orders to Chamier to hold on to his positions, and then retired to the Kimberley Club. Scott Turner, it had been reported, was advancing on Carter's Ridge.

This was to be Scott Turner's last advance. With typical daring, he led his troops to Carter's Ridge and captured three of the enemy redoubts. Then, calling to his men to follow him, he rushed forward to storm the last fort. Within minutes he was dead. 'Wonderful as it seems,' reported one of his officers, 'he gained what we thought was the front of the fort. We remained quiet almost breathless . . . I noticed the colonel seize a revolver from a man near him and deliberately take aim. He fired several shots; then he sank down, as I thought from fatigue. But it was not as we soon knew. A bullet had passed through his head.'

With Scott Turner dead, his men became demoralised. In the panic that followed, several more were killed or wounded. Finally they began to retreat. When Kekewich heard what was happening he sent frantic messages to the squadron commanders telling them to hold fast, but in the darkness all was confusion and soon the entire force was retiring.

Throughout the night the bewildered troops staggered back to Kimberley; some leading riderless horses, others supporting wounded comrades. Precisely what had happened was not clear; all the survivors could say was that they 'had not taken the gun, the fort, or anything else'. Women crowded into the streets to watch the ambulance wagons pass on their way to the hospital. 'There were few amongst us', said one of them, 'but had a father, husband, brother or son out on that dreadful day. The suspense was terrible!'

Twenty-four British died and thirty-one were wounded in the second battle of Carter's Ridge. It was the greatest disaster that besieged Kimberley had experienced. Gloom spread throughout the town, becoming all the more oppressive when it was rumoured that 'the Boers had gone round and finished off any of the wounded who were still alive'. This might or might not have been true, but it was firmly believed.

All Kimberley turned out for the mass funeral the following day. So great were the crowds that only relatives of the dead men were allowed in the cemetery. A party of Cape Police, with 'arms reversed', preceded the eight wagons that served as hearses. Scott Turner's coffin came last on a gun carriage; it was covered by a Union Jack, his helmet and sword and a huge pile of wreaths. Beside it walked Colonel Kekewich and his officers. But, it was said, 'the saddest sight of all was the riderless charger, with the riding boots reversed in the stirrups and tied fast with white ribbon. . . . The animal really looked as if he understood as he stepped quietly along.' Among those at the graveside was the deeply affected Cecil Rhodes.

Scott Turner had been a personal friend of Rhodes's. He had landed up in Kimberley from Rhodesia and was one of the few soldiers whom Rhodes admired. His death had sent Rhodes hurrying to Kekewich's headquarters full of bitter complaints. The military, he said, had bungled the sortie against Carter's Ridge; the attack had been launched by too small a force; it should never have been made. He also resented the fact that Kimberley troops were being employed on this type of sortie. 'Remember,' he stormed, 'you are not in command of a lot of "Tommies", but of men with family responsibilities, whose lives you have no right to risk.'

What could Kekewich say? He, as much as Rhodes, was distressed by Scott Turner's death. He, as much as Rhodes, regretted the outcome of the sortie. He felt that he had been let down by his subordinates but, as a loyal officer, this was not something he was prepared to discuss with an officious civilian. The rift between the two men deepened.

What no one could understand was why the Relieving Column had failed to show up. Days passed without a sign of Lord Methuen's force. 'We felt', sighed Annie Kingwill, 'that something had gone quite wrong, else our men would not have returned so soon, and the question was, "Where was the Column?" ' They were soon to find out.

Some two weeks later, on 11 December, Kimberley was wakened early by the distant rumble and roar of gunfire. The effect on the town was electrifying. Men and women rushed into the streets, carts, horses and bicycles were seized and crowds stampeded to the southern boundaries of the town – the direction from which the firing was coming. There was no doubt in anyone's mind as to what was happening. At last the Relief Column had broken through. Lord Methuen was on his way. Now it was not *whether* he would arrive, only *when*. Straining to catch their first glimpse of the advancing British troops, the townsfolk waited.

They could see little. The booming of the guns continued; puffs of smoke appeared on the horizon, above the Magersfontein hills; a war balloon was spotted rising lazily in the distance. It was rumoured that Methuen had driven the Boers into the Orange Free State and 'done other impossible things'. The wounded, it was said, would soon be coming in. Everyone was tense. But hours passed without a sign of the wounded, let alone the troops. Finally the firing stopped and the dispirited crowds dispersed.

It was days later before the truth of what had happened was generally known. Even Kekewich was badly informed about Methuen's unexpected defeat. For defeat it had been – defeat on an unprecedented scale. Advancing across the open plains towards Kimberley, the British troops had been mown down by gunfire from Boers concealed in trenches at the foot of the Magersfontein hills. Taken by surprise in the semi-darkness, Methuen's force had become completely confused. Many of the men had been killed instantly; others had been left to lie in the veld, exposed to the blistering sun throughout the day. It was one of the greatest disasters of the war. The following day Methuen had retired to the Modder River, having lost almost a thousand men, killed, wounded, captured or missing.

(4)

Christmas Day 1899 was one of the hottest days of the year in Kimberley. Nevertheless everyone was determined to enjoy themselves. Earlier in the siege people had joked about entertaining the relieving troops to Christmas dinner; now that there seemed little hope of those troops arriving until well into the new year, the joke, as Dr Ashe remarked, did not 'seem quite so excruciatingly funny'. It did, however, help to lend a touch of defiance to the Christmas festivities. Relief or no relief, Kimberley was not to be cheated out of some badly needed cheer.

Morale was given a boost when, on Christmas morning, the *Diamond Fields Advertiser* published greetings from Queen Victoria. The message had been brought to the town by a runner and it wished the townsfolk and troops a happy Christmas. Ironic as this might have seemed, patriotic Kimberley regarded it with pride. Nothing could have better emphasised the role they were playing in the war. They might have been isolated but they had not been forgotten.

Soldiers were visited by their families in the trenches, where Cecil Rhodes provided plum puddings, and Father Christmas handed out toys to the children. Most people managed to scrape together a creditable Christmas dinner. So well did they eat that the newspaper suggested that, if the wind wafted the smell of spicy food to the enemy, Kimberley would have been taken by storm. 'We made the most of that dinner,' claims one inhabitant, 'knowing that the next week we were to be "rationed", and it might be many a day before we saw anything "good" again.'

Everyone, including the military authorities, had similar thoughts. The food situation, if not yet desperate, was becoming increasingly serious. At the start of the siege it had been estimated that Kimberley had sufficient food to last anything up to three months. At the time that had seemed ample. It was confidently expected that the town would be relieved in a matter of weeks and could easily hold out. The shock of the Magersfontein reverse had made everyone think again. Although Methuen was still only a few miles away, he had informed Kekewich that he might not be able to relieve the town until mid-February or even later. There had been an immediate stocktaking, an immediate tightening up of food restrictions.

The meat ration was eventually fixed at four ounces a day for adults, and two ounces for children under the age of fifteen. Vegetables, flour, rice, sugar, tea and coffee were also rationed. A central depot was set up for the distribution of essential foodstuffs, which were only issued on the production of a permit. To obtain these permits private citizens had to make a declaration of 'the quantities of all of them' which they had in their possession. Many of those who had earlier raided the shops and brought up provisions at great expense were reluctant to apply for permits for fear that their hoarded stocks would be confiscated. Even so, the queues at the distribution centre became longer by the day. Rich and poor alike had to wait hours on end to obtain their meagre rations.

'It is very funny', said Dr Ashe, 'to see all the town's big swells either fetching their meat themselves or sending a member of their family for it. Parsons, lawyers, doctors, business men, are all there, and it is a huge joke that we are all in the same boat, but it is to be hoped that the joke won't last too long. Previous to this, we have all thought that as long as there was a decent balance at the bank nothing could go far wrong, but now we find that the balance is of very little use.'

Lack of grazing space and the shortage of cattle made it difficult, even with rationing, to eke out the meat supply. Starving Africans and impoverished whites soon began to look elsewhere for animal flesh – mules, donkeys and even dogs mysteriously disappeared from the streets. An enterprising China-man earned considerable notoriety by offering to buy up cats at 2s. 6d. each. On 8 January, the authorities began selling horseflesh at a slightly reduced price. This was eaten by the less squeamish blacks and whites, usually minced and cooked as 'meat balls'.

'I shall never', admitted Annie Kingwill, 'see a "fricadelle" in the future without thinking of that time. . . . We were not too hungry to prevent us making fun about the skinny cab horse and his food, that we had demolished. Horseflesh really tastes no different to other flesh, but is of a much darker colour, and some people fancied it to be a bit sweeter. I, however, found no difference, but preferred mule flesh. But one has to eat with determination, and not allow one's thoughts to travel!! No one knows what they can eat until they have been in a siege.'

The *Diamond Fields Advertiser* first suggested that a soup kitchen be set up. Cecil Rhodes immediately took up the idea. He put the efficient Tim Tyson, secretary of the Kimberley Club, in charge of the kitchen, which proved a huge success. Meat and every type of available vegetable – including prickly pears – were boiled up and ladled out to the destitute. So thick was the soup that, it is said, at times it had to be eaten with a knife and fork. On the first day the kitchen opened, some 3,000 pints of soup were distributed; by the end of the siege 8,000 pints were being served daily.

How to exist on a starvation diet became one of the major preoccupations of Kimberley. The *Diamond Fields Advertiser* was bombarded with letters from helpful correspondents offering advice. 'A crank', says the editor, George Green, 'asked to be permitted to belaud in our columns the virtues of vege-tarianism. Yet another sought to ventilate his crazy notion that the High Command should despatch war balloons to the Diamond Fields for the purpose of dropping 500 lbs of butter into the town two or three times a week.' Hard-pushed as he was for copy, Green was unable to use these contributions. Instead, he sent to the Public Library for Napier's history of the Peninsular War and published some of the more stirring chapters under the heading: 'Historic Achievements of the British Army. By a local Student of Military History.' The effect of these articles on the Town Guard, he says, 'was electri-cal'.

Certainly the town was in need of rousing reading. In the middle of January the shelling was stepped up. There were still few casualties, but the damage to property increased. It all added to the growing feeling of helplessness and isolation. The time was long overdue for another morale-boosting gesture. It was provided, not surprisingly, through the agency of the ever-resourceful George Labram.

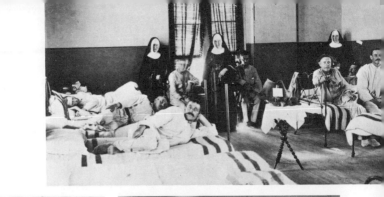

During the siege Nazareth House was used as a hospital for the sick and wounded. (M)

De Beers Mine headgear, used by Colonel Kekewich as a conning-tower during the siege. (M)

George A.L. Green, editor of the *Diamond Fields Advertiser* during the siege, and father of the South African author Lawrence Green. (K)

The famous 'Long Cecil' just after its completion in the De Beers workshops. This 28-pounder breech-loading gun was designed by the American engineer George Labram, who stands with his arm resting on the wheel. (M)

That the Kimberley guns were mere seven-pounders, and not powerful enough to retaliate Boer shelling, had always been a matter of grave concern. Towards the end of December it was decided to do something about this. George Labram was consulted and asked whether it would be possible to construct a more effective weapon. It was a tall order, but one which Labram was more than eager to tackle. At the De Beers workshops he consulted all the available books and manuals and started to work. In the incredibly short period of twenty-four days he had manufactured, from a piece of shafting, a gun of 4.1-inch bore, capable of throwing a 28-pound shell. Named 'Long Cecil' after Rhodes – there was a suggestion that it be called 'St Cecilia' – it was to become one of the wonders of Kimberley.

Everyone in the town was aware that the gun was being built and there was great excitement when, on 18 January, it was rolled out on its gun carriage. Three days later, after some preliminary trials, it was officially introduced to the enemy by a woman, not Mrs Rochfort Maguire, who usually presided at Rhodes's entertainments, but a Kimberley woman – the popular Mrs William Pickering. The success of 'Long Cecil' was instantaneous. The first shell, laconically inscribed 'With C.J.R.'s Comps', landed in the middle of the enemy camp at the Intermediate Pumping Station. It took the Boers completely by surprise. Used as they were to Kimberley's ineffective artillery, they 'could not believe their eyes' when a 28-pound shell burst among them. From the Conning Tower, Kekewich saw the bewildered enemy scattering in all directions.

From then on, 'Long Cecil', moved to different positions each day, kept up a regular bombardment. Only the shortage of suitable material prevented Labram from making companion pieces for the gun. Even so, his singular achievement was justly regarded as one of the great feats of the siege. 'Of all the things that I have personally seen and read in the annals of war,' remarked a hardened war-correspondent, 'the most remarkable is the making of this gun in a mining workshop in the centre of Africa.'

But it was a feat which was to cost Labram and Kimberley dearly. As was to be expected, the Boers lost no time in answering 'Long Cecil'. The shelling of the town became more fierce, more determined. On 24 January Kimberley was subjected to a terrifying bombardment. For forty-eight hours shells rained into the centre of the town without a break. One young woman and two children were killed and many other civilians were seriously wounded by shrapnel. More bomb-proof shelters were hastily built; only the brave or the reckless ventured into the streets. There was, as most people realised, worse to come.

It came in the form of a formidable new weapon. A six-inch gun, known as 'Long Tom' and manned by Boers and French mercenaries, was dispatched to Kimberley, via Pretoria, from the Boer lines surrounding besieged Ladysmith in Natal. Installed on a debris heap outside the town, it commenced shelling on 7 February. It was far and away the most frightening onslaught the townsfolk had experienced. 'We were startled', claims one of them, 'by a loud report, followed immediately by a "whirring" noise like an explosion, and then heard the shell burst. At first we thought it was our own gun "Long Cecil", but soon discovered our error . . . what dismayed us most of all was the size of the shell, and to hear that it could penetrate twelve feet of earth. Imagine our terror!'

The terror increased. Shells continued to crash into streets and buildings. A menacing fire raged in the centre of the town. More women and children were killed, others were tragically mutilated. At the hospital, doctors and nurses worked day and night amid shell fumes and shrapnel to tend the wounded. 'Long Cecil' was repositioned to counteract the new threat; the following day Kekewich introduced a new warning system – immediately a distant puff of smoke was seen, a flag was waved and bugles and whistles sounded warning people to take cover. It did little to soothe fears or quieten the panic.

The new crisis led to another clash between Rhodes and Kekewich. Two days after 'Long Tom' came into action, Rhodes informed the new Mayor, H.A. Oliver, that he intended calling a public protest meeting. With the relieving troops only a few miles away, it seemed madness that Kimberley should be exposed to such relentless shelling without any apparent effort being made to draw off the Boer force. At the beginning of January, Lord Roberts had arrived at Cape Town to take over as Commander-in-Chief in South Africa and Rhodes intended that those attending the meeting should protest to Roberts about the slackness of the relieving troops. When Kekewich heard of this he was horrified.

Kekewich was only too aware that in Kimberley there were a large number of Boer sympathisers. Messages, and even newspapers, were known to be smuggled to the enemy almost daily. What would happen if the Boers heard that a large meeting was to be held? Would it not provide them with a tempting target? The idea was foolish in the extreme. Later that morning he met Rhodes and told him as much. He could not, he said, allow such a meeting. According to O'Meara, Rhodes was furious. 'Before Kimberley surrenders,' he shouted, 'I will take good care that the English people shall know what I think of all this.' With that he stormed out of Kekewich's office.

But Kekewich had undoubtedly acted wisely. The shelling that day was particularly heavy. Several buildings were hit. One shell crashed into a room where a sick woman was in bed; it broke the bedstead but failed to explode and the woman miraculously escaped unharmed. However, not everyone was so lucky. The last shell of the day caused one of Kimberley's greatest tragedies: it killed George Labram.

Labram, having spent the day directing 'Long Cecil', had just come off duty. He had gone to his room on the top floor of the Grand Hotel in the Market-square to get ready for dinner. The shell struck while he was standing at the wash basin. Death was instantaneous. 'He was shockingly mauled,' says Dr Ashe, 'half his head being caved in, also his chest and abdomen, and both his thighs were so smashed up that they just hung on by a few shreds.' Incredibly, a hotel servant who was in the room survived without a scratch.

Few men had done more for besieged Kimberley than George Labram; few men were more deeply mourned. Because of the heavy shelling, his funeral was postponed until eight o'clock the following night. Huge crowds gathered at the graveside, thinking that in the darkness they would be safe. But they were wrong. The shelling suddenly started again. It was rumoured that a traitor had signalled to the enemy, who immediately commenced firing at the cemetery. 'I shall never forget that dreadful, dreadful misery,' lamented one of the mourners. 'We were unable to go home, and just slept where we were in any position, expecting every second to be killed. Those hideous sounds will live with me to my dying day.'

Labram's funeral was not reported in the *Diamond Fields Advertiser*. The newspaper had closed down. That morning the editor had published, at Rhodes's instigation, a vituperative leader attacking the military command. Kekewich, not unnaturally, had been highly incensed. He had informed the editor that in future everything he wrote would have to be censored. Major O'Meara, however, was to blow this incident up out of all proportion. He claimed that Kekewich ordered that the editor, G.A.L. Green, be arrested but that this order could not be carried out as Rhodes had spirited Green away and hidden him at the bottom of a mine. This Green was heatedly to deny. 'Nothing of the sort happened,' he says. 'I was never down a Kimberley mine in my life.' According to Green the newspaper was closed partly as a protest against censorship but largely because the heavy shelling made it impossible for the printing works to operate. This has not prevented ill-informed chroniclers from repeating O'Meara's 'arrest' story.

Newspaper or no newspaper, Rhodes's battle with the military went on. That same afternoon he had another stormy meeting with Kekewich. It seems that, having been stopped from holding his public meeting, Rhodes had consulted twelve leading Kimberley citizens and drawn up a strongly worded message to be sent to Lord Roberts, demanding immediate relief. Kekewich, thinking that it might be intercepted by the Boers, objected to the length and wording of the message. According to O'Meara, this made Rhodes so angry that he lunged at Kekewich across his desk and was only prevented from punching him full in the face because a staff officer and the Mayor stood between the two men.

However, as a result of this meeting, a coded and condensed version of the message was finally sent to Lord Roberts. Coming as it did from a civilian, it was – however one looks at it – extremely high-handed.

'Your troops', it protested, 'have been for more than two months within a distance of little over twenty miles from Kimberley.... These towns with a population of over 45,000 people have been besieged for 120 days and a large portion of the inhabitants has been enduring great hardships.... During the past few days the enemy has brought into action from a position three miles from us a 6-inch gun, throwing a 100-pound shell, which is setting fire to our buildings and is daily causing death among the population. As you are aware the military guns here are totally unable to cope with this new gun ... it is absolutely essential that immediate relief should be afforded to this place.'

A reply from Roberts was flashed back almost immediately. The Commander-in-Chief was obviously not impressed by Rhodes or his demands. He curtly informed Kekewich that any person, no matter how influential, who threatened to interfere with the military should be placed under arrest. Relief operations, he said, were about to commence. The town was urged to hold out a little longer.

(5)

Rhodes had attended George Labram's funeral with Gardner Williams, the General Manager of De Beers, and William Pickering, the Secretary of De Beers. They were accompanied by Colonel Kekewich and, on the way to the cemetery, had discussed a plan which had long been under consideration. It concerned those women and children who were without proper bomb-proof shelters. Rhodes suggested that arrangements be made to send them down the mines. Kekewich agreed. The following day placards, signed by Rhodes, were posted throughout the town.

'I recommend', they read, 'women and children who desire complete shelter to proceed to Kimberley and De Beers shafts. They will be lowered at once in the mines from 8 o'clock throughout the night. Lamps and guides will be provided.'

This humane gesture gave O'Meara another opportunity for attacking Rhodes. He claimed that Kekewich had not been consulted and the sudden appearance of the placards created widespread panic. The townsfolk were convinced that Rhodes had secret information that another serious bombardment was about to take place. There was a stampede to the mines which resulted in complete chaos. People were lowered down the mine without any thought being given to feeding them or to providing the minimum of comfort. Sanitation was non-existent. How different, sighed O'Meara, would things have been had the military been consulted.

Once again O'Meara's observations are open to question. Alpheus Williams – son of Gardner Williams – was in charge of arrangements at the Kimberley Mine. He had a great many tart things to say about O'Meara. 'From personal knowledge,' he writes, 'I can state positively that there was no panic in carrying out the arrangements. . . . An elaborate water-borne system of latrines was provided, in fact, a far more sanitary arrangement than existed in any part of Kimberley.' His father, who was in charge of arrangements at De Beers Mine, agrees with him.

So does Annie Kingwill, who took refuge in the Kimberley Mine. She agrees there was an initial panic – which would have happened anyway – but that at the mines everything was orderly. Some of the women, loaded down with mattresses and blankets, had to wait hours before they could be lowered down the shafts but they were patient and good-humoured. The well-lit galleries and tunnels of the mine were crowded and damp, but everyone managed to find a place to sleep.

'The first thing next morning,' says Annie Kingwill, 'pails of hot milk arrived for the babies, and were brought up by the ambulance men. Then came coffee, tea and bread for the older people. Even fans and smelling salts were thought of, and sent down with raisins for the children. For dinner huge tubs of soup and baskets of bread and sandwiches were sent. . . . Mr Rhodes and De Beers directors had done their utmost for our comfort, the former even sending grapes and other fruit down each day. The Medical Officer of Health and other doctors also visited the Mines regularly. . . . Two children were born down there.' Rhodes was an extremely difficult man to deal with, but he was by no means the monster that O'Meara and others have made him out to be.

Conditions in the mines were undoubtedly cramped. Annie Kingwill stayed only one night and left the following day to make room for others. But hundreds of women and children remained underground until the Relief Column arrived. Luckily, they had not long to wait. A couple of days later a huge column of dust, or smoke, was sighted on the horizon. It seemed to be advancing towards the town.

On 14 February it was learnt that Alexandersfontein had been evacuated and a contingent of the Beaconsfield Town Guard rushed out to seize the position. They were joined by troop reinforcements and two guns. Within a few hours a fight started which lasted until early the next morning.

Later that morning Kekewich sent out more troops to harass the departing Boers. Then he left the town himself, hoping to meet up with General French, who was commanding the relieving force. But in the general confusion the two officers missed each other. General French was met by the Mayors of Beaconsfield and Kimberley and then escorted to the Sanatorium, where Rhodes was waiting for him.

Crowds rushed into the streets to greet the dusty, begrimed troops. In the frenzy which followed, the long, dispiriting days of the past few months were forgotten. 'Men cheered,' it was said, 'boys screeched, and women waved their handkerchiefs, while tears streamed down their cheeks. All felt like embracing those dirty tired riders, who had undergone so many hardships to come speedily to our rescue.' By the time Kekewich returned to Kimberley most of the excitement was over. Rhodes, not the sorely-tried commander, was the hero of the hour.

The siege had lasted four months. In that time some 8,500 shells had been fired into the town. Most deaths, however, had been caused by disease and malnutrition. Infant mortality had been particularly high: a rough estimate put it as one out of every two infants born during the siege. Precise figures are difficult to arrive at, but it is said that the general death-rate was 48 per thousand for Europeans and 138 per thousand for other races.

Kimberley had made an heroic stand. But it had entailed great sacrifices. 'We all feel', commented Dr Ashe, 'what a friend said to me tonight: "If ever I am in a country where they begin to talk about war again, I shall take the first boat to the far side of the world, and stop when I get there." '

21

'Who is to take his place?'

Two weeks after the siege of Kimberley ended, another beleaguered town was relieved. On 28 February 1900, an advance party of British troops entered Ladysmith in Natal. Ladysmith had endured worse hardships than Kimberley. When the relieving army made its triumphal entry into the town a few days later, it was greeted by rows of hollow-eyed inhabitants; weary and apathetic, many of them were too sick to rejoice.

Among the sick was Dr Leander Starr Jameson. During the siege Jameson had contracted typhoid while nursing his manservant. By the time the siege was raised he was so ill that he had to be carried to Durban, put on a steamer for Cape Town, and sent to Groote Schuur – Cecil Rhodes's home – to convalesce.

After two months' rest, he had begun to recover. 'I am practically all right again,' he wrote to his brother Sam, on 25 April, '– only a little groggy in legs and head. . . . I am going to do the De Beers and Kimberley seat and shall wait here for C.J.R(hodes)., then at once to Kimberley where I have taken a house.' What this meant was that Jameson had accepted a directorship of De Beers and agreed to election as a Member for Kimberley of the Cape House of Assembly. It was a momentous decision.

Since the fiasco of his disastrous Raid, Dr Jameson had been in disgrace. Among a large section of the English community he still enjoyed a certain popularity and had, in fact, twice been invited to contest parliamentary constituencies in the Cape. But, somewhat reluctantly, he had refused to stand; his political friends had considered the invitations premature. Now, however, a Kimberley seat had become vacant – through the resignation of a sitting member, Dr Rutherfoord Harris – and Jameson had decided to accept nomination. Where better to test his popularity than in his 'home town'?

As soon as he was well enough he went to Kimberley. He arrived there in the middle of May and found the place swarming with soldiers, still disorganised from the siege. The military hospitals were particularly chaotic and he was soon doing battle with the army medical authorities. 'Kimberley', he wrote to Sam, 'is simply a typhoid breeding machine. However, I like rows with them, and at present the town is simply full of khaki. Mafeking relieved, which we heard yesterday, is a great comfort, and another fortnight or so ought to see the end of the beastly war.'

He was wrong, of course. The beastly war was to continue for another two years. Although Kimberley was not directly involved, large numbers of troops from the Diamond Fields were to be engaged in the fighting. Many of the men who had distinguished themselves in the siege – men such as Major Robert G. Scott, Major Thomas H. Rodger, Captain William Pickering, Captain T.L. Angel and Captain F. Mandy – were later awarded the D.S.O. Others, among them Lieutenant-Colonel David Harris, Lieutenant-Colonel R.A. Finlayson, Major Thomas C. Peakman and Major Thomas J. May, earned the C.M.G. Kimberley could be proud of its war record.

But Jameson was right in choosing Kimberley for his political début. His election was assured. On 22 May, the *Diamond Fields Advertiser* published an impressive petition signed, it was said, 'by all the leading citizens' calling upon him to fill the parliamentary vacancy. He was unopposed and made only one important speech. In it he reminded his audience that he had lived and worked in Kimberley continuously for twelve years. Then, to everyone's horror, he launched straight into the taboo subject of the Raid. He emphatically denied that it had been racially inspired. The intention, he claimed, had been to replace the intolerant Kruger régime with a more reasonable Afrikaner administration. It was not the Raid that was responsible for racial animosity, but it was racial animosity that had led to the Raid. That, he implied, was what the present war was all about.

The Kimberley electors evidently agreed. 'Have just come back from nomination and was duly elected,' Jameson wrote on 25 June. 'No opposition. That, I hope, is the last clearing up of the Raid business.' He was, perhaps, being over-optimistic; but the Kimberley election did mark another turning-point in his career. He represented the town for the next three years. Then, in 1904, he fought and won a strongly contested election at Grahamstown. That same year he became Prime Minister of the Cape. If the 'Raid business' had not been cleared up, Jameson had at least survived its effects.

This is more than could be claimed for Cecil Rhodes. After the Raid, Rhodes had told a friend that it would take him at least ten years to regain his lost prestige. He was not given that long. Unlike Jameson, he did not even survive the war.

In the months following the siege of Kimberley, Rhodes divided his time travelling between Europe and Rhodesia. He was far from well. The strain of the Jameson Raid, its aftermath, and the siege, had seriously aggravated his chronic heart disease. Nor was his ill-health helped by the intrigues of the notorious Princess Catherine Radziwill. For some three years this Russian-born adventuress had pursued Rhodes for personal and political gain. Her relentless persecution ended only when she was arrested for forging Rhodes's name to several promissory notes. It was to expose these forgeries that Rhodes, in January 1902, returned to South Africa from Europe against the advice of his doctors. He was warned that the heat of the Cape summer would adversely affect his heart and might even kill him. But he brushed the warnings aside, and arrived at the Cape in the sweltering February heat. In less than two months he was dead.

He died, attended by Dr Jameson and surrounded by his friends, at three minutes to six on 26 March 1902 in his seaside cottage at Muizenberg. Nowhere did the news of his death come as a greater shock, or cause more grief, than in

Kimberley. A telegram announcing his death was received at the Kimberley Club shortly after seven o'clock that evening. Within a matter of hours, the balconies and stoep of the club were draped in black bunting, and members were hurrying all over the town with the news. A continuous stream of telegrams, giving details of Rhodes's last hours, began pouring into the offices of the *Diamond Fields Advertiser*. By daybreak the following morning, all work on the mines had stopped, shops were firmly shuttered and the Theatre Royal announced that it would be closed for the next three nights.

'Amongst the employees of the Consolidated Mines,' it was reported, 'from the departmental heads down to the humblest labourer, the news was received with heartfelt and very genuine sorrow. Among the natives deep-drawn "Hau's" of shocked astonishment betokened their concern at the passing of a Great Chief. . . . The noisy iron-tongued clatter of the machinery ceased, as it never ceases, save on Christmas day, and the sun rose upon many workmen, serious faced, hastening sombrely homeward. A great silence had fallen on the busy mining city. . . . One by one the principal firms shrouded their buildings in mournful trappings of woe, and the main thoroughfares of the town assumed a sad funereal aspect.'

Rhodes died two months before his forty-ninth birthday. He had been associated with Kimberley for over thirty years. Starting as a humble digger he had risen, amid fierce competition, to dominate the town. For most people it was impossible to think of Kimberley without him. So great was the shock of his death that few could bring themselves to speak of it. 'It was discussed very little,' says the Mayor, 'and to the oft repeated question "Who is to take his place?" came the mournful answer "Ah! who indeed?" '

It would perhaps have been fitting for Rhodes to have been buried in the town that he had made his own. But he had decided otherwise. Some years earlier he had chosen a spot-known as 'The World's View'-in the Matoppo hills in Rhodesia as his last resting-place. This had been stipulated in his will. His grave, he had stated, was to be a square cut in the rocks of the Matoppos and marked by a plain brass plate inscribed: 'Here lie the remains of Cecil John Rhodes.' His instructions were faithfully observed.

The purple-and-black-draped funeral train, taking Rhodes's coffin north, drew into Kimberley station at four o' clock in the morning of 5 April 1902. Even before the train arrived, crowds had assembled on the De Beers railway bridge; each tram arriving from Beaconsfield and Kenilworth brought more people. By four o' clock, thousands of mourners had gathered outside the station, which, like most buildings in the town, was hung in black 'with here and there a touch of white relieving the monotony'. Kimberley was intent on honouring the passing of its most distinguished son.

A guard of honour, drawn from the Kimberley Regiment and commanded by Lieutenant-Colonel Finalyson, lined the entire length of the platform, while the Brigade Band took up a position close to the funeral coach. They waited in solemn silence until six o' clock. Then, as the band played the 'Dead March', a procession, headed by the acting Mayor-R.H. Henderson-filed slowly along the platform 'past the carriage . . . inside which lay the remains of the man who has been a very real friend to the people of Kimberley. The window of the car was lowered and the massive coffin surmounted by the Union Jack and various wreaths was plainly visible.'

For over four hours the crowd continued to shuffle slowly along the platform. Men and women were in tears; bewildered children were held up to peer at the coffin. Over 15,000 people are said to have passed along the platform that morning. When, shortly after ten o'clock, the train steamed slowly out of the station the crowds had not dispersed.

'Who is going to feed us,' a child was heard to say, 'now that Mr Rhodes has gone.'

(2)

The signing of the Peace of Vereeniging, which ended the Anglo-Boer War, was celebrated in Kimberley by a mass meeting on Memorial Hill on 4 June 1902.

Later that same month, the town held a more formal ceremony. At the first post-war function to be organised in the Town Hall, the man who had relieved Kimberley, General French, was presented with an ornate sword – the tip of its handle was a horse's head, studded with rough diamond eyes – encased in a gold scabbard. The blade was inscribed: 'Presented to Major General J.D.P. French, by the citizens of Kimberley, as a token of their gratitude and admiration of his gallant relief of the town on February 15th, 1900.' Accompanying the sword was a silver casket, topped by an equestrian statuette, which contained a laudatory address on parchment. (Some sixty years later this casket was discovered by a London jeweller who, after visiting Kimberley, presented it to De Beers in appreciation of the hospitality he had received.)

General French was not the only soldier to be honoured. A month after his visit, the town's former commander – the long-suffering Colonel Kekewich himself – arrived at Kimberley station to be met by an impressive delegation of civic dignitaries. The feud between Rhodes and Kekewich during the siege had for the most part been more a matter of regret than of partisanship. That Kekewich had earned Kimberley's admiration there could be no doubt; his welcome was every bit as enthusiastic as that given to General French. He was fêted at a Gala Ball and presented with a sword of honour. The women of the town showed their gratitude by subscribing towards a gold cigarette case containing diamonds. It was one of the few unalloyed highlights of Kekewich's tragic career. Whether or not Rhodes's hostility, as some maintain, contributed to his eventual downfall is uncertain. But twelve years later, at the outbreak of the First World War, plagued by ill-health and professional neglect, he committed suicide by shooting himself. In Kimberley he continued to be remembered with affection. The townsfolk, wrote R.H. Henderson in 1944, 'admired Colonel Kekewich as the "perfect specimen of an English gentleman and soldier" '.

Memorials to the siege, honouring the dead on both sides, continued to be erected in and around Kimberley for many years. The most imposing, however,

Cape Police Memorial in Lodge Road Kimberley, erected in honour of members of the Cape Police who died in the siege, and unveiled on 17 April 1904. (M)

Unveiling of the Rhodes Statue in Dutoitspan Road, Kimberley, by Sir Walter Hely Hutchinson on 4 December 1907. (K)

Drawing by Sir Herbert Baker, the architect of the Honoured Dead Memorial, which was inspired by the ruined Nereid monument at Xanthos in Asia Minor. The memorial was dedicated on 28 November 1904. (K)

Kimberley Town Hall illuminated for the coronation of King Edward VII in 1902. (K)

was the one built at the instigation of Cecil Rhodes. The idea that a monument of some sort should be built to commemorate Kimberley's heroic stand, had occurred to Rhodes during the last days of the siege. Soon after his return to Cape Town he had discussed the idea with his architect, Herbert Baker. His plans at that stage were highly romantic. The memorial was to take the form of a bath or 'Nymphaeum'–a rectangular pool of water, fed by a fountain and surrounded by white marble columns, the whole neo-Grecian bath being set in a garden of canna lilies, orange trees and red-flowering eucalyptus. But for one reason and another this rather delightful scheme never materialised. Kimberley was deprived of what Herbert Baker described as 'Rhodes's "sunny pleasure-dome and sinuous rills" . . . for the enjoyment of the people'.

Instead, there arose a hardly less impressive monument–the Honoured Dead Memorial – based on the ruined Nereid monument at Xanthos in Asia Minor. Designed by Herbert Baker and fashioned out of stone from the Matoppos where Rhodes was buried, the monument rises on a circle at the junction of five roads. A massive base supports a cluster of columns; into the stone on the west side is cut a verse by Kipling and on the stylobate stands the famous 'Long Cecil'. Beneath the blue Kimberley sky, the monument stands like some ancient terracotta-coloured tomb or temple. Many regard it not merely as a symbol of the siege, but of the town itself.

The dedication of the Honoured Dead Memorial took place on 28 November 1904, the fifth anniversary of the death of Colonel Scott Turner at Carter's Ridge. It was a solemn occasion. In a way, the monument was Rhodes's last tribute to the town that had made him–a tribute he never lived to see completed. But Kimberley was never to forget the man responsible for this symbolic monument. The citizens had, in turn, ensured that Cecil Rhodes should remain visibly among them.

Shortly after his death, a special committee had been formed to collect funds for an appropriate Rhodes memorial. An equestrian statue, it was finally decided, would be the most suitable. It was a curious choice, for Rhodes was no horseman and rode rarely and then only for exercise. But an equestrian statue it was and Hamo Thorneycroft–the celebrated Victorian sculptor, responsible for the statue of General Gordon in Trafalgar Square and that of Cromwell at Westminster–was chosen to execute it. Likenesses of British worthies by Thorneycroft dotted the British Empire, but his handsome 'Rhodes on horseback' at Kimberley was considered by many to be his *chef d'oeuvre*. De Beers offered to donate a site for the statue, and the scheme went ahead. Then, unfortunately, a formidable snag presented itself. The memorial committee decided that the site offered by De Beers was unsuitable and, having spent all their funds on commissioning the statue, they were unable to purchase a new site. They wanted the statue to stand at a junction, just off the Dutoitspan road, a stone's throw from the cottage once shared by Rhodes and Jameson. This had been the site of the original Jewish synagogue but, with the development of Kimberley, property values had soared and the purchase price was beyond the resources of the memorial committee. It looked as if a familiar Kimberley deadlock had been reached.

However, at this crucial stage, Alfred Beit arrived in town. As one of the trustees of Rhodes's will, he was actively engaged in sorting out the problems of various memorial committees. He was accompanied by the new Chairman of De Beers, Sir Lewis Michell' - Rhodes's former banker and future biographer - who found Beit's business methods both entertaining and highly instructive. When a delegation of the Kimberley committee presented their particular problem, says Michell, 'Beit replied simply that "he would look into it", a formula which often means nothing at all. But the next morning he went with me to the place and approved of it, went to the owners and bought it at a high figure, and then handed it over to the committee. Yet an hour later he had in my presence an amusing altercation with a cab-driver over a shilling. It was an apt illustration of the old adage "Take care of the pence. . .".'

Actually, arrangements for the purchase of the site were not completed until the end of 1903. When it was finally placed on the chosen spot, the equestrian statue faced northwards - towards the hinterland of Africa. It was formally unveiled, on 4 December 1907, by the Governor of the Cape, Sir Walter Hely-Hutchinson.

Together with the Honoured Dead Memorial, the Rhodes statue could be said to mark not merely the passing of remarkable Kimberley men but the end of an era in Kimberley's turbulent history.

(3)

But hardly had one era ended than another began. It could be said to have begun, in fact, a few months after Rhodes's funeral train steamed out of Kimberley station in April 1902.

Despite the competition of the Transvaal gold mines and the De Beers monopoly, new men continued to arrive and chance their luck in Kimberley. They did not come in great numbers, nor were they the reckless fortune hunters who had flocked to the diamond fields in the early days. For the most part they were industrious, experienced and hard-headed businessmen who knew enough about diamonds to appreciate the complexities of the industry. Most of them were connected, in one way or another, with the Diamond Syndicate - the vast diamond-marketing organisation which had been established a few years after amalgamation to regulate the price of diamonds. 'The Syndicate', as it was known, had been Rhodes's creation and it revolved around De Beers, but associated with it were a number of smaller diamond-buying companies who had representatives in Kimberley. It was an employee of one of these companies who was destined to become the next great financial genius of the South African diamond industry.

He arrived at Kimberley, aged twenty-two, in November 1902. A neatly dressed, modest, and apparently shy young man, he seemed an unlikely candidate to challenge the, by now, all-powerful hierarchy of the diamond fields. When he stepped off the train at Kimberley station, he had, it is said, little more than £50 to his name. But it was a name which was to count: it was Ernest Oppenheimer.

The name of Oppenheimer was by no means new to Kimberley. Earlier, two of young Ernest's brothers–Bernard and Louis–had established reputations for themselves in the town as diamond buyers. Bernard, the elder of the brothers, had been the first of the family to come to South Africa; he had been joined, in 1886, by Louis. They had both acted as representatives for Anton Dunkelsbuhler–a distant relative and former Kimberley diamond merchant.

Anton Dunkelsbuhler's association with the diamond fields dated back to the days of New Rush. He had arrived at the diggings in 1872 as the representative of Mosenthal's, a well-known Port Elizabeth firm. According to David Harris, who knew him well, Dunkelsbuhler was at one time considered 'the largest and most generous of buyers on the fields'. Like Alfred Beit he was something of a mathematical genius, and rumour had it that he slept with a ready reckoner. However, at the beginning of 1876 – shortly after the Black Flag rebellion – Dunkelsbuhler had returned to Europe and set up his own diamond business in London. One of his early employees had been the then-youthful Bernard Oppenheimer, whom he had placed in charge of his Kimberley office.

It was largely through the influence of his brothers that Ernest Oppenheimer joined the Dunkelsbuhler firm. The Oppenheimer family was large – there were six boys and four girls – and opportunities for young men in the little German town of Friedberg in Hesse, where they were born, were limited. Bernard, in fact, had left home at the early age of thirteen. His father, Eduard Oppenheimer, was a middle-class cigar merchant but his business was evidently not prosperous enough to support his growing family. Ernest was sixteen when he was apprenticed to Dunkelsbuhler's head office in London.

By all accounts young Ernest started in the diamond trade at a distinct disadvantage. His timid manner tended to make him appear nervous and at times enraged his irritable and exacting employer. The story is often told of a disaster which occurred when, in a fit of nervousness, he accidentally spilt some ink over old Dunkelsbuhler while filling an inkpot.

'Diamond expert!' fumed the bespattered tycoon. 'Diamond expert! Why you wouldn't even make a good waiter.'

But such mishaps could not disguise Oppenheimer's obvious talents. Not only did he have a natural flair for diamond sorting, but he loved his work. For him diamonds were far more than stones to be sold at a profit; they were objects of rare beauty to be relished for their own sakes. He had, from the very outset, all the true instincts of a connoisseur. Industrious and painstaking, he soon made his mark. He might have been awkward but his good judgement was such that it could not be ignored. It was not merely family connections which earned him his promotion as Dunkelsbuhler's representative in Kimberley.

His arrival in the town went practically unnoticed. He had none of the push and bombast that had singled out successful diamond buyers in the early days. He was neither a wit like Ikey Sonnenberg, nor an exhibitionist like Moritz Unger. When, many years later, his associates were asked to give their impressions of the young Ernest Oppenheimer, many of them had difficulty in remembering him. One of the few who could recall him working in the sorting rooms, was struck not by his outstanding personality but by his exceptionally muscular arms. 'It was 1902,' he said, 'a warm summer day. His sleeves were rolled up, and I noticed his arms immediately. . . . Well, I asked the man in charge of the office, "Who's that fellow with the big arms?" and he said it was a new man, Ernest Oppenheimer, who'd just been sent out from London. He said, "I don't think very much of him from what I've seen so far. He's terribly shy, and he doesn't seem to be very bright.'

Yet, in a way, neither the shyness nor the apparent lack of personality was exceptional. As a youngster, Rhodes had always been considered a solitary dreamer, and Alfred Beit had been written off as a dull nonentity. Of all the flamboyant characters produced by Kimberley, only Barney Barnato had really proved outstanding. Whether anybody realised it or not, Ernest Oppenheimer was set on a very familiar course.

But it was a lonely course. Kimberley was a hospitable town but, for a man as diffident as Ernest Oppenheimer, it was not an easy place in which to settle. People were sociable enough but one needed the right degree of bonhomie and assertiveness to break into established circles. Anyone who appeared gifted but retiring was treated with suspicion. At first Oppenheimer found it difficult to make friends. According to George Green, the editor of the *Diamond Fields Advertiser*, he lived a somewhat solitary life. 'There was not enough work to keep him busy,' says Green, 'and he often dropped into my office for a chat. In those easygoing days the "old codgers" who ruled the roast in Kimberley did not favour the intrusion of young men of marked ability and soaring ambition and the newcomer had to bide his time with such patience as he could command.'

One of the 'old codgers' with whom he did become acquainted was Dr Jameson, who was then still a Kimberley member of the Cape Assembly. Oppenheimer was living with relatives whom Jameson often visited. He is said to have given the ostracised young man some useful, if strange, advice. When Oppenheimer confessed that, although he worked hard at the office sorting diamonds, his employees did not appear to respect him because he was so young, Dr Jim promptly put him right. 'Of course they don't respect you for working hard,' he said. 'Don't sort diamonds: let them do the sorting.'

This apparently solved Oppenheimer's employment problems. He took Jameson's advice, left the sorting to his workmen and concentrated on buying and selling diamonds. All the same, it seems an odd solution to offer to a newcomer working in what – as far as the whites were concerned – was considered the most democratic town in South Africa. In the old days any employer who did not roll up his sleeves and pitch in with his workers would have been thought to be putting on airs. Kimberley had changed in more than its outward appearance.

But Oppenheimer's greatest friend was probably the relative with whom he was living, Fritz Hirschhorn. It was through Hirschhorn that young Ernest learnt about the old days in Kimberley and the great personalities of the past. Hirschhorn had known them all. Born in Frankfurt, Germany, in 1867 – he was related to Ernest Oppenheimer's mother – Hirschhorn had come to

Kimberley as a young man and started his career as the representative of Julius Pam, one of the early merchants. Establishing himself on the then-neglected river diggings, he had quickly made a fortune. There was little about diamonds that Fritz Hirschhorn did not know. Rhodes, it is said, had a high opinion of Hirschhorn's knowledge and often consulted him, as he was 'recognised to be one of the finest authorities on diamond matters' in South Africa.

A heavily built, slow-speaking man with an assumed gruffness, Fritz Hirschhorn was not only one of the richest but one of the most generous of Kimberley's magnates. He was also one of the most hospitable. When Ernest Oppenheimer came to stay with him, he was living in a large house 'The Grange', Lodge Road, close to the Sanatorium. He had never married but, as a *bon viveur,* he was noted for his lavish entertainments and his sense of fun. It is said, for instance, that once he invited several friends to eat with him and then expressed shocked surprise when they turned up. After explaining that they had come on the wrong night and there was nothing in the house to eat, he offered to take the party to a local hotel for a simple meal. When the embarrassed guests arrived at the hotel they discovered it was all a typical Hirschhorn hoax. They were ushered into the dining-room where a full orchestra played while they ate the splendid dinner previously ordered for them by their host. This was the sort of thing Fritz Hirschhorn delighted in. He could never resist springing surprises; most of his lavish donations to charity were spontaneous and secret.

For Ernest Oppenheimer, living in Hirschhorn's house undoubtedly had its advantages. There he was able to meet visiting celebrities as well as most of Kimberley's well-known personalities, men like Dr Jameson, David Harris, Gardner Williams, William Pickering and Solly Joel. If he did not make many close friends, he gained some worth-while insights into the diamond industry. Hirschhorn was an alternate director of De Beers – and became a member of the Executive Committee in 1905 – and his position as representative of Wernher Beit and Company made him a key figure in the Diamond Syndicate. Before long the quiet, unobtrusive Oppenheimer was accompanying Fritz Hirschhorn to meetings of the De Beers directors. That, in itself, proved an education.

But Oppenheimer's lonely bachelor days in Kimberley did not last long. At the end of his first three years as Dunkelsbuhler's representative, he returned to London on long leave. There he re-met and married Mary (or May, as she was known) Pollak, the younger sister of his brother Louis's wife. The newly-weds returned to South Africa and, after living temporarily in a flat in the centre of Kimberley, arranged to build themselves a house. It was an unpretentious red-brick villa in Lodge Road, Belgravia. By the time they moved in, Ernest Oppenheimer had become a firmly established, if unobtrusive, Kimberley personality.

Directors and staff of De Beers Consolidated Mines Limited, 1902: standing left to right, Captain Tim Tyson, P.A. Robbins (Chief Electrical Engineer), Irvine R. Grimmer (Assistant Secretary), Alpheus F. Williams (Assistant General Manager), William Pickering (Secretary), R.B. Carnegy (Chief Accountant); sitting left to right, F. Hirschhorn (alternate to Alfred Beit), C.E. Nind, Francis Oats, M.L.A., Captain H.M. Penfold, Colonel David Harris, M.L.A., H.P. Rudd (alternate to C.J. Rhodes). Names without designation are directors. (K)

Elections in Kimberley were often lively occasions. This photograph shows a typical election meeting in 1904. (K)

A. Goose, The Jones Street Butchery, about 1903. The shop stood at 64 Jones Street and was typical of its period. (K)

(4)

Plus ca change, plus c'est la même chose, could have served as Kimberley's motto.

By the early 1900s the town had changed considerably both in appearance and in atmosphere. The sprawling, solidly built suburbs had given a semblance of bourgeois respectability to the former mining camps. De Beers Consolidated Mines had not only stabilised but unified the town. The days of warring factions and cut-throat competition were, to all intents and purposes, over. Everybody now had a common interest and there seemed no reason why Kimberley should not develop as a prosperous community.

But, as always, things were not quite what they seemed. Behind Kimberley's somewhat staid facade lay many of the uncertainties of the early days. The town still centred on the diamond industry and was still susceptible to the vagaries of a luxury trade. Amalgamation had succeeded in regulating Kimberley's diamond output, but it had not eliminated external threats. One such threat had come with the development of a diamond mine in the Transvaal, a little way from Pretoria.

This mine, known as the Premier, had proved far more productive than had at first been considered possible. The very thought of its potential had so shocked Alfred Beit in 1903 that, it is said, he suffered a mild stroke. It appeared to challenge all that he and Rhodes had worked for. Two years later the Transvaal mine attracted world-wide attention when the famous Cullinan diamond – later presented to King Edward VII – was discovered there. De Beers was forced to recognise that, once again, it faced a powerful competitor. Kimberley was by no means as stable, nor as complacent, as it appeared.

To make matters worse, this new threat coincided with an international slump. There was an immediate decline in the demand for diamonds. To keep up the price, the Syndicate – with a huge surplus stock on hand – was forced to stop buying stones. De Beers had to cut production and lay off hundreds of workers. The year 1906 found Kimberley in the midst of yet another crippling depression. A Mayor's Fund was started to assist the destitute, and De Beers instituted relief work for the unemployed by organising road parties at Beaconsfield and Newton. The Syndicate contributed substantially to the hard-pressed charitable organisations. It is said that this, his first experience of a Kimberley slump, decided Ernest Oppenheimer to enter public life. Such widespread hardships obviously could not be dealt with by private individuals. So on 1 January 1907, he became – like so many magnates before him – a Kimberley Town Councillor.

Yet, as had so often happened in the past, poverty and progress seemed to go hand in hand. The depression years of 1906 and 1907 were crowded with gala events and festivities of one kind or another. To the casual visitor, Kimberley seemed to be not merely weathering the economic crisis but ignoring it.

'Kimberley', wrote a correspondent of the *Transvaal Leader* at the end of 1906, 'remains the most prosperous town south of the Zambesi. It is worth going to Kimberley if only to shake off the feeling of utter depression which sits like a nightmare upon every other town in the country . . . one does not find an overgrown town, with buildings towering to the sky, all gaping for tenants. Building is certainly going on, but the places in course of erection are churches or residences, giving evidence of the fact that Kimberley is a settled community, and that the people regard the place as home. Inquiries reveal the fact that business is on a sound commercial basis. Kimberley is essentially a steady place.'

Not only did it appear steady, but the succession of public functions made it appear extremely lively. The town was still capable of responding enthusiastically to any social occasion.

One of the most important of these took place, outside of Kimberley, at the beginning of 1906. On 5 April, the High Commissioner for South Africa, Lord Selborne, officially opened the railway line between Fourteen Streams and Klerksdorp. This was a great day for the diamond fields. It meant that Kimberley was now linked directly with Johannesburg by rail, cutting out hours of train travel by the previous circuitous route.

De Beers saw to it that the event was celebrated in style. A special train, with two 'palatial saloons' attached, left the gaily beflagged Kimberley station at 9.30 a.m. with 'a large and representative party of gentlemen' from all over the Cape Colony aboard. They arrived at Fourteen Streams shortly before Lord Selborne and cheered themselves hoarse as the High Commissioner's train steamed in to break a bottle of champagne hanging over the starting-point of the new line. After luncheon in the Fourteen Streams goods shed - organised by the proprietor of the Alexandersfontein Hotel - the De Beers train returned to Kimberley station heralded by a series of fog signals. Half the town had turned out to welcome Lord Selborne and cheer him on his way to the Sanatorium.

Hardly had the High Commissioner left than more distinguished visitors arrived. On 16 May, the Governor of the Cape and his wife, Sir Walter and Lady Hely-Hutchinson, visited Kimberley on their return journey from the Victoria Falls. They were immediately caught up in a whirl of activity. A Mayor's garden party at Alexandersfontein was followed by a banquet at the Sanatorium; the following day the Governor laid the foundation stone of a new preparatory school in Belgravia and unveiled a handsome memorial statue of Queen Victoria in the public gardens. The visit ended with a huge ball-'one of the largest and most brilliant functions ever held in Kimberley'-given by the directors of De Beers and attended by over 600 guests.

And so it went on. Depression or no depression, Kimberley was determined to live up to its reputation as the town that had 'made South Africa great and prosperous'. This is how a visitor described it in December 1906, and this is how many Kimberleyites thought of the town. They were proud of its importance as the hub of the country's mining industry. For, despite the growth of the Transvaal goldfields, Johannesburg still relied on Kimberley as an essential link with the rest of the country. Now that the two centres had been directly joined by rail, Kimberley's geographical significance had been emphasised. It became doubly so when, on 18 December 1906, that indefatigable opener of railways, Lord Selborne, returned to the diamond

The Synagogue, Memorial Road, erected in 1902. (K)

Architect's drawing of the Christian Brothers College, erected in 1905. (K)

Beit House, a boarding-house for girls of the Kimberley High School, was built from the £7,500 allocated to the Kimberley School Board from the Beit Bequest. (M)

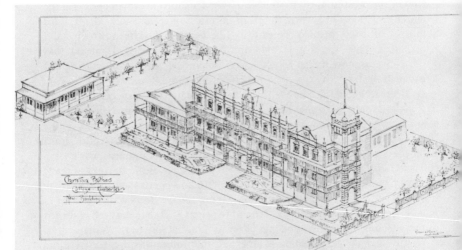

fields to turn the first sod of a railway extension which was to link Kimberley with Bloemfontein.

But the town's pride was not confined to its industrial role. There was hardly an aspect of South African life to which Kimberley was not contributing. This was particularly true of sport: Kimberley's sportsmen were acclaimed throughout the country. In 1906, for instance, when the first South African Rugby side–known then as the 'Springbokken'–toured Britain, no less than five players from Griqualand West were included in the team. The return of these local heroes in February 1907 gave Kimberley another cause for cele- bration. Not only did the town thrill to reports of the South African team's progress, but huge crowds had packed the Town Hall and cheered lustily as their five players–F.J. Dobbin, S.C. de Melker, A.F.W. Marsberg, J.W.E. Raaff and W.C. Marthize – flickered across the screen of Mr Wolfram's recently introduced 'bioscope'. The welcome given to the returning rugby players was as spirited as it was lavish. They were fêted at a splendid banquet given by the Mayor, W. Sagar, in the Town Hall as well as at an 'At Home' held at Alexandersfontein.

The Alexandersfontein hotel (expertly managed by Mr Eaton) was now, more than ever, a setting for gala occasions. Since the electrification of the Kimberley–Alexandersfontein tramway, in April 1905, it had become a favourite spot for public and private parties. Crowds would flock there at the week-end to enjoy tea with watercress sandwiches and, on Sunday afternoons, to listen to Mr Rybnikar conducting his Viennese band. The Saturday night dances, which spilled out into the gaily lit grounds, were to linger in the memory of many a young Kimberley girl; these were nights when, for them, the name Alexandersfontein spelled romance.

The year 1907 saw the opening of another famous Kimberley institution–the McGregor Museum. Two years earlier Mrs Margaret McGregor – widow of Alexander McGregor, a former mayor – had written to the Town Council offering to erect a museum in Chapel Street as a memorial to her husband. She had already bought the site and once the building was complete 'intended to hand it over to the inhabitants of Kimberley'. Her offer, needless to say, had been snapped up.

As the building of this stylish brick museum (its pediment rather daringly adorned with two reclining, seductively draped ladies) progressed, so was considerable thought being given to the arranging of a suitable opening function. It was a successful exhibition held in Kimberley by the well-known Cape artist, Hugo Naudé, that decided the matter. If the public showed such interest in one artist, why not give them a collection of painters? The McGregor Museum would be opened with an art exhibition such as Kimberley had never before seen. A committee was formed to arrange the exhibition. The chairman was J.J. Christie but, as everybody acknowledged, the real driving-force behind the committee was Captain Tim Tyson.

Tim Tyson had developed into quite a character. A balding bachelor, with a drooping moustache, Tyson was known to everyone and had a hand in every- thing. There was hardly a committee in Kimberley with which he was not

Statue of Queen Victoria, unveiled by the Governor of the Cape, Sir Walter Hely-Hutchinson, in 1906. The statue first stood in Queen's Park and was moved to its present site, outside the Art Gallery, in the 1950s. (K)

Captain Tim Tyson, the popular secretary of the Kimberley Club. (K)

Alexander McGregor Museum, Chapel Street, presented to the citizens of Kimberley by Mrs Margaret McGregor, as a memorial to her husband in 1907. (M)

connected – the Public Library, the Public Gardens, the Kimberley Hospital, the Pirates Club, the Griqualand West Cricket Union, the Kimberley Theatre Company – all had his extremely active support. Captain Tim Tyson was irrepressible.

He had been a great friend of Cecil Rhodes and, after his resignation as secretary of the Kimberley Club in 1902, he had been appointed a director of De Beers. This, however, had not ended his long association with the Club. In 1907 he was elected chairman of the Club Committee, and his little house – known as 'The Workman's Cottage' – was in Currey Street, almost opposite the Club's back entrance. It was one of the best-known houses in Kimberley.

Tim Tyson's parties, whether for members of the Kimberley Regiment, a team of cricketers or a troupe of actors, were famous. Almost as famous was his extraordinary collection of silver-ware and *objets d'art*, which he displayed on his huge dining-room table. He could never resist a bargain and haunted the Kimberley auction rooms. His most prized possession was a magnificent marble bath, which, in defiance of military orders, he had smuggled into Kimberley just after the siege. This, or so it is said, had resulted in near-disaster. When Lord Kitchener, then the Commander-in-Chief, got to hear that his hard-pressed transport was being used for such frivolities, he was so incensed that 'he put the town for a time on short rations, which unfortunate contretemps caused a slight set-back in Tim's amazing popularity'.

If this is true, the set-back did not last long. After the war Tim Tyson was as popular as he had ever been. He was also as active. When it came to arranging the art exhibition for the McGregor Museum, nobody worked harder than he. The result was a huge success. 'Not even', reported the *Diamond Fields Advertiser,* 'at the time of the Kimberley Exhibition were the local public privileged to see such a collection of pictures in their own town.'

The formal handing over of the title deeds by Mrs Margaret McGregor was performed in the brilliantly lit, but far from complete, museum building on 24 September 1907. Not until the following afternoon, however, was the art exhibition formally opened. The ceremony was presided over by the Mayor, but it was Councillor Ernest Oppenheimer who stole the show.

For some reason the chairman of the art committee was unable to attend, so Councillor Oppenheimer, as vice-chairman, took over. It gave him an opportunity to prove himself as a public speaker. On the whole, he acquitted himself well. Having first introduced the Mayor, he went on – in true South African fashion – to thank everyone remotely connected with the exhibition. The list was endless. It was enough to fluster anybody; it flustered Councillor Oppenheimer. He managed to squeeze in a special word of thanks for Tim Tyson – 'who is always to the front in anything affecting the well-being of Kimberley' – but almost forgot the guest of honour. 'There is one other matter . . .' he added hastily at the end of his speech, 'which perhaps should have been mentioned first of all – that is, it is due to Mrs McGregor that we are able to have this exhibition at all.'

His audience was indulgent. If anyone noticed Councillor Oppenheimer's *faux pas,* no comment was made. He had, after all, much to learn about public life.

Not all Oppenheimer's duties were to prove as pleasant as this one. Despite impressions gained by casual visitors, the economic depression continued. By the end of 1908, Councillor Ernest Oppenheimer was among those helping to organise the distribution of soup, to impoverished whites and coloureds, from the Kimberley Town Hall. This was one of the measures taken by the Council to alleviate the widespread distress caused by unemployment. The crippling slump was to last for another two years.

Kimberley might be changing, but the diamond industry remained as fickle as ever.

22

Mayor Oppenheimer

On the afternoon of 22 June 1911, a huge crowd gathered at the Kimberley race-course. It was a clear, sunny day and the citizens of Kimberley were in a festive mood. They were celebrating the coronation of King George V. There had been a number of entertainments arranged for the holiday–a children's party, a display of Japanese daylight fireworks, a Zulu war dance and a 'Fancy Fair' in the Town Hall–but the most sensational event had yet to take place. The final item in the afternoon's programme promised to be the highlight of the day. A crowd of some 20,000 people were to witness one of the marvels of the age. They had been promised that a certain John L. Weston would defy the laws of gravity and take to the air in a flying machine. Incredible as it seemed, they were not to be disappointed.

John (later Admiral) Weston was one of the pioneers of South African aviation. In 1907 he had constructed, at Brandfort in the Orange Free State, the first flying machine to be built in South Africa the 'Weston-Farman biplane'. Although this machine had not been flown in South Africa - it had been shipped to France, where, after several modifications, it had made some successful flights the building of it had focused attention on John Weston. His visit to Kimberley with a Bristol biplane was regarded as a singular honour for the town.

Excitement was running high when, to the applause of the crowd, a contingent of Boy Scouts wheeled Weston's machine onto the course. In fact, the excitement was such that it held up proceedings. Anxious to get a good view, the crowd swarmed round the fragile-looking plane and refused to give way. It took some time to get the course cleared. Once Weston had been given the word to go ahead, however, the crowd fell silent.

'There was a hush of expectancy,' reported the *Diamond Fields Advertiser,* 'whilst the engine was being tested; then Mr Weston signalled "all right", and started his Bristol machine. He ran along the ground until a good pace had been attained, and then rose, beautifully, opposite the grand stand, amid an outburst of applause. He attained a height of about 50 feet, and circled the Racecourse at that altitude, flying splendidly and maintaining a beautiful control of the machine.'

The performance might not quite have come up to expectations, but it was startling enough. Having made his circuit of the course, Weston returned to his starting-point to be greeted by deafening cheers. His second attempt was not so successful. The plane wobbled along the course, rose a few feet, and then flopped disappointingly at the far end of the race track. Immediately the ever-helpful Boy Scouts rushed to the rescue. The machine was speedily wheeled back and Weston started the engine for a third try. This time he took off beautifully, circled the race-course twice at a height of forty-five feet and landed with ease. The spectators went wild. 'Other flights', it was reported, 'would have been at any rate attempted by Mr Weston had it been possible to keep the crowd clear of the aerodrome.'

Weston's flight was not the first to be made in South Africa. In December 1909 a Belgian, Albert Kimmerling, had successfully demonstrated his 'Flying Matchbox' at East London and, less impressively, performed a few 'hops' at Johannesburg the following year. But Weston's performance at Kimberley was not without significance. It was to single out the town as a possible centre for aviation. The surrounding flat, bare veld seemed ideally suited for experiments in flying and it was not long before Kimberley was being spoken of as a 'natural aerodrome'. Equally important, John Weston's demonstration aroused tremendous local enthusiasm. Flying became very much a Kimberley craze. The young men (and even the young women) of the town could talk of little else. Their lively interest was soon to be rewarded.

Shortly after John Weston's demonstration, a young English flyer named Cecil Compton Paterson arrived in South Africa. With him came Captain Guy Livingstone and Evelyn 'Bok' Driver, a South African-born pilot. They were members of the recently formed African Aviation Syndicate and had come to the Cape to promote interest in flying. 'This objective', Captain Livingstone informed a Cape newspaper, 'we intend to achieve by giving exhibitions. We hope, if sufficient interest is taken, it will be possible to establish one or two schools of aviation in suitable centres.' The first of these schools was started at Alexandersfontein at the beginning of 1912.

Why, they were asked, had they chosen Kimberley? Captain Livingstone was quick to explain. His answer was very much what might have been expected. 'De Beers', he said, 'have very kindly placed at our disposal a large tract of land outside the Alexandersfontein Hotel which is eminently suited for testing purposes, and they have allowed us to erect our tents inside the ground. De Beers are also going to assist us with some of the finer work that I don't think could have been done elsewhere in South Africa.' There was, however, another reason. According to Cecil Compton Paterson, Kimberley was chosen for strategic purposes. The importance of aviation to any defence scheme had already been recognised and the diamond fields were seen as 'geographically situated to become a military pivot'. It was the hope of the African Aviation Syndicate that the South African Government would eventually form an aviation corps, with their school as a training base.

But first they had to prove themselves.

They started by giving exhibitions, Paterson flying a biplane and Driver a somewhat rickety monoplane. Success was by no means instantaneous. Although Paterson constantly astonished the townsfolk by circling the Honoured Dead Memorial, the luckless Driver had great difficulty in getting his plane off the ground. 'The question was on everybody's lips,' complained a spectator, ' "Will Driver fly?" ' More often than not the crowds which flocked to Alexandersfontein were disappointed. Even the most dedicated enthusiasts began to lose heart.

But Paterson more than redeemed the Syndicate's honour when, during the Easter holidays, he staged 'the most brilliant aviation display ever seen on the Diamond Fields'. He started by challenging Arthur Wright to race him on a motor cycle from Alexandersfontein to the Kimberley race course. According to newspaper reports the race ended in an easy victory for Paterson, but some Kimberley residents were to claim that Wright came in first. To offset any doubts, Paterson went on to demonstrate the use of aircraft in warfare. Flying over the race-course, he proceeded to 'bomb' an imaginary camp with musk melons. This, and the fact that Paterson flew back to Alexandersfontein and landed in the dark, seemed to impress even the hardened sceptics.

Paterson followed up this success by making aviation history. At the beginning of April, he accomplished the first cross-country flight ever made in Southern Africa. Taking off from Kimberley he flew to Klerksdorp in the Transvaal – a distance of 210 miles – in four hours and forty-two minutes flying time. The actual journey, however, took much longer. Buffeted by wind, and constantly running into air pockets, he was forced to make repeated landings. Reaching Kingswood at 6.25 in the evening, he spent the night in a hotel after 'tethering his machine to the horse post'. Next morning he completely lost his way, landed in the veld, and terrified a group of women who, when he climbed out of the plane, rushed into a cottage and bolted all doors against him. It was not until after six o'clock that evening that he reached Klerksdorp. For all that, it was – as everyone agreed – a remarkable feat.

But if Paterson pleased the public, he did not please his partners. A quarrel among the members of the syndicate resulted in the liquidation of their company in September 1912. Driver and Livingstone left Kimberley, and Paterson announced that he would buy the biplane and carry on by himself. But this, as it happened, was not necessary. Despite its many failures, the syndicate had made a great impression on local enthusiasts. Two young sportsmen in particular – Tom Hill and Louis Lezard – were determined that Kimberley should retain its place as a centre for aviation. They were quick to offer Paterson assistance. Hill took over the biplane, and Lezard was active in forming a new company.

This company – the Paterson Aviation Syndicate – was registered on 1 July 1913. Among the directors were some well-known Kimberley names: Alpheus Williams, Herbert Harris (son of David Harris), Tom Hill, Dr Charles May, George Ronaldson, David Macgill and Ernest Oppenheimer. Louis Lezard acted as the company's solicitor and De Beers promptly offered special facilities for the establishment of an aerodrome. Paterson was back in business again.

But it was business with a difference. The new enterprise attracted the favourable attention of the South African Government. Earlier Paterson had succeeded in interesting General Christiaan Beyers, the recently appointed Commandant-General of the Defence Force, in his activities. So much so that, during the parliamentary session of 1913, Beyers had supported a move to have selected candidates trained at Kimberley as military pilots. The scheme was to start with ten pupils. 'If they show that they are likely to develop into useful aviators,' announced Beyers, 'the intention is to send them on to military schools here. In Mr Paterson I think we have a good man.'

To have been chosen as the launching-ground for the South African Aviation Corps was a tremendous triumph for Kimberley. Here was proof indeed that the town's pioneering days were not over. 'In a short time,' declared the *Diamond Fields Advertiser*, 'Kimberley is likely to be famous not only for producing diamonds from the mine, but also diamonds of the air in the form of skilled military aviators, such as will play an important part in the warfare of the future.' Once again fame had come to Kimberley from out of the blue.

Paterson lost no time in getting started. While the new company was being formed, he left for England to whip up further support. On his return in the middle of August, he was accompanied by Edward Cheeseman, an Australian-born pilot. The 29-year-old Cheeseman was to assist with the tuition. The first batch of military pupils arrived a few days later and training began immediately.

Everything that happened at the school was avidly reported in the local press. The students, it was announced, were receiving daily lectures in the technical and practical aspects of aviation and taken on practice flights by their tutors. There were also classes in the construction and tuning of aircraft. It all sounded very professional, but to benefit from the training the pupils needed to have the right instincts. One of the officer candidates – the future Major-General Kenneth van der Spuy – was to claim that he learned to fly 'as you learn to ride a bicycle, "by feel" '

There were, by the beginning of October, nine Government and three private students attending the school. One of these private students was a 'well-known Kimberley lady', Marie Bocciarelli, who was to become South Africa's first aviatrix. (If local gossip is believed, this was not Miss Bocciarelli's only claim to Kimberley fame. Rumour had it that earlier she had acted as a model for the reclining female figures on top of the McGregor Museum.) By October also there was talk of an 'Aero Club' being formed and of special classes to train Boy Scouts in the handling of aircraft. Already Kimberley had become accustomed to the sight and sound of planes circling the outskirts of the town.

But the novelty was not to be enjoyed for long. The promising start made by the Paterson Aviation Syndicate ended in tragedy. On Saturday 11 October, Edward Cheeseman crashed the biplane. It was the fourth flight that Cheeseman had made with a pupil that morning and, despite uncertain weather, he had set off confidently. The plane had risen to 100 feet before it hit a treacherous air pocket which caused it to topple and hurtle to the ground. Pilot and pupil were dragged from the wreckage and rushed to the Kimberley Hospital. Although Cheeseman had broken his thigh, his condition was not at first thought to be serious. Indeed, he might have recovered had he not been weakened by malaria. But the combination of shock and fever proved fatal. His death, four days later, was the first in the history of South African aviation.

Transporting the famous Paterson bi-plane to Kimberley by mule wagon. (M)
Cecil Compton Paterson and one of his pupils at the controls of the first aero-
plane purchased by the government of the Union of South Africa. (M)
Pupils at the Kimberley Flying School in 1913. Included among them is Marie
Bocciarelli, the first South African woman to be trained as a pilot. (M)

The crash more or less put an end to the flying-school. The Government pupils were transferred to Tempe, near Bloemfontein, and Paterson returned to England in March the following year. Kimberley, however, never lost its enthusiasm for flying. In 1930 it became a recognised stop for the first Trans-Africa Air Service and, four years later, staged a spectacular air rally. For many years its tiny airport was regarded as a model of its kind. The town's claim to be the 'cradle' of South African aviation is well justified.

(2)

The failure of the Paterson Aviation Syndicate was a sad blow to Kimberley. During its brief existence the flying-school had provided the town with a renewed sense of progress and modernity. It had emphasised the fact that Kimberley had more to offer than its underground riches. For, although old-timers remained proud of the town's turbulent past, a new generation now had its eyes fixed firmly on the future. It was a future which promised great things. Kimberley was growing up rapidly. Nothing illustrated this more than its recent rise in status. In the year 1912 the former mining town was officially proclaimed a city.

It had been a slow process. There had long been talk of making Kimberley a city but, for one reason or another, nothing had come of it. This, however, had not prevented plans being made and hopes fostered. From the time of the amalgamation of the mines, institutional and public buildings had been designed on a much grander scale and the centre of the town had lost much of its makeshift character. Kimberley, in fact, had consciously cultivated a civic dignity to match its importance as a permanent industrial centre in the northern Cape.

With the Union of South Africa, in May 1910, the need for the town to assert itself had become more apparent. The constitution of the Union had decreed that Cape Town should be the legislative capital, Pretoria the administrative capital, and Bloemfontein the judicial capital – leaving Kimberley very much out on a limb. If it was to play a part in the new dispensation, Kimberley required some sort of official recognition. One way of obtaining that recognition was for the town to be proclaimed a city. Moves to this end had taken on a new urgency.

A lead of sorts had already been given by the Anglican church. In 1907 the Anglican community had replaced their old wood and iron church of St Cyprian in Jones Street with an altogether more substantial building in the Dutoitspan Road. This stately redbrick edifice – designed by D.W. Greatbatch, the architect of the Kimberley Exhibition – was obviously intended to be more than a parish church. It had about it the look of a cathedral and only required a Bishop to make it one. Few people were therefore surprised when, at a meeting held in the Town Hall in July 1911, it was formally resolved that 'the Western portion of the Diocese of Bloemfontein be constituted a new and separate Diocese with Kimberley as its Cathedral Town'.

The election of Kimberley's first Bishop was left to Bishop Chandler of

Bloemfontein, Canon T.C. Robson and the Reverend G.M. Lawson. They were unanimous in their choice. At the beginning of 1912, it was announced that Dr Wilfred Gore-Brown was to be the Bishop of the newly formed Diocese of Kimberley and Kuruman.

Although little was known about Gore-Brown at that time, his election proved extremely popular. The son of a former Governor of New Zealand, and then in his early fifties, the new Bishop promised to be the type of down-to-earth priest that Kimberley needed. He had worked in South Africa for ten years and, as a young man, had served as a private in the British army in order to understand 'the needs and aspirations of the man in the ranks'. He appeared to have little of the snob about him. Equally important, he was, as he announced at his enthronement in June, an ardent admirer of Cecil Rhodes. All in all, a better choice could hardly have been made. Nor could the election have been more timely. For, having its own Bishop, Kimberley could now begin to think of itself as a city.

With the enthronement of Bishop Gore-Brown, St Cyprian's Church was elevated to a cathedral. Mellowed by time and graced by a bell tower, it was to become one of the most distinguished buildings in Kimberley. That a madonna-like statue of Sister Henrietta should one day stand in front of St Cyprian's was appropriate. The Anglican community had undoubtedly contributed much to the development of the town – was not Cecil Rhodes the son of an Anglican parson? – but few were more deserving of a memorial than Henrietta Stockdale. She was an outstanding member of her church. It is unfortunate that she did not live to see the first Bishop installed. A few months earlier – in October 1911 – she had died, aged 64, after a sudden attack of paralysis.

'Loved by all for her unselfish devotion to duty,' said the *Diamond Fields Advertiser* in its obituary, 'admired for her wonderful endurance, and the centre of legions of friends, Sister Henrietta's death leaves a void in the Life of Kimberley which it is impossible to fill.' Conventional as this tribute might seem, it did not exaggerate. There would never be another Sister Henrietta. Her stature as a nurse and teacher had been acknowledged throughout South Africa. She had worked tirelessly for the nursing profession. Like Florence Nightingale, with whom she was inevitably compared, she was a woman of few illusions. A stern disciplinarian, exacting and abrasive, her approach to nursing did not allow for sentimentality. Her students were inclined to regard her with awe rather than affection. This severity, however, was largely responsible for her success. Nurses trained at the Kimberley Hospital invariably commanded respect. They were regarded as a special breed. Inspired by Sister Henrietta's example, Kimberley nurses went out to found other hospitals, other training-centres. To their duties they brought a sense of dedication which helped to raise nursing standards throughout southern Africa.

But perhaps Sister Henrietta's greatest triumph was in securing legal recognition for her profession. Largely through her determined efforts, an Act was passed by the Cape parliament, in 1891, which made provision for the state registration of nurses and midwives. The passing of this Act made medical history: South Africa, it is said, became the first country in the world to give professional respectability to its nurses.

'Sister Henrietta', claimed Dr Jameson, 'has done more for South Africa than any one woman.' He may well have been right. If Kimberley did not – as some people think – name a street after her, it had every reason to be proud of her achievements.

Of its own achievements it was still uncertain. By the middle of 1912, Kimberley had its own Bishop and its own cathedral but it had not been officially recognised as a city. There was an important issue to be settled before that could happen. It centred on an old and familiar problem – that of amalgamation. This time it was the proposed amalgamation of Kimberley with neighbouring Beaconsfield. Not until the two townships had been welded together could 'greater Kimberley' come into being.

There had been a great deal of heated argument about this amalgamation. Many of the rivalries and jealousies of the early camp days had been re-awakened. Beaconsfield – the former Dutoitspan – prided itself on its independence and was suspicious of the mating noises being made by Kimberley councillors. How, it was asked, would Beaconsfield be represented? Would it not be swallowed up by Kimberley? How much say would the Beaconsfield representatives have over their own affairs? The debate had dragged on, both in private and in public, for months.

Few men in Kimberley were more keen to see the amalgamation accomplished than Councillor Ernest Oppenheimer. In the last year or so he had made a considerable impact on civic affairs. After resigning from the council at the beginning of 1909 – shortly after the birth of his first son, Harry Frederick – he had again stood for election when a vacancy occurred the following year. Since then he had emerged as a convinced champion of greater Kimberley.

Oppenheimer's arguments had done much to allay the fears of the Beaconsfield councillors. It was pointed out that there was no question of Beaconsfield surrendering its independence. The township would retain its name, and its representatives would have equal rights on the joint council. What was being sought was a union, not an annexation. The debate was wearisome, but the Kimberley councillors persevered. They won in the end.

In October 1912, a notice in the *Cape Provincial Gazette* announced that the municipalities of Kimberley and Beaconsfield were to be combined. Two councillors would be elected from eight new wards and they would sit as members of the 'Municipality of the City of Kimberley'. The merger was to come into effect on 2 December 1912.

And that in fact is what happened. There was only one snag. For some reason, the election of the city's new mayor was slightly delayed. For the first couple of weeks of its existence the combined council was presided over by the former mayor of Kimberley. When the mayoral election did take place, however, it was a mere formality. Of the fifteen councillors present, fourteen voted for Ernest Oppenheimer and one abstained. The election result was announced

Wilfred Gore-Brown, first Anglican Bishop
of Kimberley and Kuruman. (K)

Sir Ernest Oppenheimer in his mayoral
robes. He arrived in Kimberley in 1902 and
was elected Mayor in 1912. (K)

The indomitable Sister Henrietta Stockdale
and staff, some time after 1904. (K)

as unanimous.

After being invested with his robe and chain, Oppenheimer addressed his colleagues. His speech was short and to the point. 'Efficiency', he declared, 'rather than new ventures must be the watchword.'

(3)

Fittingly enough, it was during one of its rare boom periods that Kimberley was proclaimed a city. With the recent slump successfully overcome, Kimberley moved into that halcyon, prosperous period that typified the world before the First World War. One had only to stroll around the Market-square on a Saturday morning to appreciate the city's revived affluence. The Market teemed with people. In the shade of the corrugated-iron canopies, Indian and Coloured stall-holders presided over colourful heaps of fruit and vegetables. Out in the sunshine, sweating auctioneers stood high above a jumble of second-hand goods. On the north side of the square, dominated by the 'Town Clock' with its handsome tower, sprawled the various Government buildings–the High Court, Magistrates Court, Civil Commissioner's Office, Customs and Public Works Department. On the east side were the Post and Telegraph Offices. The other two sides were a close-packed mass of shops, crammed to bursting-point with goods and people.

Even busier was Jones Street. Where it crossed the partly tarred Dutoitspan Road, it formed the business hub of the city – Gowies' Corner. From here the trams went rattling past the shops and cafes, and at night the whole area became a brightly-lit magnet for the crowds. There were the wonders of plate-glass and electric light and, most alluring of all, the places of entertainment. In time, the ever-popular Theatre Royal was to be joined by the picture palaces with their splendidly evocative names – the Vaudette, the Olympia and the Trocadero.

The liveliness of the city was matched by the vitality of its new Mayor. Ernest Oppenheimer was as good as his word. He had promised efficiency and, during his first term of office, efficiency is what he produced. There were few innovations but a great deal of tightening up, both in the administration and in the electoral procedure. Hardly had the Council met than it set about reforming itself. A new system of auditing was introduced. Arrangements were made for the Council to be represented on the Health Board. The existing eight wards, with two representatives each, were consolidated into four wards, with three representatives each. Women's suffrage was extended to include all Kimberley instead of, as formerly, only Beaconsfield. . . . That Ernest Oppenheimer meant business was obvious to all. No wonder then that at the next mayoral election, in September 1913, he was again returned to office. This time he had another well-known businessman, John Orr, as his deputy.

Having reformed the Council, Oppenheimer, with the help of De Beers, set about overhauling Kimberley's public-transport system. This was long over-due. Since being taken over by the Gibson Brothers, the tramways had passed through several stages of development. In 1892 the original mule-drawn coaches had been replaced by electric cars, powered by accumulators; these, in turn, had given way to steam traction and in 1906 an overhead trolley system had been introduced. Mechanical progress, however, had not always been accompanied by administrative efficiency. The various routes were ill-coordinated, erratically managed and the fares were disproportionately high. Demands that the municipality take over the tramways had been a feature of every local election. Now, Oppenheimer decided to make good the vague promises of his predecessors.

After a number of lengthy debates, the Council agreed to purchase the tramways from Gibson Brothers for £35,000. A loan for this amount was to be made by De Beers. However, during the negotiations it was realised that a more efficient service could be operated if De Beers ran the tramways. The company already subsidised the line to Kenilworth and was able to supply electricity at a low cost. On 1 July 1914, therefore, De Beers took over the tramway concession. The public had little cause to complain: not only was there an immediate drop in fares, but a decided increase in efficiency. Ernest Oppenheimer could chalk up another success. Unfortunately it was shortlived. A month later the First World War broke out.

Once again Kimberley's prosperity was shattered by outside events. The diamond industry, always vulnerable to international crises, was paralysed by the war. Mining ground to a halt. All work in the Kimberley Mine ceased on 4 August–the day Britain declared war on Germany–and, apart from the pumping of water, the 'Big Hole' was put permanently out of action. An era which had begun with the storming of Colesberg Kopje was ended with the march of German soldiers into Belgium. The effect on Kimberley was catastrophic.

For the first few days of the war, the city was said to be on the brink of anarchy. Thousands of Africans were thrown out of work, there was talk of threatened riots in the compounds and extra police were hastily recruited. But the scare passed. Arrangements were made to send the majority of labourers home, and De Beers put the rest of its employees on half pay. A Mayor's Relief Fund was established and the Council started public-works projects to absorb the unemployed from subsidiary industries. The situation was not unfamiliar. Kimberley had learned to cope with panic.

Not so smoothly overcome were the problems facing Ernest Oppenheimer. As the German-born mayor of a fervently patriotic Kimberley, he became the target for a small, but vociferously hostile, group of political opponents. Not only his loyalty but his personal integrity were questioned.

The trouble started immediately after the September municipal elections. When the Council met in open session to choose a new mayor, Oppenheimer, who had intended to resign, allowed his name to be put forward. There were no other nominations. Had it not been for the intervention of Councillor Fred Hicks, the election would have been unanimous. Hicks, however, decided to voice an objection. Now that the British Empire was at war, he said, he thought it would be a 'graceful act' if Oppenheimer stood down. He was careful not to be too specific, but there was no mistaking his implications. Oppenheimer certainly had no doubts. Leaping to his feet, he declared that he was as much a citizen of the British Empire as Fred Hicks. The rest of the Council agreed. Loud applause greeted Ernest Oppenheimer's election as Mayor. Only Councillor Hicks voted against the motion. The following day the *Diamond Fields Advertiser* lectured Hicks on his lack of good taste.

But the squabble did not end there. Two days later the Kimberley branch of the South African Labour Party passed a resolution protesting against Oppenheimer's appointment as Mayor and the 'scurrilous personal attack on Councillor Hicks' in the *Diamond Fields Advertiser*. The resolution implied that Oppenheimer was in some way responsible for the acts of 'barbarism inflicted on non-combatant British subjects in German territory'. Irrational as it was, this attack—which was published in the press—encouraged Hicks to raise the matter again at the next meeting of the Council. This time he became downright abusive and Oppenheimer, as Mayor, did not hesitate to rule him out of order. But Hicks refused to be silenced; he was still muttering insults when the meeting adjourned. The rest of the councillors gave Oppenheimer their wholehearted support.

So did the majority of Kimberley citizens. When the Council met again, a deputation from the Ratepayers' Association presented Oppenheimer with a glowing message of congratulation on his election as Mayor. It praised his past achievements, as well as his work in relieving the distress caused by unemployment, and expressed full confidence in his ability to carry out his duties. Even more impressive was the lengthy petition of support, signed by some 5,000 citizens, which was formally tabled by the Town Clerk. That Councillor Hicks and his political cronies were very much in the minority there could be no doubt.

In the meantime, Kimberley had been gearing itself for war. At the beginning of August the Kimberley Regiment mustered on the showgrounds and went into training. One of Ernest Oppenheimer's first official duties after his election was to inspect a battalion of volunteers leaving for South West Africa via the Cape. They were to join the South African troops who had been ordered to capture important German wireless stations at Luderitzbucht and Swakopmund. A huge crowd had gathered to cheer them on their way. Oppenheimer, dressed in his mayoral robes, made the most of the occasion. 'We know you will be a credit to Kimberley,' he told the troops in his farewell speech, 'and to the Empire of which Kimberley is a part.' There was no mistaking where his loyalties lay.

During the next few months no one worked harder than Ernest Oppenheimer in support of Kimberley's war effort. He arranged for parcels to be sent to the men on active service and sent each one of them a personally signed Christmas card, decorated with the arms of Kimberley and the Union Jack; he canvassed funds for the Red Cross and personally 'raised' a second battalion of the Kimberley Regiment. His staff at the Town Hall were devoted to him. 'It was always a thrill', one of them recalled, 'to be sent along the wide passageway to the blue and red furnished Mayor's parlour to have letters signed. Ernest Oppenheimer was a popular Mayor and well-liked by everyone.'

Yet the hostile murmurings continued. The animosity sparked off by Fred Hicks never completely disappeared. At times it manifested itself in vicious handbills, distributed secretly throughout the town. One such handbill was a reprint of a news item published by the *Rand Daily Mail*: headed *A Lesson in Manners for Mr Oppenheimer*, it reported the resignation of the German-born Mayor of Coventry. There was little that Oppenheimer could do to counteract this underhand propaganda. Popular, hard-working and undoubtedly loyal as he was, he could not defend himself against unreasoning racialism.

For all that, his opponents made little real impression in Kimberley. They might eventually have given up had they not been encouraged by outside events. Things were brought to a climax in an unexpected way.

On 7 May 1915, the trans-Atlantic liner *Lusitania* was torpedoed by a German U-boat off the west coast of Ireland. Some 1,300 people, including women and children, were drowned in what was widely considered a cowardly and unprovoked attack. Reports of the tragedy resulted in anti-German riots breaking out in cities throughout the British Empire. South Africa was no exception.

When news of the sinking was published, mobs in Johannesburg and Durban went on the rampage. Shops and business premises of anyone having, or suspected of having, German connections were burnt or ransacked. In a single night's rioting the frenzied crowds in Johannesburg were reported to have caused a quarter of a million pounds worth of damage; in Durban there was wholesale destruction of shops and warehouses. The slightly delayed Kimberley riots were no less terrifying. Prominent among the victims of the Kimberley mob was, of course, the city's Mayor.

Ernest Oppenheimer had anticipated trouble. As soon as the *Lusitania* disaster was reported he had consulted with his deputy, Thomas Pratley. The following day he had formally resigned both as Mayor and as a City Councillor. He made no mention of the racial opposition and he might, in fact, have welcomed the opportunity of stepping down. His letter of resignation made it quite clear that he had only agreed to stand for a third term at the urgent request of his fellow councillors and that he now felt he had fulfilled his obligations. His many achievements spoke for themselves.

Impressive as they were, however, they could not save him from the mob.

The Kimberley riots started late in the evening, with small groups of people meeting in the Market-square. As the bars and theatres emptied, the groups became larger and more disorderly. Agitators went to work, shouting anti-German slogans and singing 'Rule Britannia'. Soon one of the groups broke away and making straight for Dunell Street, proceeded to smash the windows of Mr Pfeffer's barbershop. Then the nearby African Lion Bar was attacked: stones were hurled through the plate-glass windows, doors were broken down, lamps, bottles and mirrors were shattered. The place was a complete wreck by the time the rioters moved on. From then on there was no stopping them. Uniformed members of the Defence Force joined the mob as it surged through the centre of the city. The police stood by helpless, afraid for the most part to draw their batons.

The rioters ran wild. Stalls in the Market-square were ripped to pieces; warehouses in Stockdale Street were ransacked and a liquor store set on fire. Flaming trails of alcohol spread along the street gutters, threatening the entire business area. Thugs and hooligans, drunk with loot from the plundered buildings, combed the streets looking for more victims. The Grand Hotel was spared only by the prompt action of its proprietor, who pinned a notice at the bar entrance stating that he was Russian-born and a British subject. Other British subjects were not so lucky. Any business house bearing a German-sounding name became a target for attack.

No one was more alive to the danger than Ernest Oppenheimer. When news of the rioting reached Belgravia, he evacuated No. 7 Lodge Road and took refuge with his wife and children in Irvine Grimmer's house a few doors away. There they were joined by Fritz Hirschhorn. That the rioters would carry out their threat to burn down Oppenheimer's house there seemed no doubt. But the expected attack did not materialise. A cordon of police - some mounted, some on foot - headed off the mob before they could reach Lodge Road and drove them back to the centre of town. Here rioting continued until the early hours of the morning. Exhaustion, rather than force, finally dispersed the mob.

But all was not over. The following day, Oppenheimer packed his family off to Cape Town and arranged for the police to guard his house. Similar guards were placed at other threatened houses. Kimberley was quiet, but far from settled. Further outbreaks of violence were expected. The question was: when, where and how would the rioters strike?

The answer came later that day as Ernest Oppenheimer was driving through the centre of town. He was spotted by a crowd of thugs who began to pelt his car with stones. The windscreen was smashed and Oppenheimer was badly cut by the glass. Blood was pouring from his forehead as he staggered from the car and, pursued by the crowd, dashed into the nearest building.

As luck would have it, the building was a convent belonging to the nuns of the Holy Family. Not even a bunch of hooligans dared violate such a sanctuary. Once the door had closed behind him, Oppenheimer was safe.

The nuns were all concern. They bathed and dressed Oppenheimer's wound, saw that he reached home safely and earned his lasting gratitude. When, many years later, he arranged for the Sanatorium - or the Belgrave Hotel as it then was - to be taken over by the Holy Family, few doubted that he was repaying a debt of kindness.

He had no such tender thoughts for the rest of Kimberley. The sudden outburst of hatred was as sickening as it was inexplicable. He was to brood over it for years. That night there was more rioting, and Oppenheimer, shut up in his closely guarded house, recognised the futility of remaining in Kimberley. The following day he left to join his family at the Cape.

Even Oppenheimer's opponents acknowledged that he had been shabbily treated. At the next Council meeting, when Thomas Pratley was elected Mayor, Fred Hicks was forced to admit that the behaviour of the rioters had been, as he put it, 'un-British'. Everyone, it seemed, could be made to wear a racial tag.

(4)

'The roses that year were too wonderful, but when you walked down the street you did not see a soul. So much beauty and such desolation; it was tragic.'

This is how William Pickering's daughter, Cecile-or Dolly, as she was called-remembered the closing months of the First World War. October and November 1918 were two of the most frightening months in Kimberley's history. It is estimated that during those two months 4,483 people - or 8.85 per cent of the entire population - died and some 40,000 people were stricken by disease in the Kimberley urban area. They were victims of the terrifying influenza epidemic which swept, not only South Africa, but the entire world.

How and where the epidemic started has never been satisfactorily explained. In different countries it was given different names. The Germans called it the 'blitz katarrh'; to the Japanese it was 'wrestler's fever'; British Tommies in the trenches on the Western Front dubbed it the 'Flanders Grippe'; and wits in Hong Kong, imitating the pidgin-English of the locals, joked about 'the too-muchee-hot-inside sickness'. But the name by which it became known to history was 'Spanish Flu'. And as 'Spanish Flu' it invaded South Africa.

Kimberley was the first inland centre to be struck by the epidemic. Cases were detected in the mine compounds as early as 23 September 1918. Joe Sperber, who worked in William Cooper's chemist shop, was to remember receiving conflicting prescriptions from Dr Ashe (of siege fame) for a young patient in the compounds in September. From the medicine ordered on two occasions, it seemed as if the city's best-known physician was at a loss to know precisely what he was treating. He and the chemists were soon to find out. The initial symptoms - a headache, followed by bouts of giddiness, a rise in temperature and pains in the chest, back and limbs-were to become all too familiar in the days ahead.

By the beginning of October the epidemic had Kimberley in its grip. At the Dutoitspan Mine alone, 2,000 cases were reported and the death toll rose to 150. The figures for other crowded centres in the city were almost as alarming. Men and women - particularly men between the ages of 25 and 45 years of age - dropped in the street and were carried off to bed to be nursed by those members of their families who were still on their feet. The few doctors who had escaped the disease themselves, could not begin to cope with the incessant demands for attention. They were forced to confine themselves to groups who were helpless to tend themselves. Instructions were issued to households where the entire family was stricken, to hoist a red flag in a prominent position so that a doctor could be summoned. Makeshift red signals of every type - From hot-waterbottle covers to red bathing-drawers - were soon seen dangling from houses throughout Kimberley.

'The doctors', said David Harris, 'described the outbreak as pneumonic plague, but from descriptions of the Great Plague in London in the seventeenth century, and having seen the condition of many local sufferers it appeared to my lay mind that the scourge was identical.'

Many others thought the same. If there were not actually cries of 'Bring out your dead', echoing through the streets, it was merely because more effective means of communication were available. A Burial Committee for whites was formed and its regulations were published in the press. Undertakers were assisted with the manufacture of plain coffins, and arrangements were made to convey the dead to the cemetery. 'All Roman Catholic and Wesleyan funerals', it was decreed, 'to be held at 9 a.m. and 3.30 p.m. All Church of England and Dutch Reformed Church at 10 a.m. and 4.30 p.m. All Presbyterians and Baptists at 11 a.m. and 5.30 p.m.'

It became impossible to dig graves fast enough. So great was the pressure at the cemeteries that burial services often had to be conducted at night, lit by the headlights of motor cars. When the gravediggers were stricken, De Beers miners had to be employed to take their place. All other work was brought practically to a standstill.

Public buildings, schools and communal institutions were closed, shops were run with skeleton staffs and few policemen were seen in the streets. The tramways, so recently a cause for pride, were badly hit. Of the 100 men employed by the tramway service, 'only one solitary individual was left to fill the role of driver'. But somehow De Beers managed to keep a tram running. The service was irregular, there were no conductors, and passengers travelled free, but the tram ran throughout the emergency.

It .was the shortage of trained medical staff that presented the greatest problem. A local committee, headed by Alpheus Williams, was formed to harness the city's resources but there were simply not enough doctors and nurses to go round. On 14 October, Colonel A.J. Orenstein–the Director of Medical Services for the Union Defence Department–arrived from Pretoria to help with the organisation but even he was handicapped by the lack of medical supplies. Volunteer workers with only a minimum of experience found themselves confronted with appalling tasks. 'Most of us', remembered Mrs Florence Roos, 'were from St John's Ambulance Association and although we had our Home Nursing Certificates there was quite a lot we had not been trained for–giving injections and laying out the dead, for instance.'

Three years earlier the Kimberley Hospital had been enlarged and a new main block added, but it could not begin to cope with the massive intake of patients. To help out, the Belgrave Hotel (Sanatorium) was hastily converted into a nursing-home, manned by volunteer nurses. It got off to a bad start. Hardly had it opened than the chef was stricken and died. There was no one to cook for either the patients or the staff until David Harris sent his housekeeper to take over the catering. The nurses were left to do the best they could without a trained supervisor.

The few professional nurses not employed at the Kimberley Hospital were kept fully occupied in the mine compounds. Here conditions were at their worst: the crowded dormitories had proved a natural breeding-ground for an infectious disease. 'Labourers were dying fast,' says Florence Roos, 'and no sooner was a bed vacated than another patient was brought in. In one ward the floor was covered with sick and dying Africans.'

Inevitably the high death-rate among the mine workers led to panic. At the beginning of October the African labourers began to agitate for permission to return home. They would rather die in their kraals, they said, than in Kimberley. Efforts to dissuade them, so as to prevent a mass exodus spreading the disease, had no effect; by the middle of the month they were threatening to break out of the compounds, even at the risk of being shot. Eventually, after the medical authorities had been consulted, it was agreed that those fit enough to travel could leave in batches of 200 at a time. The depleted railway service could not handle larger numbers. The seriously sick, however, were forced to remain.

The heroine of the compound medical staff was undoubtedly Sister Jessie Tyre. Then in her early fifties, this redoubtable nurse was a well-known Kimberley personality. She had first arrived in the city in 1900, shortly after the siege, and trained as a private nurse under Sister Henrietta. A few years later she had opened her own nursing-home and achieved local fame as a midwife (by the time she died, in 1954, it was estimated that she had brought some 11,000 Kimberley babies into the world). But it was her work among the African labourers during the influenza epidemic which singled Jessie Tyre out as a true disciple of Sister Henrietta. Such was her devotion to duty that she not only set an example to the volunteer workers but earned the lasting gratitude of De Beers, who awarded her a pension. Kimberley had every reason to be proud of its nurses.

Other local traditions were also upheld. Alpheus Williams, then the General Manager of De Beers, worked tirelessly to relieve the widespread distress. He was assisted by the acting-Mayor, Colin Lawrence, and the steward of the Kimberley Club, J. Harper, who undertook to feed the needy. Crowds of impoverished men and women flocked to the soup kitchen at the City Hall every day. Feeding them was a harrowing task. 'Some of the callers for soup', it is said, 'were already in the grip of the influenza, and it was most dramatic to see one or two of them obtain their rations and then drop down dead but a few yards away.'

With medicine in short supply, many people resorted to 'home cures' and superstitious remedies. Among the coloured community, for instance, it was widely believed that relief could be obtained from the leaves of pepper trees. 'You would see the people', remembered Mrs Hendrickse, 'walking about with their heads covered with pepper leaves, but sometimes you would hear the very next day that they had died. It seemed to work for some, not others. It was a terrible time.' The slightly better informed, took to their beds with hot-waterbottles, hoping to sweat out the fever. But there was no sure cure.

According to David Harris, it was the hooters blown on Armistice Day (11 November 1918) which signalled the beginning of the end of the epidemic. At the sound of the long-drawn blasts, convalescents forgot their aches and pains and rushed into the streets to celebrate the end of the war. 'A finer tonic could not have been dispensed by any chemist,' says Harris. 'The stimulating news brought about a different atmosphere; invalids soon became healthy people.' This is perhaps as good an explanation as any for the strange ending of a mysterious sickness.

23

Capital of the Northern Cape

The Armistice hooters blew; the influenza epidemic ended; and Kimberley men came home from the war. By the beginning of May 1919, a sufficient number had returned for the city to organise an official 'welcome home' parade. Troops, headed by Colonel T.H. Rodger of the 2nd Battalion Kimberley Regiment, marched through the crowded streets from the Drill Hall and assembled outside the City Hall. Every branch of the armed forces was represented: the Royal Navy, the Royal Air Force, the Imperial Army, the South African Field Artillery, the South African Engineering Corps, the 1st South African Infantry Brigade, the Army Service Corps, the South African Railways and Harbours Regiment. . . . Rarely had the city witnessed such an imposing military display.

Kimberley was proud of its war record. The 1st and 2nd Kimberley Regiment had first served in South West Africa (the 2nd distinguishing itself at Trekkopjes). After returning to Kimberley, the Regiment was split between those who went to German East Africa and those who joined the 1st South African Infantry Brigade, which fought first in Egypt and then trained in England to join the forces in France. Among the Kimberley heroes were Captain (later Lieutenant-Colonel) H.F. Lardner Burke, D.S.O., M.C., Private (later Captain) W.F. Faulds, V.C., Captain (later Colonel) T. Ormiston, D.S.O., and Lieutenant-Colonel Alex Smith, who as a non-commissioned officer had won the D.C.M., M.M. and the French Croix de Guerre. A few – such as Andrew Kiddie and Clair Harrison – had upheld Kimberley's aeronautic traditions by distinguishing themselves in the infant Royal Flying Corps.

Andrew 'Cam' Kiddie was, in fact, typical of Kimberley's far-roaming volunteers. He was the son of Andrew Kiddie, who in 1898 had established what was to become Kimberley's best-known bakery. At the outbreak of war, young Andrew Kiddie had first served in South West Africa and then joined the Royal Flying Corps in England, becoming a flight-commander. Besides earning the Belgian Croix de Guerre, he and Clair Harrison were among the first South Africans to be awarded the Distinguished Flying Cross. In later years, Andrew Kiddie was to be described as one of the most popular men in Kimberley. Both as a businessman (people would travel miles to buy farm sausages at Kiddie's Bakery) and as a polo player he was to contribute much to the social life of the city.

But not all Kimberley's heroes returned. During the immediate post-war years, much thought was given to the problem of erecting a suitable memorial to those who had lost their lives in the war. That such a memorial - quite distinct from that honouring the dead of the siege - should be erected there was little doubt; it was merely a matter of deciding what form it should take. There was no shortage of ideas. When the War Memorial Committee publicly canvassed for an appropriate design it was inundated with weird and wonderful suggestions. These ranged from the building of an Art Gallery 'in the form of a Gothic Cross' to the establishment of a club for young men with 'a first class Restaurant, to be conducted strictly on temperance lines' or a statue of King George V surrounded by four figures representing 'Courage, Endurance, Tenacity and Sacrifice'. Perhaps the most ambitious suggestion, however, was that a replica of the Eiffel Tower should straddle the existing Honoured Dead Memorial, with lifts passing 'through the centres of pillars of the tower for elevating and convenience of visitors to refreshment rooms'.

None of these suggestions seem to have found favour with the committee. Instead, it was announced in the middle of 1920 that a more orthodox memorial would be built in the Market-square. Even this uninspired scheme ran into trouble and, for one reason or another, the building of the memorial was delayed for several years. Not until July 1928 was a conventional stone cenotaph unveiled, by Colonel T. Ormiston, D.S.O., M.C., in the Dutoitspan Road.

But Kimberley had more to worry about in the post-war years than the building of a memorial. The diamond industry was again feeling the pinch of international upheavals. Although the Kimberley Mine had ceased operations at the beginning of the war, the other mines were reopened in 1919; but production was erratic and uncertain. There were many reasons for this.

Kimberley's pre-eminence as the diamond-producing centre in South Africa had been severely shaken before the outbreak of the war by the discovery of vast diamond deposits in South West Africa. The immediate result of these discoveries had been the establishment in Berlin of the 'Diamond Régie of South West Africa', which sought to monopolise the output from these new alluvial fields. At first De Beers had been inclined to scoff at their new rivals. They thought that, as had so often happened, the South West African finds would soon peter out and that, in any case, the smallness of the stones found there minimised the threat to their own output. But they were wrong. The new fields covered a wide area and proved very rich indeed. Moreover, the monopoly of the Diamond Régie in Berlin menaced the control exercised on the market by the Diamond Syndicate in London. The fear that deadly competition would ruin the industry again loomed large. The hard-fought amalgamation of the Kimberley mines appeared to have been brought to nothing.

For the next few years, the rivalry between the Berlin Régie - selling its stones through a syndicate in Antwerp - and the London Syndicate became a matter of extreme importance to the industry as a whole. The German government had soon recognised the need to limit the output of diamonds and, in 1913, fixed production at an all-over figure of £1 million carats. A further climax had been reached the following year when the London Syndicate put in a tender for £1 half million carats of the Régie's diamonds, in an attempt to outbid the syndicate at Antwerp. For De Beers this had proved a serious setback. The Diamond Syndicate was their only marketing outlet; if it now bought diamonds from their rivals, their own position would be gravely undermined.

A solution to the *impasse* had come not from the diamond fields but from the battle fields. When South Africa took over German South West Africa during the war, it was arranged for the diamond output to be channelled through the London Syndicate on a profit-sharing basis until the war was over. This arrangement continued after the war. Under the peace terms South Africa had been given control of the former German Colony as a Mandated Territory and, in 1919, a five-year agreement was signed between the main diamond producers of the Union of South Africa and the Administrator of South West Africa. The Berlin Régie had been eliminated by the war, and the London Syndicate again had a free hand.

The happenings in South West Africa had not escaped the notice of Ernest Oppenheimer, who, after leaving Kimberley, had eventually settled in Johannesburg. Helped by American backing, he had taken over large German and other interest on the goldfields and, in May 1917, established the soon-to-be-powerful Anglo American Corporation. Ever interested in the diamond industry, he now – backed by the American banker, J.P. Morgan – worked through the Anglo American Corporation to bring about an amalgamation of the diamond producers of South West Africa. This he more or less achieved with the establishment, in 1920, of the Consolidated Diamond Mines of South West Africa Limited. Amalgamation had always been the key to success as a diamond magnate and Oppenheimer's breakthrough in South West Africa ensured his eventual dominance of the industry. His position was further enhanced when, in recognition of his war work (particularly for raising the 2nd Brigade of the Kimberley Regiment), he was knighted by King George V.

These developments had, however, proved cold comfort for Kimberley. The regulating of the diamond industry had resulted in the output of the Kimberley mines being severely reduced. Hard-headed economics simply did not permit the flooding of the market with stones from South West Africa and Griqualand West. Nor was the position helped when, after the war, the new Russian Government began to throw large quantities of diamonds – jewellery taken from Russian aristocrats during the revolution – onto the already precarious market. It only needed a world financial depression in 1920 for Kimberley's economy to be again disrupted. Work on the recently opened mines was immediately curtailed and in 1921 De Beers was forced to stand off thousands of its employees. Among the white workers alone the employment figures dropped from 3,020 to 1,865.

It was obvious to everyone that, if it was to survive, Kimberley could no longer rely solely on its diamond mines. Alternative industries of some sort were needed to buttress the city at times of financial depression. The question was: how and by whom could such industries be established? It was the old, all-

Kimberley and Alexandersfontein tramway termini in front of the City Hall.
View taken from the top of the new Post Office in the late 1920s. (S.A. Railways
and Harbours) (K)

Stockdale Street looking from New Main Street intersection towards Cheapside
in the late 1920s. (S.A. Railways and Harbours) (K)

Jones Street, about 1937, looking past Dutoitspan Road intersection towards the
Plaza Cinema on Market-square. (K)

too-familiar problem. Kimberley had faced it, in one form or another, for many years. No solution had ever presented itself, despite endless discussion. One of the troubles was, of course, that the city had become a victim of its unnatural history: diamonds had made Kimberley and, without the diamond industry, Kimberley appeared to have no *raison d' être*. The future, as well as the past, seemed to be rooted in the mines. Arguments about the city's prospects tended to go round in circles.

But not all the talk was sterile. One proposal in particular was regarded as both feasible and promising. This was that Kimberley should become the South African Amsterdam, a diamond-cutting centre. It seemed madness that a major diamond-producing country such as South Africa should not process the stones that it mined before exporting them. If industries were needed in Kimberley, why not an industry directly connected with the diamond trade? In this way the city would be able to combine tradition with progress and retain its importance as a diamond-producing centre even after its mines were exhausted. The idea was not new, but during the 1920s it was discussed more purposefully. It was fervently championed by Councillor James Moir, Chairman of the City Council's Industries Committee, and it was largely through his efforts that the first diamond-cutting factory was established in Kimberley in August 1928. Although far from answering the city's problems, it was decidedly a step in the right direction. 'The 3rd August 1928', noted the Mayor, after laying the foundation stones of the factory, 'will always stand out as a red letter day in the history of Kimberley.'

There were other hopeful signs, not the least being the election, in December 1929, of Sir Ernest Oppenheimer as Chairman of De Beers. Oppenheimer's importance as a diamond magnate had been assured by his involvement in the South West Africa diamond fields, and this in turn had led him to renew his contacts with Kimberley. These contacts were not confined to his business interests. In 1924 he had been persuaded by General Smuts to contest the parliamentary seat for the South African Party. He had won the election with a handsome majority, and this victory had helped to restore his sorely tried affection for the diamond city. 'I thank Kimberley,' he had declared when the result was announced, 'which gave me my start in business, and which has now given me my start in political life.' Addressing his supporters later that night, he had stressed his awareness of the city's traditions. His election, he said, was 'a clarion call that will go through South Africa. It will show South Africa and the whole British Empire that we are true to Cecil Rhodes and that we stand for the British Empire. I stand for equal rights for all civilised men.' He had had little difficulty in retaining his seat in the 1928 election.

The diamond industry was still far from stable. Further diamond discoveries – first in Namaqualand, then at Lichtenburg in the Transvaal – had posed further threats to Kimberley's precarious economy. The establishment of a single diamond-cutting factory was not sufficient to offset such threats: a strong hand was needed to control the vagaries of an increasingly fickle trade. With Ernest Oppenheimer's election to the position once occupied by Cecil Rhodes there seemed a chance that a solution of some sort might be found. His

election had not been welcomed by everyone, but few doubted his determination to succeed.

Unfortunately the odds were against him. Two months before his election,
the world had been plunged into unprecedented economic disaster by the great
Wall Street crash. As was to be expected, this stock exchange calamity
completely paralysed the diamond industry. Kimberley was seized in the icy
grip of the Great Depression.

(2)

To think of Kimberley in the 1920s solely in terms of economic catastrophe
would be misleading. The uncertainty of the diamond industry undoubtedly
created many problems and threatened the long-term prosperity of the city but,
by and large, life went on much as usual. Most people were inclined to regard
the recurring setbacks as temporary - crises which could, and would, eventually be overcome. Kimberley had survived similar misfortunes in the past
and would no doubt do so again. The development of the city was slowed down
but otherwise there were few outward signs of retrogression.

The diamond city retained its importance as a tourist attraction and few
newcomers to South Africa missed the opportunity of visiting Kimberley.
Among the more important of these visitors in 1924 was the newly appointed
Governor-General, the Earl of Athlone, and his wife Princess Alice. They
arrived in September and were given a welcome reminiscent of the gala
occasions of earlier years. The highspot was a ball given in their honour by De
Beers at the Alexandersfontein Hotel. This glittering event was one of the most
spectacular ever held in the city. Dolly Pickering, one of the guests at the ball,
was to recall it vividly many years later. 'The whole place had been made to
look like fairyland,' she claimed, 'the wisteria, which was in bloom, was lighted
by mauve lights and the climbing red roses were lit with red lights. Down on the
pond the island was all lighted as was a little model ship floating on the water.
Champagne was the drink and the most perfect supper was provided by the
best chefs in town. The ballroom had huge baskets, filled with dozens and
dozens of the most beautiful gladioli, hanging from the ceiling. Men in tails and
very elegantly dressed ladies fitted perfectly into this setting.'

The following year Kimberley welcomed another royal visitor. This time it
was the dashing Prince of Wales - later King Edward VIII - who visited the
city for two days in July 1925 during his whirlwind tour of South Africa.
Despite the shortness of his visit, De Beers went to the expense of building on a
new wing to the Hotel Belgrave to accommodate the royal party. It was, all
things considered, a quixotic gesture. At that time De Beers were running both
the Hotel Belgrave and the Alexandersfontein Hotel at an enormous loss. In
1923 the debts incurred by the Alexandersfontein Hotel alone amounted to
£56,522 and pressure had been brought on De Beers to close the place down.
But the De Beers Board, conscious of the need to bolster faith in Kimberley,
had refused to abandon Alexandersfontein on the grounds that the hotel was
the most attractive spot within easy reach of the city.

Lounge and staircase of Hotel Belgrave (formerly the Sanatorium). Photograph taken in the late 1920s by Charles Leonard. (K)

Typical Sunday afternoon scene on the stoep of the Alexandersfontein Hotel in the late 1920s. Photograph by Charles Leonard. (K)

De Beers was also largely responsible for the few public building projects launched during the bleak decade. In 1926 they erected, at the cost of £12,000, a large new sports stadium close to the old De Beers Mine and donated a further £3,500 to the Kimberley Public Library for alterations to the buildings. The following year they assisted the Kimberley Athletic Club to enlarge its grounds with a grant of £2,500 and, in September 1929, agreed to advance £136,000 to the City Council for town improvements.

Gestures such as these had helped to give Kimberley a semblance of normality. No one in their right mind would have claimed that the city was thriving but on the surface, at any rate it appeared to be weathering a serious trade recession. Times were bad but they had not yet become desperate.

It was not until the calamitous depression of the 1930s had set in that the scales were tipped and Kimberley was turned into a 'ghost town'.

That fateful decade opened, portentously, with one of the worst fires in the city's history. It started late in the evening of 17 February 1930, in a small wood-and-iron shop opposite Gowies' Corner, whose owner was rumoured to be in serious financial difficulties. Whether, as many suspected, it was a case of arson is not certain but there could be no doubt about the result. A candle left burning in the closed shop sparked off a fire which soon threatened all the surrounding buildings. One of the first to burst into flames was the Theatre Royal, some fifty yards away. Despite the valiant efforts of the fire brigade hampered, as always, by inadequate equipment the theatre was completely gutted; as were some other buildings, including John Orr's shop. Only by training their hoses on buildings on the other side of the street were the firemen able to prevent the fire from spreading farther. As it was, the flames blazed all night, leaving one side of the Dutoitspan Road and part of Jones Street a blackened ruin.

To the superstitious the fire was indeed an omen, heralding disastrous days ahead. Although not as dramatic nor as instantaneous as the night-long fire, the depression proved even more ruinous. There was hardly a business in Kimberley that was not badly hit. Tradesmen and merchants suffered alongside the beleaguered diamond industry; the unemployment figures reached new heights. Those who had placed their hopes in auxiliary industries were quickly disillusioned. By 1931 the much-vaunted diamond-cutting factory had ceased operations and, despite attempts to reopen it, the company went into liquidation two years later. Even the morale-boosting props provided by De Beers could no longer be maintained. At the beginning of 1933 the Belgrave Hotel was, at Sir Ernest Oppenheimer's instigation, handed over to the nuns of the Holy Family for educational purposes.

Limited as it had been, all work in the mines came to a halt. There was another mass exodus from the city, a further decline in population. Kimberley streets were silent and deserted. During the early 1930s, it was said, a man could place a deck-chair in the middle of Dutoitspan Road and sit there undisturbed all morning. 'Have had during the year', noted the despairing Mayor in 1933, 'to watch the worst economic condition of our City go from bad to worse.'

Dan Jacobson, the novelist, whose family arrived in Kimberley during these bleak years was never to forget the impression of utter desolation that the city made on him as a child. Forlorn and forsaken, it was a place where 'Everything glared: the sky, the iron roofs, the sand on which the town sprawled.' He found it difficult to reconcile the legends of Kimberley's hectic past with this sad and ghost-like city. Had men once arrived there filled with hope and ambition? Were fortunes made in those huge, silent holes? Had the streets once been crowded, the bars packed? What possible connection was there between these assertive buildings and pompous monuments and the emptiness of the earth and sky about them? 'It was impossible', he writes, 'to avoid developing a sense of the tenuousness of the human settlement around me, of its dislocation, of the fortuitousness of its birth, early growth and sudden decline.'

Efforts were being made to arrest the decline. All the old stop-gap remedies of the past were being employed. In 1932 the City Council received a substantial loan from the South African Government – De Beers agreeing to pay the interest over the next ten years – and embarked on a programme of relief work. By the end of that year it was estimated that some £240 a month was being spent on rations and blankets for the destitute, apart from the wages paid to casual labourers. But it was not enough and, to help meet the growing expenses, deductions were made on a sliding scale from the wages of regular municipal employees. Even so the exodus from Kimberley continued: white mechanics left for the Rand, black labourers tried to find work on outlying farms.

The relief work, inadequate as it was, did some good. Kimberley, in the midst of the depression, was given a face lift. 'The remark is often made,' wrote the Mayor in 1934, 'and indeed with justification, that Kimberley owes its good roads and many other definite improvements to its periodical periods of misfortune when work has to be provided for those unfortunately thrown out of work. Whether this is the whole reason or not our main arterial roads and streets are now as good as will be found anywhere in South Africa.'

Kimberley's fortunes had indeed been reversed. Once notorious for its riches and rough roads, it could now, in its poverty, take pride in its pavements.

(3)

The old-timers were thinning out: there were not many left now who remembered Kimberley as a mining camp. Young men who had arrived hopeful and healthy at New Rush and Dutoitspan were – those who had survived – in their eighties by the 1930s. They grew fewer by the year.

Nor was it time alone that accounted for the gaps in the ranks of the early pioneers. Fortune, or the lack of it, had played a significant part. Those diggers who had been lucky enough to strike it rich in the early days had long since swapped the heat, the dust and the droughts of Griqualand West for the comforts and sea breezes of the coastal towns. Some of the very wealthy – the diamond millionaires – had retired to end their days in luxury in London, Paris and Berlin: Kimberley's *nouveaux riches* had become a recognised, if not always acceptable, element of international society. There were others, of course, who had turned from diamonds to gold and had gone on to enlarge their fortunes on the Witwatersrand. Johannesburg had also claimed a large majority of the less fortunate – those who had trekked to the goldfields during the periodic slumps. For whatever reason they left, only a handful had returned. Kimberley had proved an uncertain haven for the elderly.

Nevertheless, there were a few stalwarts who had remained loyal. They may have wavered at times, they may not have been exceptionally optimistic or hardy, but their love for Kimberley had overcome all. One such devotee was David Harris, the cousin of Barney and Harry Barnato. He had arrived at Dutoitspan, aged 19, in 1871 with only a few pounds in his pocket. His early career had been erratic but he had survived to become rich and respected. In time he had been made a director of De Beers, a Lieutenant-Colonel of the Griqualand West Brigade and had succeeded Rhodes as Honorary Colonel of the Kimberley Regiment. For thirty-two years, he had represented first Kimberley and then Beaconsfield in the Cape Parliament. His was a Kimberley success story which was climaxed in 1911 when he was knighted and became Sir David Harris, K.C.M.G. What many an ambitious digger had dreamed about, he had achieved; he was only too aware of the debt he owed to the people of Kimberley. 'I can never adequately repay them', he wrote, 'for their confidence and consideration. They have showered honours on me greater than I deserve. . . . I have frequently refused to accept many tempting offers to settle down in England, preferring to remain in Kimberley, where I am happy and contented, and among whose good people I hope to end my days.' His wish was granted. He died in Kimberley, aged ninety, on 23 September 1942. His services to the city are acknowledged by a small bust erected in his honour, close to the Drill Hall.

Not every pioneer was as fortunate. Loyalty and hard work were not always so handsomely rewarded. There were some, however, who had managed to carve a niche for themselves and so gained local recognition. An outstanding example of these lesser-known pioneers was George Beet, who died in October 1935.

Although George Beet never acquired a knighthood, he had by the time of his death earned the unofficial title of Kimberley's 'Grand Old Man'. For many he epitomised the eccentricities and the virtues of the city's turbulent past. This was not so much for what he had done as for what he had observed; his popularity was derived largely from his dedication in recording the city's history. He had lived through it all.

There were few important events that George Beet had not witnessed since his arrival on the diamond fields, aged nineteen, in 1872. Early in his career he had joined the staff of the *Diamond News* and was working on the newspaper at the time of the Black Flag Rebellion. Later he had emerged as a champion of the rebellious diggers during the Great Strike and, for a while, had acted as a stockbroker. In 1889 he had joined the trek to the Witwatersrand but, having no luck, had eventually returned to Kimberley. It was not a remarkable career but in many ways his experiences mirrored the vicissitudes of life on the diamond fields. They had provided him with ample material for the books and articles he wrote on early Kimberley. His output was enormous and his writings, both published and unpublished, reflect a deeply felt love of the city. If he tended to rely a little too heavily on memory and lack the discipline of a professional historian, this was more than made up for by his unbounded enthusiasm. He did much to make a later generation of Kimberleyites aware of their far from ordinary heritage.

Greybearded George Beet, wearing his old-fashioned high-crowned hat, was a familiar figure in Kimberley during the last years of his life. A devout Catholic, he was to be seen at daily Mass, which he boasted he had not missed attending in over fifty years. But he was no prude and had known most of the outstanding figures who had contributed to Kimberley's history – from Cecil Rhodes to the fiery Dan O'Leary. His anecdotes recalled the profligate as well as the pious and reflected the strange mixture of recklessness and respectability that distinguished Kimberley from other mining towns. It seemed only fitting that, on the day of his funeral, flags flew at half-mast as a tribute 'to one who was not only a personage but a personality'.

But all was not death and decay. Already, by the 1930s, Kimberley was undergoing a subtle change. New personalities were making their mark. It was a slow, almost incidental process which had nothing to do with the prevailing economic problems, but – quite unintentionally – it was to play an important part in the city's development. After years of bemoaning their isolation, the people of Kimberley were beginning to give closer attention to the wilderness by which they were surrounded. They discovered, somewhat to their surprise, that it was rich in more than diamonds. For the botanist, the geologist, and the archaeologist it proved to be a region of endless fascination.

Largely responsible for these new developments was the energetic curator of the McGregor museum – Maria Wilman.

Maria Wilman was by any standards an exceptional woman. Born at Beaufort West in the heart of the Karoo, she was a true South African – her father was English, her mother Afrikaans – and she had a deep love of the land. She also had a passion for learning. At the age of eighteen, after attending the Good Hope Seminary in Cape Town, she embarked on a course of scientific studies at Newnham College, Cambridge. Her choice of subject was a mark of her independence. For a young Victorian woman to enter university life was remarkable enough; to have opted to take a science tripos in geology, mineralogy and chemistry was little short of extraordinary. So much so that her sex prevented her from qualifying for a degree and, on completing her studies, she was merely awarded a certificate. It was not until November 1931 that a Master of Arts degree was belatedly conferred upon her. Infuriating as this must have been, it did not prevent her from taking a second course at Cambridge, this time with botany as her chief study. Armed with her certificates, she returned to South Africa, determined to put her training to good use.

It was not easy. Scientific posts were at that time almost as difficult for women to obtain as were university degrees. For the next few years she was

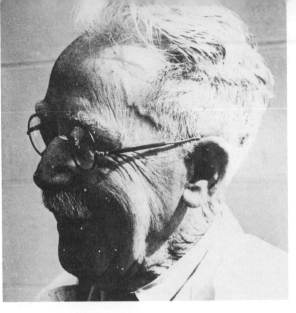

Kimberley's 'Grand Old Man', a cartoon of George Beet, historian of the diamond fields, by 'Bart', from the *Diamond Fields Advertiser*, 30 May 1923. (K)

Alfred Martin Duggan-Cronin, pioneer photographer and fervent champion of African culture, whose remarkable collection is housed in the Duggan-Cronin Bantu Gallery, formerly 'The Lodge', Kimberley. (K)

Miss Maria Wilman (driving) setting out on a research trip in her 'uncertain little Austin. The car was given to her by Mrs Margaret McGregor. (M)

obliged to work at the South African Museum in Cape Town on a voluntary basis. Not that this bothered her unduly. She was happy in her work and learnt much from the celebrated Dr G.S. Corstorphine, who was then conducting a geological survey of the Cape of Good Hope. But it was not until 1908 when, aged forty-one, she was appointed the first Director of the Alexander McGregor Museum that her exceptional talents were fully realised.

She faced a gigantic task. The McGregor Museum, for all the generosity of its founder, was inadequately equipped and sparsely stocked. It is said that, when Maria Wilman took over, a meagre range of exhibit cases contained 'not more than a dozen specimens'. To remedy this became her first concern.

She set about scouring Griqualand West for rock and mineral samples, for prehistoric relics, artefacts and tools. She roped everyone into the search: farmers, labourers, government officials, land surveyors and prospectors. Diggers, scratching out a living along the banks of the Vaal, were 'taught by her to recognise, and preserve for the Museum, bones and tools from the gravel terraces and beds' of the river. Her quest was as far-ranging as it was tireless. It uncovered buried remains and neglected curiosities; it awakened new interests. She became captivated by Bushman culture and was soon writing learned articles on rock paintings and engravings for scientific journals. She befriended Dorothea Bleek, the celebrated lexicographer and authority on Bushman languages, and accompanied her on her research expeditions. There was not an aspect of Griqualand West and its peoples that did not come under the scrutiny of Maria Wilman. 'That she managed', says a friend, 'to keep so many irons in the fire, and all aglow, remains a marvel.'

But perhaps her greatest love was botany. On her many research trips she collected specimens of the local flora and eventually compiled an invaluable list of the grasses and plants of the region. The rock garden she planted along one boundary of the Public Gardens – it stretched 1,330 feet – was said to contain more than 200 varieties of grass as well as succulents, shrubs and flowering plants. This rock garden was both her pride and her hobby. She worked on it two afternoons a week, but this afternoon work often continued well into the evening. Once she had a trowel in her hands she became oblivious of time 'and of the chauffeur-assistant, anxious to get her safely home and on pins and needles lest the uncertain little Austin, getting colder and colder, should refuse to start'. She lived in fear that, when her back was turned, some over-diligent municipal gardener would clear away some of her rare 'weeds'. The garden soon developed into one of Kimberley's unexpected sights.

Kimberley benefited in other ways from Maria Wilman's love of the land. She it was who introduced the handsome mesquite tree to the city (and to South Africa) and made the drought-resisting Australian kurrajong a feature of Kimberley streets, replacing the straggling pepper trees. Her knowledge of grass-seed enabled her to play an important part in improving the pasturage of the surrounding district and won her international acclaim. 'Our grasses', she could claim, 'have gone to Mexico, then South America and St Helena – in fact they are putting a girdle round the earth.' Her pioneer work was, in time, to change the face of Kimberley. It transformed the dust-blown desert city into an attractive, lushly green oasis.

Maria Wilman, an eminently practical and quietly spoken woman, could be formidable in her enthusiasms. She did not suffer fools gladly and never hesitated to say so. Some people found her quite frightening. But her sharp tongue and caustic observations were deceptive; to those she admired she was not only a generous friend but a source of inspiration. No one was more aware of this than Alfred Duggan-Cronin, another of Kimberley's latter-day personalities. It was Maria Wilman who was largely responsible for launching Duggan-Cronin on his remarkable career.

Alfred Martin Duggan-Cronin was a sandy-haired Irishman who had first arrived in Kimberley in 1897. A gentle, professorial-looking man, with the eyes of a visionary, he seemed ill-suited to the rough and tumble of a mining town. He looked in fact not unlike the priest that, as a youngster, he had intended to become. He was in his early twenties when he decided that he had no vocation for the priesthood and, for some unknown reason, decided to emigrate to South Africa and work for De Beers. Strange as his choice of a new career appears, it proved to be both opportune and decisive. In Kimberley he discovered an alternative vocation, a vocation which had nothing to do with religion and was only incidentally connected with mining. Fresh from Ireland, he became an inspired recorder of African tribal life.

How and when he became interested in photography is not certain. Different people were to tell different stories. The most popular version has it that, on a return visit to England in 1904, he bought a cheap box-camera and took his first snap – of a duck pond – in Madeira. However that may be, there can be no doubt about the outcome. He was employed as a guard in the De Beers compounds and, with little to amuse him, began to photograph his surroundings. Inevitably the mine workers featured prominently. Coming as they did from various tribes – each with its own customs, dress, weapons and peculiarities – these migrant labourers fascinated Duggan-Cronin. There was nothing condescending about his photographs; they reflected a deep and passionate interest in African culture.

What started as a hobby quickly developed into a mission. He became obsessed with the necessity to record every aspect of tribal life before it was destroyed by an alien civilisation. A later generation might have called his interest paternalistic, but that was not how he saw it. 'In order', he was to say, 'fully to understand the Natives among whom we work and live, it is necessary to know what they have been and done and suffered.' This was his credo. It took him beyond the confines of the compounds to the nearby kraals and villages. His photographic collection grew both in size and purpose.

But it was not until after the First World War – when he returned from serving in South West and East Africa – that his work became widely appreciated. That it blossomed was, in no small measure, due to the influence of Maria Wilman. She it was who persuaded – some would say bullied him to travel farther afield, to photograph the Bushmen of the Langebergen in Griqualand West. It was good advice. So successful was this Bushman venture that, in June 1919, the Union Research Grant Board showed interest in his activities and agreed to finance his photographic expedition among the Bechuana tribes. In this way his life's interest was decided. During the next twenty-five years he was to photograph every major tribe in Southern Africa and build up a unique record of vanishing African customs.

The first display of his work was held at the Wembley Exhibition in London in 1924. A year later he established a permanent exhibition of his photographs in a mine manager's house at Kamferdam, a few miles outside Kimberley. This aroused such interest that an offer from Bloemfontein to buy the collection at last awakened Kimberley to its worth. Duggan-Cronin was persuaded to decline the Bloemfontein offer and present his pictures to Kimberley. He did so on the condition that the photographs were suitably housed. Once again it was De Beers who provided the necessary building. They offered to display the Duggan-Cronin collection in J.B. Currey's old house, 'The Lodge'. Since Currey's departure this house had been the home of William Pickering's family and, as Pickering was a Director of De Beers, it had become a recognised social centre in the city. Many an old Kimberley citizen was to remember with affection the parties and receptions held there. After Pickering's death, in 1933, De Beers had used 'The Lodge' as a guest house and were now able to convert it into the famous Duggan-Cronin Bantu Gallery. In its new role it was to become one of the outstanding attractions of Kimberley.

Duggan-Cronin's work took him all over Africa. It demanded tremendous energy, patience and dedication. 'Once,' he told a friend, 'I had to travel over 600 miles up the Zambesi River, and some of my photos of the strange and mystic rites during initiation have been taken in enclosures where few white men have ever set foot. I have often been asked how I get my studies. Well, really, I do not know, unless perhaps it is by kindness of manner. To the Natives in the mine compounds I was known as the Englishman; while the Matabele gave me the name of Tana Bantu (Friend of Natives).'

No doubt his sympathy and tact ensured his success but, as he would have been the first to admit, he was helped in other ways. Not the least of his many assets was his African assistant, Richard Madela. This remarkable Fingo had been employed by Duggan-Cronin in 1929 when he was a mere schoolboy. He was hired originally as an odd-job boy but his talents as a linguist and diplomat were such that he became an invaluable friend, if not partner, of his devoted employer. Duggan-Cronin, who, despite his dedication, was unable to speak an African language, relied on Richard Madela to smooth his way with suspicious tribesmen. It was Richard who overcame the Africans' fear of the camera, who bribed rapacious chiefs and, when necessary, took photographs that a white man could not obtain. 'It is just as well you do not understand what the Natives are saying,' he once told Duggan-Cronin, 'for they say some funny things about you.' Their unusual, mutually protective relationship lasted for over twenty years.

The Duggan-Cronin Bantu Gallery was opened in 1937. That same year work was resumed in the Bultfontein and Wesselton mines; small-scale operations had commenced at Dutoitspan in the previous March. Despite rumours of another trade recession, there were definite signs that the crippling depression years were coming to an end. But, as had happened so often before, hope was tempered by doubt. Economic recovery could only be achieved in a stable world and the world was far from stable. There was little chance of a watery financial sun penetrating the gathering clouds of war.

(4)

At the outbreak of the Second World War the young men of Kimberley were quick to volunteer for service. By October 1939 the Kimberley Regiment was 900 strong. After a period of training, the volunteers were mobilised for garrison duty throughout the country. Later, after the formation of the 6th South African Division, they were sent to Egypt and amalgamated with the Imperial Light Horse. The combined battalion, under the command of Lieutenant-Colonel R. Reeves Moore, was to distinguish itself in the hard-fought Italian campaign. The Kimberley Regiment, it is said, almost invariably led the South African Division during the campaign 'and saw more action – and suffered more casualties – than any other unit in the Division'. In this, the third major war in which Kimberley men had served, the city had every reason to be proud of its military traditions.

Nor was Kimberley's wartime involvement confined to these achievements of the Kimberley Regiment. As the men of 21 Air School, the No.2 Air Recruiting Depot, and the Cape Corps were all trained in Kimberley, there was a hive of military activity.

But the war left Kimberley's economy in a shocking state. Having staggered through the declining years of the 1930s, it had reached a point of near collapse. Hopes of recovery were completely shattered by the outbreak of war and its inevitable effects on the diamond industry. The future seemed bleak indeed. Kimberley, quipped a cynical visitor, was rapidly becoming a city of 'Death, dumps and decay'.

The remark was hardly original. It had been said, in a variety of ways, time and time again. Every international crisis seemed to herald the eclipse of Kimberley, every depression had produced its prophets of doom. The situation was, for many, only too familiar. What could anybody do about it? Had it not been discussed, debated and argued about *ad nauseam?* What had been the result? With each new crisis the population of Kimberley had dwindled. It would keep on dwindling until the place became a backwater. This had to be accepted. There could be no solution to the insoluble problem. Kimberley, built as it was on faulty foundations, was bound to crumble.

Such counsels of despair were all too common in Kimberley during the early years of the war. Any attempt to counter them was dismissed as futile. Yet there remained a few optimists who refused to succumb to the prevailing pessimism. Despite all the mistakes of the past, they believed that it was still possible to cast Kimberley in a new role. What was needed, they argued, was less talk and more action. War or no war, a start had to be made.

The move to halt the erosion of Kimberley started, it is claimed, with a casual conversation. Seated in a car parked outside the City Hall on a rainy night in 1941, two men – Graham S. Eden, a Kimberley businessman and future

Mayor, and H.A. Morris, the City Electrical Engineer – discussed the future. They were anxious to find a solution to Kimberley's long-standing problems. Graham Eden came up with a plan. In essence it was simplicity itself. 'The town was in a bad way,' Eden said later. 'I was convinced Kimberley had to be the "big brother" to all farming interests and local authorities in the region. In other words, from being only a diamond city, Kimberley must be transformed into a regional capital. 'The problem', said Eden, 'was how to do it.' It was a problem which Morris was more than willing to help him tackle.

The two of them decided to consult the Mayor, Russell Elliott, to see what could be done. In Elliott they found an invaluable ally. Not only did he welcome their plan but agreed to place it before the City Council. In his opinion it was first necessary, if Kimberley was to assume a new status, to improve the look of the city. Shortage of money, apathy, and an inflexible resistance to any increase in rates had in recent years resulted in an alarming decline in public facilities. The roads had again fallen into disrepair and there was an absence of many basic civic amenities. Kimberley was beginning to look like the defunct town that many predicted it would become. To remedy this became the immediate concern of Russell Elliott and his supporters. They set about reforming the various municipal departments, and the 'town improvement' programme became top priority at the monthly meetings of the City Council.

Overcoming widespread scepticism and opposition was a lengthy business. It took tremendous patience, as well as organisation, to win public support for what appeared to be yet another ill-conceived 'rescue' operation. But the long struggle was to prove worth-while. 'Municipal officials', says Russell Elliott, 'were so used to cheeseparing that they found it difficult at first to adapt themselves to the new outlook but when they did the progress was phenomenal. Somehow the public came to accept the necessity for increasing rates if the town was to progress. . . . As a result the City Council in the year 1944, with the approval of the current ratepayers, authorised more capital expenditure than had been authorised in the previous twelve years combined. In 1945 a similar amount was authorised. Much of this expenditure was required to rectify existing deficiencies and lay foundations for future development. Foundations are not conspicuous at the time but are essential. Much of the progress that took place in subsequent years was based on these foundations.'

One of the immediate results of the improvement scheme was the clearance of the Malay Camp. This sprawling, overcrowded settlement – which had existed since the earliest camp days – had long been a source of shame to Kimberley. Its vulnerability to disease had been only too apparent during the various epidemics that had plagued the town and, not without reason, it was generally considered to be 'one of the worst slums in South Africa'. In 1939, De Beers, who had owned the site of the camp, had transferred their freehold rights to the City Council on condition that the land be cleared and all leases terminated within ten years. Now, four years later, the slum clearance began. It was planned to use the vacant land as the site for an imposing civic centre.

Graham Eden had, by this time, become Mayor. He made the slum clearance project his own. It was no easy undertaking. Squalid as it was, the Malay Camp was the home of a large section of the coloured community and, despite promises of compensation, there was active opposition to the scheme. This was only to be expected. Slum clearances are rarely effected without heartbreak: uprooting people, individuals or families, invariably causes distress. It was largely due to the energy and tact of Graham Eden – he was later to represent the coloured community in Parliament – that the many obstacles faced by the City Council were successfully, if slowly, overcome. Work on the new civic centre went ahead: gardens were laid out, buildings and roads were planned. A new Kimberley was coming into being.

For, valuable as they were, the civic improvements merely reflected the outward signs of revival. They were incidental to the all-over plan envisaged by the Kimberley reformers. The essence of this plan was that Kimberley should not depend exclusively on the diamond industry but realise its potential as the centre of a large and far from unproductive region. This had been the main concern of the originators of the scheme. To awaken interest in the region had called for extensive planning.

It was H.A. Morris who first thought of naming the region the Northern Cape. His initiative led to the formation of the Northern Cape and Adjoining Areas Regional Development Association. The Association was headed by Russell Elliott, assisted by Graham Eden, and H.A. Morris served as secretary; its purpose was to promote the widely defined territory as an entity.

In a pamphlet issued in June 1943, Morris had set out the Association's aims. He pointed out that Griqualand West, dependent on the diamond industry, had 'never had a soul of its own'. Prior to the Union of South Africa in 1910, the Northern Cape – 'this large territory from the Orange River right up to Mafeking' – was part of the Cape Colony; since Union it had been part of the Cape Province. Theoretically it was administered from Cape Town, some 700 miles away, but 'in practice, mostly from Bloemfontein in another province'. The region had a right to more autonomy. In size it was larger than the Orange Free State or Natal. There were some 365,000 people living between the Orange and Molopo rivers. It was rich ranching country and had already proved its worth in beef exports and dairy produce. Irrigation schemes had already been started and, if extended, would revitalise farming: the region was intersected by the Vaal, the Orange, the Riet, the Modder and the Harts rivers – there was no shortage of water. Mineral deposits in the Northern Cape – iron, manganese and lime – had scarcely been tapped. There was plenty of scope for development. With Kimberley as its 'capital' the region would forge ahead.

A thousand copies of this pamphlet were circulated throughout the Northern Cape. The response to it was remarkable. 'Practically every public body', says Russell Elliott, 'in that portion of the Cape Province north of the Orange River and in the adjoining areas of the Free State joined the Association and the volume of work was so great that it had to be divided amongst four sub-committees. . . . As a result the whole atmosphere of the region altered from one of beggardom to one of self-respect and constructive endeavour.' Gone were the local jealousies which had plagued the region in the past; in their place grew a sense of unity and purpose which could not be

ignored. State authorities began to take notice and offer assistance.
Conferences were held and the objectives of the Association – road and rail
development, the utilisation of water from the Vaal and Orange rivers, the
harnessing of mining resources and the decentralisation of industry – became
matters of national concern. Kimberley took on a new and vigorous lease of
life. *The impossible had happened.

It did not, of course, happen at once. There were the inevitable delays,
setbacks and disappointments. But, slow as it was, the progress of the Northern
Cape over the next two decades was impressive. By the end of the 1960s
Kimberley, as the central point of the developing region, had been
transformed.

Perhaps the most noticeable advance was that made by the railway system in
the Northern Cape. It is estimated that some £90,000,000,00 was spent in
capital rail improvements alone. These included the electrification of the lines
from Kimberley to Klerksdorp and Kamferdam to Hotazel and the doubling of
lines from Fourteen Streams to Kimberley and on to De Aar. A new
marshalling-yard and welding-depot was established at Beaconsfield, and an
impressive railway administration building rose outside the Kimberley station.
A large proportion of the 6,000 whites and 6,000 other races employed by the
Northern Cape railway system were resident in Kimberley. In the same period
over 700 miles of road were tarred in the region at a cost of R23,75 million and
R745,000 was paid in road subsidies by the Kimberley City Council. In 1950
Escom took over De Beers Central Power and inaugurated the Cape Northern
Undertaking 'to give a bulk supply of electricity to both De Beers and the
Kimberley City Council and develop the whole Northern Cape electrically'.
Between 1960 and 1969 the total population of the Kimberley Magisterial
District rose from 86,295 to 125,200 and property values soared (in 1942 the
municipal value of buildings in Kimberley was R6,5 million; twenty-five years
later they were valued at R75 million).

The increase in population proved a boon to local agriculture and ensured
Kimberley's importance as a commercial and supply centre for the region.
While the hopes of establishing auxiliary industries were never fully realised,
the existence of a large clothing factory, a major brickfield, various engineering works and nearby iron ore, manganese and asbestos mines, has absorbed
much of Kimberley's labour force.

Yet, extraordinary as its development has been, Kimberley has retained its
position as the hub of the South African diamond industry. That it has done so,
despite the slowing down of work in its famous mines, is due to the resolute
policy of De Beers Consolidated Mines. Both Sir Ernest Oppenheimer and
later his son Harry Oppenheimer have seen to it that the city which gave birth
to the first of South Africa's major industries continues to act as the centre of
that industry. Progress has been welded to tradition.

As a young man Harry Oppenheimer served his apprenticeship in the
diamond trade at Kimberley. After coming down from Oxford he spent a year
in the city learning to sort diamonds. Although he never developed his father's
aesthetic passion and connoisseur's knowledge of the precious stones, his

experience at the sorting-tables proved invaluable. It helped to bias him in favour of the diamond industry. Once, when asked if he had a preference between gold and diamonds, he did not hesitate to reply. 'Diamonds every time,' he said. 'I think people buy diamonds out of vanity and they buy gold because they're too stupid to think of any other monetary system which will work – and I think vanity is probably a more attractive motive than stupidity.' To such reasoning Kimberley owed its existence.

For many years, however, Kimberley played only an incidental part in Harry Oppenheimer's life. He had left the city of his birth at the age of six and spent his youth in Johannesburg and England. His year in Kimberley as a diamond sorter was merely an enjoyable interlude in his active career. On leaving the city he had returned to Johannesburg and started work with the Anglo American Corporation. The war years saw him fighting in North Africa. Not until 1948, when at the age of forty he decided to enter politics, did he become more involved with Kimberley. Then he was elected as the city's Member of Parliament. He stood as a candidate for General Smuts's United Party against two Independents – one being Fred Hicks, the councillor who had opposed his father as Mayor – and won the election handsomely. He was to act as the city's representative for the next ten years.

But it was probably on becoming chairman of De Beers, after his father's death in 1957, that his association with Kimberley deepened. He had bought a farm, Mauritzfontein, outside the city – where he kept first polo ponies, then horses – and this now became a regular retreat.

'I always take the opportunity to stay at my farm,' he told a journalist. 'I love the Karoo-like country, particularly in the mornings and evenings. My farm faces east and I like to look out at the distant hills across the Free State. I am trying to preserve game there.' Familiarity bred affection: Harry Oppenheimer became a fervent champion of Kimberley.

The Dutoitspan, Bultfontein and Wesselton mines continued to operate and, in 1963, De Beers Mine – which had been closed since 1908 – was reopened. In the early 1960s a new mine was discovered by Allister Fincham, when he was searching for asbestos, near Lime Acres in the Kimberley district. This mine, the Finsch, was eventually acquired by De Beers – Fincham being paid R2,400,000 – and so increased the company's output of local diamonds.

But it is not for production alone that Kimberley remains an important diamond centre. The city is, of course, the headquarters of De Beers and as such handles the company's entire South African output. 'Kimberley', declared Harry Oppenheimer, 'is the only real diamond town in the world, in the sense that it produces diamonds as well as handles them. No other diamond mine anywhere has a big place like Kimberley to go with it. . . . The city will continue to be the centre to which all diamonds in this part of the world are taken for sorting and evaluation.' His faith in Kimberley has been emphasised by the erection, in the centre of the city, of an impressive new diamond-sorting building bearing his name.

Perhaps it was, however, a casual remark made by Harry Oppenheimer in 1973 that best illustrates Kimberley's change of role and fortune. He was about to be made a Freeman of Kimberley and was asked whether there was a possibility of new diamond mines being discovered.

'Oh, it could happen, you know,' he replied. 'But remember that while South Africa has many kimberlite pipes only a few are payable. . . . If it did happen, it would be quite something for Kimberley.' The spectres of the past have vanished.

(5)

Side by side with the economic revival, there continued Kimberley's social, cultural and architectural development.

The post-war era opened with a royal fanfare. In 1947 the British Sovereign, King George VI, with Queen Elizabeth and their daughters, Princess Elizabeth and Princess Margaret, toured South Africa. The Royal Family spent only one day, 18 April, in Kimberley, but it was a crowded, exciting, memorable day. There was a reception in the gardens of the Duggan-Cronin Gallery, a luncheon at the Kimberley Club, a parade of ex-servicemen and a rally of schoolchildren. Sir Ernest Oppenheimer showed the royal visitors over the De Beers buildings and the Big Hole, and his grand-daughter, Harry's little daughter, Mary Oppenheimer, presented each of the princesses with a magnificent diamond.

Another distinquished visitor was the Governor-General of South Africa, Dr E.G. Jansen, who opened a new theatre on 28 November 1953. This well-appointed building was attached to the new Northern Cape Technical College, which had itself been opened the year before by the Minister of Education, Arts and Science, Mr. J.H. Viljoen. The Technical College, together with the famous and unique Elizabeth Conradie School for physically handicapped children, boosted Kimberley's reputation as one of South Africa's leading educational centres.

Standing beside the Northern Cape Technical College, and opened in the same year, 1952, by Harry Oppenheimer, was the William Humphreys Art Gallery. Here was a cultural acquisition indeed. Kimberley's William Benbow Humphreys had been an enthusiastic collector of paintings, furniture and objets d'art all his life and he now had the satisfaction of seeing his valuable collection properly housed. Some twelve years after the opening of the gallery, a new wing was added, so enhancing the gallery's reputation as one of the liveliest and most progressive in the country. Another name closely linked with the city's artistic life is that of one of her best-known artists, William M. Timlin.

Basil Humphreys, son of William Benbow Humphreys, also played an outstanding role in Kimberley's cultural development. Not only was he chairman of the gallery but he was largely responsible for the arrangement of the superb museum established by De Beers at the Big Hole, or Open Mine. Here, on some four acres, has been reconstructed the Kimberley of the great days of the diamond diggings. Old houses, shops, offices, halls, a pub and a church have been salvaged and re-erected on the site, so that visitors, strolling through the streets, can be transported back into the city's past. On display also

The Kimberley Mine Museum. A reconstructed street of the early days, showing the Wernher, Beit & Co.'s office, an old pub and Barney Barnato's Boxing school. Photograph by Pat Sydie in 1976. (M)

Basuto Hat Church, erected in the mid-1950s, at the De Beers Dutoitspan Hostel for African mineworkers. (K)

An aerial view of the 'Big Hole' – Kimberley Mine – in 1970. (K)

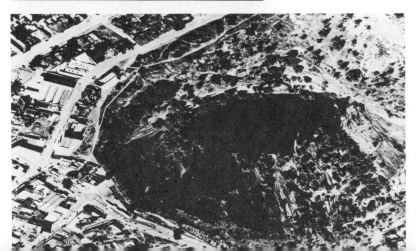

is the De Beers directors' private railway coach; part of the first 'pulsator' building; towering mine headgear; and photographic, mining and transport exhibitions. Even Gowies' Corner Building, lovingly restored, lifts its famous clock tower proudly into the sunshine once more. All in all, the Mine Museum is one of the most exciting and evocative tourist attractions in South Africa.

The McGregor Museum, too, has developed considerably. In 1955 a new building was erected in Chapel Street but even this proved inadequate. The Museum, particularly renowned for its scientific, anthropological and ecological exhibits, is now housed in the magnificently refurbished Sanatorium, or Belgrave Hotel, thus giving this grandiose old building a new lease of life. Kimberley's other renowned hotel, Alexandersfontein, has been similarly transformed: it is now part of the Danie Theron Combat School, one of South Africa's major military training centres.

These post-war years of cultural progress saw a new name – Dan Jacobson – added to the list of writers associated with Kimberley, who have made their mark in the literary world. Among them were, and are, such names as the internationally known author, Sarah Gertrude Millin; one of the first black South African novelists, Sol Plaatje; Lawrence Green, Benjamin Bennett and Gerald Gordon.

All this activity, whether cultural or economic, has meant considerable alteration to the face of the city. Inevitably much of the mining-camp atmosphere – which persisted until well after the Second World War – has been lost. And so, of course, has much of the charm. 'The town is being improved all the time,' Harry Oppenheimer once mused, 'although for me in a way that is rather sad. I suppose that it is inevitable that it must start to lose its old Wild West atmosphere with corrugated iron buildings gradually disappearing. It isn't so easy to visualise it as the place that was created out of the diamond fields.'

The cast iron, the corrugated iron, the pediments, the pillars, the pilasters, the decorative stonework, the stained-glass fanlights, the arched sash windows, the riotously ornate gables, have almost all gone. So have many of the long-established little family businesses. In their place has come the largely anonymous architecture of cities all over the world: multi-storied blocks of flats and offices, massive municipal complexes, supermarkets, filling-stations, parking-lots, mile upon mile of soulless suburban sprawl.

Admittedly, there have been improvements. There are the undoubted conveniences of highways, made-up pavements, escalators, air-conditioning. The new city is unexpectedly green. There are tree-lined streets, acres of lush lawns, superbly tended public gardens and islands of bright flowers down the centres of the more important roads. On the site of the old Malay Camp stands the great new Civic Centre; outside lies the Oppenheimer Memorial Gardens with its fountain and its bust of Sir Ernest; opposite lies the William Humphreys Art Gallery. The square outside the station boasts the vast, glitteringly white S.A.R. Administration Building; an impressive new hotel towers above Dutoitspan Road; the black and gleaming glass of the Trust Bank reflects the dramatically clouded skies; the soaring Harry Oppenheimer House adds a touch of elegance to the modern architecture.

Yet in spite of these often impressive changes, vestiges of the past remain. Nothing will ever rid Kimberley of its essential character. Its centre remains a haphazard, unplanned, confusing place. The streets remain short, narrow, set at all angles. The Big Hole – or Open Mine – still yawns in the heart of the city. All around, the blue-grey mine dumps lie like a range of miniature mountains. Nothing can alter its table-top flatness, its utter lack of topographical variety, its monotonous but strangely attractive setting: the limitless, grass-grown, camelthorn-studded veld. Nothing can change its incomparable skies.

But even among the buildings there are remnants of the past. The splendidly constructed Open Mine Museum is not the only reminder of the mining-camp days. The old Town Hall on the Market-square has been restored to its full Victorian Renaissance glory. The mellow red brick of the old De Beers building still graces Stockdale Street. The Public Library, the old McGregor Museum, the Kimberley Club, the Magistrates Court, the Sanatorium, the churches, the statues, the war memorials and many of the romantically turreted and balconied old houses still stand.

And here and there, among the impersonal blocks of flats and ubiquitous garages, one will suddenly come across a house that evokes Kimberley of a hundred years ago – a small, shabby, corrugated-iron structure, hung with creepers and set in a dusty, sun-scorched patch of earth. To look at it is to be carried back to the days when Kimberley was one of the most stimulating, most exciting and most extraordinary places on earth.

It is precisely because of this once-romantic past that Kimberley continues to intrigue and attract. More than any other city can Kimberley claim to be the womb of modern industrial South Africa. This is a fact that its civic leaders should always remember. As a modern city, Kimberley can never hope to be remarkable; only its associations with the great days of the diamond diggings make Kimberley one of South Africa's foremost tourist attractions. What remains of those once-turbulent days should be preserved, cherished and enhanced. For it is this, and only this, which makes the Diamond City unique among the cities of the world.

Bibliography

UNPUBLISHED SOURCES

Beet: The Diamond Fields Pioneer Association: History of the Diamond Fields, edited by George Beet. Kimberley Public Library.

Currey: Half a Century In South Africa, typescript of J.B. Currey's autobiography. South African Library, Cape Town.

Elliott: Typescript memorandum: The Development and Progress of Kimberley During the Last Thirty Years, by R.C. Elliott. R.C. Elliott, Kimberley.

Farrer & Mackenzie: The Good Old Days In Kimberley, typescript of a talk given to the Ladies' Section of the Kimberley Club on 2 June 1966 by Mrs C.H. Farrer (née Pickering) and Mrs P. Mackenzie (née Harris). In the possession of Mrs J. Hoare, Kimberley.

Grimmer: Notes from De Beers Consolidated Mines Annual Reports, compiled by Irvine R. Grimmer. De Beers Archives, Kimberley.

Hawthorne: Digging For Diamonds: Kimberley and Its Story, compiled (largely from contemporary newspaper accounts) by Sydney Charles James Hawthorne. Kimberley Public Library.

Mayors' Minutes: Copies of mayoral reports. Kimberley Public Library.

Michell: The Memoirs, Diaries etc of Sir Lewis Michell. Private Accession 540. Cape Archives, Cape Town.

Pickering: Letter by N.E. Pickering. In the possession of Mrs C.H. Farrer, Kimberley.

Scott: The Papers of Colonel R.G. Scott, V.C. In the possession of Mrs D. Pitchford, Grahamstown.

Southey: The Southey Papers. Private Accession 611. Cape Archives, Cape Town.

Stow: Memoir of the Formation of the De Beers Mining Company Limited, and Its Subsequent Transformation into De Beers Consolidated Mines Limited with Five Life Governors, by F. Philipson-Stow. McGregor Museum, Kimberley.

PRINTED BOOKS

Algar, F., *The Diamond Fields* (privately printed), London, 1872

Anderson, Ken, *... and So They Talked,* Howard Timmins, Cape Town, 1963

Angove, John, *In the Early Days,* Handel House, Kimberley and Johannesburg, 1910

Anon, *Life on the Diamond Fields* (privately printed), London, 1875

Ashe, E. Oliver, *Besieged by the Boers,* Hutchinson, London, 1900

Babe, Jerome L., *The South African Diamond Fields,* David Wesley, New York, 1872

Baker, H., *Cecil Rhodes by His Architect,* Oxford University Press, 1934

Balfour, Alice, *Twelve Hundred Miles in a Waggon,* Edward Arnold, London, 1895

Barlow, T., *The Life and Times of President Brand,* Juta, Cape Town, 1972

Beet, A.J., and C.B. Harris, *Kimberley Under Siege,* Diamond Fields Advertiser, Kimberley, (n.d.)

Beet, George, *Grand Old Days of the Diamond Fields,* Maskew Miller, Cape Town, 1931

Beit, Sir Alfred, *The Will and the Way,* Longmans, London, 1957

Boyle, Frederick, *To the Cape for Diamonds,* Chapman & Hall, London, 1873

Bryce, James, *Impressions of South Africa,* Macmillan, London, 1897

Buchanan-Gould, V., *Not Without Honour,* Hutchinson, London, 1948

Burrows, E.H., *A History of Medicine in South Africa,* Balkema, Cape Town, 1958

Carter, Thomas, *A Narrative of the Boer War,* Macqueen, London, 1896

Cartwright, A.P., *Gold Paved the Way,* Macmillan, London, 1967
Cary, Robert, *Charter Royal,* Howard Timmins, Cape Town, 1970
Chilvers, H.A., *The Story of De Beers,* Cassell, London, 1939
— *Out of the Crucible,* Juta, Johannesburg, 1948
Churchill, Lord Randolph, *Men, Mines and Animals in South Africa,* Sampson Low, London, 1892
Cohen, Louis, *Reminiscences of Kimberley,* Bennett, London, 1911
Collier, R., *The Plague of the Spanish Lady,* Macmillan, London, 1974
Collins, William W., *Free Statia,* Struik (reprint), Cape Town, 1965
Colquhoun, Archibald, *Dan to Beersheba,* Heinemann, London, 1908
Colvin, Ian, *The Life of Jameson,* Edward Arnold, London, 1922
Cronwright-Schreiner, S.C., *Letters of Olive Schreiner,* T. Fisher Unwin, London, 1924
Cumberland, Stuart, *What I Think of South Africa,* Chapman & Hall, London, 1896
Curson, H.H., *The History of the Kimberley Regiment,* Northern Cape Printers, Kimberley, 1963
De Kiewiet, C.W., *The Imperial Factor in South Africa,* Cambridge University Press, 1937
Dixie, Lady Florence, *In the Land of Misfortune,* Bentley, London, 1882
Doughty, Oswald, *Early Diamond Days,* Longmans, London, 1963
Emden, Paul H., *Randlords,* Hodder & Stoughton, London, 1935
Farini, G.A., *Through the Kalahari,* Sampson Low, London, 1886
Fort, G.S., *Alfred Beit,* London, 1932
— *Chance or Design? A Pioneer Looks Back,* Robert Hale, London, 1942
Froude, J.A., *Two Lectures on South Africa,* Longmans, London, 1880
Graumann, Sir Harry, *Rand, Riches and South Africa,* Simpkin Marshall, London, 1936
Green, G.A.L., *An Editor Looks Back,* Juta, Cape Town, 1947
Gutsche, Thelma, *The Microcosm,* Howard Timmins, Cape Town, 1968
Hancock, W.K., *Smuts: The Sanguine Years,* Cambridge University Press, 1962
Harris, Sir David, *Pioneer, Soldier and Politician,* Sampson Low, London, 1931
Henderson, R.H., *An Ulsterman in Africa,* Unie-Volkspers, Cape Town, 1944
Herrman, Louis, *A History of the Jews in South Africa,* South African Jewish Board of Deputies, Cape Town, 1935
Hocking, Anthony, *Oppenheimer and Son,* McGraw Hill, Johannesburg, 1973
Jackson, Stanley, *The Great Barnato,* Heinemann, London, 1970
Joel, Stanhope, *Ace of Diamonds,* Muller, London, 1958
Johnson, Frank, *Great Days,* Bell, London, 1940
Jourdan, Philip, *Cecil Rhodes,* Bodley Head, London, 1910
Kingwill, Annie, *The Siege of Kimberley,* (privately printed) Graaff-Reinet (n.d.)
Klein, H., *Stagecoach Dust,* Nelson, London, 1937
Kruger, Rayne, *Good-bye Dolly Gray,* Four Square Books, London, 1964
Laidler, P.W., and M. Gelfand, *South Africa: Its Medical History,* Struik, Cape Town, 1971
Le Sueur, Gordon, *Cecil Rhodes,* John Murray, London, 1913
Lewinsohn, Richard, *Barney Barnato,* Routledge, London, 1937
Lewsen, Phyllis, *The Correspondence of J.X. Merriman 1870-1890,* Van Riebeeck Society, Cape Town, 1960
Little, J.S., *South Africa: A Sketch Book,* Swan Sonnenschein, London, 1887
Lockhart, J.G. and C.M. Woodhouse, *Rhodes,* Hodder & Stoughton, London, 1963
McDonald, J.G., *Rhodes: A Life,* Chatto & Windus, London, 1941
Macmillan, Mona, *Sir Henry Barkly,* Balkema, Cape Town, 1970
MacNeill, J.G. Swift, *What I Have Seen and Heard,* Arrowsmith, London, 1925
McNish, A.T., *The Road to El Dorado,* Struik, Cape Town, 1968
— *Graves and Guineas,* Struik, Cape Town, 1969
— *The Glittering Road,* Struik, Cape Town, 1970
Matthews, J.W., *Incwadi Yami,* Sampson Low, London, 1887
Maurois, André, *Cecil Rhodes,* Collins, 1953
Meintjes, Johannes, *Olive Schreiner,* Keartland, Johannesburg, 1965
Michell, Sir Lewis, *The Life of the Right Hon. Cecil John Rhodes,* Edward Arnold, London, 1910
Millin, S.G., *Rhodes,* Chatto & Windus, London, 1933
Morton, W.J., *South African Diamond Fields,* American Geographical Society, New York, 1877
Murray, R.W., *South African Reminiscences,* Juta, Cape Town, 1894
Oberholzer, H., *Pioneers of Early Aviation,* National Museum, Bloemfontein, 1974
O'Meara, W.A.J., *Kekewich in Kimberley,* Medici Society, London, 1926
Pakenham, Elizabeth, *Jameson's Raid,* Weidenfeld & Nicolson, London, 1961

Payton, Charles, *The Diamond Diggings of South Africa,* Horace Cox, London, 1872
Phillips, Lionel, *Some Reminiscences,* Hutchinson, London, 1924
Phillips, Mrs. L., *Some South African Recollections,* Longmans, London, 1899
Plomer, W., *Cecil Rhodes,* Nelson, London, 1933
Raymond, Harry, *B.I. Barnato: A Memoir,* Ibister, London, 1897
Reunert, Theodore, *Diamonds and Gold in South Africa,* Juta, Cape Town, 1893
Robertson, Marian, *Diamond Fever,* Oxford University Press, Cape Town, 1974
Rosenthal, Eric, *River of Diamonds,* Howard Timmins, Cape Town, (n.d.)
   —*Gold! Gold! Gold!,* Collier Macmillan, Johannesburg, 1970
Rose Innes, James, *Autobiography,* Oxford University Press, 1949
Rossmore, Lord, *Things I Can Tell,* Eveleigh Nash, London, 1912
Rouillard, Nancy, *Matabele Thompson,* Faber & Faber, London, 1936
Sauer, Hans, *Ex-Africa,* Bles, London, 1937
Scully, W.C., *Reminiscences of a South African Pioneer,* T. Fisher Unwin, London, 1913
Searle, Charlotte, *History of Nursing in South Africa 1652-1960,* Struik, Cape Town, 1965
Smithers, Elsa, *March Hare,* Oxford University Press, 1935
Smuts, J.C., *Jan Christian Smuts,* Cassell, London, 1952
Sonnenberg, Max, *The Way I Saw It,* Howard Timmins, Cape Town, (n.d.)
Statham, F.R., *South Africa As It Is,* T. Fisher Unwin, London, 1897
Steyn, M.M., *The Diary of a South African,* Juta, Cape Town, (n.d.)
Streeter, E.W., *Great Diamonds of the World,* George Bell, London, 1882
Taylor, J.B., *A Pioneer Looks Back,* Hutchinson, London, 1939
Taylor, W.P., *African Treasures: Sixty Years among Diamonds and Gold,* John Long, London, 1932
Thorne, Eudore, *Indomitable Spirit,* Historical Society of Kimberley and Northern Cape, 1971
Trollope, Anthony, *South Africa* (abridged edition), Longmans, London, 1938
Uys, C.J., *In the Era of Shepstone,* Lovedale, South Africa, 1933
Van der Heever, C.M., *J.B.M. Hertzog,* A.P.B., Johannesburg, 1946
'Vindex': *Cecil Rhodes: His Political Life and Speeches,* Bell, London, 1900
Walker, E.A., *W.P. Schreiner,* Oxford University Press, 1937
Warner, Constance, *History of the Kimberley Club* (privately printed), Kimberley, 1965
Warren, Sir Charles, *On the Veldt in the Seventies,* Ibister, London, 1902
Weinthal, Leo, *Memories, Mines and Millions,* Simpkin Marshall, London, 1929
Williams, A.E., *Some Dreams Come True,* Howard Timmins, Cape Town, 1948
Williams, Basil, *Cecil Rhodes,* Constable, London, 1921
Williams, G.F., *The Diamond Mines of South Africa,* Macmillan, London, 1902
Williams, W.W., *The Life of Sir Charles Warren,* Blackwell, London, 1941
Wilmot, A., *The Life and Times of Sir Richard Southey,* Sampson Low, London, 1904
Wilson, H.W., *With the Flag to Pretoria,* Harmsworth, London, 1901
Wilson, Lady Sarah, *South African Memories,* Edward Arnold, London, 1909
Wrench, J.E., *Alfred Lord Milner,* Eyre & Spottiswoode, London, 1958
Wright, H.M., (ed.) *Sir James Rose Innes, Selected Correspondence,* Van Riebeeck Society, Cape Town, 1972

GENERAL

Theal, G.M., *History of South Africa,* Swan Sonnenschein, London, 1889
Walker, E.A., *History of South Africa,* Longmans, London, 1957
Wilson, Monica, and Leonard Thompson, *The Oxford History of South Africa,* Oxford University Press, London, 1969
Dictionary of South African Biography, vols 1 and 2, Nasionale Boekhandel, 1968; Tafelberg-Uitgewers, 1972

PERIODICALS AND PAMPHLETS

Diamond Field Keepsake (1873), *Diamond News* (magazine), *South African Mining and Engineering Journal* (1929), *Tramway System of Southern Africa* by W.D. Howarth (Kimberley Library), *Northern Cape* by H.A. Morris (Kimberley Library), *Government Gazette, Statute Law of Griqualand West,* vol. 1 (1875), *Leaflet on Presentation to General French* (De Beers Office),

Griqualand West Hebrew Congregation: *Service of Thanksgiving* (1973), *Geological Magazine* (London 1869), *Transactions of the Royal Society of South Africa*, *John Bull* (London 1906), *Life, Sport and Drama* (Johannesburg 1921-22), *South Africa* (London), *The Listener* (London 1972).

NEWSPAPERS

Bechuanaland News, Cape Argus, Cape Times, Daily Graphic (London), *Diamond Field, Diamond Fields Advertiser, Diamond News, Diamond Times, Eastern Province Herald, The Friend* (Bloemfontein), *Grahamstown Journal, Independent, Sunday Times* (Johannesburg), *The Times* (London), *The Winning Post* (London), newspaper cuttings (Kimberley Library).

NEWSPAPER ABBREVIATIONS

B.N. –*Bechuanaland News;*
C.A. –*Cape Argus,* Cape Town;
C.T. –*Cape Times,* Cape Town;
D.F. –*Diamond Field,* Kimberley;
D.F.A. –*Diamond Fields Advertiser,* Kimberley;
D.N. –*Diamond News,* Kimberley;
D.T. –*Diamond Times,* Kimberley;
E.P.H. –*Eastern Province Herald,* Port Elizabeth;
G.J. –*Grahamstown Journal,* Grahamstown;
Ind. –*Independent,* Kimberley;
S.A. –*South Africa,* London;
W.P. –*Winning Post,* London.

References

1: THE FIRST FINDS
5: 'keep his eyes open', Robertson, p. 81; 'here be diamonds', Boyle, p. 84.
6: 'hollow dug by', Robertson, p.59; 'to find out what it really was', Robertson, p. 69; 'dozen of beer', *B.N.*, 2 June 1894: 'a dull, rounded', Robertson, p. 73.
7: 'Stranger things', Robertson, p. 40.
10: 'least known, most insignificant', Robertson, p. 21; 'The reason why', Robertson, p. 117.
11: 'My suspicions . . . were at once', *G.J.*, 5 February 1869; 'I made a very lengthy', *Geological Magazine*, Jan. 1869.
12: 'The parties concerned', ibid, May 1869: 'lazy man', Robertson, p. 175.
13: 'I am quite willing', Robertson, p. 177.
14: 'anything to show', Robertson, p. 189; 'swell the funds', Robertson, p. 191; 'I can no longer', Robertson, p. 194.

2: THE RIVER DIGGINGS
16: 'a small mud cottage', *D.F. Keepsake*, 1873.
17: 'It was a most marvellous', *S.A.*, 23 Dec. 1893; 'In six weeks', ibid; 'there were sixty or seventy', *Stow*; 'diamonds are found', Robertson, p. 220.
18: 'farming and the ghost', *D.F. Keepsake*, 1873.
19: 'This is not a bad', Robertson, p. 225.
20: 'Who follows me', *Beet*; 'Seeing that no shots', *Beet*; 'We heard him', *Beet*; 'We signed the undertaking', *Beet*; 'an additional 12s. 6d.', *D.N.*, 4 Feb. 1871.
21: 'The Vaal, there is no doubt', Robertson, p. 220.
23: 'Butchers, bakers, sailors', G.

Williams, p. 127; '*These* diggings', *Mackenzie*; Wits. University (quoted by M. Robertson in mss); 'Otherwise . . . all would go', *Southey*; 'welcomed all comers', G. Williams, p. 162; 'a straggling chain', Boyle, p. 79; 'There were very few', Doughty, p. 11.
24: 'We may challenge', *D.N.*, 1 July 1871; 'When digging for diamonds', Angove, p. 111.
25: 'While the stuff', Payton, pp. 8–9; 'liquor up' and 'Pickaxes . . . Cocktails', *D.N.*, 1 July 1871; 'The quietude of these', Angove, p. 16.
27: 'the proclamation of British', *Southey*, 22 Sept. 1870.
29: 'would be charged' and 'through the river', Babe, p. 36.
30: 'They would most certainly', A. Williams, p. 108; 'a courteous gentleman' and 'rougher elements', G. Beet, p. 38; 'Their bumptiousness', *Southey*, 1 Sept. 1870; 'strongly of opinion', *Southey*, 15 Sept. 1870; 'In short', *Southey*, 22 Sept. 1870.
31: I hope', Wilmot, p. 194; 'until Campbell . . . comes', *Friend*, 1 Dec. 1870; 'Parker of the strong arm', ibid; 'You must not lose sight', ibid.
32: 'In justice to Mr Parker', Boyle, p. 58; 'bearing the well-selected', *Friend*, 22 Dec. 1870.

3: THE DIAMOND FARMS
33: 'a great number of people', *Friend*, 24 Nov. 1870; 'veritable gems', *Friend*, 11 Aug. 1870; 'were plastered' and 'If that . . . is not philanthropy', *Friend*, 18 Aug. 1870.
34: 'From Bultfontein', *Friend*, 11 Aug. 1870; 'By diggers' law', *D.N.*, 4 Feb. 1871; 'equally rich', *Friend*, 24 Nov. 1870.
35: 'I am here', Chilvers, *Story of De*

Beers, p. 16; 'Accompanied by', *Friend*, 22 Dec. 1870; 'Claims . . . were marked up', Boyle, pp. 92–3; 'Mr Hurley has come', *Friend*, 22 Dec. 1870.

36: 'We are anxious', ibid; 'in the name of the Government', *Friend*, 29 Dec. 1870.

37: 'organise, if possible' and 'clear out', *Friend*, 5 Jan. 1871.

38: 'afraid of a personal encounter', *D.N.*, 18 Feb. 1871; 'no chance', *Friend*, 19 Jan. 1871; 'resisting a Government', *D.N.*, 28 Jan. 1871.

39: 'At Pniel', ibid; 'The Free State boers', *Friend*, 26 Jan. 1871; 'bloodshed', ibid.

40: 'The meeting became so excited', *D.N.*, 22 April 1871.

41: 'The eyes of all', *D.N.*, 13 May 1871; 'pay a royalty', ibid; 'one of the largest', *D.N.*, 20 May 1871.

42: 'Mr Lilienfeld . . . was as welcome', ibid; 'expressed great satisfaction', ibid; 'it was under actual', Boyle, p. 94.

43: 'the Government Inspector shall', Boyle, p. 401; 'He has no privileges', Boyle, p. 93; 'pretty well decided', *D.N.*, 11 March 1871. For Jackson's account see *Beet* mss, Kimberley Library. He says he first heard of the 'lone digger' in May 1871, but this is obviously an error. Contemporary newspaper reports show that diggers were actively working De Beers at the beginning of May. Jackson must have heard about the digger some time in April.

45: 'Everyone knows', *D.N.*, 6 May 1871.

46: 'sifting the surface gravel', G. Beet, p. 74; 'was diffident as to', *Hawthorne*, vol. 1, pp. 52–3; Giddy's report, G. Beet, pp. 75–7.

49: 'The claims are selling', *Friend*, 10 Aug. 1871; 'The "Colesberg Rush" ', *Friend*, 17 Aug. 1871.

50: 'and afterwards lay out a town', ibid; 'There are at least', *Friend*, 7 Sept. 1871; 'It was pathetic', *Beet*; Jackson's account.

4: 'A GENTLEMAN'S DIGGINGS'

53: 'All the seats', Boyle, p. 50.

54: 'by storm', *D.N.*, 7 Oct. 1871; 'A very few words', Boyle, p. 50; 'The farmer', Boyle, p. 60.

55: 'What a frightful', Boyle, p. 58; 'No object', Boyle, p. 62; 'My ankles', Boyle, p. 72; 'There were, and are', Boyle, p. 64; 'quite pretty', Boyle, p. 76; 'after the troops have', Boyle, p. 78.

56: 'Through the straggling purlieus', Boyle, pp. 111–12.

58: 'swellest of swells', Boyle, p. 80; 'Boers do not come', Boyle, p. 118.

59: 'submit to the decision', Theal; 'measures of resistance', ibid; 'I was glad to find', Wilmot, p. 197.

60: 'Her Majesty's government', Theal; 'not consist of British', ibid.

61: 'I had not a single', ibid; 'To this transaction', ibid.

62: 'Her Majesty is compelled', *Statute Law of Griqualand West*, vol. 1, p. 4: 'so far as the same', ibid; 'I hereby command', ibid.

63: 'There was not an obstacle', Doughty, p. 209; 'All contemplated with alarm', Boyle, pp. 39–40; 'in so far as the same', ibid.

64: 'rough-and-ready', Boyle, p. 94; 'Something in this style', Boyle, p. 169.

65: 'I am a digger', Boyle, pp. 182–3; 'chasing negroes', ibid; 'By the action of Government', *D.N.*, 30 Dec. 1871.

66: 'A man having a white face', *D.N.*, 3 Feb. 1872.

67: 'Bottles of French brandy', *D.N.*, 20 July 1872; 'the gallant officer', ibid; 'Too late to go', ibid.

68: 'for increasing the means', ibid; 'weak, bad, revengeful', Boyle, p. 413.

69: 'I have met men', Macmillan, p. 213; 'antiquated Conservatives', Macmillan, p. 212; 'among the first', Macmillan, p. 214.

5: DUST, DROUGHT AND FLIES

70: 'The four great mines', *S.A. Mining and Engineering Journal*, Sept. 1929.

71: 'This time last year', *D.F. Keepsake*, 1873.

74: 'Just fancy', *Friend*, 21 Sept. 1871; 'And the flies!', Angove, p. 38; 'Dishes and drink', Boyle, p. 110; 'The wells', Payton, p. 153; 'The newcomer',

Payton, p. 154.

75: 'and more promised', *D.N.*, 16
Sept. 1871; 'a poor man who', *Beet.*

76: 'These primitive buildings', *D.N.*,
9 March 1872; 'merely the trunk',
Matthews, pp. 102–3; 'brown wall
coming on', *Beet*; Alice Stockdale
account.

77: 'The dust of the dry', *D.N.*, 11
Nov. 1871; 'My nose is peeled', ibid;
'Fancy sleeping in', Payton, p. 149.

78: 'We had many nice', *Beet*; 'The
consequence is', *D.N.*, 29 April 1871;
'the boy holding up', *Beet*; 'It is perfectly', *D.N.*, 23 Sept. 1871.

79: 'I would advise no one', Babe,
p. 62; 'Every visit . . . impresses', Boyle,
pp. 285–9.

80: 'by far the most pleasant', *D.F.
Keepsake*, 1873; 'It is a pretty', ibid;
'Such an immense number', Payton,
p. 26.

82: 'Even the *Diamond News*',
Friend, 7 Sept. 1871; 'there are never
less', ibid; 'Many of the residences',
D.F. Keepsake, 1873; 'The centre of a
country', Boyle, pp. 154–5.

83: 'It is true that', Doughty, p. 166;
'subscribed *at once*', *D.N.*, 21 Feb. 1872.

84: 'There was a goodly', Angove,
p. 53; 'A shipment of these', Lewsen,
vol. 1, p. 6; 'A great many of them',
Payton, p. 146.

87: 'The sudden riches', Doughty,
p. 127; 'excessive indulgence' and
'curse', Matthews, p. 100; 'the two
great social evils', Matthews, p. 117;
'The difference . . . between', ibid;
'Just as I had finished', Harris, pp. 34–5.

88: 'It is desirable', Payton, p. 162;
'The over-and-under', Angove, pp. 44–5;
'Some of those women', Angove, p. 46;
'turf swindling', *Hawthorne*, vol. 1,
p. 129.

89: 'There were no sitting out', news-
paper cutting, Kimberley Library;
'What with white ants', ibid; 'Signor
Marcellino, the Fire King', *D.N.*, 27
March 1872; 'planks, having gin boxes',
D.N., 11 Nov. 1871.

90: 'This dramatic first born', *Life,
Sport and Drama*, 27 May 1921; 'a very
fine hall', *D.N.*, 27 April 1872; 'to supply a want', ibid; 'Great Wizard' and
'Royal Family', *D.N.*, 31 Oct. 1872.

91: 'The wizard's performance', *Life,
Sport and Drama*, 23 May 1921; 'The
cry is "Still" ', *D.N.*, 21 Nov. 1872;
'His Great Feat', *D.N.*, 24 Dec. 1872.

6: A COLLECTION OF
   CHARACTERS
92: 'still sporting his', Beet, p. 60;
'in a sort of' and 'This lady', Boyle,
p. 307.

93: 'He was certainly very down',
Rossmore, p. 222; 'Oh come now',
Rossmore, pp. 222–3.

94: 'had the audacity', Rossmore,
p. 223; 'Amsterdam house' and 'He is
not', Payton, p. 114;'The Empress
Eugénie', *D.N.*, 15 July 1871.

95: 'If I had not', *D.N.*, 9 Sept. 1871;
'his name as Unger', ibid; 'appeared to
have been', ibid; 'It is to be regretted',
ibid.

96. 'started as a timber merchant',
Sonnenberg, p. 14; 'there was no ill
feeling', A. Williams, p. 254; 'Although
he was as cunning', Cohen.

97: 'Good God, man', A. Williams,
p. 255; 'I felt', Rossmore, p. 227; 'a
match for anyone', A. Williams, p. 255;
'The whole town . . . loved him', Cohen;
'strongly marked oriental', *Ind.*, 7 July
1886; 'a noted "card" ', Harris, p.31.

98: 'So intent was he', ibid; 'Whenever he was selling', Payton, p. 132;
'Well . . . he is apt', *Beet*; 'Gentle in
manner', *Ind.*, 14 July 1886.

99: 'the derelicts of other', Millin,
p. 17.

101: 'As a public man', *D.F.A.*, 22
Aug. 1892; 'If ever . . . a man', *S.A.*,
23 Dec. 1893.

102: 'Diamond Merchant . . . having',
D.N., 5 June 1872; 'Mr J.B. Robinson',
ibid; 'I remember . . . just before', *D.N.*,
8 May 1875.

103: 'The pliant whip', ibid, 3 Oct.
1872.

105: 'The camp is' and 'Nothing is',
Lewsen, vol. 1, pp. 6–7; 'governing
class', ibid, p. xi; 'picked and sweated',
Walker, p. 51.

106: 'that she first began', Buchanan-
Gould, p. 40; 'When the camp below',
O. Schreiner, *Undine*; 'his indignation',
Van der Heever, p. 20.

107: 'No, I never', Van der Heever,

p. 22; 'The vicious language', Van der Heever, p. 20; 'his course was set', Van der Heever, p. 22.·

108: 'a tall, lanky', B. Williams, p. 11; 'Shouldn't do that', B. Williams, p. 40; 'Mr Rhodes of Natal', Payton, p. 215.

109: 'a nasty habit' and 'the great proportion', B. Williams, p. 29.

7: GOVERNOR SOUTHEY
111: 'where bridal pairs', Murray, p. 200; 'all hustle and bustle', Murray, pp. 200-1.

112: 'just in the nick of time', *D.F.*, 16 Jan. 1873; 'met with good wishes', Murray, p. 201; 'Currey made the bullets', *Ind.*, 10 Nov. 1890.

113: 'By common consent', *Currey*, ch. II, p. 1; 'for the first time', ibid; 'object of curbing' and 'Mining Boards', *Currey*, p. 16; 'determine more definitely', *Statute Law of Griqualand West*, vol. 1, p. 83; 'to keep or to frequent', ibid, p. 85.

115: 'The Americans who had', *Currey*, ch. XII, p. 9; 'must receive' and 'declined to', ibid, pp. 16-17.

116: 'We certainly do not', *D.F.*, 19 July 1873; 'encouragement of properly', ibid.

117: 'I could . . . say a good deal', Lewsen, vol. 1, pp. 10-11.

118: 'Then . . . many men forsook', *Hawthorne*, vol. 1, 1873, p. 84; 'little above the peasant', Wilmot, p. 256; 'uprightness and integrity', *D.F.A.*, 20 Nov. 1889.

119: 'All . . . seemed to be', *Currey*, ch. XII, p. 18; 'It was . . . the destruction', ibid.

120: 'talk over and conciliate', Lewsen, vol. 1, p. 11; 'I should consider it', Matthews, p. 279.

122: 'were really quitrent', Wilmot, p. 254; 'You cannot drown the market', Boyle, pp. 376-7.

123: 'Too late, boy, too late', there are many versions of this story, for example Jackson, p. 22, Raymond, p. 16, Emden, p. 127; 'one of the jolliest', Raymond, p. 16; 'diggers have gone down', *D.F.*, 3 Dec. 1873.

125: 'I have read with much', Wilmot, p. 411.

127: 'To see this fine structure', *D.N.*,

1 Oct. 1874; 'The worst feature', ibid; 'a large Roman Catholic church', Anon, *Life on the Diamond Fields*, p. 34; 'a temporary or loose', Hebrew Congregation pamphlet, 9 Sept. 1973, p. 8; 'We are astonished', *D.N.*, 26 Nov. 1874.

128: 'It looks exceedingly', *D.N.*, 7 Nov. 1874; 'next door to Sangers', *Hawthorne*, vol. 1, p. 82; 'The ladies . . . were', ibid, p. 104; 'series of athletic sports', *D.N.*, 22 Dec. 1874.

129: 'The Christmas season 1874', *Hawthorne*, vol. 1, p. 105.

8: THE BLACK FLAG REBELLION
130: 'repeal, alter or mutilate', *Hawthorne*, vol. 1, p. 98; 'brother diggers and brother sufferers', ibid.

131: 'I was on a Yankee', Carter, p. 101; 'Fenians were afraid', Uys, p. 331; 'eyes of a dark', *C.A.*, 19 June 1926.

132: 'Up the Free State', *D.F.*, 14 Nov. 1872; 'What an abominable', Lewsen, vol. 1, p. 11; 'A little bloodshed', De Kiewiet, p. 55.

133: 'was to admire and respect', Murray, p. 197; 'diggers from America', Froude.

134: 'The great creature', Lewsen, p. 12; 'Mr Southey the Governor', Macmillan, p. 223; 'The only point', Lewsen, p. 9; 'Ruin, financial ruin', *D.F.*, 28 Nov. 1874.

135: 'privilege to white persons', Macmillan, p. 209; 'a political organization', Wilmot, p. 265; 'The paper appeared', *D.F.A.*, 21 Feb. 1930; 'to assemble with their', *Hawthorne*, vol. 1, p. 108.

136: 'These are stirring times!', Lewsen, p. 13; 'taking illegal oaths', Wilmot, p. 278; 'I am glad to find', Wilmot, p. 413; 'to discuss eleven matters', Wilmot, p. 281.

137: 'It was apparent', A. Williams, p. 191; 'I addressed the armed men', A. Williams, p. 192.

138: 'the insanely injudicious', De Kiewiet, p. 55; 'a few names of', A. Williams, p. 193.

139: 'It is much to be', *D.N.*, 8 May 1875; 'Troops arrived', *E.P.H.*, 9 July 1875.

9: CIVIC BEGINNINGS

141: 'he had been told', *D.N.*, 6 Jan. 1876; 'what he considered', ibid; 'was the last man', ibid.

142: 'My character was', *Beet*; 'There was an end', De Kiewiet, p. 58.

143: 'It is perhaps idle', De Kiewiet, pp. 58-9; 'they were induced to make', *Hawthorne*, vol. 1, p. 21.

144: 'All that is revolting', Little, p. 43; 'The first holders', *Hawthorne*, vol. 1, p. 154.

145: 'The want of', Angove, p. 123; 'Cordial greetings' and 'much pleasure', Angove, p. 125; 'Comparatively poverty-stricken', *Hawthorne*, vol. 1, p. 119.

146: 'whether municipal', *D.N.*, 20 Jan. 1872; 'to consider the advisability', *D.N.*, 25 May 1876.

147: 'Whether it is in the air', Murray, p. 191; 'Could bunting have', *D.N.*, 6 July 1876; 'Shows one can never', *Beet*.

148: 'its very smart appearance', Angove, p. 98; 'a source of amusement', Angove, p. 97.

149: 'battle royal' and 'Those were the', Steyn, p. 210; 'When it became known', Cohen, p. 55.

150: 'It rather interested', *W.P.*, 22 Feb. 1908; 'If you can make', Cohen, p. 55; 'cradle of the', ibid; 'some of the most', ibid.

151: 'When we saw', *Ind.*, 11 Jan. 1876; ' 'Ow the dogs', Cohen, p. 335; 'The lady who was', *Life, Sport and Drama*, 23 April 1921; 'The Junoesque goddess', ibid.

152: 'I fought him', ibid; 'the first drama ever', *Life, Sport and Drama*, 7 May 1921; 'called me into', ibid.

10: ENTER DOCTOR JIM

153: 'business on the lines', Lockhart, p. 81; 'were two very different', Murray, p. 193; 'His Honour could turn', Murray, p. 192.

155: 'the Home Government', De Kiewiet, p. 91; 'so troublesome a crown colony', Matthews, p. 291; 'The Imperial Government', Murray, p. 192.

156: 'I like Major Lanyon', Warren, p. 305; 'We had a good show', Warren, p. 301; 'The news of this', Matthews, p. 303.

157: 'he had seen nothing', Warren, p. 302; 'was due to the' and 'uppish', Warren, p. 304; 'Diamonds are looking up', Warren, p. 308; 'premier on the Fields', *D.F.A.*, 18 Feb. 1930; 'Whether a man had', ibid; 'Prices here are awful', Warren, p. 307.

158: 'they could not afford', B. Williams, p. 46; 'His friends once', Michell, vol. 1, p. 67.

159: 'Anthony Trollope has arrived', Warren, p. 364; 'Dust so thick', Trollope, p. 173; 'I sometimes thought', Trollope, p. 174; 'I do not think', Trollope, pp. 174-5.

160: 'The rooms are generally', Trollope, pp. 175-6; 'I could but say', Trollope, pp. 176-7; 'I thought that I could', Trollope, p. 184.

161: 'The simple teaching' and 'one of the', Trollope, p. 171; 'And as the nice', Trollope, p. 184; 'that I was speaking to', Trollope, p. 185.

162: 'teaching was not', Laidler & Gelfand, p. 359; 'came from all parts', Burrows; 'the most beautiful', Warren, p. 210; 'angel carved in' and 'Sir', Burrows.

162-3: 'The Kimberley system', Burrows.

163: 'Dr Prince begs to', *Ind.*, 23 Jan. 1879; 'The diamond may have', Colvin, vol. 1, p. 11; 'With the fair sex', *W.P.*, 2 May 1908.

165: 'I knew a chap', ibid.

11: COMPANY MINING

166: 'very melancholy to look at', Trollope, pp. 158-9.

167: 'Even the candidates', *Hawthorne*, 1877, p. 204; 'It was evident', ibid.

168: 'for the mere sake', *D.N.*, 26 Nov. 1878.

169: 'An edifying spectacle', *D.N.*, 5 April 1879; 'members who had', *Ind.*, 29 Jan. 1879; 'You immediately feel', Trollope, p. 161.

170: 'The ground, which', Boyle, p. 172; 'a red-letter day', Angove, p. 117; 'on account of', Angove, p. 120; 'rights' and 'good government', Angove, p. 119; 'for there you will see', *C.T.*, 8 April 1880; Massett's description of Kimberley, ibid.

173: 'I should imagine', ibid.

175: 'Whether Mr Robinson', *Ind.*, 15 Dec. 1879; 'usurper' and Mr Robinson should', *Ind.*, 22 Dec. 1879; 'It is to be', *D.N.*, 27 Dec. 1879.

177: 'gone to the expense', Trollope, p. 165.

178: 'Messrs Barnato Brothers', *Ind.*, 10 March 1881; 'To secure the amalgamation', *Ind.*, 22 Oct. 1881.

179: 'wonderful changes and 'There is every', Lewsen, vol. 1, p. 81.

12: PROGRESS AND A THREAT

183: 'In redemption of', Matthews, p. 314; 'electrified' and 'into a sense', ibid; 'the expiring stage', Rose Innes, p. 47; 'would be detrimental', Matthews, p. 314.

184: 'We are evidently', Lewsen, vol. 1, pp. 81–2; 'I feel like a man', Matthews, p. 317.

186: 'a capital brass band', *Ind.*, 15 March 1881; 'The unlimited expenditure', Matthews, p. 319; 'the place' and 'The old time', *W.P.*, 10 April 1909.

187: 'There is every prospect', *Ind.*, 7 July 1881; 'vast straggling' and 'Our first', Dixie, p. 182; 'room or outhouse', ibid.

189: '66 surgical', Laidler & Gelfand, p. 399; 'men as well as women', Dixie, p. 286.

190: 'Mr Lynch may safely', *Ind.*, 15 April 1882; 'soon . . . there would be', *Hawthorne*, vol. 2, p. 98.

193: 'It beats anything', *Pickering* letter.

194: 'After a morning of', Rose Innes, p. 47; 'The place was', Colquhoun, p. 257; 'Books to suit', *Ind.*, 15 April 1880; 'the public had not', *Hawthorne*, 1882, p. 44; 'a resort for young men', ibid.

195: 'to accept charge', ibid; 'Why try to enjoy', Trollope, p. 176; 'The name of such Municipality', *Government Gazette*, 15 June 1883; 'the work of a few days', Angove, p. 173.

197: 'built of rough', newspaper cutting, Kimberley Library; 'The various offices', Matthews, p. 247; 'had a hail storm', Matthews, p. 248.

198: 'arbitrary and injudicious',

Matthews, p. 253.

199: 'blood poisoning consequent', *Hawthorne*, 1882, p. 81; 'There's your law', Sauer, p. 38.

13: I. D. B.

201: 'It is the fashion', *Ind.*, 21 Feb. 1881; 'intelligible Registers', *Statute Law of Griqualand West*, vol. 1, p. 26; 'not exceeding three', ibid, p. 28.

202: 'I had been intimidated', Graumann, pp. 3–4; 'I can conscientiously say', Matthews, p. 219; 'the fraternity of', Matthews, p. 231.

203: 'those in prison', *Hawthorne*, 1882, p. 43.

204: 'had for its object', *Ind.*, 25 March 1880; 'I had a long discussion', ibid.

205: The licensed diamond buyers', Angove, p. 180.

206: 'I have seen cases', *D.F.A.*, 12 April 1882; 'As regards the system', ibid; 'you might as well', Weinthal, p. 82.

207: 'Justice for Licensed', *D.F.A.*, 26 June 1882; 'into the hearts', *Hawthorne*, 1882, p. 49; 'The 19th of April, 1882', *D.F.A.*, 28 June 1882.

209: 'I decidedly objected', Matthews, p. 216; 'We had great difficulty', *S.A.*, 23 Dec. 1893.

210: 'in an endeavour', *Ind.*,15 Sept. 1883; 'the first step', ibid; 'By their efforts', *Ind.*, 25 Sept. 1883; 'A law of exceptional', Churchill, p. 82.

211: 'He showed remarkable', *D.F.A.*, 26 Nov. 1888.

14: THE GREAT STRIKE AND SMALLPOX

214: 'for the searching', Matthews, p. 215.

215: 'Rules and Regulations', *Hawthorne*, 1883, p. 120; 'Fashionable Tailor' and 'all of one', *D.F.A.*, 26 Jan. 1883; 'The number and expense', Matthews, p. 215.

216: 'looked upon as farcical', *Hawthorne*, 1883, p. 137; 'it would be a disgraceful', ibid, p. 183.

217: 'the objection to', ibid, pp. 198–9; 'Whenever a crowd', *D.F.A.*, 20 Oct. 1883.

218: 'a bulbous disease', Sauer, p. 72;

'In the first place', ibid; 'is smallpox as we', Colvin, vol. 1, p. 31.

219: 'Needless to say', Sauer, pp. 78–9.

219–20: Phillips's speech, Colvin, p. 33.

220: 'The woman has her', Warren, pp. 369–70.

221: 'I happened', Matthews, p. 408; 'To my intense delight', ibid; 'for his successful', ibid; 'With many disasters', *Hawthorne*, 1883, pp. 216–17.

222: 'thunderous and fearful', *Ind.*, 11 Jan. 1884; 'The violent trembling', Angove, p. 162.

223: 'it was evident', Sauer, p. 84; 'a woman of strong', Sauer, p. 85;

224: 'This request', ibid; 'found several dead', Sauer, p. 86; 'he had no hesitation', *Hawthorne*, 1884, p. 235.

225: 'This judgement', Sauer, p. 87; 'Why does the', Colvin, p. 35; 'it was not', Colvin, p. 36; 'the spread of the', *Hawthorne*, 1884, p. 262.

226: 'The outcome of all', *Beet*.

228: 'I used to dread', Smithers, p. 135; 'A party of strikers', Smithers, pp. 135–6; 'The reason for this', *Beet*.

229: 'pick-handles, crow bars', ibid; 'When Schute and I', *Ind.*, 6 May 1884; 'Rush the bastards', *Beet*; 'This poor fellow's', ibid.

230: 'he was personally', *Hawthorne*, 1884, p. 249; 'the white as well', ibid; 'the employer got more', *Grimmer*; 'I attended the opening', Matthews, pp. 218–19.

231: 'When the natives' time', *Grimmer*; 'I do not think', *Beet*.

15: THE RAILWAY ARRIVES

232: 'The suicidal mania', Lewsen, vol. 1, p. 123; 'The fact is', *D.T.*, 14 May 1883; 'The decline in', Matthews, p. 254; 'Scrip rose', *Ind.*, 7 July 1886.

233: 'A kindlier man', *S.A.*, 4 Aug. 1917; 'I wish to let', A. Williams, p. 172.

234: 'the ruinously low', *Ind.*, 3 July 1883.

235: 'I have had', Lewsen, p. 110; 'Crawling Trains', *Beet*; 'What, *more* cattle', Balfour, p. 33.

236: 'as distant a resemblence', Farini, p. 2; 'excellent model', *Ind.*, 30 Nov. 1885.

237: 'under the shelter', *Hawthorne*, 1885; p. 410; 'sparkling gems' and 'a

huge necklet', ibid, p. 411; 'The railway even in', Matthews, p. 101.

239: 'The seats are luxuriously', *D.F.A.*, 3 Aug. 1885; 'to be worked either', *Ind.*, 16 Sept. 1885; 'the Diamond Fields would', Angove, p. 166.

240: 'It may be relied upon', *D.F.A.*, 17 July 1886; 'There has seldom', *D.F.A.*, 23 July 1886.

241: 'When I reached Kimberley', *John Bull*, 28 July 1906.

242: 'I did not know', *John Bull*, 4 Aug. 1906.

244: 'Corrugated iron is', Cumberland, p. 41.

245: 'most pleasing . . . with a great', Warner, p. 20; 'that the time was ripe', Warner, p. 38.

246: 'many of the mining', A. Williams, p. 387; 'young females of', *S.A.*, 2 April 1892; 'of an emasculated', Matthews, p. 396; 'the smallest bishop', A. Williams, p. 388.

247: 'Nothing in the annals', *Hawthorne*, 1886, p. 112.

248: 'The Rugby Union', ibid.

16: AMALGAMATION

249: 'some of the thorns', *D.F.A.*, 28 June 1884.

250: 'Hullo, do you never', Fort, *Alfred Beit*, p. 72.

251: 'like that of an undergraduate', MacNeill, p. 264.

253: 'message of salvation', Lewsen, vol. 1, p. 202; 'Personally I am', ibid.

254: 'We felt that' and 'However, in', *D.F.A.*, 7 May 1887.

255: 'I feel now', *D.T.*, 17 July 1885.

256: 'It sounded . . . as if', *D.F.A.*, 8 July 1887.

257: 'Well Mr Rhodes', G. Williams, p. 287.

258: 'as a better offer', *D.F.A.*, 22 Sept. 1887; 'You can go', 'Vindex'.

259: 'If only we can', ibid.

260: 'Well, you've had', B. Williams, p. 102.

261: 'Some people', Lockhart, p. 120; 'If they do not', 'Vindex'.

263: 'The powers of the', Michell, vol. 1, p. 185; 'This town', Wilson, p. 14.

17: THE FIFTH MINE

267: 'fit and proper person', *Ind.*, Oct.

1888; 'the worst mining disaster', Chilvers, *Story of De Beers*, p. 75.

269: 'Gold Mines are all', Lewsen, vol. 2, p. 12.

270: 'existence and domination', B. Williams, p. 107; 'The handsome rooms', *Ind.*, 19 April 1890; 'At the present time', *D.F.A.*, 3 May 1890.

271: 'those wretched', *Beet*; 'my hobby', ibid; 'To see the orchard', ibid.

274: 'The debris heaps', Angove, p. 103; 'permits to wash', *Mayor's Minutes*, 1890.

275: 'He is not as well off', *Ind.*, 5 Dec. 1890; 'The people of Kimberley', Rouillard, p. 50.

276: 'No, I only want', Le Sueur, p. 194; 'The expansion of British', *D.F.A.*, 18 April 1890; 'a remarkably fine', *D.F.A.*, 5 May 1890.

277: 'When at last I found', B. Williams, p. 150; 'He followed it up', Chilvers, *Story of De Beers*, p. 191; 'a hole at random', G. Williams, pp. 345–6; 'riding over the', *D.F.A.*, 19 Jan. 1891.

278: 'It was always recognised', *Ind.*, 9 Feb. 1891; 'The excitement', *Ind.*, 7 Feb. 1891.

279: 'The huge crowd', *Ind.*, 24 Feb. 1891; 'begged Mr Barnato' and 'the influence', ibid.

280: 'It is contended', *D.F.A.*, 19 March 1891.

281: Sister Henrietta's letter, *see Ind.*, 6 Jan. 1891.

282: 'straggling, haphazard', Churchill, p. 36; 'At Kimberley', Churchill, p. 38; 'On returning from', Churchill, p. 44; 'If a man walking', Churchill, pp. 45–6; 'At De Beers mine', *Daily Graphic*, 21 July 1891.

283: 'All for the vanity', *Grimmer*.

18: THE EXHIBITION

284: 'being situated on the borders', *S.A.*, 21 May 1892; 'promised to give', *S.A.*, 23 Jan. 1892.

285: 'a gentleman with', ibid; 'The object of this', *S.A.*, 20 Feb. 1892; 'Haberdashery and millinery', ibid; 'If a shed', *S.A.*, 2 Jan. 1892; 'which might subsequently', ibid.

286: 'with the proverbial', *S.A.*, 14 May 1892; 'On the whole', *S.A.*, 21 May 1892.

288: 'Rather! There will be', *S.A.*, 18 June 1892.

289: Opening of Exhibition, *S.A.*, 8 Oct. 1892.

290: 'Instead of the profit', Henderson, pp. 59–60; 'I have a very', *Mayor's Minutes*, 1892.

291: 'Kimberley was "going to the dogs" ', *S.A.*, 31 Dec. 1892; Exhibition was its 'last kick', ibid; 'This little town', *S.A.*, 27 Aug. 1892.

292: 'blade by blade', *Beet*; 'What scenes of life', *S.A.*, 31 Dec. 1892.

293: 'We have spent', Balfour, p. 67.

294: 'Of course', *S.A.*, 31 Dec. 1892; 'a demand for the support', Lewsen, vol. 2, p. 55.

295: 'I know nothing', *S.A.*, 9 July 1892; 'One powerful corporation', Bryce, p. 246; 'De Beers is the', Cumberland, p. 61.

19: PRELUDES TO WAR

298: 'Life has never been', Cronwright-Schreiner, pp. 222–3.

299: 'the stronghold', Wright, p. 154; 'large and representative', *D.F.A.*, 30 Oct. 1895; 'In the conduct of', ibid.

300: 'as a legislative', *D.F.A.*, 31 Oct. 1895; 'that a politician of such', Smuts, p. 32; 'as though the wife', Lockhart, p. 324; 'No upheaval of Nature', Wilson, p. 18.

301: 'he was too uncertain', *Mayor's Minutes*, 1894; 'One heard perfect', Wilson, p. 18; 'The Mayors of Kimberley', *E.P.H.*, 6 Jan. 1896; 'and the town resounded', ibid.

302: 'We the undersigned', ibid; 'Loud and deep', Wilson, p. 21; 'In times of political', *E.P.H.*, 6 Jan. 1896.

303: 'clemency be shown', *Mayor's Minutes*, 1896; 'It has', Cumberland, p. 41.

304: 'it takes about', ibid; 'to be sent to Parliament', *Ind.*, 3 July 1890.

305: 'Speaking of performances', Cumberland, pp. 50–2.

306: 'simply to hear', ibid; 'Always wind up', Cumberland; 'My reception everywhere', Wrench, p. 189.

308: 'this most English', Cumberland, p. 47.

308–9: 'The Sanatorium is' and 'The number of', *Beet.*

309: 'to meet the growing', ibid.

310: 'We batted', *D.F.A.*, 26 July 1971; 'We know', ibid; 'This Conference', Walker, p. 481.

311: 'I was convinced', Harris, p. 153; 'for the sole purpose', Harris, p. 155; 'Are you afraid', Harris, p. 156; 'disloyal British', O'Meara, p. 14; 'he did not see', A. Beet, p. 9.

312: 'At this time', O'Meara, p. 15; 'The need for troops', O'Meara, p. 17; 'silence of death', A. Beet, p. 12.

20: BESIEGED

313: '*Fearful* excitement', Scott; 'Men on horseback', ibid; 'I do feel so anxious', ibid; 'ran around frightening', Ashe, p. 5; 'The three death-like', Kingwill, p. 2.

314: 'The poor garden', *Scott*; 'No one is allowed out', ibid; 'Paraffin which had', Ashe, p. 10; 'Citizens generally feel', Michell, vol. 2, p. 268.

315: 'We dined', *Scott*; 'Without his presence', Henderson, p. 71; 'I really do not', Kingwill, p. 11.

316: 'Gardens were laid out', Harris, p. 158; 'I told him', Henderson, p. 76.

317: 'I was so glad', Henderson, p. 77; 'an evil influence', Henderson; 'Suspicious and cynical', Harris, p. 173; 'In case Your Honour', Wilson, vol. 2, p. 373.

318: 'We had a pretty', Ashe, p. 19.

319: 'No one felt particularly', Kingwill, p. 4; 'soon began to treat', Ashe, p. 43; 'There was quite a small', Kingwill, p. 4.

320: 'We were, of course', Jourdan, p. 112; 'in every way willing', O'Meara, p. 55; 'If you had had', Henderson, p. 78; 'One Saturday morning', Kingwill, p. 5.

322: 'news that the Relief Column', ibid; 'Our hearts were heavy', Kingwill, p. 6; 'Of course they all knew', Ashe, p. 69.

323: 'Wonderful as it seems', A. Beet, p. 43; 'had not taken', Ashe, p. 67; 'There were few', Kingwill, p. 6; 'the Boers had gone', Ashe, p. 68; 'the saddest sight', Kingwill, p. 8.

324: 'Remember you are not',

O'Meara, p. 77; 'We felt that something', Kingwill, p. 9; 'done other impossible', Kingwill, p. 10.

325: 'We made the most', Kingwill, p. 11; 'the quantities of all', Ashe, p. 93; 'It is very funny', Ashe, p. 102.

326: 'I shall never', Kingwill, p. 12; 'A crank', Green, pp. 80–1.

328: 'could not believe', Jourdan, p. 12; 'Of all the things', A. Beet, p. 51; 'We were startled', Kingwill, pp. 16–17.

329: Before Kimberley', O'Meara, p. 111; 'He was shockingly', Ashe, p. 163.

330: 'I shall never forget', Kingwill, p. 21; 'Nothing of the sort', Green, p. 86; 'Your troops', O'Meara, p. 115.

331: 'From personal knowledge', A. Williams, p. 275; 'The first thing next', Kingwill, pp. 23–4.

332: 'Men cheered, boys screeched', Kingwill, pp. 24–5; 'We all feel', Ashe, p. 209.

21: 'WHO IS TO TAKE HIS PLACE?'

333: 'I am practically all right', Colvin, vol. 2, pp. 193–5; 'Kimberley is simply', Colvin, p. 195.

334: 'Have just come back', Colvin, p. 199.

335: 'Amongst the employees', *Mayor's Minutes*, 1902; 'It was discussed', ibid; 'with here and there', *D.F.A.*, 7 April 1902; 'past the carriage', ibid.

336: 'Who is going to', ibid; 'Presented to Major General', *Leaflet on Presentation to General French* (De Beers Office); 'admired Colonel Kekewich', Henderson, p. 75.

338: 'Rhodes's sunny pleasure-dome', Baker, p. 51.

339: 'Beit replied simply', *Michell.*

340: 'The largest and most', Harris, p. 41; 'Diamond expert!', Hocking, p. 18.

341: 'It was 1902', Hahn, p. 127; 'There was not enough', Green, p. 104.

342: 'recognised to be one', *Diamond News* (magazine), Oct. 1947.

344: 'Kimberley remains', *S.A.*, 5 Jan. 1907.

345: 'palatial saloons' and 'a large

party', *Mayor's Minutes*, 1906; 'one of the largest', *S.A.*, 16 June 1906; 'made South Africa great', ibid.

347: 'intended to hand it over', *Mayor's Minutes*, 1905.

349: 'he put the town', Green, p. 112; 'Not even at the time', *D.F.A.*, 25 Sept. 1907; 'who is always' and 'There is one', *D.F.A.*, 26 Sept. 1907.

22: MAYOR OPPENHEIMER
351: 'There was a hush', *D.F.A.*, 23 June 1911.

352: 'Other flights', ibid; 'This objective we intend', *D.F.A.* (supplement p. 31), 17 July 1971; 'De Beers have very kindly', ibid; 'geographically situated', Oberholzer, p. 42; 'The question was', *D.F.A.*, 9 April 1912.

353: 'tethering his machine', *D.F.A.*, 11 April 1912.

354: 'If they show', *S.A.*, 25 Oct. 1913; 'In a short time', *D.F.A.*, 18 Aug. 1913; 'as you learn to ride', *Sunday Times*, 12 Oct. 1975.

356: 'the Western portion', *Mayor's Minutes*, 1911.

357: 'the needs and aspirations', *S.A.*, 27 July 1912; 'Loved by all', *D.F.A.*, 7 Oct. 1911.

358: 'Sister Henrietta has done', A. Williams, p. 386.

360: 'Efficiency rather than', *S.A.*, 18 Jan. 1913.

362: 'scurrilous personal attack', *D.F.A.*, 12 Sept. 1914; 'barbarism inflicted', ibid; 'We know you will', Hocking, p. 54; 'It was always a thrill', *D.F.A.* (supplement), 17 July 1971.

365: 'The roses that year', personal information; 'The doctors described', Harris, pp. 287–8.

366: 'All Roman Catholic', Harris, p. 287; 'only one solitary', Harris, p. 290; 'Most of us', *D.F.A.* (supplement), 17 July 1971; 'Labourers were dying', ibid.

367: 'Some of the callers', Harris, p. 289; 'A finer tonic', Harris, p. 293.

23: CAPITAL OF THE NORTHERN CAPE
368: 'one of the most popular men', *D.F.A.*, 29 June 1964.

369: Suggestions for War Memorial, see *D.F.A.* (supplement), 24 June 1919.

372: 'The 3rd August 1928 will', *Mayor's Minutes*, 1928; 'I thank Kimberley', *D.F.A.*, 18 June 1924; 'a clarion call', ibid.

373: 'The whole place', *Farrer and Mackenzie*.

375: 'Have had during the year', *Mayor's Minutes*, 1933.

376: 'Everything glared', *The Listener*, 30 Nov. 1972; 'It was impossible', ibid; 'The remark is often', *Mayor's Minutes*, 1934.

377: 'I can never adequately', Harris, pp. 251–2.

378: 'to one who was', *D.F.A.*, 19 Oct. 1935.

380: 'not more than a dozen', *D.F.A.*, 10 Nov. 1957; 'taught by her to recognise', *Transactions of the Royal Society of S.A.*, vol. xxxv (part lv); 'That she managed to keep', ibid; 'and of the chauffeur-assistant', ibid; 'Our grasses have gone', ibid.

381: 'In order fully to understand', *D.F.A.* (supplement), 25 Aug. 1964.

382: 'Once I had to travel', *D.F.A.*, 26 Aug. 1954; 'It is just as well', ibid.

383: 'and saw more action', *D.F.A.* (supplement), 17 July 1971; 'Death, dumps and decay', *Elliott*.

384: 'The town was in', *D.F.A.*, 29 Nov. 1961; 'Municipal officials', *Elliott*.

385: 'never had a soul of its', *Northern Cape* (pamphlet); 'this large territory' and 'in practice', ibid; 'Practically every public body', *Elliott*.

386: 'to give a bulk supply', ibid.

387: 'Diamonds every time', Anderson, p. 39; 'I always take', *Sunday Times* (magazine), 2 Sept. 1973; 'Kimberley is the', ibid.

388: 'Oh, it could happen', ibid.

390: 'The town is being', ibid.

Index